# HANDBOOK OF RETURN MIGRATION

ELGAR HANDBOOKS IN MIGRATION

The Elgar Handbooks in Migration series provides a definitive overview of recent research in all matters relating to the study of Migration, forming an extensive guide to the subject. This series covers research areas including internal migration, the global impact of human trafficking and forced labour, and international migration policy, and constitutes an essential new resource in the field. Each volume is edited by an editor recognized as an international leader within the field and consists of original contributions by leading authors. These *Handbooks* are developed using an international approach and contribute to both the expansion of current debates within the field, and the development of future research agendas.

Titles in the series include:

Handbook of Culture and Migration
*Edited by Jeffrey H. Cohen and Ibrahim Sirkeci*

Handbook on the Governance and Politics of Migration
*Edited by Emma Carmel, Katharina Lenner and Regine Paul*

Handbook of Citizenship and Migration
*Edited by Marco Giugni and Maria Grasso*

Handbook of Migration and Global Justice
*Edited by Leanne Weber and Claudia Tazreiter*

Research Handbook on International Migration and Digital Technology
*Edited by Marie McAuliffe*

Handbook on Migration and Welfare
*Edited by Markus M.L. Crepaz*

Handbook of Return Migration
*Edited by Russell King and Katie Kuschminder*

# Handbook of Return Migration

*Edited by*

Russell King

*Professor of Geography, University of Sussex, UK*

Katie Kuschminder

*Senior Researcher, University of Amsterdam, the Netherlands*

ELGAR HANDBOOKS IN MIGRATION

Cheltenham, UK • Northampton, MA, USA

© Russell King and Katie Kuschminder 2022

Cover image: Jr Korpa on Unsplash

All rights reserved. No part of this publication may be reproduced, stored in a retrieval system or transmitted in any form or by any means, electronic, mechanical or photocopying, recording, or otherwise without the prior permission of the publisher.

Published by
Edward Elgar Publishing Limited
The Lypiatts
15 Lansdown Road
Cheltenham
Glos GL50 2JA
UK

Edward Elgar Publishing, Inc.
William Pratt House
9 Dewey Court
Northampton
Massachusetts 01060
USA

A catalogue record for this book
is available from the British Library

Library of Congress Control Number: 2021949011

This book is available electronically in the **Elgar**online
Sociology, Social Policy and Education subject collection
http://dx.doi.org/10.4337/9781839100055

Printed on elemental chlorine free (ECF)
recycled paper containing 30% Post-Consumer Waste

ISBN 978 1 83910 004 8 (cased)
ISBN 978 1 83910 005 5 (eBook)
Printed and bound in the USA

# Contents

*List of figures* vii
*List of tables* viii
*List of contributors* ix
*Acknowledgements* xvi

1 Introduction: definitions, typologies and theories of return migration 1
  Russell King and Katie Kuschminder

PART I   THEORISING AND CONCEPTUALISING RETURN MIGRATION

2 The economics of return migration 24
  Jackline Wahba

3 Return and transnationalism 38
  Özge Bilgili

4 Gendering return migration 53
  Russell King and Aija Lulle

5 Theorising voluntariness in return 70
  Marta Bivand Erdal and Ceri Oeppen

6 Departheid: re-politicising the inhumane treatment of illegalised migrants in so-called liberal democratic states 84
  Barak Kalir

7 Return visits and other return mobilities 96
  Md Farid Miah

PART II   THE POLITICISATION OF RETURN MIGRATION

8 Critical reflections on assisted return programmes and practices 108
  Ine Lietaert

9 The contours of deportation studies 122
  Martin Lemberg-Pedersen

10 The Return Directive: clarifying the scope and substance of the rights of migrants facing expulsion from the EU 137
   Alan Desmond

11 The return industry: the case of the Netherlands 153
   Marieke van Houte

| 12 | The legitimisation of the policy objective of sustainable reintegration<br>*Rossella Marino and Ine Lietaert* | 167 |
| 13 | Corruption and return migration<br>*Erlend Paasche* | 185 |

## PART III    EXPERIENCES OF RETURN AND REINTEGRATION

| 14 | Reintegration strategies<br>*Katie Kuschminder* | 200 |
| 15 | Labour migrants and the retirement–return nexus<br>*Claudio Bolzman* | 212 |
| 16 | Return migration and psychosocial wellbeing<br>*Zana Vathi* | 226 |
| 17 | The return migration of children: (re)integration is not always plain sailing<br>*Daina Grosa* | 241 |
| 18 | Student mobility: between returning home and remaining abroad<br>*Elisa Alves* | 255 |
| 19 | Returning lifestyle migrants<br>*Katie Walsh* | 270 |
| 20 | Revisiting second-generation 'return' migration to the ancestral homeland<br>*Nilay Kılınç* | 283 |
| 21 | Return migration experiences: the case of Central and Eastern Europe<br>*Anne White* | 299 |

## PART IV    RETURN MIGRATION AND DEVELOPMENT

| 22 | Exploring the return migration and development nexus<br>*Russell King* | 314 |
| 23 | Diaspora return and knowledge transfer<br>*Charlotte Mueller* | 331 |
| 24 | Return migration, entrepreneurship and development<br>*Giulia Sinatti* | 344 |

*Index*     358

# Figures

| | | |
|---|---|---|
| 3.1 | Manifold associations between imaginary return, return mobilities and return migration | 44 |
| 3.2 | Reintegration as a consequence of transnational engagement and belonging | 47 |

# Tables

| | | |
|---|---|---|
| 3.1 | Types, categories and dimensions of transnationalism | 41 |
| 3.2 | Linking return and transnationalism | 43 |
| 12.1 | Overview of evolution and development of sustainable reintegration | 170 |
| 14.1 | Reintegration strategies | 203 |
| 14.2 | Structural and cultural environment for return | 205 |
| 14.3 | Potential to vernacularise based on the reintegration strategy and conditions of the structural and cultural environment | 207 |
| 15.1 | Typology of return migration and transnational geographical mobility | 215 |
| 15.2 | Share of Italian, Portuguese and Spanish immigrants leaving Switzerland (Geneva) between 2011 and 2016 (average annual scores) | 216 |
| 20.1 | A classification of migratory generations | 284 |

# Contributors

**Elisa Alves** is Associate Researcher at IGOT/CEG (the Institute for Geography and Spatial Planning/Centre of Geographical Studies) at the University of Lisbon since 2015. Before that, she was an Associate Researcher at CIES-IUL (the Centre for Research and Studies in Sociology, at the University Institute of Lisbon) and she was consultant at the Border and Immigration Service (SEF), the Portuguese National Contact Point for the European Migration Network (EMN). Her main publications have covered international student mobility in the Lusophone space, the meaning of the concept of international student and their social and spatial trajectories, with a focus on future mobility projects, which also includes the topic of return migration.

**Özge Bilgili** is Assistant Professor of Interdisciplinary Social Science at Utrecht University, where she is a member of the European Research Centre on Migration and Ethnic Relations (ERCOMER). Since 2016, she has been the Chair of the Dutch Association for Migration Research (DAMR), a board member of IMISCOE and its Standing Committee on Migrant Transnationalism, an affiliated researcher at United Nations University–MERIT and a nominated member of Utrecht Young Academy. Previously, she was a Post-Doctoral Researcher at the Maastricht Graduate School of Governance, a Senior Researcher for the Migrant Integration Policy Index 2015 project and Thomas J. Alexander Fellow at the Education and Skills Department of the Organisation for Economic Co-operation and Development (OECD). Her research is at the intersections of migrant integration, transnationalism, mobility and development studies and benefits from a wide range of disciplines including Sociology, Political Science, Economics and (Social) Psychology. As a migration scholar, she regularly conducts research for international organisations and national governments.

**Claudio Bolzman** is Honorary Professor of Sociology at the University of Applied Sciences and Arts Western Switzerland (HES-SO) and Visiting Professor in Migration Studies at the University of Valencia. He is also a member of the Swiss National Centre of Competence in Research 'LIVES – Overcoming Vulnerability: Life Course Perspectives' and Associate Researcher at the Centre for the Interdisciplinary Study of Gerontology and Vulnerability (CIGEV, University of Geneva). He has held visiting appointments, among others, at the University of Lyon 2, the University of Seville, El Colegio de la Frontera Norte (Mexico) and the University of Sherbrooke. His main research interests are on migration and transnational mobilities. He has researched and published extensively on ageing and return migration, including papers in leading sociological and migration journals such as the *International Journal of Comparative Sociology*, the *Journal of Ethnic and Migration Studies* and *Population, Space and Place*.

**Alan Desmond** is Lecturer in Law at the University of Leicester and a member of the University's Migration, Mobility and Citizenship Network (MMCN). Before joining Leicester Law School in September 2016 he worked at third-level institutions in Ireland, Italy and Poland. He is the editor of *Shining New Light on the UN Migrant Workers Convention* (PULP, 2017) and of a special issue of the *International Journal of Law in Context* (2020) on the

Global Compact for Migration. His work has appeared in journals including the *European Journal of Migration and Law*, the *Human Rights Law Review* and the *European Journal of International Law*. He has been a Visiting Researcher at Yaşar University in Izmir, the Centre of Migration Research at Warsaw University, Harvard Law School and the UCLA School of Law. He is Deputy Editor of the *Journal of Immigration, Asylum and Nationality Law*. Before entering legal academia, Alan worked as a freelance print and broadcast journalist in Poland and wrote a number of award-winning Irish language books.

**Marta Bivand Erdal** is Research Professor in Migration Studies at the Peace Research Institute Oslo (PRIO), where she is Co-Director of the PRIO Migration Centre. As a Human Geographer she is interested in the impacts of migration and transnationalism in both emigration and immigration contexts. This has led to research on the interactions of migrant transnationalism and integration; remittances, migration and development; return mobilities; citizenship, nation and diversity; and migration and religion. Marta's work draws on interview, focus group and survey data, paying critical attention to the use of categories. Her empirical focus is on European and Asian contexts. She has published extensively on themes connected with international migration in Geography and Migration Studies journals, among others *International Migration*, the *International Migration Review*, the *Journal of Ethnic and Migration Studies, Gender, Place and Culture, Political Geography* and *Population, Space and Place*.

**Daina Grosa** is a Migration Researcher at the Institute of Philosophy and Sociology, University of Latvia and a PhD candidate in Migration Studies at the University of Sussex. She has a Master's degree in Applied Linguistics from Monash University, Australia. Her research interests include bilingualism, heritage language acquisition and maintenance, return migration and diaspora studies. She has been involved in researching the diaspora Latvian community worldwide from an education perspective as well as Latvian return migrants and their children's integration into the education system of the homeland. Her research has been included in Latvian publications, disseminating the work of Latvian migration researchers on diaspora life, identity and language maintenance and the challenges faced on return to Latvia. Community activism in the Latvian diaspora in Australia as well as the implementation of support mechanisms for return migrant children in Latvia have given her hands-on experience with her topics of research.

**Barak Kalir** is an Anthropologist based at the University of Amsterdam. He has recently rounded off an European Research Council (ERC)-funded project entitled: 'The Social Life of State Deportation Regimes' in which, together with a team of researchers, he ethnographically documented and analysed the views, motivations and practices of state bureaucrats and civil-society actors directly involved in the detention and deportation of illegalised migrants in several countries around the world. Among his recent publications are: 'To deport or to adopt' (2020, *Ethnography*), 'Departheid: the draconian governance of illegalized migrants in Western states' (2019, *Conflict and Society*), 'Repressive compassion: deportation caseworkers furnishing an emotional comfort zone in encounters with illegalized migrants' (2019, *PoLAR: Political and Legal Anthropology Review*) and two journal special issues: 'Nonrecording states: between legibility and looking away' (2017, *Focaal: Journal of Global and Historical Anthropology*) and 'Re-searching access: what do attempts at studying migration control tell us about the state?' (2019, *Social Anthropology*).

**Nilay Kılınç** is a Post-Doctoral Fellow at the University of Helsinki. Her current research is on highly skilled Turkish migrants' social and professional networks in the Nordic region. She obtained her PhD from the University of Surrey and her MA from Lund University. Her PhD thesis explored the second-generation Turkish-Germans' lifestyle-motivated 'return' migration and their post-'return' lives in Antalya, Turkey. Since 2012, she has been working on return migration, through her MA thesis (on gendered narratives of return) and her academic collaboration with the-then Willy Brandt Professor, Russell King, at Malmö University. During her post-doctoral fellowship at New Europe College Bucharest and the University of Leipzig, she worked on forced return migration from Germany to Turkey and published on this topic in the *Nordic Journal of Migration Research*. She has published several book chapters and journal articles on return migration in relation to identity, home, belonging, nostalgia and translocality.

**Russell King** is Professor of Geography at the University of Sussex and Visiting Professor in Migration Studies at Malmö University, where he was the Willy Brandt Professor 2012–13. Before moving to Sussex in 1993 he was Professor of Geography at Trinity College Dublin and Lecturer, then Reader, in Geography at the University of Leicester. He has held visiting appointments at the University of Malta, Ben Gurion University of the Negev and Cornell University. He has long-standing interests in the study of migration and has written extensively on return migration. Among his books on this topic are his edited *Return Migration and Economic Problems* (Croom Helm, 1986, republished Routledge, 2015) and his co-authored (with Anastasia Christou) *Counter-Diaspora: The Greek Second Generation Returns 'Home'* (Harvard University Press, 2014). He was editor of the *Journal of Ethnic and Migration Studies*, 2001–13 and continues to publish widely on migration topics in leading geography and migration journals.

**Katie Kuschminder** is Senior Researcher in the Department of Political Science at the University of Amsterdam. She was formerly Associate Professor at Maastricht University and United Nations University–MERIT. From 2016 to 2018 she was a Rubicon Research Fellow at the European University Institute in Florence. In 2020, she received a European Research Council Starting Grant for her project on Reintegration Governance. She has been working on return migration for the past decade. In 2017, she published *Reintegration Strategies: Conceptualizing How Return Migrants Reintegrate* in the Palgrave Macmillan/Springer 'Migration, Diaspora, and Citizenship' series. She has completed work on return migration for the Dutch Ministry of Foreign Affairs, German Development Cooperation, the International Organization for Migration, the International Labour Organization, the World Bank and the United Nations High Commissioner for Refugees. Her work on return migration has also been published in journals such as *International Migration* and *Migration Studies*.

**Martin Lemberg-Pedersen** is Honorary Associate Professor at the Department of Politics and International Studies, University of Warwick and Head of Policy and Society for Amnesty International, Denmark. He has been working for more than a decade on various dimensions of European border control, actors, networks, political economic dynamics and humanitarian consequences. This includes a particular focus on contested European plans to deport unaccompanied minors, in collaboration with the Danish Institute for International Studies and the Refugee Studies Centre, University of Oxford, among others. He has conducted work and consultations concerning border control and deportation politics for the Danish Refugee

Council, the Danish Red Cross, the European Parliament LIBE Committee, the Norwegian Ministry of the Interior and the Royal Danish Defence College. He is a member of the EU Horizon 2020 project 'Advancing Alternative Migration Governance' (AdMiGov). His work has been published in journals such as the *Journal of Borderlands Studies*, *Citizenship Studies* and *Global Affairs*.

**Ine Lietaert** is Assistant Professor of Migration Governance and Regional Integration Studies at the United Nations University–CRIS where she coordinates the Migration and Social Policy research cluster. She is also affiliated, as Professor of International Social Work, to the Department of Social Work and Social Pedagogy, Ghent University. She is a research member of the Centre for the Social Study of Migration and Refugees and the UNU Migration Network. Her research interest mainly focuses on the impact of international/regional and national policies on social work and social welfare practices, with particular reference to the governance of 'mobile' groups in vulnerable situations (e.g. return migrants and internally displaced persons (IDPs)) and the impact of mobility and different types of borders and policies on their lives. She has published on the topic of return migration and reintegration in highly ranked peer-review journals from different disciplines, including Social Work, Anthropology, Geography and Demography.

**Aija Lulle** is Lecturer in Human Geography at Loughborough University and Adjunct Professor of Migration and Mobility Studies at the University of Eastern Finland. Before joining the Loughborough Geography Department in 2018, she worked as the post-doctoral researcher on the EU Horizon 2020 'YMOBILITY' project at the University of Sussex, researching youth mobilities across Europe (2015–18). She was also a post-doctoral researcher at the University of Eastern Finland where she researched transnational migrant children and families in Baltic-Nordic spaces (2016–18). She has published on migration and related topics in a wide range of leading journals. She has edited special issues of the *Journal of Ethnic and Migration Studies*, the *Nordic Journal of Migration Research*, *Sexualities* and the *Journal of Rural Studies*.

**Rossella Marino** is a PhD student in the Department of Social Work and Social Pedagogy at Ghent University and a PhD Fellow at the United Nations University–CRIS (UNU-CRIS). Her PhD revolves around the institutional dynamics arising from the externalisation of EU migration management to the Gambia. Before starting her PhD, she was a research intern at the Institute for European Studies of Vrije Universiteit Brussel (VUB) and UNU-CRIS. Her university education took place in Italy and Denmark. Her research interest in migration issues has corresponded with a practical engagement with asylum-seekers and theatre representation in the Italian city of Trento.

**Md Farid Miah** is a Post-Doctoral Research Fellow at the University of Sussex, working on the Horizon 2020 Twinning for Excellence project titled 'Migration and Integration Research and Networking' (MIRNet). He is also a Tutor in the School of Global Studies at Sussex, where he teaches interdisciplinary undergraduate modules covering Human Geography, Cultural Studies and Global Migration. He has an interdisciplinary academic background which consists of a BA in History from Dhaka University, an MBA from Cardiff Metropolitan University and an MSc in Tourism and Business Studies from Sunderland University. Having completed his PhD in Human Geography at Sussex in 2019 on the bilateral transnational visiting mobilities of Bangladeshi migrants and non-migrants, he has published his research findings in journals such as *Population, Place and Space* and *Contemporary South Asia*. He has also contributed a co-authored chapter in the book *Memory, Migration and Travel* (Routledge, 2018).

**Charlotte Mueller** is a PhD Fellow with the Migration and Development Research Group at Maastricht University and United Nations University–MERIT. Her main research interests focus on return migration, diasporas and knowledge transfer. Since 2016 she has been working in collaboration with the International Organization for Migration on the evaluation of the 'Connection Diaspora for Development' project, for which she has conducted fieldwork in Afghanistan, Ethiopia, Ghana, Somalia and Sierra Leone. At present, she is the Assistant Coordinator for the United Nations University Migration Network. She holds an MSc in Public Policy and Human Development with a specialisation in Migration Studies from United Nations University–MERIT/Maastricht University and a BA in International Cultural and Business Studies from the University of Passau.

**Ceri Oeppen** is Senior Lecturer in Human Geography at the University of Sussex and Co-Director of the Sussex Centre for Migration Research. From 2014 to 2020 she was a Global Fellow at the Peace Research Institute Oslo (PRIO). She has been working on return migration, particularly in the context of transnationalism, for over a decade, specialising in ethnographic research about the experiences of people from Afghanistan, including for the large international project 'Possibilities and Realities of Return Migration' (PREMIG), led by PRIO. More recently, she has also conducted research analysing the reintegration of returnees in West Africa. She is co-editor of *Beyond the 'Wild Tribes': Understanding Modern Afghanistan and Its Diaspora* (University of Columbia Press/Hurst, 2010) and has published papers in *Global Networks*, the *Journal of Ethnic and Migration Studies* and *Race and Class*.

**Erlend Paasche** is Senior Researcher at the Norwegian Institute for Social Research. He has conducted sociological research on return and reintegration for over a decade, with fieldwork experience in Syria, Iraq, Kosovo and Nigeria. He has taken part in a string of evaluations of assisted return to various origin states – commissioned by the Norwegian Directorate of Immigration – and evaluated migration control by border police at Norwegian airports for the European Commission. He was previously affiliated with the Centre of Excellence in the Study of Civil War (CSCW) and the Peace Research Institute Oslo (PRIO), as well as the Department of Sociology and Human Geography and the Department of Criminology and Sociology of Law at the University of Oslo, where he also taught Migration Studies. Currently, he coordinates the project 'Deporting Foreigners' (2021–24), which examines the international relations of return and readmission from Europe to major origin states.

**Giulia Sinatti** is Assistant Professor in Social and Cultural Anthropology at Vrije Universiteit Amsterdam, where she has been since 2014. Previously, she held positions at the Università di Milano-Bicocca (Italy), the Université Cheick Anta Diop de Dakar (Senegal), the London School of Economics and Goldsmiths College (United Kingdom) and Erasmus University Rotterdam. An ethnographer with a background in Anthropology, Sociology and Human Geography, her research has focused extensively on return migration, from the perspective of both mobility experiences among African migrants and of the governance of migration between Africa and Europe. She has published widely on the subject of return migration and her work has appeared, among others, in *African Studies*, *Ethnic and Racial Studies*, *Population, Space and Place* and *Open House International*.

**Marieke van Houte** is a Researcher at Erasmus University Rotterdam. Before going to Rotterdam she was a Marie Skłodowska-Curie Fellow (2015–16) at the International Migration Institute (IMI), University of Oxford. She holds a PhD (2014) from the Maastricht Graduate School of Governance, Maastricht University. Her research is on the relationship between migration, change, conflict and development, from the perspective of migrants and policy. Return migration is a key theme in her work, alongside the transnational engagement of migrants and processes of structure and agency in mobility. Her work is grounded in empirical fieldwork in a variety of contexts. Her book *Return Migration to Afghanistan: Moving Back or Moving Forward?* was published by Palgrave Macmillan in 2016. Her work on return migration has also been published in leading migration journals, including *Migration Studies*, the *International Migration Review, Population, Space and Place, Citizenship Studies* and *International Migration*.

**Zana Vathi** is Reader in Social Sciences at Edge Hill University, UK, and has been doing research on migration since 2005. She is the author of *Migrating and Settling in a Mobile World* (Springer, 2015) and co-editor of *Return Migration and Psychosocial Wellbeing* (Routledge, 2017, with Russell King). Her work has been published in leading international journals such as, inter alia, the *Journal of Ethnic and Migration Studies, International Migration, Ethnic and Racial Studies, Urban Studies* and *Childhood*. She has served as an international expert for the International Organization for Migration, Terre Des Hommes and the World Bank. Since 2018 she has founded and directs the work of the Migration Working Group – North West. In the period 2019–20 she acted as the Research Coordinator of RET-MIG – 'Revisiting Return Migration in Shifting Geopolitics' – an international research initiative and network funded by IMISCOE.

**Jackline Wahba** is Professor of Economics at the University of Southampton. She was appointed Officer of the Order of the British Empire (OBE) in the 2020 Queen's Birthday Honours for services to Economic Policy. She obtained her PhD from the Department of Economics at the University of Southampton. She leads the migration research strand within the ESRC Centre for Population Change at the University of Southampton. She has served as an advisor to international organisations. She is a Research Fellow of IZA, CReAM and ERF. She is also a member of the editorial board of the journal *World Development*. She was a member of the UK Migration Advisory Committee between 2012 and 2021 and is an elected member of the Council of the Royal Economic Society (2020–25).

**Katie Walsh** is Reader in Human Geography at the University of Sussex. In 2018 she published *Transnational Geographies of the Heart: Intimate Subjectivities in a Globalizing City* (Wiley, 2018) based on ethnographic research with British migrants in Dubai. She is also co-editor of the edited volumes: *British Migration* (2018, with Pauline Leonard), *Transnational Migration and Home in Older Age* (2016, with Lena Näre) and *The New Expatriates* (2012, with Anne-Meike Fechter). Her work on return migration has been published in these edited volumes, as well as in a co-edited special issue of *Area* (2018) on 'Geographies of the ageing–migration nexus'.

**Anne White** is M.B. Grabowski Professor of Polish Studies at University College London, School of Slavonic and East European Studies (SSEES). Before moving to SSEES in 2014 she was at the University of Bath. Her contributions to return migration research include analyses of EU sending-country migration cultures characterised by assumptions that 'return is easy'; 'double return migration', where returnees hope to settle in their country of origin only to realise that 'home' is now the country to which they had migrated; and the unsuccessful livelihood strategies of would-be migrants with little capital of any kind existing on the fringes of migration networks. Most recently, she has been working on social remittances and how they contribute overall to social change in sending countries.

# Acknowledgements

Producing a large edited Handbook is a challenging logistical exercise whose success depends on help, collaboration and respect all round. We have been hugely fortunate in our choice of contributors. Despite the fact that their writing of chapters coincided with the worst of the Covid-19 pandemic in Europe, with attendant disruptions to their academic and personal lives, all the chapter authors were able to deliver their contributions pretty much according to our original schedule, including suggested revisions. We thank them all in celebrating this remarkable collective effort. We are also very grateful to Daniel Mather at Edward Elgar for his encouragement and advice and for his obvious genuine interest in the project. Finally, we thank Jenny Money, who did a superb job cross-checking all the references – a vital element of the Handbook – and helping to copy-edit the final text.

Russell King and Katie Kuschminder

# 1. Introduction: definitions, typologies and theories of return migration

*Russell King and Katie Kuschminder*

## INTRODUCTION

More than twenty years ago, one of us wrote: 'Return migration is the great unwritten chapter in the history of migration' (King, 2000, p.7). Is this bold assertion still true? Almost certainly not. Over the past two decades, return migration has evolved to take its place as a cornerstone in the field of migration studies. There is now a rich and wide-ranging literature covering many types, geographies, temporalities and other nuances of return migration and its effects. The *Handbook of Return Migration* aspires to be both a state-of-the-art and an agenda for opening up new debates and avenues of research, including new theories and conceptualisations of return migration.

Yet, despite significant growth in the scholarship on return migration in recent years, it remains relatively overlooked in much of the mainstream migration studies literature. Given that, according to Azose and Raftery (2019), around a quarter to a third of migrants subsequently return, this lack of proportionate attention to return migration is surprising. If we take a sample of recent textbooks on migration, concentrating on those which take a global view of the phenomenon, we find that none of them have a dedicated chapter on return (see Cohen and Sirkeci, 2011; de Haas et al., 2020; de Lima, 2017, Linhard and Parsons, 2019; Martiniello and Rath, 2012; Mavroudi and Nagel, 2016; Samers and Collyer, 2017). To find out what they say about return, one has to go to the index and trace through the scattered mentions – if indeed there is an index entry on return migration.

On the other side, there has been a recent flurry of books dedicated to return migration, most of them edited collections which follow the earlier volumes edited by King (1986a) and Ghosh (2000). Such studies include those which are mainly historical (Harper, 2005), others which focus on 'ethnic' or 'diasporic' return (Conway and Potter, 2009; Tsuda, 2009), two which use the trope of 'homecoming' (Long and Oxfeld, 2004; Markowitz and Stefansson, 2004) and others which have a more specific geographic or thematic focus – for instance Potter et al. (2005) on the Caribbean, Åkesson and Baaz (2015) on Africa, Nadler et al. (2016) on Europe, Kuschminder (2017) on return and reintegration, Vathi and King (2017) on psychosocial aspects of return and Anghel et al. (2019) on transnational return. Alongside this recent expansion of books on return has been a much larger-scale production of journal articles, far too numerous to reference here; many of them are cited in the various chapters of this Handbook.[1]

The *Handbook of Return Migration* is structured into four parts, each comprising several chapters. Part I is on 'Theorising and Conceptualising Return Migration' and consists of six chapters which, between them, map the general field of return migration – as both a timespace event and a process – and contribute a range of theoretical and conceptual insights. Return is viewed, in turn, as an economic process with economic impacts (Wahba, Chapter 2), as an important element of transnationalism (Bilgili, Chapter 3) and as an inescapably gendered phenomenon (King and Lulle, Chapter 4). Erdal and Oeppen (Chapter 5) theorise and question 'voluntariness' in return, setting the scene for Kalir's (Chapter 6) exposé of the inhumanity and violence of forced return, denoted as 'Departheid'. Part I concludes with Miah's (Chapter 7) overview of return visits, which draws on the 'mobilities' framework.

Part II of the Handbook examines the politicisation of return migration and also contains six chapters. Building on Chapters 5 and 6, which exposed the false dichotomy between voluntary and forced migration and the contested terrain of deportation, Lietaert (Chapter 8) critically assesses so-called 'assisted return' programmes as a governance tool of the European Union (EU) to repatriate 'unwanted' migrants such as rejected asylum-seekers and undocumented migrants. This is followed by a sequence of chapters which focus on deportation (Lemberg-Pedersen, Chapter 9), the legal ramifications of the EU's 2008 Return Directive (Desmond, Chapter 10) and the 'return industry' in the Netherlands (van Houte, Chapter 11). In Chapter 12, Marino and Lietaert explore the policy objective of 'sustainable return', tracing an evolution from success being judged on the simple criterion of the absence of re-emigration to more nuanced psychosocial dimensions and the exercise of choice over future (im)mobility plans. Finally, Chapter 13 (Paasche) looks at the under-researched domain of corruption in return migration. Corruption in the home country is a disincentive to return and a battle to be faced for many returnees.

Part III explores the important theme of reintegration, above all questioning two notions: that return to the homeland is the 'natural' thing for migrants to aspire to and that reintegration is a straightforward process for returnees since they are back where they 'truly belong' in familiar surroundings. Eight chapters cover a variety of dimensions and experiences across a range of social and demographic types of return. The part opens with a review of reintegration strategies and processes (Kuschminder, Chapter 14). The succeeding chapter (Bolzman, Chapter 15) looks at labour migrants' options of mobility at the 'retirement–return' nexus: stay put, return for good and intermediate strategies of post-retirement transnational mobility. This is followed by an examination of the psychosocial aspects of return migration (Vathi, Chapter 16). Four chapters then explore the return modalities and reintegration experiences of a variety of socio-demographic groups: school-age children (Grosa, Chapter 17), third-level students (Alves, Chapter 18), older lifestyle migrants (Walsh, Chapter 19) and second-generation 'returnees' (Kılınç, Chapter 20). In the last of these chapters, the protagonists are arguably not true returnees since they are not returning to their country of birth but to an ancestral and imagined 'homeland'. Part III is rounded off by a review of the recent return-and-reintegration experiences of migrants from the post-communist Central and East European countries (White, Chapter 21).

Part IV is about the impact of return migration on development in the migrants' countries of origin; three chapters here. Chapter 22 (King) unpacks the 'return migration and development nexus' and links different development outcomes to different theorisations of (return) migration, as well as surveying existing empirical research on development impacts in various parts of the world. The final two chapters investigate more specific aspects of the return–development nexus: knowledge transfer (Mueller, Chapter 23) and entrepreneurship (Sinatti, Chapter 24). All three chapters show that return impacts are contingent on time and place and on the distinction between 'top-down' programmes organised at state or supra-national level and the 'bottom-up' initiatives of the migrants/returnees themselves.

## DEFINING RETURN MIGRATION

Is return migration a meaningful, valid and unambiguous concept? At first glance, yes. Its common sense meaning would appear to be self-evident and therefore not to need further discussion. Perhaps this is why there have been relatively few attempts to define the phenomenon. It is also the case that many other terms have been used in the literature to connote return, including counterstream migration, reverse migration, U-turn migration, homeward migration and the confusing word 're-migration'.[2]

The apparent straightforwardness of the notion of return migration evaporates when we attempt to pin down a simple, all-encompassing definition. Here is a selection of definitions taken from some of the key literature:

> when people return after emigration for the first time to their country (or region) of origin, then and only then we will use the term *return migration*. (Bovenkerk, 1974, p.5, emphasis in the original)

> Return migration is defined as the movement of emigrants back to their homeland to resettle. (Gmelch, 1980, p.136)

> Return migration is when people return to their country or region of origin after a significant period abroad or in another region. (King, 1986b, p.4; also 2000, p.8)

> The return of migrants to their country of origin – sometimes as a fulfilment of original intentions, sometimes as a consequence of revised intentions. (Bartram et al., 2014, p.121)

> Return migration … refers to the movement of migrants back to a country of origin, following an absence of at least one year. (Erdal, 2017, p.104)

A close reading of this sample of definitions, arranged in chronological order, reveals some of the complexities involved. Bovenkerk, whose 1974 extended essay can be seen as the first systematic analysis of the concept of return migration, was railing against the plethora of competing terms for return but his definition reveals a rigid view of migration as a one-time event, an impression reinforced by Gmelch, for whom return means resettlement. Both Bartram et al. and Erdal see return only in terms of international migration, overlooking the relevance of return in internal migration, especially in big countries like China or the United States. King's definition might be criticised by the vagueness of the phrase 'significant period abroad' (cf. Kuschminder, 2017, p.3). Erdal is precise – 'an absence of at least one year' – but this would exclude return from a shorter-term migration, for instance from a seasonal job or the case of a rejected asylum-seeker.

This does not exhaust the complexities involved in trying to define return migration. Another issue concerns the precise location of the return. If return is 'movement in space, a going back to where one started', then it must be recognised that 'place of origin is a rather fluid category' (Pauli, 2021, p.97). An early demographic study of Puerto Rican return migration by Hernández Alvarez (1967) showed that only half of the returnees from the United States returned to their place of origin; the remainder returned to a different location. Typically, these were rural-origin migrants who returned to San Juan, the capital, where their economic and social prospects were better.

To be satisfactory, a definition of return migration must remain broad so as to include the various types and circumstances of return and to encompass the differing perspectives of researchers in different disciplines, as well as policy-makers and practitioners. We endorse the definition of King (1986a, 2000), above, with the proviso that the 'significant period abroad' can be varied according to context. In their field survey of return migration to Southern Italy carried out in the early 1980s, King et al. (1984, 1985, 1986) specified a dual temporal threshold: at least one year spent abroad and at least a year spent back in the home community, in order to exclude temporary return visitors. Kuschminder's more recent research on return migration and reintegration in Ethiopia considered a minimum of three months for the stay abroad – on the argument that this allowed for short-term contract migration and student migration – and in the belief that this length of time still allows for 'exposure to another culture and context to have an impact on individuals' values and behaviours' (2017, p.5).

## TYPOLOGIES OF RETURN

The pioneering essay by Bovenkerk (1974) on the sociology of return migration sets out some basic but important classifications of types of return. Below, we elaborate on these, blending in contributions from subsequent authors who build on his analysis (Gmelch, 1980; King, 1986b; and, more recently, Battistella, 2018; Conway et al., 2009, pp.2–3; Kuschminder, 2017, pp.5–8). These typologies give an insight into the diversity of return migration as an event and a process.

A first typology is by the *level of development of the countries involved* (low, middle or high income) and the *skill level of the migrant*. This creates a diversified matrix of migrations and, hence, returns. Typical cases include low-skilled migrants moving from poor to richer countries, either as a survival strategy to support family members at home or as 'target' migrants to accumulate savings and experience prior to return; high-skilled migrants moving in the same direction (brain drain and brain return); professional and business migrants moving between high-income countries for career and lifestyle reasons; or to low-income countries for expat placements, followed by return.

Recognising that all forms of migration and mobility can be regarded as timespace phenomena (Mavroudi et al., 2017), *temporal and geographical* criteria create a series of typologies. *Time* enters the equation regarding the length of the return stay – ranging from short visits to temporary stays of several months, longer stays lasting many years followed by re-migration, to a 'return for good'. Another aspect of the return matrix is biographical and generational time and the constitution of the returning demographic unit – individuals or families; adults, children or retirees; and first-generation migrants or their descendants ('diaspora return', cf. Tsuda, 2009).

*Distance* is another element contributing to the heterogeneity of forms of return migration. Rural–urban internal migration may lead to a 'return to the village' on retirement. With international migration, return moves are more likely where countries are close by, so that transnational contacts are easy to maintain both before and after return. With long-distance, intercontinental migration, the economic, social and psychological separation between host and home countries and long-term residence abroad make return less likely, although not impossible.

The *motivations and circumstances* of return – including varying degrees of voluntariness and forced return – are also fundamental in conceptualising and categorising return. Return can take place for multiple, often combined, reasons relating to family, life-stage, (un)employment, business/investment opportunities, nostalgia, expulsion etc. This leads to more complex and integrated typologies. Probably the most well known is Cerase's (1974) fourfold typology which links stage of integration in the host society (United States) with the type of development stimulus which returnees can effect in their homeland (Southern Italy). A quick return is the *return of failure*; the migrant failed to adapt to the new life in the United States and hence brought nothing back to Southern Italy. A return after a few years brings the *return of conservatism*: something tangible is brought back, mainly savings, but this is invested in land and housing, seen to confer social prestige in the eyes of the local community. Cerase's *return of innovation* comes after ten or more years abroad: long enough for the migrant to have absorbed the 'modernising' and 'business' values of American society but not too long, so that he or she is able to 'innovate' upon return. The final type, the *return of retirement*, is self-explanatory.

A different fourfold typology is proposed by Battistella (2018). The first type is the *return of achievement*. The migrant returns voluntarily at the end of the migration project having achieved the purpose for which he or she went abroad (which might be a work contract, a period of education or training or a target sum of capital saved). Second, the *return of completion* is rather similar to the first type – after completing a contract or secondment – but the return is not voluntary because the migrant would like to stay abroad longer. Third, the *return of setback* is a hybrid voluntary/forced return. In this type, the migrant faces obstacles such as unemployment, unhappiness, homesickness or family obligations in the home country – such as the illness or death of a close relative – and has to return before the return project is completed. Finally, the *return of crisis* or *forced return* arises due to situations such as political upheaval, environmental disaster, repatriation due to criminal acts or the failure of an asylum application.

## THEORISING RETURN MIGRATION

Cassarino's seminal 2004 article remains the key statement on theorising return migration. It offers a concise overview of how return can be re-thought through the application of several of migration's existing theoretical frames – neoclassical economics, the new economics of labour migration, structuralism, transnationalism and social network theory. All of these theories yield valuable insights, albeit some of them from contradictory standpoints. Their value, however, is often speculative rather than empirically proven, due to the lack of reliable data on return.

The *neoclassical approach* rests on wage differentials between sending and receiving areas/countries and the migrant's expectation of significantly higher earnings in the destination, sufficient to trigger the move and to defray the costs of moving (Todaro, 1969). In this view, return migrants are those who somehow miscalculated the balance of costs and benefits or whose migration project failed in some other way. In the rarified world of neoclassical economies, return migration is thus an anomaly.

By contrast, under the *new economics of labour migration* (NELM), return migration is the norm – the expected outcome of a successfully implemented strategy of migrating, earning, remitting, saving and, finally, returning back to a more secure and comfortable life. Unlike the individualised economic calculations of the neoclassical model, the NELM approach conceptualises migration and return as a family-level strategy to both maximise and diversify income and resources and hedge against the failure of one of them (Stark, 1991; Taylor, 1999). It assumes the mutual interdependence of family members, whereby one or more migrates (and returns) and others stay put; at a later phase of the family/household cycle, another member may migrate to continue the support of the remaining household. Cassarino (2004, p.260) concludes that 'migrants go abroad for a limited period of time, until they succeed in providing their households with the liquidity and income they expect to earn ... Thus return represents the logical outcome of migration and the achievement of success, not failure.'

Cassarino is arguably less thorough in his coverage of the *structural approach to return migration*, limiting himself to social and institutional factors in the country of origin and falling back on Cerase (1974) and Gmelch (1980) for support. For sure, this context is absolutely important, as it helps to understand how the motivations and expectations of return are matched with opportunities and realities in the home-country setting and therefore whether the return experience can be deemed a success or a failure (Cassarino, 2004, p.258). Although Cassarino makes passing reference to the unequal relationship between the migrant-sending and the migrant-receiving country, there is more to say about the way in which migration and return are embedded in global and regional core–periphery structures and relationships. In a nutshell and following Delgado Wise and Márquez Covarrubias (2009; see also King, Chapter 22), periphery-to-core migration and core-to-periphery return are elements of the reproduction of global spatial inequality and of the subservient dependency of the peripheral, less-developed countries on the economic hegemony of the global North, including the oil-rich states of the Gulf. In this historical-structural framework, returnees are those who are 'expelled' by the richer countries because they are no longer useful, for instance due to old age or sickness or during a recession when they become unemployed.

Next up on the list of theoretical frameworks for analysing return is *transnationalism*. According to Cassarino (2004, p.261), transnationalism constitutes a lens to capture and understand better the strong economic, social and cultural links between migrants' host and home countries, including their return moves. Launched by a series of interventions by Glick Schiller and her colleagues in the early 1990s (see Glick Schiller et al., 1995 for an accessible summary), the transnational paradigm attracted some of the most prominent scholars in migration studies (e.g. Faist, 2000a; Portes, 1999; Portes et al., 1999; Vertovec, 1999) but was not without its critics (notably Mitchell, 1997; Waldinger and Fitzgerald, 2004). As proposed by Glick Schiller et al. (1995, p.48), 'transmigrants' are migrants whose lives 'exhibit multiple and frequent connections across international borders and whose identities are configured in relation to more than one country'. Undoubtedly, return migration is part and parcel of transnationalism's back-and-forth system of social and economic relationships and exchanges but the surprising thing is that most of the canonical writings on transnationalism make rather scant reference to return migration. The main attempts to systematically analyse what we might call the 'transnationalism–return nexus' are by Carling and Erdal (2014) and Bilgili (Chapter 3). For instance, Bilgili points out that return migration is not just about physical return moves but also about myths, ideologies and imaginaries of return. Cassarino (2004, p.262) suggests that migrants use return visits to prepare for their more definitive return and reintegration at home, although this is only one type of link between transnational behaviour and return migration. One might then assume that, once return and reintegration take place, transnationalism ceases but, as King and Christou (2011, 2014) have shown, returnees often engage in 'reverse transnationalism' by retaining strong links back to their former host countries.

Carling and Erdal (2014, pp.2–3) write that transnationalism and return migration are, both conceptually and practically, entwined with each other in complex ways, as befits their 'nexus' relationship. To give one example: regular return visits, the preferred way of living for many established migrants, may be a precursor to and a preparation for return; or they may be a substitute for permanent return, which may be seen as problematic or impossible. Or another example: intention to return, born out of ongoing transnational links to the homeland, may not actually result in return, which is constantly deferred. Carling and Erdal also demonstrate how the transnationalism–return nexus is recursive. Thus, if migrants have strong transnational attachments that boost their intention to return, it is also likely that this intention will, in turn, accentuate their transnational practices (2014, pp.3–4).

Much of the above discussion connects the transnational view of return to the *mobilities framework*.[3] The transnational approach acknowledges that return to the country of origin is not the end of the story; the door is not closed on future migrations, either of the returnees themselves or perhaps of their returned children who may want to continue their adult lives in the country of their birth and upbringing. Meantime, periodic returns, of varying duration, are part of transnational life for many migrants and, hence, it is often more appropriate to speak of *return mobilities* (King and Christou, 2011). Return visits are a specific – but highly variegated – form of return mobility, analysed by Miah (Chapter 7), alongside the more specific case of diasporic visits for knowledge transfer (Mueller, Chapter 23).

*Social network theory* is another framework proposed by Cassarino (2004, pp.265–8) to deepen our thinking about return migration. Like the transnational approach, social networks encompass migrants and returnees who maintain strong linkages – material, personal, emotional – to both their 'home' and their 'host' countries and communities. Here the stress is on family and other social networks, which act as conduits for the decision to return, the return move itself and what happens after return. Although there is some similarity with the near-identical notions of transnational social spaces (cf. Faist, 2000b) and transnational social fields (Glick Schiller and Fouron, 1999), social networks are more dependent on links between a defined set of persons who possess the attributes (kinship, social capital, cultural and economic resources, identity etc.) necessary to be part of the given network (Cassarino, 2004, pp.266–7). In other words, networks are *relational*, made up of social actors involved in relational ramifications leading towards return and which may constitute a distinctive 'returnee identity'.

Our final framework for theorising return migration draws on Cassarino's (2004, pp.271–5) notion of *return preparedness* and on the *aspiration–ability* model proposed by Carling (2002; also Carling and Schewel, 2018). Combining these perspectives reveals the dynamism, fluidity and uncertainty of return as an evolving process rather than a simple 'event'.

Setting aside the 'forced' or 'assisted' return of refugees, failed asylum-seekers and undocumented migrants, the *preparedness* of migrants to return depends on two elements – their *willingness* to do so and their *readiness* to make the move. The distinction here is that migrants may want to return but not be ready to do so. Also critical in Cassarino's framework is the *mobilisation of resources* for return, which pertains to both tangible resources (financial capital, a place to stay etc.) and intangible resources (contacts, relationships, skills – in other words, human and social capital). Efficient resource mobilisation for return is more likely to result in a 'successful' return, one that has the potential to contribute to the development of the country and community of origin.

The aspiration–ability framework, applied by Carling (2002) to the emigration of Cape Verdeans, can easily be applied to return migration. In this scenario, return is a two-step process, not unlike the 'willingness-readiness' model of Cassarino. First, then, migrants must have the *aspiration* to return (which in forced or unplanned migration is not there); if this aspiration is not translated into action, the result is a kind of 'myth' or 'fantasy' of return (cf. Anwar, 1979; Bolognani, 2016). Aspirations to return may also differ within a family or household along gender and generational lines: typically, the first generation are more likely to want to return than their second-generation children (see Grosa, Chapter 17; but also Kılınç, Chapter 20 for a different view) and men seem more oriented to return than women (King and Lulle, Chapter 4). Second, the *ability* to return relies very much on possessing the resources to do so; hence the connection to Cassarino's (2004) framework. A somewhat analogous two-stage model is developed by Carling et al. (2015) in a large research project on the *possibilities* and *realities* of return migration.[4]

## EVOLUTION OF A GROWING FIELD

The chapters in this Handbook illustrate the rich subfield of return migration within migration studies and across several disciplines including sociology, human geography, anthropology, economics, political science and history. In this section, we explore four ways in which return migration scholarship has expanded over the past two decades. These are (i) the widening geographical range of research on return, (ii) broadening the conceptualisation of return, (iii) the increasing politicisation of return, and (iv) the post-return effects of return migration.

**Expanding Geographies of Return**

Early studies of return migration were published in a sporadic and geographically scattered way, reflecting the transatlantic and colonial heritages of early mass migrations. Pioneering books of this era were *The Western Educated Man in India* (Useem and Useem, 1955), *They Remember America: The Story of the Repatriated Greek-Americans* (Saloutos, 1956) and *Peasants No More* (Lopreato, 1967), the last of these a study of the remaking of social class in a South Italian village as a result of return migration from the United States and elsewhere.

Looking back, we see the 1960s as the 'take-off' period for return migration literature. Two main geographical arenas accounted for the bulk of the studies in this era. The first was the United States, with research on returns to Italy (Cerase, 1967, 1974; Lopreato, 1967) and Puerto Rico (Hernández Alvarez, 1967). The second was the British-Caribbean migration system, with studies on return migration to what was then known as the 'West Indies' (Davison, 1969; Patterson, 1968).

Return migration literature swelled in the 1970s, the turning-point being the oil crisis of 1973/74 when countries like West Germany and France stopped recruiting migrant workers and implemented policies to encourage return migration. The result was a plethora of studies on return to Southern European countries, some of them statistical but many of them based on detailed field-survey and ethnographic research (see, inter alia, Abadan-Unat et al., 1976; Baučić, 1972; Brettell, 1979; Kayser, 1972; King, 1977; Lianos, 1975; Rhoades, 1978, 1979). This genre of post-oil crisis research on return migration, associated with industrial restructuring and the decline of the Fordist system but also shaped by other factors such as personal and family considerations, as well as by economic growth in Southern Europe, continued into the 1980s (for examples, see King et al., 1986; Lever-Tracey, 1989; Lewis and Williams, 1986; Papademetriou, 1985; Saraceno, 1986).

The 1990s and, even more, the twenty-first century, have seen the expansion of return migration research to a global range, concomitant with the globalisation of migration – one of Castles and Miller's key trends in their *The Age of Migration* (2003, pp.7–9), alongside the acceleration, diversification, politicisation and feminisation of migration on a world scale. The Caribbean has continued to attract attention as a theatre for return (Gmelch, 1992; Potter, 2005; Potter et al., 2005; Thomas-Hope, 1999) but much of the more recent focus of research has been on Africa, both North and sub-Saharan, and is cast within a development context – what King (Chapter 22) calls the 'return–development nexus'. Highlights of this African literature include Åkesson and Baaz's (2015) edited book on return migration and African development, Ammassari's (2009) monograph on high-skilled returnees in Ghana and Côte d'Ivoire and a series of papers on Morocco (de Haas et al., 2015) and on various West African countries (Diatta and Mbow, 1999; González-Ferrer et al., 2014; Kleist, 2020; Mezger Kveder and Beauchemin, 2015; Sinatti, 2015). A fuller indication of the extent of the 'new' return literature sited in the global South is given in Chapter 22 in the Handbook.

Finally, the Central and East European (CEE) region – the 'global East' – has also seen a rise in return migration, especially since the post-2008 economic crisis as well as in the light of Brexit and the onset of the Covid-19 pandemic. White (Chapter 21) explores the changing nature of return to this region and the differentiated experience across time, space and generations of returnees. Poland has been the main focus of return to CEE countries (Anacka et al., 2013; Cieślik, 2011; Dzięglewski, 2016; Parutis, 2014), though studies are not lacking on other countries, including Romania and Latvia (Aspite-Berina et al., 2020), Lithuania (Barcevičius, 2016) and Estonia (Saar and Saar, 2020).

**Broadening the Conceptualisation and Theorisation of Return**

There has been a significant expansion in approaches to conceptualising return. Prior analysis (Bovenkerk, 1974; Cerase, 1974; Gmelch, 1980) primarily examined the return of labour migrants, including seasonal workers, plus some attention to brain drain and return and the return of retirement. Over the past twenty or so years we observe an increasing diversity of types and forms of return and this variety is fully represented in the following 23 chapters of this Handbook. Seeing return as an increasingly diversified phenomenon leads to more complex and nuanced theorisations.

First, *international student migration*, which has doubled over the past two decades, has attracted increasing scholarly attention as a key element of global mobility, including return (see Findlay et al., 2017; also Alves, Chapter 18 for an original typology of returning students). A second focus for recent research has been the return challenges facing *children* who are taken to their parental homeland within the ambit of family return migration (cf. Vathi and King, 2021). In Chapter 17, Grosa takes a child-centred approach and argues for children to be given greater voice in sharing their specific experiences and challenges of return, especially as regards educational (re)integration and youth wellbeing. Third, the return of the *adult second generation* to the country of origin of their parents is a 'migration chronotope' (King and Christou, 2010) which has seen a flourishing of research in recent years (Christou and King, 2014; Conway and Potter, 2009; Teerling, 2014; Wessendorf, 2013; see also Lee, 2018 on the return of the '1.5 generation'). Kılınç (Chapter 20) addresses the core paradox of second-generation return: how can we call it 'return' when individuals settle in a country that they were not even born and raised in? The answer, for many such 'returnees', is that they experience ontological belonging to an ancestral homeland and thus a pull to 'return' there. Post-return outcomes, however, often do not live up to expectations and disillusionment results – a generalisation found to be applicable to many experiences with other types of return migration. Fourth, *lifestyle migration*, which includes international retirement migration, has attracted a lot of scholarly attention in recent years, spearheaded by the research of Benson (see Benson, 2011; Benson and O'Reilly, 2009; Benson and Osbaldiston, 2014). However, lifestyle migrants' return migration has been overlooked; Walsh (Chapter 19) rectifies this. She demonstrates that, although lifestyle migrants have high levels of agency when they migrate, this may not be the case when they return, driven by ill-health or financial problems, leading often to a difficult reintegration process. Fifth, there has been a reconceptualisation of return migration as a *gendered process* (Kuschminder, 2017). Albeit belatedly, it is now widely recognised that gender dynamics within and beyond families play a pivotal role in return decision-making and in post-return experiences (King and Lulle, Chapter 4). Finally, there has been a '*psychosocial turn*' in the study of return and reintegration, based on an appreciation of the importance of subjective perceptions of wellbeing. Gmelch and Gmelch (1995) were among the first to stress return migrants' subjectivities. The volume edited by Vathi and King (2017) provides an overall assessment of the psychosocial dimension of return migration, arguing for a migrant-centred approach to wellbeing and mental health on return (also Vathi, Chapter 16).

Certain chapters in the Handbook, especially those in Part I, contribute to ongoing theorisations of return migration which extend the overview provided by us in an earlier section of this chapter. Bilgili (Chapter 3) sees return as 'migration, mobility and imaginary' and as an option experienced by migrants differently throughout their migration trajectory and their lifecourse. Interactions between actual return migration, various temporally defined return mobilities and imaginaries of return are analysed by Bilgili to produce a variety of (non-)return processes and outcomes. In Chapter 6, Kalir advances the theoretical notion of 'Departheid' to capture the hegemonic doctrine present in many 'so-called liberal democratic states' which 'illegalises' and racialises certain categories of migrants in order to force their return. This politicised theory of return adds considerably to our understanding of how certain types of return take place. Kalir goes on to give examples from Europe, the United States and Australia to demonstrate how the faultlines of global mobility are drawn between the North and the South, representing the protracted coloniality of power exercised often along racialised lines. Hence it is the non-white racialised 'other' from poor, ex-colonial countries who is either prevented from entering or forced to return from rich Western states. The role of race and (post-)coloniality in deportation politics is further analysed by Lemberg-Pedersen (Chapter 9), operationalising Foucauldian governmentality and Agambian biopolitics. Theorising reintegration, especially the elusive notion of 'sustainable reintegration', is advanced through the combined contributions of several chapters in the Handbook (see, especially, Marino and Lietaert, Chapter 12 and Kuschminder, Chapter 14). Kuschminder's 'reintegration strategies' framework (see also Kuschminder, 2017) highlights the heterogeneity of returnees and return migration processes. This is a framework which has not only theoretical significance but also relevance for policy-makers dealing with return migration.

Collectively, this review of new conceptualisations and theoretical perspectives on return, bolstered by cross-references to selected chapters in the Handbook, widens considerably the scholarly field of return migration studies. We stress the importance of understanding the needs and experiences of different types of return migrants across gender, age, generation, race, class, education and other intersectionalities.

**The Politicisation of Return**

There has been a clear policy turn in return migration, stemming from an increased politicisation of return over the past two decades. Part II of the Handbook is devoted to this important aspect.

Increasing returns of migrants without rights to stay have become a central policy objective of the EU. Deportations and so-called assisted voluntary return (AVR) have increased substantially since around 2000 and this has led to new policy ambitions such as 'sustainable return and reintegration' (Marino and Lietaert, Chapter 12). This is exemplified by the 2018 Global Compact for Migration wherein states commit to facilitating 'safe and dignified return … to create conducive conditions for personal safety, economic empowerment, inclusion and social cohesion in communities, in order to ensure that integration of migrants upon return to their countries of origin is sustainable'.[5] Despite the increasing prominence of such programmes, there has been a striking lack of evaluation. However, the critical academic research reviewed in this Handbook has increased significantly in recent years, examining political structures and motivations, the various actors and their agency, the experiences of migrants and human-rights aspects.

Taken together, several chapters in the Handbook make significant contributions not only to the politics and policy of different types of return, including the vexed distinction (in reality, a continuum) between voluntary and forced return (cf. Erdal and Oeppen, Chapter 5) but also to theorising returns which are not actioned by the migrants themselves and thus not 'explained' by economic and social network theories. Key terms in this array of theoretical ideas allied to forced and semi-forced migration include *deportability*, the *illegalisation* of migrants, *Deportheid* and the misnomer of *assisted voluntary return* (see De Genova, 2002, 2010; Kalir, 2019, also his Chapter 6 in this volume; Lemberg-Pedersen, Chapter 9; Lietaert, Chapter 8).

Within the 'deportation space', an important advance is made by De Genova's (2002, 2010) theory of 'deportability', linked to the establishment of a 'deportation regime'. Both De Genova and Kalir (2019) critically analyse the notion of migrant 'illegality' (no migrant, nor any person, is by nature 'illegal'); this leads on to a discussion of the 'illegalisation' of migrants (hence their deportability) which is produced by repressive state policies including bureaucratic rules (often impossible for migrants to understand or comply with), police actions and deportation practices. Making migrants 'illegal' creates enduring vulnerability, reproducing the internal borders of the nation state in everyday life (cf. Mezzadra and Neilson, 2012). Vulnerability is often paired with uncertainty and 'waiting', which are important emerging concepts in the temporal turn in migration studies, which focuses on the temporalities of migrants and migration regimes (Jacobsen et al., 2021; Mavroudi et al., 2017).

The politicisation of return also has far-reaching implications for returnees post-return. As noted above, the issue of what constitutes a 'sustainable reintegration' is politicised in that, for the countries driving the return, this means no further re-migration. A more rights-based or capabilities view would argue that a successful reintegration is more about access to choice, including the option of further mobility. The politics of return and reintegration are also, in many countries, heavily imbued with corruption (Paasche, Chapter 13). Returnees and returned refugees are often faced with the dilemma: to try to counter the corrupting structures in the society of origin or to reintegrate by 'playing the game' in order to survive.

Repatriated asylum-seekers who have had their claims rejected face particular challenges. Not only do they return to the material and social conditions which they sought to escape from but they also bear the stigma of 'failure' and may be rejected, even by their own families, who expected them to succeed abroad and to support them. In the Afghan context, Schuster and Majidi (2013) have shown that reintegration is exceptionally difficult for deportees and other forced returnees. Issues of shame have to be faced by those who return empty-handed and the situation is even worse for those who still need to repay debts incurred to fund the asylum trip, as research on forced return from Libya to Ghana has shown (see Kleist, 2017, 2020).

**Impacts and Effects of Return Migration**

The effects of return migration can be considered under many headings – social, demographic, political, cultural and, above all, economic. The term *return–development nexus*, coined by King in Chapter 22, sets a framework for examining the actual and potential developmental impacts of return migration – through, for instance, the return of skills (human capital gain and 'brain return'), the incorporation of new ideas ('return of innovation' – Cerase, 1974; 'social remittances' – Levitt, 1998) and the productive investment of accumulated savings and remittances (see Wahba, Chapter 2).

Following landmark papers by de Haas (2010, 2012) and Gamlen (2014), the relationship between (return) migration and development has been variously viewed through optimistic versus pessimistic lenses, oscillating like a pendulum swing. During the optimistic phase of growth and modernisation in the 1950s and 1960s, returnees were argued to have a positive impact on their countries of origin by bringing back capital and skills. A new phase of optimism arose during the neoliberal era of the 1990s and 2000s, when remittances, savings and entrepreneurship were seen as potential drivers of home-country development. During the intervening decades of the 1970s and 1980s, when global recession and economic restructuring sparked multiple waves of return, migrants returned to face unemployment and depression in their home countries, whilst remittances and savings were seen as 'wasted' on unproductive investments and conspicuous consumption. Gamlen (2014) then foresaw an era of neo-pessimism starting in the 2010s and based on critiques of hidden political and economic agendas and neoliberal views of migrant potentialities as 'buzz and spin'.

The overall conclusion is that, for returnees to have the potential to contribute to development, there must be advantageous conditions in the country of return; above all profitable investment opportunities free of corruption. A favourable economic climate and an open structural and cultural environment give the best chances for returnees to exercise their own capabilities and agency in promoting development-oriented activities, including knowledge transfer (Mueller, Chapter 23) and business development (Sinatti, Chapter 24). Sinatti's contribution exemplifies the multi-level approach of returnee entrepreneurship, acknowledging the distinction between 'top-down, state-driven' development objectives to foster returnee investment versus 'bottom-up, migrant-centred' initiatives. This comparison highlights differences in 'economic growth' versus 'human development' perspectives. Sinatti argues for a combined approach to return migration and development that both incorporates a critical analysis of macro-level structural conditions and acknowledges the potential for change brought by migrants and their transnational economic and social practices.

However, whilst recognising that return migrants can have a positive impact, this should not be demanded of all returnees and migrants should not be made to feel duty-bound to be agents of development – for two reasons. First, not all migrants have the human, social and financial capital required to effect development. Second, placing the responsibility for stimulating development on migrants should not be used as an excuse or a replacement policy for the lack of action from governments.

## LOOKING FORWARD: NEW IMPLICATIONS OF RETURN

The contributions in this Handbook stress the need for further research on return migration and articulate some key issues that should be considered, both for research and for policy and practice. We identify four such areas: first, the need to critically assess terminology and, in particular, to bridge several terminological dichotomies; second, the issue of inequality in return migration, as both cause and effect; third, the multiple interfaces between return and economic, social, cultural and political change; and, finally, issues pertaining to gender, age, generations and intersectionality.

### Refining Terms and Bridging Dichotomies

One of the recurrent themes in the Handbook is the need to address the shortcomings of terminology, to avoid imprecision, ambiguity, stereotypes and the use of the same term to mean two different things. The confusing word 're-migration' has already been remarked upon earlier in this chapter. For different reasons, we also reject the word 'illegal' to describe any migrant. As Kalir (Chapter 6) points out, migrants are labelled thus through state policies of categorisation and exclusion, so that migrants are 'illegalised'. 'Reintegration' is another slippery concept in the context of return migration (Kuschminder, 2017, pp.8–13; also Chapter 14 in the Handbook).

These examples open up a wider debate on the many dichotomous terms which abound in the field of (return) migration studies.[6] Resonating through the Handbook are the following dichotomous pairs of return-related terms. The most recurrent is the forced vs voluntary division, which we have already critiqued as inherently problematic with, in reality, many shades in between which descriptors such as semi-forced or semi-voluntary might be used to connote. Even the apparently simply returnee vs non-returnee (or vs non-migrant) comparison is flawed since migrant non-returnees may return at some future point and non-migrants may migrate (and then return) in the future. Analogous to this is the temporary vs permanent return binary; again, this discounts future actions – the intending temporary returnee may end up staying permanently in the home country and the intending permanent returnee may up sticks and move again.

Another important dichotomy rooted in return migration, which comes periodically to the fore in this Handbook, is the politicised framing of returnees as 'deserving' or 'undeserving'. It appears that there is one contingent of 'virtuous' returnees who are expected to contribute something to their origin country or who are classed as deserving of help through accepting a return assistance package. On the other hand, there are those deemed undeserving and who struggle through their return process as somehow 'unworthy' and 'unaccepted'. There is a need for further reflection on this dichotomy. How can return migration research be inclusive within this polarisation? What does this particular dichotomy mean for typologies of return? How should our research engage with and, where necessary, challenge this and other politicised dichotomies?

Our final dichotomy is this: are returnees successes or failures? Put another way, are they positively or negatively selected from the stock of migrants from which they are drawn? In the Handbook, this issue is analysed by Wahba (Chapter 2) and King (Chapter 22). The answer is far from straightforward. Empirical evidence exists for both positive and negative return selection, depending on the economic and geographical context and also on the distribution of incomes between and within countries. Wahba quotes research (notably by Borjas and Bratsberg, 1996) that suggests that the type of selection in return migration effectively reinforces the selectivity of the initial migration flow. This means that, if the initial migrants were positively selected (i.e. above-average in terms of their education and skills), return migrants will be the lesser-skilled because those who stay in the country are the most able and highly rewarded income-wise. The migrant origin country thus suffers a 'double whammy': it loses its higher-skilled migrants but then gets back a negative selection of these migrants. Conversely, if the initial migrants were negatively selected (representing a bias towards below-average education and skills), returnees are likely to be the more highly skilled amongst this group. A more qualitative overview, partially consistent with the above finding, is given in the classic paper on return migration by Gmelch (1980, pp.141–2). According to evidence reviewed by him, returnees are neither the most successful, since that success is best experienced and advanced in the host country, nor abject failures, since failed migrants are reluctant to return to the shame that this entails and want to stay abroad until at least some measure of success in their migration project is achieved.

**New Implications of Return**

Moving on from the dichotomies discussed above, we now look at some wider implications of return migration within changing global processes. First is the complex relationship between *return migration and inequality*. Taking return out of the equation for a moment, the relationship between migration and inequality is subject to contradictory theoretical interpretations. According to neoclassical equilibrium theory, migration takes place from low-wage, high-unemployment regions and countries to high-wage, low-unemployment destinations. The transfer of surplus labour recalibrates the supply and demand of labour in each location, leading to wage equalisation, when migration stops. However, according to the Marxist-inspired historical-structural model, migration serves only to reproduce the structural inequality between poor, peripheral countries and regions – which are reservoirs of surplus labour – and the destination 'core' regions and countries whose growth is further enhanced by supplies of cheap labour (King, 2018). Hence migration drives and exacerbates spatial and social inequality.

How is return factored into these relationships? As is demonstrated in several chapters in the Handbook, certain forms of return migration create systemic vulnerabilities for returnees, thereby exacerbating global and local inequalities. Many deportees and assisted voluntary returnees fit this mould. Schuster and Majidi's (2013) research on deportees in Afghanistan shows how they are regarded as 'contaminated' and are ostracised by the society of return, driving them into isolation and further situations of vulnerability. Lemberg-Pedersen (Chapter 9) stresses the globalising nature of the 'deportation turn', reflected in empirical research in several countries worldwide, including Ethiopia (Kuschminder et al., 2021), Afghanistan (Schuster and Majidi, 2013), Jamaica (Miller, 2008) and the Dominican Republic (Ceciliano-Navarro and Golash-Boza, 2021). In all these studies, returnees are frequently found to be worse off post-return, due to economic failure, sudden forced return or other circumstances. As a result, they are propelled into vulnerability, thereby increasing inequalities and posing further challenges for poverty eradication and the achievement of sustainable development goals. Very different is the experience of retired lifestyle migrants who, at some stage, may be forced to return to their home countries in distressed circumstances following illness, the loss of a partner or financial difficulties (Walsh, Chapter 19).

In other theoretical and empirical scenarios, return migration can have a more socially equalising function. The NELM framework foresees migrants escaping poverty and building up a profile of remittances and savings abroad which can then help to boost the family's economic and social wellbeing upon return. Poverty in the home country – or at least in the regions and communities affected by this migration-and-return process – is therefore reduced. However, in a different subplot to this scenario, other outcomes may result. For instance, when some people are too poor to migrate (since there are inevitable costs attached to migration – getting a passport, paying for travel etc.) and only the better-off can afford to leave, then migration exacerbates inequality, especially when the departing migrants are able to return better-off than when they left.

The second theme which we signal for further research is the role that return migration can play in advancing *cultural globalisation and development*. Bilgili (Chapter 3) demonstrates the important connections between return migration and transnationalism, including the flow of social remittances (new ideas and behaviours; Levitt, 1998) and knowledge transfer (Mueller, Chapter 23). Cultural globalisation can be an important stimulus towards recognising human rights, women's rights and the acceptance of other cultures, religions and lifestyles. This can occur across multiple types of return – labour migrants, brain return, returning students, second-generation return and lifestyle return. Moreover, it should not be assumed that this is a purely North-to-South return flow of cultural change; it has the potential to occur in all of the global 'compass' migrations – North–North, South–South and South–North. Likewise, it is not restricted to any temporal mode of return but can occur across all return mobility types – permanent, temporary, transnational visits, even virtual return (Skype calls, other social media etc.).

However, the spread of new values, ideas and behaviours through return migration is not automatic and is subject to certain conditions, which include the ability of migrants to absorb some elements of cultural change in the host country and to transmit such change to their home society. Returnees should be able to translate international and global ideas into locally meaningful concepts that can be understood and accepted (see Kuschminder, Chapter 14).

The final theme we wish to signpost for future research springs out of Chapter 4 on gendering return migration, where King and Lulle point to the need for developing an intersectional approach to combinations of socio-demographic variables – gender, age, generation, class, race, health status, education/skill, disability and sexual orientation – which shape the return migration experience. Whilst some of these variables are dealt with in individual chapters (King and Lulle, Chapter 4, on gender; Bolzman, Chapter 15, on retirement migration; Grosa, Chapter 17, on returning children; Alves, Chapter 18, on returning university students; Walsh, Chapter 19, on the later-life return of lifestyle migrants; Kılınç, Chapter 20, on second-generation return), what is missing is the intersectionality of these and other returnee characteristics. Amelina and Lutz (2019) have recently pushed for an intersectional approach to transnational migration; this optic now needs to be turned more specifically towards return migration as an embodied and complex experience.

The intersectionally related return-migrant characteristics listed above are felt and experienced by the returnees themselves as part of their evolving personal and group identity, but are also part of how they are perceived by the society of return. In research terms, this is a work still in progress but there are several indications that this work is moving in interesting directions. For instance, Potter and Phillips (2006) describe returnees from Britain to Barbados as 'both black and symbolically white', a hybrid ethno-racial returnee identity which refers not to their skin colour but to acquired cultural attributes such as their 'British' accents, reputation for professionalism and punctuality, and enhanced social status. Another example: issues of sexual identity are brought out as part of Christou and King's (2014) research on second-generation Greek-American and Greek-German 'return' to Greece. Specifically, they highlight the case of gay men who, perhaps counter-intuitively, have relocated to Athens to escape the homophobia of the more closed ethnic 'Greektown' communities of the host societies where they were brought up (2014, pp.80–1, 156–7).

## CONCLUSION: A 'RETURN TURN'?

Recent years have seen increased attention paid to return migration, so that we can detect a 'return turn' in literature and policy. As Åkesson and Baaz (2015, p.5) have pointed out in the context of return to Africa, this policy attention is politically charged: the issue of return reflects the management and control of migration by governments and their anti-immigration electorates. Policies worldwide encourage migrants to return to their home countries: this has been especially the case in Trump's USA and in Europe in the wake of the so-called refugee crisis of 2015–16.

Policy and politics apart and thanks to the combined research efforts of anthropologists, sociologists and human geographers, 'a comparative ethnography of return has taken shape' (Pauli, 2021, p.95). Drawing on many hundreds of studies, this Handbook has attempted to portray the richness and diversity of this comparative ethnography across the globe. However, it has to be acknowledged that most studies of return migration are not comparative but based on single case studies (Carling, 2004; Kuschminder, 2017, p.8). The work of synthesis and theorisation in which we and our authors have engaged is built both from the bottom up – by detailed comparison of case studies – and from top-down a priori theorisations. Both approaches are amply evidenced in the Handbook.

Many chapters warn against deploying sedentary, essentialised and teleological assumptions when discussing return. In short, there is no return to the situation as it once was: the place has changed, along with the people who live there; and so have the migrants themselves. Everyone is older than before and many have moved on with their lives. The challenges of reintegration are therefore considerable and perhaps greater than the obstacles which migrants faced in adapting to the host society. Yet, return migration does not necessarily close the migration cycle – far from it. Pauli (2021, p.104) writes that return is always a new beginning; a special kind of beginning 'permeated with memories, hopes, desires, anxieties and longings'. These memories and hopes are both about what has been left behind and in anticipation of the future.

# NOTES

1. As part of the PREMIG project ('Possibilities and Realities of Return Migration') based at the Peace Research Institute Oslo (PRIO), Carling et al. (2011) surveyed more than 1,100 publications on return migration, the vast majority of them journal articles. Whilst acknowledging gaps and omissions, the compilers justifiably claim that their literature survey 'constitute[s] a reasonable representation of the literature on return migration' (2011, p.4). Literature on 'the return decision' and on 'reintegration post-return' constitutes the bulk of the items referenced. Now ten years out of date, this remarkable survey has not been repeated: one can only guess the scale of growth in the return migration literature since then. If we take literally the statement by Carling et al. (2011, p.4) that 'a handful of publications [on return migration] are coming out every week', we might estimate the addition of at least another thousand items by 2021.
2. 'Re-migration' is confusing because it has been used in the literature to mean different types of movement. Especially those writing in German or Dutch, who also transpose this term when writing in English (e.g. Davids and van Houte, 2008; Unger, 1981), use re-migration to mean return migration. For others, re-migration means re-migration, that is, a new migration following an earlier migration episode. The chapters in this Handbook avoid the word re-migration and carefully distinguish between return migration and re-migration (or re-emigration). Actually, the story does not end there since some return migrants who re-migrate 'return' to their former host country. As Pauli (2021, p.97) writes, 'the returnee returns again, away from the country of origin and back to the host country'. White (2014; also Chapter 21 in this volume) calls this 'double return migration'; an alternative term would be 're-return' but, at this stage, the directionality of the move becomes unclear.
3. The mobilities framework was not mentioned by Cassarino (2004), largely because its main protagonists published slightly later (see Cresswell, 2006; Urry, 2007). Having said that, 'return' mobilities did not feature prominently in the writings of the mobilities school.
4. This was the PREMIG project, whose final report (Carling et al., 2015) and annotated bibliography (Carling et al., 2011) are useful resources for scholars of return migration.
5. See Global Compact for Safe, Orderly and Regular Migration, 2018. Available from: Global Compact for Safe, Orderly and Regular Migration to Be Adopted at High-Level Conference in Marrakech, Morocco, 10–11 December | Meetings Coverage and Press Releases (un.org).
6. In earlier writings, Cohen (1995, pp.5–7) called them 'migration dyads', whilst King (2002, pp.91–4) used the term 'migration binaries'. Cohen nominated six dyads: internal vs international migration, forced vs free migration, settler vs labour migration, temporary vs permanent migration, legal vs illegal migration and planned vs flight migration. King discussed these further and added two more: the act of migration and its subsequent effects; and the notion of whether migration should be regarded as 'exceptional' or 'the norm' in societal terms. Many of these binaries can be applied to return migration but here, too, they need to be questioned, blurred and deconstructed.

# REFERENCES

Abadan-Unat, N., Keleş, R., Penninx, R., van Renselaar, H., van Velsen, L. and Yenisey, L. (1976) *Migration and Development. A Study of the Effects of International Labour Migration on Boğazliyan District*, Ankara: Ajans-Turk Press.

Åkesson, L. and Baaz, M.E. (eds) (2015) *Africa's Return Migrants: The New Developers?*, London: Zed Books.

Amelina, A. and Lutz, H. (2019) *Gender and Migration: Transnational and Intersectional Prospects*, London: Routledge.

Ammassari, S. (2009) *Migration and Development: Factoring Return into the Equation*, Newcastle-upon-Tyne: Cambridge Scholars Publishing.

Anacka, M., Matejko, E. and Nestorowicz, J. (2013) 'Ready to move: liquid return to Poland' in B. Glorius, I. Grabowska-Lusinska and A. Kuvik (eds), *Mobility in Transition: Migration Patterns after EU Enlargement*, Amsterdam: Amsterdam University Press, pp. 277–308.

Anghel, R.G., Fauser, M. and Boccagni, P. (eds) (2019) *Transnational Return and Social Change: Hierarchies, Identities and Ideas*, London: Anthem Press.

Anwar, M. (1979) *The Myth of Return: Pakistanis in Britain*, London: Heinemann.

Aspite-Berina, E., Manea, M.-E. and Berzins, M. (2020) 'The ambiguity of return migration: prolonged crisis and uncertainty in the life strategies of young Romanian and Latvian returnees', *International Migration*, **58** (1), 61–75.

Azose, J.J. and Raftery, A.E. (2019) 'Estimates of emigration, return migration, and transit migration between all pairs of countries', *PNAS*, **116** (1), 116–22.

Barcevičius, E. (2016) 'How successful are highly qualified return migrants in the Lithuanian labour market?', *International Migration*, **54** (3), 35–47.

Bartram, D., Poros, M.V. and Monforte, P. (2014) *Key Concepts in Migration*, London: Sage.

Battistella, G. (2018) *Return Migration: A Conceptual and Policy Framework*, Rome: Scalabrini Migration Center.

Baučić, I. (1972) *The Effects of Emigration from Yugoslavia and the Problems of Returning Emigrant Workers*, The Hague: Nijhoff.

Benson, M. (2011) *The British in Rural France: Lifestyle Migration and the Quest for a Better Way of Life*, Manchester: Manchester University Press.

Benson, M. and O'Reilly, K. (eds) (2009) *Lifestyle Migration: Expectations, Aspirations and Experiences*, Farnham: Ashgate.

Benson, M. and Osbaldiston, N. (eds) (2014) *Understanding Lifestyle Migration: Theoretical Approaches to Migration and the Quest for a Better Way of Life*, Basingstoke: Palgrave Macmillan.

Bolognani, M. (2016) 'From myth of return to return fantasy: a psychosocial interpretation of return imaginaries', *Identities*, **23** (2), 193–209.

Borjas, G. and Bratsberg, B. (1996) 'Who leaves? The outmigration of the foreign-born', *Review of Economics and Statistics*, **78** (1), 165–76.

Bovenkerk, F. (1974) *The Sociology of Return Migration: A Bibliographic Essay*, The Hague: Nijhoff.

Brettell, C.B. (1979) 'Emigrar para voltar: a Portuguese ideology of return migration', *Papers in Anthropology*, **20** (1), 1–20.

Carling, J. (2002) 'Migration in the age of involuntary immobility: theoretical reflections and Cape Verdean experiences', *Journal of Ethnic and Migration Studies*, **28** (1), 5–42.

Carling, J. (2004) 'Emigration, return and development in Cape Verde: the impact of closing borders', *Population, Space and Place*, **10** (2), 113–32.

Carling, J. and Erdal, M.B. (2014) 'Return migration and transnationalism: how are the two connected?', *International Migration*, **52** (6), 2–12.

Carling, J. and Schewel, K. (2018) 'Revisiting aspiration and ability in international migration', *Journal of Ethnic and Migration Studies*, **44** (6), 945–63.

Carling, J., Mortensen, E.B. and Wu, J. (2011) *A Systematic Bibliography on Return Migration*, Oslo: PRIO.

Carling, J., Bolognani, M., Erdal, M.B., Ezzati, R.T., Oeppen, C., Paasche, E., Pettersen, S.V. and Sagmo, T.H. (2015) *Possibilities and Realities of Return Migration*, Oslo: PRIO.

Cassarino, J.-P. (2004) 'Theorising return migration: the conceptual approach to return migrants revisited', *International Journal on Multicultural Societies*, **6** (2), 253–79.

Castles, S. and Miller, M.J. (2003) *The Age of Migration: International Population Movements in the Modern World*, Basingstoke: Palgrave Macmillan (3rd edition).

Ceciliano-Navarro, Y. and Golash-Boza, T. (2021) 'Social, human and positive psychological capital in the labour market re-integration of people deported to the Dominican Republic', *International Migration*, **59** (2), 221–38.

Ceiślik, A. (2011) 'Where do you prefer to work? How the work environment influences return migration decisions from the United Kingdom to Poland', *Journal of Ethnic and Migration Studies*, **37** (9), 1367–83.

Cerase, F.P. (1967) 'A study of Italian returning migrants from the United States', *International Migration Review*, **1** (3), 67–74.

Cerase, F.P. (1974) 'Migration and social change, expectations and reality: a study of return migration from the United States to Italy', *International Migration Review*, **8** (2), 245–62.

Christou, A. and King, R. (2014) *Counter-Diaspora: The Greek Second Generation Returns 'Home'*, Cambridge MA: Harvard University Press.

Cohen, J.H. and Sirkeci, I. (2011) *Cultures of Migration: The Global Nature of Contemporary Mobility*, Austin TX: University of Texas Press.

Cohen, R. (ed.) (1995) *The Cambridge Survey of World Migration*, Cambridge: Cambridge University Press.

Conway, D. and Potter, R.B. (eds) (2009) *Return Migration of the Next Generations: 21st Century Transnational Mobility*, Farnham: Ashgate.

Conway, D., Potter, R.B. and Phillips, J. (2009) 'The experience of return: Caribbean return migrants' in R.B. Potter, D. Conway and J. Phillips (eds), *The Experience of Return Migration: Caribbean Perspectives*, Aldershot: Ashgate, pp. 1–25.

Cresswell, T. (2006) *On The Move: Mobility in the Modern Western World*, New York: Routledge.

Davids, T. and van Houte, M. (2008) 'Remigration, development and mixed embeddedness: an agenda for qualitative research?', *International Journal on Multicultural Societies*, **10** (2), 169–193.

Davison, B. (1969) 'No place back home: a study of Jamaicans returning to Kingston', *Race and Class*, **9** (4), 499–509.

De Genova, N. (2002) 'Migrant "illegality" and deportability in everyday life', *Annual Review of Anthropology*, **31**, 419–47.

De Genova, N. (2010) 'The deportation regime: sovereignty, space and the freedom of movement' in N. Peutz and N. De Genova (eds), *The Deportation Regime*, Durham NC: Duke University Press, pp. 33–68.

de Haas, H. (2010) 'Migration and development: a theoretical perspective', *International Migration Review*, **44** (1), 227–64.

de Haas, H. (2012) 'The migration and development pendulum: a critical review on research and policy', *International Migration*, **50** (3), 8–25.

de Haas, H., Fokkema, T. and Fihri, M.F. (2015) 'Return migration as failure or success? The determinants of return migration intentions among Moroccan migrants in Europe', *Journal of International Migration and Integration*, **16** (2), 415–29.

de Haas, H., Castles, S. and Miller, M.J. (2020) *The Age of Migration: International Population Movements in the Modern World*, London: Red Globe Press (6th edition).

de Lima, P. (2017) *International Migration: The Wellbeing of Migrants*, Edinburgh: Dunedin Press.

Delgado Wise, R. and Márquez Covarrubias, H. (2009) 'Understanding the relationship between migration and development: toward a new theoretical approach', *Social Analysis*, **53** (3), 85–105.

Diatta, M.A. and Mbow, N. (1999) 'Releasing the development potential of return migration: the case of Senegal', *International Migration*, **37** (1), 243–66.

Dzięglewski, M. (2016) 'Return migration and social change in Poland: "closures" to migrants' non-economic transfers', *Central and Eastern European Migration Review*, **5** (2), 167–88.

Erdal, M.B. (2017) 'Timespaces of return migration: the interplay of everyday practices and imaginaries of return in transnational social fields' in E. Mavroudi, B. Page and A. Christou (eds), *Timespace and International Migration*, Cheltenham, UK and Northampton, MA, USA: Edward Elgar Publishing, pp. 104–18.

Faist, T. (2000a) 'Transnationalism in international migration: implications for the study of citizenship and culture', *Ethnic and Racial Studies*, **23** (2), 189–222.

Faist, T. (2000b) *The Volume and Dynamics of International Migration and Transnational Social Spaces*, Oxford: Clarendon Press.

Findlay, A., Prezeras, L., McCollum, D. and Packwood, H. (2017) '"It was always in the plan": international study as "learning to migrate"', *Area*, **49** (2), 192–9.

Gamlen, A. (2014) 'The new migration-and-development pessimism', *Progress in Human Geography*, **38** (4), 581–97.

Ghosh, B. (ed.) (2000) *Return Migration: Journey of Hope or Despair?*, Geneva: UN and IOM.

Glick Schiller, N. and Fouron, G. (1999) 'Terrains of blood and nation: Haitian transnational social fields', *Ethnic and Racial Studies*, **22** (2), 340–66.

Glick Schiller, N., Basch, L. and Blanc-Szanton, C. (1995) 'From immigrant to transmigrant: theorizing transnational migration', *Anthropology Quarterly*, **68** (1), 48–63.

Gmelch, G. (1980) 'Return migration', *Annual Review of Anthropology*, **9**, 135–59.

Gmelch, G. (1992) *Double Passage: The Lives of Caribbean Migrants Abroad and Back Home*, Ann Arbor: University of Michigan Press.

Gmelch, G. and Gmelch, S.B. (1995) 'Gender and migration: the readjustment of women migrants in Barbados, Ireland and Newfoundland', *Human Organization*, **54** (4), 470–3.

González-Ferrer, A., Baizan, P., Beauchemin, C., Kraus, E., Schoumaker, B. and Black, R. (2014) 'Distance, transnational arrangements and return decisions of Senegalese, Ghanaian and Congolese migrants', *International Migration Review*, **37** (6), 666–99.

Harper, M. (ed.) (2005) *Emigrant Homecomings: The Return Movement of Emigrants, 1600–2000*, Manchester: Manchester University Press.

Hernández Alvarez, J. (1967) *Return Migration to Puerto Rico*, Berkeley CA: University of California Institute of International Studies.

Jacobsen, C., Karlsen, M. and Khosravi, S. (2021) *Waiting and the Temporalities of Irregular Migation*, London: Routledge.

Kalir, B. (2019) 'Departheid: the draconian governance of illegalized migrants in western states', *Conflict and Society*, **5** (1), 19–40.

Kayser, B. (1972) *Cyclically Determined Homeward Flows of Migrant Workers*, Paris: OECD.

King, R. (1977) 'Problems of return migration: a case study of Italians returning from Britain', *Tijdschrift voor Economische en Sociale Geografie*, **68** (4), 241–6.

King, R. (ed.) (1986a) *Return Migration and Regional Economic Problems*, London: Croom Helm.

King, R. (1986b) 'Return migration and regional economic development: an overview' in R. King (ed.), *Return Migration and Regional Economic Problems*, London: Croom Helm, pp. 1–37.

King, R. (2000) 'Generalizations from the history of return migration' in B. Ghosh (ed.), *Return Migration: Journey of Hope or Despair?*, Geneva: UN and IOM, pp. 7–55.

King, R. (2002) 'Towards a new map of migration', *International Journal of Population Geography*, **8** (2), 89–106.

King, R. (2018) 'Is migration a form of development aid given by poor to rich countries?', *Journal of Intercultural Studies*, **39** (2), 114–28.

King, R. and Christou, A. (2010) 'Cultural geographies of counter-diasporic migration: perspectives from the study of second-generation "returnees" to Greece', *Population, Space and Place*, **16** (2), 103–19.

King, R. and Christou, A. (2011) 'Of counter-diaspora and reverse transnationalism: "return" mobilities to and from the ancestral homeland', *Mobilities*, **6** (4), 451–66.

King, R. and Christou, A. (2014) 'Second-generation "return" to Greece: new dynamics of transnationalism and integration', *International Migration*, **52** (6), 85–99.

King, R., Strachan, A.J. and Mortimer, J. (1984) 'Return migration and tertiary development: a Calabrian case-study', *Anthropological Quarterly*, **57** (3), 112–24.

King, R., Strachan, A.J. and Mortimer, J. (1985) 'The urban dimension of European return migration: the case of Bari, southern Italy', *Urban Studies*, **22** (3), 219–35.

King, R., Strachan, A.J. and Mortimer, J. (1986) 'Gastarbeiter go home: return migration and economic change in the Italian Mezzogiorno' in R. King (ed.), *Return Migration and Regional Economic Problems*, London: Croom Helm, pp. 38–68.

Kleist, N. (2017) 'Disrupted migration projects: the moral economy of forced return from Libya to Ghana', *Africa*, **87** (2), 322–42.

Kleist, N. (2020) 'Trajectories of involuntary return to Ghana: forced relocation processes and post-return life', *Geoforum*, **116**, 272–81.

Kuschminder, K. (2017) *Reintegration Strategies: Conceptualizing How Return Migrants Reintegrate*, Cham: Palgrave Macmillan.

Kuschminder, K., Ogahara, Z. and Rajabzadeh, I. (2021) 'Evaluations of return within a mass deportation: Ethiopians' experiences of return after expulsion from Saudi Arabia', *International Migration*, **59** (2), 167–85.

Lee, J.Y. (2018) *Transnational Return Migration of 1.5 Generation Korean New Zealanders: A Quest for Home*, Lanham MD: Lexington Books.

Lever-Tracey, C. (1989) 'Return migration to Malta: neither failed immigrants nor successful guestworkers', *Australia and New Zealand Journal of Sociology*, **25** (3), 428–50.

Levitt, P. (1998) 'Social remittances: migration driven local-level forms of cultural diffusion', *International Migration Review*, **32** (4), 926–48.

Lewis, J. and Williams, A. (1986) 'The economic impact of return migration in central Portugal' in R. King (ed.), *Return Migration and Regional Economic Problems*, London: Croom Helm, pp. 100–28.

Lianos, T.P. (1975) 'Flows of Greek outmigration and return migration', *International Migration*, **13** (3), 119–33.

Linhard, T. and Parsons, T.H. (eds) (2019) *Mapping Migration, Identity and Space*, Cham: Palgrave Macmillan.

Long, L.D. and Oxfeld, E. (eds) (2004) *Coming Home? Refugees, Migrants and Those Who Stayed Behind*, Philadelphia: University of Pennsylvania Press.

Lopreato, J. (1967) *Peasants No More*, San Francisco: Chandler.

Markowitz, F. and Stefansson, A.H. (eds) (2004) *Homecomings: Unsettling Paths of Return*, Lanham MD: Lexington Books.

Martiniello, M. and Rath, J. (eds) (2012) *An Introduction to International Migration Studies: European Perspectives*, Amsterdam: Amsterdam University Press.

Mavroudi, E. and Nagel, C. (2016) *Global Migration: Patterns, Processes and Policies*, London: Routledge.

Mavroudi, E., Page, B. and Christou, A. (eds) (2017) *Timespace and International Migration*, Cheltenham, UK and Northampton, MA, USA: Edward Elgar Publishing.

Mezger Kveder, C. and Beauchemin, C. (2015) 'The role of international migration experience for investment at home: direct, indirect and equalising effects in Senegal', *Population, Space and Place*, **21** (6), 535–52.

Mezzadra, S. and Neilson, B. (2012) 'Borderscapes of differential inclusion: subjectivity and struggles on the threshold of justice's success' in E. Balibar, S. Mezzadra and R. Samaddar (eds), *The Borders of Justice*, Philadelphia: Temple University Press, pp. 181–204.

Miller, O.A. (2008) *Migration Can Fall Apart: Life Stories from Voluntary and Deportee Return Migrants*, Lanham MD: University Press of America.

Mitchell, K. (1997) 'Transnational discourse: bringing geography back in', *Antipode*, **29** (2), 101–14.

Nadler, R., Kovács, Z., Glorius, B. and Lang, T. (eds) (2016) *Return Migration and Regional Development: Mobility Against the Stream*, London: Palgrave Macmillan.

Papademetriou, D.G. (1985) 'Emigration and return in the Mediterranean littoral', *Comparative Politics*, **18** (1), 21–39.

Parutis, V. (2014) 'Returning "home": East European migrants' discourses of return', *International Migration*, **52** (5), 159–77.

Patterson, H.O. (1968) 'West Indian migrants returning home: some observations', *Race and Class*, **10** (1), 69–77.

Pauli, J. (2021) 'Return migration' in J.H. Cohen and I. Sirkeci (eds), *Handbook of Culture and Migration*, Cheltenham, UK and Northampton, MA, USA: Edward Elgar Publishing, pp. 95–109.

Portes, A. (1999) 'Towards a new world – the origins and effects of transnational activities', *Ethnic and Racial Studies*, **22** (2), 463–77.

Portes, A., Guarnizo, L.E. and Landolt, P. (1999) 'The study of transnationalism: pitfalls and promise of an emergent research field', *Ethnic and Racial Studies*, **22** (2), 217–37.

Potter, R.B. (2005) '"Young, gifted and back": second-generation transnational return migration to the Caribbean', *Progress in Development Studies*, **5** (3), 213–36.

Potter, R.B. and Phillips, J. (2006) 'Both black and symbolically white: the "Bajan-Brit" return migrant as a post-colonial hybrid', *Ethnic and Racial Studies*, **29** (5), 901–27.

Potter, R.B., Conway, D. and Phillips, J. (eds) (2005) *The Experience of Return Migration: Caribbean Perspectives*, Aldershot: Ashgate.

Rhoades, R.E. (1978) 'Intra-European return migration and rural development: lessons from the Spanish case', *Human Organization*, **37** (2), 136–47.

Rhoades, R.E. (1979) 'From caves to main street: return migration and the transformation of a Spanish village', *Papers in Anthropology*, **20** (1), 57–74.

Saar, M. and Saar, E. (2020) 'Can the concept of lifestyle migration be applied to return migration? The case of Estonians in the UK', *International Migration*, **58** (2), 52–65.

Saloutos, T. (1956) *They Remember America: The Story of the Repatriated Greek-Americans*, Berkeley CA: University of California Press.

Samers, M. and Collyer, M. (2017) *Migration*, London: Routledge (2nd edition).

Saraceno, E. (1986) 'The occupational resettlement of returning migrants and regional development: the case of Friuli-Venezia Giulia, Italy' in R. King (ed.), *Return Migration and Regional Economic Problems*, London: Croom Helm, pp. 69–78.

Schuster, L. and Majidi, N. (2013) 'What happens post-deportation? The experience of deported Afghans', *Migration Studies*, **1** (2), 221–40.

Sinatti, G. (2015) 'Return migration as a win–win–win scenario? Visions of return amongst Senegalese migrants, the state of origin and receiving countries', *Ethnic and Racial Studies*, **38** (2), 275–91.

Stark, O. (1991) *The Migration of Labour*, Oxford: Blackwell.

Taylor, J.E. (1999) 'The new economics of labour migration and the role of remittances in the migration process', *International Migration*, **37** (1), 63–86.

Teerling, J. (2014) *The 'Return' of British-Born Cypriots to Cyprus: A Narrative Ethnography*, Brighton: Sussex Academic Press.

Thomas-Hope, E. (1999) 'Return migration to Jamaica and its development potential', *International Migration*, **37** (1), 183–207.

Todaro, M.P. (1969) 'A model of labor migration and urban unemployment in less developed countries', *American Economic Review*, **59** (1), 138–48.

Tsuda, T. (ed.) (2009) *Diasporic Homecomings: Ethnic Return Migration in Comparative Perspective*, Stanford CA: Stanford University Press.

Unger, K. (1981) 'Greek emigration to and return from West Germany', *Ekistics*, **48** (290), 369–74.

Urry, J. (2007) *Mobilities*, Cambridge: Polity.

Useem, J. and Useem, R.H. (1955) *The Western Educated Man in India*, New York: Dryden Press.

Vathi, Z. and King, R. (eds) (2017) *Return Migration and Psychosocial Wellbeing: Discourses, Policy-Making and Outcomes for Migrants and Their Families*, Abingdon: Routledge.

Vathi, Z. and King, R. (2021) 'Memory, place and agency: transnational mirroring of otherness among young Albanian returnees', *Children's Geographies*, **19** (2), 197–209.

Vertovec, S. (1999) 'Conceiving and researching transnationalism', *Ethnic and Racial Studies*, **22** (2), 447–62.

Waldinger, R. and Fitzgerald, D. (2004) 'Transnationalism in question', *American Journal of Sociology*, **109** (5), 1177–95.

Wessendorf, S. (2013) *Second-Generation Transnationalism and Roots Migration: Cross-Border Lives*, Farnham: Ashgate.

White, A. (2014) 'Double return migration: failed returns to Poland leading to settlement abroad and new transnational strategies', *International Migration*, **52** (6), 72–84.

# PART I

# THEORISING AND CONCEPTUALISING RETURN MIGRATION

# 2. The economics of return migration
*Jackline Wahba*

## INTRODUCTION

Not all international migration moves are permanent as millions of migrants return to their country of origin every year. However, most return migration is not recorded since statistics on outflows from host countries are not regularly and systematically collected. Moreover, not all outflows are necessarily return to the country of origin but could be migration to a third country. At the same time, records on return migrants conducted in the country of origin tend to have many shortcomings as they are seldom regular and representative of all return migrants. Thus, the statistics on the size of return migration are far from capturing the full extent of the flows and stocks of return migrants. Recent estimates suggest that return migration could have been about 26–31 per cent of all global movements between 2010 and 2015, highlighting its significance (Azose and Raftery, 2019).

Although in some policy circles, return migration is more about 'repatriation' and 'assisted returns', indeed the academic economic literature is more concerned about planned return which is the most prevalent pattern of return – that is, migrants choosing to return to their country of origin on their own accord because they planned to migrate temporarily all along or due to a change in circumstances that resulted in them changing their initial migration plans. The economic literature frames the return migration choice as a decision individuals make as part of an optimal strategy that maximises their lifetime utility. Individuals decide whether to migrate and/or return based on the expected costs and benefits over the life cycle. Hence, this chapter aims to provide a review of the economic literature on the determinants of return migration, and the consequences of return for the returnee and the country of origin. It focuses on two main questions from an economic perspective: Why do immigrants return to their country of origin? What are the implications of return migration? It also highlights the empirical challenges in studying return migration and the gaps in the existing economic literature.

The chapter is structured as follows. The next section discusses the determinants of return migration, both from theoretical and empirical perspectives. The succeeding one reviews the main consequences of return migration for both the host and home countries. The final section concludes by summarising the main findings of the economic literature on return migration and highlighting gaps for future research.

## REASONS FOR RETURN MIGRATION

### Theoretical Literature

Return migration has typically been viewed as a puzzle by economists who argue the prime determinant of international migration being the wage differential between origin and destination. Migrants move to destinations where wages are higher, and thus moving back to where wages are lower might seem counterintuitive. As a result, several theoretical propositions have been put forward to explain return migration as an optimal strategy. Within this theoretical framework, temporary migration is modelled as a planned move to maximise utility over the life cycle. People migrate for a period to accumulate resources for future consumption and investment later when they return to their country of origin. Several different theoretical reasons have been put forward to explain the reasons behind return migration, which are listed below.

- *Preference for consumption in the home country.* Return migration might be driven by higher utility from consumption in the home country; that is, migrants prefer consumption in their home country to consumption overseas. Migrants experience a marginal cost from being overseas which is greater than the decreasing marginal utility of overseas earnings; see for example Djajic and Milbourne (1988) and Stark et al. (1997).
- *High purchasing power in the home country.* Return migration might also be motivated by lower prices in the country of origin when the host country's currency can have a higher purchasing power than that of the host country. Thus, migrants can increase their lifelong consumption if they save while overseas and then return to consume in their country of origin where prices are cheaper.
- *Target savings.* One of the main reasons behind temporary migration is the accumulation of savings. Migrants move abroad temporarily to save in order to ease credit constraints. Migrants use their savings for consumption, and investment later when they return; see for example, Dustmann and Kirchkamp (2002) and Mesnard (2004). Hence, migrants would stay overseas until the marginal utility cost of overseas work is equal to the marginal benefit from higher savings overseas (and higher lifetime consumption).
- *Accumulation of skills.* Another determinant of temporary migration is skill acquisition. Individuals move in order to acquire skills overseas that are well rewarded in the home country. Hence, people might move overseas for a period to accumulate human capital that leads to higher productivity (higher wages) on return, for example, Dustmann et al. (2011).
- *Shocks.* Return migration might also be a response to failure to achieve the planned earnings and savings or due to experiencing worse than expected outcomes. Borjas and Bratsberg (1996) show that erroneous information and uncertainty about the economic conditions in the host country would lead to return migration. Although it might be optimal to immigrate initially, negative shocks in the host country like unemployment might affect the gains from immigration and therefore make it more optimal to return faster.

Overall, this literature put forward several potential theoretical motives for return migration based on a calculation of the benefits and costs of staying overseas versus going back to the home country while taking into consideration the potential preference for living in the home country.

**Empirical Evidence**

Empirical evidence on the determinants of return migration is scarce as typically this requires observing immigrants in the host country prior to leaving and then identifying accurately those who left as opposed to those who dropped from the sample due to survey attrition and disentangling the various reasons for their return. Alternatively, one would like to observe all the returnees at the country of origin and be able to distinguish between the main motives for their return, which is not typically feasible. Several empirical investigations have attempted to identify the return motives using various ways.

A few studies examine the determinants of return migration using data in the home country. For example, Yang (2006) relies on data from four linked household surveys conducted by the National Statistics Office of the Philippine government, covering a nationally representative household sample. He uses the large exchange rate shocks generated by the 1997 Asian financial crisis as a quasi-experiment to shed light on the motives of return migration. He finds that Philippine migrants are less likely to return when they experience more positive exchange rate shocks, which he explains as evidence in support of life-cycle motivations rather than target-earnings explanations for return migration. Life-cycle migrants accumulate savings that help raise their future consumption levels, and they return in order to consume. Target earners are credit constrained and work overseas only until they have saved the minimum investment level, after which they return immediately and invest in entrepreneurial enterprises.

On the other hand, most studies examining the motives for return migration are based on the host country. For example, Abarcar (2017) employs data from the Longitudinal Survey of Immigrants to Australia, a nationally representative study of principal immigrant applicants issued permanent visas offshore and who arrived in Australia between 1993 and 1995. Like Yang (2006), Abarcar (2017) uses exogenous exchange rate shocks arising from the 1997 Asian financial crisis to examine the competing motives of immigrants to return to their home country. He attempts to distinguish between two competing return motives: a life-cycle explanation (consumption) versus target-earners' motivation (investment). He argues that a positive exchange rate shock of the host country's currency with respect to the origin country's currency raises the marginal benefit of staying overseas as it increases the origin country value of foreign wages and would lead to less return migration. On the other hand, positive exchange rate shocks would make target earners more likely to return home as they become more likely to have reached the minimum investment threshold. He finds that a depreciation in a migrant's home-country currency leads to a reduction in the probability of return migration of immigrants in Australia, which supports the life-cycle return motive.

Indeed, useful insights about the determinants of return migration can also be gained from the host country where the source of variation is the countries of origin, and where potentially all immigrants (stayers and returnees) can be observed. Several studies have used the German Socio-Economic Panel (GSOEP) which is a rich longitudinal data set of households in Germany that includes an oversampled group of immigrants. Using the GSOEP, Kirdar (2009) tests the savings accumulation hypothesis using exogenous variation in purchasing power parity and examines how labour market outcomes like unemployment and retirement influence the return migration decision. He finds that purchasing power parity is an important determinant of return migration from Germany and that immigrants return when the marginal benefit of higher savings falls below the marginal cost of staying, which supports the conjecture that savings accumulation is an important motive for temporary migration.

Focusing on the role of labour market shocks, in particular unemployment, a few studies find that unemployment is an important push factor. Kirdar (2009) finds a positive impact of unemployment on return migration. Bijwaard et al. (2014) use a unique administrative panel for the entire population of immigrants to the Netherlands between 1999 and 2007 and find that unemployment raises the return probability, while employment spells following unemployment delay the return for most migrants. Importantly, they address the potential endogeneity between unemployment and return migration and thus are able to quantify the causal impact of labour market dynamics such as unemployment on migration duration. They also highlight the impact of unemployment for different migrants based on region of origin and duration of migration. They show that across all immigrant groups, except for those from the new European Union (EU) countries, the longer the immigrants are unemployed the higher the probability that they leave the Netherlands.

A third though small group of papers use data from both host and home countries. Zaiceva and Zimmermann (2016) use several sources of data of both home and host countries (EU Labour Force Survey (LFS), Eurobarometer and European Economic Survey) to examine the impact of macroeconomic shocks as opposed to individual shocks on return. They study the impact of the economic crisis on the accelerated return of migrants from the new EU countries in 2011. However, they find that since several of the new EU member states were hit relatively more than the destination countries, return migration may have been delayed. Also, the results underscore that, particularly within the EU, return migration might not be permanent but rather part of repeat and circular migration in post-enlargement Europe.

Using innovative data that successfully tracked a high proportion of the very top performers in secondary school over the period 1976 to 2004 from three Pacific countries (Tonga, Papua New Guinea and New Zealand), Gibson and McKenzie (2011) find evidence of high levels of return migration. They find that income gains or economic incentives for migrating play a very minor role in determining which of the highly skilled migrate and return and which do not. They argue that the income maximisation framework is not the appropriate model for analysing the first-order determinants of return migration of the best and brightest, and non-income aspects such as family, personal connection to the home country and lifestyle reasons play a more important role in the return decision of that group.

Indeed, it is not realistic to expect that there is only one motive for return or that only economic factors matter for return decisions. Constant and Massey (2003) find that return migration was strongly influenced by both economic and social ties to the origin country. The roles played by social networks, family and personal reasons are acknowledged to be very significant determinants that might be driving the preference for home consumption. Albeit, disentangling or quantifying all the competing motives for return migration is typically constrained by the availability of adequate data.

## IMPLICATIONS OF RETURN MIGRATION

Understanding the implications of return migration is important for both the host and the home country. The economics of migration literature is typically concerned about who returns, in other words the selectivity of return and whether the return migration decision is exogenous or endogenous as those two aspects have differential impacts on the consequences of return migration, as described below.

### Empirical Challenges

**Selectivity of return: selectivity bias**
Migrants are not random, and neither are returnees. Thus, if migrants are positively selected, they would have favourable characteristics that would allow them to earn higher wages in the host country, while if they are negatively selected then they would typically struggle in the

host country as they would exhibit lower human capital. Borjas (1987) extends Roy (1951) in showing that the composition of migratory flows depends on the relative distribution of incomes between the origin and destination countries, and average returns on human capital. Thus, although immigrants consider the average expected wage when deciding to migrate, their decision is also determined by the income dispersion in the home and host countries. So, for a given host country (e.g. the US), a larger income dispersion in the origin country implies a higher US-origin wage differential for low-skilled workers, and hence a higher incentive to migrate compared to high-skilled workers. This is referred to as negative selection of immigrants, as the low-skilled (those with below-average earnings) migrate. The reverse follows as, when the income variance at origin is low, the high-skilled are taxed to insure the lower-skilled, so high-skilled workers are more likely to migrate as they gain more from migrating. Hence immigrants would be positively selected as the high-skilled (those with above-average earnings) immigrate.

As Borjas and Bratsberg (1996) show, return migration reinforces the type of selection that initially generated the immigrant flow. Thus, if immigrants are positively selected, so that they have above-average skills, return migrants will be the least skilled amongst the immigrants; that is, those who stay in the host country are the most able. In contrast, if immigrants are negatively selected, return migrants will be the most skilled amongst immigrants; that is, the least able are the ones who stay in the host country. In theory, return migrants may be negatively selected if 'failures' in the host country return, or they may be positively selected if successful immigrants return. In general, the type of selection in return migration would impact both the host and the home countries.

It is important, however, to note that more than one type of selectivity might operate at the same time in the same host country, depending on their immigrants' country of origin. Bijwaard and Wahba (2014) examine whether high- or low-income immigrants leave sooner where income is a proxy for skill. Focusing only on labour immigrants from developing countries in the Netherlands, they find evidence of both negative and positive selection.

**Endogeneity of return: simultaneity bias**
Another concern in the economic literature on migration is the endogeneity of the return migration decision. Migrants' behaviour in the host country is typically not exogenous to the return decision. Immigrants' performance and economic outcomes are interdependent with the return plan and hence this simultaneity in decisions and behaviours need to be addressed to ensure that the causal impact of return on outcomes is disentangled from the effect of the outcome on return. For example, if return migrants are observed to have poor labour market outcomes, it is important to model whether this leads to return migration or, because migrants were planning to return, they had weak attachment to the labour market. A recent paper by Bijwaard and Wahba (2019) addresses this challenge: namely that out-migration might be correlated with the labour market status in the host country and the overseas earnings of immigrants. Their results highlight the importance of addressing the endogeneity of the labour supply and out-migration when estimating immigrant earnings profiles or economic performance. Indeed, assuming that the labour market performance of immigrants is exogenous would lead to biased estimates of immigrants' earnings growth.

We discuss below how those two challenges are addressed in the economic literature on return migration. The quest for establishing causal evidence on the relationship, rather than mere correlation, has advanced this literature.

## Before Return

Temporary migrants behave differently than permanent migrants. In addition, those planning to return might behave differently from those migrants who plan to stay for good in the destination country. Thus, return plans affect immigrants' behaviour and their performance in the destination country.

### Economic behaviour

There is growing evidence that return intentions affect migrants' behaviour while overseas. Return intentions affect whether, and to what extent, immigrants invest in the host country, both in terms of specific human capital and physical capital. Thus, return plans might impact immigrants' work effort. Galor and Stark (1991) show that migrants' work effort is higher than that of comparable native-born workers due to differences in incentives rather than differences in characteristics.

Migrants might be less likely to invest in physical capital, such as housing or businesses in the destination, because of the limited asset-return period. At the same time, migrants might focus their investment on the country of origin through accumulating more savings and sending more remittances. For example, the evidence suggests that temporary migrants tend to remit more than permanent migrants (e.g. Merkle and Zimmermann, 1992). Dustmann and Mestres (2010) also find that the remittance behaviour of immigrants is affected by their return migration plans. They control for the possible reverse causality and still document a substantial magnitude of the effects of temporary versus permanent migration on remittance behaviour.

Chabé-Ferret et al. (2018) analyse the relationship between return plans and immigrants' behaviour in the host and origin countries, addressing the potential endogeneity between return plans and different investment decisions. They also investigate the potential trade-off and complementarities between various immigrants' investment behaviours in the host and origin countries. They find that temporary migrants are more likely to remit and finance projects at origin, but less likely to invest in housing in the host country. The findings highlight that there is no trade-off between immigrants' investment in the home and in the host country but those who plan to return tend to behave differently from those migrants planning to stay permanently.

### Assimilation and integration

Another aspect of immigrants' behaviour that is affected by their return intentions is the incentive for assimilation in the host country. On the one hand, migrants who plan to return might have little incentive to assimilate or to invest in host-country-specific human capital such as language learning. On the other hand, temporary migrants might invest in language skills if the returns to human capital accumulated abroad are high. Dustmann (1999) explores the effects of return migration on investments in the host country's language (German), and finds that permanent migrants have a 10 per cent higher probability to be fluent in German than migrants who intend to return. Chabé-Ferret et al. (2018) find that those immigrants who plan to leave France are less likely to have experienced improvements in proficiency of the French language compared to immigrants who intend to stay, even after controlling for the level of French language proficiency upon arrival and whether the country of origin and France share French as an official language. Hence, investing in assimilation might be too costly for those immigrants who are staying temporarily and are planning to return to their home country.

## After Return

The economic literature has also highlighted the contribution of returnees to the economic development of their countries of origin through several channels (see also King's Chapter 22). First, returnees bring back overseas savings which they use to set up businesses. Second, they bring back new skills and human capital. Third, returnees also bring back new ideas and norms, commonly referred to as social remittances (Levitt, 1998). There is a growing literature on the economic impact of return migration. Earlier studies focused on documenting the association between return migration and various outcomes, but the recent literature is more concerned about establishing causal relationships. In an ideal situation, one would like to see the counterfactual: what would have happened if the same individuals had not migrated? Would return migrants have behaved in the same way if they did not migrate? Alas, in many cases estimating those counterfactuals is not feasible, so the literature aims to test the causal impact in a variety of other ways discussed below.

### Entrepreneurship

Many studies have documented the relationship between return migration and entrepreneurship (see also Sinatti, Chapter 24). Typically, in the economics literature migration is seen as an opportunity to accumulate savings to overcome credit constraints. Earlier papers focus only on returnees and find that returnees who accumulated overseas savings were more likely to become entrepreneurs rather than waged workers: see inter alia, McCormick and Wahba (2001); Dustmann and Kirchkamp (2002); Mesnard (2004). This literature also differentiates between self-employment and setting up businesses with the aim of highlighting that indeed return migrants are entrepreneurs who invest their savings in micro-enterprise development but that their occupational choice involves entrepreneurial skills. Piracha and Vadean (2010) examine the occupational choice of returnees in Albania, comparing returnees to non-migrants, and control for the selection bias associated with return migration. They explicitly differentiate between the propensities of returnees to become self-employed as own account workers versus entrepreneurs (i.e. owners of firms with paid employees). However, Kveder and Flahaux (2013) find that Senegalese return migrants resort to self-employment as a 'last resort' if they were unable to accumulate capital overseas. On the other hand, there is evidence that return migration significantly improves the chances of survival of their entrepreneurial activities in Egypt (see Marchetta, 2012). This might be due to having fewer credit constraints, but also the result of utilising newly acquired skills, ideas and entrepreneurial knowledge throughout their migration experience to start and successfully manage micro-enterprises. Overall, this literature portrays the occupational choice of returnees as a positive contribution to micro-enterprise development and therefore to the economic development of the country of origin.

Later papers have attempted to tackle the two main empirical challenges mentioned above. For example, Wahba and Zenou (2012) dealt with the endogeneity problem of entrepreneurship and return migration, while Piracha and Vadean (2010) and Batista et al. (2017) have addressed the selectivity problem; that is, return migrants being a selected group. The evidence underscores that, even after addressing the endogeneity and selectivity problems, return migration has indeed increased entrepreneurship and micro-enterprise development in origin countries.

**Brain gain**

Another important benefit of migration is the acquisition of human capital: new skills. A strand of the literature on return migration highlights the impact of overseas migration on wages of return migrants and attempts to quantify the returns to migrants' wages from overseas working experience. Earlier studies investigate whether migrants benefit from their overseas migration by earning a higher wage after they return by analysing the wages differences between return migrants and non-migrants. As mentioned, this simple comparison confounds the two challenges mentioned above, which are that the observed relationship between earnings and migration experience reflects the self-selection of individuals into return migration, and the endogeneity of migration duration. A priori, failing to control for the unobserved ability (selectivity) of migrants produces an unclear bias in the estimation of the impact of migration as there is no consensus in the literature about whether migrants are positively or negatively selected.

The evidence on 'returns to returning', as it is often called, is rather mixed. Co et al. (2000) find no significant wage premium for returning men, but a positive one for women in Hungary. Barrett and O'Connell (2001) find a return migration wage premium for men but not for women in Ireland. However, when Barrett and Goggin (2010) control for selectivity of migration, they find a positive wage premium for returnees of both genders in Ireland.

Most of the papers attempt to control for the selectivity of return migration in some way, or to estimate counterfactual wage distributions of migrants if they did not emigrate. Lacuesta (2010) finds that return migrants earn significantly more than non-migrants in Mexico, but this premium is the result of pre-migration differences in ability and not human capital gains derived from migration. On the other hand, Reinhold and Thom (2013) find a significantly positive effect of return migration on workers' wages after their return to Mexico and argue that this is driven by occupation-specific job experience overseas. The return to migration experience is largest for migrants who worked in occupations in the US that match their current occupation in Mexico.

Several studies show that controlling for self-selection into migration changes the results. For example, De Vreyer et al. (2010) find that migrants are negatively selected in their population of origin and that overseas work experience leads to a wage premium for West African migrants returning from an Organisation for Economic Co-operation and Development (OECD) country but not for other return migrants returning from non-OECD countries. De Coulon and Piracha (2005), who study the selectivity and performance of Albanian return migrants, find that return migrants are negatively selected and that if the non-migrants would have migrated and returned, they would have earned more than twice the wage of actual return migrants. However, Ambrosini et al. (2015) use census and survey data to identify the return wage premium and the selection of recent Romanian migrants and returnees. They control for selection into temporary migration and find the premium to return migration increases with migrants' skills.

Wahba (2015) highlights the importance of controlling for the various selectivity problems when quantifying the impact of return migration on the wages of returnees to Egypt. She estimates the wages of return migrants controlling for several selectivity biases arising from the various decisions, namely: emigration, return migration, labour force participation and occupational choice following return. The findings provide strong evidence that overseas temporary migration results in a wage premium upon return, even after controlling for the various potential selection biases. However, the estimates underscore the significance of controlling for both emigration and return migration selections. Ignoring the double selectivity in migration would overestimate the impact of return migration on the wage premium of returnees, as Egyptian migrants are positively selected relative to non-migrants but returnees are negatively selected among migrants.

**Occupational mobility**
Another measure of human capital acquisition is occupational upgrading. The existing literature on the impact of return on upward mobility is very scarce. Carletto and Kilic (2011) estimate the impact of return migration on the occupational mobility of returnees compared to non-migrants in Albania. They control for the non-random nature of emigration and return using instrumental variables and find that past migration experience increases the probability of upward occupational mobility. On the other hand, Masso et al. (2014) rely on online job search data in Estonia to show that temporary overseas experience does not have any significant effect on upward occupational mobility.

Elmallakh and Wahba (2021) examine whether temporary international migration enables returnees to climb the occupational ladder. Using data from Egypt, they investigate the occupational mobility of returnees relative to non-migrants and control for the endogeneity of the temporary migration decision. They find evidence that return migration increases the probability of upward occupational mobility. The findings underscore the role played by temporary migration in dampening potential brain drain concerns through the human capital enhancement of return migrants.

On the other hand, Coniglio and Brzozowski (2018) highlight that the benefits of return migration depend on the success of the overseas work experience as well as the ability of returnees to reintegrate in the labour market of the country of origin. Using data on a representative sample of returnees in one of the regions in Poland, Silesia, they estimate the determinants of unsuccessful return defined as skill waste upon return, economic inactivity, experiencing hardships and job-related difficulties. They show that a skill mismatch overseas is often correlated with a skill waste upon return, although they also find that some soft skills acquired overseas provide returnees with a competitive advantage relative to non-migrants.

**International knowledge transfer**
Migrants spread ideas, technology and knowledge across countries. Although there is an established economic literature on the impact of international migration on international trade and foreign direct investment (FDI), many of those important dimensions are also observed to flourish as a result of return migration, since returnees with already established links in the destination country foster trade, FDI and innovation upon return. The evidence suggests that return migration is a catalyst in international knowledge diffusion and a major input to increases in productivity (see also Mueller, Chapter 23). For example, Bahar et al. (2019) exploit data from a natural experiment on return migration to post-conflict Yugoslavia and show how return migrants positively impact the performance of the same export sectors in which they had worked while abroad. Choudhury (2016) studies how knowledge production is facilitated by local employees working at geographically distant R&D locations in India. He tests whether local workers with return migrant managers file higher numbers of patents than local workers with local managers. He finds that return migrants have higher prior patent grants and file more patents compared with local hires. Also, the results show that local

employees who have return migrant managers file more patents. Overall, the findings suggest that return migrants may act as a 'bridge' for transferring knowledge.

**Social and political norms**
When individuals emigrate, they become exposed to different cultures, norms and political ideologies which they might then absorb and transfer to their country of origin. Indeed, in many cases, those new ideas and norms are transferred back to the country of origin by the diaspora and return migrants. Those norms span social, economic and political spheres. Although social scientists have been studying social remittances, a term coined by Levitt (1998), for a while, economists have only relatively recently been investigating the causal relationship between migration and social and political norms. Aiming to establish more than simple correlation, this strand of the economic literature has been innovative in its use of data.

Return migrants transmit back to their home country political ideas regarding the quality of political institutions, raising awareness and demands for political accountability and increasing direct participation in political life. Spilimbergo (2009), using a comprehensive panel data set on foreign students globally over 50 years, finds that foreign-educated individuals bring about democratic change at home if they acquired foreign education in democratic countries. Similarly, Mercier (2016) studies the impact of political leaders who had studied abroad on the level of democracy in their country during their tenure. She builds an original database on the personal background of 932 politicians who were at the head of the executive power in a developing country over the 1960–2004 period. She finds a positive correlation between leaders who studied abroad and the change in the score of democracy in their home country during their tenure, for leaders who reach power in initially autocratic settings and who studied in high-income OECD countries.

Migrants might experience different and potentially better-quality and more democratic institutions while they are abroad and hence, upon return, would both demand similar high-quality institutions and accountability and also participate more in the political process. One of the early papers by Batista and Vicente (2011) examines the impact of migration on the demand for political accountability in Cape Verde. They devised a simple 'experiment' to capture demand for better governance at home. They offered respondents to a survey on perceived corruption in public services in Cape Verde the opportunity to anonymously make the results available in the national media by giving them a prepaid postcard to post if they wished the conclusions of the survey to be made public. The respondents were also told that at least 50 per cent of the postcards would have to be returned for the information to be released in the media. The authors found that international emigration positively affects the demand for improved political accountability, with stronger effects for migrants to countries with better governance and for return migrants relative to current migrants as returnees can directly influence their networks in the home country.

Another issue raised by the economic literature is whether the norms adopted by return migrants diffuse to their origin households and communities. Chauvet and Mercier (2014) use electoral and census data from Mali in order to study the link between return migration and political outcomes. They control for the endogeneity of migration and find a positive impact of return migration on participation rates and on electoral competitiveness, driven by returnees from non-African countries. Interestingly, the impact of returnees on turnout goes beyond their own participation as they affect electoral outcomes in neighbouring areas where non-migrants are poorly educated, which the authors interpret as evidence of a diffusion of political norms from returnees to non-migrants.

Migration also affects social behaviour and norms, such as fertility and gender inequality. Returnees adjust their fertility choices to the norms that prevail in their previous country of destination. Bertoli and Marchetta (2015) have examined how the prevailing social norms in the countries of destination of Egyptian migrants affect their fertility choices upon return. They focus the analysis on Egyptian men who migrate predominantly to other Arab countries characterised by a higher number of children per woman. They control for the endogeneity of the migration decision and show that return migrants are likely to have high fertility rates, similar to the fertility norms in their country of destination. Returnees also absorb gender norms of destination. Tuccio and Wahba (2018) exploit unique data on female empowerment to construct several measures of gender norms in Jordan on the role of women, female freedom of mobility and female decision-making power. Controlling for both emigration and return migration selections, they find that women with a returnee family member are more likely to bear traditional gender norms than women in households with no migration experience. The results are driven by returnees from more conservative Arab countries, suggesting a transfer of conservative norms from destinations with highly traditional gender roles. They also show that return migration not only affects perceptions but also outcomes such as female labour force participation, education and fertility.[1]

More recently, Tuccio et al. (2019) examine the impact of international migration on the transfer of political and social norms. Exploiting unique data on Morocco, they study whether households with return and current migrants bear different political preferences and behaviours to non-migrant families. They control for the double selection into emigration and return migration and also for the destination choice. This is the first paper in the economic literature where the country of destination selection is addressed. This is an important issue since most of the previous literature finds that the country of destination matters for the adoption of norms, but does not address this selection. Hence a critical issue is whether migrants move to a particular destination because they have a preference for the norms of that country; for example, more conservative migrants move to Arab countries while more liberal individuals migrate to a Western country, which would imply that any transfer of norms is not exogenous. Controlling for the various selectivity biases including the country of destination, they still find that having a returnee in the household increases the demand for political and social change, which is driven by returnees mostly from Western European countries.

To sum up, this growing strand of the economic literature suggests that both return plans and return migration affect migrants' behaviour and their performance in the host country while overseas, and more importantly, in the home country after return.

## CONCLUSION

Although the economic literature on return migration is fundamentally examining very similar questions and issues to those studied by other social sciences, the economic approach has been more preoccupied with establishing causal relationships of the determinants and the consequences of return migration. Great advances in this literature have been made. Overall, the economic literature views return migration as part of an optimal strategy, and as such the focus is on migrants who choose to return to their country of origin on their own accord. Thus, many studies examine the various determinants of return migration and try to disentangle the push and pull factors in the host and home countries. Most of this literature, though, focuses on the impacts of return migration and shows that return migrants bring back financial capital, human capital and new norms. Also, the effects of return migration spill over to their households, communities and beyond. Overall, the evidence suggests that return migration plays a positive role in stimulating economic development of the origin country.

Reviewing the economic literature on return migration underscores several gaps in our knowledge. First, there is a need to better record return migration. Collecting data on the previous location of individuals in censuses and labour force surveys should be common practice to ensure we have adequate records on returnees. This would enable researchers to understand better the determinants and consequences of return. Second, it is important for future research to attempt to quantify the macro impact of return migration on the country of origin to highlight the significance of return and its consequences beyond just a few case studies. Third, there is a need to study the return implications of different types of migrants such as refugees or undocumented migrants. Finally, better understanding of the impact of both the overseas migration experience and the policies in the origin countries on the success of the return is needed to ensure that the potential of return migration is maximised.

## NOTE

1. The results discussed in this paragraph refer to the particular situation where returnees to Egypt and Jordan are coming back from more conservative Arab countries. In Chapter 4 of this Handbook, King and Lulle present examples of a different scenario, where the migration process is from more socially conservative, patriarchal countries to destinations which have higher degrees of gender equality and female empowerment. In this migration situation, which is probably more common on a global scale, return migration has the potential to carry back to the country of origin the social remittance of greater gender equality.

## REFERENCES

Abarcar, P. (2017) 'The return motivations of legal permanent migrants: evidence from exchange rate shocks and immigrants in Australia', *Journal of Economic Behaviour and Organisation*, **144**, 62–77.

Ambrosini, J.W., Mayr, K., Peri, G. and Radu, D. (2015) 'The selection of migrants and returnees in Romania', *Economics of Transition*, **23** (4), 753–93.

Azose, J.J. and Raftery, A.E. (2019) 'Estimation of emigration, return migration, and transit migration between all pairs of countries', *PNAS*, **116** (1), 116–22.

Bahar, D., Özgüzel, C., Hauptmann, A. and Rapoport, H. (2019) *Migration and Post-Conflict Reconstruction: The Effect of Returning Refugees on Export Performance in the Former Yugoslavia*, Paris: Paris School of Economics.

Barrett, A. and Goggin, J. (2010) 'Returning to the question of a wage premium for returning migrants', *National Institute Economic Review*, **213** (1), R43–R51.

Barrett, A. and O'Connell, P.J. (2001) 'Is there a wage premium for returning Irish migrants?', *Economic and Social Review*, **32** (1), 1–21.

Batista, C. and Vicente, P.C. (2011) 'Do migrants improve governance at home? Evidence from a voting experiment', *World Bank Economic Review*, **25** (1), 77–104.

Batista, C., McIndoe-Calder, T. and Vicente, P.C. (2017) 'Return migration, self-selection and entrepreneurship', *Oxford Bulletin of Economics and Statistics*, **79** (5), 797–821.

Bertoli, S. and Marchetta, F. (2015) 'Bringing it all back home: return migration and fertility choices', *World Development*, **65**, 27–40.
Bijwaard, G.E. and Wahba, J. (2014) 'Do high-income or low-income immigrants leave faster?', *Journal of Development Economics*, **108**, 54–68.
Bijwaard, G.E. and Wahba, J. (2019) 'Immigrants' wage growth and selective out-migration', *Oxford Bulletin of Economics and Statistics*, **81** (5), 1065–94.
Bijwaard, G.E., Schluter, C. and Wahba, J. (2014) 'The impact of labor market dynamics on the return migration of immigrants', *Review of Economics and Statistics*, **96** (3), 483–94.
Borjas, G. (1987) 'Self-selection and the earnings of immigrants', *American Economic Review*, **77** (4), 531–53.
Borjas, G. and Bratsberg, B. (1996) 'Who leaves? The outmigration of the foreign-born', *Review of Economics and Statistics*, **78** (1), 165–76.
Carletto, C. and Kilic, T. (2011) 'Moving up the ladder? The impact of migration experience on occupational mobility in Albania', *Journal of Development Studies*, **47** (6), 846–69.
Chabé-Ferret, B., Machado, J. and Wahba, J. (2018) 'Remigration plans and migrants' behaviour', *Regional Science and Urban Economics*, **68**, 56–72.
Chauvet, L. and Mercier, M. (2014) 'Do return migrants transfer political norms to their origin country? Evidence from Mali', *Journal of Comparative Economics*, **42** (3), 630–51.
Choudhury, P. (2016) 'Return migration and geography of innovation in MNEs: a natural experiment of on-the-job learning of knowledge production by local workers reporting to return migrants', *Journal of Economic Geography*, **16** (3), 585–610.
Co, C., Gang, I. and Yun, M.-S. (2000) 'Returns to returning', *Journal of Population Economics*, **13** (1), 57–79.
Coniglio, N.D. and Brzozowski, J. (2018) 'Migration and development at home: bitter or sweet return? Evidence from Poland', *European Urban and Regional Studies*, **25** (1), 85–105.
Constant, A. and Massey, D.S. (2003) 'Self-selection, earnings and out-migration: a longitudinal study of immigrants', *Journal of Population Economics*, **16** (4), 631–53.
De Coulon, A. and Piracha, M. (2005) 'Self-selection and the performance of return migrants: the source country perspective', *Journal of Population Economics*, **18** (4), 779–807.
De Vreyer, P., Gubert, F. and Robilliard, A.-S. (2010) 'Are there returns to migration experience? An empirical analysis using data on return migrants and non-migrants in West Africa', *Annals of Economics and Statistics*, **97–8**, 307–28.
Djajic, S. and Milbourne, R. (1988) 'A general equilibrium model of guest worker migration: a source-country perspective', *Journal of International Economics*, **25** (3–4), 335–51.
Dustmann, C. (1999) 'Temporary migration, human capital, and language fluency of migrants', *Scandinavian Journal of Economics*, **101** (2), 297–314.
Dustmann, C. and Kirchkamp, O. (2002) 'The optimal migration duration and activity choice after remigration', *Journal of Development Economics*, **67** (2), 351–72.
Dustmann, C. and Mestres, J. (2010) 'Remittances and temporary migration', *Journal of Development Economics*, **92** (1), 62–70.
Dustmann, C., Fadlon, I. and Weiss, Y. (2011) 'Return migration, human capital accumulation, and the brain drain', *Journal of Development Economics*, **95** (1), 58–67.
Elmallakh, N. and Wahba, J. (2021) 'Upward or downward: occupational mobility and return migration', *World Development*, **137**, January, 105203.
Galor, O. and Stark, O. (1991) 'The probability of return migration, migrants' work effort, and migrants' performance', *Journal of Development Economics*, **35** (2), 399–405.
Gibson, J. and McKenzie, D. (2011) 'The microeconomic determinants of emigration and return migration of the best and brightest: evidence from the Pacific', *Journal of Development Economics*, **95** (1), 18–29.
Kirdar, M.G. (2009) 'Labor market outcomes, savings accumulation, and return migration', *Labour Economics*, **16** (4), 418–28.
Kveder, C.L.M. and Flahaux, M.-L. (2013) 'Returning to Dakar: a mixed methods analysis of the role of migration experience for occupational status', *World Development*, **45**, 223–38.
Lacuesta, A. (2010) 'A revision of the self-selection of migrants using returning migrant's earnings', *Annals of Economics and Statistics*, **97–8**, 235–59.

Levitt, P. (1998) 'Social remittances: migration driven local-level forms of cultural diffusion', *International Migration Review*, **32** (4), 926–48.

Marchetta, F. (2012) 'Return migration and the survival of entrepreneurial activities in Egypt', *World Development*, **40** (10), 1999–2013.

Masso, J., Eamets, R. and Mõtsmees, P. (2014) 'The effect of migration experience on occupational mobility in Estonia', *International Journal of Manpower*, **35** (6), 753–75.

McCormick, B. and Wahba, J. (2001) 'Overseas work experience, savings and entrepreneurship amongst return migrants to LDCs', *The Scottish Journal of Political Economy*, **48** (2), 164–78.

Mercier, M. (2016) 'The return of the prodigy son: do return migrants make better leaders?', *Journal of Development Economics*, **122**, 76–91.

Merkle, L. and Zimmermann, K. (1992) 'Savings, remittances, and return migration', *Economics Letters*, **38** (1), 77–81.

Mesnard, A. (2004) 'Temporary migration and capital market imperfections', *Oxford Economic Papers*, **56** (2), 242–62.

Piracha, M. and Vadean, P.F. (2010) 'Return migration and occupational choice: evidence from Albania', *World Development*, **38** (8), 1141–55.

Reinhold, S. and Thom, K. (2013) 'Migration experience and earnings in the Mexican labor market', *Journal of Human Resources*, **48** (3), 768–820.

Roy, A. (1951) 'Some thoughts on the distribution of earnings', *Oxford Economic Papers*, **3** (2), 135–46.

Spilimbergo, A. (2009) 'Democracy and foreign education', *American Economic Review*, **99** (1), 528–43.

Stark, O., Helmenstein, C. and Yegorov, Y. (1997) 'Migrants' savings, purchasing power parity, and the optimal duration of migration', *International Tax and Public Finance*, **4** (3), 307–24.

Tuccio, M. and Wahba, J. (2018) 'Return migration and the transfer of gender norms: evidence from the Middle East', *Journal of Comparative Economics*, **46** (4), 1006–29.

Tuccio, M., Wahba, J. and Hamdouch, B. (2019) 'International migration as a driver of political and social change: evidence from Morocco', *Journal of Population Economics*, **32** (4), 1171–203.

Wahba, J. (2015) 'Selection, selection, selection: the impact of return migration', *Journal of Population Economics*, **28** (3), 535–63.

Wahba, J. and Zenou, Y. (2012) 'Out of sight, out of mind: migration, entrepreneurship and social capital', *Regional Science and Urban Economics*, **42** (5), 890–903.

Yang, D. (2006) 'Why do migrants return to poor countries? Evidence from Philippine migrants' responses to exchange rate shocks', *Review of Economics and Statistics*, **88** (4), 715–35.

Zaiceva, A. and Zimmermann, K. (2016) 'Returning home at times of trouble? Return migration of EU enlargement migrants during the crisis' in M. Kahanec and K. Zimmermann (eds), *Labor Migration, EU Enlargement, and the Great Recession*, Berlin: Springer, pp. 397–418.

# 3. Return and transnationalism
## Özge Bilgili

## INTRODUCTION

In the early days of the Corona pandemic, I found myself tweeting:

> I am now drafting a book chapter on #return and #transnationalism. Return, not possible. Virtual transnationalism more than ever before. This forced #immobility due to #COVID-19 has shaken how we think about it all ...

Indeed, the conditions under which we have been relating to the concepts of return and transnationalism have changed. However, this extreme situation that constrains our mobility will not last forever. The inherent need for movement and our nature will demand the continuation of our movements across borders. With the impossibility of return mobilities and interpersonal contact comes the need to connect through other means, including telephone calls, apps and social media – whether with our friends, family or acquaintances who are living elsewhere. Hence, it would not be unrealistic to argue that these conditions create unprecedented levels of virtual transnationalism, while putting a halt on return.

This chapter will not be able to account for the new perspectives which we will develop over time on return and transnationalism due to the Corona pandemic but will rely on what we already know and have researched as academics. My main objective is to provide a discussion on the ways in which return and transnationalism are interlinked. I do so first by defining the different types of return, including return mobilities, imaginary return and return migration. Second, I lay out the different elements of transnationalism by focusing on the behavioural and emotional dimensions. Next, bringing these two together, I discuss how different types of return can be considered as an element, a determinant and a consequence of transnational (social, economic and political) engagements and belonging. Accordingly, I propose two conceptual models relating to return migration and reintegration processes. Finally, following a review of the existing literature, I point to the the currently missing links between return and transnationalism and highlight ideas for future research.

It should be noted that when using the concept of 'return', I do not refer to a one-time definite return, which is often considered as the end of the migration cycle (Black and Koser, 1999; Sinatti, 2015). Moving away from this deterministic and linear approach to migrants' mobility patterns, I see return as an option considered and experienced by migrants throughout their migration trajectory, a trajectory that is permanently in evolution and subject to changing conditions. I emphasise return not only as an act but also as an option because the 'myth of return' can be equally significant in the lives of migrants. The idea, hope, aspiration, intention or plan to return are all part of the discussion of return as a concept (King and Christou, 2011). The question of return appears and disappears over the lifecourse of migrants and is reconsidered at times as a place of saviour and home, as well as a last resort or even an unwanted destination. It

## UNDERSTANDING RETURN AS MIGRATION, MOBILITIES AND IMAGINARY

The theoretical analysis of return migration as we understand it today dates back to nearly half a century ago when Bovenkerk (1974) wrote *The Sociology of Return Migration*. Later, one of the earliest definitions of return migration was proposed by Gmelch (1980). Although Gmelch recognised the analytical difficulty in making a distinction between those who return temporarily and those who go back home only for short-term visits,[1] in the core of his definition return migration refers to a permanent resettlement in the country of origin: 'Return migration is defined as the movement of emigrants back to their homelands to resettle' (1980, p.136). In a way, return is considered as the end of a migration cycle. With the increased prevalence of return in national and international policies, definitions introduced by international organisations have also become commonly used (Sinatti, 2015; see also IOM, 2019; United Nations, 1998).

In the more recent academic literature, one of the most commonly used definitions of return is given by Cassarino (2008) who highlights the significance of time and the voluntariness of return. As much as his definition has its strengths in referring to various dimensions for return migration, it remains limited in a number of ways. It is certainly of great importance to recognise the various time dimensions and the voluntariness of return; however, return is more of a process that takes place within the migration trajectories of people. The fluidity and temporary nature of migratory movements cannot be ignored (Peixoto et al., 2019). Therefore, we need to situate return within the larger discussion on im/mobility patterns in a person's life, which includes multiple reasons for return, the localities of return and the intention to re-migrate when discussing it. Also, as mentioned in the introduction, it is a helpful analytical approach to think of return along the spectrum of both an imaginary and a lived experience. This comes close to how King and Christou (2011, p.452) define return as 'a broader concept which includes return migration and repatriation (where the return is forced) but which can also be imagined or provisional, encompassing various short-term visits such as holidays'. Conceptualising return in these ways is crucial for understanding its different meanings in the lives of migrants (see also Sinatti, 2015). Against this backdrop, the main question I am concerned with in this chapter is: How are return and transnationalism interlinked? Before answering this question, I first define transnationalism and its dimensions, which will help to identify the points of discussion in relation to return.

## DEFINING TRANSNATIONALISM AND ITS DIMENSIONS

Basch and her colleagues (1994, p.7) defined transnationalism as 'the process by which immigrants forge and sustain multi-stranded social relations that link together their societies of origin and settlement'. Transnationalism as an approach is one that aims to observe and understand better the new realities of migrant lives, such as living in the host country while maintaining meaningful relationships with the home country. A variety of terms is used to define migrants' transnational behaviour and identifications. For instance, the term 'transnationality' introduced by Thomas Faist and his colleagues is defined as 'the degree to which families and individuals are engaged in transactions across borders and this may depend highly on and change over the life course' (Faist et al., 2013). Snel et al. (2006) use the term 'transnational involvement' as the total of the transnational activities and identifications of individuals. Guarnizo (2003, p.670) alternatively discusses transnational ways of living, referring to 'an active, dynamic field of social intercourse that involves and simultaneously affects actors (individuals, groups, institutions) located in different countries'. Vertovec (2004) also considers transnational practices as such to the extent that transformation in the sociocultural, political and economic domains takes place. Additionally, Itzigsohn et al. (1999) highlight the level of institutionalisation, the involvement of people in the transnational field and the movement of people in transnational geographical space, distinguishing between 'narrow' and 'broad' forms of transnationality.[2]

Finally, Levitt (2008) conceptualises the wide range of border-crossing activities as 'transnational ways of being', in contrast to 'transnational ways of belonging', which refers more specifically to migrants' multiple identifications and feelings of attachment. The transnational ways of being, referring to migrants' involvement in activities oriented towards their homeland, encompass different arenas of life. One can generally distinguish between social, economic and civic/political transnational engagements (Table 3.1). In the economic domain, we mainly refer to financial and in-kind remittances, investments in the home country (e.g. house, business, land), the purchase of government bonds or entry to government programmes and charitable donations made either directly to the country of origin or in a community organisation in the country of residence. The political/civic activities oriented towards the home country include participation in elections or membership in political parties there, on the one hand, and, on the other hand, participating in political demonstrations or the mobilisation of political contacts in the host country for affairs related to the home country (Al-Ali et al., 2001; Guarnizo et al., 2003).

Within the social domain, we include social relationships maintained through visits to friends and family in the origin country or contact through telephone calls, letters, e-mails, links with homeland or diaspora organisations and attendance at social gatherings with the ethnic community in the host country (King-O'Riain, 2015). In addition, individuals' participation in cultural events (e.g. concerts, theatre and exhibitions) relating to their country of origin or the consumption of media, art and other cultural products can be included as practices in this domain (Bilgili, 2014).

In addition to these relatively concrete and measurable aspects, there also exists a more subjective and identity-related dimension of transnationalism, namely, 'transnational ways of belonging'. Transnational identities emerge and are recreated as a result of individuals' memories, cultural productions and feelings of belonging. These are conscious demonstrations reflecting individuals' sense of belonging to a certain group or groups (Morawska, 2007). In their definition of 'transnational ways of belonging', Levitt and Glick Schiller (2004) refer not only to an awareness of belonging and identification but also to actions that signify these identifications (e.g. wearing a Christian cross or Jewish star, flying a flag). Within transnational social fields, transnational ways of belonging occupy as significant a place as transnational ways of being.

*Table 3.1    Types, categories and dimensions of transnationalism*

| Type | Category | Dimension |
|---|---|---|
| *Transnational ways of being* Behavioural aspects, including different forms of engagement and involvement | Social transnationalism | Virtual connections online |
| | | Telephone conversations |
| | | Social-media usage |
| | | Return mobilities |
| | Economic transnationalism | Sending/receiving financial remittances |
| | | Sending/receiving goods |
| | | Making investments in the home country |
| | Political transnationalism | Extraterritorial voting |
| | | Engagement in diaspora organisations/hometown associations |
| *Transnational ways of belonging* Emotional aspects, including feelings of identification and attachment | Transnational identification | Homeland attachment and feelings of belonging |
| | | Identification with home country |
| | | Feelings of nostalgia and wish to return |

*Source:* Author's own creation based on the work of Levitt (2008) and Al-Ali et al. (2001).

All in all, even though transnational engagements and identifications cannot be considered as new social phenomena, their nature, frequency and meaning for the individuals and society at large have changed. This is primarily due to the often-referred-to changes in communication technologies, fast and cheaper travel and increasing interaction between communities across countries (Vertovec, 2001). In other words, the circumstances attributable to globalisation have contributed to the establishment of transnational social fields. Within these latter, mobilities of return also take on new, diverse and important meanings. The two dimensions of transnationalism that explicitly overlap with the understanding of return as seen above are return mobilities (social transnationalism) and return intentions (transnational identification).[3] These two dimensions are obviously meaningful for those migrants or their descendants who reside primarily in the countries of destination.

It is, however, important to mention that transnationalism may be part of returnees' lives as well. Returnees may use their transnational social networks as well as their cultural capital upon return for various purposes, as we will see in the next section. In this regard, there is possibly a continuity in the transnational engagements and belongings of migrants wherever they may be located. In the following section, I discuss how return mobilities, imaginaries of return and return migration are all affected by but also become elements of transnational belonging and being. It is these inherent linkages between transnationalism and return that make the topic such a compelling one.

# EXISTING RESEARCH ON RETURN AND TRANSNATIONALISM

Even though transnationalism has been one of the dominant approaches within migration studies in the past couple of decades and the term return frequently appears in empirical studies with a transnational approach, there is a lack of systematic discussion about the linkages between the two. Carling and Erdal (2014) have started the conversation on this topic by looking at how transnationalism interacts with return intentions, actual plans for return migration, post-return experiences and future re-migration. This is, indeed, in line with how return migration and transnationalism are interlinked in much of the literature and is one way to think about how return and transnationalism are linked.

In addition, the increasing research linking return and transnationalism helps us to understand how these associations change over the lifecourse of migrants and depend on diverse conditions across time and space. These include the legal, political, economic and sociocultural conditions in both countries of origin and of destination as well as the characteristics of the migrant communities of which migrants are a part, as this influences the depth and rootedness of transnational social fields in a given context (Duval, 2004). Looking at the existing literature that intersects return and transnationalism, we observe that there is a variety of attention points and discussions around these factors.

Some research focuses on migrants who are abroad and discusses what return means for them. These include earlier works on imaginaries of return (al-Rasheed, 1994; Chavez, 1994; Ramji, 2006; Wessendorf, 2007), decisions of older migrants, retirement and return migration (Bolzman et al., 2006; de Bree et al., 2010; de Coulon and Wolff, 2005; de Haas and Serow, 1997; Hunter, 2011), return mobilities among second-generation immigrants (Fokkema, 2011; King and Christou, 2008, 2011; Reynolds, 2008; Vathi and King, 2011; Wang, 2016), return and repatriation in the context of forced migration (Brees, 2010; Ruben et al., 2009; van Meeteren, 2012; Wahlbeck, 1998) and other work generally on return mobilities (Ali and Holden, 2006; Duval, 2004; Ley and Kobayashi, 2005; Oeppen, 2013; O'Flaherty et al., 2007). More recent research has discussed the ways in which the return mobilities of both first- and second-generation immigrants can be seen as preparation for return (Erdal et al., 2016; Grasmuck and Hinze, 2016; Hunter, 2015; Kunuroglu et al., 2018; Pelliccia, 2017; Wahlbeck, 2015). The return literature has also often been linked to homemaking and belonging in the past few years (Bell and Erdal, 2015; Botterill, 2016; Buffel, 2017; Čapo, 2015; Fábos, 2015; Koh, 2015; Tharmalingam, 2016; Zontini, 2015). Other researchers have focused on the experiences of migrants in the post-return period and reintegration (Gu and Schweisfurth, 2015; Lietaert et al., 2017; Setrana and Tonah, 2016). In the remainder of this chapter, I discuss what these different lines of research tell us and reflect on how transnationalism supports a better understanding of return.

## INVESTIGATING RETURN THROUGH A TRANSNATIONAL LENS

I propose mapping out how different types of return, including the post-return period, relate to transnational engagements and belonging (Table 3.2). Briefly, different types of return can be considered as an element, a determinant or a consequence of transnational engagements and belonging. I make a distinction between return mobilities, the imaginary of return, and return migration and the post-return period. The last of these is indicated separately as it refers to the distinct process of the reintegration of returnees. Following Table 3.2, in the remainder of this section I focus on the description of different types of return and reintegration as elements, determinants and consequences of transnational engagement and belonging.

*Table 3.2*     *Linking return and transnationalism*

|  | Type of return | Link with transnational engagement | Link with transnational belonging |
|---|---|---|---|
| *Return mobilities* | Return visits (holidays, business trips, ancestral visits) | Element of transnational (social) engagement | Determinant of transnational belonging |
|  | Return as temporary relocation |  |  |
| *Imaginary return* | Intention and plan to return | Determinant of transnational engagement | Element of transnational belonging |
|  | Aspiration, hope, wish to return |  |  |
| *Return migration* | Long-term return | Consequence of transnational engagement | Consequence of transnational belonging |
|  | Ancestral return |  |  |
| *Post-return* | Reintegration process | Consequence of transnational engagement | Consequence of transnational belonging |

*Note:* Author's own creation.

## Return Mobilities and Imaginary Return as Elements of Transnational Engagement and Belonging

Within return mobilities I consider short return visits – such as holidays, business trips and ancestral visits for the children of migrants – and temporary relocations, which include, for example, the longer stays of retirees for part of the year in their communities of origin (King and Christou, 2011; see also Miah, Chapter 7). These activities can be considered as elements of transnational engagement (see Table 3.2, column 2). For imaginary return, I make a distinction between the more objective and emotional aspects of return ideas. I refer to intentions and plans to return as part of the migratory plan, ideals and objectives of the individual. For example, for a student migrant, investing in education abroad can be ideal for finding a job upon return and is a natural part of the migration plan (Gu and Schweisfurth, 2015). With aspiration, hope and a wish to return, I aim to encompass the more emotional and affective dimensions of the return idea. Both types of imaginary return, in fact, have a close association with how transnational belonging is understood and measured and therefore I place them as elements of it (see Table 3.2, column 3).

## Imaginary Return as a Determinant of Return Mobilities (Transnational Engagement)

What does transnationalism mean for different types of return? In the first instance, I propose an association between imaginary return and return mobilities (see left side of Figure 3.1). Namely, *the intention and aspiration to return among migrants and their descendants may be positively or negatively related to their return mobilities.* To explain, primarily, we can argue that, if a migrant has a plan to go back to the origin country after a certain period of time, she or he may want to keep the social contacts close and active (see Bell and Erdal, 2015). This may result in more frequent return visits but also engagement in more intense and regular social, economic and political activities oriented towards the origin country. Perhaps less likely, imaginary return may also have no or a negative relation with return mobilities. If the migration project is temporary and has a very independent goal, migrants may refrain from return mobility. For example, if a lifestyle migrant is looking for new experiences elsewhere, their interest in return mobilities may be non-existent or even negative (see Hayes, 2015). They may prefer not to have much contact with home or deliberately avoid maintaining strong connections. Independent of the ability to do so, a similar argument can be made for student migrants who plan to be abroad for a short period and choose not to go back to the country of origin for visits.

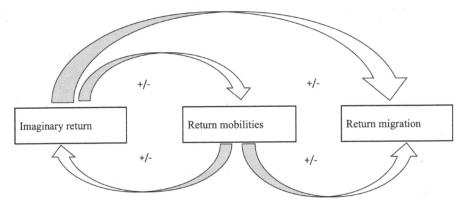

*Note:* Author's own figure.

*Figure 3.1*    Manifold associations between imaginary return, return mobilities and return migration

**Return Mobilities as a Determinant of Imaginary Return (Transnational Belonging)**

Following the first proposal and the highlighting of a bidirectional approach, I suggest that *return mobilities may be positively or negatively related to the intention and aspiration to return among migrants and their descendants* (see left side of Figure 3.1). For example, Duval (2004) conceptualises return mobility as a process of identity negotiation between origin and destination societies which both allows migrants to position themselves in relation to the two contexts and influences their desire and incentives to remain connected. In some instances, this effect of return mobilities can be positive and increase migrants' intentions of and aspiration to return back to the origin country. However, the effect of these visits may also function in a different way and could confront migrants with the idea that they would rather remain 'visitors' than become returnees in the future. For instance, in their study among Polish migrants, Bell and Erdal (2015) suggest that, for those migrants who engage in return visits, these visits reconfirm that life carries on and that their permanent return may simply be an illusion (see also Bell, 2016).

**Return Migration as a Consequence of Return Mobilities and Imaginary Return**

Duval (2004, p.54) asked, almost two decades ago, 'Can the return visit, as a transnational exercise bridging identities and facilitating the maintenance of social networks and fields, indeed facilitate return migration?' I argue that *return mobilities and imaginary return may positively or negatively affect the voluntariness and preparedness of migrants and may or may not lead to return migration* (see right side of Figure 3.1). In this proposition, I see return migration as an outcome of return mobilities and the intentions and aspirations for return.

Given the oft-argued mismatch between imaginaries of return and return migration (Bilgili and Siegel, 2017) and because return intentions do not necessarily translate into actual return migration, one has to bear in mind both the positive, the negative or the absence of a relationship between them.

On the one hand, those who engage more in return visits and who have higher levels of intentions and aspirations for return migration may be more prepared for it. Aspirations for return may function as an emotional resource and the plan to return may help migrants to seek out resources and conditions that help them to execute their return migration. Moreover, temporary return visits may help migrants to sustain the necessary social bonds with family and friends in the origin country and increase the wishes, aspirations and hopes to one day return long-term. Zontini (2015) argues that annual visits are important in strengthening connections and fostering a sense of belonging among Italian migrants who are compelled to consider the idea of return at some point and saw the close contact with families and friends back home as a preparation for their future return (see also Baldassar, 2007; Bolzman et al., 2006). Bell and Erdal (2015) similarly suggest that return visits are important because they help to maintain and gain more shared experiences and memories (see again Miah, Chapter 7).

Some also see return mobilities as 'testing grounds' for more permanent return or a form of ancestral return. As Duval (2004) puts it, migrants get a chance to observe the changes in their origin country during their visits and relate to these accordingly. Sometimes the visits may allow them to assess their career prospects upon return or help them to see how they would be able to position themselves within the wider social context. In short, return visits help migrants to reaffirm social ties, rebuild relationships and reacquaint themselves with the place of return. In this way, return visits not only increase the wish to return but also help to realise the plan (Duval, 2004).

Return mobilities, however, may also substitute for return migration and, therefore, may also have no or a negative relation to return migration. Return visits may make it possible to exercise a life simultaneously embedded in both the origin and the destination country, without having to return permanently. Particularly if the migrants' legal status allows them to easily make trips to the community of origin, these return mobilities may take away the deeper need to return and enable migrants to sustain a transnational life which excludes the option of a long-term or permanent return. In her study among older Turkish immigrants living in Brussels, Buffel (2017) has shown that migrants were entangled between living in Brussels and Turkey but primarily preferred to 'age in place'. They believed that Brussels provided better healthcare and social-security support yet they still had opportunities to maintain ties through back-and-forth travel or regular phone calls. Even though the longing to return to the homeland as an idea persisted among these migrants, they opted for growing older in their Belgian neighbourhood which they transformed into a transnational social space.

As the evidence suggests, the association between return mobilities, imaginaries of return and return migration can be complex and multi-layered. Moreover, the strength and the direction of these associations may change over the lifecourse as, for many migrants, mobility and sedentarism intersect at different points of their lives (Ralph and Staeheli, 2011). Botterill (2016) also argues that these associations depend on differentiated (classed, gendered and familial) opportunities and limitations that emerge in time. Furthermore, beyond the individual-level conditions across time and space, community, national and international-level circumstances are also crucial. Duval (2004) argues that the relationship between return visits and return migration depends on the transnational nature of the migrant communities within which the individuals are situated. The research on return and transnationalism needs to do more digging into these kinds of mechanism and create a more comprehensive overview of the dynamics and also the factors that come into play when thinking about return mobilities, imaginaries of return and return migration.

## POST-RETURN: REINTEGRATION AS A CONSEQUENCE OF TRANSNATIONAL ENGAGEMENT AND BELONGING

This section discusses what role there is for transnational engagements and belonging in the post-return period that involves the reintegration process (see final row of Table 3.2). Most research with a transnational lens focuses on the ties which migrants have with their country of origin while being abroad. This emphasis overshadows the idea that the linkages with the previous country of settlement do not need to be resolved after return.[4] As a matter of fact, many returnees, including repatriated refugees and rejected asylum-seekers, maintain transnational connections (Weima, 2017). During their migration experience, they make new social contacts and acquire knowledge, know-how and experiences which they take back with them upon return. When transnational connections become part of the daily activities and relationships of migrants when they are abroad, they are more likely to continue after return. The more institutionally embedded these connections are (e.g. hometown associations, religious groups), the easier it is to sustain them (Levitt and Glick Schiller, 2004). Moreover, legal advantages such as having dual citizenship may make it easier for migrants to maintain strong contacts with the previous host society even after return migration (Levitt and Nyberg Sørensen, 2004). Some research has used Boccagni's (2012) conceptualisation of everyday transnationalism by focusing on interpersonal, institutional and emotional ties with past life experiences abroad to see how transnational connections also continue after return migration. For example, Lietaert et al. (2017) have taken into account personal relationships with a significant other abroad (through cross-border communication), interactions with institutions – for example, (diasporic) civil-society organisations – abroad that are relevant for their life upon return and symbolic ties that help to reproduce a part of their identity (e.g. certain consumption patterns or ways of dressing).

It goes beyond the scope of this chapter to discuss in detail how transnational engagements and belonging relate to different dimensions of the reintegration process.[5] However, I briefly highlight that reintegration as a concept is one that is often questioned and lacks a universally accepted definition (see Kuschminder, Chapter 14). It is often discussed in combination with 'sustainable return' and has the underlying assumption that individuals who are reintegrated do not re-migrate (Bilgili and Fransen, 2019). I strongly object to this definition, which is closely interlinked with political objectives; instead I prefer to see reintegration rather as a process that has a multi-dimensional character. Similar to long-lasting discussions on immigrant integration and inclusion, I think this term also calls for a holistic approach that takes into account structural and sociocultural dimensions (Arowolo, 2000; Bilgili and Fransen, 2019). As can be seen in Figure 3.2, I propose that transnational engagements and belonging may have an impact on returnees' reintegration processes: *reintegration may be hindered or facilitated by returnees' sustained transnational engagements or belonging*, depending on which dimension of reintegration we are focusing on and under what conditions. However, there is, thus far, very limited research that systematically looks at how transnational engagements and belonging relate to these dimensions.

There is some research that links transnational engagements and belonging with reintegration processes. For example, Gu and Schweisfurth (2015) discuss how, through transnational education, Chinese students accumulate social and cultural capital that translates into a diasporic consciousness characterised by multiple identities and fosters their social and economic advantage within Chinese society. Their transnational connectedness should not be understood merely by the relations they have with those who are in the former country of settlement but also those they have with other returnees who have similar experiences. The authors state that, with other alumni with similar experiences, they become part of a transnational imaginary that keeps them connected across a range of networks. They refer to these as 'transnational bubbles' within a wider local and national context. The returnee students reintegrate in China not despite but through the help of these networks of which they are proud members and which give a meaning to the interpersonal and intercultural relationships in their daily lives.

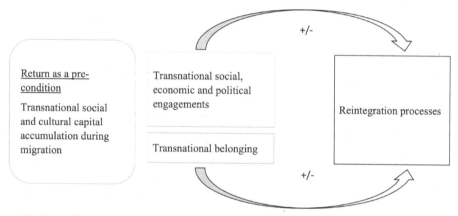

Note: Author's own figure.

Figure 3.2    Reintegration as a consequence of transnational engagement and belonging

In their study among Ghanaian returnees, Setrana and Tonah (2016) also illustrate that the returnees utilise their connections in the prior host country for developing businesses and other benefits which may not be readily available in Ghana. It is important to note, though, that this is, in many instances, in line with 'migrant projects' as a livelihood strategy. For instance, Asiedu (2005) and Mazzucato (2005) have both shown how a considerable share of migrants send remittances to invest in businesses in Accra and Kumasi. Upon return, too, they utilise not only financial resources but also their transnational social networks for these businesses. Grant (2009) considers many returnees as 'transnational entrepreneurs' who are involved in the import–export trade upon return and utilise their connections abroad to both develop and sustain their businesses.

My review of the literature in this field has shown that much of the research focuses on those who are more easily involved in the transnational social field and who place themselves more on the voluntary side of the voluntary and forced return spectrum (Sinatti, 2015, 2019). There is much less research on the transnational connections of those who return under more disadvantaged conditions and what it means for them (Weima, 2017). Lietaert and her colleagues (2017) have addressed this topic by studying the experiences of Georgian and Armenian migrants who returned back from Belgium through a voluntary assistance and reintegration programme. They have shown that, for voluntary assisted-return migrants in Armenia and Georgia, transnational connections have been crucial for their emotional well-being. These connections may function as a coping strategy both emotionally and financially. At the same time, reliance on these connections is found to remind the returnees of their hardship and dependence on external support, which gives an ambivalent meaning to transnational connections (see also Chapter 8 by Lietaert and Chapter 12 by Marino and Lietaert). In this regard, it is important to consider the potentially negative impact of sustained transnational links for reintegration, especially on the more emotional and affective side.

## CONCLUSION

This chapter has provided some conceptually valid associations between return and transnationalism and referred to the already existing literature in the field. By conceptualising return as return mobilities, imaginaries of return and return migration, I aimed to show the complete picture by acknowledging the more latent and intangible aspects of return and its meanings for individuals (see Table 3.1). This approach mirrored adequately the behavioural and emotional aspects of transnationalism. By considering return mobilities and imaginaries of return as elements of transnationalism, I wanted to highlight the inherent linkages between the two. Moreover, by suggesting a relationship between the two as the determinants and consequences of each other, I nurtured the idea that we cannot think of the links between the two as unidirectional and that we can carve out potentially diverse meanings and bidirectional associations between them. It was also important to make consequential links not only to return migration but also to reintegration processes in the post-return period in order to illustrate the continuity in transnational linkages for returnees. As Weima (2017, p.116) argues, 'Returnee transnationalisms contribute to a less state-centric and non-sedentarist understanding of returnee lives and shed new light into the links between return, reintegration and transnationalism.'

All in all, I conclude by emphasising that, in the past couple of decades, there has been a vast amount of research which, in one way or another, has linked return and transnationalism. Yet, the empirical evidence is complex and hard to summarise in a simple manner. This is an inevitable consequence of the varied experiences of migrants and their equally diverse and changing contexts. What I believe lies in the future of research that studies return through a transnational lens is an understanding and further theorisation of the mechanisms through which the associations I proposed (see Figures 3.1 and 3.2) come about. Doing this should challenge some of the troubling sedentary binaries in migration research such as origin/destination, temporary/permanent and forced/voluntary migration. Especially at a time when return is reduced to being a solution to unwanted migration among policy-makers, situating and understanding return as part of the mobilities of individuals with a transnational lens is imperative.

## NOTES

1. According to Gmelch (1980, p.136), 'Migrants returning for a vacation or an extended visit without the intention of remaining at home are generally not defined as return migrants, though in some settings it is difficult to distinguish analytically the migrants returning home for a short visit or seasonally from those who have returned permanently.'
2. See also Portes et al. (1999) for a discussion on transnationalism 'from above' – associated with multinationals or nation-state institutions – and 'from below' – associated with migrants and grassroots organisations.
3. When thinking of the extent to which migrants develop and maintain a sense of belonging to their home country, researchers often refer to feelings of nostalgia and a wish to return as a proxy for attachment (see Itzigsohn and Saucedo, 2002).
4. Return does not necessarily happen back to the community of origin but perhaps to another place in the region where the migrant may consider returning in the wider sense (Duval, 2004).
5. I follow Cassarino's (2004) definition; he made a distinction between economic, social, legal and cultural reintegration. In his view, economic reintegration refers to successful participation in the labour market, access to employment and the ability to create a sustainable livelihood. Social reintegration encompasses participation in organisations, engaging in social interactions with other society members and acceptance among family and friends. Legal reintegration denotes the establishment of citizenship and rights in the country of return, including the ability to participate in local elections and judicial processes. Finally, cultural reintegration refers to participation in local cultural events and an acceptance of the norms and values of the society.

## REFERENCES

Al-Ali, N., Black, R. and Koser, K. (2001) 'The limits to "transnationalism": Bosnian and Eritrean refugees in Europe as emerging transnational communities', *Ethnic and Racial Studies*, **24** (4), 578–600.

al-Rasheed, M. (1994) 'The myth of return: Iraqi Arab and Assyrian refugees in London', *Journal of Refugee Studies*, **7** (2), 199–219.

Ali, N. and Holden, A. (2006) 'Post-colonial Pakistani mobilities: the embodiment of the "myth of return" in tourism', *Mobilities*, **1** (2), 217–42.

Arowolo, O. O. (2000) 'Return migration and the problem of reintegration', *International Migration*, **38** (5), 59–82.

Asiedu, B.A. (2005) 'Some benefits of migrants' return visits to Ghana', *Population, Space and Place*, **11** (1), 1–11.

Baldassar, L. (2007) 'Transnational families and aged care: the mobility of care and the migracy of ageing', *Journal of Ethnic and Migration Studies*, **33** (2), 275–97.

Basch, L., Glick Schiller, N. and Szanton Blanc, C. (1994) *Nations Unbound: Transnational Projects, Postcolonial Predicaments and Deterritorialized Nation-States*, London: Routledge.

Bell, J. (2016) 'Migrants: keeping a foot in both worlds or losing the ground beneath them? Transnationalism and integration as experienced in the everyday lives of Polish migrants in Belfast, Northern Ireland', *Social Identities*, **22** (1), 80–94.

Bell, J. and Erdal, M.B. (2015) 'Limited but enduring transnational ties? Transnational family life among Polish migrants in Norway', *Studia Migracyjne-Przegląd Polonijny*, **41** (3), 77–98.

Bilgili, Ö. (2014) 'Migrants' multi-sited social lives', *Comparative Migration Studies*, **2** (3), 283–304.

Bilgili, Ö. and Fransen, S. (2019) 'Return, reintegration and the role of state' in M. Czaika, L. Rössl, F. Altenburg and T. Pfeffer (eds), *Migration and Integration 8-Dialogzwischen Politik, Wissenschaft und Praxis*, Krema: Donau Universität Krems, pp. 129–39.

Bilgili, Ö. and Siegel, M. (2017) 'To return permanently or to return temporarily? Explaining migrants' intentions', *Migration and Development*, **6** (1), 14–32.

Black, R. and Koser, K. (eds) (1999) *The End of the Refugee Cycle? Refugee Repatriation and Reconstruction*, Oxford: Berghahn.

Boccagni, P. (2012) 'Rethinking transnational studies: transnational ties and the transnationalism of everyday life', *European Journal of Social Theory*, **15** (1), 117–32.

Bolzman, C., Fibbi, R. and Vial, M. (2006) 'What to do after retirement? Elderly migrants and the question of return', *Journal of Ethnic and Migration Studies*, **32** (8), 1359–75.

Botterill, K. (2016) 'Diminished transnationalism? Growing older and practising home in Thailand' in K. Walsh and L. Näre (eds), *Transnational Migration and Home in Older Age*, New York: Routledge, pp. 113–26.

Bovenkerk, F. (1974) *The Sociology of Return Migration*, The Hague: Martinus Nijhoff.

Brees, I. (2010) 'Refugees and transnationalism on the Thai–Burmese border', *Global Networks*, **10** (2), 282–99.

Buffel, T. (2017) 'Ageing migrants and the creation of home: mobility and the maintenance of transnational ties', *Population, Space and Place*, **23** (5), e1994.

Čapo, J. (2015) '"Durable solutions", transnationalism, and homemaking among Croatian and Bosnian former refugees', *Refuge: Canada's Journal on Refugees*, **31** (1), 19–29.

Carling, J. and Erdal, M.B. (2014) 'Return migration and transnationalism: how are the two connected?', *International Migration*, **52** (6), 2–12.

Cassarino, J.P. (2004) 'Theorising return migration: the conceptual approach to return migrants revisited', *International Journal on Multicultural Societies*, **6** (2), 253–79.

Cassarino, J.P. (2008) *Return Migrants to the Maghreb Countries: Reintegration and Development Challenges*, Florence: European University Institute.

Chavez, L.R. (1994) 'The power of the imagined community: the settlement of undocumented Mexicans and Central Americans in the United States', *American Anthropologist*, **96** (1), 52–73.

de Bree, J., Davids, T. and de Haas, H. (2010) 'Post-return experiences and transnational belonging of return migrants: a Dutch-Moroccan case study', *Global Networks*, **10** (4), 489–509.

de Coulon, A. and Wolff, F.-C. (2005) *Immigrants at Retirement: Stay/Return or 'Va-et-Vient'?*, London: London School of Economics and Political Science, Centre for Economic Performance Discussion Paper CEPDP0691.

de Haas, W.H. and Serow, W.J. (1997) 'Retirement migration decision making: life course mobility, sequencing of events, social ties and alternatives', *Journal of the Community Development Society*, **28** (1), 116–30.

Duval, D.T. (2004) 'Linking return visits and return migration among Commonwealth Eastern Caribbean migrants in Toronto', *Global Networks*, **4** (1), 51–67.

Erdal, M., Amjad, A., Bodla, Q.Z. and Rubab, A. (2016) 'Going back to Pakistan for education? The interplay of return mobilities, education, and transnational living', *Population, Space and Place*, **22** (8), 836–48.

Fábos, A. (2015) 'Microbuses and mobile homemaking in exile: Sudanese visiting strategies in Cairo', *Refuge: Canada's Journal on Refugees*, **31** (1), 55–66.

Faist, T., Fauser, M. and Reisenauer, E. (2013) *Transnational Migration*, Cambridge: Polity Press.

Fokkema, T. (2011) '"Return" migration intentions among second-generation Turks in Europe: the effect of integration and transnationalism in a cross-national perspective', *Journal of Mediterranean Studies*, **20** (2), 365–88.

Gmelch, G. (1980) 'Return migration', *Annual Review of Anthropology*, **9**, 135–59.

Grant, R. (2009) *Globalizing City. The Urban and Economic Transformation of Accra, Ghana*, Syracuse NY: Syracuse University Press.

Grasmuck, S. and Hinze, A.M. (2016) 'Transnational heritage migrants in Istanbul: second-generation Turk-American and Turk-German "returnees" in their parents' homeland', *Journal of Ethnic and Migration Studies*, **42** (12), 1959–76.

Gu, Q. and Schweisfurth, M. (2015) 'Transnational connections, competences and identities: experiences of Chinese international students after their return "home"', *British Educational Research Journal*, **41** (6), 947–70.

Guarnizo, L.E. (2003) 'The economics of transnational living', *International Migration Review*, **37** (3), 666–99.

Guarnizo, L., Portes, A. and Haller, W. (2003) 'Assimilation and transnationalism: determinants of transnational political action among contemporary migrants', *American Journal of Sociology*, **108** (6), 1211–48.

Hayes, M. (2015) 'Introduction: the emerging lifestyle migration industry and geographies of transnationalism, mobility and displacement in Latin America', *Journal of Latin American Geography*, **14** (1), 7–18.

Hunter, A. (2011) 'Theory and practice of return migration at retirement: the case of migrant worker hostel residents in France', *Population, Space and Place*, **17** (2), 179–92.

Hunter, A. (2015) 'Empowering or impeding return migration? ICT, mobile phones, and older migrants' communications with home', *Global Networks*, **15** (4), 485–502.

IOM (2019) *Key Migration Terms*, Geneva: International Organization for Migration, https://www.iom.int/key-migration-terms (accessed 12 March 2021).

Itzigsohn, J. and Saucedo, S.G. (2002) 'Immigrant incorporation and sociocultural transnationalism', *International Migration Review*, **36** (3), 766–98.

Itzigsohn, J., Cabral, C.D., Medina, E.H. and Vazquez, O. (1999) 'Mapping Dominican transnationalism: narrow and broad transnational practices', *Ethnic and Racial Studies*, **22** (2), 316–39.

King, R. and Christou, A. (2008) *Cultural Geographies of Counter-Diasporic Migration: The Second Generation Returns 'Home'*, Brighton: University of Sussex, SCMR Working Paper 45.

King, R. and Christou, A. (2011) 'Of counter-diaspora and reverse transnationalism: return mobilities to and from the ancestral homeland', *Mobilities*, **6** (4), 451–66.

King-O'Riain, R.C. (2015) 'Emotional streaming and transconnectivity: Skype and emotion practices in transnational families in Ireland', *Global Networks*, **15** (2), 256–73.

Koh, P. (2015) 'You can come home again: narratives of home and belonging among second-generation Việt Kiều in Vietnam', *SOJOURN: Journal of Social Issues in Southeast Asia*, **30** (1), 173–214.

Kunuroglu, F., Yagmur, K., van de Vijver, F.J. and Kroon, S. (2018) 'Motives for Turkish return migration from Western Europe: home, sense of belonging, discrimination and transnationalism', *Turkish Studies*, **19** (3), 422–50.

Levitt, P. (2008) *Taking Culture Seriously: Unexplored Aspects of the Migration–Development Nexus*, New York: SSRC Migration and Development Conference Paper No. 13.

Levitt, P. and Glick Schiller, N. (2004) 'Conceptualizing simultaneity: a transnational social field perspective on society', *International Migration Review*, **38** (3), 1002–39.

Levitt, P. and Nyberg Sørensen, N. (2004) *Global Migration Perspectives: The Transnational Turn in Migration Studies*, Geneva: Global Commission on International Migration, Global Migration Perspectives No. 6.

Ley, D. and Kobayashi, A. (2005) 'Back to Hong Kong: return migration or transnational sojourn?', *Global Networks*, **5** (2), 111–27.

Lietaert, I., Broekaert, E. and Derluyn, I. (2017) 'The boundaries of transnationalism: the case of assisted voluntary return migrants', *Global Networks*, **17** (3), 366–81.

Mazzucato, V. (2005) *Ghanaian Migrants' Double Engagement: A Transnational View of Development and Integration Policies*, Geneva: Global Commission on International Migration, Global Migration Perspectives No. 48.

Morawska, E. (2007) 'Transnationalism' in M.C. Waters and R. Ueda (eds), *Harvard Encyclopedia of the New Americans*, Cambridge MA: Harvard University Press, pp. 149–63.

O'Flaherty, M., Skrbis, Z. and Tranter, B. (2007) 'Home visits: transnationalism among Australian migrants', *Ethnic and Racial Studies*, **30** (5), 817–44.

Oeppen, C. (2013) 'A stranger at "home": interactions between transnational return visits and integration for Afghan-American professionals', *Global Networks*, **13** (2), 261–78.

Peixoto, J., Candeias, P., Ferreira, B., de Oliveira, I.T., Azevedo, J., Marques, J.C., Santana, P., Malheiros, J., Madeira, P.M., Schiltz, A., Ferro, A. and Santana, E. (2019) 'New emigration and Portuguese society: transnationalism and return' in C. Pereira and J. Azevedo (eds), *New and Old Routes of Portuguese Emigration*, Cham: Springer, pp. 49–72.

Pelliccia, A. (2017) 'Ancestral return migration and second-generation Greeks in Italy', *Journal of Modern Greek Studies*, **35** (1), 129–54.

Portes, A., Guarnizo, L. and Landolt, P. (1999) 'The study of transnationalism: pitfalls and promises of an emergent research field', *Ethnic and Racial Studies*, **22** (2), 217–37.

Ralph, D. and Staeheli, L.A. (2011) 'Home and migration: mobilities, belongings and identities', *Geography Compass*, **5** (7), 517–30.

Ramji, H. (2006) 'British Indians "returning home": an exploration of transnational belongings', *Sociology*, **40** (4), 645–62. DOI: 10.1177%2F0038038506065152.

Reynolds, T. (2008) *Ties That Bind: Families, Social Capital and Caribbean Second-Generation Return Migration*, Brighton: University of Sussex, SCMR Working Paper No. 46.

Ruben, R., van Houte, M. and Davids, T. (2009) 'What determines the embeddedness of forced-return migrants? Rethinking the role of pre- and post-return assistance', *International Migration Review*, **43** (4), 908–37.

Setrana, M.B. and Tonah, S. (2016) 'Do transnational links matter after return? Labour market participation among Ghanaian return migrants', *The Journal of Development Studies*, **52** (4), 549–60.

Sinatti, G. (2015) 'Return migration as a win–win–win scenario? Visions of return among Senegalese migrants, the state of origin and receiving countries', *Ethnic and Racial Studies*, **38** (2), 275–91.

Sinatti, G. (2019) 'Return migration, entrepreneurship and development: contrasting the economic growth perspective of Senegal's diaspora policy through a migrant-centred approach', *African Studies*, **78** (4), 609–23.

Snel, E., Engbersen, G. and Leerkes, A. (2006) 'Transnational involvement and social integration', *Global Networks*, **6** (3), 285–308.

Tharmalingam, S. (2016) 'Making a space a home: role of homeland-based cultural practices in home-making of Tamils and Somalis in Norway', *International Journal of Social Science Studies*, **4** (6), 84–93.

United Nations (1998) *Recommendations of Statistics on International Migration, Revision 1*, New York: United Nations Department of Economic and Social Affairs, Statistics Division.

van Meeteren, M. (2012) 'Transnational activities and aspirations of irregular migrants in Belgium and the Netherlands', *Global Networks*, **12** (3), 314–32.

Vathi, Z. and King, R. (2011) 'Return visits of the young Albanian second generation in Europe: contrasting themes and comparative host-country perspectives', *Mobilities*, **6** (4), 503–18.

Vertovec, S. (2001) 'Transnationalism and identity', *Journal of Ethnic and Migration Studies*, **27** (4), 573–82.

Vertovec, S. (2004) 'Migrant transnationalism and modes of transformation', *International Migration Review*, **38** (2), 970–1000.

Wahlbeck, Ö. (1998) 'Transnationalism and diasporas: the Kurdish example', Paper presented at the International Sociological Association XIV World Congress of Sociology, Montreal, 26 July–1 August.

Wahlbeck, Ö. (2015) 'The Finnish and Swedish migration dynamics and transnational social spaces', *Mobilities*, **10** (1), 100–18.

Wang, L.K. (2016) 'The benefits of in-betweenness: return migration of second-generation Chinese American professionals to China', *Journal of Ethnic and Migration Studies*, **42** (12), 1941–58.

Weima, Y. (2017) 'Refugee repatriation and ongoing transnationalisms', *Transnational Social Review*, **7** (1), 113–17.

Wessendorf, S. (2007) '"Roots migrants": transnationalism and "return" among second-generation Italians in Switzerland', *Journal of Ethnic and Migration Studies*, **33** (7), 1083–102.

Zontini, E. (2015) 'Growing old in a transnational social field: belonging, mobility and identity among Italian migrants', *Ethnic and Racial Studies*, **38** (2), 326–41.

# 4. Gendering return migration
## Russell King and Aija Lulle

## INTRODUCTION

Except in a few dark corners of migration studies where gender-blindness and patriarchal interpretations still hold sway, with migrants implicitly assumed to be male or treated as genderless units of labour, it is now accepted that migration is a fundamentally gendered phenomenon. Over the past three decades, gender has progressively been 'mainstreamed' into the study of migration, albeit this process has been uneven and has proceeded in stages.

One aspect of the wider phenomenon of migration which has received less attention from a gendered perspective is return migration. On the one hand, the literature on gender and migration tends to overlook the return stage of the migration cycle. If we scan the standard texts on gender and migration, we find that they mainly or even exclusively deal with the initial structural, network, family and individual factors framing the act of migration, and the gendered roles, divisions, tensions and changes which take place amongst migrant communities in their destination settings.[1] On the other hand, if we examine the literature on return migration, we discover that gender is given scant attention.[2]

One further general remark is crucial to make at the outset: the conflation of gender in migration with attentiveness solely to the experience of women. For a time, especially in the 1980s and 1990s but also occasionally since then, this seemed to be an almost automatic assumption. Take, for example, the title of an important edited collection by Anthias and Lazaridis (2000): *Gender and Migration in Southern Europe: Women on the Move*. Or the revealing index entry in Urry's (2007) landmark book *Mobilities:* 'gender: see women'. It needs to be emphasised that gendered experiences of migration and return are about the experiences of *both* women *and* men (and of other gendered identities). Such roles and experiences are *relational*, conditioned by power-laden dynamics across the gender divide, both within and outside the family. Moreover, these relational dynamics also exist *within* genders, formed by power hierarchies and other relations shaped by generation, ethnicity, race, culture, class and employment status.

In the next section of the chapter we briefly recount the incorporation of a gender lens into the field of migration, including return. We sketch out a typical assumptive model of gender dynamics throughout the migration process, from departure to return and post-return. We then examine in more detail the gendered motivations for return migration. The succeeding section deals with the more specific phenomenon of forced return, based on selected case studies from the literature, which illustrate how masculinities and femininities are affected by this form of return. The penultimate section examines gender roles after return to the home country. The conclusion sums up key messages from the chapter and identifies avenues of research for future attention.

## GENDER IN MIGRATION AND RETURN

Most of the general textbooks on migration published recently acknowledge that migration is a gendered phenomenon (e.g. Castles et al., 2014, pp.61–2, 257–8; Samers, 2010, pp.98–103). These texts and those of other authors who chart the evolution of gender in migration studies (e.g. King et al., 2006; Marchetti, 2018) point to the 1980s as the 'lift-off' period when the relevance of gender to migration was recognised, even if at this stage attention was focused exclusively on women. Two pioneering studies are frequently highlighted: Phizacklea's *One Way Ticket: Migration and Female Labour* (1983), and a paper by Morokvaśic (1984a) intriguingly titled 'Birds of passage are also women', published in a special issue of the *International Migration Review* on 'Women in migration' (Morokvaśic, 1984b). The title of Morokvaśic's paper was a direct riposte to an important book, *Birds of Passage* (Piore, 1979), which was a broadly Marxist analysis of the role of migrant labour in the growth of capitalist industrial production in Europe and North America. Phizacklea and Morokvaśic challenged the hegemonic model of labour migration as a male-led process with women either remaining behind in the home country or following on later as part of family-reunion migration. According to these two authors, women were not mere followers of men in migration but were often pioneers in constructing their own female-led migration chains, as the Irish, Caribbean and Filipino cases demonstrated.

Thus started an intellectual and activist initiative, resulting from the intersection of migration with the nascent field of 'Women's studies', towards the *feminisation* of migration and of ways of thinking about migration (Buijs, 1993; Phizacklea, 1998; Pojmann, 2006). This initiative had both a quantitative and a qualitative aspect (Marchetti, 2018, pp.444–5). At a quantitative level, it was belatedly realised that women made up very nearly one half of all international migrants globally. At a qualitative level, the agency and independence of women migrants were emphasised, as well as their multiple layers of disadvantage – as women, as migrants and as often racialised foreigners (Lazaridis, 2000). This bifurcated experience of women in migration – as either 'victims' or 'heroes', reluctant followers or independent pioneers – feeds through into return migration, as we shall see shortly.

The male-led migration model of the early postwar decades, during which millions of migrant workers from poor countries were recruited to labour in construction, heavy industry and manufacturing, was relatively short-lived. Economic restructuring in the 1970s and 1980s, followed by the collapse of the communist bloc in Europe in 1989–91, opened up new geographies and typologies of migration flows and returns which also had new gendered characteristics. Especially since the removal of the Iron Curtain as a barrier to migration, the domestic help and care-work sectors, as occupational destinations for migrant women within Europe, grew rapidly. Similar large-scale flows built up in North America. The result was a flurry of classic studies published in the years bridging the new millennium (Andall, 2000; Anderson, 2000; Ehrenreich and Hochschild, 2002; Hondagneu-Sotelo, 2001; Momsen, 1999; Parreñas, 2001). In fact, across the richest countries of the world, not only in North America and Europe but also the Gulf States, Singapore and elsewhere, migrant domestic and care-workers have formed an expanding category of gendered and racialised labour shaped by broader processes of global and national labour market segmentation.

The most recent phase in the theorisation of gender and migration is marked by a series of important papers by feminist migration scholars who adopt an interdisciplinary approach combining sociology, anthropology, history and human geography (see especially Donato et al., 2006a; Mahler and Pessar, 2001a, 2006; Silvey, 2004, 2006).[3] Whilst much of this more recent debate still entails a concentration on women-centred studies, these papers constitute a new focus on gender as a socially constructed analytical category permeating the whole migration process, including return. Moreover, they also foregrounded new research on the shifting masculinities of men involved in migration processes (see, e.g., Ahmad, 2015; Datta et al., 2009; Donaldson et al., 2009; Elmhirst, 2007; Gallo and Scrinzi, 2016; Hoang and Yeoh, 2011; Osella and Osella, 2000).

From the insights provided by the literature reviewed thus far, we extract three conceptual ideas which are relevant to our analysis of return migration as a gendered phenomenon. These are gender as a *relational* concept, the debate on *intersectionality* and the notion of *gendered geographies of power*.

The relationality of gender has many ramifications (Anthias, 2000). Gender is a central organising principle of social relations. The behaviour, constraints and opportunities of one gender in migration are predicated on the behaviour and power dynamics exercised by the other gender; but this also applies to within-gender relations such as that between the generations. Relationality can be expressed within family and kinship networks – between husbands and wives, parents and children, brothers and sisters and so on – and is also subject to the 'gender regimes' within broader society, based on what is seen as 'acceptable' or 'desirable' behaviour between men and women of different ages and statuses. There are two further dimensions of gender relations to be considered for migrant men and women: those within their own ethnic community, and those played out in relation to the dominant group in the host society. Finally, it must be appreciated that the relationship between migration and gender relations is two-way: gender helps to explain how emigration, immigration and return migration are organised; but the reverse is also true – migration and return can fundamentally change gender relations.

This last statement provides a link to 'gendered geographies of power' (Mahler and Pessar, 2001a). By 'geographies' is meant the various spaces and territories through which migrants move and in which they become socially embedded as well as the multiple spatial and social scales involved. These scales range from the body (migration being self-evidently an embodied experience) through the family to the wider local or regional community, and finally up to national scales (e.g. gendered rules on migration and citizenship) and the global level of gendered global labour markets. Another important component in Mahler and Pessar's model is 'social location'. This refers to people's positions within 'hierarchies of power created through historical, political, economic, geographic, kinship-based and other socially stratifying facts' (2001a: pp.445–6). These positionalities are gendered and have the potential to shift across various stages of the migration cycle, according to migrants' ability to effect change in their social situation. However, such hierarchies are based not just around gender but are complexly entwined with nationality, race, class, sexuality and so on – which implies an intersectional approach.

Intersectionality, which had its origins in feminist Black scholars' writings on the multiple oppressions of African-American women in the 1980s, has spread latterly into gendered analyses of the experiences of migrant women in a variety of global contexts (Amelina and Lutz, 2019, pp.7–9; Marchetti, 2018, pp.447–8). Indeed, Bastia (2014, p.240) asks: Are female migrants the new quintessential intersectional subject? 'Intersectional thinking' criticises the sole focus on gender and makes the case for an interlocking analysis of gender, initially alongside class and race/ethnicity. Other social categories added include age/generation, education/skills, sexuality and 'disability'. The intersectional approach specifically focuses on 'axes of inequality' which intertwine in the production and reproduction of unequal life chances across the gendered migrant lifecourse as it moves in a spatial trajectory from origin to destination(s) and back to origin (Amelina and Lutz, 2019, pp.49–51).

## FROM ORIGIN TO DESTINATION AND THEN RETURN: A MODEL OF SHIFTING GENDER DYNAMICS

As a prelude to the more detailed examination of the gendered dynamics of return migration, we present a heuristic model as a template. Although we do not cite any literature to back this up, we have in mind the two largest global flows from lower to higher income countries in recent decades – from Mexico to the United States and from Turkey to Germany. Our model is based on a typical migration cycle (emigration, immigration, return migration, post-return) of labour migrants, incorporating family migration (or family-reunion migration, or family formation abroad), prior to the return. We link the model to the theoretical ideas of relationality, intersectionality and gendered geographies of power.

Labour migration in the early postwar decades – the *Gastarbeiter* programme in Germany or the *bracero* scheme for the United States and Mexico – mostly involved male workers in their initial phases, and hence the frequent returns were also of circulating men. The shift to a more family-based model of migration, facilitated by host-country social legislation on family reunion and rights to family life, or achieved by irregular means, brought women and children into the picture. Here we see a diversity of situations unfold. In some settings, women remained confined to childcare and home management roles, and so became isolated from the host society and deprived of the extended family support they had enjoyed in the home country. However, if migrant women were able to access work, then this could be a force for change in gender relations, improving their social location in the hierarchies of power within their family, ethnic community and the wider society. Having their own income (provided they were able to have some control over how it was spent) elevated their status within the household and gave them enhanced confidence at a personal and relational level. On the downside, their disadvantaged position in a gendered, segmented and often racialised labour market meant that their employment ambitions would be frustrated, arguably more so than migrant men, by a ceiling made of concrete rather than glass.

Taking our heuristic model to the next stage, return, we observe that, on the whole, women are less desirous of returning than men, a finding which reflects their respective gendered power relationships and identities in the two geographical settings. Women are reluctant to return-migrate because they feel emotionally closely linked to their children and the latter's wellbeing and are unwilling to sacrifice whatever empowerment they have achieved through earning an income and absorbing some of the gender-equality norms and behaviours of the host society. If they returned, they would be drawn back into the more patriarchal society of the home country and perhaps become geographically and socially isolated in rural settings. They would miss the social, retailing and health facilities of an urban centre in the destination country. Men, on the other hand, are more open to return as they see this as a way of reclaiming their social status, and even enhancing it as a 'successful' returned migrant. Returning to a rural or small-town environment, men generally fit more comfortably back into village life and can engage in homosocial activities in the streets, squares, cafés and bars, and participate in hobby farming, hunting, fishing and other male-based leisure activities.

The model outlined above is only relevant for certain types of migration and return. It is less applicable to highly skilled migration, or independent female migration where it is the men who stayed behind. Clearly the gendered experiences of return are highly contingent, dependent on the geographical, developmental and temporal contexts. The rest of this chapter explores these more varied outcomes, based on a review of empirical case studies.

## MOTIVATIONS AND DECISIONS TO RETURN

The gendering of decisions to return is influenced by the pattern of gender relations in three reference settings: the country of origin, the country of destination and, easily overlooked, the migrants' ethnic community in the destination country. In the stylised model presented above, the society of origin is more traditional and socially conservative, that of destination more liberal and socially advanced, whereas the social forms created by the migrant community might be hypothesised as a hybrid between the two. All these assumptions need to be nuanced, even overturned, by different real-world situations. Moreover, in most if not all societies, gender relations are not static but undergoing change. This change is not always or inevitably in a 'progressive' direction.

People return 'home' in multiple gendered roles: as women, men, wives, husbands, mothers, fathers, daughters, sons, brothers, young, middle-aged and old, higher- and lower-skilled and with diverse sexual identities. They return as individuals or with other family members; families and households may be split or reunited through return. Even those who return on their own are likely to be involved in ongoing transnational social, economic and care relationships with family members in different locations (see Bilgili, Chapter 3).

Several empirical studies carried out over recent decades, including some classic monographs (e.g. Grasmuck and Pessar, 1991; Levitt, 2001), reveal a consistent, time-proven trend: women are more reluctant than men to return (see Girma, 2017; Le Mare et al., 2015; Pérez, 2005; Potter and Conway, 2005; Sondhi and King, 2017; Vlase, 2013). All of the above are qualitative studies based on interviews and ethnographic fieldwork. We pick out two examples to illustrate some concrete perspectives. Writing about the gendering of return to the Caribbean, Potter and Conway (2005, p.285) report that female returnees regret 'the loss of gendered gains made in metropolitan societies' in the UK and elsewhere. Returning women realise that they have less access to work in their home countries and are therefore more dependent on their husbands. As a consequence, they spend more time on domestic work and child rearing, thereby conforming to local norms of what married women should do, including what is 'respectable' behaviour.

In the second example, on the return of Indian students after they have completed their studies in Canada, Sondhi and King (2017) find marked contrasts between men and women. Male former students consider their return to be 'natural' and expected to remain in India permanently, except for a minority who aspire to develop an academic career outside India. Pressures for men to return come from patrilineal family norms whereby sons continue the family lineage, get married, and cater to the needs of their ageing parents. Whilst female students, too, are under an expectation to return, many are reluctant to do so, having experienced a measure of independence from their families and hence reconfigured their personal gendered geographies of power (cf. Mahler and Pessar, 2001a). Those who have returned lament their decision and seek ways to move abroad again. Not only are they subject to renewed control by their parents, they also face gendered barriers in the Indian professional job market.

Complementary insights into the gendering of return are also revealed by quantitative surveys. One of the first was by Waldorf (1995) who used repeat survey data on the main 'guestworker' populations in Germany over the period 1970–89. The survey included a question on intention to return within four years. For the initial years of the survey, gender differences were minimal, except for Yugoslavian women, who expressed lower return intentions, reflecting a more rapid integration in Germany than the other groups surveyed – Italians, Greeks, Spaniards and Turks. The main trend over time was for women to rapidly become less willing to return. Other studies are more explicit in finding women less prone to express an intention to return compared to men: for example, Paparusso and Ambrosetti (2017) on Moroccans in Italy, and Snel et al. (2015) on Central and Eastern Europeans in the Netherlands. The latter study found male respondents three times more likely than females to intend to return within two years.

The male perspective on return, generally under-researched, is uncovered in a series of qualitative studies on Somaliland (Gullbekk Markussen, 2020; Hansen, 2008; Kleist, 2010). Whilst Somali women are reluctant to return from (relatively) egalitarian societies in Europe and North America, men are more geared to return as a response to the loss of masculinity suffered during migration, when they were either unemployed or performing what they regarded as demeaning jobs. Returning to Somaliland, male returnees hope to reassert their masculine identity in patriarchal families and lineages in their homeland.

Economic factors can differentially affect gendered returns. In general, women returning to a poorer country with a patriarchally structured labour market face greater challenges than men in getting a job, as studies in Morocco and the Caribbean have shown (see de Haas and Fokkema, 2010; Phillips and Potter, 2005). Instead, women from low- and middle-income countries may need to remain abroad in order to support their extended families back home. Their return would disrupt the transborder household economy maintained by remittances, especially where they are the main income-earner for their families – the case for many female-led migrations. The economic influence over the gendering of return migration became particularly evident during and following the global financial crisis, especially in southern European Union countries severely affected by recession (Martínez-Buján, 2019; Michail, 2013). The crisis hit male-dominated sectors of employment, such as construction and factory work, harder than female migrant work in the care sector; male unemployment increased faster than female job loss. Gender norms amongst many of the migrant groups (e.g. Albanians in Greece) made it unacceptable for gender-role switching whereby men would become home-makers and child-carers, and women the sole breadwinners (van Boeschoten, 2015). In any case, it was generally impossible to sustain the migrant household on just the woman's wage, which would often be based on part-time employment. Men tended therefore to return to their countries of origin to try to find work there, or pick up their small farm holdings, whilst women held on to their jobs in the host country. This pattern of transborder family separation, well documented in the case of Albania and Greece (Michail, 2013), also allowed the children of the migrants to continue their education and stay with their peers in the host country.

Following another line of economic thinking, return migration might be stimulated when the country of origin enters a period of strong development and offers its emigrants both an improved standard of living and a better quality of life (see Wahba, Chapter 2, and King, Chapter 22). The gender dimensions of this kind of economically motivated return are not so clear; in many cases such returns are more related to lifecourse stage although they may be underscored by 'traditional' ideals of heteronormative family life. This is what Ní Laoire (2008) found in her study of 'Celtic tiger' Ireland, seen as the 'natural' place for emigrants to return to raise their young families. Similar findings are evident in recent Estonian return migration of young graduates from London (Saar and Saar, 2020). A newly buoyant Estonian economy has coincided with the passage from one life-stage (young single workers) to another (married with young children born or planned), when the superior lifestyle and lower cost of living of their Baltic homeland exerts a strong pull influence.

A different set of perspectives for engendering return migration motives arises from considerations of family networks, emotions and care concerns. Thomson (2005), in his study on the return migration of British postwar emigrants to Australia, found homesickness to be more prevalent amongst women, mainly because they reacted less well than their menfolk to the challenging 'macho' world of Australia in the early postwar decades. However, in a subtle twist, Thomson also noted how some men wanting to move back to Britain 'blamed' their decision on the homesickness of their wives rather than recognise publicly their own struggles with masculinity and identity in the Australian context.

Much more common is the situation where women are more often pulled to return than men due to their gendered responsibilities and pressures to care for family members, especially elderly parents (Baldassar et al., 2007). In a joint-authored monograph (Lulle and King, 2016), we have documented the pressures on middle-aged Latvian migrant women in the UK to return, or to make frequent return visits, to care for elderly or frail relatives. Our research also reveals another angle on gendered return: Latvian mature women work in the UK long enough to accumulate savings and a pension which gives them the economic freedom to choose whether to return or not, independent of their husbands (many such women are widows, divorced or separated).

Going back to our heuristic model elaborated earlier, it would be a mistake to oversimplify the bilateral contrast between the society of the home country as rigidly patriarchal and hostile to the lives of returning women, and the host-country society as more liberal, egalitarian and open-minded. In some migrant communities in destination countries, patriarchal structures travel with the migrants and survive intact: Walton-Roberts (2004, p.366) calls them 'transnational patriarchies'. This happens particularly when migrants originate from socially conservative rural areas and reproduce in a static form the values and behaviours of those rural areas as they were when they left. Indeed, partly as a reactive defence mechanism against what are seen as the too-liberal values of 'Western' society, the dictatorial level of patriarchal control exercised by male family heads over female family members, especially wives and daughters, may be even greater than that in the home country, which meantime might be liberalising to some extent. Research on second-generation Greeks 'returning' to Greece from the United States and Germany (Christou and King, 2014) and on second-generation Turks relocating from Germany to Turkey (King and Kılınç, 2013) documents numerous instances where young women move to their parents' home country as a legitimate escape-route from oppressive and sometimes physically abusive parental behaviour. Christou and King (2014) also report cases whereby gay men have relocated to the anonymity of a big city, Athens, to escape homophobia amongst the tightly knit 'Greektown' where they were brought up in the United States or Germany.

## CHANGING MASCULINITIES AND FEMININITIES IN FORCED RETURN

Gendered roles and effects in return migration must also be unpacked through a critical understanding of the (un)free will of the return. Forced return imposes extra layers of compulsion and vulnerability over gendered negotiations about the return move. As the literature reviewed below suggests, expected performances of masculinity in migration are compromised, female exploitation deepened, and ongoing quests for a new identity ruptured and reshaped.

In a pioneering study revealingly titled *Migration Can Fall Apart*, Miller (2008) documents in raw detail the life-stories of deportees from the United States to Jamaica. Most of the deportation stories presented are of young men whose low levels of capital – social, cultural, educational, economic and so on – have rendered them vulnerable throughout their lives. Many are from poor, fragmented families, typically moving to the United States as young children or teenagers and failing to properly establish themselves and integrate there. The result, repeated in many tragic stories described in the book, is a descent into alienation, substance abuse, gangster life and criminality, followed by arrest and deportation to a country which is even less familiar and more alienating to them, where they are rejected by Jamaican society.

One of Miller's chapters is headed 'You look like a fool returning with nothing' (2008, pp.51–71), and this is a theme picked up by other writers on involuntary return migration. Kleist's (2017) study of Ghanaian male migrants deported from Libya during and after that country's civil war reveals their sense of shame and social inadequacy. Returning home sometimes with nothing more than the clothes on their backs, they are seen as a burden to the family whom they originally set out on the migration trail to financially support. This was their role in the moral economy of a society dependent on emigration; however, their forced return shatters this masculine ideal.

The predominance of young males amongst deportees is evident both from statistics and from research on this kind of forced return. Young men tend to be the majority in flows of irregular migration, such as those from Central and South America to the United States or from Africa to Europe. Their undocumented status and presence at border crossings, public spaces and job locations such as construction sites makes them visible to the official eye and therefore easy to pick up, arrest and deport (Hagan et al., 2008, p.71). Others are deported via the prison system. According to Golash-Boza and Hondagneu-Sotelo (2013), the targeting of Black and Latino men by US police authorities is nothing short of a 'gendered racial removal program', which can leave wives, partners and US-born children in a state of separation.

Similar findings are revealed in the different geographical context of Cape Verde, where the deportation mainly of men from the United States and Europe, has multiple effects on the long-established Cape Verdean tradition of mobility and transnational living (Drotbohm, 2015). Here, too, the deportees are seen as a disappointment to everybody connected to them, consistent with the syndrome of the migrant who returns 'empty-handed' and is thus a failure and a burden. Even more problematic are the impacts on female partners and children left behind, who without their principal breadwinner, have somehow to fend for themselves both economically and emotionally, in a kind of reversal of the normal pattern of migratory family lives. Drotbohm's in-depth ethnography of deportees also uncovered other gendered outcomes: the even greater exclusion and stigmatisation of the few deportee women; and amongst some men, a macho emphasis on the brutality of the crimes committed abroad in order to project an image of 'hardness' (2015, pp.661–2).

For research which looks specifically at female involuntary returns we turn to a recent paper by Nisrane et al. (2020) on Ethiopian domestic workers in the Arabian Gulf countries. Under the prevailing *kafala* system, domestic workers are assigned to an employer and kept in often slave-like conditions for the duration of their contract, usually 2–3 years. Verbal, psychological, physical and sexual abuse are commonplace. The *kafala* system offers two advantages to the receiving country: it prevents migrants' long-term settlement, and it guarantees employers a live-in worker for the contract period. The worker is tied to the employer, who generally holds her passport. In desperation, many Ethiopian women escape their abusive employers but in doing so they break their contract, become 'illegal' and are subject to deportation. As well as documenting horrific cases of abuse, including beatings, rape, starvation and 18-hour working days, Nisrane et al. (2020) focus attention on coping mechanisms post-return. These comprise 'sense-making' and 'benefit-finding'. Sense-making strategies mainly involve attributing 'otherness' to Arabs and thereby 'normalising' their violence towards women as 'it is part of their nature'. In terms of the 'benefits' of such a brutal experience, the women first thank God that they survived and were made stronger by their suffering, unlike many of their co-nationals who had breakdowns or committed suicide. Second, they appreciate that such an exploitative system at least enabled them to support their families via remittances.[4]

We end this part of the chapter with a happier story. Research by Kılınç (2019) in the Turkish tourist city of Antalya shows how deported second-generation German-Turkish young men, sent back to Turkey because of their criminal activities in Germany, are able to reinvent themselves in this 'tourist paradise'. They make use of their languages (Turkish, German, English) to become tourist guides, waiters, shop owners, translators, even real-estate entrepreneurs. Although none has family origins there, they find in Antalya an ideal place for their self-healing; a cosmopolitan environment where they can forge a new purpose in their lives and develop a new spatial belonging. They reject their macho, criminal past and embrace a new masculine identity based on sociality and entrepreneurship. The example of one of the participants is particularly revealing of the remaking of masculinity: previously a gang member, drug dealer and violent criminal in Germany, now the owner of a hair salon who 'talks about hair all day with middle-aged German women!' (2019, p.250).

## GENDERED ROLES AFTER RETURN

Like all stages of the typical migration cycle described earlier, the post-return experiences of migrants are subject to the intersectional and power-laden dynamics of gender relations. For many migrants, a future return was always in their sights, and to that end homeland family ties and contacts with former neighbours, school friends and work colleagues were maintained. Hence, the return is embedded in these transnational ties, some strong and others weaker, which become reactivated after the return takes place. However, after return the direction of ongoing transnational ties is reversed. 'Reverse transnationalism' (King and Christou, 2011) builds on the nostalgia felt by returnees for their relatives, friends and colleagues who remain in the host country.

The possible changes in gender roles and relations after return can be considered an important element of 'social remittances' – the 'ideas, behaviors, identities and social capital that flow from migrant-receiving countries back to migrants' home communities' (Levitt, 1998, p.927). In this scenario a kind of 'battle' develops between the generally more liberal gender norms brought back from the host society and the more 'traditional' gender relations which characterise the country of origin and return. These contrasts are likely to be exacerbated if the migration was to a large metropolitan centre abroad, and the return to a rural village or provincial small town.

Sakka et al. (1999) statistically compared gender-role attitudes between return migrants and a group of non-migrants in villages in Greece. The key variables were sharing household tasks and attitudes towards gender within the family. Questionnaires were administered to samples of 85 returnees and 70 non-migrants. Results showed that task-sharing behaviour had changed to greater equality as a result of living abroad in a different socio-cultural environment (mainly Germany). Gender-role attitudes changed to a lesser extent, and only when these changes were congruent with the financial aims of the family or consistent with the living conditions in rural Greece upon return. Indeed, on the specific question of the participation of women in family decision-making, returned migrants seemed to adopt a more 'traditional' attitude than non-migrants. This could be explained by several influences. First, return migration could be biased towards those migrants with more 'traditional' values. Second, the pace of social change within enclaved Greek migrant labour communities abroad might actually be slower than in rural areas back home, which are more under the influence of national and global trends towards gender equality. Third, the rural employment situation in Greece offers few possibilities for women (unlike in Germany), and so women are forced back into a more subservient role in family decision-making as a result of no longer being income-earners.

Other studies confirm this last point. Vlase (2013) offers a nuanced analysis of the gendered tensions evident within the Romanian migrant household when they return from Italy. Male returnees regain bargaining power within families since they once again become the main or sole breadwinners (instead of joint earners in Italy), and the community of origin also assigns them enhanced social status in recognition of their autonomous economic activities. Many of them used their savings and work experience from Italy to establish small businesses in Romania. Women are keenly aware of their nominally reduced power within the family following return, since they are 'returned' to a largely domestic role. However, they do their best to counter the asymmetric balance of power, for instance by encouraging their young daughters to be independent and develop their own careers, leading to more balanced gender roles over the longer term. Another option for returned women is to retain their transnational network connections to Italy and to go there for occasional short-term work assignments.

In the Asian literature on higher-skilled gendered returns, educated women are more reluctant to return precisely because of their pragmatic unwillingness to accept the strong prevailing gender divisions in their home countries (e.g. Sondhi and King, 2017). Where high-skilled women do return, they have to confront existing gender hierarchies and expectations in academic, professional and management positions (Ge et al., 2011). Their ability to mobilise social remittances against entrenched, professionalised (but also unfair and corrupt) gender norms is limited. Moving away from Asia, Wong's (2014) study of the gendered geographies of skilled return migration to Ghana reveals more varied outcomes, including marital separation in order to preserve career aspirations or the educational prospects of children, reflecting in turn Ghanaian society's more matrifocal nature.

In contrast to all the literature reviewed thus far, more traditional gender norms can also 'travel' across international borders via returning migrants. Evidence for this comes from two quantitative studies based on panel survey data for Jordan (Tuccio and Wahba, 2018) and Egypt (Samari, 2021). This reinforcement of traditional gender roles in the family and in society at large happens when male migrants from these two countries migrate to more conservative Arab countries, specifically Saudi Arabia and the Gulf States, where there is large-scale demand for migrant labour at all skill levels. Their wives and families remain behind, waiting for the men to return. In the Jordanian study, which is the most statistically detailed of the two, the main part of the analysis is focused around a composite index which aggregates several indicators on women's perception of their own status in society. Three key subvariables regard women's views on their leadership roles, their role in family decision-making and their freedom of mobility outside the home. More concrete data relate to family size (number of children) and the proportion of daughters dropping out of school due to patriarchal decisions. The basic comparison is between women in households with a male returnee, and women in households without a returnee. Across the board, Tuccio and Wahba (2018) find a negative impact of return migration. Their conclusion is unequivocally that migration widens the gender gap in Jordan. For Egypt, Samari (2021, p.1115) produces an almost identical conclusion: 'return migration from Arab countries is associated with less egalitarian beliefs and more restrictive gender norms for women'.

A completely different line of analysis is revealed by studies of how returnee women are perceived, and treated, by the societies to which they return, especially where these societies are characterised by aggressive forms of macho behaviour. The most explicit study of this genre is by Alcalde (2020) on street sexual harassment in Lima, Peru. Peruvian returnee women from the United States and Europe had got used to not having to endure this treatment, so it is a shock for them to find that harassment and lewd remarks on the streets and groping (or worse) on buses are daily occurrences in Lima.

Other studies which focus on the gendered, sexualised treatment of returnee women – of different ages – come from the Caribbean and Southern European regions. Research in various Caribbean islands, including Barbados (Phillips and Potter, 2005) and Puerto Rico (Pérez, 2005), explores the contrasting gendered and racialised identities of young men and women, and the different ways they are perceived by the wider societies of these territories. In Barbados, where Phillips and Potter concentrate on the returnee second generation who were born and brought up in Britain, their female research participants complained about the excessive attention paid to them by local men who were constantly 'hitting on them'. On the other hand, local young women saw their return-migrant counterparts, with their metropolitan ways and British accents, as 'unfair competition' for boyfriends and future marriage partners. Somewhat analogous findings emerged in Puerto Rico (Pérez, 2005), except here the gendered performances of young returnees are commented on disparagingly mainly by the older generation (many of whom, ironically, had been themselves migrants earlier in their lives). Young returnee men, with their hip-hop, 'gangsta' clothes, piercings and tattoos, are regarded as feckless and lazy, whilst young women are criticised for their provocative clothing, allegedly loose morals and other behavioural characteristics associated with being *de afuera*, 'from abroad' and therefore not authentically Puerto Rican.

A final example of the intersection between return migration and the sexual stereotyping of returnee women comes from a study of second-generation Italian-American and Greek-American women 'returning' to their ancestral homelands in Italy and Greece (Isaakyan and Triandafyllidou, 2019). The authors focus especially on the sexual stigmatisation of these mostly mature-aged women, who are seen as 'sexual tourists' by local men of all ages, for whom an affair with an American woman enhances their masculinity, both in their own eyes and those of their male friends. The case studies presented in the paper go some way towards challenging the stereotype of the 'easy foreign woman' and shed light on how second-generation women are routed to their parental homelands and negotiate their new gendered belonging there.

As we saw earlier, return motivations and post-return experiences are fundamentally gendered through care responsibilities. Women's traditional tasks to care for family members are an element of universal patriarchy, which assigns to women the major responsibility and expectation to 'take care of care'. Such expectations are more intense in some cultures than others; they are manifested through the gendered duties and obligations inscribed into a society's norms, but also reinforced through internalised guilt and shame if, in a migration situation, necessary hands-on care at crucial life-stages cannot be provided. This is one of the most important reasons for return, especially for women. So the question arises: what happens after the return? Whilst some families, or women on their own, return to countries with well-developed welfare states which include comprehensive care arrangements for older and frail people, the majority of the migrant-sending countries do not fall into this category. Even when they do, as in the UK and the Netherlands, women abroad still feel the burden of responsibility for arranging the healthcare of their ageing family members left behind, and the obligation to return when things get impossible to manage from afar (Baldassar et al., 2007). In most migrant-sending countries, social protection for people who are in need of personal or institutionalised care is patchy, non-existent or too expensive. A good illustration of this is a study by Núñez-Carrasco et al. (2011) on South Africa, where many migrants with ill-health, including HIV-related problems, return home. Who provides the care? Women, of course: either those who also returned with the sick person or those who always stayed behind. Either way, women's productive livelihoods are disrupted. Even where return takes place as the 'logical' end to the migration cycle, it is the women who returned who usually provide whatever care is needed, having often always fulfilled a care role whilst abroad (Olwig, 2012). In this sense the story comes full circle: women who migrated often did so in order to be part of a more gender-equal society, including better economic opportunities, but upon return much of this empowerment is lost.

## CONCLUSION AND WAYS FORWARD

This chapter has explored a relatively little-researched yet vitally important aspect of return migration: how that process is gendered. Gender roles, relations and power dynamics are imbricated in all types of return across all economic and socio-cultural contexts, where gendered identities are intersectionally combined with race, class and other dimensions of the human condition.

Research evidence across multiple geographical settings and time periods consistently shows that women are more reluctant than men to return. This is explained by the personal autonomy and economic empowerment that women are generally able to achieve abroad relative to their situation before migrating. No wonder, then, that they are hesitant about returning to the *status quo ante*, with oppressive gender roles resurrected. Wherever they are, women are pressed to provide care; this is a more-or-less universal social norm which in a migration context can also be their main income-earning opportunity, caring for others outside their families, as well as shouldering care responsibilities for their own family members.[5] Family care duties generally take on an important role following return, partly due to life-stage but also to comply with the gender-norm expectations of the society of origin. However, if care obligations can be sustained transnationally, women are less compelled to return, preferring to continue working abroad to generate remittances which home-based family members can use to support themselves and care for others. If the woman returns, the remittance flow ceases, which can impact the whole family.

Extending the discussion by Girma (2017), several important gaps need to be investigated in future research on the changing gender dynamics of return migration. One of these relates to the impact on men and women who never migrated. How do their lives change when some family members return home? Second, there is scope for focusing in more detail on the ways that the specific social remittance associated with revised gender relations travels across transnational space when return takes place. Third, the intersections of gender with age, ethnicity, family status and so on need further unpacking in the context of return. For instance, age, generation and marital status are key demographic variables which, combined with gender, will have different effects in shaping returns. Fourth, there needs to be a rebalancing of research to move away just from a focus on women to embrace gendered experiences of men in return decisions and outcomes. Fifth, we make a plea for more quantitative studies of the type engaged in by Samari (2021), Tuccio and Wahba (2018) and Waldorf (1995), in order to achieve more statistically robust results. Sixth, there is scope for widening the geographical range beyond studies which focus on the return of migrants from more to less developed countries. This is necessary to move beyond the standard (and sometimes false) dichotomy of emigration being empowering for women and return being disempowering for women and empowering for men. Studies on migration and return between countries within the global South, or in other global settings such as the Middle East, can surely reveal other gendered patterns. Finally, research can be extended longitudinally to examine what happens 'post-post-return'. Are the gendered 'successes' and 'failures' of the return project succeeded by further migrations or by other forms of internal or transnational mobility?

# NOTES

1. There are several books, including edited collections, entitled *Gender and Migration* (see, inter alia, Amelina and Lutz, 2019; Anthias and Lazaridis, 2000; Donato and Gabaccia, 2015; Kofman et al., 2000; Piper, 2009; Timmerman et al., 2018) but none of them engage in an effective treatment of gendering return migration – in retrospect a surprising oversight.
2. Edited books on return migration, including its variants of ethnic and diasporic return, have proliferated since the mid-2000s (Anghel et al., 2019; Harper, 2005; Long and Oxfeld, 2004; Markowitz and Stefansson, 2004, Nadler et al., 2016; Potter et al., 2005; Tsuda, 2009). These volumes generally pay little attention to gender, which sometimes is not even an index entry (the case with Anghel et al., 2019; Markowitz and Stefansson, 2004; Tsuda, 2009). However, in some of these edited books, individual chapters do spotlight gendered differences in the return process (King and Kılınç, 2016 in Nadler et al., 2016; Pérez, 2005 and Phillips and Potter, 2005 in Potter et al., 2005; Thomson, 2005 in Harper, 2005) and we pick these insights up at various points later in our chapter.
3. As with the earlier-cited special issue of *International Migration Review* on 'Women in migration' (Morokvaśic, 1984b), many of these new analyses of gender and migration were associated with special issues of journals, notably *Identities* (Mahler and Pessar, 2001b) on 'Gendering transnational social spaces' and *International Migration Review* (Donato et al., 2006b) on 'Gender and migration revisited'.
4. The findings of Nisrane et al. (2020) are borne out by Kuschminder's (2017) much broader study on Ethiopian return migration, in which she addresses three returnee groups: domestic workers, stu-

dents and professionals. Her focus is on reintegration, a topic treated in more detail in her Chapter 14 in this Handbook.
5. Like most generalisations, there are exceptions to this one. Kuschminder (2017) found that professional women wanted to return to Ethiopia so they would *not* have care responsibilities and therefore could have 'time for themselves'. In Ethiopia they could afford nannies, cooks and cleaners, whereas in the United States they themselves were responsible for these domestic duties.

# REFERENCES

Ahmad, A.N. (2015) *Masculinity, Sexuality, and Illegal Migration: Human Smuggling from Pakistan to Europe*, Karachi: Oxford University Press.
Alcalde, M.C. (2020) 'Gender, autonomy and return migration: negotiating street harassment in Lima, Peru', *Global Networks*, **20** (1), 25–41.
Amelina, A. and Lutz, H. (2019) *Gender and Migration: Transnational and Intersectional Prospects*, London: Routledge.
Andall, J. (2000) *Gender, Migration and Domestic Service: The Politics of Black Women in Italy*, Aldershot: Ashgate.
Anderson, B. (2000) *Doing the Dirty Work: The Global Politics of Domestic Labour*, London: Zed Books.
Anghel, R.G., Fauser, M. and Boccagni, P. (eds) (2019) *Transnational Return and Social Change: Hierarchies, Identities and Ideas*, London: Anthem Press.
Anthias, F. (2000) 'Metaphors of home: gendering new migrations to southern Europe' in F. Anthias and G. Lazaridis (eds), *Gender and Migration in Southern Europe: Women on the Move*, Oxford: Berg, pp. 15–47.
Anthias, F. and Lazaridis, G. (eds) (2000) *Gender and Migration in Southern Europe: Women on the Move*, Oxford: Berg.
Baldassar, L., Baldock, C.V. and Wilding, R. (2007) *Families Caring Across Borders: Migration, Ageing and Transnational Caregiving*, Basingstoke: Palgrave Macmillan.
Bastia, T. (2014) 'Intersectionality, migration and development', *Progress in Development Studies*, **14** (3), 237–48.
Buijs, G. (ed.) (1993) *Migrant Women: Crossing Boundaries and Changing Identities*, Oxford: Berg.
Castles, S., de Haas, H. and Miller, M.J. (2014) *The Age of Migration: International Population Movements in the Modern World*, Basingstoke: Palgrave Macmillan.
Christou, A. and King, R. (2014) *Counter-Diaspora: The Greek Second Generation Returns 'Home'*, Cambridge MA: Harvard University Press.
Datta, K., McIlwaine, C., Herbert, J., Evans, Y., May, J. and Wills, J. (2009) 'Men on the move: narratives of migration and work among low-paid migrant men in London', *Social and Cultural Geography*, **10** (8), 853–73.
de Haas, H. and Fokkema, T. (2010) 'Intra-household conflicts in migration decision making: return and pendulum migration in Morocco', *Population and Development Review*, **36** (3), 541–61.
Donaldson, M., Hibbins, R., Howson, R. and Pease, B. (eds) (2009) *Migrant Men: Critical Studies of Masculinities and the Migration Experience*, New York: Routledge.
Donato, K.M. and Gabaccia, D. (eds) (2015) *Gender and International Migration*, New York: Russell Sage.
Donato, K.M., Gabaccia, D., Heldway, J., Manalansan, M. and Pessar, P.R. (2006a) 'A glass half full? Gender in migration studies', *International Migration Review*, **40** (1), 3–26.
Donato, K.M., Gabaccia, D., Holdaway, J., Manalansan, M. and Pessar, P.R. (eds) (2006b) 'Gender and migration revisited', special issue of *International Migration Review*, **40** (1), 1–249.
Drotbohm, H. (2015) 'The reversal of migratory family lives: a Cape Verdean perspective on gender and sociality pre- and post-deportation', *Journal of Ethnic and Migration Studies*, **41** (4), 653–70.
Ehrenreich, B. and Hochschild, A.R. (eds) (2002) *Global Woman: Nannies, Maids and Sex Workers in the New Economy*, New York: Henry Holt.

Elmhirst, R. (2007) 'Tigers and gangsters: masculinities and feminised migration in Indonesia', *Population, Space and Place*, **13** (3), 225–38.
Gallo, E. and Scrinzi, F. (2016) *Migration, Masculinities and Reproductive Labour: Men of the Home*, New York: Palgrave Macmillan.
Ge, J., Resurreccion, B.P. and Elmhirst, R. (2011) 'Return migration and the reiteration of gender norms in water management politics: insights from a Chinese village', *Geoforum*, **42** (2), 133–42.
Girma, H. (2017) 'The salience of gender in return migration', *Sociology Compass*, **11** (5), e12481.
Golash-Boza, T. and Hondagneu-Sotelo, P. (2013) 'Latino immigrant men and the deportation crisis: a gendered racial removal program', *Latino Studies*, **11** (3), 271–92.
Grasmuck, S. and Pessar, P. (1991) *Between Two Islands: Dominican International Migration*, Berkeley CA: University of California Press.
Gullbekk Markussen, M.K. (2020) '"Nobody comes to Baba for advice": negotiating ageing masculinities in the Somali diaspora', *Journal of Ethnic and Migration Studies*, **46** (7), 1442–59.
Hagan, J., Eschbach, K. and Rodriguez, N. (2008) 'US deportation policy, family separation, and circular migration', *International Migration Review*, **42** (1), 64–88.
Hansen, P. (2008) 'Circumcising migration: gendering return migration among Somalilanders', *Journal of Ethnic and Migration Studies*, **34** (7), 1109–25.
Harper, M. (ed.) (2005) *Emigrant Homecomings: The Return Movement of Emigrants, 1600–2000*, Manchester: Manchester University Press.
Hoang, L.A. and Yeoh, B. (2011) 'Breadwinning wives and left-behind husbands: men and masculinities in the Vietnamese transnational family', *Gender and Society*, **25** (6), 717–39.
Hondagneu-Sotelo, P. (2001) *Doméstica: Immigrant Workers Cleaning and Caring in the Shadows of Affluence*, Berkeley CA: University of California Press.
Isaakyan, I. and Triandafyllidou, A. (2019) 'Transatlantic repatriation: stigma management of second-generation Italian and Greek women "returning home"', *European Journal of Cultural Studies*, **22** (2), 180–94.
Kılınç, N. (2019) 'From vagabond to tourist: second-generation Turkish-German deportees' narratives of self-healing and well-being', *Nordic Journal of Migration Research*, **9** (2), 239–55.
King, R. and Christou, A. (2011) 'Of counter-diaspora and reverse transnationalism: "return" mobilities to and from the ancestral homeland', *Mobilities*, **6** (4), 451–66.
King, R. and Kılınç, N. (2013) *'Euro-Turks' Return: The Counterdiasporic Migration of German-Born Turks to Turkey*, Malmö: Malmö University, Willy Brandt Series of Working Papers in International Migration and Ethnic Relations 2/13.
King, R. and Kılınç, N. (2016) 'The counter-diasporic migration of Turkish-Germans to Turkey: gendered narratives of home and belonging' in R. Nadler, Z. Kovacs, B. Glorius and T. Lang (eds), *Return Migration and Regional Development in Europe: Mobility Against the Stream*, London: Palgrave Macmillan, pp. 167–94.
King, R., Thomson, M., Fielding, T. and Warnes, T. (2006) 'Time, generations and gender in migration and settlement' in R. Penninx, M. Berger and K. Kraal (eds), *The Dynamics of International Migration and Settlement in Europe*, Amsterdam: Amsterdam University Press, pp. 233–67.
Kleist, N. (2010) 'Negotiating respectable masculinity: gender and recognition in the Somali diaspora', *African Diasporas*, **3** (1), 185–206.
Kleist, N. (2017) 'Disrupted migration projects: the moral economy of involuntary return to Ghana from Libya', *Africa*, **87** (2), 322–42.
Kofman, E., Phizacklea, A., Raghuram, P. and Sales, R. (2000) *Gender and International Migration in Europe*, London: Routledge.
Kuschminder, K. (2017) *Reintegration Strategies: Conceptualizing How Return Migrants Reintegrate*, Cham: Palgrave Macmillan.
Lazaridis, G. (2000) 'Filipino and Albanian women migrant workers in Greece: multiple layers of oppression' in F. Anthias and G. Lazaridis (eds), *Gender and Migration in Southern Europe: Women on the Move*, Oxford: Berg, pp. 49–79.
Le Mare, A., Promphaking, B. and Rigg, J. (2015) 'Returning home: the middle-income trap and gendered norms in Thailand', *Journal of International Development*, **27** (2), 285–306.
Levitt, P. (1998) 'Social remittances: migration driven local-level forms of cultural diffusion', *International Migration Review*, **32** (4), 926–48.

Levitt, P. (2001) *The Transnational Villagers*, Berkeley CA: University of California Press.
Long, L.D. and Oxfeld, E. (eds) (2004) *Coming Home? Refugees, Migrants, and Those Who Stayed Behind*, Philadelphia: University of Pennsylvania Press.
Lulle, A. and King, R. (2016) *Ageing, Gender, and Labour Migration*, New York: Palgrave Macmillan.
Mahler, S.J. and Pessar, P.R. (2001a) 'Gendered geographies of power: analysing gender across transnational spaces', *Identities*, **7** (4), 441–59.
Mahler, S.J. and Pessar, P.R. (eds) (2001b) 'Gendering transnational social spaces', special issue of *Identities*, **7** (4), 440–663.
Mahler, S.J. and Pessar, P.R. (2006) 'Gender matters: ethnographers bring gender from the periphery to the core of migration studies', *International Migration Review*, **40** (1), 27–63.
Marchetti, S. (2018) 'Gender, migration and globalisation: an overview of the debates' in A. Triandafyllidou (ed.), *Handbook of Migration and Globalisation*, Cheltenham, UK and Northampton, MA, USA: Edward Elgar Publishing, pp. 444–57.
Markowitz, F. and Stefansson, A.H. (eds) (2004) *Homecomings: Unsettling Paths of Return*, Lanham MD: Lexington Books.
Martínez-Buján, R. (2019) 'Here or there? Gendered return migration to Bolivia from Spain during economic crisis and fluctuating migration policies', *Journal of Ethnic and Migration Studies*, **45** (16), 3105–22.
Michail, D. (2013) 'Social development and transnational households: resilience and motivation for Albanian immigrants in Greece in the era of economic crisis', *Southeast European and Black Sea Studies*, **13** (2), 265–79.
Miller, O.A. (2008) *Migration Can Fall Apart: Life Stories from Voluntary and Deportee Return Migrants*, Lanham MD: University Press of America.
Momsen, J.H. (ed.) (1999) *Gender, Migration and Domestic Service*, London: Routledge.
Morokvaśic, M. (1984a) 'Birds of passage are also women', *International Migration Review*, **18** (4), 886–907.
Morokvaśic, M. (ed.) (1984b) 'Women in migration', special issue of *International Migration Review*, **18** (4), 881–1314.
Nadler, R., Kovacs, Z., Glorius, B. and Lang, T. (eds) (2016) *Return Migration and Regional Development in Europe: Mobility Against the Stream*, London: Palgrave Macmillan.
Ní Laoire, C. (2008) 'Settling back? A biographical and life-course perspective on Ireland's recent return migration', *Irish Geography*, **41** (2), 195–210.
Nisrane, B.L., Ossewaarde, R. and Need, A. (2020) 'The exploitation narratives and coping strategies of Ethiopian women return migrants from the Arabian Gulf', *Gender, Place and Culture*, **27** (4), 568–86.
Núñez-Carrasco, L., Vearey, J. and Drimie, S. (2011) 'Who cares? HIV-related sickness, urban–rural linkages, and the gendered role of care in return migration in South Africa', *Gender and Development*, **19** (1), 105–14.
Olwig, K.F. (2012) 'The "successful" return: Caribbean narratives of migration, family and gender', *Journal of the Royal Anthropological Institute*, **18** (4), 828–45.
Osella, F. and Osella, C. (2000) 'Migration, money and masculinity in Kerala', *Journal of the Royal Anthropological Institute*, **6** (1), 117–33.
Paparusso, A. and Ambrosetti, E. (2017) 'To stay or return? Return migration intentions of Moroccans in Italy', *International Migration*, **55** (6), 137–55.
Parreñas, E. (2001) *Servants of Globalization: Women, Migration and Domestic Work*, Stanford CA: Stanford University Press.
Pérez, G.M. (2005) 'A gendered tale of Puerto Rican return: place, nation and identity' in R.B. Potter, D. Conway and J. Phillips (eds), *The Experience of Return Migration: Caribbean Perspectives*, Aldershot: Ashgate, pp. 183–205.
Phillips, J. and Potter, R.B. (2005) 'Incorporating race and gender into Caribbean return migration: the example of second-generation "Bajan-Brits"' in R.B. Potter, D. Conway and J. Phillips (eds), *The Experience of Return Migration: Caribbean Perspectives*, Aldershot: Ashgate, pp. 69–88.
Phizacklea, A. (ed.) (1983) *One Way Ticket: Migration and Female Labour*, London: Routledge and Kegan Paul.
Phizacklea, A. (1998) 'Migration and globalisation: a feminist perspective' in K. Koser and H. Lutz (eds), *The New Migration in Europe*, London: Macmillan, pp. 21–38.

Piore, M.J. (1979) *Birds of Passage: Migrant Labor and Industrial Societies*, New York: Cambridge University Press.
Piper, N. (ed.) (2009) *New Perspectives on Gender and Migration*, London: Routledge.
Pojmann, W. (2006) *Immigrant Women and Feminism in Italy*, Aldershot: Ashgate.
Potter, R.B. and Conway, D. (2005) 'Experiencing return: societal contributions, adaptions and frustrations' in R.B. Potter, D. Conway and J. Phillips (eds), *The Experience of Return Migration: Caribbean Perspectives*, Aldershot: Ashgate, pp. 283–7.
Potter, R.B., Conway, D. and Phillips, J. (eds) (2005) *The Experience of Return Migration: Caribbean Perspectives*, Aldershot: Ashgate.
Saar, M. and Saar, E. (2020) 'Can the concept of lifestyle migration be applied to return migration? The case of Estonians in the UK', *International Migration*, **58** (2), 52–66.
Sakka, D., Dikaiou, M. and Kiosseoglou, G. (1999) 'Return migration: changing roles of men and women', *International Migration*, **37** (4), 741–63.
Samari, G. (2021) 'Coming back and moving backwards: return migration and gender norms in Egypt', *Journal of Ethnic and Migration Studies*, **47** (5), 1103–18.
Samers, M. (2010) *Migration*, London: Routledge.
Silvey, R. (2004) 'Power, difference and mobility: feminist advances in migration studies', *Progress in Human Geography*, **28** (3), 490–506.
Silvey, R. (2006) 'Geographies of gender and migration: spatializing social difference', *International Migration Review*, **40** (1), 64–81.
Snel, E., Faber, M. and Engbersen, G. (2015) 'To stay or return? Explaining return intentions of Central and Eastern European labour migrants', *Central and Eastern European Migration Review*, **4** (2), 5–24.
Sondhi, G. and King, R. (2017) 'Gendering international student migration: an Indian case-study', *Journal of Ethnic and Migration Studies*, **43** (8), 1308–25.
Thomson, A. (2005) '"My wayward heart": homesickness, longing and the return of British post-war immigrants from Australia' in M. Harper (ed.), *Emigrant Homecomings: The Return Movement of Emigrants 1600–2000*, Manchester: Manchester University Press, pp. 105–30.
Timmerman, C., Fonseca, M.L., Van Praag, L. and Pereira, S. (eds) (2018) *Gender and Migration: A Gender-Sensitive Approach to Migration Dynamics*, Leuven: Leuven University Press.
Tsuda, T. (ed.) (2009) *Diasporic Homecomings: Ethnic Return Migration in Comparative Perspective*, Stanford CA: Stanford University Press.
Tuccio, M. and Wahba, J. (2018) 'Return migration and the transfer of gender norms: evidence from the Middle East', *Journal of Comparative Economics*, **46** (4), 1006–29.
Urry, J. (2007) *Mobilities*, Cambridge: Polity.
van Boeschoten, R. (2015) 'Transnational mobility and the renegotiation of gender identities: Albanian and Bulgarian migrants in Greece' in H. Vermeulen, M. Baldwin-Edwards and R. van Boeschoten (eds), *Migration in the Southern Balkans*, Cham: Springer, pp. 162–82.
Vlase, I. (2013) '"My husband is a patriot!": gender and Romanian family return migration from Italy', *Journal of Ethnic and Migration Studies*, **39** (5), 741–58.
Waldorf, B. (1995) 'Determinants of international migration intentions', *Professional Geographer*, **47** (2), 125–36.
Walton-Roberts, M. (2004) 'Transnational migration theory in population geography: gendered practices in networks linking Canada and India', *Population, Space and Place*, **10** (5), 361–73.
Wong, M. (2014) 'Navigating return: the gendered geographies of skilled return migration to Ghana', *Global Networks*, **14** (4), 438–57.

# 5. Theorising voluntariness in return
*Marta Bivand Erdal and Ceri Oeppen*

## INTRODUCTION

The distinction between forced and voluntary return is a key categorisation in studies of return migration. Like all binaries, the reality is usually more complicated than it initially appears. This is reflected in the controversies surrounding 'Assisted Voluntary Return' (AVR) programmes, which are often targeted at migrants without a legal right to stay, meaning many of those who supposedly 'voluntarily' return, in practice have little other choice (Carling et al., 2015; Koser and Kuschminder, 2017; Leerkes et al., 2017; Webber, 2011; see also Lietaert, Chapter 8). Can such returns really be described as voluntary, in any meaningful way? There are several other scenarios where a return that might be labelled – or at first appear as – voluntary, might in fact be coerced, even if the migrant has had some agency in the decision-making process. In this chapter, we explore how scholars might understand voluntariness in the decision to return in a variety of different contexts, from the perspective of migrants, as well as those of policy-makers.

Our point of departure is an acknowledgement that, when considering return migration, there are several different potential outcomes and that a variety of different agents may be involved in shaping and influencing the decision to return. We unpack the notion of voluntariness in relation to return, reviewing the wider literature on voluntariness as well as building on our previous work, which has looked at agency and post-return mobility (Erdal and Oeppen, 2017) and the notion of voluntariness in relation to the decision to migrate more generally (Erdal and Oeppen, 2018).

In keeping with contemporary approaches in migration studies, we aim to go beyond the labelling of a migrant's return as *either* voluntary *or* non-voluntary and instead look at the different ways in which a theoretical understanding of voluntariness, as well as empirical observations of migrants' return decision-making and experiences, can lead to a more nuanced understanding of what voluntariness means in relation to return migration. Applying Olsaretti's (1998, 2004, 2018) philosophical work on voluntariness to return migration, we suggest that analysing the voluntariness of return requires a full understanding of the context in which decisions are made, including the acceptability of possible alternatives from which to choose.

We start with a theoretical discussion of what constitutes 'voluntariness'. We then look at voluntariness in relation to the different types of return managed by states' immigration authorities and international organisations; such returns are often targeted at those who do not have a legal right to remain. We then consider voluntariness in relation to liquid migration (the relatively unconstrained migration that characterises intra-European Union (EU) labour mobility) and other forms of migration regularised by states, before outlining the potential roles of non-state actors such as family and community in return migration decision-making. We draw these sections together by reflecting on the way in which voluntariness, agency, force and coercion can operate at different scales, in different places and at different stages of the migration experience.

## WHAT IS VOLUNTARINESS?

Before exploring voluntariness directly in relation to return migration, we first look at the theorisation of volition – or voluntariness – in a more general sense. This is important because migratory decisions and actions that can be considered 'voluntary' in a theoretical sense are not necessarily the same as migrations that are *labelled* 'voluntary' by those involved in migration policy-making and the management of return migration (Erdal and Oeppen, 2018; Webber, 2011). We also look beyond the migration studies literature because, as Ottonelli and Torresi (2013) suggest, voluntariness has not been paid the attention it might have been, given how important the terms 'voluntary' and 'forced' are to categorising types of migration, including return migration.

Acting by choice, without compulsion and with free will, are ways of thinking about voluntariness. However, looking at the term in more depth, questions quickly emerge. Do we consider a choice to be voluntary *only* if it is taken from a totally free range of options? What happens if someone chooses the least-worst option from a limited range; is their choice then still voluntary – for example, if someone chooses to migrate to get a better job because the employment options available to them in their current location are limited or do not match their qualifications and aspirations? What happens if someone chooses the only reasonable option available to them; are they making a voluntary choice – for example, if someone chooses to migrate out of a war zone, because the alternative is being injured or killed? Depending on how we think about and theorise voluntariness, these different scenarios might be considered more, or less, voluntary. These questions are, in turn, related to wider sociological considerations of agency. In the case of the person leaving the war zone, we might highlight that they have exercised agency in leaving and see them as advantaged over those who were unable to leave and were staying involuntarily (Black and Collyer, 2014) but, simultaneously, most would not see the person leaving the war zone as migrating voluntarily, even if they had exhibited agency in doing so.

This leads us to consider that it is not just the act of making a choice but the range of options available to the choice-maker and the context in which that choice takes place, that are key to understanding voluntariness. In relation to the context in which a choice is being made, the libertarian philosopher Nozick (1974) proposes that voluntary decisions are those made when an individual's rights to life, liberty and property are *not* being infringed upon by another individual or state institution. As soon as someone's rights are being infringed then we can consider any choices they make to be coerced (Nozick, 1974). Putting this theorisation into practice, it becomes clear that the observer's definition of 'rights' will have a significant impact on their understanding of voluntariness. Consequently, we suggest that the identification of whether a choice is called voluntary or coerced cannot be made without consideration of its normative context.

For example, an individual who meets the criteria of the 1951 Refugee Convention definition (with 1967 protocol) has had their rights to life and/or liberty infringed by persecution and the failure of their state to protect them from that persecution. As such they could be seen as the archetypal opposite of a voluntary migrant. So what about someone whose access to livelihoods, adequate sustenance, education or healthcare has been infringed? Under Nozick's very minimalist understanding of rights (Kymlicka, 2002), as long as someone in that position is not imprisoned or enslaved, they are still free to make voluntary choices; therefore, if they choose to migrate they are not being forced to do so and their choice is a free one. However, we, along with others (see Long, 2013), consider Olsaretti's (1998, 2004, 2018) more expansive consideration of the conditions that lead to non-voluntary decisions to be more appropriate. Whereas Nozick would argue that, as long as someone is free, they cannot be coerced, Olsaretti (1998) argues that freedom and voluntariness do not necessarily coincide and, instead, theorising voluntariness should consider the alternative possibilities available to the decision-maker, where the alternatives are either acceptable options or the lack of options is acceptable to the person making the choice. In Erdal and Oeppen (2018, p.986), we apply Olsaretti's (1998, p.71) ideas to some fictional migration-relevant examples to illustrate this further. In more-recent work, Olsaretti (2004, 2018) has emphasised the importance of context and the impact of normative judgements about what is and is not an acceptable option, as well as the need to consider options in relation to some objective standard of well-being. Related to context is the role of agents, both those taking an action (voluntary or otherwise) and those who shape the possibilities of those actions and their alternatives (Zimmerman, 1981). To Olsaretti's work, Colburn (2008) adds that perceptions of *alternatives* are not just about normative judgements of acceptability but are also reliant on access to information about alternatives.

The above brief outline of some of the philosophical debates around voluntariness indicates the challenge of applying theoretical discussions of voluntariness in the complex context of migrant decision-making, including the decision to return as well as the initial emigration. Philosophical discussions of the condition of voluntariness based on hypothetical individuals choosing between a small number of alternatives do not adequately mirror the complexity of migrant decision-making, which will probably include household (or other group) decision-making, as well as a weighing up of possibilities in both country of origin and of destination, as well as elsewhere. For return migrants, additional complexities could be considered relating to temporal and spatial frames of reference. For example, is the return intended to be temporary, long-term or 'for good'? How does a migrant's return link to past experiences – is it a return to a place previously lived in or somewhere where parents might have lived but the migrant has never been? Spatially, is the return intended to represent resettlement or could it involve leading a transnational life between different locations (Harpviken, 2014; Iaria, 2014)? These are important considerations that might affect how we think about the voluntariness of return and the possible alternatives to return which the migrant might have.

In general, contemporary migration studies tend to highlight the 'messiness' of labels and categories such as 'forced' and 'voluntary' and, instead, refer to spectrums of experience (see Fussell, 2012; Richmond, 1993), concepts such as mixed migration (Van Hear et al., 2009) or the migration–displacement nexus (Koser and Martin, 2011), rather than delving more deeply into the conditions of voluntariness. However, philosophical discussions of voluntariness have, to some extent, been picked up on in the migration studies literature (Bartram, 2015; Erdal and Oeppen, 2018; Ingram, 2012; Ottonelli and Torresi, 2013), including in relation to return migration (Long, 2013).

Ottonelli and Torresi (2013, p.792) make the case for a more political, less metaphysical, approach to voluntariness than that implied by philosophical discussions trying to define the conditions for a choice being either voluntary *or* non-voluntary. Nevertheless, the influence of ideas raised by political philosophers such as Olsaretti are apparent in Ottonelli and Torresi's conception of voluntariness through their emphasis on non-coercion and what they call 'sufficiency' in the country of origin, or what Olsaretti might term 'acceptable alternatives'. The theme of alternatives is also integral to Bartram's (2015) paper on forced migration, which posits forced migration as a rejection of non-migratory alternatives; and highlights the normative decisions made around what types of rejected alternatives (e.g. changing religion, death) constitute refugee status, rather than other migrant statuses.

In our own work, we have looked at the role of acceptable available alternatives to migration – as well as the agency to act upon those options – as key to understanding whether or not migration is voluntary (Erdal and Oeppen, 2018). However, as we also suggest, whether someone's decision to migrate is described as voluntary or not in legal, policy and practice terms very much depends on who is doing the describing – or labelling – of that decision and the available alternatives, rather than a philosophical concept of voluntariness.

Although she is not writing specifically about migration, Olsaretti's (2018) emphasis on voluntariness being both a normative issue and one that can only be considered with an understanding of the presence or not of alternative options, as well as full contextual understanding, has shaped how we have used the idea of voluntariness in our own work on migrant decision-making. We now examine how voluntariness might be understood in relation to the institutions attempting to manage, compel or assist return migration.

## VOLUNTARINESS AND MANAGED RETURNS

The management of return migration is integral to many aspects of migration policy regimes, particularly those related to refugees and asylum-seekers, as well as policies related to controlling migration. The principle of *non-refoulement* – not returning a refugee if it would endanger their life or liberty – is at the heart of international law relating to refugees. Meanwhile, the return of rejected asylum-seekers and other migrants who do not have permission to stay is seen as an essential component of managed migration in liberal democracies (IOM, 2004a; Koser and Kuschminder, 2017). There are two main arenas in which return is 'managed': individualised return (e.g. returns assisted or mandated by governments where a migrant's right to stay has expired or been refused or the migrant requires assistance to return – see also Lietaert, Chapter 8); and larger-scale mass return movements, such as the post-conflict repatriations managed by international organisations like the United Nations Refugee Agency (UNHCR). The voluntariness, or otherwise, of these managed returns is an essential component of how they are viewed by society, individuals and institutions (Cleton and Chauvin, 2020; Collyer, 2012).

There are some kinds of managed return where their non-voluntary nature is not debatable, because of the way in which government authorities restrict the returnees' agency in decision-making, thereby forcing them to return. For example, the deportation of foreign-national prisoners at the end of their prison sentence, or the forced removal of rejected asylum-seekers after they have exhausted their rights of appeal. The voluntariness of other types of managed return is more complex, in particular the 'pay-to-go' schemes that are offered to incentivise migrants to return to their country of origin. To complicate matters further, whilst the exact terminology varies to some extent between countries, and between institutions, such schemes are usually referred to as 'assisted *voluntary* return' (AVR) programmes. Despite the name, the extent to which these programmes are genuinely voluntary has been debated extensively in the critical migration studies literature (Ashutosh and Mountz, 2011; Lietaert et al., 2017; Webber, 2011).

In some cases, migrants may approach the International Organization for Migration (IOM), or other institutions mandated by governments to manage AVR programmes because they have decided that they wish to go home but cannot do so without assistance (e.g. financial support or help with travel documents). However, our previous work (Carling et al., 2015; Erdal and Oeppen, 2017; Oeppen and Majidi, 2015) and that of others (Leerkes et al., 2017; van Houte, 2014) would suggest that the uptake of AVR services does not necessarily mean that the service-user wants to return. AVR programmes are often targeted at those who would otherwise be considered deportable (i.e. irregular migrants, rejected asylum-seekers) or those who may be in the future (i.e. asylum-seekers). For example, in the UK, around 40 per cent of applications for AVR are made from immigrant removal (detention) centres (Morris and Salomons, 2013).

This is why considering voluntary decisions to be those made when there are available acceptable alternatives can shed light on why the voluntariness of AVR has been so heavily questioned. AVR could be considered as what Zimmerman (1981) calls a 'coercive offer'. As the immigration authorities offering AVR are also the agents who set the boundaries of who is and who is not legally allowed to remain (and therefore constrict the alternative options available to the migrant), this results in intentional coerced return on the part of those offering AVR programmes, following Zimmerman's (1981) discussion of coercion. In other words, if AVR is 'offered as a less painful alternative to continued destitution followed by (inevitable) compulsory return' (Webber, 2011, p.103), in the absence of other acceptable alternatives, then we cannot consider it to be fully voluntary. This contradiction has been recognised by those facilitating AVR, such as the IOM who, in a training manual, refer to 'voluntary [return] under compulsion' and 'voluntary [return] without compulsion' (IOM, 2004b, p.4). Leerkes et al. (2017) consequently refer to AVR as 'soft deportation', whilst refugee rights' organisations such as the European Council on Refugees and Exiles (ECRE) prefer 'mandatory return with consent'.

Whilst the majority of recent work on managed returns has focused on deportations and assisted return from Europe, it is also important to consider the extent to which voluntariness can be assessed in larger-scale managed repatriations, such as those usually overseen by the UNHCR in collaboration with other humanitarian agencies and the governments of 'host countries' and 'countries of origin'.[1] The UNHCR makes the formal distinction between 'facilitating' return (i.e. assisting refugees who choose to return, whatever the circumstances) and 'promoting' return – that is, encouraging return movements, particularly in post-conflict contexts, when it views peace as durable (UNHCR, 2004). It also stresses that all returns of refugees and internally displaced persons must be voluntary. Interestingly, in earlier 'return handbooks', the UNHCR has implicitly drawn on similar ideas to Olsaretti (2018), in terms of the importance of the context in which the decision is made, as well as the necessity of available acceptable alternatives to return as a pre-condition for voluntary decisions – see UNHCR, 1996, Section 2.3:

> The difficulty of identifying true 'voluntariness' enhances the need to scrutinize objectively the refugees' situation ... If refugees are legally recognized as such, their rights are protected and if they are allowed to settle, their choice to repatriate is likely to be truly free and voluntary. If, however, their rights are not recognized, if they are subjected to pressures and restrictions and confined to closed camps, they may choose to return, but this is not an act of free will.

Despite this recognition of the challenges of truly voluntary return, the UNHCR has been criticised for submitting to political pressures and 'promoting' return inappropriately, for example, when peace is probably neither durable nor sustainable (Turton and Marsden, 2002). The UNHCR and other agencies such as the World Food Programme, as well as 'host-country' governments, have also overseen the implementation of 'push factors' aimed at promoting so-called voluntary return, such as the reduction in food rations in refugee camps which has led to returns which, if not entirely forced, could certainly be considered as coerced (Hathaway, 2005; Johnson, 2014).

Whilst it is clear that, in some cases, potential returnees may have a genuine aspiration to return but need assistance to do so, we should also pay attention to how discourse and labels such as 'voluntary' can shape potential returnee aspirations (Erdal and Oeppen, 2018), as can institutional intermediaries such as AVR counsellors (Cleton and Schweitzer, 2020). Theorising voluntariness in return requires us not only to understand the conditions of voluntariness but also the purposes which voluntariness serves to those using the term. For migration management, the use of the term 'voluntary' can be seen as giving legitimacy to coerced returns (Cleton and Chauvin, 2020; Collyer, 2012; Kalir and Wissink, 2016; Leerkes et al., 2017).

## VOLUNTARINESS AND RETURN IN REGULAR AND LIQUID MIGRATION CONTEXTS

The 'managed return' of migrants without regular status to legally stay raises particular considerations about voluntariness where, despite migrants' active decision-making, it may not be appropriate to label such return migration as 'voluntary'. However, the vast majority of migration internationally is of a regular nature, where migrants hold the relevant entry visas and obtain the required permits for stay, frequently related to work or family members in the countries to which they migrate (de Haas et al., 2019; Kofman, 2004). In these circumstances, too, we may ask how and under what circumstances return may be considered to be voluntary or not.

Applying the understanding of voluntariness discussed above, we can consider which alternatives are open to migrants – whether they are free to weigh the pros and cons – and the acceptability of different alternatives. For instance, Nicole[2] is a Filipina with a temporary visa tied to her role as an *au pair* in Denmark. Her situation is shaped, first, by a regular migrant status and second, by a temporary permit (see, e.g., Valenta et al., 2020; Vianello et al., 2019; Wyss, 2019). The implication is that, upon the expiry of her *au pair* visa, she either needs to be in the possession of a further permit, in Denmark or indeed elsewhere, or she will be expected to return to the Philippines.

Theorising the voluntariness of Nicole's return depends on what her alternatives are, as well as on how she assesses their acceptability and the extent to which she is, in fact, able to make the choice freely. If voluntariness in return involves the ability to freely choose *between* acceptable alternatives, for Nicole this might, on the one hand, mean that return to the Philippines could be described as 'voluntary' but, on the other hand, might not. This would depend on *context*: whether a further extension of her visa in Denmark was an alternative and whether this was acceptable. The same can be said for the option to move elsewhere and significantly also in relation to the circumstances awaiting Nicole in the Philippines, which could either be perceived as a second-best option – such as foreseeing a future working in a call centre – or be a non-alternative, for example, due to an abusive family situation. In the latter case, return to the Philippines would not be an acceptable alternative for Nicole and could not be considered a voluntary choice (see also Anderson, 2009; Pratt, 2012), even if made freely.

We might consider voluntariness in return, similarly, using the example of a Bangladeshi construction worker in one of the Gulf States, a Zimbabwean labour migrant in South Africa or an Ethiopian domestic worker in the Middle East (see, e.g., Kuschminder, 2016; Moniruzzaman and Walton-Roberts, 2018; Nzima and Moyo, 2017). All of these are, in different ways, regulated cases of migration, where the question of return may be contract-bound, rendering the question of voluntariness to very particular constraints. Yet, if the migrant in question has voluntarily accepted the pre-conditions of migrating for work in this way, how we understand the issue of voluntariness – and its relation to freedom – is fundamental to how we would evaluate the degree of voluntariness that different modes of return (or the lack of) might offer.

A contrasting example might be that of Filip, a Polish labour migrant in the Netherlands. Given the free mobility within the EU, he works in the Netherlands but, to a great extent, 'lives' in Poland (see Bygnes and Erdal, 2017; Engbersen et al., 2015; Friberg, 2012). How would we consider the voluntariness of return in Filip's case? This example serves to illustrate the point that return is not always simply return; instead return might be closely linked to transnational living arrangements and sustained mobility to secure a livelihood (see also Erdal and Oeppen, 2017). This is referred to as open-ended or 'liquid migration' in the context of the EU, based on Zygmunt Bauman's work on modernity as 'liquid' in an era of globalisation (Bauman, 2000) and free mobility in the EU but also the empirical insight that many intra-European migrants have an open-ended plan for their migration projects, closely related to the fact that no permits – and hence no permit end-dates – are involved (Engbersen et al., 2010; Goździak, 2014).

While not all intra-European migrants adopt an open-ended approach to their migration projects, for those that do, how would we consider voluntariness in relation to return in such cases? If migration is understood as open-ended, return may be seen as a contradiction in terms, as ongoing mobility might better describe their reality. However, there may also be circumstances whereby, for example, a Polish labour migrant in another European country is 'trapped' in liquid migration (Bygnes and Erdal, 2017). Filip might prefer to return and live with his partner and their children in Poland but this does not constitute an acceptable alternative, due to his inability to gain employment there with a salary that would cover the family's expenses. In Filip's case, his ongoing mobility is open-ended despite his desires, yet no one else is forcing him to continue to migrate for work. No individual or institution is forcing him to not return, yet he does not see any other acceptable alternatives. Instead, he chooses the only alternative which he deems acceptable considering his circumstances and responsibilities (Erdal and Oeppen, 2017).

## VOLUNTARINESS AND NON-STATE SOURCES OF COERCION

The state is generally seen as the main agent of force and coercion in relation to return. In this section we look at other types of coercion, outside of the state. For Nicole, our Filipina *au pair* in Denmark, we might consider the household hosting her, who may or may not opt to renew the *au pair* arrangement, as constituting a potential non-state source of coercion in relation to the alternatives open to her – and how or when her return migration might occur. As a parallel, employers of different kinds and sizes are evidently a key source of coercion, sometimes in conjunction with states in relation to managing migration and thus also in relation to questions of decision-making and voluntariness in return.

The example of Filip points in the direction of a different non-state source of 'force' – namely, family, and family obligations. In the context of free mobility within the EU, family obligations are a source of force that acts independently of the state regulation of mobility. By contrast, in cases of family migration requiring visas and permits, where one person's legal status depends on that of other family members, state regulation and family relationships and obligations constitute an interwoven set of constraints and opportunities for mobility, residence rights and return. The question of voluntariness in return – whether in relation to the decision to return or not or to the journey itself or the experience post-return – here interacts with a range of different potential agents of force which might exert themselves on the individual.

We have pointed to family relationships and obligations and thus to the family as a potential source of coercion in relation to the voluntariness of return. Life-stage events (births, marriages, deaths) can be the catalyst for return migration that would otherwise not have taken place. Empirical accounts suggest that the death of a migrant's parent(s) in particular can mean that they are compelled to return before they would otherwise choose to do so (see, e.g., Guzman Elizalde, 2017). It is obvious that considering gender and gender dynamics is especially relevant in this context (cf. King and Lulle, Chapter 4). In some cases, patriarchal structures will hold sway and exert huge pressure on individuals to act in particular ways, where the question of which alternatives are acceptable to the individual is really not one that may be considered only at the individual level but also at some collective level. Simultaneously, it is not uncommon that individual and collective interests, also in collectivist-oriented societies, do not perfectly align. Thus, there is a potential for a mismatch in evaluations of the existing 'acceptable alternatives' to return and perhaps also in views on the degree to which the individual is free to choose among them in the first place – independent of, for example, the family.

Power hierarchies within families also relate closely to generation and age. Thus, for children and youth, questions of voluntariness in return are particularly pertinent (e.g. Zúñiga and Hamann, 2015; see also Grosa, Chapter 17). Whereas for children autonomy is limited, for young people – as autonomy increases – the question of voluntariness in return and acceptable alternatives can become especially pressing. For young people, the issue of voluntariness in return may also raise existential questions about belonging and identity.

Meanwhile, there are other potential agents which may also have a role in coercing return, such as clan, caste or *biraderis*. Such collectives, often based on extended kinship networks, can exert power through expectations that lock in individuals' scope of agency, based on shared identity and common group membership. Meanwhile – and on the flip-side – such collectives simultaneously also offer a safety net in many circumstances where other safety nets do not exist. Thus, such group membership can both enable and constrain access to acceptable alternatives, depending on group and individual views of what is acceptable. Similar effects might occur with other groupings – with, for example, religious identity – in the case of conversions or sexual orientation, where collectives might exert force by actively constraining the space in which the individual can exert the agency to choose between acceptable alternatives.

## LOCATING VOLUNTARINESS

In this final section, we draw together themes from the discussion above to reflect on the ways in which degrees of voluntariness and constraints on it might operate at different scales, in different locations and at different stages of the return migration decision-making, journey and experience. There is a clear scale of actors involved, from the individual to the family (or household), to the community, to state immigration authorities and international organisations; all of which may both enable and constrain voluntariness in a practical sense and also shape normative discourse about what is and is not considered an acceptable alternative to return – the presence of which, as we have discussed, is a pre-condition for return to be chosen voluntarily. Below, we reflect on locating voluntariness discursively and politically, locating voluntariness in a temporal sense and locating voluntariness spatially, as well as raising questions for future theorising around voluntariness in return.

For migration studies scholars, understanding voluntariness in return migration is further complicated by the difficulties of decoupling the labels used by policy-makers and the way in which they use the term 'voluntary return' from a more philosophical understanding of what constitutes a truly voluntary action. We have discussed this in more detail in relation to migration more generally (Erdal and Oeppen, 2018) but it is particularly pertinent in relation to return migration where the term 'voluntary' has been used to legitimise returns that would largely not be considered voluntary in a theoretical sense or by migrants' rights activists (see also Cleton and Chauvin, 2020). The label 'voluntary' when used in relation to migration carries a normative weight (Erdal and Oeppen, 2018) which, in turn, may also have significant implications on how migrants are treated by immigration authorities (Ottonelli and Torresi, 2013).

Although, in this chapter, our main focus has been on voluntariness in relation to a somewhat artificially defined 'decision to return', we should also remember that contemporary migration scholars consider return to be more of a *process* than a one-off decision or movement. Thus, we can also think about theorising voluntariness in relation to return as something that affects the whole process rather than solely at the point of physical return. For example, the circumstances of initial migration are difficult to separate from the voluntariness of return migration, particularly when considering the role of immigration authorities in constraining the voluntariness of return. An Afghan asylum-seeker in the UK is much more likely to be subject to explicit disciplinary control from the UK government in relation to their return than a German highly skilled labour migrant. However, both the Afghan asylum-seeker and the German migrant might have family obligations shaping their migratory experience and aspirations for eventual return, whatever their status in relation to UK immigration regulations. As return is a process, we also need to consider what happens *after* the actual physical return. Ottonelli and Torresi (2013) argue that an 'exit option' is a necessary condition for a voluntary migration. They are referring to the opportunity to change status after migrating – for example, from exploitative labour conditions to a more acceptable position (2013, pp.801–2) – but the same point is relevant after return. Can a return migration be considered voluntary, in a philosophical sense if, after return, there is no available alternative of re-migration or other onward mobility? This is a highly relevant question in a practical sense, too, as empirical studies suggest that return migrants who have returned against their will are much more likely to want to re-migrate (Schuster and Majidi, 2015).

Considering return as a process spanning different times not only points us in the direction of the future but also in that of the past. If, in relation to migration decisions, we consider a two-step process, acknowledging both aspiration and ability to migrate (Carling, 2002; Carling and Schewel, 2018), we should do the same when considering return migration (see also Cleton and Schweitzer, 2020). Voluntariness, then, not only plays a role in the decision to return (or not) but is also a significant factor in the preceding stages of return aspirations. The reason why distinguishing between aspiration and ability to migrate is important, also in relation to return migration, is that we may find that return is not possible, even when it is desired for some, thus creating a situation of non-voluntary immobility. A more extreme case of the impossibility of return migration is presented by the case of Palestinian refugees and others who do not have a state to which to return. By contrast, as we have discussed in relation to AVR programmes and deportations, we may find cases of non-voluntary return mobility. It is also worth noting that, for many potential returnees – just like other potential migrants – voluntary *immobility* may be the correct descriptor.

The degree of voluntariness in return migration is further complicated by potential conflicts between different actors. For example, migrants might be forced to return because their situation has become irregular; however, their family wants them to stay and send remittances. Immigration authorities might deem internal relocation in the country of origin an acceptable alternative for a rejected asylum seeker but the latter might have fuller information about the spatial variations in risk on return. A temporary migrant whose permit to stay expires might choose to move to a larger city where their irregular status is less likely to be detected, even if they risk arrest, as they see that as an acceptable alternative to returning to their country of origin. Conflicts between different actors add political complexity to the degree of voluntariness; arguably, the very presence of permits, visas and other regulations in the first place can itself be a source of coercion in return decision-making (after Zimmerman, 1981). A migrant may also choose *not* to return, despite wishing to, for fear of the shame upon return through not meeting expectations in the origin community. The perceived success of a 'migration project' affects returnees' status and social embeddedness (Cerase, 1974) and is thus salient for understanding the degree of voluntariness in their return decision, as well as the alternatives they had to choose from. Relatedly, returnee preparedness and resource mobilisation (Cassarino, 2004) may also be factors explaining the choices that migrants make between potential return alternatives.

In structuring this chapter, we have made a distinction between state and non-state actors although, in reality, the judgements and decisions of these actors are also often intertwined. To add further complexity, although our focus has been on those with an active stake in the return migration decision, there are also external factors and structures which will affect the decision to return (e.g. the economy or the climate). Further work on theorising voluntariness in return may also want to consider these external forces.

To theorise voluntariness in return migration we need to consider the spatial location of potential alternatives to return – they could be in the country of migration, the country of origin or elsewhere. Also, migrants may reflect on and evaluate the alternatives in various locations differently post-return, compared to before the return decision and journey. Increasingly, in contexts of regular migration and where individuals hold dual citizenship, the reality of transnational lives is becoming pertinent. Here, questions of voluntariness must be considered primarily, if not solely, in relation to non-state agents of coercion. Thus, considerations of the different factors which we need to take into account to deem a return migration to be voluntary or non-voluntary are wide-ranging, both politically, temporally and spatially. How return is labelled as voluntary or not and by whom is significant for unpacking the effects of voluntariness in return migration.

Meanwhile, efforts to theorise voluntariness in return – as with migration in general – gain much from conceptual clarity: how terms such as force and coercion, choice and freedom are used matters. Following Olsaretti (2018) and others, we have theorised that voluntariness in return requires the availability of acceptable alternatives, their suitability in relation to an objective standard of well-being, as well as a contextual understanding of the circumstances in which voluntary choices are made or non-voluntary actions are taken. However, the availability, or otherwise, of acceptable alternatives cannot, in practice, be separated from normative judgements about what constitutes acceptable or the amount of information an individual subject has about those alternatives.

For scholars of international migration – and specifically return migration – we therefore suggest that it is important to reflect on the use of different terminologies of return and seek to maintain high levels of precision in their application. Too often policy categories, such as 'assisted voluntary return', become analytical categories, without the necessary caution about the risk of analytical slippage. For analytical purposes, studies of managed return migration might be more interested in the 'managed' aspects (e.g. when analysing policy and policy effectiveness) or in the 'return migration' aspects (e.g. when analysing broader migration processes in a particular country of origin or, indeed, destination) and it is important to be explicit about the way in which and in what contexts the term 'voluntary' is being used. As we have sought to show in this chapter, in order to investigate the ways in which a return migration decision – or the return migration process as a whole – might be deemed voluntary or not, there is a need for substantial contextual information in order to assess the existence of plausibly acceptable alternatives; it is not enough to rely on an administrative label.

## NOTES

1. The UNHCR includes supporting the return of internally displaced persons (IDPs) in their mandate but the bulk of the literature on large-scale returns focuses on the repatriation of refugees across national borders.
2. Nicole (and Filip, mentioned later) are hypothetical examples based on our real-life observations of migrant individuals during previous field research.

## REFERENCES

Anderson, B. (2009) 'What's in a name? Immigration controls and subjectivities: the case of au pairs and domestic worker visa holders in the UK', *Subjectivity*, **29** (1), 407–24.

Ashutosh, I. and Mountz, A. (2011) 'Migration management for the benefit of whom? Interrogating the work of the International Organization for Migration', *Citizenship Studies*, **15** (1), 21–38.

Bartram, D. (2015) 'Forced migration and "rejected alternatives": a conceptual refinement', *Journal of Immigrant and Refugee Studies*, **13** (4), 439–56.

Bauman, Z. (2000) *Liquid Modernity*, Cambridge: Polity.

Black, R. and Collyer, M. (2014) 'Populations "trapped" at times of crisis', *Forced Migration Review*, **45**, 52–6.

Bygnes, S. and Erdal, M. (2017) 'Liquid migration, grounded lives: considerations about future mobility and settlement among Polish and Spanish migrants in Norway', *Journal of Ethnic and Migration Studies*, **43** (1), 102–18.

Carling, J. (2002) 'Migration in the age of involuntary immobility: theoretical reflections and Cape Verdean experiences', *Journal of Ethnic and Migration Studies*, **28** (1), 5–42.

Carling, J. and Schewel, K. (2018) 'Revisiting aspiration and ability in international migration', *Journal of Ethnic and Migration Studies*, **44** (6), 945–63.

Carling, J., Bolognani, M., Erdal, M.B., Tordhol Ezzati, R., Oeppen, C., Paasche, E., Vatne Pettersen, S. and Heggli Sagmo, T. (2015) *Possibilities and Realities of Return Migration* (Final Report), Oslo: PRIO.

Cassarino, J.-P. (2004) 'Theorising return migration: the conceptual approach to return migrants revisited', *International Journal on Multicultural Societies*, **6** (2), 253–79.

Cerase, F.P. (1974) 'Expectations and reality: a case study of return migration from the United States to Southern Italy', *International Migration Review*, **8** (2), 245–62.

Cleton, L. and Chauvin, S. (2020) 'Performing freedom in the Dutch deportation regime: bureaucratic persuasion and the enforcement of "voluntary return"', *Journal of Ethnic and Migration Studies*, **46** (1), 297–313.

Cleton, L. and Schweitzer, R. (2020) *Using or Inducing Return Aspirations? On the Role of Return Counsellors in the Implementation of 'Assisted Voluntary Return' Policies in Austria and the Netherlands*, Amsterdam: International Migration Institute, IMI Working Paper No. 160.

Colburn, B. (2008) 'Debate: the concept of voluntariness', *Journal of Political Philosophy*, **16** (1), 101–11.

Collyer, M. (2012) 'Deportation and the micropolitics of exclusion: the rise of removals from the UK to Sri Lanka', *Geopolitics*, **17** (2), 276–92.

de Haas, H., Castles, S. and Miller, M.J. (2019) *The Age of Migration: International Population Movements in the Modern World*, London: Red Globe Press (6th edition).

Engbersen, G., Snel, E. and de Boom, J. (2010) '"A van full of Poles": liquid migration from Central and Eastern Europe' in G. Engbersen, R. Black, M. Okólski and C. Panţîru (eds), *A Continent Moving West? EU Enlargement and Labour Migration from Central and Eastern Europe*, Amsterdam: Amsterdam University Press, pp. 115–40.

Engbersen, G., Snel, E. and Faber, M. (2015) 'To stay or return? Explaining return intentions of Central and Eastern European labour migrants', *Central and Eastern European Migration Review*, **4** (2), 5–24.

Erdal, M.B. and Oeppen, C. (2017) 'Forced to return? Agency and the role of post-return mobility for psychosocial wellbeing among returnees to Afghanistan, Pakistan and Poland' in Z. Vathi and R. King (eds), *Return Migration and Psychosocial Wellbeing: Discourses, Policy-Making and Outcomes for Migrants and Their Families*, London: Routledge, pp. 39–55.

Erdal, M.B. and Oeppen, C. (2018) 'Forced to leave? The discursive and analytical significance of describing migration as forced and voluntary', *Journal of Ethnic and Migration Studies*, **44** (6), 981–98.

Friberg, J.H. (2012) 'The stages of migration: from going abroad to settling down: post-accession Polish migrant workers in Norway', *Journal of Ethnic and Migration Studies*, **38** (10), 1589–605.

Fussell, E. (2012) 'Space, time, and volition: dimensions of migration theory' in M.R. Rosenblum and D.J. Tichenor (eds), *The Oxford Handbook of the Politics of International Migration*, New York: Oxford University Press, pp. 25–52.

Goździak, E.M. (2014) 'Polish migration after the fall of the Iron Curtain', *International Migration*, **52** (1), 1–3.

Guzman Elizalde, L. (2017) *Return to Mexico: Exploring the (Re)Integration Experience*, Brighton: University of Sussex, unpublished PhD thesis.

Harpviken, K.B. (2014) 'Split return: transnational household strategies in Afghan repatriation', *International Migration*, **52** (6), 57–71.

Hathaway, J.C. (2005) *The Rights of Refugees under International Law*, Cambridge: Cambridge University Press.

Iaria, V. (2014) 'Post-return transnationalism and the Iraqi displacement in Syria and Jordan', *International Migration*, **52** (6), 43–56.

Ingram, D. (2012) 'The structural injustice of forced migration and the failings of normative theory', *Perspectives on Global Development and Technology*, **11** (4), 50–71.

IOM (2004a) *Return Migration: Policies and Practices in Europe*, Geneva: International Organization for Migration.

IOM (2004b) *Return Migration (Volume Three of Essentials of Migration Management: A Guide for Policy Makers and Practitioners)*, Geneva: International Organization for Migration.

Johnson, H.L. (2014) *Borders, Asylum and Global Non-Citizenship: The Other Side of the Fence*, Cambridge: Cambridge University Press.

Kalir, B. and Wissink, L. (2016) 'The deportation continuum: convergences between state agents and NGO workers in the Dutch deportation field', *Citizenship Studies*, **20** (1), 34–49.

Kofman, E. (2004) 'Family-related migration: a critial review of European Studies', *Journal of Ethnic and Migration Studies*, **30** (2), 243–62.

Koser, K. and Kuschminder, K. (2017) 'Assisted voluntary return and reintegration of migrants: a comparative approach' in M. McAuliffe and K. Koser (eds), *A Long Way to Go: Irregular Migration Patterns, Processes, Drivers and Decision-Making*, Canberra: ANU Press, pp. 255–76.

Koser, K. and Martin, S. (eds) (2011) *The Migration–Displacement Nexus: Patterns, Processes and Policies*, Oxford: Berghahn.

Kuschminder, K. (2016) 'Strong ties, weak ties: exploring the role of networks in domestic worker migration from Ethiopia to the Middle East', *Asian and Pacific Migration Journal*, **25** (4), 401–21.

Kymlicka, W. (2002) *Contemporary Political Philosophy: An Introduction*, Oxford: Oxford University Press (2nd edition).

Leerkes, A., van Os, R. and Boersema, E. (2017) 'What drives "soft deportation"? Understanding the rise in assisted voluntary return among rejected asylum seekers in the Netherlands', *Population, Space and Place*, **23** (8), e2059.

Lietaert, I., Broekaert, E. and Derluyn, I. (2017) 'From social instrument to migration management tool: assisted voluntary return programmes – the case of Belgium', *Social Policy and Administration*, **51** (7), 961–80.

Long, K. (2013) *The Point of No Return: Refugees, Rights, and Repatriation*, Oxford: Oxford University Press.

Moniruzzaman, M. and Walton-Roberts, M. (2018) 'Migration, debt and resource backwash: how sustainable is Bangladesh–Gulf circular migration?', *Migration and Development*, **7** (1), 85–103.

Morris, H. and Salomons, M. (2013) *Difficult Decisions: A Review of UNHCR's Engagement with Assisted Voluntary Return Programmes*, Geneva: United Nations High Commissioner for Refugees.

Nozick, R. (1974) *Anarchy, State and Utopia*, Oxford: Blackwell.

Nzima, D. and Moyo, P. (2017) 'The new "diaspora trap" framework: explaining return migration from South Africa to Zimbabwe beyond the "failure-success" framework', *Migration Letters*, **14** (3), 355–70.

Oeppen, C. and Majidi, N. (2015) *Can Afghans Reintegrate after Assisted Returns from Europe?* Oslo: PRIO, Policy Brief 7/2015.

Olsaretti, S. (1998) 'Freedom, force and choice: against the rights-based definition of voluntariness', *Journal of Political Philosophy*, **6** (1), 53–78.

Olsaretti, S. (2004) *Liberty, Desert and the Market: A Philosophical Study*, Cambridge: Cambridge University Press.

Olsaretti, S. (2018) 'Voluntariness, coercion, self-ownership' in D. Schmidtz and C.E. Pavel (eds), *The Oxford Handbook of Freedom*, Oxford: Oxford University Press, pp. 439–55.

Ottonelli, V. and Torresi, T. (2013) 'When is migration voluntary?', *International Migration Review*, **47** (4), 783–813.

Pratt, G. (2012) *Families Apart: Migrant Mothers and the Conflicts of Labor and Love*, Minneapolis: University of Minnesota Press.

Richmond, A.H. (1993) 'Reactive migration: sociological perspectives on refugee movements', *Journal of Refugee Studies*, **6** (1), 7–24.

Schuster, L. and Majidi, N. (2015) 'Deportation stigma and re-migration', *Journal of Ethnic and Migration Studies*, **41** (4), 635–52.

Turton, D. and Marsden, P. (2002) *Taking Refugees for a Ride? The Politics of Refugee Return to Afghanistan*, Kabul: Afghanistan Research and Evaluation Unit.

UNHCR (1996) *Voluntary Repatriation: International Protection (Handbook)*, Geneva: United Nations High Commissioner for Refugees.
UNHCR (2004) *Handbook for Repatriation and Reintegration Activities*, Geneva: United Nations High Commissioner for Refugees.
Valenta, M., Knowlton, K.E., Jakobsen, J., Al Awad, M. and Strabac, Z. (2020) 'Temporary labour-migration system and long-term residence strategies in the United Arab Emirates', *International Migration*, **58** (1), 182–97.
Van Hear, N., Brubaker, R. and Bessa, T. (2009) *Managing Mobility for Human Development: The Growing Salience of Mixed Migration*, Oxford: United Nations Development Programme.
van Houte, M. (2014) *Moving Back or Moving Forward? Return Migration After Conflict*, Maastricht: Maastricht University, unpublished PhD thesis.
Vianello, F.A., Finotelli, C. and Brey, E. (2019) 'A slow ride towards permanent residency: legal transitions and the working trajectories of Ukrainian migrants in Italy and Spain', *Journal of Ethnic and Migration Studies*, DOI: 10.1080/1369183X.2019.1590187.
Webber, F. (2011) 'How voluntary are voluntary returns?', *Race and Class*, **52** (4), 98–107.
Wyss, A. (2019) 'Stuck in mobility? Interrupted journeys of migrants with precarious legal status in Europe', *Journal of Immigrant and Refugee Studies*, **17** (1), 77–93.
Zimmerman, D. (1981) 'Coercive wage offers', *Philosophy and Public Affairs*, **10** (2), 121–45.
Zúñiga, V. and Hamann, E.T. (2015) 'Going to a home you have never been to: the return migration of Mexican and American-Mexican children', *Children's Geographies*, **13** (6), 643–55.

# 6. Departheid: re-politicising the inhumane treatment of illegalised migrants in so-called liberal democratic states

*Barak Kalir*

## INTRODUCTION

The systemic violence against unarmed migrants and refugees in Western countries poses a pertinent challenge to scholars interested in the governance of human mobility in the twenty-first century. We can agree that certain restrictions on the mobility of non-citizens are the prerogative of sovereign nation states and that, at times, they might be necessary in regulating the movement of people. We cannot, however, accept that the administrative regulation of mobility directly causes the death of tens of thousands of people at the maritime borders of the European Union (EU) or at the land borders between Mexico and the United States. We can also not accept that the inability to meet the administrative requirements for a legal status in Western states leads to the incarceration of millions of illegalised migrants in detention centres or to their confinement in concentration camps. Nor can we accept the deportation or so-called 'voluntary' return of migrants and refugees from some of the richest countries in the world back to life-threatening conditions in places that are undergoing war, civil unrest and/or severe economic crisis.

Advancing the notion of Departheid is an attempt to capture a hegemonic governing doctrine, imposed in so-called liberal democratic states, that promotes and legitimises the rejection, containment and deportation of illegalised migrants at all costs. The category of illegalised migrants refers to people who are denoted an illegal status by the state authorities and are thereby rendered deportable. It includes unauthorised or irregular migrants and so-called 'failed' or 'bogus' asylum-seekers. Speaking of illegalised migrants is meant to stress the process that leads to illegalisation, rather than seeing this as a legalistic given.

Recognising Departheid is a move to re-politicise the disproportionate violence inflicted within the 'migration apparatus' (Feldman, 2012) on racialised migrants and refugees from the Global South. In a fundamental way, Departheid reveals the reconfiguration of colonial power structures in our contemporary world order (cf. Saucier and Woods, 2014). As scholars of (forced) mobility, we must account for a distinctive 'racial cruelty' (Reddy, 2011) that is evident in the humiliating and dehumanising treatment of undesired migrants and refugees by civil servants and frontline bureaucrats in Western states.

This chapter[1] expounds on the definition of Departheid and elaborates on the economic and political interests that propel its establishment and consolidation as a hegemonic paradigm for governing mobility. Highlighting the disproportionate harm caused to millions of non-Western, non-White migrants and refugees, the chapter uncovers the ideological work of White Supremacy in preventing any 'legitimacy deficit' (Ugelvik, 2016) from surfacing in the implementation of Departheid. The final section of the chapter outlines five concrete academic and political fronts in which the notion of Departheid can help advance research and activism around oppressive mobility regimes.

## DEFINING DEPARTHEID

The essence of Departheid is an exercise in spatial engineering *allegedly* geared towards the distancing of all illegalised migrants from the national territory of any specific state. The word *allegedly* is crucial to the definition of Departheid because the production of deportable people – who are unprotected, disenfranchised and readily exploitable – is, in fact, one of Departheid's goals (De Giorgi, 2010). Departheid is constituted through operations in three interlocking sites. First, at the point of entry, states fortify and protect borders to pre-emptively deny entrance to those who, it is suspected, will become illegalised migrants; second, inside their sovereign territory, states segregate and confine illegalised migrants to specially designated 'waiting zones' – neighbourhoods, camps, hot spots, prisons and detention facilities – from where surveillance and controlled removals can be more easily managed; third, at the point of exit, states oblige illegalised migrants to 'voluntarily leave' or force them to 'return' to their country of origin, country of departure or any other so-called third country.

The treatment of illegalised migrants in all three sites is marked by the deployment of legal, psychological and physical violence. Legal violence is pertinent to the definition of Departheid. According to Menjívar and Abrego (2012, p.1380), it is important to 'use the analytic category "legal violence" to capture the normalized but cumulatively injurious effects of the law'. In other words, while certain bureaucratic procedures in Western countries are anchored in the letter of the law – for example, the illegalisation of migrants or their forceful removal – they might nevertheless be illegitimate in inflicting disproportional harm on those subjected to them. One only needs to be reminded that deportations of Jews, Blacks and Roma to concentration and extermination camps under Nazi Germany were all done legally, following detailed manuals and careful registrations. The equation of legality with legitimacy should thus always be seen as an achievement of a hegemonic, oppressive mobility regime (Kalir, 2019a). Accordingly, endorsing the fortification of physical borders and sacralising exclusionary definitions of citizenship in Western states are legalistic expressions of a successfully constituted Departheid and not its foregoing legitimate origins, as some of its advocates claim.

Departheid is nowadays operative in many countries all over the world. It is important, however, to locate its origins, both historically and geographically. The consolidation of Departheid has occurred in Western states since the early 1990s. It is around that time, after the Cold War has virtually ended, that we witness how an increased mobility of migrants and refugees from the Global South is met with a violent, criminalising and, overall, dehumanising assault by Western states, often using 'illiberal practices' (Bigo, 2002), especially since the 9/11 terrorist attacks.

Oppressive mobility regimes have clearly been in place throughout history across the world. It is, however, around the early 1990s that we see a particular investment in the restrictive governance of mobility along specific fault lines that separate the West from the Rest in a unidirectional asymmetric fashion. Under the guise of globalisation, cross-state flows of goods, technologies, information and people have been encouraged and even celebrated (Ohmae, 1991). As for the flow of people, while citizens of Western states are able to enter and often also to work in almost all other parts of the world, the reversed flow is severely hindered. By limiting legal immigration and restricting visa applications – especially for people from the Global South and predominantly along the lines of nationality as a proxy for class and race – Western states render unauthorised border-crossing the only option available to millions of migrants and refugees (Neumayer, 2006).

Concurrently, since the early 1990s, Western states began investing heavily in the fortification of borders, the identification of illegalised migrants and their detention and deportation. For example, according to the US Department of Homeland Security, compulsory removals of non-citizens stood at 869,646 people from 1993 to 2000 under the Clinton administration, at 2,012,539 from 2001 to 2008 under the Bush administration and at 3,094,208 from 2009 to 2016 under the Obama administration. In this same period, the United States administered nearly 27 million apprehensions by immigration enforcement officers (Chishti et al., 2017). To grasp this massive apprehension phenomenon, we should consider that 'on any given day, the country has some 30,000 people in administrative immigration detention' (GDP, 2016). The overall budget of the two agencies responsible for migration in the United States – Border Patrol and Immigration and Customs Enforcement – stood at nearly $20 billion in 2016 (DHS, 2017).

In Europe, according to a Eurostat (2018) report, between 2008 and 2016 more than 6.8 million people were apprehended for 'illegal presence', more than 4.6 million were ordered to leave and about 3.5 million non-EU citizens were refused entry at the border. As for deportation, about 1.75 million people were 'returned' to a non-EU member state in this period. According to independent sources, around 200,000 illegalised migrants are detained each year (GDP and AIE, 2015, p.23; see also GDP, 2019). In addition, in 2005 the EU established the European Border and Coast Guard Agency (Frontex) to coordinate and implement a more effective protection of EU borders and a swifter 'return' of illegalised migrants from member states. The annual budget of Frontex operations grew exponentially from 6 million euros in 2005 to 230 million euros in 2018 (Nielsen, 2018). The implementation of an oppressive mobility regime is, by 2005, also part and parcel of the EU enlargement plan, with new member states (most recently, Poland, Romania and Bulgaria) obliged to restrictively modify their immigration laws and to heavily invest in establishing the required infrastructure for the prevention of entry, the detention and the deportation of illegalised migrants (Anderson et al., 2013; Rigo, 2005).

In Australia, mandatory detention was introduced in 1992 – initially as a temporary measure to confront the increased arrival of Indochinese 'boat people' – but was soon after permanently extended to all 'unlawful' non-citizens. Australia moved from detaining 188 illegalised migrants in 1991–92 to 19,376 detainees in 2011–12, a rise of more than 10,000 per cent in 20 years (Phillips and Spinks, 2013, pp.5–6). The detention and deportation of illegalised migrants was partly replaced around 2004 with offshore processing procedures. Australia has invested heavily in deploying its navy to intercept incoming boats and escort them to offshore locations on poor islands (Manus, Papua New Guinea and Nauru), where processing asylum claims and administering detention and 'return' were subcontracted to private companies at a cost of AU$2 billion in only four years of operation (Jabri, 2013; Magner, 2004). The conditions in Australian-sponsored detention centres have been criticised repeatedly as inhumane, leading to recurrent riots, self-harm and suicide attempts by detainees (Pickering and Weber, 2014).

To recognise that the borderlines of contemporary human mobility are drawn between the rich Global North and the poor Global South is to recognise that Departheid is distinctively constituted along colonial vectors of structural and symbolic violence. Whether we choose to talk of a post- or a neo-colonial world order, it must be clear that the coloniality of power (Mignolo, 2012) is continuously present in shaping the freedom of movement and the treatment of migrants and refugees around the world along racialised lines. The establishment of Departheid is best viewed in direct continuity with colonial configurations for restricting the mobility of 'subject races', a term coined by the British colonial regime to derogatorily refer to native populations as 'backward', 'primitives' or 'savages'. Under colonial regimes, 'subject races' were vehemently dehumanised and distinctively considered to be an inferior 'race'. The mobility of 'subject races' was severely controlled by the colonisers (Mitchell, 1991).

If not to the protracted coloniality of power, how otherwise should we account for systemic violence against unarmed border-crossers? For the fact that migrants and refugees who have not (yet or fully) complied with administrative requirements set by Western states end up in concentration camps or being subjected to police raids, lengthy detention periods, family separation and violent deportation to life-threatening places? How can we explain that billions are invested in barricading borders but so little is done to find solutions for minors who enter Europe seeking asylum and end up sleeping rough and selling sex for survival in capital cities all across the continent?

There are two more crucial observations with respect to the 'racial cruelty' (Reddy, 2011) involved in the constitution of Departheid: desertion and death. According to minimalist statistics, more than 34,000 people have died since 2000 trying to enter Europe.[2] At the US border with Mexico, more than 7,200 deaths have been recorded in the past 20 years (CBP, 2018). The actual numbers are likely to be much higher, as many deaths remain unaccounted for. Death also occurs during violent forced deportations and in detention centres, where detainees often engage in self-harm and suicide. In Australia, for example, 'between January 2011 and February 2013 there were 4,313 reported incidents of actual, threatened and attempted serious self-harm in immigration detention facilities' (Triggs, 2013, p.721). In the United Kingdom, in 2018, there were two suicide attempts every day in detention-for-deportation centres (Taylor et al., 2018).

Illegalised migrants, who refuse to 'voluntarily' return and manage to evade deportation, are being deserted by the authorities. States undo their responsibility towards illegalised migrants, who often end up living without access to some of the most basic provisions such as medical care, shelter, food and education for their children (Kalir and van Schendel, 2017). The constant fear of random detention and deportation and the possibility of families breaking up weighs heavily on the mental and physical health of illegalised migrants (Cavazos-Rehg et al., 2017). Insidiously, making the lives of illegalised migrants unbearable is often the deliberate goal under Departheid (Kalir, 2017a). Numerous policy-makers and politicians in Western states believe that this is the only way to force illegalised migrants to 'voluntarily' return and to deter future illegalised migrants from trying to enter. This belief appears unshaken by studies showing that restrictive migration policies and desertion are largely futile in preventing or deterring further unauthorised migration (Wong, 2015).

It is perplexing to recognise that huge budgets are allocated for the implementation of Departheid in spite of its proven futility in achieving its purported goals (cleansing states of the presence of illegalised migrants) and the enormous harm it causes to the well-being of millions of people (Golash-Boza, 2015; Nevins, 2001).[3] In order to understand the persistence of Departheid, we need to expose the economic, political and ideological motivations that consolidate it as a hegemonic system for governing mobility.

## UNCOVERING DEPARTHEID: MONEY-MAKING AND WHITE SUPREMACY

The most obvious interests that fuel the establishment and the intensification of Departheid are economic gains to multiple actors. As exposed in the previous section, states invest heavily in installing and maintaining Departheid. This money is allocated mostly to private companies that provide for the fencing of borders, surveillance technologies, building and running of detention facilities, deportation flights and so on (Arbogast, 2016). Various state institutions are also allocated large budgets to purchase equipment and hire, train and retain personnel for the implementation of Departheid. One can think here of border guards, with their transport, arms and telecommunication equipment, as well as the multiple police forces that are deployed to inspect suspected illegalised migrants, organise raids, detain to-be-deported migrants and operate deportations. Sustaining Departheid also means an expensive investment in the time of numerous other state officials: advisors and clerks in several ministries and public institutions, judges, prosecutors, state attorneys and so on.

The national economies of Western states benefit enormously from the cheap labour that disenfranchised, unprotected and readily exploitable illegalised migrants are forced to sell under the most unfavourable conditions: from big industrial and agricultural companies, to middle-sized employers in the retail and service sectors, to millions of ordinary citizens who can outsource domestic work and child/elderly care to illegalised migrants. Having no access to the formal market, illegalised migrants are also regularly dependent on local brokers who charge an exorbitant commission for arranging accommodation and employment.

Some of the investment in Departheid is also increasingly allocated to civil-society organisations for the administration of all sorts of 'voluntary return' programmes or what can be called 'soft deportation' (Kalir, 2017b). Both the International Organization for Migration (IOM) and a series of local and international non-governmental organisations (NGOs) have been recruited by Western states to promote and implement assisted and/or non-assisted return programmes, whereby illegalised migrants receive money and/or guidance and training in preparation for return to their country of origin or for resettlement in a third country. Many illegalised migrants who end up taking part in 'voluntary return' programmes do so because they face extremely vulnerable circumstances, including severe medical conditions (for which they are sometimes offered treatment in return for going back to their country of origin).

Economically speaking, then, the foregrounding of Departheid as the championed modality for the governance of illegalised migrants is beneficial to the state apparatus, business elite, civil society and large sections of the citizenry. The losing party is the millions of exploited illegalised migrants who have no political say about their marginalisation in the society where they live and work. Notably, however, it is taxpayers' money that finances most activities that constitute Departheid. Legitimacy for Departheid must therefore be shored up in wide political and public circles.

There is probably no better way for states to furnish support for Departheid than to turn the entire issue of governing human mobility into a national security one. Unsurprisingly, then, since the 1990s, the 'securitization of migration' (Huysmans, 2000) has been a defining development in framing people's right to exercise mobility across state borders as a security risk for the physical safety and cultural integrity of national populations. Framing the administration of mobility as a security issue and branding illegalised migrants as a new 'state enemy' are effective not only in sanctioning enormous investments in Departheid but also in diverting public attention from other political fronts on which many Western states are failing to deliver: affordable and reliable healthcare systems, gender equality, effective control over the financial markets, unemployment benefits and so on.

Under processes of globalisation that partly undermine the sovereign power of individual states, fighting weak migrants and refugees serves as a pretext for states to beef up agencies such as the police, border guards, the army, the diplomatic mission and state bureaucracy. States can thus reinforce their overall importance and, specifically, their image as protectors of the national population. It is disturbing to note that, in recent years, there is not a single mainstream political party in Europe, the United States or Australia that has called for a deceleration in the securitisation of migration. Electorally speaking, being anti-immigration is decisively a winning ticket in the Western world.

There is, however, one thorny hurdle over which Western states must jump in their aggressive push towards an ever-more securitised and oppressive mobility regime: the fact that migrants and refugees are not the 'enemy' that politicians, the media and opinion-makers would have the public believe. Studies have consistently shown that immigration historically correlates with economic growth (Friedberg and Hunt, 1995; Peri, 2012), that Western states have a much greater capacity to receive refugees than they do currently (Bauböck, 2018) and that migrants and refugees are not involved in terrorism in any remotely significant sense and are, in fact, extremely law-abiding (Wortley, 2009).

To explain the arresting grip of Departheid on Western societies, we must turn our attention to the ideological work that underlies it. More specifically, we need to account for the ways in which the governance of mobility in Western states is always (still) directly aligned with (post)colonial geopolitical and mental configurations that are impelled by White Supremacy. As a first step, we should recognise that the treatment of migrants and refugees in the West is impregnated with racial profiling, institutional racism and all sorts of racialising technologies (Albahari, 2006; Fekete, 2009; Hyndman and Mountz, 2008; Khosravi, 2009; Schuster, 2003; van Houtum, 2010). Studies have shown that policies and practices that constitute Departheid are selectively applied along specific racial and racialising lines (e.g. Bloch and Schuster, 2005; Collyer, 2012; Golash-Boza and Hondagneu-Sotelo, 2013). Departheid is hardly ever applied to White people, either because their mobility is always already legally permitted or because they are not considered to be threatening, even when administratively lacking the right documentation.[4]

As a second step we must recall that, under colonialism, the European colonisers drew a marked distinction between White 'masters' who were classified as citizens and the non-White 'natives' who were reduced to the status of 'subject races'. Under this racialised imperial order, 'subject races', seen as 'backward', 'primitive' or 'savages', were subjugated as minorities in their own territory to extreme forms of control over their physical movement as well as their social and economic mobility (Mitchell, 1991). It is, in fact, within the colonial rule that the notion of citizenship first developed as a crucial marker to keep out 'subject races' from the realm of European law, with all the entitlements and protections that it endowed on the colonisers (Isin, 2016).

It is important to note that, historically, tying processes of racialisation in Europe to regimes of mobility in the service of capitalism preceded colonial expansion (Robinson, 2000[1983]). The colonial configuration of racialised mobility was predicated on an entrenched European model, whereby racist ideologies legitimised the subjugation of 'inferior' races as serfs to the 'nobles'. An ideology of White Supremacy dominated the colonial encounter and justified the killing and enslavement of non-White people. In the twentieth century, racist policies to govern mobility were atrociously at work under Nazi Germany but were also evident in the United States with the Jim Crow laws or in Australia with its White immigration policy that restricted non-European mobility up to the mid-1970s. In South Africa, Apartheid, openly basing itself on White Supremacy, was still in operation until the early 1990s.

Departheid should therefore be seen as the latest mutation of long-standing oppressive governing ideologies for the spatial management of racialised populations. Under Departheid, in similarity with colonial modalities, a certain category of non-citizens is exploited, dehumanised and legally subjected to surveillance, confinement and deportation. Just like under Apartheid, non-White subjects have no political representation and are denied the right to vote, even when they have lived in the state territory since forever – or for decades – as is the case with many illegalised migrants.

Nowadays, however, White Supremacy is not openly advocated as the ideological ground on which Western mobility regimes are formed. This is the case because, given the entrenched coded racial matrix that structures global mobility in a neo-colonial world order, there is no need for an explicit recourse to White Supremacy and racial classifications in reproducing the colonial order (Mezzadra and Nielson, 2013; Ngai, 2014; Rigo, 2005). The economic domination of Western states over ex-colonies and, more generally, over the Global South, dictates a vicious cycle whereby many of those who populate exploited and depleted territories in the South are bound to seek livelihood and safety in the North (Balibar, 2001; Golash-Boza, 2015). In Western states, all operations under Departheid are based on laws and regulations that carry the stamp of liberal and democratic procedures. These laws and regulations, however, always already include racialising and exclusionary logics, so that state bureaucrats can then 'simply' apply them as the caretakers of law and order in the society. Departheid should therefore be conceived as a form of structural racism that is not directly predicated on the racist thinking of all the individuals and groups who work in its service.

## DEPARTHEID: WHAT IS IT GOOD FOR?

Advancing the notion of Departheid can contribute to academic and political work on five concrete fronts. The first three fronts are within the realm of studying and understanding the workings of contemporary oppressive mobility regimes. The last two fronts are geared more directly towards political activism to bring about the demise of Departheid.

First, as an act of naming, Departheid can raise attention and amass critical assessment of a phenomenon that otherwise might not be conceived in its fullness and lead different critics to believe that they work in and on different fields that too easily get fragmented across disciplinary, methodological and national lines. Indeed, one of the most substantial achievements of any oppressive hegemonic ideology – which Departheid clearly is – is the ability to deflect attention from its unitary form and thereby to prevent distinctive portents from pointing in a singular direction.

Second, as an alternative analytical point of departure, Departheid can resolve a prevailing sense of puzzlement that underlines many studies on the inhumane treatment of illegalised migrants in Western states. This sense of puzzlement is rooted in taking for granted democratic and liberal values to mark the (self-proclaimed) moral position of Western states. From this point of departure, critical studies often end up, quite insidiously, reproducing a false notion of a humane Western governing regime that has gone astray and is simply in need of corrective reforms. In contrast, Departheid postulates that Western states intentionally implement a racialised mobility regime. It therefore asks us to evaluate, for example, the deaths of migrants and refugees at borders, their months-long confinement in detention centres and their forced removal and 'voluntary' return, as deliberate violence and not as the unintended consequence of otherwise humane policies.

Third, Departheid calls for a reorientation of research within migration and refugee studies, setting our focus more persistently on the work and normative views of policy-makers, civil servants and street-level bureaucrats in institutions charged with implementing oppressive migration policies. Not taking anything away from a focus on the agentic and creative capacities of illegalised migrants, we need more and better accounts of the dehumanising management of migration and borders from the side of the oppressor (e.g. Aas and Gundhus, 2014; Bosworth, 2014; Hall, 2010).

Fourth, by coining Departheid as a racialising and racist regime for governing migrants and refugees, we prepare the ground for legal action to demand its abolition and claim reparation for those who have been subjugated to its unjust procedures: violation of the 1951 Refugee Convention, confinement in conditions that fail to meet basic human-rights standards, physical and mental injuries, deportation to unsafe places and death. Taking Departheid to court, as it were, is a mighty task (Kanstroom, 2012). Unlike Apartheid, which was condemned by most states around the world, Departheid is endorsed by almost all nation states and is predicated, internationally, on agreements and collaboration between states regarding the 'returning' of citizens to the national territory to which they belong.

Fifth, exposing the humiliating, racist and inhumane treatment of migrants and refugees under Departheid might shame those who work in its service. We should insist on the direct responsibility of state actors and street-level bureaucrats, as it is only through their daily work that Departheid exists. Recalling Arendt's (1963) 'banality of evil', we must recognise that people in general and bureaucrats in particular are not evil but that racist state projects are evil and those who serve them can and should be charged for their thoughtlessness and carelessness (Kalir, 2019b; Vrăbiescu and Kalir, 2018). Many NGOs and other civil-society actors who assist in the operation of Departheid, albeit with a humane approach, should also be called to assume responsibility and re-evaluate their stance (Kalir, 2017b; Kalir and Wissink, 2016).

## THE FIRST CRACKS?

Resistance to Departheid takes on different forms in different places. Concerned individuals, social movements, grassroots organisations and combative NGOs engage in multiple actions to disrupt the operation of Departheid and to uncover the structural and racial violence that is embedded in its functioning. Sabotaging deportation flights, campaigning for the closure of detention centres, assisting migrants and refugees to cross borders, publicly denouncing acts of police violence, offering rights to illegalised migrants at a city level, building sanctuaries and offering legal advice and protection to fight injustices in court are just some examples of the growing attempts to shake the legalistic and operational foundations of Departheid.

Western states fight back, trying to assert Departheid in a more forceful fashion, by inflicting even greater arbitrary and immoral violence on border-crossers (as in the case of family separation at the US–Mexico border), expanding the budget and authority of border guards (as in the case of Frontex), forbidding rescue operations of boats with migrants and refugees in the Mediterranean Sea and much more. Yet, the most telling indication for the acute legitimacy deficit from which Departheid suffers can be found in the move to criminalise solidarity with migrants and refugees in some European states (PICUM, 2017; Tazzioli and Walters, 2019). An attempt to gain legitimacy for the oppressive operations of Departheid by increasingly resorting to legalistic measures and by banning and censoring opposing voices might, in fact, reveal the deeply immoral basis of this mobility regime to more and more people. Similarly, the populist and racist rhetoric that some politicians and public intellectuals must use in order to blame migrants and refugees for the ills of Western societies becomes phantasmagoric, to a point that many might start to doubt the lucidity of the push behind Departheid. Of course, there is also the very real possibility that populist and even authoritarian tendencies will have the upper hand in this battle for freedom of movement and dignity for all. This is why not politicising an academic debate on 'return' policies is a luxury that scholars cannot afford.

## NOTES

1. Parts of this chapter first appeared in 2019 in my article 'Departheid: the draconian governance of illegalized migrants in western states', *Conflict and Society*, **5** (1), 19–40.
2. See, for example, http://15years.morizbuesing.com (accessed 8 March 2021).
3. There are exceptions where an enormous investment coupled with the brutal treatment of illegalised migrants has led to the relative 'success' of Departheid. In Australia, the harsh offshore regime – and its physical remoteness – together ensured that the numbers of arriving migrants and asylum-seekers became relatively low in comparison with other Western states. Israel is another example where considerable investment in fencing borders and an utter disregard for basic human rights and international conventions led to a relatively 'efficient' implementation of Departheid (Amit, 2020; Kalir, 2010).
4. Notably, some EU member states, mostly Germany and, to some extent, the United Kingdom and France, deport considerable numbers of White people. Yet, interestingly, most White deportees are Europeans who come either from non-EU states and are predominantly Muslim (Albania and Bosnia-Herzegovina) or from peripheral, late-comer states to the EU (Poland, Romania and Bulgaria) whose citizens are often racialised.

## REFERENCES

Aas, K.F. and Gundhus, H.O. (2014) 'Policing humanitarian borderlands: Frontex, human rights and the precariousness of life', *British Journal of Criminology*, **55** (1), 1–18.
Albahari, M. (2006) *Death and the Modern State: Making Borders and Sovereignty at the Southern Edges of Europe*, San Diego: UC San Diego Center for Comparative Immigration Studies Working Paper 137.
Amit, I. (2020) *Between the Excessive and the Effective: The Everyday Life of the Israeli Deportation Regime*, Amsterdam: University of Amsterdam, unpublished PhD thesis.
Anderson, B., Gibney, M.J. and Paoletti, E. (2013) *The Social, Political and Historical Contours of Deportation*, Berlin: Springer.
Arbogast, L. (2016) *Migrant Detention in the European Union: A Thriving Business*, Brussels: Migreurop/Rosa Luxemburg Stiftung.
Arendt, H. (1963) *Eichmann in Jerusalem: A Report on the Banality of Evil*, New York: Viking.
Balibar, E. (2001) 'Outlines of a topography of cruelty: citizenship and civility in the era of global violence', *Constellations*, **8** (1), 15–29.

Bauböck, R. (2018) 'Refugee protection and burden-sharing in the European Union', *Journal of Common Market Studies*, **56** (1), 141–56.

Bigo, D. (2002) 'Security and immigration: toward a critique of the governmentality of unease', *Alternatives*, **27** (1), 63–92.

Bloch, A. and Schuster, L. (2005) 'At the extremes of exclusion: deportation, detention and dispersal', *Ethnic and Racial Studies*, **28** (3), 491–512.

Bosworth, M. (2014) *Inside Immigration Detention*, Oxford: Oxford University Press.

Cavazos-Rehg, P.A., Zayas, L.H. and Spitznagel, E.L. (2017) 'Legal status, emotional well-being and subjective health status of Latino immigrants', *Journal of the National Medical Association*, **99** (10), 1126–31.

CBP (2018) *Southwest Border Deaths by Fiscal Year*, Washington DC: US Customs and Border Protection, https://www.cbp.gov/sites/default/files/assets/documents/2019-Mar/bp-southwest-border-sector-deaths-fy1998-fy2018.pdf (accessed 7 March 2021).

Chishti, M., Pierce, S. and Bolter, J. (2017) *The Obama Record on Deportations: Deporter in Chief or Not?* Washington DC: Migration Policy Institute, 26 January, https://www.migrationpolicy.org/article/obama-record-deportations-deporter-chief-or-not (accessed 7 March 2021).

Collyer, M. (2012) 'Deportation and the micropolitics of exclusion: the rise of removals from the UK to Sri Lanka', *Geopolitics*, **17** (2), 276–92.

De Giorgi, A. (2010) 'Immigration control, post-fordism, and less eligibility', *Punishment and Society*, **12** (2), 147–67.

DHS (2017) *Budget-in-Brief: Fiscal Year 2016*, Washington DC: US Department of Homeland Security.

Eurostat (2018) 'Enforcement of immigration legislation statistics', *Statistics Explained*, https://ec.europa.eu/eurostat/statistics-explained/pdfscache/37449.pdf (accessed 10 March 2021).

Fekete, L. (2009) *A Suitable Enemy: Racism, Migration and Islamophobia in Europe*, London: Pluto Press.

Feldman, G. (2012) *The Migration Apparatus: Security, Labor, and Policymaking in the European Union*, Stanford CA: Stanford University Press.

Friedberg, R.M. and Hunt, J. (1995) 'The impact of immigrants on host country wages, employment and growth', *Journal of Economic Perspectives*, **9** (2), 23–44.

GDP (2016) *United States Immigration Detention Profile*, Geneva: Global Detention Project.

GDP (2019) *European Union: Organization and Alliances Countries Grid*, Geneva: Global Detention Project.

GDP and AIE (2015) *The Uncounted: The Detention of Migrants and Asylum Seekers in Europe*, Geneva: Global Detention Project and Access Info Europe.

Golash-Boza, T.M. (2015) *Deported: Immigrant Policing, Disposable Labor, and Global Capitalism*, New York: New York University Press.

Golash-Boza, T. and Hondagneu-Sotelo, P. (2013) 'Latino immigrant men and the deportation crisis: a gendered racial removal program', *Latino Studies*, **11** (3), 271–92.

Hall, A. (2010) '"These people could be anyone": fear, contempt (and empathy) in a British immigration removal centre', *Journal of Ethnic and Migration Studies*, **36** (6), 881–98.

Huysmans, J. (2000) 'The European Union and the securitization of migration', *Journal of Common Market Studies*, **38** (5), 751–77.

Hyndman, J. and Mountz, A. (2008) 'Another brick in the wall? Neo-refoulement and the externalization of asylum by Australia and Europe', *Government and Opposition*, **43** (2), 249–69.

Isin, E.F. (2016) *Citizenship after Orientalism: Transforming Political Theory*, Berlin: Springer.

Jabri, P. (2013) 'Australia's Pacific asylum-seeker camps to cost $2bn', *Business Recorder*, 17 December, https://www.brecorder.com/2013/12/17/149148 (accessed 7 March 2021).

Kalir, B. (2010) *Latino Migrants in the Jewish State: Undocumented Lives in Israel*, Bloomington: Indiana University Press.

Kalir, B. (2017a) 'State desertion and "out-of-procedure" asylum seekers in the Netherlands', *Focaal: Journal of Global and Historical Anthropology*, **77**, 63–75.

Kalir, B. (2017b) 'Between "voluntary" return programs and soft deportation: sending vulnerable migrants in Spain back "home"' in Z. Vathi and R. King (eds), *Return Migration and Psychosocial Wellbeing*, London: Routledge, pp. 56–71.

Kalir, B. (2019a) 'Repressive compassion: deportation caseworkers furnishing an emotional comfort zone in encounters with illegalized migrants', *PoLAR: Political and Legal Anthropology Review*, **42** (1), 68–84.

Kalir, B. (2019b) 'On the universal and the particular in studying oppressive mobility regimes', *International Journal of Migration and Border Studies*, **5** (4), 409–16.

Kalir, B. and van Schendel, W. (2017) 'Nonrecording states between legibility and looking away', *Focaal: Journal of Global and Historical Anthropology*, **77**, 1–7.

Kalir, B. and Wissink, L. (2016) 'The deportation continuum: convergences between state agents and NGO workers in the Dutch deportation field', *Citizenship Studies*, **20** (1), 34–49.

Kanstroom, D. (2012) *Aftermath: Deportation Law and the New American Diaspora*, Oxford: Oxford University Press.

Khosravi, S. (2009) 'Sweden: detention and deportation of asylum seekers', *Race and Class*, **50** (4), 38–56.

Magner, T. (2004) 'A less than "pacific" solution for asylum seekers in Australia', *International Journal of Refugee Law*, **16** (1), 53–90.

Menjívar, C. and Abrego, L. (2012) 'Legal violence: immigration law and the lives of Central American immigrants', *American Journal of Sociology*, **117** (5), 1380–421.

Mezzadra, S. and Neilson, B. (2013) *Border as Method, or, the Multiplication of Labor*, Durham NC: Duke University Press.

Mignolo, W. (2012) *Local Histories/Global Designs: Coloniality, Subaltern Knowledges, and Border Thinking*, Princeton NJ: Princeton University Press.

Mitchell, T. (1991) *Colonising Egypt*, Berkeley CA: University of California Press.

Neumayer, E. (2006) 'Unequal access to foreign spaces: how states use visa restrictions to regulate mobility in a globalized world', *Transactions of the Institute of British Geographers*, **31** (1), 72–84.

Nevins, J. (2001) *Operation Gatekeeper: The Rise of the 'Illegal Alien' and the Remaking of the US–Mexico Boundary*, London: Routledge.

Ngai, M.M. (2014) *Impossible Subjects: Illegal Aliens and the Making of Modern America*, Princeton NJ: Princeton University Press.

Nielsen, N. (2018) 'Frontex: Europe's new law enforcement agency?', *Eurobserver*, 22 February.

Ohmae, K. (1991) *The Borderless World: Power and Strategy in the Interlinked Economy*, New York: Harper Perennial.

Peri, G. (2012) 'The effect of immigration on productivity: evidence from US states', *Review of Economics and Statistics*, **94** (1), 348–58.

Phillips, J. and Spinks, H. (2013) *Immigration Detention in Australia*, Canberra: Department of Parliamentary Services Research Paper.

Pickering, S. and Weber, L. (2014) 'New deterrence scripts in Australia's rejuvenated off-shore detention regime for asylum seekers', *Law and Social Inquiry*, **39** (4), 1006–26.

PICUM (2017) *Help Is No Crime: People Share Their Stories of Being Accused, Intimidated and Punished for Helping Migrants*, Brussels: Platform for International Cooperation for Undocumented Migrants, website of testimonies: Help Is No Crime: People share their stories of being accused, intimidated and punished for helping migrants • PICUM (accessed 7 March 2021).

Reddy, C. (2011) *Freedom with Violence*, Durham NC: Duke University Press.

Rigo, E. (2005) 'Citizenship at Europe's borders: some reflections on the post-colonial condition of Europe in the context of EU enlargement', *Citizenship Studies*, **9** (1), 3–22.

Robinson, C. (2000[1983]) *Black Marxism: The Making of the Black Radical Tradition*, Chapel Hill NC: University of North Carolina Press.

Saucier, P.K. and Woods, T.P. (2014) 'Ex aqua: the Mediterranean basin, Africans on the move, and the politics of policing', *Theoria*, **61** (141), 55–75.

Schuster, L. (2003) 'Common sense or racism? The treatment of asylum-seekers in Europe', *Patterns of Prejudice*, **37** (3), 233–56.

Taylor, D., Walker, P. and Grierson, J. (2018) 'Revealed: two suicide attempts every day in UK deportation centres', *The Guardian*, 11 October.

Tazzioli, M. and Walters, W. (2019) 'Migration, solidarity and the limits of Europe', *Global Discourse*, **9** (1), 175–90.

Triggs, G. (2013) 'Mental health and immigration detention', *Medical Journal of Australia*, **199** (11), 721–2.

Ugelvik, T. (2016) 'Techniques of legitimation: the narrative construction of legitimacy among immigration detention officers', *Crime, Media, Culture*, **12** (2), 215–32.

van Houtum, H. (2010) 'Human blacklisting: the global apartheid of the EU's external border regime', *Society and Space*, **28** (6), 957–76.

Vrăbiescu, I. and Kalir, B. (2018) 'Care-full failure: how auxiliary assistance to poor Roma migrant women in Spain compounds marginalization', *Social Identities*, **24** (4), 520–32.

Wong, T.K. (2015) *Rights, Deportation, and Detention in the Age of Immigration Control*, Stanford CA: Stanford University Press.

Wortley, S. (2009) 'Introduction. The immigration–crime connection: competing theoretical perspectives', *Journal of International Migration and Integration*, **10** (4), 349–58.

# 7. Return visits and other return mobilities
## Md Farid Miah

## INTRODUCTION

Return visits were 'completely overlooked' (Baldassar, 2001, p.5) within studies on migration for a long period of time. Earlier theorisation of migration as a one-way journey that ends with settlement and migrants' eventual assimilation in the destination country did not leave any space for the many types of return mobilities. In fact, migration theory lacked a 'vocabulary' and 'framework' to address the transnational 'to-and-fro' mobilities of migrants (King et al., 2013). However, this understanding has since been shifted. Following the transnational turn of the 1990s and then the mobilities turn of the 2000s, the conceptualisation of migration has loosened to accommodate more short-term, circular and sequential types of human spatial movement. Short-term visiting mobilities are temporally enfolded within longer-term migrations and relocations. This is explicitly depicted in the return side of the migration coin. The earliest thoughts on return visits can be traced back to the theorisation of return migration. For example, King (2000, pp.10–11) noted migrants' occasional, seasonal and temporary return visits in his generalised account of the history and typology of return migration. Return visits can also be seen as a 'substitute' for return migration, where frequent visits are a way of 'compensating' for migrants' lengthy absence from their home country and subsequent non-return in the event of permanent settlement elsewhere (King and Lulle, 2015).

The nuances of migrants' return visits to their home country have increasingly been receiving scholarly attention, resulting in a relatively large volume of recent and current literature. Most notably, Baldassar's (2001) pioneering book, *Visits Home*, provided a thick ethnographic account of such visits undertaken by migrant Italians in Australia to San Fior, one of their main 'home' villages in the Alps. Subsequently, return visits between other spatially distant places across the globe have also been studied by many scholars. Examples of such studies of return visits range widely across multiple global contexts, including the Caribbean (Conway et al., 2009; Duval, 2004a, 2004b; Stephenson, 2002), Africa (Asiedu, 2005; Sagmo, 2015; Wagner, 2008), Asia (Bolognani, 2014; Cressey, 2006; Miah and King, 2018; Oeppen, 2013; Sterling and Pang, 2013; Zeitlyn, 2012) and Europe (Humbracht, 2015; King and Lulle, 2015; King et al., 2011; Lulle, 2014; Mueller, 2015; Vathi and King, 2011). These inherently interdisciplinary and cross-border studies reveal multiple and diverse characteristics, trajectories, experiences and social, cultural and economic impacts of such visits in different spatial and temporal contexts.

It is well documented that transnational migration creates new 'spatial arrangements' of social relationships (Williams and Hall, 2000). Kinship networks have become spatially stretched and many families, individuals and groups live geographically dispersed lives. Return visits, often assisted by cheap air and coach travel, enable migrants to overcome this spatial decoupling of kinship, locality and culture. Although widely available digital communication technologies such as social media apps allow instant virtual exchanges, they do not erode people's 'compulsion to proximity' (Urry, 2002, p.263). Corporeal visits to meet families and friends face-to-face is irreplaceable, as these physical encounters produce 'thick, embodied socialities where people are uniquely accessible, available and subject to one another' (Larsen et al., 2006, p.280). The visits are doubly embedded: within the micro-spatialities of the diaspora experience and within the life-course of the individuals concerned. Such visits are performative encounters of kinship and belonging (Fortier, 1999, 2000), often with more-or-less predefined choreographies. As research on British-Bangladeshi migrants has shown, complex gender and generational relationships are also played out, often across an unequal social and geopolitical field, during the visits (Miah and King, 2018, 2020; Zeitlyn, 2012).

## DEFINING RETURN VISITS

A precise definition of the notion of return visits does not exist. This is mainly due to the combination of inherent interdisciplinary overlap and voids. The act of visiting comprises a set of activities and practices that have been the subject of both Tourism and Migration studies, both of them highly interdisciplinary but also potentially fragmented fields. Certain forms of tourism, such as 'diaspora tourism' (Huang et al., 2016), 'ethnic tourism' (King, 1994) and 'VFR (visiting friends and relatives) tourism' (Janta et al., 2015), also incorporate some aspects of migrants' return visits. Janta et al. (2015) noted that visits intricately link tourism with migratory phenomena. The 'functional interlinkages' between two 'human spatial mobilities' – tourism and migration – have also been recognised by migration scholars (King et al., 2013). While tourism scholarship tends to lay stress on the economic significance of such visits by measuring the size and volume of visits and associated economic expenditure, including in commercial accommodation, migration scholars consider it as a 'fundamental part' of the migrant's experience and life-course (King, 2015; Mueller, 2015).

Return visits can be viewed as an important characteristic of the phenomenon of migration. It might not be universal but at least the 'desire to return' (Baldassar, 2001, p.11) is present among the vast majority of migrants. The visits are always in the making. There are moral and cultural obligations that constantly remind migrants of their duty to return to their hometown and provide care for their relatives by being physically co-present. Cultural obligations are also reciprocated by the visitors and hosts. While the migrants are obliged to return periodically, relatives and friends in the home country fulfil their duty of providing hospitality for the visitors. For many migrants, such as Italians settled in Australia, return visits also come as an opportunity to relieve their nostalgia or homesickness and to reinvigorate their cultural identities. As Baldassar (2001, p.323) famously argued:

> [The] visit 'home' is a secular pilgrimage of redemption in response to the obligation of child to kin, townsperson to town. In the case of the second-generation emigrant, the visit is a transformatory rite of passage brought about by the development of ties to one's ancestral past.

Migrants' return visits are symbolised by their collection of materials and tokens from the homeland, which has similarity with 'the relics brought back from religious pilgrimages' (Baldassar, 2001, p.149). These collections are special mementos displayed in their houses in their country of settlement and through which a symbolic link with home-country places and people is maintained. Visiting relatives and friends occasionally back in the home villages and towns strengthens this tie and rejuvenates the migrants' cultural identity. There is also a spatial dimension to their cultural identity renewal process. Return visits are not merely about cultural renewal and fulfilling care obligations to relatives and friends; they are also 'a state of mind' (Stephenson, 2002, p.392). The homeland visit is about the ability to be physically present in the place of one's memory, where one can 'smell the air, touch the soil and test the produce, hear the bell tower or the call to prayer' (Baldassar, 2008, p.262). The return visits constitute an embodied and psychological reification of those memories (Miah and King, 2018, p.220). Long-held memories of people and places are revisited and reconstructed through back-and-forth visits during migrants' life-course. For the second and subsequent migrant generations, who are born in the host country, visits work as a rite of passage, a process of diffusing cultural knowledge and heritage of the ancestral place and people by one generation to another. Return visits lead the second generation and other diasporic migrants to develop personal ties to their ancestral past through this process. Their hybrid cultural identities are affirmed and informed by the visits.

Return visits can also be defined based on their frequency and duration. Duval (2004a, p.51) defined return visits as a form of 'periodic, but temporary, sojourn made by members of diasporic communities' to their homeland. Visits are a specific 'space–time phenomenon' (King and Lulle, 2015), an expression of mobilities between a diasporic and a home place and often carefully planned and timed to coincide with an important cultural event such as a wedding, childbirth, a funeral, Eid and Christmas. What makes return visits different from other forms of short-term mobility, such as tourism, are pre-existing 'significant social ties' (Duval, 2004b, p.51). The frequency and length of return visits are also dependent upon many other factors such as geographical proximity, strength of familial and personal relationships, affordability and leisure or business interest. Spatial proximity is as important as timing. Visits are relatively frequent and of short duration where there is close geographical proximity. Intra-continental visits, such as within Europe, happen more frequently compared to inter-continental visits, such as between North America and Asia. For example, the young German migrants researched by Mueller (2015) chose England as their destination precisely for the geographical proximity that enables them to maintain transnational friendship and family connections through frequent visits – for instance, for one or two weekends every month. Return visits tend to be relatively less frequent, more costly and of longer duration in other distant geographical contexts, such as visits from the UK to South Asian countries or the Caribbean examples cited earlier. Regardless of their frequency, duration, spatial proximity and affordability, all return visits are meaningful and integral to the maintenance of transnational familial, social and cultural ties.

## A TYPOLOGY OF RETURN VISITS

The many characteristics of return visits, associated activities and embedded practices can be addressed better through a typology of visits. Drawing mainly from the Italian-Australian experience, Baldassar et al. (2007, p.139) presented a fivefold typology of home-country visits, which are: care visits, duty and ritual visits, routine visits, special visits and tourist visits. Following in similar footsteps but in a somewhat different geographical context, based on British-Pakistani practices, Bolognani (2014, pp.106–13) also noted five types of visit: roots visits, holiday visits, health visits, family visits and business visits. As the names suggest, there are both similarities and differences between these two typologies. Perhaps the differences are reflective of the fact that migrants' return visits are constitutive of diverse practices and vary across different spatio-temporal contexts. Janta et al. (2015, p.587) listed the five most important practices of visiting mobilities, namely: social relationships, the provision of care, affirmations of identities and roots, the maintenance of territorial rights and, finally, leisure tourism. Following on from these types of visit and other studies of visiting mobilities, I now provide an extended and updated eightfold typology of return visits. As a caveat, the list is neither exhaustive nor has rigid boundaries, as visitors often engage in multiple activities on their homeland trips.

**Routine Visits**

Migration and subsequent settlement in a new country do not necessarily diminish migrants' ties to the birth country. Regardless of geographical distance and length of absence, the nostalgia for the home country never really leaves them. This is the case particularly for most first-generation emigrants, who have nostalgic 'memoryscapes' (Miah and King, 2018) of childhood and growing up in the home country before their migration journey began. For many of them, return visits are a routine part of their immigrant life. Depending on affordability, they visit regularly and continue to plan one visit home after another. This was the case, as noted by Baldassar (2001), for many of the long-term settled and successful first-generation Italian migrants in Australia. Return visits are also a fundamental characteristic of the intra-European migration experience. Regular return visits are undertaken the most frequently by those migrants who enjoy free-movement rights. Budget airlines and cheap coach travel make such visits relatively inexpensive. Lulle (2014) examined such frequent visits commencing between the British Channel Island of Guernsey and Latvia. Latvian labour migrants' visits to their home country are driven by the necessity of a corporeal co-presence with left-behind family and friends in their home country and are underpinned by the 'sensory and emotional' experience which they long for (Lulle, 2014, p.127).

**Ritual Visits**

Ritual visits require migrants to attend and participate in key life-cycle events or family rituals such as childbirth, weddings, funerals and special anniversaries. Unwritten rules of kinship mean that the home-country society, culture, relatives and friends expect their migrant counterparts to be present at such rituals, wherever this is possible. Migrants are also morally obliged to fulfil their duty by being physically present to take part in these events. Such visits are relatively less frequent and last longer than the regular or routine visits. Celebratory or commemorative events and anniversaries are generally well prepared and carefully timed. Since the visitors often travel with their family on these visits, they often coincide with official holidays or vacations. Ritual visits also provide a rare opportunity for extended networks of relatives and friends to meet each other. This may also pave the way for meeting prospective brides or grooms. During family emergencies, such as sudden severe illness or death, visits can also happen at short notice, although they will probably soon be followed by a formal ritual with the presence of extended family and kinship networks.

## Care Visits

The discharging of care obligations, especially to children and elderly or sick parents by visiting in person is also common among migrants (King and Lulle, 2015). In fact, these caregiving activities are a 'fundamental feature of transnational family life' (Baldassar and Merla, 2013, p.25). Care visits require both emotional and physical labour. For migrant parents, visiting to care for their left-behind children in order to sustain 'familyhood' can be both challenging and stressful. Although care can be provided distantly by delegation, by sending remittances and via digital communication tools, visits are still required. Co-present sociality, body language, eye contact and simply 'being there' are necessary for building and maintaining trustworthy, respectable, intimate and meaningful relationships (Janta et al., 2015). Care visits can also involve a migrant's own personal care, often utilising cheaper and relatively affordable provisions, such as 'visiting doctors and dentists' (King and Lulle, 2015, p.605) in the home country. Similar visits by second-generation British Pakistanis to their parental country for 'spiritual, mental and physical wellbeing' can also be evidenced (Bolognani, 2014, p.108).

## Roots Visits

Return visits, as discussed earlier, can offer the opportunity for transnational migrants to make personal ties with their ancestral roots. Migrants' identities are thus shaped by their journeying between places of origin and destination and back again. For second and subsequent generations, visits to the ancestral home can lead to the confirmation and reshaping of their ethno-national identity. In the Italo-Australian case, Baldassar (2001) noted that most of the second generation witness a certain transformation of their hybrid cultural identities through visits to Italy. Identity and roots visits reveal a more complex and fluid picture than other forms of return visiting. Depending on the migrant communities, their geographical proximity, the strength of cultural ties and the level of socio-economic contrast, some of the second generation may feel a stronger sense of identity and belonging with their ancestral heritage, while others feel a sense of rejection or experience a hybrid construction of multi-ethnic and national identities. In the Pakistani case, the second-generation visitors often journey to Pakistan to pay sacred visits to their family graves and build ties with their heritage. However, young female visitors, in particular, can develop a sense of alienation from their parental homeland due to male treatment and harassment (Bolognani, 2014). Similarly, American-Afghan visitors in Kabul feel disorientated from their distorted country and culture and see their Americanness reaffirmed (Oeppen, 2013). In the British-Bangladeshi case, second-generation children construct a mixed or fluid combination of their cultural identities. Identity-seeking and roots visits depict a complex and shifting trajectory of identity and belonging across different spaces, times and generations. Rather than the binary combination of home and host society and culture, migrants' roots visits can also include journeys to a third place, such as a place of religious importance (DeHanas, 2013).

## Rights Visits

The assertion and maintenance of several forms of territorial rights, such as citizenship, voting, renewing passports, preferential access to health checks and other public social services, often require residential attachments in order to qualify (Janta et al., 2015). This can only be achieved through physical visits to the home country. Besides, most migrants have their inheritance, such as land, a house and other material resources there. Many of the first-generation migrants buy land and build houses with their savings and remittances. These houses function as an anchor during their return visits. The properties require regular return visits from migrants for multiple reasons: for regular maintenance in order to keep them habitable, in the event of ownership transfer or selling or mitigating any disputes that can arise during their absence (Miah, 2021). Disputes around these properties can prompt emergency visits as a physical presence is required to deal with the complicated issues. Frequent visits or a more prolonged stay might be necessary where solving such issues involves slow-moving bureaucratic processes (Miah and King, 2018).

**Pre-return Visits**

Pre-return visits are closely connected with subsequent return migration; a kind of step-wise temporality well documented by research in the Caribbean. Frequent return visits are used as a prior strategy for return migration, whereby the individuals and families visit their friends and relatives before deciding to return to their homeland (Conway et al., 2009; Duval, 2004b). Regular visits enable migrants to keep up to date with social, cultural and economic transformations in the home country. 'Benchmarking' those changes, including 'conjuring up mental maps' of places and people in the home country, equips migrants with the skills that are required for a successful return (Duval, 2004b, p.60). Return visits are thus often integral to the process of return migration. It is not just about keeping oneself familiar with the ancestral cultural heritage and subsequent changes over time; it is also about being able to fully reintegrate into the home society. In the Caribbean context, the degree of acceptance back into the home community is, in many ways, dependent upon migrants' ability to properly decipher the norms and rules expected and practised in the social sphere. From this perspective, return visits can be viewed as 'a mechanism' fostered by migrants and to be deployed in the event of return and reintegration into the home country (Duval, 2004b, p.64). However, the application of the mechanism might be straightforward for first-generation migrants but it becomes more complex for the second and subsequent generations. In a slightly different context, for second-generation Greek-Germans and Greek-Americans, childhood visits do not necessarily facilitate their return and reintegration process in Greece in their adulthood (Christou and King, 2014). This is because such visits, undertaken usually as holidays during the summer, when their relatives and friends are also in a relaxed and welcoming mood, give a distorted perception of life in the ancestral homeland. Permanent return often brings disillusionment and frustration.

**Economic Visits**

Return visits can also serve business and economic purposes for some migrants. Many ethnic businesses in the host country are linked to or dependent on the supply of materials from the home country. Return visits enable migrants to take up investment opportunities in addition to visiting relatives and friends. Investment visits are relatively more popular with second-generation migrants than with their first-generation parents. For example, second-generation British Pakistanis source their garments from Pakistan for their clothing shops in Birmingham (Bolognani, 2014). There are other examples, too. Asiedu (2005) noted British-Ghanaian migrants' investment, expenditure and donation activities in Ghana during visits. Active involvement in philanthropic activities – including donating money, medical supplies, vehicles, computers, educational materials, clothing and food items as well as involvement with home-town associations and developmental activities – require British-Ghanaians to visit their home country occasionally. Economic visits can also include visits to the home country as an employee of an external organisation. Such visiting opportunities for America-born Afghans were brought about by the lucrative interpreting job offers from the US forces in Kabul (Oeppen, 2013).

**Leisure Visits**

Visits can also be an opportunity to step out of the routine and hectic work life in the host country. During home-country visits, migrants often take part in leisure and tourism-related activities. Engaging in place-bound consumption and touristic practices, in the form of sight-seeing, boat trips, shopping and so forth, can be a key part of the migrant's visiting experience. Sometimes, migrants' trips to tourist sites are accompanied by their hosts as part of the longer itinerary of visits. On other occasions, once the reunion meetings are completed with the extended network of relatives and friends and all duties and obligations are fulfilled, brief side trips are made by the migrants, independently, to popular touristic sites. Shopping trips to buy artefacts, souvenirs and clothes are also made. In the context of family return visits, these side trips are fondly remembered by the younger-generation visitors and are designed by their first-generation parents in the hope that their children and grandchildren will continue to visit and maintain ties with the ancestral country. Childhood visits to the diasporic homeland (King et al., 2011; Zeitlyn, 2012), coinciding often with the summer holidays, give children a relative freedom to roam free in their parental country that is not permitted in the diaspora. Children remember these trips as fun times with frequent references to sun, sea, beaches, idyllic villages, nature, the countryside and generous hospitality and friendship from their home-country cousins and relatives.

## NOT A LEVEL PLAYING FIELD

Although return visits are generally a positive experience for many migrants, by no means do such visits take place across a 'level playing field' (King et al., 2013). A mismatch between expectations and the actual experience, gendered boundaries, generational gaps, politics, tension and power imbalances in the form of economic and wealth gaps are also played out during visits. Migrants' nostalgia and idealised recollection of the homeland are rarely reciprocated by the hosting relatives and friends. This is partly because migrants and non-migrant relatives and friends are differently positioned in the 'moral dimensions of migration and transnationalism' (Carling, 2008, p.1453). Return visits may have significant emotional, sensory and bodily implications for the migrants; for their hosting relatives and friends, visits are considered as a repayment for 'the debt of communality' (Carling, 2008, p.1458). Migrants' long absence from the home country means that their return visits are a moral entitlement for the left-behind relatives and friends. The lack or absence of visits is considered a sign of distancing, a lack of care and thought, and ingratitude.

There is also a generational gap. Second-generation Australian Italians in Baldassar's (2001) study were disappointed by the lack of enthusiasm and empathy and the reluctance to take them sight-seeing on the part of their older-generation relatives in Italy. Besides, scant disregard for their birth-country of Australia as a land of 'kangaroos, drought and desert', along with the constant assertion of the cultural and economic superiority of Italy, disillusioned them. While first-generation migrants mostly ignore these reactions or are less affected by this political and cultural jousting, the second generation can hardly do the same. The generational differences in return visits are also clearly evident through the different types of activity undertaken by the visitors. While the second generation highly regards these visits as a holiday, often part of their planned multi-country trips, the first generation considers them as an important aspect of their transnational familyhood and cultural ties to their home-country places and people. This difference is enhanced further by the perception of second-generation migrants as 'outsiders' (Wagner, 2015) or 'foreigners', distinguished by their accents, attitudes and dress, both by their relatives and by the 'home' society at large.

Visiting experiences are also highly gendered, as the Bangladesh case illustrates (Miah and King, 2018). Female visitors are expected to conform to the gendered norms of the host families and societies and maintain gendered boundaries by adhering to the prescribed dress and behavioural codes. Visitors are often considered as a part of the extended host family and hence are their 'responsibility'. Failure to conform to these unwritten rules of hospitality can create tension as the host family is worried about their reputation within the local social sphere. This is particularly visible where the migrants' home-country society is more socially and culturally conservative and patriarchal than their diasporic location. In a patriarchal social setting, male visitors tend to enjoy the freedom of sole sojourning while female visitors are often escorted in the public arena by their host counterparts. While some visitors find this uncomfortable and see it as a loss of freedom, others happily conform during the short duration of the visits.

There are also power asymmetries between the visitors and their hosts, often manifested in resource inequalities – including wealth gaps, legal entitlements to mobility and cultural and linguistic resources (Carling, 2008). Migrant visitors engage in uneasy competition to show off their economic wellbeing to their relatives and friends in the home country. However, in a highly unequal transnational context, such as between the UK and Bangladesh, migrants are in a position of power – due to their relative economic wealth and freedom of mobility facilitated by their new citizenship – over their relatives and friends in the home country (Miah and King, 2018; Zeitlyn, 2012). The complex positionality of migrants, characterised by the apparent 'mismatch between being low-income in London and a king in Bangladesh' (DeHanas, 2013, p. 463), can lead to uneasy class relations and raise unrealistic expectations on the part of the home-country relatives and friends. This is reflected in the material cultural practice of exchanging gifts during return visits. Relatives and friends often expect expensive gifts, including the latest models of smartphones and laptops. Subtle tensions and disillusionment can arise in the absence of such expensive gifts being distributed to them. In exchange for these rather expensive gifts, the visitors receive homemade and handcrafted local items high in symbolic rather than material value.

## CONCLUSION

Return visits are a fundamental part of the migration experience. Migrants' mobility between places characterises their transnational way of life (see also Bilgili, Chapter 3). The rhythm of their movement, the journey between places and the pilgrim-like status of the return visit are part of their spatial self-identity – the identity of being a migrant. Visits allow them to reaffirm the elements of this identity by being both 'here' and 'there'. The process of identity construction through return visiting continues from one generation to another and becomes a rite of passage. Second-generation children are introduced to their ancestral culture and heritage through visits. However, the identity trajectory of second-generation migrants is more complex and fluid compared to that of their first-generation parents. The shifting trajectories of second-generation identities and sense of belonging can also include reference to a 'third' space or 'hybrid' culture beyond their diasporic and home locations.

These visits can take the shape of a temporary stay or a more prolonged sojourn in the home country. While some visits take place frequently and spontaneously, others can be occasional. Geographical proximity often influences the frequency and length of visits. An intimate personal relationship with the left-behind country and the memories of place and people are maintained through such visits. Visits include a set of practices, ranging from fulfilling the family cultural obligation of providing care for relatives by being physically co-present, to holidaying or checking up on business opportunities in the home country. These activities vary according to various spatio-temporal contexts. Experiences of visits also reveal unequal relationships and associated politics and tensions. Our understanding of the migration phenomenon would be incomplete without a comprehensive understanding of the complex ways in which migrants maintain personal, familial and social ties to their home country through return visits.

## REFERENCES

Asiedu, A. (2005) 'Some benefits of migrants' return visits to Ghana', *Population, Space and Place*, **11** (1), 1–11.

Baldassar, L. (2001) *Visits Home: Migration Experiences between Italy and Australia*, Melbourne: Melbourne University Press.

Baldassar, L. (2008) 'Missing kin and longing to be together: emotions and the construction of co-presence in transnational relationships', *Journal of Intercultural Studies*, **29** (3), 247–66.

Baldassar, L. and Merla, L. (2013) 'Locating transnational care circulation in migration and family studies' in L. Baldassar and L. Merla (eds), *Transnational Families, Migration and the Circulation of Care: Understanding Mobility and Absence in Family Life*, Abingdon: Routledge, pp. 25–58.

Baldassar, L., Baldock, C. and Wilding, R. (2007) *Families Caring Across Borders: Transnational Migration, Ageing and Long Distance Care*, London: Palgrave Macmillan.

Bolognani, M. (2014) 'Visits to the country of origin: how second-generation British Pakistanis shape transnational identity and maintain power asymmetries', *Global Networks*, **14** (1), 103–20.

Carling, J. (2008) 'The human dynamics of migrant transnationalism', *Ethnic and Racial Studies*, **31** (8), 1452–77.

Christou, A. and King, R. (2014) *Counter-Diaspora: The Greek Second Generation Returns 'Home'*, Cambridge MA: Harvard University Press.

Conway, D., Potter, R.B. and St Bernard, G. (2009) 'Repetitive visiting as a pre-return transnational strategy among youthful Trinidadian returnees', *Mobilities*, **4** (2), 249–73.

Cressey, G. (2006) *Diaspora Youth and Ancestral Homeland: British Pakistani/Kashmiri Youth Visiting Kin in Pakistan and Kashmir*, Leiden: Brill.

DeHanas, D.N. (2013) 'Of Hajj and home: roots visits to Mecca and Bangladesh in everyday belonging', *Ethnicities*, **13** (4), 457–74.
Duval, D.T. (2004a) 'Conceptualizing return visits: a transnational perspective' in T. Coles and D.J. Timothy (eds), *Tourism, Diasporas and Space*, London: Routledge, pp. 50–61.
Duval, D.T. (2004b) 'Linking return visits and return migration among Commonwealth Eastern Caribbean migrants in Toronto', *Global Networks*, **4** (1), 51–67.
Fortier, A. (1999) 'Re-membering places and the performance of belonging(s)', *Theory, Culture and Society*, **16** (2), 41–64.
Fortier, A. (2000) *Migrant Belongings: Memory, Space, Identity*, Oxford: Berg.
Huang, W.J., Ramshaw, G. and Norman, W.C. (2016) 'Homecoming or tourism? Diaspora tourism experience of second-generation immigrants', *Tourism Geographies*, **18** (1), 59–79.
Humbracht, M. (2015) 'Reimagining transnational relations: the embodied politics of visiting friends and relatives mobilities', *Population, Space and Place*, **21** (7), 640–53.
Janta, H., Cohen, S.A. and Williams, A.M. (2015) 'Rethinking visiting friends and relatives mobilities', *Population, Space and Place*, **21** (7), 585–98.
King, B. (1994) 'What is ethnic tourism? An Australian perspective', *Tourism Management*, **15** (3), 173–6.
King, R. (2000) 'Generalizations from the history of return migration' in B. Ghosh (ed.), *Return Migration: Journey of Hope or Despair?*, Geneva: United Nations, pp. 7–55.
King, R. (2015) 'Migration comes of age', *Ethnic and Racial Studies*, **38** (13), 2366–72.
King, R. and Lulle, A. (2015) 'Rhythmic island: Latvian migrants in Guernsey and their enfolded patterns of space–time mobility', *Population, Space and Place*, **21** (7), 599–611.
King, R., Christou, A. and Teerling, J. (2011) '"We took a bath with the chickens": memories of childhood visits to the homeland by second-generation Greek and Greek Cypriot "returnees"', *Global Networks*, **11** (1), 1–23.
King, R., Lulle, A., Mueller, D. and Vathi, Z. (2013) *Visiting Friends and Relatives and its Links with International Migration: A Three-Way Comparison of Migrants in the UK*, Malmö: Malmö Institute for Studies of Migration, Diversity and Welfare, Willy Brandt Series of Working Papers in International Migration and Ethnic Relations, 4/13.
Larsen, J., Axhausen, K.W. and Urry, J. (2006) 'Geographies of social networks: meetings, travel and communications', *Mobilities*, **1** (2), 261–83.
Lulle, A. (2014) 'Spaces of encounter-displacement: contemporary labour migrants' return visits to Latvia', *Geografiska Annaler, Series B: Human Geography*, **96** (2), 127–40.
Miah, Md.F. (2021) 'Transnational land and property disputes: the British-Bangladeshi experience', *Contemporary South Asia*, DOI: 10.1080/09584935.2021.1886249.
Miah, Md.F. and King, R. (2018) 'Memoryscapes of the homeland by two generations of British Bangladeshis' in S. Marschall (ed.), *Memory, Migration and Travel*, London: Routledge, pp. 213–33.
Miah, Md.F. and King, R. (2020) 'When migrants become hosts and nonmigrants become mobile: Bangladeshis visiting their friends and relatives in London', *Population, Space and Place*, **27** (2), e2355.
Mueller, D. (2015) 'Young Germans in England visiting Germany: translocal subjectivities and ambivalent views of "home"', *Population, Space and Place*, **21** (7), 625–39.
Oeppen, C. (2013) 'A stranger at "home": interactions between transnational return visits and integration for Afghan-American professionals', *Global Networks*, **13** (2), 261–78. DOI: 10.1111/glob.12008.
Sagmo, T.H. (2015) 'Return visits as a marker of differentiation in the social field', *Mobilities*, **10** (4), 649–65.
Stephenson, M.L. (2002) 'Travelling to the ancestral homelands: the aspirations and experiences of a UK Caribbean community', *Current Issues in Tourism*, **5** (5), 378–425.
Sterling, S. and Pang, C.L. (2013) 'Managing multi-mobility and multi-layered identity in China: how ethnic Chinese-Venezuelan returnees cope with Chinese language, culture and identity', *Asian Ethnicity*, **14** (4), 511–24.
Urry, J. (2002) 'Mobility and proximity', *Sociology*, **36** (2), 255–74.
Vathi, Z. and King, R. (2011) 'Return visits of the young Albanian second generation in Europe: contrasting themes and comparative host-country perspectives', *Mobilities*, **6** (4), 503–18.
Wagner, L. (2008) 'Diasporic visitor, diasporic tourist', *Civilisations*, **57** (1–2), 191–205.

Wagner, L. (2015) 'Shopping for diasporic belonging: being "local" or being "mobile" as a VFR visitor in the ancestral homeland', *Population, Space and Place*, **21** (7), 654–68.
Williams, A.M. and Hall, C.M. (2000) 'Tourism and migration: new relationships between production and consumption', *Tourism Geographies*, **2** (1), 5–27.
Zeitlyn, B. (2012) 'Maintaining transnational social fields: the role of visits to Bangladesh for British Bangladeshi children', *Journal of Ethnic and Migration Studies*, **38** (6), 953–68.

# PART II

# THE POLITICISATION OF RETURN MIGRATION

# 8. Critical reflections on assisted return programmes and practices
*Ine Lietaert*

## INTRODUCTION

Assisted return (AR) programmes refer to governmental support programmes, developed by migrant host states, which provide counselling and administrative, logistical and/or financial support to encourage and facilitate the return and reintegration of migrants in their country of origin. The first programmes to support the return of migrants from Europe go back to the 1970s; however, mainly from the 1990s onwards, they have grown in popularity (Kuschminder, 2017; Lietaert et al., 2017a). Over past decades, this has resulted in a steep growth in the number of programmes and of actors involved, an increase in countries developing such programmes and those receiving assisted returnees and a real expansion of the budget dedicated to AR programmes (IOM, 2019). Moreover, through the European Union EU Return Directive (see Desmond, Chapter 10) and with the support of the EU Return Fund, AR became established as a central component of EU migration policy and its different member states (EMN, 2016). With the emphasis on safe and dignified return and sustainable reintegration in the Global Compact for Migration, including a call to guarantee that returning migrants are assisted in their reintegration processes, AR took its place on the international migration governance agenda as well (see Marino and Lietaert, Chapter 12).

The (EU) policy narrative on assisted return is quite solid and has changed little over time (EC, 2015; European Parliament and Council of the European Union, 2007, 2008). AR is seen as an indispensable link in the chain of migration management. It is one of the measures designed to encourage and facilitate the return of non-EU nationals without legal residence. As such, AR targets rejected asylum applicants and undocumented migrants. These latter's return is presented as essential to protect fair and credible asylum procedures and deter irregular migration. AR is considered to be politically more appealing for both host countries and countries of return and a more realistic, humane, cost-effective and sustainable solution than forced removal (Black et al., 2011; Kuschminder, 2017). Post-return reintegration support should facilitate economic and social reintegration in the country of return and accordingly increase the sustainability of return and discourage possible re-emigration to Europe (Black et al., 2011; EMN, 2016). Reintegration support is said to function as an extra incentive for migrants to return voluntarily.

However, this AR policy narrative is overloaded with criticism, for being merely a legitimisation for forced removal, ignoring the reality of return processes, lacking evidence for many of its central claims and even challenging fundamental rights obligations (Baldaccini, 2009; Lietaert, 2016; Vosyliūtė, 2019). What is more, insights are lacking into how, exactly, AR is translated into practice (Ellerman, 2006; Feneberg, 2019; Kalir and Wissink, 2016; Lietaert, 2019). In this chapter, I argue that the uniform narrative that is shared among many EU states conceals the existing variation in the way in which the practice is designed in different countries and implemented by different actors. Therefore, this chapter focuses on the operationalisation of AR by analysing available policy documents, academic literature and research reports on the evolution and implementation of AR in the Netherlands, Belgium and Germany. These particular countries form an interesting base as they have well-established AR programmes which were closely connected when being initiated (Mommers and Velthuis, 2010), though the different country contexts and policies clearly induce differences in the realisation of AR. By investigating these three contexts, I aim to disentangle the factors that shape the implementation of AR and critically reflect on the impact that this has on its content and meaning – as an essential first step towards more comparative research. Before presenting the analysis of AR in the three target countries, some critical reflections are set out on the meaning of 'return', 'voluntariness' and 'assistance' – the three central concepts of AR.

**Return**

People returning through AR programmes are a small subgroup within the huge variety of return mobilities. It is a group that returns under very particular circumstances, being explicitly selected and targeted by migration policies because they are not allowed to stay in the host country.

Yet, it is clear that this legal obligation to return does not equal an easy, straightforward or even feasible return process. People were often engaged in long, fragmented and dangerous migration journeys before they reached the 'destination' country and were confronted with precarious living conditions both during and after the journey (Collyer, 2010; de Haas et al., 2018). Returning can mean reconnecting with family, with a sense of agency and feelings of belonging. At the same time, it might imply losing social contacts and a sense of belonging, access to protection, security and remittances (which provide for the extended family) and nullifying the emotional, social and financial sacrifices that have been made (Lietaert, 2020). Hence, returning is a complex and difficult process that cannot be simply equated with 'follow the law'. Returning, too, with few resources and little capital, often to post-return contexts with challenging economic conditions, hampered access to services and sometimes realistic security threats, makes reintegrating de facto challenging (Cassarino, 2008).

**Voluntariness**

The voluntary character of so-called assisted *voluntary* return (AVR) has been contested for many years (Blitz et al., 2005; Webber, 2011) and is also critically appraised in other chapters in this Handbook (Erdal and Oeppen, Chapter 5; Kalir, Chapter 6). Scholars have argued that the label 'voluntary return' is instrumentalised by governments to legitimise their return policy towards international organisations, the wider public and migrants themselves (Cleton and Chauvin, 2020; Noll, 1999). It is indicated that AR is actually supporting the involuntary return of migrants who have no residence permit and return because this is the least-worst option (van Houte, 2014). Indeed, evaluations of voluntariness need to be related to the available alternatives (Erdal and Oeppen, 2018). However, framing all assisted returns as 'forced' based on the absence of a legal status in the host country disregards the complex ways in which returnees and their communities experience diverse elements of force and choice, even beyond their legal status (Lietaert, 2016; Wanki and Lietaert, 2019). The dichotomy also ignores the possibility that AR might create to label return as 'a choice' and, as such, rationalise the return decision (Lietaert et al., 2017b) and the possible salutogenic power of experiencing a restored sense of self-competence in making decisions and regaining control over life, even in restricted contexts (Veronese et al., 2020). That said, this chapter shows how voluntariness also depends on the consequences that are linked to not choosing the option of AR, such as losing access to support or becoming deportable. Therefore, voluntariness is linked to the accessibility criteria set for AR and its link with forced return.

The discussion on the impact of experiences and labels of voluntariness on mobility is still far from settled and the topic warrants further investigation (Erdal and Oeppen, 2018). Nonetheless, the fact that several countries no longer use the term 'assisted voluntary return' but 'assisted return', instead, is already an important step forward in recognising its reality (Kuschminder, 2017). Such a change might be more problematic when 'voluntariness' is one of the core principles in discourses on AR, as within EU policy, with the result that the terminology endures.

**Assistance**

Return assistance covers an immense diversity of meanings. Most AR programmes are built as a stepwise system of increasing support, the first step being 'return' or 'travel' support – supporting the physical return (Lietaert et al., 2017a). As such, this involves *pre-return assistance* which can contain (a combination of) information provision, counselling regarding the return decision, administrative support to enable return (e.g. attaining travel documents, birth certificates of children or medical documents), the booking and payment of transportation to the country of origin, shelter during counselling or in attendance of the return and skills training or the preparation of reintegration projects (EMN, 2016). Return support can be complemented with 'reintegration support' – *post-return assistance* to reintegrate in the country of origin. When moving up to higher levels of support, access becomes more restricted. Only a minority of assisted returnees receives post-return reintegration support, while the frequently used term assisted voluntary return (and reintegration) or AVR(R) includes both groups (Kuschminder, 2017) and thus incorporates a wide variety. Besides the content, the way in which the support is given, by whom and within which timeframe and socio-economic post-return context, also impacts on what 'assisted' means. Thus far this has received little research attention (Feneberg, 2019), allowing for an implementation black box in this field.

These reflections on AR's central terms highlight the need for a detailed contextualisation of assisted return processes and show how concealing language, combined with a lack of insight into the concrete content and meaning of support in this quickly growing and evolving field, only adds to the relevance of understanding the organisation and implementation of AR. In what follows, I set out my analysis of how pre-return support is organised and implemented in the three focus countries.

## PRE-RETURN ASSISTANCE

For many years, the core focus of pre-return assistance was to provide information about AR to the target group and arrange the travel of those who signed up (EMN, 2016). Recently, however, attention has shifted to the development of *return counselling* (EMN, 2019). Return counselling can, according to EU policy documents, comprise all previously summarised

*Critical reflections on assisted return programmes and practices* 111

forms of pre-return assistance (i.e. information provision, counselling regarding the return decision, administrative and financial support to enable the physical return, skills training or the preparation of reintegration projects). This counselling is ascribed a dual objective: on the one hand, it should support informed decision-making; on the other, it strives to ensure compliance with migration policies (EMN, 2019). Consequently, it balances between the logics of support and control. Which objective gains the upper hand differs between countries. My analysis of AR in the three target countries highlighted the variation in the combination, prioritisation and implementation of these objectives and revealed three factors playing a significant role therein. It became clear that the objective of AR was influenced by and tangible through, first, its institutional positioning and linkages with forced return and, second, the way in which access to the programme is managed. Third, the composition of the field of actors involved in counselling is shaped by the previous two factors; it then, in turn, shapes the context and meaning of AR in practice.

**Institutional Positioning**

Research has indicated that host countries follow different institutional logics and set different priorities within their return policy, building on certain social norms, the prevailing discourse about migration and the country's historical, political, economic and institutional context (Ellermann, 2006; Leerkes and van Houte, 2020). This has implications for the institutional positioning of AR, both within state policy and in relation to forced return. The call for efficiency in return-migration management has installed a 'dual-track policy' towards return in the three countries (EMN, 2015a; Lietaert et al., 2017a; Mommers and Velthuis, 2010). This dual track refers to the connection between AR return and forced return based on the reasoning that no 'voluntary' return policy is possible without forced return measures. Both are unavoidably complementary and the more tied their connection, the more efficient removal will be.

In the Netherlands, this interwovenness between AR and forced return was installed from the outset (Mommers and Velthuis, 2010). It was definitely institutionalised through the establishment of the Repatriation and Departure Service (DT&V), which has the mandate to coordinate and implement Dutch return policy (assisted and forced return) and is positioned under the authority of the Ministry of Justice and Security (DT&V, 2020a). This return policy is implemented through return counselling via 'case managers' – government employees who have regular meetings with rejected asylum applicants to discuss and prepare their return. Accordingly, the Dutch authorities describe their return counselling as explicitly aimed at ensuring compliance with their national return policies (EMN, 2019). DT&V civil servants have the authority and the discretion to include or exclude people from AR and direct 'a case' to forced removal when people are insufficiently cooperating with their return. They are also trained to use several techniques to steer and influence the return decision of their clients (Cleton and Chauvin, 2020; Kalir and Wissink, 2016).

This creates a different context compared to Germany and Belgium, where the authorities responsible for AR – respectively, the Federal Office of Migration and Refugees (BAMF; Federal Ministry of the Interior) and the Federal Agency for the Reception of Asylum-Seekers (Fedasil; State Secretary of Migration) – combine several tasks of the state's migration policy, such as organising the asylum reception system and implementing the integration policy (EMN, 2007; Fedasil, 2020a). Analysis of the Belgian AR programme showed that the call for a more integrated return policy, as introduced and stimulated through the EU return policy, encouraged the institutional integration of all aspects of migration and asylum policies into one responsible ministry (Lietaert et al., 2017a). As such, in Belgium, a much closer connection between assisted and forced return was installed. In Germany, each state locally decides whether to allocate the authority regarding AR and forced return to one central authority or to separate ones, resulting in a variation of the link between AR and forced return between regions (EMN, 2015a; Feneberg, 2019). Yet still, in both countries, return counselling has no direct link with forced return and both the German and the Belgian government departments responsible for AR situate the aim of return counselling as 'in between' supporting informed decision-making and ensuring compliance, which creates a different manifestation of counselling in practice compared to the Netherlands (EMN, 2019; Vandevoordt, 2017).

**Accessibility**

People's legal status (broken down into asylum applicants, rejected asylum applicants and people who never applied for asylum – who are referred to as undocumented migrants) and nationality (non-EU citizens) were, from the outset, the two main criteria that regulated the access to all AR programmes. Yet, each EU country makes different subdivisions within the target group and has been including additional criteria that regulate access to the programme, which displays different accents and objectives within return policies. Analysis of the Dutch, Belgian and German AR policy showed that access to AR in these countries depends on the combination of criteria based on people's legal status and administrative procedure, the timeframe within which a person decides to return combined with their nationality and their state of destitution or vulnerability.

**Legal status and administrative procedure**
When AR was first introduced in the three countries, it only included travel support; rejected asylum applicants were the main target group. However, accessibility was enlarged beyond asylum applicants in order to cater for the needs of vulnerable migrants, meaning that undocumented migrants from outside the EU were included when they were 'lacking financial means', 'in a situation of destitution' or 'welfare dependent' (EMN, 2009; Mommers and Velthuis, 2010). This made AR programmes accessible to a wide group of people right from the start.

The moment that reintegration support was added to AR schemes, a clearer divide in accessibility was installed based on legal status. From the outset, reintegration support was principally designed for migrants who had applied for asylum (Mommers and Velthuis, 2010). To date, in the Netherlands and Germany, reintegration support is only accessible for (rejected) asylum applicants from particular countries of origin (BAMF, 2020; BMZ, 2020; DT&V, 2020b); in the German context, it is also limited to migrants living in the state which organises the project. In Belgium, while the reintegration support was accessible for both (rejected) asylum applicants and undocumented migrants at first, nowadays the Belgian AR programme also excludes from reintegration support people who had never applied for asylum (Fedasil, 2020b).

After some years of focusing on rejected asylum applicants and restructuring and professionalising return counselling in the asylum system, the group of undocumented migrants entered the picture again. With the Netherlands as front runner, all three countries started to develop 'outreach activities' in order to reach people who were 'not in contact with the authorities' and offer them return counselling (EMN, 2015b; Mommers and Velthuis, 2010). The aim was to increase the presence and availability of counsellors in a bid to reach undocumented migrants living in large cities and, more recently, migrants in transit. There was a common understanding that this is a 'hard-to-reach' target group and several innovative approaches were initiated to enable return counselling – such as offering shelter and training or involving counsellors originating from the countries of origin of the target group, migrant communities, peers or outreach community workers. Yet, it is important to remember that this group remained excluded from reintegration support. This shows a pattern for an increase in means for and power of return counselling, while the access to reintegration support is steadily declining and the amount of financial support for the migrants remains low (Dünnwald, 2013; Feneberg, 2019; Lietaert et al., 2017a). Exceptions to this trend, however, are the more recent AR projects involving cooperation between national migration and development agencies in all three countries. Within these programmes, in particular the German cooperation between the Ministry of the Interior and the Ministry of Economic Cooperation and Development, larger levels of reintegration assistance are combined with campaigns against irregular migration and the creation of job advice centres and services before and after return, targeting countries from where particularly large numbers of migrants, who are not entitled to stay in Germany, originate (BMZ, 2020).

**Time-dependent criteria and nationality**
At different moments in time, all three countries additionally introduced criteria considering the timeframe in which the decision to return is made as a determinant for access. Yet, this was equally introduced as a measure to decrease the gap between those to whom a return decision was issued and those actually returning, so as to increase the efficiency of return policy by including AR explicitly into the migration management chain. In the Netherlands, an 'all-encompassing decision' was instituted in 2000 (Mommers and Velthuis, 2010). Through this, the rejection of an asylum claim would automatically invoke the responsibility for the applicant to return to the origin country within 28 days and allowed the government to enforce return once this period has ended. Exceeding the period of voluntary departure closes access to AR. The same philosophy – of more automatically issuing return decisions and a stricter follow-up of compliance so that a removal can be enforced after the period of voluntary departure – became a legal obligation for all EU member states through the 2008 Return Directive (2008/115/EC). This installed a very important procedural guarantee that people are granted a period of voluntary departure. In addition, it also resulted in the access to AR being linked to this period of voluntary departure. Consequently, migrants who are not granted such a period from the outset (e.g. because of the risk of them absconding) or are granted a shorter period (often based on their nationality and/or the administrative procedures) are excluded from AR.

All AR programmes were designed for non-EU citizens from the outset, with people able to enter visa-free gradually being excluded from reintegration support in all three countries. Both Germany and the Netherlands restrict access even further, by working with a predefined list of countries where reintegration support is possible, which means that nationality overshadows any other consideration. Moreover, in both countries reintegration support is provided through projects temporarily targeting specific nationalities and therefore access to reintegration support depends on whether there are projects available focusing on that particular country of origin (DT&V, 2020b; Feneberg, 2019). In Belgium, instead of nationality, it is the timing in which a rejected asylum applicant applies for AR, within or beyond the period for voluntary departure, that regulates the access to reintegration support (Lietaert et al., 2017a).

**Destitution and vulnerability**

Finally, people's needs still regulate some access to AR. In Germany, proof of destitution is required for each application although in Belgium and the Netherlands this is not the case. Yet, in all three countries, when people can access AR, vulnerable persons can receive additional financial support (EMN, 2016). All three countries also more recently developed separate reintegration projects tailored specifically to meet the needs of vulnerable people or focused on the adaptation of return counselling to the needs of specific vulnerable persons (EMN, 2019).

Belgium, notably, has an extended system of case-by-case exceptional access to AR (travel and reintegration support) for 'vulnerable' people who would normally be excluded based on the administrative, time-dependent or nationality criteria (EMN, 2016). This list of vulnerability criteria is open-ended, which importantly reverts to AR again based on needs and gives some tools to counsellors to enable return. However, the way in which this functions in practice – whereby migrants get support based on exceptions – and what this implies for the standard accessibility criteria, has not yet been investigated. In the Netherlands, there is no such systematic scheme available and access to AR is determined by the criteria set by DT&V. Still, judgements of 'vulnerability' do play a role. Several researchers have shown that 'deserving migrants' are often granted more leeway and time to arrange for their AR (Cleton and Chauvin, 2020). These are often people who are classified as vulnerable (such as families, the elderly or the sick) and for whom the counsellor has empathy and can understand the difficulties in the return processes and the fact that returning takes time.

**The Field of Actors**

The organisational field of AR has become progressively more complex and diversified. The differing involvement of actors has created models of AR which vary between and even within countries. The main actors in each country are the national government, civil-society organisations such as non-governmental organisations (NGOs) and the International Organization for Migration (IOM). This chapter has investigated the implementation of AR by the first two only, since little detailed information could be found on the functioning of the IOM in these countries, despite its central role; this importantly illustrates how the available data on AR implementation remains scattered.

My analysis has shown that differences between actors in (1) agendas, values and priorities, (2) expertise and resources, and (3) mandate and credibility allow for different implementations of support. Importantly, this occurs within the boundaries of the institutional context and accessibility criteria set up in each country. It also depends on the role attached to civil-society organisations and their relationship with the state, which also differs between countries (McGhee et al., 2016). As such, the political context shapes and limits the potential of civil-society organisations to negotiate and realise the differences in AR (Wiktorowicz, 2000). The concrete implementation of AR by different actors also highlights the ethical dilemmas within return policy as a field inherently imbued with fierce opposing interests and a strong symbolic rhetoric (Vandevoordt, 2017).

## Agendas, values and priorities

As illustrated earlier, different objectives are attributed to return counselling, which not only depends on the programme's institutional positioning but also on the implementing actors. Different agendas connect to the values and priorities of actors and impact on the way in which they engage with AR. Research in Belgium and Germany has shown that, for civil-society organisations that set the objective to start from a person-centred approach and support every migrant in need, engagement within return counselling is justifiable in the quest for a humane solution for people in destitute situations (Dünnwald, 2013; Vandevoordt, 2018). Return counselling cannot be refused because of the restrictive policy framework reducing people's choices. These organisations often explicitly distinguish their activities from governmental return objectives. This materialises in return counselling with an 'open-ended' approach, implying broader counselling that explores the different options of the migrant, amongst which return is one. For organisations that solely focus on return counselling, it implies that there are no consequences when the counselling does not result in return (EMN, 2015a; Feneberg, 2019), although the latter might be beyond the actors' control. Still, it remains the case that the goal of many civil-society organisations (increase the wellbeing of individuals) differs from that of most state agencies (increase return rates), which means that the composition of the field impacts on the way in which counselling is implemented (EMN, 2015a; Feneberg, 2019).

Yet, it remains clear that any representation of state actors versus non-state actors is far too simplistic (Kalir and Wissink, 2016). State actors are not one uniform group (Bonjour, 2011). Local authorities, for example, have different priorities, which translates into different policies towards rejected asylum applicants and undocumented migrants (Leerkes and van Houte, 2020). Research in the Belgian context has argued that the implementation of AR by local social-welfare services, although being local state institutions, can be considered as similar to that of civil-society actors, given their substantial autonomy in the Belgian context (Vandevoordt, 2017). What is more, it appeared that social workers in local social services refrained from return counselling when push factors to return are consciously embedded in the way in which support is organised, since their professional values as social workers conflicted with return enforcement aims (Lietaert, 2017). Yet, between state agencies responsible for return policy, differences in agendas, priorities and approaches also exist (Vandevoordt, 2017). All this indicates that professional backgrounds and organisational values play a role as well, which again goes beyond a state versus non-state divide. Moreover, whether other elements – such as different origins and institutional compositions within organisations (faith-based organisations, intergovernmental organisations etc.) and the values that accompany this positionality – also impact on the way in which assistance is implemented is something that needs further investigation.

However, the extent to which civil-society organisations in all three countries can pursue their own goals and can be critical towards the state's return policy has been rightfully questioned (Feneberg, 2019; Kalir and Wissink, 2016; Vandevoordt, 2017) – certainly when they are financially dependent on state-sponsored projects, which brings us to debates on resource dependency, instrumentalisation and isomorphism between state and non-state actors. Research within the Dutch context concluded that the desire to be recognised by the state as a discussion partner and to influence policy-making reduces the space for civil-society organisations to think and negotiate alternatives to current return policy (Kalir and Wissink, 2016). In the Belgian context, it was shown that it was precisely the close relationship between state and civil actors and the considerable autonomy of the latter that enabled policy influencing and, at the same time, might lead to instrumentalisation (Vandevoordt, 2017).

A final difference appeared to be how much or until which point – both geographically and temporally – actors take responsibility for supporting people's return processes (Feneberg, 2019; Lietaert, 2017). The states' main interest is people's departure and, despite a strong discourse on efforts to work towards the sustainable reintegration of returnees (Marino and Lietaert, Chapter 12), they rarely took responsibility beyond their borders. In all three countries, the mandate to implement reintegration support was from the outset outsourced to the IOM and civil-society organisations (EMN, 2009; Mommers and Velthuis, 2010) and both actors have, indeed, had a big influence on the launching, broadening and improving of the quality of post-return assistance – thereby transforming managing migration goals into humanitarian ones (Dünnwald, 2013; Mommers and Velthuis, 2010; Vandevoordt, 2018). Setting high standards in individual assistance is also a way in which civil-society organisations in these countries differentiate themselves from state agencies (Dünnwald 2013; Vandevoordt, 2017).

**Expertise and resources**
A second important element of the diversity between the actors in these countries is their experience and resources. A lack of experience with AR makes it difficult for actors to engage with return counselling (EMN, 2015a; Feneberg, 2019; Lietaert, 2017). When the field of AR actors constantly changes because support is financed through short-duration projects, this creates a situation in which non-state actors have little opportunity to be critical (see *supra*) and build the needed expertise. This volatility for civil actors is the case in Germany and the Netherlands while, in Belgium, the nationally and EU-funded reintegration programme has a more permanent character and thus allows for continuity in capacity-building among civil-society actors (Lietaert et al., 2017a). Yet, in all three countries, it has been the expertise of the state that has been notably expanding, with civil servants being increasingly trained in return counselling (Cleton and Chauvin, 2020; Feneberg, 2019).

Specialisation in return counselling might be needed given the demanded insights into post-return conditions to start a conversation about perspectives after return. Research in Belgium has shown that such specialisation creates the challenge that social workers in generalist services, who are the people who are in contact with the broad target group of AR, lose the feeling of responsibility to engage with the topic (Lietaert, 2017). Separating the counselling of the emotional decision to return from preparing and supporting the return of those who made the decision also leads to the fading of the moral dilemmas inherent to AR (Vandevoordt, 2018). Research in Germany has shown that specialisation might also lead to a narrowing of the counselling on the topic of return and away from a broad counselling approach (Feneberg, 2019). As such, a balance between general and specialised counselling seems important.

**Mandate and credibility**
Relatedly, actors clearly differ in the mandate they have and receive within AR. States recognise that civil-society organisations are more likely to be trusted by migrants (EMN, 2015b) and, as such, recognise the essence of trust in an actor who is to be considered as a reliable partner to discuss return. This mandate to talk about return is more easily ascribed to civil-society actors because of their independence from the government and their open-ended counselling, which increases the trustworthiness of information about support (EMN, 2015a).

The continuity of care also appears important here, both for the confidence of counsellors to engage with return counselling as well as for the perception of their credibility. Research in Belgium has shown that, if social workers can stay in touch with people who have returned, thus continuing their relationship with clients beyond return and knowing about the welfare of returnees (including their struggles), this can create confidence in a person's own abilities to talk about return (Lietaert, 2017). In contrast, only hearing 'success stories' can create suspicion and feelings of deception. For reintegration counsellors who are engaged in both pre-return counselling as well as the follow-up to reintegration projects, this connection is obvious and gives the counsellors the tools and the mandate to talk about return (Vandevoordt, 2017). As such, the continuity of care strengthens the mandate and credibility of an actor; whether this is arranged within one organisation or the extent to which connections are made differs between the various actors. Moreover, creating a continuity of care should be a priority of host-country governments as well, as this might enhance their ability to monitor their return policy.

Finally, the field of actors is subjected to rapid changes. An evolution noticeable in the three countries is that state agencies systematically increase the role they are taking up as coordinators and implementors of AR, both pre- and post-return. This shifts the relations between the different actors swiftly and warrants close follow-up on the impact of AR (Feneberg, 2019; Vandevoordt, 2017). Different 'new' actors are also entering the field while not-so-new actors take up new roles within return policies (i.e. Frontex, the European Return and Reintegration Network, national development agencies); these are significant changes, the impact of which is yet to be investigated.

## EVOLUTION IN THE CONTENT, MEANING AND OUTCOME OF AR

Despite obvious differences in the meaning of AR in the three countries under study, the analysis above also reveals the evolution towards making AR more conditional and exclusive, steered by the call to make return policy more effective. This section reflects on how this evolution leaves aside many essential questions about the conditions needed to enable (assisted) return and reintegration in the development of AR pre-return, as such creating inconsistencies and disconnections between policy objectives and outcomes and between return policies and reintegration policies.

The analysis of accessibility has shown that, by connecting the period of voluntary departure issued through the return decision with access to AR – an evolution unfolding across Europe – the programme becomes a reward for the quick departure of certain groups of migrants and operates independently of people's needs. When this becomes the sole focus, AR abandons its potential to be a tool to remove obstacles and enable return. The link with needs comes in again through the renewed focus on vulnerability. However, assistance is only granted to certain groups of 'deserving' vulnerable migrants, while AR programmes *in se* target a group of vulnerable migrants, people who return under disadvantaged conditions for a successful reintegration process (Cassarino, 2008). This restricted access clearly goes against the call for broad access to AR return schemes and efforts to increase the sustainability of returnees' reintegration, two principles that are emphasised in standards of EU and global return policy (Council of Europe, 2016; UN, 2018).

These changes in AR to increase the effectiveness of return policy, translated into accelerating return procedures as a shared trend in the three countries, also place the responsibility to return within the set timeframe entirely with the migrant. Through this, non-return becomes just a matter of disobedience (Mommers and Velthuis, 2010). This viewpoint disregards the complex nature of returning, the external factors that complicate the process and any role and responsibility of the host country in these factors through the crucial role of entry policies and asylum systems (Schuster, 2020; Vosyliūtė, 2019). Thus, there is no evidence that more time pressure or exclusion from welfare rights increases compliance to return. On the contrary, in fact, there is more and more concrete evidence that hardship and deprivation in the host country and mobility bans decrease people's willingness to return (Bastia, 2011; Crawley et al., 2011; UNDP, 2019; Veronese et al., 2020) and some basic conditions and mental space are needed to consider and prepare a return (EMN, 2015a; Lietaert, 2016).

The exploration of differences in the mandate and credibility of the actors highlighted the centrality of trust and continuity of care for return counselling, which is clearly hindered by the pressure that is created by time-dependent criteria and the conditionality of support. Moreover, quick and unprepared departure increases vulnerabilities after return (Cassarino, 2008; Lietaert, 2016). What is more, it seems so easily forgotten that the decision to return can have an impact on the possibilities and life chances of the returnee and his/her entire family (Kleist, 2018), which cannot simply be equated with 'following the law'. Return might be surrounded with emotional distress and it often demands time and space to redefine individual and familial plans, goals and dreams. It remains clear that the way in which returnees, their families and their communities in the host and home countries use, interpret, embrace, reject or evaluate the meaning, impact and usefulness of assisted return is an essential layer that needs to be added to understandings of AR programmes. Moreover, the complexity of accessibility is never displayed through websites or flyers and, as such, only becomes clear within return counselling, making that the moment at which a person learns what can be expected within AR. Often, it means that people have to readjust their expectations, for which they have very little time, which might lead to absconding rather than return. Although summaries of what works in practice to enable return mention 'providing time to the migrant to reflect on the decision about return' (EMN, 2015b) and the 'access to reintegration support' (EMN, 2018), analysis has shown that this seems to receive very little attention in the designing of policies of pre-return assistance. This even totally disappears in the recasting of the Return Directive, where time pressure and exclusion from AR is, in fact, sharpened (Vosyliūtė, 2019; also Desmond, Chapter 10).

## CONCLUSION

This chapter began by noting the expansion of AR programmes and their associated solid and unifying policy narrative. One of the more topical issues emerging is the lack of insight into the actual practice of assisted return. This chapter contributes to these insights by analysing the concrete design and implementation of AR in three countries, in order to distinguish the various factors that create variation and influence the meaning and impact that AR might have. The results highlight a complex interplay of different factors shaping AR in the pre-return context, with a principal influence of the institutional positioning of AR, its accessibility scheme and the composition of its field of actors – factors which are, moreover, subjected to constant and rapid changes.

This review started with the operationalisation of pre-return assistance, focusing on the policy and actors concerning AR in the pre-return phase. Obviously, this is only one part of the story. Similar insights into the implementation of post-return assistance, and the connection between the two, are urgently needed. The content of post-return reintegration support equally spans an immense variety of elements. Given the enormous impact of social, economic, cultural and political realities and safety and stability dimensions in countries on the usefulness of support and their meaning of return and reintegration, analysing the post-return implementation of return assistance might even be more complex. Though the same framework could be applied as a starting point, it obviously needs adaption and enlargement. Questions about the institutional positioning of AR require investigation of, amongst others, the existence of national policies towards returning migrants, which might include assisted returnees or focus on other returning nationals, the position of the government towards EU policy and the relation between national migration policies, EU return policies and other internal (e.g. labour-market policy) or external policy fields (e.g. development cooperation). As the results showed, the accessibility of support is determined by the host states designing the programme. However, AR projects are arising which also include return migrants post-return. Moreover, it is clear that the access to property, rights and services in the country of return and the institutional capacities and resources are central to reintegration processes and might interact with AR support. Finally, the field of actors involved in post-return is booming. New state and non-state actors at different levels – local, national, regional and international – are joining well-established players in the field and the role and impact of informal actors and networks is increasingly recognised. Who takes which role, with which agendas and priorities, expertise and resources, mandate and credibility, as well as the power relations between the actors and other support mechanisms, needs to be investigated.

# REFERENCES

Baldaccini, A. (2009) 'The return and removal of irregular migrants under EU law: an analysis of the returns directive', *European Journal of Migration and Law*, **11** (1), 1–17.

BAMF (2020) 'Voluntary return and reintegration programmes', https://www.returningfromgermany.de/en/programmes (accessed 10 March 2021).

Bastia, T. (2011) 'Should I stay or should I go? Return migration in times of crises', *Journal of International Development*, **23** (4), 583–95.

Black, R., Collyer, M. and Sommerville, W. (2011) *Pay To Go Schemes and Other Noncoercive Return Programs: Is Scale Possible?*, Washington DC: Migration Policy Institute.

Blitz, B.K., Sales, R. and Marzano, L. (2005) 'Non-voluntary return? The politics of return to Afghanistan', *Political Studies*, **53** (1), 182–200.

BMZ (2020) 'The BMZ's programme "Returning to New Opportunities"', https://www.bmz.de/en/issues/Sonderinitiative-Fluchtursachen-bekaempfen-Fluechtlinge-reintegrieren/deutsche_politik/perspektive_heimat/index.jsp (accessed 19 March 2021).

Bonjour, S. (2011) 'The power and morals of policy makers: reassessing the control gap debate', *International Migration Review*, **45** (1), 89–122.

Cassarino, J.-P. (2008) 'Conditions of modern return migrants', *International Journal on Multicultural Societies*, **10** (2), 95–105.

Cleton, L. and Chauvin, S. (2020) 'Performing freedom in the Dutch deportation regime: bureaucratic persuasion and the enforcement of "voluntary return"', *Journal of Ethnic and Migration Studies*, **46** (1), 297–313.

Collyer, M. (2010) 'Stranded migrants and the fragmented journey', *Journal of Refugee Studies*, **23** (3), 273–93.

Council of Europe (2016) *Non-Binding Common Standards for Assisted Voluntary Return (and Reintegration) Programmes Implemented by Member States*, Brussels: Council of Europe.

Crawley, H., Hemmings, J. and Price, N. (2011) *Coping with Destitution: Survival and Livelihood Strategies of Refused Asylum Seekers Living in the UK*, Oxford: Oxfam GB.

de Haas, H., Natter, K. and Vezzoli, S. (2018) 'Growing restrictiveness or changing selection? The nature and evolution of migration policies', *International Migration Review*, **52** (2), 324–67.

DT&V (2020a) *Dienst Terugkeer & Vertrek: OverDT&V*, The Hague: Dienst Terugkeer & Vertrek, https://www.dienstterugkeerenvertrek.nl/over-dtv (accessed 19 March 2021).

DT&V (2020b) *Terugkeerprojecten*, https://www.infoterugkeer.nl/terugkeerprojecten/overzicht-projecten/.m (accessed 19 March 2021).

Dünnwald, S. (2013) 'Voluntary return: the practical failure of a benevolent concept' in M. Geiger and A. Pécoud (eds), *Disciplining the Transnational Mobility of People*, London: Palgrave Macmillan, pp.228–49.

EC (2015) *Communication on an EU Action Plan on Return, COM(2015)453 Final*, Brussels: European Union.

Ellermann, A. (2006) 'Street-level democracy: how immigration bureaucrats manage public opposition', *West European Politics*, **29** (2), 293–309.

EMN (2007) *Voluntary and Forced Return of Third Country Nationals from Germany*, Nuremberg: German National Contact Point for the European Migration Network, Research Study 2006.

EMN (2009) *Programmes and Strategies in Belgium Fostering Assisted Voluntary Return and Reintegration in Third Countries*, Brussels: European Migration Network.

EMN (2015a) *Dissemination of Information on Voluntary Return: How to Reach Irregular Migrants*, Nuremberg: German National Contact Point for the European Migration Network, Working Paper No. 65.

EMN (2015b) *Dissemination of Information on Voluntary Return: How to Reach Irregular Migrants Not in Contact with the Authorities*, Brussels: European Migration Network, EMN Inform.

EMN (2016) *Overview: Incentives to Return to a Third Country and Support Provided to Migrants for their Reintegration*, Brussels: European Migration Network, EMN Inform.

EMN (2018) *The Effectiveness of Return in Belgium: Challenges and Good Practices Linked to EU Rules and Standards*, Brussels: European Migration Network.

EMN (2019) *Policies and Practices on Return Counselling for Migrants in EU Member States and Norway*, Brussels: European Migration Network, EMN Inform.

Erdal, M.B. and Oeppen, C. (2018) 'Forced to leave? The discursive and analytical significance of describing migration as forced and voluntary', *Journal of Ethnic and Migration Studies*, **44** (6), 981–98.

European Parliament and Council of the European Union (2007) 'Establishing the European Return Fund for the period 2008 to 2013 as part of the General "Solidarity" and Management of Migration Flows', *Official Journal*, L 144, 6 June, p. 45.

European Parliament and Council of the European Union (2008) 'Directive 2008/115/EC on common standards and procedures in Member States for returning illegally staying third-country nationals', *Official Journal*, L 348, 24 December, pp. 98–107.

Fedasil (2020a) *About Fedasil*, Brussels: Federal Agency for the Reception of Asylum Seekers, https://www.fedasil.be/nl/over-fedasil (accessed 11 March 2021).

Fedasil (2020b) *Reintegration*, Brussels: Federal Agency for the Reception of Asylum Seekers, https://www.fedasil.be/nl/vrijwillige-terugkeer/re-integratie (accessed 11 March 2021).

Feneberg, V. (2019) 'Ich zwinge niemanden, freiwillig zurück zu gehen. Die institutionelle Umsetzung der Politik der geförderten Rückkehr durch staatliche und nicht-staatliche Akteure', *Zeitschrift für Flucht- und Flüchtlingsforschung*, **3** (1), 8–43.

IOM (2019) *Return and Reintegration: Key Highlights 2018*, Geneva: International Organization for Migration.

Kalir, B. and Wissink, L. (2016) 'The deportation continuum: convergences between state agents and NGO workers in the Dutch deportation field', *Citizenship Studies*, **20** (1), 34–49.

Kleist, N. (2018) 'Trajectories of involuntary return migration to Ghana: forced relocation processes and post-return life', *Geoforum*, **116**, 272–81.

Kuschminder, K. (2017) *Taking Stock of Assisted Voluntary Return from Europe: Decision Making, Reintegration and Sustainable Return – Time for a Paradigm Shift*, Fiesole: Robert Schuman Centre for Advanced Studies, EUI Working Paper.

Leerkes, A. and van Houte, M. (2020) 'Beyond the deportation regime: differential state interests and capacities in dealing with (non-)deportability in Europe', *Citizenship Studies*, **24** (3), 319–38.

Lietaert, I. (2016) *Perspectives on Return Migration: A Multi-Sited, Longitudinal Study on the Return Processes of Armenian and Georgian Migrants*, Ghent: Ghent University, unpublished PhD thesis.

Lietaert, I. (2017) 'Transnational knowledge in social work programs: challenges and strategies within assisted voluntary return and reintegration support', *Transnational Social Review*, **17** (2), 158–73.

Lietaert, I. (2019) 'The usefulness of reintegration support: the dual perspectives of returnees and caseworkers', *British Journal of Social Work*, **49** (5), 1216–33.

Lietaert, I. (2020) 'Migrants' post-return wellbeing: a view from the Caucasus', *International Migration*, DOI: 10.1111/imig.12777.

Lietaert, I., Broekaert, E. and Derluyn, I. (2017a) 'From social instrument to migration management tool: assisted voluntary return programmes – the case of Belgium', *Social Policy and Administration*, **51** (7), 961–80.

Lietaert, I., Broekaert, E. and Derluyn, I. (2017b) 'Time heals? A multi-sited, longitudinal case study on the lived experiences of returnees in Armenia' in Z. Vathi and R. King (eds), *Return Migration and Psychosocial Wellbeing: Discourses, Policy-Making and Outcomes for Migrants and their Families*, London and New York: Routledge, pp. 165–81.

McGhee, D., Bennett, C. and Walker, S. (2016) 'The combination of "insider" and "outsider" strategies in VSO–government partnerships: the relationship between Refugee Action and the Home Office in the UK', *Voluntary Sector Review*, **7** (1), 27–46.

Mommers, C. and Velthuis, E. (2010) *Leaving the Netherlands: Twenty Years of Voluntary Return Policy in The Netherlands (1989–2009)*, The Hague: International Organization for Migration.

Noll, G. (1999) 'Rejected asylum seekers: the problem of return', *International Migration*, **37** (1), 267–88.

Schuster, L. (2020) 'Fatal flaws in the UK asylum decision-making system: an analysis of Home Office refusal letters', *Journal of Ethnic Migration Studies*, **46** (7), 1371–87.

UN (2018) *Global Compact for Safe, Orderly and Regular Migration, A/RES/73/195*, New York: United Nations.

UNDP (2019) *Scaling Fences: Voices of Irregular African Migrants to Europe*, New York: United Nations Development Programme.

van Houte, M. (2014) *Moving Back or Moving Forward? Return Migration after Conflict*, Maastricht: Maastricht Graduate School of Governance, unpublished PhD thesis.

Vandevoordt, R. (2017) 'Between humanitarian assistance and migration management: on civil actors' role in voluntary return from Belgium', *Journal of Ethnic Migration Studies*, **43** (11), 1907–22.

Vandevoordt, R. (2018) 'Judgement and ambivalence in migration work: on the (dis)appearance of dilemmas in assisting voluntary return', *Sociology*, **52** (2), 282–97.

Veronese, G., Pepe, A., Addimando, L., Sala, G. and Vigliaroni, M. (2020) '"It's paradise there, I saw it on TV": psychological wellbeing, migratory motivators, and expectations of return among West African migrants', *Nordic Psychology*, **72** (1), 33–50.

Vosyliūtė, L. (2019) *Increasing Efficiency of Return Policy: Role of Evidence and Policy Alternatives*, Brussels: Research Social Platform on Migration and Asylum, ReSOMA Policy Brief, http://www.resoma.eu/sites/resoma/resoma/files/policy_brief/pdf/POB2.1%20Return.pdf (accessed 10 March 2021).

Wanki, P. and Lietaert, I. (2019) '"Bushfalling": the ambiguities of role identities experienced by self-sponsored Cameroonian students in Flanders (Belgium)', *Identities*, **26** (6), 725–43.

Webber, F. (2011) 'How voluntary are voluntary returns?', *Race and Class*, **52** (4), 98–107.

Wiktorowicz, Q. (2000) 'Civil society as social control: state power in Jordan', *Comparative Politics*, **33** (1), 43–61.

# 9. The contours of deportation studies
*Martin Lemberg-Pedersen*

## INTRODUCTION

Across the world, deportation politics is a topic of both urgent and long-standing political concern. In the United States (US), the Trump election-campaign promise of deporting millions of irregular immigrants led to the Immigration and Customs Enforcement (ICE) operations deporting more than 300,000 so-called unauthorised immigrants to Central and South American countries such as Mexico, Puerto Rico and Brazil in 2018. Yet, these operations were still smaller in scale than under the Obama administration, where an annual average of around 400,000 were deported between 2012 and 2014 (Gramlich, 2020). Similarly, the European Commission's (EC) 2020 Migration Pact described the upscaling of deportations from the Schengen space as 'a fresh start [that strikes] a new balance between responsibility and solidarity' (Stevis-Gridneff, 2020). This, even though the Commission had voiced a similar focus many times in the previous years – for instance when the controversial European Union (EU)–Afghanistan Joint Way Forward statement aimed at deporting at least 80,000 rejected Afghan asylum-seekers from European asylum systems (EEAS, 2016). So-called Western countries have been instrumental in facilitating this 'deportation turn' whereby governments increasingly rely on the technology of the forced removal of asylum-seekers as a way of addressing domestic political controversy. However, countries from the so-called Global South, including Thailand, India and South Africa, have also recently been upscaling the use of this political technology. In 2016, for instance, an estimated 1 million people were deported to Afghanistan, a number which included more than 400,000 and 250,000 people from Iran and Pakistan, respectively (Majidi, 2017, pp.4, 8–9).

Among the international organisations (IOs) working with humanitarian and migration management operations, the 'repatriation' of people has long been among the staples of standard durable solutions. This has the effect of narrating the deportations of irregular migrants, refugees and asylum-seekers as misplaced anomalies reinserted into the state-based international system and its 'national order of things' (Malkki, 1995). Consequently, as a political technology enforcing socio-normative boundaries between membership and non-membership, the differential ascriptions of rights, duties and the legitimacy of the use of force, deportation gives rise to crucial political, ideological and ethical debates, as Kalir forcefully argues in Chapter 6 of the Handbook.

Through five interlinked sections, the present chapter introduces central conceptualisations and discussions through which the interdisciplinary field of deportation study has evolved. After a brief introductory literature overview, the first section sketches a central approach in deportation studies – namely, regimes of sovereign biopolitics. The second section then moves on to discussing deportation in terms of continuums and corridors. The third section adds to this a new perspective on deportation politics as markets and technologies, before the fourth section discusses issues of race and postcoloniality in deportation. The fifth section relates the previous discussions to the assumptions and positionalities that dominate liberal theorising on deportation. Finally comes the conclusion.

## DEPORTATION REGIMES AND SOVEREIGN BIOPOLITICS

The study of deportation is a subset of the wider field of border studies and its heterogeneous family of inter- and multidisciplinary studies takes on the histories, regimes, lived experiences and materialities of border politics. Here, deportation studies denote the more particular focus on the forcible movements of people out of a territory. Thus, deportation can be seen as the imposing of a certain directionality of displacement upon individuals or groups of individuals. This can be enacted by state authorities or by agents acting on behalf of them. As such, instances of forced migration have many implications on the sociopolitical lives of those deported and the redesign of fluid categories such as membership and non-membership of communities (cf. Coutin, 2015).

Scholars have examined deportation politics from historical, genealogical and postcolonial inquiries (Kanstroom, 2007; Walters, 2002). Others have unfolded sociological and political theoretical reflections on the relation between deportation, membership and citizenship (Anderson et al., 2011). Others, again, have developed ethnographic-juridical analyses of how the immigration laws reconfigure certain populations into criminalised 'illegals' (de Genova, 2002). The geopolitics of deportation also include interstate relations between actors trying to deport people and those states to which they wish to deport them through complex webs of readmission agreements, such as those between European and Asian and African countries. Between EU member states and non-European countries, these agreements increased from 33 in 1986 to 156 in 1995, 186 in 2004 and 216 in 2010 (Cassarino, 2010, p.11). This political dimension of deportations links to questions about transnational transport infrastructures, such as commercial vessels, harbours, airlines and airports around the world (Walters, 2017).

More recently, ethnographic and anthropological works have focused on the social and economic stigmatisation of people after deportation and their challenge of building new lives – or the perceived necessity of abandoning this goal and instead undertaking multiple attempts to re-migrate (Schuster and Majidi, 2015; cf. Khosravi, 2018). Studies of deportation from the EU, Iran or Pakistan to Afghanistan have also dealt with the clashes between deporting states' grand visions of national communities 'taking back' populations and the actual impact on the stability of local communities and their informal, mobile and transnational ways of living when they are turned into deportation dumping zones (Majidi, 2017).

These discussions illustrate how the study of the deportation field has evolved in new and productive ways over recent decades. The scholarship on immigration ethics, which deals with questions about the normative legitimacy of immigration practices across ideal and non-ideal world settings, has also evolved significantly since the 1990s (Carens, 2013; Cole, 2000; cf. Miller, 1995). Yet only a few of these works have dealt with the applied ethics *of deportation practices* in particular, instead discussing border control in the abstract (for an example, see Miller, 2013). This branch of literature has consequently contributed relatively little to the interdisciplinarity of deportation studies (for exceptions, see Cohen, 1997; Gibney, 2008, 2013; Lemberg-Pedersen, 2018; Lenard, 2015).

In deportation studies there has been convergence towards the conceptual framework of 'deportation regimes', understood as mechanisms of differentiation which redraw the sovereignty and mobility of spaces in both deporting and receiving countries (Mezzadra and Neilson, 2013; Peutz and de Genova, 2010). Those living under deportation regimes are transformed into a 'distinctly disposable commodity' through politically constructed venues of entangled national, transnational and organisational interests. 'Deportables' are therefore defined as those forced to live precariously in the shadow of deportation, withdrawn from normal societal rights and protections. Instead, they can be traded and speculated in, for instance as undocumented labour in construction, service and agricultural sectors, by networks specialising in labour recruitment, smuggling and sex work and also as symbolic capital for political campaigns and surveillance measures (de Genova, 2002). The risk of deportation, therefore, has severe implications for people's sense of identity, belonging and decision-making about the future (Kuschminder, 2018). Peutz and de Genova (2010, p.2) argue that deportation can be seen as 'the formulation and emphatic reaffirmation of state sovereignty' through the construction of matrices of political subjectivities for citizens and non-citizens.

Critical geographical analyses have sought to deconstruct the deeply embedded state-centric epistemological, ontological and methodological assumptions of national 'territorial traps' in migration politics (Agnew, 1994; Wimmer and Glick Schiller, 2002). Such constellations of assumptions have the effect of situating inquiries into the already-bounded positionalities of citizens and policy-makers, which gaze outwards through a 'sovereign monocular eye' (Ó Thuathail, 1996), perceiving migrants as misplaced individuals and populations flowing through national territories.

Several anthropological and sociological scholars have focused on the sovereign power of deportation regimes through Giorgio Agamben's extension of Foucauldian, Benjamite and Arendtian biopolitics into a complex political theology on sovereignty (Agamben, 1998, 2005; cf. Coutin, 2015; de Genova, 2010; Walters, 2002). Biopolitics can be defined as the instrumentalisation of biological processes according to political interests; biopolitical analyses therefore enquire into the 'microphysics of power' manifesting governmental power. Thus, while a geopolitical perspective asks 'why' and 'where' power is manifested in certain ways, a biopolitical perspective asks 'how' this power is realised. This brings to the foreground the concrete laws, instruments and practices through which deportations are pursued.

For Foucault, biopolitics denoted a political economy working through scientific instruments such as demographics and statistics about the population, the risks against which are pre-empted through security apparatuses. Taken together, the notions of risks and rights create a specific relationship between liberal governance and individual freedom so that, in the society of security, 'freedom is nothing else but the correlative of the deployment of apparatuses of security and circulation' (Foucault, 2007, pp.11, 42–9).

While Foucault famously analysed the Benthamite Panopticon as a formative model of such a society, Agamben controversially locates the paradigm of modern sovereignty and its suspension of law in the logics of the Nazi concentration camps. Offering a 'correction' to Foucault's biopolitics, Agamben's work is a juridical-discursive tracing of sovereign power, defined through its capacity to declare states of exception banning some human existences from societal status (Agamben, 1998; cf. Walters, 2002). Viewing the codification of lawful communities as fundamentally functioning through the exclusion of some existences, Agamben understands this exclusion as the biopolitical production of 'bare life'. In the state of exception, sovereign power generates a 'zone of indistinction' whereby those it excludes are still subsumed under the workings of power through 'inclusive exclusions' (Agamben, 1998). In this view, deportation regimes form as paradigmatic an example of inclusive exclusions as do camps, since they, as biopolitical machines, serve to target individuals or groups – in Agambenian terms 'bare life' – thereby including those excluded, such as deportables, under complex juridico-discursive webs of sovereign control (cf. de Genova, 2010).

## CONTINUUMS, ACTORS AND CORRIDORS IN DEPORTATION POLITICS

However, deportation has also been analysed through other frameworks than that of regimes. One reason for this is that, unlike state-centric political narratives on deportations, the matrices of political subjectivities in deportation politics are often characterised by messiness and cross-cutting interests. The institutional and bureaucratic realities of deportations consist of multiple intervening actors, reconfigured legislations and volatile dynamics in transnational networks between so-called sending, receiving and deporting states. Accordingly, it has been argued that notions of deportation regimes relying on Agambenian biopolitics risk reaffirming the political imaginary of states and their claim to be able to draw a clear line between norm and exception (cf. Bigo, 2007). They seem to subtly reiterate state-centric conceptions of power, reiterations which then seep back into the conceptualisation of deportation. Viewing migrants as bare life produced via the exceptional machinations of sovereign power seems to align with states' desire to reduce migrants to passive existences to be moulded in the authoritarian embraces of security regimes. Yet, people moving through deportation structures employ various strategies to navigate their situations, such as negotiations with border guards and of surveillance systems, working irregularly, dissenting, demonstrating and collaborating with grassroots or monitoring bodies. Again, the Agambenian zone of indistinction seems ill-equipped to acknowledge the agency of people in deportation corridors – including how they sometimes resist, thereby co-shaping deportation corridors. Similarly, Agamben's notion of sovereign power seems undifferentiated when it comes to the dynamic constellations of multiple actors and interests – under, at and beyond the state level – which the focus on the continuums and corridors of deportation allows for. When applied to the politics of displacement, the prevalence of an unquestioned state-centrism still generates a set of peculiar problems.

According to Kalir and Wissink (2016), some studies define a deportation regime as constituted by street-level public bureaucrats on the one hand and non-governmental organisations (NGOs) and civil-society actors on the other. Yet this is not a case of mutually exclusive activities. Rather, non-state actors supervene in, and interact with, state regimes, which aligns with the Foucauldian point that relations of power have a directly productive role. Accordingly, the authors argue, while the regime terminology is useful in analysing the implications of state sovereignty for deportation politics, an analytical framework of a 'deportation continuum' appears better suited for examining constellations of power. It is defined by a focus on the interactions of multiple stakeholders involved in the continuous crafting of political subjectivities, competing imaginaries of citizenship and alternative visions of deportation (Kalir and Wissink, 2016). This nuancing also helps to explain the dynamics, such as institutional barriers and turf wars, which continue to plague the relation between politically dictated visions of efficient deportations and the messy reality managed by street-level bureaucrats and experienced by deportables, where states are unable to realise the deportations promised to national electorates (Bosworth et al., 2018; Lipsky, 2010).

Drotbohm and Hasselberg (2015) have suggested that a framework of 'deportation corridors' can combine useful facets of the regime- and continuum-terminologies. Here we can define such corridors not as singular events of physical removal enforced by a state but, instead, as processes spanning multiple stages, spaces and scales as well as temporalities, actors and interests. This concept builds on Nyers' (2003) work on 'transnational corridors of expulsion' and Peutz's (2006) call for 'an anthropology of removal' to study daily performances of deportation. Depending on particular contexts, it can include pre-emptive arrests and encampment, return counselling by non-state actors, technological infrastructures such as biometric databases, legal reforms and administrative case work and diplomatic negotiations on readmission and aid, as well as social life (or death) after deportation. Since the 2010s, the EU's Frontex Agency has taken a more proactive role when it comes to deportations, organising joint return operations and supporting national return operations, as well as setting up a Frontex pool of monitors in 2017 from which the agency itself picks those monitors escorting flights (Frontex, 2017). The Frontex deportation flights are both in the form of single- and also multi-stop flights chartered from a group of smaller airlines. These go from participating EU member states to regions like West Africa, the Balkans and the Caucasus.

Countries receiving EU deportees then arrange their own readmission agreements with other countries, leading to chain migration in which already-deported migrants are deported once more. Certain migrant populations – often from the Global South and outside the smooth grids of capitalism, trade and tourism – are thus turned into transnational sequences of forced flows.

The focus on the intersecting interests involved in deportation continuums and corridors can be linked to the scholarship on 'humanitarian borders' that explores how various border-control actors deploy languages and instruments rights to facilitate control priorities (Chimni, 2000; Cuttitta, 2018; Fassin, 2011; Walters, 2011). This literature has focused on the ways and strategies through which humanitarian scripts can slide rapidly between nodes of care and control when it comes to policies on refugee health, asylum systems and search-and-rescue operations. However, it also applies to the discursive and bureaucratic pursuit of deportations, for instance through discourses of 'humane and safe return' and 'return and reintegration'. Or, in the case of the Commission-funded European Return Platform for Unaccompanied Minors (ERPUM), an attempted deportation corridor that ran unsuccessfully between 2010 and 2014 or how six EU member states depicted the goal of deporting separated child refugees to Afghanistan as potential 'family reunification' (Lemberg-Pedersen, 2018). In line with the 'emergency imaginary' often plaguing humanitarian action (Calhoun, 2010), the slides of metonomy between care and control instrumentalised by governments or other actors involved in deportation ascribe to particular lives the characteristics of being both *a* risk and *at* risk – that is, how these lives are un/rescuable (cf. Aradau, 2004; Ticktin, 2016). The 'humanitarianization of child deportation politics' (Lemberg-Pedersen, 2020) is therefore defined as processes whereby governments frame different deportation corridors, for instance for unaccompanied minors or sex workers, as humanitarian rescue (cf. Plambech, 2017). Through such framing, they seek to ascribe to themselves the role of saviours, while leaving crucial questions of responsibility after deportation unresolved and opaque. The instrumentalisation of humanitarian logics observable in deportation practices therefore allows for analyses of the competing and overlapping interests at stake.

This production of surveillable, forced movement in turn requires funds, personnel, technological equipment and infrastructures. The following section describes how the study of deportation has increasingly and productively turned towards new disciplinary fusions in order to engage with this development.

## DEPORTATION MARKETS AND TECHNOLOGIES

The 2000s have witnessed a fundamental reconfiguration of global border and deportation technologies, spanning biometric databases, border surveillance systems, Big Data and Artificial Intelligence. In line with the continuum of actors involved in deportation corridors, the (re)construction and governance of deportation takes place through processes of multi-levelled governance. However, beyond the state and NGO actors emphasised by Kalir and Wissink (2016), the political economy of this continuum must also include the range of commercial for-profit sectors and companies competing on markets for border control (Lemberg-Pedersen, 2013). The trajectory of deportation data is also one through continuums of technological and financial tools shaped by wider ensembles of actors, logics and interests outside state-centred logics and regimes.

The marketisation dynamics observable in deportation continuums reflect a multi-faceted and multi-sectoral market for functions in border-control infrastructures. It therefore spans a plethora of contracts for both massive transnational fintech ICT and security conglomerates and small and medium-sized businesses (SMEs) vying for local contracts concerning housing, interpretation, counselling, health, cleaning, layout/design, event organisation, office supplies or transportation. These markets, whether they be local, national or global, are highly profitable. When it comes to biometrics, the latter market is estimated to be worth €65.3 billion by 2024 (Market and Markets, 2019). On different scales, actors on the market for deportation corridors exercise a growing presence in policy-making through networking and lobbyism efforts and public–private partnerships and private rule-setting as they seek to influence the institutions and persons involved in contract tenders for deportation services and infrastructure (Lemberg-Pedersen and Halpern, 2021; cf. Baird, 2018; Jones et al., 2020). One case in point is the Jordanian company IrisGuard which, after its start in 2001, evolved into a market front-runner for deportation and displacement data through a contract with the United Arab Emirates (UAE) for the construction of a deportation database called the 'IrisFarm', followed by similar contracts with authorities from India, Jordan, Egypt and Iraq. This was followed later by lucrative partnerships with non-state actors, such as the World Bank Group and the United Nations High Commissioner for Refugees (UNHCR). The IrisFarm's purpose was to identify deportables, labelled 'expellee' workers from India, Pakistan and Bangladesh, trying to re-enter the country and then to use these data to launch their re-deportation (Lemberg-Pedersen and Haioty, 2020).

While the political-economic dimension of deportation continuums reveals the introduction of rules and norms from outside state-centric outlooks, public–private interactions are also circumscribed by the legal frameworks of state authorities. As such, the markets for deportation functions are also generated by states or by political communities such as the EU. For instance, the EC has introduced several proposals to change the regulations of the Union's border-control databases by making use of biometric data such as Eurodac, the Schengen Information System (SIS II) and the Visa Information System (VIS). Thus, in 2016, the Commission tabled a draft 'concerning the use of SIS for the return of illegally staying third-country nationals, laying down the conditions and procedures for entering alerts on return decisions in SIS II'. This was desired by the Commission as a means to accelerate 'the return of illegally staying third-country nationals' via the introduction of new alert categories into the system, among other things detailing the purposes of return and return decisions issued to so-called illegally staying third-country nationals (EC 2016, pp.2, 5). Thus, following these proposals, the EU's Agency for the Operational Management of Large-Scale IT Systems in the Area of Freedom, Security and Justice (EU-Lisa) issued several contract tenders for the evolution of the SIS II, VIS and Eurodac databases. Many commercial actors on the market for EU border control launched consortium bids on these tenders and the company Accenture won contracts for both the SIS II, alongside its partners ATOS Belgium and Hewlett-Packard Belgium – one worth, for instance, €2.8 million in 2018. To name another, the same year Accenture also won a contract for the VIS, alongside Safran and Hewlett-Packard Belgium in the Bridge Consortium, worth €54.8 million (Lemberg-Pedersen et al., 2020). This example illustrates the conjunction of the legal, political and economic interests co-shaping deportation corridors from the EU.

At the theoretical level, such biometric databases in deportation corridors can be seen as the material underpinnings of the virtual data flows accompanying the stages of expulsion. For instance, the use of technologies to scan and construct data-doubles (Bowker and Star, 1999) of deportables' biometric iris information features prominently in governments' current upscaling and expansion of the technological infrastructures of deportation corridors. The construction of such deportation data represents interventions where the flux of life is *datafied* or, in other words, translated into computerised data. These data are then used for identification and verification purposes in accordance with the targets determined for the deportation databases. Such aspects of deportation politics therefore exemplify cases of the 'dataveillance' of people, defined as the use of personal data systems to surveil – that is, monitor and collect information about – people's behaviour or communications (cf. Clarke, 1988). This can be connected to 'motivational measures' designed to condition deportables to leave voluntarily, residence sanctions for not cooperating on their own returns or the requirement to stay at certain detention facilities before an impending deportation (see Lietaert, Chapter 8).

Theoretically, this instrumentalisation of deportables' digital footprints can be described as an expanding realm of 'digital biopolitics'. This concept signifies how technologies for measurement, identification, biocoding and imaging have enhanced the biopolitical capacity of the various actors in deportation continuums to govern bodies at the refugee–technology interface (see also Ajana, 2020). Complementing Foucauldian analyses of biopolitical *dispositifs* and security devices, this understanding of some deportation technologies means that they co-constitute particular knowledge regimes. However, the technological construction of data categories is not neutral. Rather, the categories of sorting are built by epistemic communities which rely on certain cultural and normative frames of reference. These normative contours are thus already embedded and diffused through the technologies (cf. Guittet and Jeandesboz, 2010). Nevertheles, because deportation corridors are (re)configured by multiple actors, these contours are also constantly renegotiated between policy-makers, technology companies and bureaucracies, and contestation from civil society and migrants. The biopolitical function of the datafied deportation corridors 'is to codify, categorise and profile in order to manage the (perceived and constructed) risks associated with … the mobility of refugees [thereby intensifying] the culture of sorting, prediction and pre-emption that has become the norm in border security policies and practices' (Ajana, 2020, pp.468–9). The dataveillance turn in the deportation continuum also reflects the larger tendency of 'data-craving' in governance structures (Lemberg-Pedersen and Haioty, 2020) – that is, an intense and accelerating desire for the extraction, storage and processing of data about persons and their lives.

## RACE AND POSTCOLONIALITY IN DEPORTATION POLITICS

Intimate links exist between displacement politics, figures of migration and the socio-geographical imaginaries of the 'sovereign monocular eye' running back through European, global and colonial histories. This connects the study of deportation to controversial discussions of settler colonialism, racialisation and white supremacism and colonial matrices of power and knowledge (cf. Hage, 2016; Lemberg-Pedersen, 2019; Mayblin, 2017; Mignolo, 2007; Quijano, 2000). Unfortunately, however, these (post)colonial questions remained peripheral to Agamben's and Foucault's biopolitical analyses. Weheliye (2014) has argued that a peculiar blindness inhabits and inhibits biopolitical analyses of race and colonialism and, according to Rothberg (2009, pp.62–3), 'Agamben builds an artificial discursive wall around "the West" that prevents him … from seeing forces outside Europe as constitutive of modernity.'

Despite this, several scholars have developed innovative research on migration control by operationalising Foucauldian governmentality and Agambenian biopolitics to address questions of colonialism and race. Mbembe (2003) has developed a striking analysis of 'necropolitics' – that is, the subjugation of life under death – in Western migration politics, while others apply the Agambenian genealogy of camps and states of exception to a range of settler colonial exclusions, such as the British colonial rule in Kenya (cf. Bignall and Svirsky, 2012).

Nevertheless, biopolitics has been criticised for treating conceptual terms as bare life or the statistical categorisations of vitality in infrastructures as governance tools, which can be transposed across a vast variety of eras, contexts and dynamics. However, this makes for abstract categorisations severed from the gendered and racialised processes dominating actual political discourses about governable figures, both in current deportation contexts and colonial contexts such as enslavement. Biopolitics, therefore, says Weheliye, misconstrues how profoundly race and racism have shaped the modern idea of the human, favouring instead theorising about 'indivisible biological' or legal categorisations which enter analyses 'anterior to processes of racialization' (Weheliye, 2014, p.12). This is compatible with the de-selection of historicised contextual knowledge and the prioritisation and even technological acceleration of data-craving infrastructures with certain categories, actions, norms and technological regimes actionable in the here-and-now. As such, it risks performing epistemological erasure if reproducing the supervenience of deportation databases on socially discriminatory hierarchies (Vergara-Figueroa, 2018).

Weheliye suggests, instead, construing the understanding of race as a set of sociopolitical processes used to discipline and categorise humanity which, in the context of displacement and deportation, can be seen as the assumption of differences in the causes, scales and 'manageability' of refugee flows, depending on their origin. These assumptions are often realigned with existing cultural and geopolitical framings of differences between the Global North and South and postcolonial geographies of empire. These myths of origin, temporality and difference continue to demarcate the political and normative arguments in deportation politics, transforming the issue of deportation into a managerial problem to be solved, governed or converted into profit. The insider gaze of the sovereign-capitalist-citizen therefore comes replete with a particular temporality that serves to individualise events and obscure those patterns of privilege and prejudice which also serve as social boundaries for deportation practices. Kalir (2019) has argued that current Western deportation politics function through the hegemonic, oppressive and systemic production of the structural mistreatment of deportable populations on a massive societal scale (see also his Chapter 6 in this volume). The current condition of 'departheid', he says (2019, p.20), bases spatial engineering on the identification, sorting and differential treatment of racialised migrants. This forces such populations to 'depart, be deported [or] evade deportation'. This posits a crucial question for deportation studies, namely: What are the implications of postcolonial encounters such as deportation corridors for the deporting societies and their conception of rights and humanity?

This accelerating dataveillance and postcolonial insider gaze make it all the more urgent to understand the kinds of normative and epistemological contours which are used to codify the technologies of social sorting in deportation corridors.

## FEASIBILITY AND POSITIONALITY IN LIBERAL DEPORTATION ETHICS

Remarkably, while research into the ethical challenges of deportation practices has proliferated in the interdisciplinary landscape of the last decades, this has been in a manner detached from the discussions in *immigration ethics* about the legitimacy of border control. One reason for this is that the latter discipline uses political theory and applied ethics to explore normative questions about what *ought to* be done in immigration politics given certain values. A growing body of such works on immigration has emerged since the late 1980s but very few engage directly with the ethical dilemmas of deportation politics, instead revolving around principled debates between varieties of particularism, liberal nationalism, universal liberalism and cosmopolitanism. In this theoretical space discussions have turned on the justifiability of restrictions on immigration and open/closed borders and on whether border control can be justified as protecting nation states' cultural or liberal values (cf. Blake, 2002; Carens, 1987; Miller, 1995; Walzer, 1983). Other debates have concerned the democratic and liberal legitimacy of blocking free movement (Abizadeh, 2008). As such the ethical debates have remained at an ideational level, generally assuming certain liberal-democratic foundations for membership, non-membership and basic rights. However, this means that the question of the legitimacy of enforcing, for instance, deportation decisions vis-à-vis the safeguarding of rights, vanishes from sight, featuring instead indirectly as the logical, if criticised, outcome of principled state-centric immigration ethics (Moreno-Lax and Lemberg-Pedersen, 2019; cf. Sager, 2017).

The question of feasibility concerns how ethical principles can be constrained by institutional structures, politics and agency (cf. Bosniak, 2017; Carens, 1999, 2013; Lemberg-Pedersen, 2018; Miller, 2013). At the political level and among principled proponents of border control, including deportations, this discussion is often framed as one between nationalistic realists knowing of the messy non-ideal state of the world and naïve idealists arguing for the universal rights of deportables. This serves to portray those emphasising the crucial importance of basic rights as being disconnected from the actual realities of the world, including knowledge of what motivates (or not) citizen populations to support such protection (Miller, 2013). By contrast, nationalistic justifications of deportations are depicted as properly contextualised and thus more feasible. This therefore connects to discussions about idealism, non-idealism and feasibility constraints in deportation politics.

However, this understanding of feasibility in deportation ethics rests on a 'false universalism' (Cole, 2014, p.509) that is not grounded in rationally stringent criteria about the courses of action feasible in different circumstances of border control. Instead, it is based on sets of contingent and ideologically specific assumptions placating state-centrist and nationalistic world views. This means that these views are then allowed to circumscribe the possibilities for justice and the proportionality of coercive border controls, largely based on the highly specialised function of very particular borders enforced by (Western) liberal-democratic nation states. In other words, the contours posited as necessary to engage in discussions about the realism and idealism in deportation ethics turn out to map closely on to the existing legal-political deportation regimes in place in liberal-democratic Western states.

This turns the standard ethical discussions about feasibility on their head and opens up the possibility that states' deportation politics – rather than by definition being necessary and realistic – can, in fact, also be mired in idealised or utopian assumptions reaffirming particularistic and/or nationalistic ideology. Consequently, deportation politics guided by such ideals can also be criticised for lacking feasibility. This point represents one potential bridge between recent discussions in immigration ethics about the ways in which ideological interference can alter and misrepresent empirical context and findings from the larger interdisciplinary body of deportation studies about 'non-deportability' (Paoletti, 2010). Thus, many of the dominant assumptions in nationalistic political and ethical arguments for deportation fare quite poorly when compared with conditions in the real world, where European governments typically only manage to deport between one third and a quarter of the populations they have rendered deportable. This 'implementation gap' (Eule, 2018) means that many of the deportation corridors pursued by governments range from relatively to largely unsuccessful; the same can be said about the range of dysfunctional remedies, such as surveillance regimes, return counselling and 'motivation enhancing' measures trying to compel migrants to leave voluntarily (cf. Lietaert, Chapter 8). For instance, throughout the 2010s, European governments routinely ignored the deteriorating security condition in Afghanistan in their attempts to establish deportation corridors (cf. Majidi, 2017). They therefore portrayed the likelihood of successfully tracing the families of unaccompanied minor asylum-seekers from Afghanistan in a positive light, rebranding deportations of the latter as a form of family reunification in line with the best interests of the child, even though this assessment conflicts with several UN reports about threats to children and civilians in Afghanistan as well as two decades of failed European tracing experiences (Lemberg-Pedersen, 2015, 2018, 2020; Lemberg-Pedersen and Chatty, 2015). When it comes to earlier stages of deportation corridors, such as the border infrastructures of European countries, one recurring government argument has been that minimal living conditions serve to deter prospective migrants from undertaking dangerous journeys to Europe. However, if the traumatising conditions facing deportable populations are, in fact, intended by governments as a means to signal to prospective immigrants, then the inhumane violations of basic rights of those residing in the deportation infrastructure are neither necessary nor unavoidable. Instead, the deterrence argument indicates that such consequences are, in fact, predicted and accepted moral costs of nationalistic designs for deportation policy.

Inquiries into the narrowly defined feasibility constraints of deportation politics aid in addressing what has been described as a 'prevailing sense of puzzlement' with the recurring, massive humanitarian consequences of Western deportation corridors (cf. Kalir, 2019, p.21). This is because it helps to formulate the question of why, given the spread and mobilisation of nationalistic, racist and white supremacist movements across Western states, discussions about the ethics and feasibility of deportation policies still assume as a starting point that governments act from an ideal of liberal democracy and basic rights made difficult by an unrelenting and harsh world. Yet, there are profound problems with such assumptions of a liberal-democratic positionality in immigration ethics and deportation politics and this reflects a deep and radical dilemma facing liberal theory.

The positionality underpinning dominant ethical discussions about displacement and deportation has tended to assume what Phillip Cole (2017) calls 'insider theory'. This is defined as a body of theory that privileges the voice of the insider, the one who possesses privilege. With regards to deportation, this reflects a citizen positionality. At the level of justice claims, the citizen-insider is the only voice acknowledged, while the phenomena of displacement and deportability are instead inserted at another level of theorising, namely, as a problem to be managed by the citizen-insider. Such insider categorisations are not new to Western ethics and have been observable across a range of historical eras, such as feudalism, the imperial transatlantic slave trade, regimes of gender inequality or racist and other forms of discriminatory regimes. Like deportables today, certain groups have been excluded not only at the actual level of socioeconomic and political systems but also at the structural level of liberal theorising that continues to be marshalled as the normative foundation for Western governments' state-centric deportation practices.

## CONCLUSION

This chapter has provided a brief introduction to several of the most influential theorising moves when it comes to the politics of deportation. These theories have brought out certain common threads useful for building a radical-critical perspective from which to analyse deportation. This perspective grounds an interdisciplinary problematisation of the state-centric and methodological assumptions which have hidden deportation from the view of immigration ethics, excluded it from its theoretical structures and yet brought in the key features of Western border-control politics as unstated premises for ethical and political debate.

These debates mirror those in critical geography, where a 'sovereign monocular eye' grounds a citizen-manager positionality capable of viewing the phenomenon of deportation as a geo- and biopolitical problem to be managed through the production of different sequences of forced flows. However, while biopolitical theorising adds critical weight to the deconstruction of dominant deportation epistemologies, it also risks reproducing sovereign decisionism and state-centric notions of responsibility for displacement. This has unfortunate implications, one of which is the inability to pursue studies of the technological infrastructures of deportation corridors and how they seem to be accelerating a digital biopolitics characterised by a pervasive data-craving for deportation data spanning across the entirety of the deportation continuum, from states' border and deportation structures to humanitarian NGOs' operations as well as the commercial sectors of ICT, security and the military.

## REFERENCES

Abizadeh, A. (2008) 'Democratic theory and border coercion: no right to unilaterally control your own borders', *Political Theory*, **36** (1), 37–65.
Agamben, G. (1998) *Homo Sacer: Sovereign Power and Bare Life*, Stanford: Stanford University Press.

Agamben, G. (2005) *State of Exception*, Chicago: University of Chicago Press.
Agnew, J. (1994) 'The territorial trap: the geographical assumptions of international relations theory', *Review of International Political Economy*, **1** (1), 53–80.
Ajana, B. (2020) 'Digital biopolitics, humanitarianism and the datafication of refugees' in E. Cox, S. Durran, D. Farrier, L. Stonebridge and A. Woolley (eds), *Refugee Imaginaries: Research Across the Humanities*, Edinburgh: Edinburgh University Press, pp. 463–79.
Anderson, B., Gibney, M. and Paoletti, E. (2011) 'Citizenship, deportation and the boundaries of belonging', *Citizenship Studies*, **15** (5), 547–63.
Aradau, C. (2004) 'The perverse politics of four-letter words: risk and pity in the securitisation of human trafficking', *Millennium*, **33** (2), 251–78.
Baird, T. (2018) 'Interest groups and strategic constructivism: business actors and border security policies in the European Union', *Journal of Ethnic and Migration Studies*, **44** (1), 118–36.
Bignall, S. and Svirsky, M. (2012) 'Introduction: Agamben and colonialism' in M. Svirsky and S. Bignall (eds), *Agamben and Colonialism*, Edinburgh: Edinburgh University Press, pp. 1–16.
Bigo, D. (2007) 'Detention of foreigners, states of exception, and the social practices of control' in P.K. Rajaram and C. Grundy-Warr (eds), *Borderscapes: Hidden Geographies and Politics at Territory's Edge*, Minneapolis: University of Minnesota Press, pp. 3–34.
Blake, M. (2002) 'Distributive justice, state coercion, and autonomy', *Philosophy and Public Affairs*, **30** (3), 257–96.
Bosniak, L. (2017) 'Immigration ethics and the context of justice', *Ethics and International Affairs*, **31** (1), 93–102.
Bosworth, F., Franko Aas, K. and Pickering, S. (2018) 'Punishment, globalization and migration: "Get them the hell out of here"', *Punishment and Society*, **20** (1), 34–53.
Bowker, G. and Star, S.L. (1999) *Sorting Things Out: Classification and Its Consequences*, Cambridge MA: MIT Press.
Calhoun, C. (2010) 'The idea of emergency: humanitarian action and global (dis)order' in D. Fassin and M. Pandolfi (eds), *Contemporary States of Emergency: The Politics of Military and Humanitarian Interventions*, New York: Zone Books, pp. 29–58.
Carens, J. (1987) 'Aliens and citizens: the case for open borders', *The Review of Politics*, **49** (2), 251–73.
Carens, J. (1999) 'A reply to Meilaender: reconsidering open borders', *International Migration Review*, **33** (4), 1082–97.
Carens, J. (2013) *The Ethics of Immigration Policy*, Oxford: Oxford University Press.
Cassarino, J.-P. (2010) *Unbalanced Reciprocities: Cooperation on Readmission in the Euro-Mediterranean Area*, Washington DC: The Middle East Institute.
Chimni, B.S. (2000) 'Globalization, humanitarianism and the erosion of refugee protection', *Journal of Refugee Studies*, **13** (3), 243–63.
Clarke, R.A. (1988) 'Information technology and dataveillance', *Communications of the Association for Computing Machinery*, **31** (5), 498–511.
Cohen, R. (1997) 'Shaping the nation, excluding the other: the deportation of migrants from Britain' in J. Lucassen and L. Lucassen (eds), *Migration, Migration History, History: Old Paradigms and New Perspectives*, Bern: Peter Lang, pp. 351–73.
Cole, P. (2000) *Philosophies of Exclusion: Liberal Political Theory and Immigration*, Edinburgh: Edinburgh University Press.
Cole, P. (2014) 'Beyond reason: the philosophy and politics of immigration', *Critical Review of International Social and Political Philosophy*, **17** (5), 503–20.
Cole, P. (2017) 'Insider theory and the construction of statelessness' in T. Bloom, K. Tonkiss and P. Cole (eds), *Understanding Statelessness*, London and New York: Routledge, pp. 255–67.
Coutin, S. (2015) 'Deportation studies: origins, themes, directions', *Journal of Ethnic and Migration Studies*, **41** (4), 671–81.
Cuttitta, P. (2018) 'Delocalization, humanitarianism, and human rights: the Mediterranean border between exclusion and inclusion', *Antipode*, **50** (3), 783–803.
de Genova, N. (2002) 'Migrant illegality and deportability in everyday life', *Annual Review of Anthropology*, **31**, 419–47.

de Genova, N. (2010) 'The deportation regime: sovereignty, space and the freedom of movement' in N. de Genova and N. Peutz (eds), *The Deportation Regime. Sovereignty, Space and the Freedom of Movement*, Durham NC and London: Duke University Press, pp. 33–68.

Drotbohm, H. and Hasselberg, I. (2015) 'Deportation, anxiety, justice: new ethnographic perspectives', *Journal of Ethnic and Migration Studies*, **41** (4), 551–62.

EC (2016) *COM/2016/0882 final – 2016/0408 (COD)*, Brussels: European Commission.

EEAS (2016) 'Joint way forward on migration issues between Afghanistan and the EU', *ReliefWeb*, 2 October. European External Action Service, https://eeas.europa.eu/sites/eeas/files/eu_afghanistan_joint_way (accessed 25 September 2021).

Eule, T.G. (2018) 'The surprising nonchalance of migration control agents', *Journal of Ethnic and Migration Studies*, **44** (16), 2780–95.

Fassin, D. (2011) 'Policing borders, producing boundaries: the governmentality of immigration in dark times', *Annual Review of Anthropology*, **40**, 213–26.

Foucault, M. (2007) *Security, Territory, Population*, Basingstoke: Palgrave Macmillan (trans. Graham Burchell).

Frontex (2017) 'Frontex creates a new pool of return experts', 1 October, https://frontex.europa.eu/media-centre/news-release/frontex-creates-a-new-pool-of-return-experts-yWWYG1 (accessed 23 March 2021).

Gibney, M. (2008) 'Asylum and the expansion of deportation in the United Kingdom', *Government and Opposition*, **43** (2), 146–67.

Gibney, M. (2013) 'Is deportation a form of forced migration?', *Refugee Survey Quarterly*, **32** (2), 116–29.

Gramlich, J. (2020) 'How border apprehensions, ICE arrests and deportations have changed under Trump', FactTank, 2 March, https://www.pewresearch.org/fact-tank/2020/03/02/how-border-apprehensions-ice-arrests-and-deportations-have-changed-under-trump/ (accessed 23 March 2021).

Guittet, E.P. and Jeandesboz, J. (2010) 'Security technologies' in J.P. Burgess (ed.), *The Routledge Handbook of New Security Studies*, London: Routledge, pp. 229–39.

Hage, G. (2016) 'État de siège: a dying domesticating colonialism?', *American Ethnologist*, **43** (1), 38–49.

Jones, C., Kilpatrick, J. and Gkliati, M. (2020) *Deportation Union. Rights, Accountability and the EU's Push to Increased Forced Removals*, Berlin: Statewatch, Open Society Initiative for Europe (OSIFE) Report.

Kalir, B. (2019) 'Departheid: the draconian governance of illegalized migrants in western states', *Conflict and Society: Advances in Research*, **5** (1), 19–40.

Kalir, B. and Wissink, L. (2016) 'The deportation continuum: convergences between state agents and NGO workers in the Dutch deportation field', *Citizenship Studies*, **20** (1), 34–49.

Kanstroom, D. (2007) *Deportation Nation: Outsiders in American History*, Cambridge MA: Harvard University Press.

Khosravi, S. (2018) *After Deportation. Ethnographic Perspectives*, Basingstoke: Palgrave Macmillan.

Kuschminder, K. (2018) 'Afghan refugee journeys: onwards migration decision-making in Greece and Turkey', *Journal of Refugee Studies*, **31** (4), 566–87.

Lægaard, S. (2006) 'Feasibility and stability in normative political philosophy: the case of liberal nationalism', *Ethics, Theory, Morality, Practice*, **9** (4), 399–416.

Lemberg-Pedersen, M. (2013) 'Private security companies and the European borderscapes' in N. Nyberg Sørensen and T. Gammeltoft-Hansen (eds), *The Migration Industry: The Commercialization of International Migration*, New York: Routledge, pp. 152–72.

Lemberg-Pedersen, M. (2015) *The Rise and Fall of the ERPUM Pilot. Tracing the European Policy Drive to Deport Unaccompanied Minors*, Oxford: University of Oxford, Refugee Studies Centre Working Paper No. 108.

Lemberg-Pedersen, M. (2018) 'The "imaginary world" of nationalistic ethics: feasibility constraints on Nordic deportation corridors targeting unaccompanied Afghan minors', *Etikk i Praksis. Nordic Journal of Applied Ethics*, **12** (2), 47–68.

Lemberg-Pedersen, M. (2019) 'Manufacturing displacement: externalization and postcoloniality in European migration control', *Global Affairs*, **5** (3), 247–71.

Lemberg-Pedersen, M. (2020) 'The humanitarianization of child deportation politics', *Journal of Borderlands Studies*, DOI: 10.1080/08865655.2020.1835524.
Lemberg-Pedersen, M. and Chatty, D. (2015) *ERPUM and the Drive to Deport Unaccompanied Minors*, Oxford: University of Oxford, Refugee Studies Centre, Research in Brief No. 4.
Lemberg-Pedersen, M. and Haioty, E. (2020) 'Re-assembling the surveillable refugee body in the era of data-craving', *Citizenship Studies*, **24** (5), 607–24.
Lemberg-Pedersen, M. and Halpern, O.J. (2021) *Frontex and Exit Governance: Datasurveillance, Civil Society and Markets for Border Control. ADMIGOV Deliverable 2.3.*, Copenhagen: University of Copenhagen.
Lemberg-Pedersen, M., Hansen, J. and Halpern, O.J. (2020) *The Political Economy of Entry Governance. ADMIGOV-Report, Deliverable 1.3*, Copenhagen: Aalborg University.
Lenard, P.T. (2015) 'The ethics of deportation in liberal democratic states', *European Journal of Political Theory*, **14** (4), 464–80.
Lipsky, M. (2010) *Street-Level Bureaucracy: Dilemmas of the Individual in Public Services*, New York: Russell Sage Foundation.
Majidi, N. (2017) *From Forced Migration to Forced Returns in Afghanistan: Policy and Program Implications*, Washington DC: Transatlantic Council on Migration.
Malkki, L. (1995) 'Refugees and exile: from "refugee studies" to the national order of things', *Annual Review of Anthropology*, **24**, 495–523.
Market and Markets (2019) *Biometric System Market by Authentication Type (Single-Factor: Fingerprint, Iris, Palm Print, Face, Voice; Multi-Factor), Offering (Hardware, Software), Functionality (Contact, Noncontact, Combined), End user, and Region – Global Forecast to 2024*, Northbrook IL: Market and Markets Report.
Mayblin, L. (2017) *Asylum After Empire. Colonial Legacies in the Politics of Asylum Seeking*, London: Rowman and Littlefield International.
Mbembe, A. (2003) 'Necropolitics', *Public Culture*, **15** (1), 1–40.
Mezzadra, S. and Neilson, B. (2013) Border as Method, or, the Multiplication of Labor, Durham NC: Duke University Press.
Mignolo, W. (2007) 'Introduction', *Cultural Studies*, **21** (2–3), 155–67.
Miller, D. (1995) *On Nationality*, Oxford: Oxford University Press.
Miller, D. (2013) *Justice for Earthlings: Essays in Political Philosophy*, Cambridge: Cambridge University Press.
Moreno-Lax, V. and Lemberg-Pedersen, M. (2019) 'Border-induced displacement: the ethical and legal implications of distance-creation through externalization', *Questions of International Law*, **56**, 5–33.
Nyers, P. (2003) 'Abject cosmopolitanism. The politics of protection in the antideportation movement', *Third World Quarterly*, **24**, 1069–93.
Ó Thuathail, G. (1996) *Critical Geopolitics*, London: Routledge.
Paoletti, E. (2010) *Deportation, Non-Deportability and Ideas of Membership*, Oxford: University of Oxford, Refugee Studies Centre Working Paper No. 65.
Peutz, N. (2006) 'Embarking on an anthropology of removal', *Current Anthropology*, **47** (2), 217–41.
Plambech, S. (2017) 'Sex, deportation and rescue: economies of migration among Nigerian sex workers', *Feminist Economics*, **23** (3), 134–59.
Quijano, A. (2000) 'Coloniality of power and Eurocentrism in Latin America', *International Sociology*, **15** (2), 215–32.
Rothberg, M. (2009) *Multidirectional Memory: Remembering the Holocaust in the Age of Decolonization*, Stanford: Stanford University Press.
Sager, A. (2017) 'Immigration enforcement and domination: an indirect argument for much more open borders', *Political Research Quarterly*, **70** (1), 42–54.
Schuster, L. and Majidi, N. (2015) 'Deportation stigma and re-migration', *Journal of Ethnic and Migration Studies*, **41** (4), 635–52.
Stevis-Gridneff, M. (2020) 'E.U. offers cash and more deportations in new plan for migrants', *New York Times*, 23 September, https://www.nytimes.com/2020/09/23/world/europe/eu-migrants-asylum-deportation.html (accessed 23 March 2021).
Ticktin, M. (2016) 'Thinking beyond humanitarian borders', *Social Research: An International Quarterly*, **83** (2), 255–71.

Vergara-Figueroa, A. (2018) *Afrodescendant Resistance to Deracination in Colombia: Massacre at Bellavista-Bojayá-Chocó*, Basingstoke: Palgrave.

Walters, W. (2002) 'Deportation, expulsion, and the international police of aliens', *Citizenship Studies*, **6** (3), 265–92.

Walters, W. (2011) 'Foucault and frontiers: notes on the birth of the humanitarian border' in U. Bröckling, S. Krasmann and T. Lemke (eds), *Governmentality: Current Issues and Future Challenges*, New York: Routledge, pp. 138–64.

Walters, W. (2017) 'Aviation as deportation infrastructure: airports, planes, and expulsion', *Journal of Ethnic and Migration Studies*, **44** (16), 2796–817.

Walzer, M. (1983) *Spheres of Justice: A Defense of Pluralism and Equality*, New York: Basic Books.

Weheliye, A. (2014) *Habeas Viscus. Racializing Assemblages, Biopolitics and Black Feminist Theories of the Human*, Durham NC and London: Duke University Press.

Wimmer, A. and Glick Schiller, N. (2002) 'Methodological nationalism and beyond: nation-state building, migration and the social sciences', *Global Networks*, **2** (4), 301–34.

# 10. The Return Directive: clarifying the scope and substance of the rights of migrants facing expulsion from the EU

*Alan Desmond*

## INTRODUCTION

The European Union (EU) has been producing an important and ever-growing body of migration-related policy and legislation since 1999. In that year, the Treaty of Amsterdam entered into force, conferring law-making powers on the EU in the field of migration and providing the legal basis for the creation of the common EU asylum and migration policy. Efforts to forge this common policy, which forms part of the broader project of turning the EU into an area of freedom, security and justice, have been pursued in three principal areas, namely: regular migration, irregular migration and asylum. The primary response of the EU to the issue of irregular migration is to try to prevent the arrival of irregular migrants and to deport those who have managed to enter or who remain unlawfully in the EU, with EU policy on irregular migration long the subject of criticism for its prioritisation of migration control over the protection of migrants' rights (Cholewinski, 2004; Desmond, 2016). This emphasis on migration control is illustrated by the 2008 Return Directive (see *Directive 2008/115/EC*), the single most important piece of legislation adopted in the area of irregular migration, which sets out common standards and procedures in EU member states for returning irregular migrants.

In the sections which follow, I begin by providing a brief summary of the content of the Directive and of views expressed around the time of its adoption. I then provide a thematic overview of the case law of the Court of Justice of the EU (CJEU) on the Directive. The Directive has given rise to an important body of case law that clarifies the scope and substance of the rights of migrants facing expulsion from the EU. Space constraints preclude a detailed examination of each of the Directive's provisions and each of the almost 30 rulings so far issued by the CJEU concerning the Directive. I therefore examine some of the key provisions as they have been interpreted by the CJEU, thereby illuminating the content of the Directive and its implications for irregular migrants and the protection of their rights. I then turn to the issue of regularisation, arguing that it is a key feature of the Directive, despite the legislation's self-evident focus on expulsion. Finally, I briefly discuss the European Commission's proposed revision of the Directive, highlighting the reduction in rights protection that its adoption would facilitate.

It is worth clarifying at the outset some basic terms and technical issues. The Return Directive applies to the procedures for the removal from the EU of non-EU citizens, so-called third-country nationals (TCNs), who are unlawfully present. It does not cover the expulsion of an EU citizen. Neither does it cover the expulsion of a TCN who enjoys free movement rights under EU law by virtue of a family relationship with an EU citizen. Similarly, states may exclude from the scope of the Directive any TCNs who are subject to return as a criminal law sanction and TCNs who are apprehended in connection with the irregular crossing of an external border.[1] The Directive is binding on all EU member states except for Ireland and Denmark and also binds four Schengen states outside the EU – Iceland, Liechtenstein, Norway and Switzerland. For time-saving and simplification purposes, I use the terms expulsion, deportation, removal and return interchangeably throughout the chapter.

## THE RETURN DIRECTIVE: A BRIEF OVERVIEW

**Structure and Content**

The Return Directive comprises 23 Articles divided into five Chapters, in addition to the 30 paragraphs contained in the non-binding Preamble. The Directive requires states to issue a return decision to any TCN staying illegally on their territory[2] and explicitly favours allowing irregular TCNs to voluntarily leave the EU, in preference to undertaking a forced return.[3] To that end, a return decision must provide for an appropriate period for voluntary departure of between seven and 30 days; however, that time must be extended by an appropriate period if required by the circumstances of the individual case, such as children's school attendance. During the period for voluntary departure a TCN may be subjected to certain conditions to secure compliance with the return decision, such as regular reporting to the authorities or deposit of an adequate financial guarantee. Significantly, states enjoy wide discretion to grant an abridged period for voluntary departure or, indeed, none at all if there is a risk of absconding, or if the TCN concerned has made a manifestly unfounded application for a legal stay or poses a risk to public policy, public security or national security.

Despite the stated preference for voluntary return, the main body of the Directive is devoted to setting out the formalities, procedures and safeguards for enforced removal. These measures apply if no period for voluntary departure has been granted or if an individual has failed to comply with the obligation to return within the voluntary departure period. The Directive imposes a general obligation on states to issue TCNs who are not granted – or who do not avail themselves of – the possibility of voluntary return with an entry ban of up to five years, and longer in the case of a serious threat to public policy, public security or national security.[4] The life of an entry ban does not begin until the point at which the person concerned actually leaves the territory of the EU (ECJ, 26 July 2017).

In terms of procedural safeguards, return decisions and entry-ban decisions must be provided in writing and must include reasons for the decision as well as information about available legal remedies. If requested, states must provide an oral or written translation of the aforementioned information in a language which the TCN understands, though this may be denied to a TCN whose entry and stay in the state has at all times been unlawful. TCNs must have a right to appeal against return-related decisions to a judicial or administrative authority or competent body with the power to temporarily suspend return. While TCNs must have the right to obtain legal advice, representation and linguistic assistance, states must only ensure that the necessary legal assistance and/or representation is granted on request free of charge in accordance with relevant national legislation or rules regarding legal aid and may provide that such free legal assistance is subject to certain conditions.

The detention of TCNs for the purposes of removal takes centre stage in the Directive, with four of its 23 Articles devoted to this feature of the return process. When no other less coercive measures would be effective, the Directive allows states to detain irregular migrants for as short a period as possible where removal arrangements are in progress, in particular but not only where there is a risk of absconding or the TCN is hampering the removal process. Detention must be ordered in writing by administrative or judicial authorities, for an initial maximum period of six months. This period of detention may be extended for a further period of a maximum of 12 months when removal cannot be effected due to a lack of cooperation from the migrant concerned or to delays in obtaining the necessary documentation from third countries; however, such extension must be subject to the supervision of judicial authorities, not an administrative authority. Detention shall be reviewed at reasonable intervals of time and when a reasonable prospect of removal no longer exists or the risk of absconding or obstruction ceases, the person concerned shall be released immediately.

TCNs detained for the purposes of effecting their return must be held in specialised detention facilities. Where this is not possible and a state has to resort to prison accommodation, the TCNs in detention shall be kept separated from ordinary prisoners. Such TCNs have the right – on request – to establish contact with legal representatives, family members and competent consular authorities and must be provided with information on the rules of the detention facility and their rights and obligations. Particular attention shall be paid to the situation of vulnerable persons. The relevant national, international and non-governmental bodies shall have the possibility to visit detention facilities.

**Critique**

The Return Directive adopted in 2008 contained a demonstrably weaker set of rights protection provisions than the original draft legislation proposed in 2005 (Baldaccini, 2009). It is therefore perhaps not surprising that the Directive elicited trenchant criticism from scholars, civil-society actors, international organisations and non-EU countries for codifying a rights-deficient expulsion regime (Acosta, 2009; AI and ECRE, 2007; Baldaccini, 2009; OHCHR, 2008; PICUM, 2015; UNHCR, 2008). In this respect, the Directive betrays the EU's tendency to treat irregular migration as a law enforcement and security issue, with the human rights of irregular migrants treated as a secondary issue (Desmond, 2016).

The Directive's provisions on detention are particularly problematic from a human rights perspective. The very wide powers which the Directive confers on states to detain TCNs who are the subject of return procedures have facilitated the adoption of detention as a key element of migration management across the EU (PICUM, 2015). It is important to underline the self-evident but often under-appreciated point that TCNs who are subject to return procedures under the Directive have been neither charged with nor convicted of a criminal offence but may nonetheless be deprived of their liberty for an initial period of up to six months and a subsequent period of up to 12 months. This latter extension of detention may be ordered where there are delays in obtaining the necessary documentation from third countries. The end result is that an individual may be detained for up to 18 months due to difficulties – which are beyond the control of the individual concerned – in effecting the expulsion.

The Directive's time limits on detention brought an end to the unlimited pre-removal detention periods in operation in some states (Commission Communication, 2014). At the same time, however, the Directive appears to have encouraged those states whose detention periods for TCNs subject to return procedures were shorter than that sanctioned by the Directive to extend such periods. To cite just one example, Greece increased its maximum period of detention from three months to 12 (Article 48 *Law 3772/2009*; Commission Communication, 2014; PICUM, 2015). This is a striking example of the capacity for common EU measures in the field of migration to result in a reduction in human rights standards. It bears equally eloquent testimony to the punitive, securitised approach taken at the EU level to irregular migration.

At the same time, however, the Directive must comply with human rights standards, as acknowledged in the text itself. The Preamble contains explicit reference to the European Convention on Human Rights (ECHR), the Refugee Convention and the EU Charter on Fundamental Rights, while Article 1 provides that the Directive is to be applied in accordance with international human rights standards. More specifically, Article 5 provides that, when implementing the Directive, states must respect the principle of *non-refoulement* and 'shall take due account of' the best interests of the child, family life and the state of health of the TCN facing removal. During the period for voluntary departure and for the duration of any postponement of removal, states must take 'into account as far as possible' the following principles: the maintenance of family unity, the provision of emergency health care, access to basic education for minors and consideration of the special needs of vulnerable persons. The fact that the Directive is braided with such references to human rights standards provides opportunities for the CJEU to impose consequential restrictions on states' efforts to run roughshod over migrants' rights in the 'fight' against irregular migration, opportunities that, as I show presently, the CJEU has sometimes seized.

## BALANCING THE PROTECTION OF MIGRANTS' RIGHTS WITH EU EFFORTS AT MIGRATION CONTROL

The Return Directive has given rise to a significant body of case law in which the CJEU has clarified the scope and substance of the rights and safeguards conferred on irregular migrants by this signature piece of EU legislation.[5] Since the entry into force of the Directive on 13 January 2009, the CJEU has delivered nearly 30 judgments interpreting its provisions. In the following consideration of some of the key rulings, I illustrate how the Court has interpreted the Directive's provisions so as to advance the rights of irregular migrants while restricting the scope of state activity in detaining[6] and criminalising such migrants. At the same time, I highlight how such victories are often grounded not so much in a judicial concern for human rights protection as in attempts to ensure the effectiveness of EU law.

### Limiting the Detention of Irregular Migrants

The first decision of the CJEU on the Return Directive dealt with detention under Article 15 of the Directive and was delivered in Kadzoev – a Chechen apprehended by Bulgarian law-enforcement officials in 2006. When the ruling was delivered on 30 November 2009, Kadzoev had been detained for over three years. The CJEU held, first, that a TCN detained pending removal must be immediately released once there is no reasonable prospect of removing him.[7] A reasonable prospect of removal will not exist where the TCN in question is not likely to be admitted to a third country within the period of detention set out in the Directive. Second, the Court found that detention beyond the maximum 18-month period sanctioned by the Directive is prohibited. This applies even where the TCN does not possess valid documents, is aggressive and has no accommodation or means of supporting himself.[8] Furthermore, time spent in detention, even when deportation is suspended pending appeal, counts towards the Directive's time limit. *Kadzoev*'s case is therefore an important confirmation of detention safeguards for unlawfully present TCNs and illustrates how the Directive protects migrants' rights (Cornelisse, 2011).

At the same time, however, by tying the reasonable prospect of removal to the maximum period of detention permissible under the Directive, the Court in the *Kadzoev* case may, in fact, have encouraged wider recourse to prolonged detention (Majcher, 2020, p.536). It is also important to point out that the ruling in *Kadzoev* gives rise to the question of what should happen once a TCN whose expulsion cannot be effected is released from detention. The failure to address this issue is discussed later in the chapter.

**The Return Directive and Asylum-seekers**

There is an intimate connection between the legal regulation of international protection and irregular migration. Once an individual has been deemed not to qualify for refugee status or some other form of international protection and has no other claim to a legal status, s/he is essentially an irregular migrant and comes within the scope of the Return Directive.

*Arslan* concerned an individual who, while detained under the Return Directive, filed an application for asylum (ECJ, 30 May 2013). The CJEU held that, from the point at which asylum is sought under EU law (*Council Directives 2005/85/EC and 2013/32/EU*) until the outcome of the examination of the application, the Return Directive cannot apply to a TCN. Such an individual can therefore not be detained under Article 15 of the Directive.[9]

The Court went on to hold, however, that a TCN who has filed an application for international protection may continue to be detained on the basis of other relevant laws, where an assessment of all relevant circumstances suggests that the application was made solely to delay or jeopardise enforcement of the return decision and that detention is necessary to prevent the person concerned from permanently evading return. One consequence of this finding is that detention of an individual for the duration of the examination of his/her international protection application will not count towards the maximum period of detention allowed under the Return Directive,[10] with the individual exposed to the risk of being detained for a combined total period considerably in excess of 18 months.

The more recent case of *Gnandi* concerned a return decision issued to an asylum-seeker nearly two weeks after his asylum application had been rejected. The CJEU here found that states are not precluded by EU law from issuing a return decision together with or immediately after rejection of an initial asylum application (ECJ, 19 June 2018) and such unsuccessful asylum applicants are illegally staying within the meaning of the Return Directive. Crucially, however, the Court made the far-reaching finding that, if an applicant appeals against the first-instance negative decision, that appeal must have suspensive effect: 'All the effects of the return decision must be suspended during the period prescribed for bringing that appeal and, if such an appeal is brought, until resolution of the appeal.'

This entails a number of significant consequences. For example, if the appeal against the rejection of an asylum claim at first instance is not decided in the TCN's favour, the period granted for voluntary departure under the Return Directive should not start to run until the conclusion of the appeal. Furthermore, while the appeal is ongoing, the appellant is to retain his/her status as an applicant for international protection, must be allowed to remain until the outcome of the appeal and may not be detained with a view to his/her removal (ECJ, 19 June 2018, paras 62–4).

Equally significant is the CJEU's finding in *Gnandi* that TCNs must be allowed to rely on any change in circumstances that occurred after the adoption of the return decision and that may have a significant bearing on the assessment of their situation under the Return Directive and in particular in relation to *non-refoulement*, their state of health, family life and the principle of the best interests of the child. This means that, even if an application for international protection ultimately fails, an unsuccessful asylum-seeker may still be able to resist expulsion under the Return Directive.

**Resisting the Criminalisation of Irregular Migration by Reference to the Effectiveness of the Return Directive**

The CJEU has interpreted the Directive in a number of rulings to limit states' efforts to criminalise irregular migration (Mitsilegas, 2015). The *El Dridi* case, the second CJEU ruling on the Return Directive, concerned Italian legislation which had allowed the District Court in Trento to impose a one-year prison sentence in 2010 on Mr El Dridi, an irregular TCN, for failure to comply with a removal order. The CJEU found that states may not provide for a custodial sentence solely because an unlawfully staying TCN has not complied with an order to leave their territory within the time limit specified in the order. Such a penalty would be at variance with the Directive's objective of establishing an effective policy of removal of irregular TCNs, as it would delay enforcement of the return decision. Rather than imposing criminal penalties, states must seek to effect the return decision (ECJ, 28 April 2011).

The Court found that such criminal penalties would also be at odds with the requirement in Article 4(3) of the Treaty on European Union (see *Consolidated Versions*, 2016) that member states, pursuant to the principle of sincere cooperation, take any appropriate measure to fulfil their EU law obligations and refrain from measures which could jeopardise the attainment of Directives' objectives. The Italian legislation in question was therefore precluded by the Return Directive. The ruling in *El Dridi* had immediate and far-reaching consequences, both for Italian legislation on irregular migration and for the individual irregular migrants themselves (Annoni, 2019; Costello, 2016; Vavoula, 2019).

The Court in the *El Dridi* case did find, however, that, where the application of the measures set out in the Directive to facilitate the enforcement of a return decision has not led to the removal of a TCN, then states are free to adopt criminal law measures aimed at dissuading such migrants from remaining unlawfully in those states. This is an issue on which the CJEU elaborated in the *Achughbabian* case, which concerned French legislation criminalising irregular stay. The Court found that, while states may place a TCN in detention for 'a brief but reasonable time' in order to determine whether or not his/her stay is lawful, the Return Directive precludes national legislation that provides for the imposition of a criminal sanction of imprisonment solely on grounds of illegal residence. Such sanctions would undermine the effectiveness of the Directive by delaying removal.[11] It mattered not that such sanctions were rarely imposed. Instead, once the unlawful nature of stay is established, a return decision must be adopted.

It is clear, then, that a criminal sentence may not be imposed before or during return proceedings solely on the basis of unlawful presence. The Court in the *Achughbabian* case found that the Directive does not, however, preclude the imposition of penal sanctions on irregular

TCNs to whom the Directive's return procedure has been applied but who nonetheless illegally remain 'without there being any justified ground for non-return'. Thus it is only where there is no justification for the non-return of a TCN that states may criminally penalise irregular migrants whose removal has not been effected by application of the full rigours of the Return Directive, namely, the coercive measures mandated by Article 8 and the maximum period of pre-removal detention sanctioned by Article 15.

The Court in *Achughbabian* did not elaborate on what may constitute a 'justified ground for non-return' but it seems safe to assume that such grounds include a lack of cooperation from the country to which return is sought, a lack of capacity on the part of the expelling state and human rights obstacles such as a real risk of inhuman or degrading treatment in the receiving state (Costello, 2016, pp.305–6; Raffaelli, 2012, p.183). This latter point finds support in the Court's observation that the criminal punishment of TCNs in situations where non-return cannot be justified must accord with human rights obligations, particularly those set out in the ECHR. On the other hand, where removal under the Directive has not been possible because of a TCN's 'aggressive behaviour' or other form of non-cooperation and his/her detention under the Directive has therefore ceased, s/he may be criminally prosecuted as there is no justified ground for his/her non-return.

The rulings in the *El Dridi* and *Achughbabian* cases, severely curtailing states' power to criminalise migration law infractions, are important achievements from the perspective of the protection of migrants' rights. It is worth highlighting, however, that the Court's reasoning was grounded in the effectiveness of EU law, specifically the return procedures, rather than in the protection of migrants' rights or any ethical disquiet concerning the criminalisation of migration (Majcher, 2020, p.369; Raffaelli, 2011). Indeed, the CJEU appears to view the criminalisation of irregular migration per se as unobjectionable. Hence its finding that if application of the measures under the Return Directive has not produced the desired result of the removal of a TCN, states may impose a criminal sentence to dissuade that TCN from remaining irregularly on its territory.[12]

Similarly, the Court in the *Sagor* and *Mbaye* cases found that the Directive does not preclude criminal fines for irregular stay, as such penal sanctions will not delay removal and therefore will not undermine the effectiveness of the Directive (ECJ, 6 December 2012, 21 March 2013). Much more surprising, however, is the Court's finding in *Celaj* (ECJ, 1 October 2015) that the Directive does not preclude criminal incarceration for violation of an entry ban. Skerdjan Celaj had been issued with a deportation order and a three-year entry ban by the Italian authorities in 2012. He left Italy in 2012 but re-entered in 2014, breaching the entry ban. Following his arrest, criminal law proceedings were brought against him with a view to securing an eight-month sentence for his entry-ban violation. Application of the effectiveness-based logic deployed in *El Dridi* would have led to the conclusion that the Return Directive precludes such a criminal penalty as it would clearly delay the (re-)removal of the TCN in question, thereby thwarting the effectiveness of the Directive. The CJEU, however, found that there was no incompatibility between the Italian legislation in question and EU law.

The Court distinguished *Celaj* from earlier cases by noting that TCNs such as Hassen El Dridi and Alexandre Achughbabian had been subject to 'a first return procedure'. Skerdjan Celaj, on the other hand, had already been subjected to a first return procedure and now came within the category of irregular TCNs for whose non-return there was no justified ground, thereby opening the door to criminal incarceration. If the ruling in *Celaj* represents a change of tack by the CJEU, it is possibly explained by reference to the wider context in which the judgment was delivered in October 2015. The 'migration crisis', then at its peak, may have influenced the Court to take a more deferential approach to states' efforts to punish (repeat) irregular migration (Kosinska, 2016).

**The Right to be Heard Prior to the Adoption of a Return Decision and to a Decision to Extend Detention under the Directive**

The Return Directive makes no explicit mention of the right to be heard. It does provide in Article 1, however, that the return of TCNs should be carried out 'in accordance with fundamental rights as general principles of Community law' as well as international law, including human rights obligations. This has allowed the CJEU to find that irregular migrants have a right to be heard prior to the adoption of a return decision on the basis that the rights of the defence, which include the right of an individual to be heard in proceedings which significantly affect him/her, is both a fundamental principle and a general principle of EU law (ECJ, 5 November 2014, paras 42–45).

In two rulings delivered at the end of 2014, the Court fleshed out the implications of the right to be heard for irregular TCNs in the EU. In the *Mukarubega* case, the CJEU held that a TCN must have the opportunity to effectively submit his/her views as part of the procedure relating to a residence application or the legality of stay and to put forward reasons as to why s/he should be allowed to remain in the host state. If, however, the outcome of such a procedure is the adoption of a return decision, the right to be heard does not necessarily require that a TCN be heard specifically on the subject of the return decision. To find otherwise would be to 'needlessly prolong the administrative procedure' (ECJ, 5 November 2014).

The Court, in the case of *Boudjlida*, found that the right to be heard entails an opportunity for a TCN to effectively submit his point of view on the irregularity of his stay and reasons which may prevent the adoption of a return decision.[13] The TCN in question must also be heard as to whether factors such as his state of health or family life in the host state may influence the state's implementation of the Directive, as required by Article 5 (ECJ, 11 December 2014, paras 48-49).

The rulings in the *Mukarubega* and *Boudjlida* cases might at first glance appear to be favourable from the perspective of the rights of prospective deportees. Indeed, there is evidence from a number of states that these judgments have secured important protections for irregular TCNs (Moraru and Renaudiere, 2016). The Court, however, significantly limited the scope and content of the right by finding that it does not include an obligation on a state to warn a TCN 'that it is contemplating adopting a return decision with respect to him, or to disclose to him the information on which it intends to rely as justification for that decision, or to allow him a period of reflection before seeking his observations'. Furthermore, there is no right to free legal assistance, and any legal advice may be accessed only to the extent that it 'does not affect the due progress of the return procedure and does not undermine the effective implementation' of the Directive.

It is therefore perhaps not surprising that these two rulings have been criticised for eviscerating the right to be heard in the return context of any meaningful protective content (Basilien-Gainche, 2015) and for evincing a concern about the effectiveness of EU return policy at the expense of migrants' rights (Majcher, 2020, p.158). It is, however, important to point out the Article 13 safeguard that, subsequent to the adoption of a return decision, TCNs have the right to appeal and to obtain legal advice, representation and, where necessary, linguistic assistance for the purposes of such an appeal.

In the *G. and R.* case, two TCNs challenged the decision to extend their initial six-month detention under the Directive by a further 12 months on the grounds that their right to be heard had been infringed. The Dutch court accepted that the parties concerned were not properly heard before the adoption of the extension decisions (ECJ, 10 September 2013, para. 18) but was uncertain if this infringement meant that detention had to be lifted.

The CJEU ruled that national courts may lift the detention measure in such circumstances only if they consider that the non-infringement of rights would have resulted in a different outcome or, in other words, if a proper hearing would have led to a decision not to extend the detention of G. and R.[14] The automatic annulment of a detention decision on the basis of a procedural irregularity, which might in fact have had no impact on the outcome of the extension decision, would run the risk of undermining the effectiveness of the Directive (ECJ, 10 September 2013, para. 41).

The ruling in *G. and R.* has been characterised as 'orthodox, if disappointing' (Costello, 2016, p.307) and attracted attention for the Court's failure to refer to relevant case law concerning the right to liberty, including the rich body of case law concerning pre-removal detention which has been developed by the European Court of Human Rights in Strasbourg (Majcher, 2020, p.358). The ruling arguably illustrates an important feature of the criminalisation of irregular migration whereby the criminal law-type enforcement mechanisms deployed to control and manage migration are decoupled from the procedural safeguards that traditionally accompany criminal law sanctions.

## Mahdi: Mandating a Robust Judicial Supervision of Detention

The *Mahdi* case concerned a TCN without identity documents who was being held in an immigration detention centre in Sofia, Bulgaria, pending removal to Sudan. The CJEU made a number of important findings concerning the judicial supervision of the extension of detention under the Directive. The Court found that any decision on an extension of the detention period must, as in the case of the initial detention order, be in writing, with reasons being given in fact and in law. This is to allow the TCN to defend his/her rights and to allow the judicial authority to effectively carry out the review of the legality of the decision (ECJ, 5 June 2014, paras 44–45).

When considering an application for an extension of the initial period of detention, the judicial authority must engage in an in-depth case-by-case examination to ensure that one of the two grounds permitting extension – namely, the risk of absconding or lack of cooperation – are made out. The national court must consider whether detention should be extended or instead replaced with a less coercive measure or, indeed, whether the TCN concerned should be released if there is no longer any 'reasonable prospect of removal'. The judicial authority also has 'power to take into account the facts stated and evidence adduced by the administrative authority which has brought the matter before it, as well as any facts, evidence and observations which may be submitted to the judicial authority in the course of the proceedings'. Thus, the powers of the judicial authority in the context of an examination can, under no circumstances, be confined just to the matters adduced by the administrative authority concerned.

As regards the grounds permitting an extension of detention, the CJEU found that an absence of identity documents does not in and of itself automatically entail a risk of absconding grounding an extension of detention. This is instead a factor to be taken into account when conducting an individualised, case-specific examination of the request for extension. Similarly, the Court found that an absence of identity documents does not automatically amount to a lack of cooperation on the part of the TCN, justifying the extension of detention. Instead, the national court must undertake an examination of the TCN's conduct during the period of detention to ascertain whether s/he has cooperated in the implementation of the removal operation and whether 'it is likely that that operation lasts longer than anticipated because of that conduct'.

**Release from Detention When a Reasonable Prospect of Removal No Longer Exists**

The Court has made clear in cases such as *Kadzoev* and *Mahdi* that irregular TCNs must be immediately released from detention once there is no longer any reasonable prospect of removing them from the EU. What, however, is to happen to such migrants upon release? The CJEU is reluctant to take a position on this issue, noting in *Mahdi* that the purpose of the Directive is not to regulate the conditions of residence of such irregular migrants.

The Directive itself provides in the Preamble and Article 14 that irregular TCNs who cannot be removed should be provided with written confirmation of their situation so as to be able to demonstrate their specific situation in the event of administrative controls or checks. Similarly, Article 14 provides that, where a removal has been postponed, states must take into account 'as far as possible' the following principles: (a) maintaining a TCN's family unity with family members present in the state; (b) the provision of emergency health care and essential treatment of illness; (c) providing minors with access to the basic education system subject to the length of their stay; (d) the special needs of vulnerable persons.

This situation gives rise to a number of problems. First, the Article 14 'safeguards' fall far short of the rights to which irregular migrants are entitled under international human rights law (EU Agency for Fundamental Rights, 2011) and do not eliminate the state of precarity in which non-removable, non-detainable migrants may find themselves. Second, it is unclear if the safeguards apply to migrants who cannot be returned due to factors such as, for example, a lack of cooperation from the country of origin. The Directive does, however, provide a framework which might be harnessed to address the unsatisfactory state of legal limbo in which such migrants find themselves. This is discussed in the next section.

# REGULARISATION: A NECESSARY TOOL FOR ACHIEVING THE RETURN DIRECTIVE'S GOAL OF THE TERMINATION OF ILLEGAL STAY IN THE EU?

Chapter II of the Directive is entitled 'Termination of Illegal Stay'. The self-evident preference codified in the Directive for achieving this goal is the removal of irregular migrants from the EU. At the same time, however, the Directive explicitly envisages regularisation of such TCNs, a process involving conferral of a legal status on unlawfully present migrants. Specifically, Article 6(4) provides that, instead of issuing or enforcing a return decision, a state may 'at any moment decide to grant an autonomous residence permit or other authorisation offering a right to stay' to an irregular TCN. It is possible to argue that the Directive not only permits states to regularise irregular migrants but, in fact, obliges states to either issue and enforce a return decision or to confer a legal status on unlawfully present TCNs. I deal in turn with the two main, complementary grounds on which such an argument might be advanced – first, an effectiveness-based argument and, second, a human rights-based argument.

The aim of the Return Directive to eliminate the presence of irregular migrants in the EU is inferable from the text of the Directive itself. Article 6(1) requires states to issue a return decision to any unlawfully staying TCN, a provision that has been interpreted by the CJEU to mean that states must 'explicitly make provision in their national law for the obligation to leave the national territory in cases of illegal stay'.[15] The aim is also evident in the view of the Commission that the Directive ensures that 'a person is either legally present in the EU or is issued with a return decision' (Commission Communication, 2011, p.9). More recently, the Commission has referred to the obligation on states to take all necessary measures to ensure return (Commission Recommendation, 2017, p.24). Both the Commission and the CJEU have repeatedly referred to the need to ensure the effectiveness of the EU's return policy generally and of the Return Directive in particular. Both are demonstrably lacking in effectiveness, as evidenced by the fact that the majority of unlawfully present migrants are not issued with return decisions and the majority of those who *do* receive return decisions do not leave the EU (European Parliamentary Research Service, 2019a; Lutz, 2018).

Regularisation, unconditionally open to states under Article 6(4), would allow TCNs who are not or cannot be deported to remain in the EU on a legal basis, thereby reducing the ongoing chasm between the number of return decisions issued and the number effected. Embracing regularisation would transform current return policy from one that is grossly ineffective to one that would have a greater likelihood of achieving the aim of lowering the number of irregular migrants unlawfully present in the EU.

The human rights-based argument for regularisation is anchored in the belief that human rights considerations require a TCN to be allowed to remain lawfully in the EU instead of being expelled. These considerations include any family life a TCN may have in the host state, with which deportation would inevitably interfere. Similarly, the principle of the best interests of the child might mean that a child migrant should not be expelled to a country where her quality of life would be drastically lower than in the expelling state or that a TCN parent should not be expelled where expulsion would result in a separation of parent and child or removal of a child so as to accompany the deportee parent. Such considerations are, in fact, expressly acknowledged in the Directive and should, as set out in the Preamble, be primary considerations of states when implementing the Directive.

The CJEU explicitly held in *Mahdi* that there is no obligation on states under Article 6(4) to regularise TCNs for whom there is no longer a reasonable prospect of removal. Nonetheless, the explicit reference to human rights considerations in the Directive, the CJEU's increasing reference to the EU Charter for Fundamental Rights and human dignity in its case law on the Directive[16] and the wide concern with ensuring the effectiveness of the Directive and EU return policy all combine to produce a compelling argument for regularisation. Future applicants before the CJEU should revisit the Court's finding in *Mahdi* concerning Article 6(4) to make the argument concerning a regularisation obligation under this important provision of the Directive.

## PROPOSED REVISION OF THE RETURN DIRECTIVE

Despite the strong argument that can be made for regularisation under the Directive, it is clear that the EU's emphasis on return has not been diluted since the adoption of the legislation in 2008. Indeed, in recent years the Commission has prioritised the need to enhance the effectiveness of EU return policy.[17] As part of its efforts, and against the background of the 2015 migration 'crisis', the Commission in 2018 proposed significant amendments to the Return Directive[18] that, if adopted, will make the Directive even more punitive and less rights-friendly than its current incarnation.

The Commission's proposal is premised on the belief that return policy would be improved and the duration of return procedures shortened by addressing some key flaws in the current implementation of the Directive, such as the inconsistent use of detention across states and inconsistent interpretation of the risk of absconding. The Commission has therefore proposed that the legislation be revised to increase the grounds for detention of TCNs subject to a return procedure. Furthermore, the proposal to define a 'risk of absconding' would facilitate a refusal of voluntary departure and use of detention, simultaneously increasing the number of persons subject to an entry ban. The revised Directive would also require states, where necessary, to change their national laws to ensure that TCNs facing expulsion may be detained for a minimum of three months.

The Commission's proposal is objectionable not only for the adverse impacts on irregular migrants' rights that its adoption would entail. A recent report for the European Parliament also found that it would generate substantial costs for member states and the EU without any clear evidence that it would lead to a more effective return policy (European Parliamentary Research Service, Impact Assessment, 2019b). It is, of course, possible that negotiations on the text of the revised Directive will secure improvements prior to its adoption but, as proposed by the Commission, it is clearly suffering from significant weaknesses on a variety of fronts.

## CONCLUSION

The dismay evinced by those concerned with migrants' rights at the adoption of the Return Directive in 2008 will have been at least partially allayed by the rulings of the CJEU on the provisions of this piece of EU legislation. In the majority of those rulings, the Court has resolved the tension between migrants' rights and states' efforts to control migration in favour of the former. Such a resolution has, however, often appeared to be motivated by a desire to secure the effectiveness of EU law rather than human rights protection. Furthermore, even when judgments by the CJEU on the content of the Directive appear to result in a victory for migrants' rights, the Court's endorsement of the limitability of rights, as in the case of its rulings on the right to be heard, indicate such victories to be pyrrhic.

The changes to the Directive proposed by the Commission in 2018 against the background of the continuing fallout from the 2015 'crisis' will have the effect of further reducing the protection of migrants' rights. Furthermore, it appears that this reduction will not bring the EU any closer to achieving its oft-repeated goal of improving the effectiveness of its return policy. This contradictory and unsatisfactory state of affairs underscores the need, over 20 years since the entry into force of the Treaty of Amsterdam, for serious consideration to be given to regularisation as a means of addressing the presence of irregular migrants in the EU.

## NOTES

1. Article 2(2)(a) Return Directive (RD). The CJEU has held that this means individuals who have been apprehended or intercepted at the very time of the irregular crossing of the border or near that border after the crossing (see ECJ, 7 June 2016, para. 72).
2. Article 6(1) RD. Exceptions to this general rule are to be found in Article 6(2)-(5).
3. Preamble RD, Recital 10.
4. Article 11(1) and (2) RD. Article 11(3) sets out exceptions to the mandatory nature of entry bans.
5. The Directive has had an impact beyond the specific context of irregular migration. Its intersection with asylum will be discussed below. It is also worth noting that the CJEU has recently held that member states may draw inspiration from the Return Directive to designate competent authorities and to define the procedure applicable to the adoption of a decision ordering the return of an EU citizen, if this is not precluded by any provision of EU law (see ECJ, 14 September 2017, para. 52).
6. It is worth noting that the provisions on detention contained in Article 15 of the Return Directive are, in many respects, more migrant-friendly than the application of the right to liberty in Article 5 ECHR by the European Court of Human Rights in Strasbourg. For a discussion of migration detention under Article 5 ECHR, see Cornelisse (2016).
7. ECJ, 30 November 2009, para. 63. This is simply a re-statement of the requirement clearly contained in Article 15(4) RD.
8. Ibid., para. 68. The absolute nature of this 18-month limit was recently reiterated in ECJ, 14 May 2020.
9. For an in-depth discussion of the interaction of the different frameworks governing detention of irregular TCNs and international protection applicants, see Majcher (2020, pp.360–6).
10. This had already been established in ECJ, 30 November 2009, para. 48.
11. ECJ, 6 December 2011, paras 36–9 (the CJEU has made the same finding in respect of criminal sanctions for illegal entry. See ECJ, 7 June 2016).
12. ECJ, 28 April 2011, paras 52 and 60; ECJ, 6 December 2011, paras 46 and 48.
13. As set out in Article 6(2)-(5) RD. ECJ, 11 December 2014, para. 47.
14. ECJ, 10 September 2013, para. 45. This was repeated in relation to the right to be heard in the context of the process leading up to the adoption of a return decision in *Boudjlida*.
15. ECJ, 5 November 2014, para. 62.
16. For example, the CJEU held that the RD should be interpreted, as stated in Recital 2, 'with full respect for the fundamental rights and dignity of the persons concerned' in ECJ, 18 December 2014.
17. Commission Communication 2015, 2017; Commission Recommendation 2017, 1600 final; 2017, 6505.
18. Ibid.

## REFERENCES

Acosta, D. (2009) *Latin American Responses to the Adoption of the Returns Directive*, Brussels: Centre for European Policy Studies.

AI and ECRE (2007) *Letter from AI and ECRE to LIBE Committee of the European Parliament*, https://www.statewatch.org/media/documents/news/2007/dec/eu-returns-ai-ecre.pdf (accessed 10 March 2021).

Annoni, A. (2019) 'Reshaping criminalisation of irregular migration in Italy: the impact of EU law beyond the El Dridi judgment' in V. Mitsilegas, A. di Martino and L. Mancano (eds), *The Court of Justice and European Criminal Law: Leading Cases in a Contextual Analysis*, London: Bloomsbury, pp. 289–303.

Baldaccini, A. (2009) 'The return and removal of irregular migrants under EU law: an analysis of the Returns Directive', *European Journal of Migration and Law*, **11** (1), 1–17.

Basilien-Gainche, M.L. (2015) 'Immigration detention under the Return Directive: the shadowed lights', *European Journal of Migration and Law*, **17** (1), 104–26.

Cholewinski, R. (2004) 'European Union policy on irregular migration: human rights lost?' in B. Bogusz, R. Cholewinski, A. Cygan and E. Szyszczak (eds), *Irregular Migration and Human Rights: Theoretical, European and International Perspectives*, Leiden: Nijhoff, pp. 159–92.

Cornelisse, G. (2011) 'Case C-357/09 PPU, proceedings concerning Said Shamilovich Kadzoev (Huchbarov), Judgment of the European Court of Justice (Grand Chamber) of 30 November 2009', *Common Market Law Review*, **48** (3), 925–45.

Cornelisse, G. (2016) 'Immigration detention: an instrument in the fight against illegal immigration or a tool for its management?' in M.J. Guia, R. Koulish and V. Mitsilegas (eds), *Immigration Detention, Risk and Human Rights*, London: Springer, pp. 73–89.

Costello, C. (2016) *The Human Rights of Migrants and Refugees in European Law*, Oxford: Oxford University Press.

Desmond, A. (2016) 'The development of a common EU migration policy and the rights of irregular migrants: a progress narrative?', *Human Rights Law Review*, **16** (2), 247–72.

EU Agency for Fundamental Rights (2011) *Fundamental Rights of Migrants in an Irregular Situation in the European Union*, Vienna: EU Agency for Fundamental Rights.

European Parliamentary Research Service (2019a) *Data on Returns of Irregular Migrants*, Brussels: European Parliament.

European Parliamentary Research Service (2019b) *The Proposed Return Directive (Recast) Substitute Impact Assessment*, Brussels: European Parliament.

Kosinska, A.M. (2016) 'The problem of criminalisation of the illegal entry of a third-country national in the case of breaching an entry ban: commentary on the judgment of the Court of Justice of 1 October 2015 in Case C 290/14, *Skerdjan Celaj*', *European Journal of Migration and Law*, **18** (2), 243–57.

Lutz, F. (2018) 'Non-removable returnees under Union law: status quo and possible developments', *European Journal of Migration and Law*, **20** (1), 28–52.

Majcher, I. (2020) *The European Union Returns Directive and Its Compatibility with International Human Rights Law: Analysis of Return Decision, Entry Ban, Detention, and Removal*, Leiden: Brill Nijhoff.

Mitsilegas, V. (2015) *The Criminalisation of Migration in Europe: Challenges for Human Rights and the Rule of Law*, London: Springer.

Moraru, M. and Renaudiere, G. (2016) *European Synthesis Report on the Judicial Implementation of Chapter IV of the Return Directive Pre-Removal Detention*, Florence: European University Institute, Migration Policy Centre.

OHCHR (2008) *UN Experts Express Concern about Proposed EU Return Directive*, Geneva: Office of the High Commissioner for Human Rights: UN experts express concern about proposed EU Return Directive (ohchr.org) (accessed 9 March 2021).

PICUM (2015) *PICUM Position Paper on EU Return Directive*, Brussels: Platform for International Cooperation on Undocumented Migrants.

Raffaelli, R. (2011) 'Criminalising irregular immigration and the Returns Directive: an analysis of the *El Dridi* case', *European Journal of Migration and Law*, **13** (4), 467–89.

Raffaelli, R. (2012) 'Case note: the Achughbabian case: impact of the Return Directive on national criminal legislation', *Diritto Penale Contemporaneo*, **1**, 176–83.

UNHCR (2008) *UNHCR Position on the Proposal for a Directive on Common Standards and Procedures in Member States for Returning Illegally Staying Third-Country Nationals*, Geneva: United Nations High Commissioner for Refugees.

Vavoula, N. (2019) 'Criminalisation of irregular migration in the EU: the impact of *El Dridi*' in V. Mitsilegas, A. di Martino and L. Mancano (eds), *The Court of Justice and European Criminal Law: Leading Cases in a Contextual Analysis*, London: Bloomsbury, pp. 273–89.

## Cases (European Court of Justice, ECJ)

ECJ, 30 November 2009, C-357/09 PPU, *Said Shamilovich Kadzoev (Huchbarov)*.
ECJ, 28 April 2011, C-61/11 PPU, *Hassen El Dridi*.
ECJ, 6 December 2011, C-329/11, *Alexandre Achughbabian v. Préfet du Val-de-Marne*.
ECJ, 6 December 2012, C-430/11, *Md Sagor*.
ECJ, 21 March 2013, C-522/11, *Abdoul Khadre Mbaye*.

ECJ, 30 May 2013, C-534/11, *Mehmet Arslan v. Policie ČR, Krajské Ředitelství Policie Ústeckého Kraje, Odbor Cizinecké Policie*.
ECJ, 10 September 2013, C-383/13 PPU, *G. and R. v. Staatssecretaris van Veiligheid En Justitie*.
ECJ, 5 June 2014, C-146/14 PPU, *Bashir Mohamed Ali Mahdi*.
ECJ, 5 November 2014, C-166/13, *Mukarubega v. Préfet de police and Préfet de la Seine-Saint-Denis*.
ECJ, 11 December 2014, C-249/13, *Khaled Boudjlida v. Préfet Des Pyrénées- Atlantiques*.
ECJ, 18 December 2014, C-562/13, *Centre Public d'Action Sociale d'Ottignies-Louvain-La-Neuve v. Moussa Abdida*.
ECJ, 1 October 2015, C-290/14, *Skerdjan Celaj*.
ECJ, 7 June 2016, C-47/15, *Sélina Affum v. Préfet du Pas-de-Calais, Procureur Général de La Cour d'Appel de Douai*.
ECJ, 26 July 2017, C-225/16, *Mossa Ouhrami*.
ECJ, 14 Sept 2017, C-184/16, *Petrea v. Ypourgos Esoterikon kai Dioikitikis Anasygrotisis*.
ECJ, 19 June 2018, C-181/16, *Sadikou Gnandi v. État Belge*.
ECJ, 14 May 2020, Joined Cases C-924/19 PPU and C-925/19 PPU, *FMS and Others v. Országos Idegenrendeszeti Főigazgatóság Dél-alföldi Regionális Igazgatóság and Országos Idegenrendeszeti Főigazgatóság*.

**Legislation**

Article 48 *Law 3772/2009*, amending Article 76 of the *Law on Migration 3386/2005*.
*Consolidated Versions of the Treaty on European Union and the Treaty on the Functioning of the European Union* (2016) OJ C202/1.
*Council Directive 2005/85/EC of 1 December 2005 on Minimum Standards on Procedures in Member States for Granting and Withdrawing Refugee Status* (2005) OJ L326/13.
*Directive 2008/115/EC of the European Parliament and of the Council of 16 December 2008 on Common Standards and Procedures in Member States for Returning Illegally Staying Third-Country Nationals* (2008) OJ L348/98.
*Directive 2013/32/EU of the European Parliament and of the Council of 26 June 2013 on Common Procedures for Granting and Withdrawing International Protection* (2013) OJ L180/60.

# EU DOCUMENTS

Commission Communication (2011) *Communication from the Commission to the European Parliament, the Council, the Economic and Social Committee and the Committee of the Regions: Communication on Migration* COM(2011) 248 final.
Commission Communication (2014) *Communication from the Commission to the Council and the European Parliament on EU Return Policy* (COM)2014 199 final.
Commission Communication (2015) *Communication from the Commission to the European Parliament, the Council, the European Economic and Social Committee and the Committee of the Regions, A European Agenda on Migration* COM(2015) 240 final.
Commission Communication (2017) *Communication from the Commission to the European Parliament and the Council On A More Effective Return Policy in the European Union: A Renewed Action Plan* COM(2017) 200 final.
Commission Recommendation (2017) *Commission Recommendation of 7.3.2017 on Making Returns More Effective When Implementing the Directive 2008/115/EC of the European Parliament and of the Council* C(2017) 1600 final.
Commission Recommendation (2017) *Annex to the Commission Recommendation Establishing a Common 'Return Handbook' to be Used by Member States' Competent Authorities when Carrying Out Return Related Tasks* C(2017) 6505.
Directive Proposal (2005) *Proposal for a Directive of the European Parliament and of the Council on Common Standards and Procedures in Member States for Returning Illegally Staying Third-Country Nationals* COM(2005) 391 final.

Directive Proposal (2018) *Proposal for a Directive of the European Parliament and of the Council on Common Standards and Procedures in Member States for Returning Illegally Staying Third-Country Nationals (Recast)* COM(2018) 634 final.

# 11. The return industry: the case of the Netherlands

*Marieke van Houte*

## INTRODUCTION

The field of actors involved with the return of rejected asylum-seekers and other migrants without a legal right to stay is a dimension of what has been called the 'migration industry'. Synthesising the available literature, I define the migration industry as 'the expanding field of professional actors who earn an income from the facilitation and/or control of the mobility of people, which implies that they have an interest in creating the demand for their own services'. This inevitably leads to power inequalities and negotiations among and between professional agents and clients.

The case of the Netherlands is a strong example of such a *return migration industry*: it has one of the longest histories of increasing interest in and capacity to enforce the return of migrants without legal residence, through both facilitation and coercion (Ataç, 2019; Leerkes and van Houte, 2020; Rosenberger, 2019) and a comprehensive approach in which multilevel governance and non-governmental actors are involved (Leerkes et al., 2017). This has led to increased return rates that are currently among the highest in Europe (Leerkes and van Houte, 2020). Nevertheless, a wide gap still remains between those ordered to leave and those actually returning. In 2019, only approximately 39 per cent of those who were ordered to leave demonstrably left the country (calculations based on data from the Ministry of Justice and Security, 2020) – 60 per cent of this group returned to their country of origin, while most others were sent back to countries of first asylum within the European Union (EU), as per the Dublin Agreement (Leerkes and van Houte, 2020).

In this chapter, I discuss the diversity of actors in the Dutch return migration industry and the power dynamics between them, in order to better understand this paradox of (in)efficiency: while the increased incorporation of professional actors has had some effect on return numbers (Leerkes et al., 2017), part of its *in*efficiency is also ascribed to the tensions between the stakes of the different actors in the field (van der Leun and Bouter, 2015). The main question to be answered is why a state with a high enforcement interest *and* capacity (Leerkes and van Houte, 2020) develops a policy landscape that is suboptimal in generating return rates.

The chapter continues with a literature review discussing the concept of the migration industry – and the industry of return more specifically. It then provides an overview of the development of the Dutch return industry as a case study of how, through time, different goals and stakes have formed a complex landscape of interdependent governmental and non-governmental actors. In the conclusion, I argue that the paradox of (in)efficiency can be understood when we take into account the fact that, in a liberal state, return needs to be not only implemented but also legitimised and, in that sense, considering the decreased resistance against return of migrants without a legal stay, the Dutch return industry has, indeed, become increasingly efficient.

For this chapter, I rely on insights from fieldwork between 2006 and 2020 amongst return migrants, formal interviews and informal talks with government officials, civil servants, employees of the International Organization for Migration (IOM) and non-governmental organisations (NGOs), conference proceedings and policy meetings, as well as a literature and document review. While I am taking an analytical and critical perspective on the return migration industry, it cannot go unmentioned that the range of researchers, observers and evaluators, including myself, who are being paid to produce evaluations, reports and academic publications on this topic, are also part of this very industry.

## THE 'INDUSTRY' OF MIGRATION AND RETURN

The concept of the migration industry entails the industry that emerges around the facilitation and control of global migration movements – not to be mistaken for the notion of migration for the purpose of the global political economic industry (Samers, 1999). The phenomenon has been identified and discussed by scholars across geographical areas. One of the first definitions, by Castles (2004, p.859), describes its emergence as follows:

> The migration industry develops out of migration networks. Once a migration gets underway, needs arise for a variety of special services. The migration industry includes travel agents, lawyers, bankers, labor recruiters, brokers, interpreters, and housing agents. The agents have an interest in the continuation of migration and may go on organizing it even when governments try to restrict movements …

Hugo (2006, p.169) adds that 'this group of middlemen and women has been growing apace and is a key element in initiating and facilitating migration … This industry has greatly expanded and become increasingly sophisticated with globalization.'

In addition to the notion of a fast-emerging industry that develops out of migration networks, Salt and Stein (1997, p.468) specify the distinction between migration networks and the migration industry by defining the latter as networks, agents and individuals that 'stand to make a commercial gain' from migration. Similarly, Hernández-León (2005, p.1) defines the migration industry as 'the ensemble of entrepreneurs, businesses and services which, motivated by the pursuit of financial gain, facilitate and sustain international migration'.

These early conceptualisations implicitly take into account the role of the state, yet mainly argue that the migration industry facilitates migration by decreasing the risk of migration – *despite* the control by the state – through legal or illegal channels (Hernández-León, 2005).[1]

More recent literature has put the concept of the migration industry in a different light, one which mainly links to migration governance and management. This literature explicitly focuses on the industry around border control, asylum, encampment, detention and removal. Andersson (2016, p.1061) summarises this side of the migration industry as follows:

> The past 25 years have seen the consolidation of such a system or industry, involving actors such as European security forces and their African counterparts; NGOs, humanitarian groups and international bodies such as the International Organization for Migration (IOM), often working closely with the security response; and multinational defence and outsourcing companies.

In their important contribution to the discussion, Gammeltoft-Hansen and Sørensen (2013, p.i) synthesise the insights from both conceptualisations and argue that

[A] host of new business opportunities have emerged that capitalize both on the migrants' desires to migrate and the struggle by governments to manage migration. From the rapid growth of specialized transportation and labour immigration companies, to multinational companies managing detention centres or establishing border security, to the organized criminal networks profiting from human smuggling and trafficking, we are currently witnessing a growing commercialization of international migration.

It becomes clear that 'the migration industry' is 'not ... a homogeneous field of actors sharing a certain goal, but rather ... a networked entity in which objectives oppose each other, roles overlap and responsibilities shift over time' (Schapendonk, 2018, p.664). Despite the different focal areas of the literature, the academic discussion of this messy field can be synthesised into four characteristics or criteria of the migration industry:

- First, the migration industry comprises actors who facilitate migration *and* those trying to control migration. It includes travel agents, businesses producing control and surveillance equipment, coast guards and rescue providers.
- Second, the migration industry has significantly expanded. The geographical spread of these scholars' empirical work itself shows, furthermore, that this is a global phenomenon.
- Third, the concept of an industry that mediates and controls migration focuses on a level of professional involvement and relies on 'agents' (Elrick and Lewandowska, 2008) or 'specialized social actors and commercial institutions' (Garapich, 2008, p.736) that earn an income from human mobility. This implies that all actors in the migration industry have, to a certain degree, an interest in creating a demand for their own services (Åkesson and Alpes, 2019; Andersson, 2016). It includes public, private and social-service providers facilitating or controlling migration and formal and informal actors (with varying degrees of professionalism), bureaucratic institutions, private businesses, NGOs, social movements, faith-based organisations, lawyers, artists and, indeed, researchers. While profit may not drive all these actors, they do have to operate on market terms to maintain themselves (Plambech, 2017). It is the labour involved in managing, facilitating and controlling migration that makes this an industry (Cranston et al., 2018).
- Fourth, this brokerage implies power inequalities between professional agents and clients and between those who have access to these agents and those who do not (Cranston et al., 2018; Garapich, 2008; Lim, 2015), leading to a reinforcement of power inequalities based on im/mobility but also providing room for migrants' navigation and negotiation (Schapendonk, 2018). Similarly, power inequalities and negotiations also exist between the different agents of the migration industry (Vandevoordt, 2017).

Synthesising the above, I define the migration industry as 'the expanding field of professional actors who earn an income from the facilitation and/or control of the mobility of people, which implies that they have an interest in creating the demand for their own services'. This inevitably leads to power inequalities and negotiations among and between professional agents and clients. This migration industry can be conceptualised as taking place in three intersecting fields: the facilitation and control of migration movements; reception, asylum and integration; and detention, removal and repatriation (Schapendonk, 2018).

The overwhelming majority of the scholarship on the migration or mobility industry has discussed the variety of conditions of migration movements, including migration through legal channels such as labour migration and overseas recruitment (Friberg, 2016; Lindquist, 2010), skilled migrants (Harvey et al., 2018), expatriates (Cranston, 2018), educational migration

(Beech, 2018), lifestyle migrants (Hayes, 2015), elite migration (Koh and Wissink, 2018) and marriage migration (Belanger, 2016), as well as migration through irregular channels such as sex workers and human trafficking (Plambech, 2017) and asylum migration (Schapendonk, 2018). The industry concerned with managed or enforced return migration has, to a lesser extent, been conceptualised as such (but see Gammeltoft-Hansen, 2013; Peutz, 2006).

Despite the relative lack of scholarship on the return migration industry, practices and empirical research on return can be discussed through this lens, as (1) it is a telling example of a situation where the facilitation and the control of mobility go hand-in-hand; (2) the field has significantly expanded following increased state budgets to promote return (Mountz et al., 2013) as well as increased budgets and priority from the EU (Baldaccini, 2009); (3) it involves a wide range of professional actors, including public, private and social or non-profit actors (Plambech, 2017; Trujillo-Pagan, 2014); which (4) implies power inequalities and negotiations between clients and agents and among the different agents themselves. To illustrate and analyse the workings of the return industry and, in particular, the efficiency paradox discussed above, this chapter now discusses the case of the Netherlands with these four criteria of the migration industry in mind.

## THE DUTCH RETURN INDUSTRY

### The Emergence and Expansion of the Facilitation and Control of Return

The Netherlands has one of the longest histories of actively and increasingly prioritising, facilitating and enforcing the return of rejected asylum-seekers (Leerkes et al., 2017). The strong increase in the number of asylum-seekers in the 1980s and 1990s and the associated pressure on the asylum system marked a policy shift from liberal and ad hoc solutions to stricter measures with regard to migration management (Mommers and Velthuis, 2010).

Promoting 'voluntary' return became official government policy in 1989 and has been facilitated by the IOM since 1992. In 1997 and 1999, the first Return Policy notes proposed a more binding and integrated approach to deal with the challenges of return,[2] highlighting the *obligation* of rejected asylum-seekers or undocumented migrants to return. Together with the implementation of the *Koppelingswet* (Linkage Act) in 1998 which made access to the formal labour market, housing and the social-welfare system dependent on legal status and the *Vreemdelingenwet* (Aliens Act) in 2000, greater emphasis was put on the deterrence of undocumented stay and the enforcement of return of undocumented migrants (van der Leun, 2006). Although assisted return was, as it is across Europe, the preferred option because of the financial and political cost of forced deportation (Cleton and Chauvin, 2020; see also Baldaccini, 2009; Collyer, 2012; Gibney, 2008), it was emphasised that failure to comply with assisted return would lead to forced return (Leerkes et al., 2017). This issue is also dealt with by Lietaert, in Chapter 8 of this Handbook.

Despite the increased national priority, municipalities were reluctant to deny rejected asylum-seekers the right to shelter in order to avoid situations of homelessness, petty crime and social unrest. Faced with the associated difficulties in effectively returning rejected asylum-seekers, the national government increasingly took charge of the return procedure. While offering regularisation to around 28,000 rejected former asylum-seekers who fell under old legislation, the government announced that maximum efforts would be made to exclude and expel those to whom the amnesty measure did not apply (van der Leun and Bouter, 2015). To this end, the *Dienst Terugkeer & Vertrek* (Return and Repatriation Service, DT&V) was established in 2007 within the Ministry of Justice and Security. Taking over tasks from the Immigration and Naturalization Service (IND), the national police and the military police, this agency became responsible for centrally organising the 'return chain' from the moment an asylum claim is rejected or an individual is found to be illegally present until his or her eventual departure. The agency's goal was to work more efficiently across the different departments and levels of governance. Return rates did increase after 2007, which is partly ascribed to this more centralised enforcement structure (Leerkes et al., 2017).

In addition to the practical difficulties of coordinating return, locating 'removable' migrants and arranging travel documents and readmission for them, the first policy notes already identified another important challenge to the effectiveness of return policy: the sensitivity of return in the eyes of the general public. As public resistance to deportation could slow down or undo return procedures, leading to ineffective, inefficient and politically sensitive policy, creating public support for return policy was considered to be important for its successful implementation. Two strategies to achieve this implied the further expansion of the return migration industry.

First, from 1993 onwards, grassroots civil-society organisations working with undocumented migrants and rejected asylum-seekers were incorporated in the return infrastructure as implementing partners of assisted-return programmes in addition to the IOM. The first example of this was the *Knooppunt Vrijwillige Terugkeer* ('Junction of Voluntary Return', KVT), a cooperative of civil organisations working with asylum-seekers and migrants which was operational between 1993 and 1999 (Mommers and Velthuis, 2010). Later, multiple NGOs became involved, consistently labelling their return programmes as 'voluntary' and highlighting the empowering nature of their services (Cleton and Chauvin, 2020). The framework for outsourcing assisted-return programmes to multiple NGOs can also be found in Belgium, Italy and Switzerland (ICMPD and ECDPM, 2013) while most other European countries operate return through one provider, often the IOM (Kuschminder, 2017). The official role of these grassroots organisations was to establish contact with difficult-to-reach target groups, being a channel for providing information, a mediator to help get return out of the taboo sphere and potentially playing a role in facilitating return in practical terms (Mommers and Velthuis, 2010; Vandevoordt, 2017). While measurable return numbers became increasingly highlighted as a condition for funding, the consistently low contribution to return rates on the one hand and the persistent efforts by the government to still include NGOs on the other give reason to believe that their main role was to provide return with a positive image in order to enhance the legitimacy of the return policy, both in the eyes of prospective returnees and in the eyes of the general public, thereby appeasing the critical stance of these organisations by incorporating them, as discussed in more detail in the next section.

Second, and in a similar vein, return was from the outset also connected to more optimistic policy goals: a 'dual-track policy' linked migration management and development policy objectives, highlighting that returnees could contribute to the development of their country of origin with their education and skills (Mommers and Velthuis, 2010). In 2005, the Ministry of Foreign Affairs started to allocate Official Development Assistance (ODA) budgets to Migration and Development programmes, in collaboration with the Ministry of Justice and Alien Affairs. However, of the six domains that were identified in 2008 to reinforce the link between migration and development, the bulk of this budget (10 million out of a total of 13.3

million euros in 2012) was allocated to the domain of 'stimulating the voluntary, sustainable return and reintegration of ex-asylum-seekers'.[3] The assisted-return programmes of the IOM and NGOs were now not only labelled 'voluntary' but also 'sustainable'.[4] The Netherlands is among the few European countries (the others are Austria, Belgium and Switzerland) that use ODA budgets for assisted return (OECD, 2017).

After 30 years of policy development, the current Dutch return-policy landscape consists of a number of distinct but overlapping dimensions: (1) international and bilateral readmission agreements and diplomatic relations with origin and transit countries in a bid to create the legal and practical conditions for return (Cassarino, 2007); (2) measures to increase the likelihood of apprehension of undocumented migrants, including identification obligation supported by systematic control mechanisms; (3) an assisted-return infrastructure, including logistical assistance and transportation to the country of origin, cash or in-kind assistance for return, counselling or training pre- or post-return and policies that promote fair and humane treatment with which to improve legitimacy and compliance; (4) measures to increase forced return, such as identification obligations and detention facilities; (5) policies of social exclusion that seek to promote departure more indirectly, mainly through systematic exclusion from the right to employment, housing, social benefits, medical care and other services; and (6) non-return policies that deal with migrants who are unwilling and unable to return.

## A Wide Range of Professional Actors Who Earn an Income from Return and the Power Dynamics Between Them

In the return industry that has emerged in the Netherlands, many professional actors are involved in managing and facilitating return, notably several agencies within the national and local government and civil organisations; compared to other examples of the migration industry, it relies less on private companies. I now describe the different power dynamics that emerge between these agencies, based on their different goals and positions on five different moments in the return procedure.

### Apprehension

The return procedure starts when an asylum claim is rejected by the IND or when a person without legal documents is apprehended by the local police during internal controls or by military police during border controls. The individual migrant is registered at the Return and Repatriation Service (DT&V). It is the task of the DT&V to coordinate and administer both assisted return and forced departures/removals. The agency relies on and coordinates the other national and local governmental partners involved, including the Immigration and Naturalization Service (IND) and the Central Agency for the Reception of Asylum Seekers (COA), the National Police and the Royal Netherlands Marechaussee (military police), the Custodial Institutions Agency (DJI, responsible for immigrant detention), the Ministry for Foreign Affairs, municipalities and the NIDOS Foundation (guardianship organisation for minors).[5]

Although the coordination by the DT&V of all these governmental agencies has had some effect, a first issue affecting the efficiency of the return industry is the implementation gap (Czaika and de Haas, 2013) between national policy and national and local implementing agencies. For example, local police are reported to be reluctant to track down undocumented migrants who do not become a public nuisance or display criminal behaviour, as it is at odds with their main mandate to take care of public security and fight criminality (Leerkes et al., 2012). This 'implementation gap' also seems to be related to the organisational structure of the police: local police divisions work under local governance structures, making local issues of social order a priority over national border enforcement. A similar pattern of resistance is visible in Belgium, where police forces are locally organised; the Norwegian police, however, who are more centrally organised, are known for their stoicism in their law enforcement tasks (Leerkes and van Houte, 2020).

**Assisted return**
DT&V assigns to each individual migrant a case manager, whose task is to first encourage the migrant to comply with assisted return. DT&V outsources its assisted-return programmes to the IOM and non-governmental organisations and allocates and controls their budgets, which are provided by the Ministry for Foreign Affairs and the European Asylum, Migration and Integration Fund (AMIF). As discussed above, the Ministry for Foreign Affairs has been involved in the funding of assisted-return programmes on the grounds of their contribution to migration and development, adding a more positive connotation to return. As the political climate has changed and the public debate on migration has become more supportive (or less resistant) to enforcement, the migration and development goals and claims to sustainable return have slowly been downplayed. Nevertheless, assisted-return programmes are still funded through ODA budgets, while the decision-making power over the allocation of AVR funds is in the hands of the DT&V.[6] Here, it is surprising how this seemingly unfavourable arrangement for the Ministry for Foreign Affairs takes place with so *little* tension. In the changing political climate in which public support for development cooperation is decreasing, it seems that, rather than legitimising return policy through development in the 1990s and 2000s, development cooperation is currently legitimising itself through its contribution to migration management: to a domestic audience it contributes to migration management while, for an international audience, the Ministry still meets its commitments to ODA expenditure.

Although the IOM as an intergovernmental organisation which is funded by its member states to 'promote humane and orderly migration for the benefit of all' is the implementing partner for the bulk of assisted-return cases, a minority of cases are referred to NGOs such as Bridge to Better, the Goedwerk Foundation, the Stichting International Education Ter Apel (IETA), SolidRoad, the Refugee Council, World Wide Tools and ROS. NGOs have (had) different reasons to (dis)engage in the return migration industry and below I discuss a few telling examples to show this variety of reasons.

The earliest return initiatives by NGOs were not so much prompted by the government but emerged from the intrinsic mission to offer hands-on support to refugees and undocumented migrants (Mommers and Velthuis, 2010). For example, the *Rotterdam Ongedocumenteerden Steunpunt* (Rotterdam Undocumented Migrants Support Point, ROS) was founded in 2005 from a collective of small civic organisations, working with undocumented migrants, that had also offered return assistance between 2001 and 2004. Along with a manifold mission statement to support undocumented migrants through shelter, advice and education, ROS expressed the intention to continue offering return assistance *as an alternative* to the return measures by the government. They added that private funding would need to be attracted, as funding from the local government 'should not be expected' (ROS, 2006). After having been unsuccessful in attracting such funding for some years, their return project resumed in 2012, this time under the flag and funding scheme of the DT&V (ROS, 2014). Today, the funding by DT&V is worth several times that of the original funding base by private donors and small charities and the organisation has substantially grown in terms of paid staff.

Cordaid, an established development organisation linked to the international Caritas network, with its wide range of activities and funding streams, was another organisation that became involved in return at an early stage, because of its link with migration and development and its commitment to offer solutions to rejected asylum-seekers in the Netherlands. They set up their Mediation Agency for Return in 2001, which put returnees in contact with Cordaid's local development partners in their countries of origin to assist them after return. It received state funding through the Return, Migration and Development Programme of the Ministry for Foreign Affairs from 2005.[7] After some years, in which they commissioned an evaluation report of the effect of return assistance on the wellbeing of returnees (van Houte and de Koning, 2008), Cordaid decided that return should no longer be part of their development agenda.[8] The Mediation Agency continued as an independent organisation until ceasing its activities in July 2015 due to a lack of funding.[9]

With the stepping up of return policy, NGOs became increasingly and more systematically incorporated as implementers of assisted return. In 2010, several NGOs active in return were briefly united based on state subsidies in the *Stichting Duurzame Terugkeer* (Sustainable Return Foundation, SDT) which also included the IOM and the COA. However, subsidies for the platform were abruptly discontinued a year later, after having produced low return rates.[10] The funding scheme then came under the direction of the newly established DT&V, to which NGOs could apply individually. This attracted the involvement of several other NGOs, many of which (such as SMS, Pharos, Healthnet TPO, the HIT Foundation, Cordaid/Mediation Agency for Return and Beyond Borders) discontinued their activities on return at some point, either because they could not or did not want to meet the funding criteria based on return rates.

The DT&V has since continued to fund other NGO projects. While the old generation emerged from existing NGOs with a wider mandate, the 'new generation' of NGOs have been relatively recently established *for the purpose* of offering return support to rejected asylum-seekers.[11] Nevertheless, they still produce relatively low return numbers compared to the IOM.

The Dutch Refugee Council is a last and telling example of NGO involvement in the return industry. It is the most established refugee support organisation in the Netherlands and is structurally co-funded by the Dutch government, offering country-wide support in asylum procedures and integration in the Netherlands. In its position of representing the interests of refugees and asylum-seekers, the organisation has long taken a critical stance towards return. Nevertheless, the Refugee Council also saw many of their beneficiaries left in a legal limbo situation in the Netherlands and they were ambivalent about discussing return as a possible way out of undocumented life. For a long time, their role was limited to advocacy work on the one hand and informing their clients about the possibilities and referring them to organisations that offer return assistance on the other (Muus and Muller, 1999). In 2015, however, they started implementing return-assistance programmes funded through the DT&V, coordinating with the former partners of the Mediation Agency for Return.[12] Their increased involvement marks a positional shift from a critical outsider to an implementing partner of the DT&V.

Despite the fact that NGOs consistently underperformed in terms of measurable return outputs and the inefficiency in the coming and going of these small-scale initiatives, the DT&V remains committed to the inclusion of NGOs as implementation partners of assisted return. It seems that the main function of the involvement of NGOs is less instrumental than it is symbolic: from a governance perspective, their involvement offers legitimacy and credibility to return policy (Kalir and Wissink, 2016), while the available, yet unstable, funding schemes appease their resistance and keep them 'committed to the return policy as best as possible' (Brouwer et al., 2017, p.29). If not for their practical contribution to return, it is therefore still in the interest of the DT&V and the Dutch state to keep them on board.

**Forced removal and detention**

If a migrant does not comply with assisted return within the set amount of time, the DT&V attempts to organise forced return. This involves obtaining documentation from the embassy of the migrant's country of origin, arranging a flight and escort by the military police and, if deemed necessary, detention. As travel documents and renewed asylum claims are a particular challenge for forced return to happen, this process can take months or years, if it is even possible. Here, the relevant power dynamics are on the international and bilateral level; whether the state is able to create the legal and practical conditions for return depends on the diplomatic relations with the origin and transit countries, although limited research is available on the precise workings of these power dynamics (Cassarino, 2007; Leerkes and van Houte, 2020).

Immigration detention received particular attention in the discussion on the migration industry, especially in contexts where detention facilities are privatised, such as the US and the UK (Gammeltoft-Hansen, 2013; Peutz, 2006; Walters, 2002). In the Netherlands, this privatisation of detention and removal is less of an issue, as immigration detention falls under the responsibility of the Ministry for Justice and Security and removal by the military police under that of the Ministry of Defence, although private actors – including airlines – do get involved. Actors who actively resist forced return through legal or advocacy work, such as NGO workers[13] or lawyers, can also be considered to be part of the return industry, as they earn an income from people trying to avoid return policies.

**Social exclusion and non-return**

When assisted return or forced removal are not possible, a last measure of the Dutch return regime, to promote departure more indirectly, is social exclusion – mainly through exclusion from the right to employment, housing, social benefits, medical care and other services. The Netherlands takes a strict stance on this social exclusion, in particular in the areas of accommodation and allowances – a pattern related to the protection and tightening of the expenditure of the welfare state (Rosenberger, 2019). The implementation of this measure involves professionals within social services, such as doctors, teachers and employees of housing agencies, who also become actors in the return industry, saddling them with the 'dual task of being a judge and a server at the same time' (cf. Lipsky, 1980, p.74, cited in van der Leun, 2006).

Moreover, the dimension of social exclusion again highlights the friction between national and local governance: the primary responsibility of municipalities is to maintain public order and the safety of its inhabitants (van der Leun and Bouter, 2015). Faced with the reality that those who cannot or will not return will end up on their streets, leading to issues of criminality and public unrest, municipalities often continue to fund shelter arrangements for unauthorised migrants and often refuse to cooperate in the removal of rejected asylum-seekers, thereby ignoring national legislation (Leerkes et al., 2012; van der Leun and Bouter, 2015). Municipalities also engage in negotiations and lobbying in favour of undocumented migrants; this has been and continues to be a source of friction with the national government (van der

Leun and Bouter, 2015). This national–local divide has been identified by scholars in many other contexts concerning irregular migrants (Ambrosini, 2018; Bauder, 2017).

Finally, the reality that migrants who cannot be returned and are excluded from any form of livelihood would end up on the streets, causing social unrest, leads to the institutionalised provision of shelter and basic support though local governance and NGOs on the one hand and (clandestine) service-providers on the other. Although these shelter facilities are heavily contested, dealing with the people who cannot be deported is, in fact, the result of the strict approach to excluding migrants without the right to stay (Leerkes and van Houte, 2020).

## CONCLUSION: UNDERSTANDING THE RETURN INDUSTRY IN THE NETHERLANDS

The Dutch return enforcement structure is a clear example of a (return) migration industry: over the course of 30 years, an expanding field of professional multilevel governmental, non-governmental and private actors has emerged, who earn an income from the facilitation and control of return migration. Although the Dutch government has increasingly worked to direct, encapsulate and centralise this complex policy landscape following its growing priority to enforce return, its functioning seems suboptimal in terms of generating return rates. The discussion of the Dutch case shows that this can partly be ascribed to the oft-mentioned implementation gap between national policy and implementing agencies on the national and local level. However, the earliest policy notes also show a recognition that return policy has to be not only implemented but also legitimised by the general public and civil society, in order to meet the need of the liberal state to obtain legitimacy in the eyes of its citizens (Leerkes and van Houte, 2020).

This need for legitimacy explains the involvement of non-governmental actors. Compared to a single implementation partner such as the IOM, the involvement of NGOs has made the return infrastructure less cost-efficient because of their low return rates, small scale and discontinuity. Yet the reason why the state makes such an effort to keep them on board is to provide return policies with a sense of legitimacy (Webber, 2012, cited in Carr, 2014) – if a range of NGOs is involved in return assistance, it contributes to the view of potential returnees and the general public that return is an ethically and practically plausible option. The need to ensure funding in turn leads to claims of their contribution to 'hope'; 'durable solutions' adds to this legitimising language and appeases the resistance and critical stance of these NGOs towards return policies.

One could argue that NGOs contracted by the government and with government funding to assist with voluntary return become instrumentalised in the facilitation and management of return (Kalir and Wissink, 2016), while jeopardising their independence to fully represent their service users' views on government policy and legislation (Carr, 2014). However, NGOs are not all powerless players in this field. The examples discussed above show that NGOs involved in the return industry have held different positions in this power dynamic. Established organisations such as Cordaid and the Refugee Council, which do not rely on funding from return budgets as their core mandate, have been able to maintain a sense of autonomy and become (dis)engaged on their own terms. The balance between autonomy and dependency is more complicated to maintain for smaller grassroots organisations such as ROS. Becoming incorporated into state-funded programmes meant the survival and continuation of their services to undocumented migrants on the one hand and dependency on state funding and legitimising return policy on the other. Indeed, other small NGOs have had to cease their activities as an organisation when they could not or no longer wanted to meet the funding requirements. Still, by offering something that the state needs (accessing hard-to-reach target groups and offering legitimacy to return policy), some of these NGOs may enhance their practical autonomy to benefit their own goals, support their beneficiaries and strengthen their position in order to influence the policy agenda (Vandevoordt, 2017). Finally, while the first NGOs initially became involved in return independently from the national policy and were subsequently incorporated, later NGOs seemed to have been founded in response to available funding schemes and their engagement can be considered to be less critical towards the return policy and the organisation itself can be considered to have developed more as a subcontractor of the government (Cleton and Chauvin, 2020) rather than a grassroots organisation.

To conclude, the paradox of (in)efficiency can be understood when we take into account that efficiency has to be calculated in terms of both financial and political costs. The return industry that has emerged has had some, although limited, effect on return numbers, yet seems to have been increasingly successful in creating legitimacy and an appeased resistance against the return of migrants without a legal permit to stay. At the same time, the power negotiations that continue to take place between national and local governments, and between government and NGOs, show that this field is far from static.

## NOTES

1. Hernández-León (2005) recognises that some national governments actually promote emigration in order to produce remittance flows to the country of origin.
2. Tweede Kamer der Staten-Generaal 1996–1997, 25386 Nr. 1, 03-06-1997; Tweede Kamer der Staten-Generaal, 1998–1999, 26646 Nr. 1, 25-06-1999.
3. *Voortgangsrapportage migratie en ontwikkeling*, 3 July 2013.
4. Staatscourant, 10 March 2005, Nr. 49, p.9.
5. Dienst Terugkeer & Vertrek: Leidraad Terugkeer & Vertrek, 16 January 2015. See also Brouwer et al. (2017).
6. Staatscourant, 3 February 2014, Nr. 3363.
7. Tweede Kamer der Staten-Generaal 2004–2005 29693 Nr. 4, 01-07-2005.
8. Other organisations, including Healthnet TPO, an organisation for psychosocial health care in developing countries and Pharos, an expertise centre on health issues for refugees and new organisations on health issues, made similar choices: they became involved in return and in the SDT platform when they thought that it might match with the mandate of their organisation – although much lighter than Cordaid – and withdrew when they felt that the funding scheme became too restrictive to stay true to that mandate.
9. Mediation Agency for Return: Termination of the Foundation Maatwerk bij Terugkeer, 26 June 2015.
10. Kamerstuk 2011-29344-80 – terugkeerbeleid.
11. These include Bridge to Better (established end 2011), the Goedwerk Foundation (2012), the Stichting International Education Ter Apel (IETA) (2013) and SolidRoad (2014).
12. See https://www.vluchtelingenwerk.nl/wat-wij-doen/onze-projecten/onze-afgeronde-projecten/projecten-terugkeer-terug-naar-het-land-van-herkomst (accessed 30 September 2021).
13. For example, Amnesty International, which actively advocates against return policies (see their publication *Uitgezet*).

# REFERENCES

Åkesson, L. and Alpes, J. (2019) 'What is a legitimate mobility manager? Juxtaposing migration brokers with the EU', *Journal of Ethnic and Migration Studies*, **45** (14), 2689–705.
Ambrosini, M. (2018) *Irregular Immigration in Southern Europe: Actors, Dynamics and Governance*, Cham: Springer.
Andersson, R. (2016) 'Europe's failed "fight" against irregular migration: ethnographic notes on a counterproductive industry', *Journal of Ethnic and Migration Studies*, **42** (7), 1055–75.
Ataç, I. (2019) 'Deserving shelter: conditional access to accommodation for rejected asylum seekers in Austria, the Netherlands, and Sweden', *Journal of Immigrant and Refugee Studies*, **17** (1), 44–60.
Baldaccini, A. (2009) 'The return and removal of irregular migrants under EU law: an analysis of the Returns Directive', *European Journal of Migration and Law*, **11** (1), 1–17.
Bauder, H. (2017) 'Sanctuary cities: policies and practices in international perspective', *International Migration*, **55** (2), 174–87.
Beech, S.E. (2018) 'Adapting to change in the higher education system: international student mobility as a migration industry', *Journal of Ethnic and Migration Studies*, **44** (4), 610–25.
Belanger, D. (2016) 'Beyond the brokers: local marriage migration industries of rural Vietnam', *Positions: Asia Critique*, **24** (1), 71–96.
Brouwer, P., Cleton, L. and Cnossen, M. (2017) *Returning Rejected Asylum Seekers: Policy and Practices in the Netherlands*, Rijswijk: European Migration Network.
Carr, H. (2014) 'Returning "home": experiences of reintegration for asylum seekers and refugees', *British Journal of Social Work*, **44** (S1), 140–56.
Cassarino, J.-P. (2007) 'Informalising readmission agreements in the EU neighbourhood', *The International Spectator*, **42**, 179–96.
Castles, S. (2004) 'The factors that make and unmake migration policies', *International Migration Review*, **38** (3), 852–84.
Cleton, L. and Chauvin, S. (2020) 'Performing freedom in the Dutch deportation regime: bureaucratic persuasion and the enforcement of "voluntary return"', *Journal of Ethnic and Migration Studies*, **46** (1), 297–313.
Collyer, M. (2012) 'Deportation and the micropolitics of exclusion: the rise of removals from the UK to Sri Lanka', *Geopolitics*, **17** (2), 276–92.
Cranston, S. (2018) 'Calculating the migration industries: knowing the successful expatriate in the global mobility industry', *Journal of Ethnic and Migration Studies*, **44** (4), 626–43.
Cranston, S., Schapendonk, J. and Spaan, E. (2018) 'New directions in exploring the migration industries: introduction to special issue', *Journal of Ethnic and Migration Studies*, **44** (4), 543–57.
Czaika, M. and de Haas, H. (2013) 'The effectiveness of immigration policies', *Population and Development Review*, **39** (3), 487–508.
Elrick, T. and Lewandowska, E. (2008) 'Matching and making labour demand and supply: agents in Polish migrant networks of domestic elderly care in Germany and Italy', *Journal of Ethnic and Migration Studies*, **34** (5), 717–34.
Friberg, J.H. (2016) 'The rise and implications of temporary staffing as a migration industry in Norway', *Nordic Journal of Migration Research*, **6** (2), 81–91.
Gammeltoft-Hansen, T. (2013) 'The rise of the private border guard: accountability and responsibility in the migration control industry' in T. Gammeltoft-Hansen and N.N. Sørensen (eds), *The Migration Industry and the Commercialization of International Migration*, London and New York: Routledge, pp. 128–51.
Gammeltoft-Hansen, T. and Sørensen, N.N. (eds) (2013) *The Migration Industry and the Commercialization of International Migration*, London and New York: Routledge.
Garapich, M.P. (2008) 'The migration industry and civil society: Polish immigrants in the United Kingdom before and after EU enlargement', *Journal of Ethnic and Migration Studies*, **34** (5), 735–52.
Gibney, M.J. (2008) 'Asylum and the expansion of deportation in the United Kingdom', *Government and Opposition*, **43** (2), 146–67.
Harvey, W.S., Groutsis, D. and van den Broek, D. (2018) 'Intermediaries and destination reputations: explaining flows of skilled migration', *Journal of Ethnic and Migration Studies*, **44** (4), 644–62.

Hayes, M. (2015) 'Introduction: the emerging lifestyle migration industry and geographies of transnationalism, mobility and displacement in Latin America', *Journal of Latin American Geography*, **14** (1), 7–18.
Hernández-León, R. (2005) *The Migration Industry in the Mexico–U.S. Migratory System*, Los Angeles: University of California, California Center for Population Research Working Paper.
Hugo, G.J. (2006) 'Immigration responses to global change in Asia: a review', *Geographical Research*, **44** (2), 155–72.
ICMPD and ECDPM (2013) *Migration and Development Policies and Practices: A Mapping Study of Eleven European Countries and the European Commission*, Vienna and Maastricht: International Centre for Migration Policy Development and European Centre for Development Policy Management.
Kalir, B. and Wissink, L. (2016) 'The deportation continuum: convergences between state agents and NGO workers in the Dutch deportation field', *Citizenship Studies*, **20** (1), 34–49.
Koh, S.Y. and Wissink, B. (2018) 'Enabling, structuring and creating elite transnational lifestyles: intermediaries of the super-rich and the elite mobilities industry', *Journal of Ethnic and Migration Studies*, **44** (4), 592–609.
Kuschminder, K. (2017) *Taking Stock of Assisted Voluntary Return from Europe: Decision Making, Reintegration and Sustainable Return – Time for a Paradigm Shift*, Florence: European University Institute, Robert Schuman Centre for Advanced Studies Working Paper.
Leerkes, A. and van Houte, M. (2020) 'Beyond the deportation regime: differential state interests and capacities in dealing with (non-)deportability in Europe', *Citizenship Studies*, **24** (3), 319–38.
Leerkes, A., Varsanyi, M. and Engbersen, G. (2012) 'Local limits to migration control: practices of selective migration policing in a restrictive national policy context', *Police Quarterly*, **15** (4), 446–75.
Leerkes, A., van Os, R. and Boersema, E. (2017) 'What drives "soft deportation"? Understanding the rise in Assisted Voluntary Return among rejected asylum seekers in the Netherlands', *Population, Space and Place*, **23** (8), e2059.
Lim, A. (2015) 'Networked mobility in the "migration industry": transnational migration of Filipino caregivers to Israel', *Asian Women*, **31** (1), 85–118.
Lindquist, J. (2010) 'Labour recruitment, circuits of capital and gendered mobility: reconceptualizing the Indonesian migration industry', *Pacific Affairs*, **83** (1), 115–32.
Lipsky, M. (1980) *Street-Level Bureaucracy: Dilemmas of the Individual in Public Services*, New York: Russell Sage Foundation.
Ministry of Justice and Security (2020) *Rapportage Vreemdelingenketen Periode Januari–December 2019*, The Hague: Ministry of Justice and Security, Document No. 20401868.
Mommers, C. and Velthuis, E. (2010) *Leaving the Netherlands. Twenty Years of Voluntary Return Policy in the Netherlands (1989–2009)*, The Hague: International Organization for Migration.
Mountz, A., Coddington, K., Catania, R.T. and Loyd, J.M. (2013) 'Conceptualizing detention: mobility, containment, bordering, and exclusion', *Progress in Human Geography*, **37** (4), 522–41.
Muus, P.J. and Muller, P.H.A.M. (1999) *Beeldvorming onder (Uitgeprocedeerde) Asielzoekers en Vluchtelingen over Terugkeer- en Remigratie(beleid)*, The Hague: Wetenschappelijk Onderzoek- en Documentatiecentrum (WODC).
OECD (2017) *ODA Reporting of In-Donor Country Refugee Costs: Members' Methodologies for Calculating Costs*, Paris: OECD, https://www.oecd.org/fr/developpement/financementpourledeveloppementdurable/RefugeeCostsMethodologicalNote.pdf (accessed 6 April 2021).
Peutz, N. (2006) 'Embarking on an anthropology of removal', *Current Anthropology*, **47** (2), 217–41.
Plambech, S. (2017) 'Sex, deportation and rescue: economies of migration among Nigerian sex workers', *Feminist Economics*, **23** (3), 134–59.
ROS (2006). *Jaarverslag 2005*, Rotterdam: Rotterdams Ongedocumenteerden Steunpunt, Annual Report.
ROS (2014). *Jaarverslag 2013*, Rotterdam: Rotterdams Ongedocumenteerden Steunpunt, Annual Report.
Rosenberger, S. (2019) 'Navigating the representative-politics–liberal-rights dilemma: social policy designs for nonremoved migrants', *Journal of Immigrant and Refugee Studies*, **17** (1), 11–26.
Salt, J. and Stein, J. (1997) 'Migration as a business: the case of trafficking', *International Migration*, **35** (4), 467–94.

Samers, M. (1999) '"Globalization", the geopolitical economy of migration and the "spatial vent"', *Review of International Political Economy*, **6** (2), 166–99.

Schapendonk, J. (2018) 'Navigating the migration industry: migrants moving through an African-European web of facilitation/control', *Journal of Ethnic and Migration Studies*, **44** (4), 663–79.

Trujillo-Pagan, N. (2014) 'Emphasizing the "complex" in the "immigration industrial complex"', *Critical Sociology*, **40** (1), 29–46.

van der Leun, J. (2006) 'Excluding illegal migrants in the Netherlands: between national policies and local implementation', *West European Politics*, **29** (2), 310–26.

van der Leun, J. and Bouter, H. (2015) 'Gimme shelter: inclusion and exclusion of irregular immigrants in Dutch civil society', *Journal of Immigrant and Refugee Studies*, **13** (2), 135–55.

van Houte, M. and de Koning, M. (2008) *Towards a Better Embeddedness? Monitoring Assistance to Involuntary Returning Migrants from Western Countries*, Nijmegen and Amsterdam: CIDIN/AMIDSt.

Vandevoordt, R. (2017) 'Between humanitarian assistance and migration management: on civil actors' role in voluntary return from Belgium', *Journal of Ethnic and Migration Studies*, **43** (11), 1907–22.

Walters, W. (2002) 'Deportation, expulsion, and the international police of aliens', *Citizenship Studies*, **6** (3), 265–92.

Webber, F. (2012) 'UK: the real "immigration debate"', *Race and Class*, **53** (3), 91–8.

# 12. The legitimisation of the policy objective of sustainable reintegration
*Rossella Marino and Ine Lietaert*

## INTRODUCTION

The sustainable reintegration of migrants returning from host countries to their countries of origin is the goal of the so-called Assisted Voluntary Return and Reintegration (AVRR) programmes, which offer returnees support to travel home and post-return financial, vocational and psychosocial assistance (Kuschminder, 2017). These programmes have grown exponentially over the past decade, involving over 1.6 million returnees worldwide (IOM, 2019a, p.10). Assisted return and sustainable reintegration were included in the *Global Compact on Safe, Orderly and Regular Migration* (Global Compact, 2018) which is the leading text of global migration governance (Betts and Kainz, 2017). The Global Compact's Objective 21 calls for facilitating

> the sustainable reintegration of returning migrants into community life by providing them equal access to social protection and services, justice, psycho-social assistance, vocational training, employment opportunities and decent work, recognition of skills acquired abroad, and financial services, in order to fully build upon their entrepreneurship, skills and human capital as active members of society and contributors to sustainable development in the country of origin upon return. (Global Compact, 2018, p.30)

The inclusion of sustainable reintegration in the Global Compact is the culmination of an extended discursive evolution, starting with the inception of the policy objective as sustainable return. Over the years, several definitions of and interpretative frameworks for the sustainability of return and reintegration have been devised (Black et al., 2004; IOM, 2015, 2017a; Koser and Kuschminder, 2015) and more or less comprehensive reviews of those definitions and frameworks have been performed (Danish Refugee Council, 2011; Filipi et al., 2013; Strand and Aalen, 2016; Whyte and Hirslund, 2013). Nevertheless, the concept of sustainability in the context of return remains 'slippery' (Özerdem and Payne, 2019, p.404) and 'ambiguous' (Kuschminder, 2017, p.7), not least because policy concepts are by no means politically or ideologically neutral (Atkinson and Joyce, 2011; Bakewell, 2008; Boswell et al., 2011). Sustainable reintegration embodies (European) receiving countries' interest in reducing migrants on their territories (Lietaert and Van Gorp, 2019) and is thus inextricably linked with (European) migration management as a knowledge-based discourse whereby nation states differentiate between and hence govern differently 'who can be of ac/count and who cannot' (Oelgemöller, 2017, p.1).

Such a politically sensitive and increasingly relevant policy objective being surrounded by indeterminacy and opacity commands deeper investigation. Paving the way for the better assessment of policy outcomes and addressing the long-standing quest for greater clarity around the sustainability of return (Danish Refugee Council, 2008; Koser and Kuschminder,

2015; Strachan, 2019; Van Wijk, 2010), this chapter traces the evolution of sustainable reintegration from its emergence as sustainable return in the 1980s to its normalisation as a prominent policy objective of global migration governance today. More specifically, we engage in a content review of almost 100 texts addressing or conceptualising sustainable return and reintegration, retrieved from the policy, organisational and academic domains. Within these domains, the International Organization for Migration (IOM) – advancing and implementing AVRR programmes worldwide (Graviano and Darbellay, 2019) as well as producing knowledge and imparting authority upon policy approaches (Geiger and Pécoud, 2010) – has greatly contributed to the discursive formulation and promotion of sustainable return and reintegration. The sustainability of return and reintegration has long attracted the attention of NGOs and researchers who – both in cooperation with the IOM and independently – have additionally elaborated upon this concept. Finally, sustainable return and reintegration have been mentioned in normative frameworks and underpinned several international debates and fora. The documents and texts stemming from these endeavours were therefore examined in the light of Nay's (2014) framework on the normalisation, fragmentation and assimilation of policy objectives.

This chapter is structured as follows. First, we situate Nay's (2014) framework on the legitimisation of policy constructs on which we draw for our examination, along with the methods we followed to gather our corpus of documents and perform our analysis. Hereafter, the specific processes of the early normalisation, fragmentation, assimilation and renewed normalisation leading to the legitimisation of sustainable reintegration – consisting in the emergence of sustainable return, its multi-actor appropriation and discursive upgrade into sustainable reintegration and the latter's final consolidation – are individually disentangled in dedicated paragraphs. A concluding section contains our reflections on the implications of such processes for migration-related discourse and practice, with a particular focus on the need for more critical debating over the (non-)definition of sustainable reintegration.

## THEORETICAL FRAMEWORK AND METHODS

The present chapter delves into the evolution of the 'sustainability' concept since it was first attached to assisted return by disentangling the processes of normalisation, fragmentation and assimilation related to the legitimisation of policy constructs (Nay, 2014). In concrete terms, a policy concept is *normalised* after being codified, discussed in diverse fora and included in regulatory frameworks. Normalisation relies on the production of authoritative analyses by means of expert knowledge and the development of statistical appraisals and assessment tools stemming from the operationalisation of the policy objective. *Fragmentation* regards the multiplication of definitions and interpretations of the policy concept, potentially away from its initial conceptualisation and circle of emergence. Finally, the original creators of the policy concept tend to *assimilate* critical or alternative conceptions by reformulating them in conforming terms. According to Nay, these legitimising processes are bolstered by 'knowledge networks' comprising policy-implementing actors as well as various expert profiles and having 'the capacity to gather, shape, publicise and circulate the policy standards, information and knowledge used in policy making' (Nay, 2014, p.214).

For the purpose of this analysis, an elaborate search was conducted to ascertain how 'sustainability' has been used in publications on assisted return. Given the pivotal role of the

IOM, its repository was taken as a starting point to access relevant publication series, such as World Migration Reports, the IOM's Annual Reports of Activities and AVRR Key Highlights. This approach was supplemented with a general search for IOM publications mentioning the term 'sustainability', revealing interesting material from IOM central and field offices. Furthermore, we made searches in the online publication repositories of organisations and thinktanks which are active in migration-related knowledge production as well as queries in the databases of the European Union (EU) and the European Migration Network to collect significant texts and pertinent legislation and reports. The scholarly works referenced in the above material were finally added to the corpus. The combination of these searches resulted in 98 reports on which we performed a summative content analysis whereby we focused on the contextual usage of the policy objective rather than its frequency (Hsieh and Shannon, 2005). The singled-out passages were arranged chronologically, then categorised as belonging to the normalisation, fragmentation or assimilation processes and herein presented accordingly. We recognise that this method might not disclose all publications on the topic. Yet the elaborate searching method allowed for a reliable investigation of the changes in the meaning of sustainable reintegration over time.

The sections below address our findings regarding the overlapping and intertwining processes of normalisation, fragmentation and assimilation that from the conceptualisation of sustainable return have led to the formulation of sustainable reintegration. However, rather than stopping at the assimilation phase, we take the discussion one step further and explore the supplementary normalisation of such enhanced definitions. The legitimisation of sustainable reintegration is thus portrayed as a cycle resting on the productive relationship between research and policy, in which distinguishing lines are increasingly blurred. Table 12.1 contains a schematic overview of these processes, highlighting the key actors involved, the main conceptualisations, when the process occurred and the central events.

## EARLY NORMALISATION: SUSTAINABLE RETURN IS EQUATED WITH THE ABSENCE OF RE-EMIGRATION

Tracing the origins of sustainable reintegration revealed that destination countries were already providing 'incentives to return' to guestworkers in the aftermath of the 1970s recession (Rogers, 1981). In that context, some scholars pitted returnees' 're-adaptation' – which translated into socio-economic readjustment and sense of belonging – against their propensity to re-emigrate to former host countries (Gmelch, 1980). This early preoccupation with the re-emigration of returnees remained a core aspect of the discourse on the sustainability of return, which is the policy formulation that has dominated the early normalisation phase detailed below.

The interest of host countries in the return of foreigners carried on with post-conflict assisted repatriation mainly operated by the UNHCR, which was established as the preferred durable solution for refugees (Chimni, 1999). After aiding returning refugees with their basic and immediate needs, the UNHCR (1997a) sought to ensure the 'sustainability' of its activities in stimulating longer-term rehabilitation projects. In this context, the 'UNHCR's approach ha[d] become more ambitious, concerned not simply to secure physical survival but also to enable social, economic and even political processes which it sees as crucial to "sustainable return" ... which implies a situation where a constructive relationship between returnees,

Table 12.1  Overview of evolution and development of sustainable reintegration

| | Main actor(s) involved | Main conceptualisation(s) | Time frame | Relevant event(s) |
|---|---|---|---|---|
| Early normalisation | UNHCR, IOM, EU and EU member states | • Political and material reinsertion of refugees.<br>• Absence of returnees' re-emigration connected to income stability. | 1990s–2000s | • Conflicts in the 1990s.<br>• Increase in asylum applications in the 2000s.<br>• IOM International Dialogue on Migration. |
| Fragmentation | NGOs and researchers | • Individual/aggregate and subjective/objective sustainable return.<br>• 'Mobile livelihoods'.<br>• 'Mixed embeddedness'.<br>• Sustainable return as reintegration in safe and secure environment. | 2004–15 | • UK's Department for International Development workshop on the sustainability of AVR. |
| Assimilation | IOM | • Sustainable return as reintegration averting push factors.<br>• Sustainable reintegration including economic, social and psychosocial dimensions. | 2013–17 | • 2015 'migration crisis'. |
| Further normalisation | IOM and EU | • Sustainable reintegration including economic, social and psychosocial dimensions. | 2017 onwards | • Adoption of Global Compact on Migration in 2018.<br>• European Dialogue on Return and Sustainable Reintegration of Migrants in 2019. |

*Source*: Author's own creation.

civil society and the state is consolidate' (Macrae, 1999, p.3). Sustainable return, standing as a synonym for effective reintegration, was therefore initially used by the UNHCR in the frame of refugees' assisted repatriation (UNHCR, 1997b). This composite and legally based conceptualisation specific to refugees was developed in subsequent texts such as the paper of the United Nations Mission in Kosovo on minorities' right to sustainable return (UNMIK, 2003) and the UNHCR's (2004) *Handbook for Repatriation and Reintegration Activities*. However, this strand remained largely separate from the evolution of sustainable reintegration in return-migration discourse on which we focus in the present chapter.

Indeed, at the turn of the millennium, (European) governments were persuaded to extend the offer of reintegration-oriented assistance to undocumented migrants and rejected asylum-seekers present on their territories, as this approach had boosted repatriation to post-conflict Bosnia and Kosovo (IOM, 2003, 2010a; Koser, 2001). Beyond the provision of reintegration assistance, our analysis showed that the AVRR programme re-adapted discourse and language from repatriation programmes for returning refugees. It was agreed in 1997 that the IOM would tend to the return of irregular migrants and failed asylum-seekers, with a view to protecting host countries' asylum systems from non-eligible individuals (IOM, 1998; UNHCR, 2001). Wider reintegration assistance for these returnees was aimed at guaranteeing their 'economic self-sufficiency' (IOM, 2000, p.52).

Inaugurating a fruitful relationship with academia, the IOM commissioned a first comparative assessment of European AVRR programmes in 2001 (Koser, 2001). This report presented the train of thought at the basis of these programmes – namely that offering assistance for migrants' effective reintegration would render their return sustainable and therefore prevent them from re-emigrating irregularly. As such, sustainable return could translate in local development and consequently reduce emigration overall. Entering an important debate which subsequently continued, the author of the report noted that those assumptions had never been confirmed by research and it looked as though migrants enacted development if left mobile. Alongside return numbers and cost-related criteria, the comparative assessment indicated that the sustainability of return was viewed by all implementers as an important aspect through which to judge assisted-return schemes. In a specific framework, sketched to evaluate these programmes and drawn on different stakeholders' views, the indicators for sustainability consisted in '[i]ndividual and family reintegration in the short- and medium-/long-term [and] re-migration rates' (Koser, 2001, p.36). In sum, the absence of re-emigration was linked to the sustainability of return and this association generally endured. In a green paper, the EU similarly asserted that 'every sustainable return of an illegal resident is in the common interest of all Member States in order to avoid secondary movements' (European Commission, 2002, p.22).

In a first study explicitly aiming to investigate differences in the sustainability of return (IOM, 2002), income (in)stability was connected to the (un)successfulness of returnees' reintegration and hence their propensity (not) to re-emigrate. This connection was explored further in subsequent IOM research carried out under the aegis of the European Commission and scrutinising the anticipated reintegration needs of possible returnees, who had to be listened to because they possessed 'a longer-term view, i.e. a more sustainable one' (IOM, 2004a, p.65). From this survey, the IOM derived that the right reintegration assistance could prevent returnees from re-emigrating – putting its emphasis on a restrictive permanent return – as their initial reasons for leaving matched their reintegration concerns. It should be noted that, despite emigration causes and reintegration needs being broad, the IOM emphasised the provision of business-establishment aid as an overarching solution, arguably because the correction of security and political factors is beyond the scope of the circumscribed reintegration assistance it can deliver. In an extensive appraisal of European policies and practices on return migration, the IOM went further in reporting that sustainability-oriented reintegration support could convince more migrants to return and keep returnees where they are, while working towards the removal of the *general* root causes of irregular emigration (IOM, 2004b). This is relevant to the so-called migration–development nexus which commanded a tighter cooperation between migrant-receiving and -sending countries in the return and reintegration domain (Betts and Kainz, 2017).

By this time, despite sustainable return being the preferred expression, references to reintegration were also arising in relevant publications. The *World Migration Report 2003* did not define sustainable reintegration but presented it among the targets of the 'comprehensive and cooperative migration management approach' (IOM, 2003, p.54). Testifying to the related project of standardising the language around return migration, a first step towards terminological unison was made in the first IOM glossary, which defined reintegration, instead of sustainable return, as the '[r]e-inclusion or re-incorporation of a person into a group or a process, e.g. of a migrant into the society of his [*sic*] country of origin' (IOM, 2004c, p.54). Such reintegration could be cultural, economic and social.

Still sustainable return was the primary object of this normalisation drive, in which debates, discussion and conferences also played a part. Debates, discussions and conferences also played a part in this normalisation phase. Within the framework of the IOM's *International Dialogue on Migration* (IDM), a workshop on managing return migration with a focus on the sustainability of returns was attended by both states and diverse stakeholders from all over the world (IOM, 2010b). EU legislation normalised sustainable return further as the latter was mentioned (without a definition) in Directive 2008/115/EC (Official Journal of the European Union, 2008), along with the call for greater international cooperation on the matter of return migration. Nevertheless, several publications in the 2000s repeatedly mentioned sustainable reintegration and return without defining them (inter alia, IOM, 2005, 2008), signalling an increasing popularity of these expressions which was not (yet) matched by a compelling drive for terminological clarity.

In sum, stemming primarily from the European context, sustainable return derived from the multi-level conceptualisation of refugee repatriations and became entrenched in the domain of return migration through the knowledge-producing cooperations of the IOM, the formulation of normative texts and contextual international debates. In this initial phase, the policy objective – often used interchangeably with (sustainable) reintegration and not clearly or unanimously defined – largely meant the protracted presence of the migrants in their countries of origin via the assisted set-up of for-profit activities.

## APPROPRIATION BY VARIOUS ACTORS AND THE PROLIFERATION OF REINTERPRETATIONS: SUSTAINABLE RETURN IS FRAGMENTED

As sustainable return figured in IOM publications, normative texts and discussion fora, it attracted the interest of scholars and NGOs which – mainly independently from the IOM in this case – reinterpreted and rendered more sophisticated the originally normalised equation with returnees permanently staying in their countries of return. This trend originated again in the field of refugee return to then spill over into the return-migration domain more generally. In particular, towards the end of the 1990s and in relation to refugee repatriation, some scholars began to criticise the story of an unproblematic homecoming for returnees which was narrated by international organisations and some pundits alike (Strand and Aalen, 2016). This contention applied particularly to the undefined 'sustainable minority return' to post-conflict environments, which entailed various degrees of redress (Black, 2001; Mesić and Bagić, 2010; OHR, 1999; Williams, 2006).

The experience of post-conflict return to the Balkans was also the subject of a seminal report that provided the very first multidimensional, research-based, rigorous and measurable definition of sustainable return (Black et al., 2004). This report by Black and his colleagues unearthed a series of crucial reflections which laid the basis for all subsequent discussions on the matter of sustainable return. As refugee return impacted on communities of origin as a whole, the aggregate dimension of sustainable return was explored alongside the individual one, although the former is more difficult to actually measure and is therefore generally overlooked (Fransen, 2017). Aggregate sustainable return occurred 'if socio-economic conditions and levels of violence and persecution [for the home country or region] are not significantly worsened by return, as measured one year after the return process is complete', whereas individual sustainable return existed 'if returnees' socio-economic status and fear of violence or persecution is no worse, relative to the population in the place of origin, one year after their return' (Black et al., 2004, p.39). According to the authors, sustainability – which could be physical, socio-economic or political – encompassed returnees' individual perceptions, their objective conditions and the broader return context. Due to the post-conflict setting of the study, the report stressed the political dimension of return as the incidence of violence, persecution and conflict. Remarkably, this dimension has received virtually no attention in the subsequent literature on the sustainable return of illegalised migrants and rejected asylum seekers, signifying a deep and uncritical rift between the policy and academic approaches to refugee and non-refugee return (Strachan, 2019). Moreover, Black and his colleagues importantly and clearly explained that the absence of re-emigration – subsumed under the category of physical sustainability and known as the narrow interpretation of sustainability (Black and Gent, 2006) – was not explicitly cited in their definitions because the socio-economic and security factors contained therein would precisely push any returnee not to re-emigrate. Alongside some indicators of sustainable return based on the above definitions and layers, the factors influencing the sustainability of return – age, migration experience, return decision and assistance – were sketched out. Some later studies expanded this list (Koser and Kuschminder, 2015; Kuschminder, 2017). Finally, the report drew on the concept of sustainable livelihood as an additional variation of sustainability, referring to an existence which 'can be maintained without external inputs, and ... sufficiently robust to withstand external shocks' (Black et al., 2004, p.26). This significant concept was used in later publications, too (Mesić and Bagić, 2010; Ruben et al., 2009).

Still within the context of refugee returns, Black and his colleagues' research was featured in a workshop on the sustainability of AVR to the Balkans, organised by the UK's Department for International Development. In the introduction to the workshop, it was contended that sustainable return is '[m]ore than return because physical return may not be sustainable on its own, and policies to promote return should seek a sustainable solution. Less than return because integral to a sustainable solution for returnees and countries of origin ... is the re-opening of choice' (DRC, 2004, p.3). This was taken further by Stepputat (2004), who saw sustainable return as involving 'mobile livelihoods'. More specifically, Stepputat maintained that 'the question of local integration, resettlement or return is a political question of conflicting interests between countries of asylum and countries of origin, a problem that technical and economic programmes of return and sustainable integration cannot do away with' (Stepputat, 2004, p.21), referring to the inconsistency between the thorny politics of return migration and the technical machine of migration management. This political predicament might be a reason why the dimension of the reopening of choice, for returning refugees and migrants, has found more favour among the academic community than that of the policy-makers. Nevertheless, others denoted that a degree of permanence by returnees is essential in ensuring the improvement of countries of origin which, in turn, renders return palatable (Black and Gent, 2006).

Some then considered sustainability as yet another trendy word in global politics (Mesić and Bagić, 2010), which had become almost meaningless (Black and Gent, 2006). Yet, it represented 'an important starting point for dialogue between donors and migrants' countries of origin, and between interior and cooperation/development ministries, each with different perspectives on how "success" can best be judged' (Black and Gent, 2006, p.33). This difference in perspectives on sustainability was exemplified in a report by the Austrian element of the European Migration Network, namely, the pool of EU experts on migration. When the relevant actors were asked to voice their own interpretation of sustainable return, some referred to the lack of re-emigration, whereas others – for instance the NGO Caritas – put its emphasis on the access to basic services and items (National Contact Point Austria, 2006).

By that time, generalising the debate beyond refugee returns, the normalised correlation between return migration and development was disputed. It was argued that returnees could hardly spur development in origin countries as they struggled on both a societal and a personal level (van Houte and Davids, 2008). Accordingly, some called for greater attention to be given to social and personal sustainability (DRC, 2004). Trying to account for this deeper dimension, Ruben et al. (2009) substituted reintegration with 'mixed embeddedness', as the latter concept captured more accurately the multidimensionality of return migration. Having economic, social network and psychosocial dimensions, it 'refers to the ways how individuals find and define their position in society, feel a sense of belonging and possibilities for participation in society' (Ruben et al., 2009, p.910). This publication introduced the crucial idea of the multifaceted identity underpinning returnees' embeddedness, which cannot easily re-adapt to original values and norms.

Still within the debate on whether reintegration can lead to development and/or re-emigration, a significant contribution edited by Cassarino (2008) – building on a previous expansion of existing theories on return migration (Cassarino, 2004) – underscored the impact of return preparation, viewed as the intermixing of the willingness and readiness to return, the ability to mobilise resources for returning and the migration experience (Cassarino, 2008, p.19). Cassarino (2014) subsequently read return preparedness in conjunction with the degree of completion of the migration cycle and the annexed motives to return. On this note, coercive and standardised assisted-return programmes not respecting migrants' willingness and stressing their feeble capacity to develop countries of origin could, in themselves, jeopardise sustainability (Danish Refugee Council, 2008; Whyte and Hirslund, 2013).

Beyond the strictly academic domain, some confrontation around sustainability also arose within the EU framework. In 2010, the HIT Foundation related that, despite the term featured in many European policy papers and norms, no common and authoritative definition of it existed at EU level. However, the foundation was able to collect a few relevant conceptualisations, such as '"[s]ustainability" means that returnees: ... go and never come back to the individual member state ... go and never come back to any other member state of the European Union ... establish a new livelihood in their country and can sustain their family ... contribute to economic and social development of the country of return ... decide to use legal and official means of migration in the future' (Van Wijk, 2010, p.8). Within this definition range, the normalised correlation endured, as it was repeated that '[s]ustainable return can have several definitions, but it generally implies the absence of re-migration after return because the returnee is fully integrated socially and economically in the home community' (European Commission et al., 2012, p.7). Echoing earlier assumptions on the relationship between return and overall development which could counter the aggregate root causes for migration, the European Migration Network portrayed sustainable return as 'return which deters new irregular migration of the returnee and – where possible – of other third-country nationals in the Country of Return' (European Migration Network, 2016, p.9). Expanding on this reasoning, the European Parliament (2017) finally understood sustainable return 'not only as [an] absence of re-emigration, but also as a returnee's positive impact on the development of their communities of origin' (2017, p.1).

With the interest in the terminological dimension of sustainability mounting, new questions arose as to whether there could be one universal definition of and approach to sustainable return (Cherti and Szilard, 2013; Whyte and Hirslund, 2013). The substantial review of AVRR performed by Koser and Kuschminder (2015) and published by the IOM sought to bring some clarity to this debate. The authors devised a specific definition of sustainable return, occurring when '[t]he individual has reintegrated into the economic, social and cultural processes of the country of origin and feels that they are in an environment of safety and security upon return' (Koser and Kuschminder, 2015, p.49), on which they based a composite return and reintegration index. The authors notably questioned the equation between sustainable return and the absence of re-emigration, arguing that 'people may re-migrate even if their circumstances upon return are demonstrably better than when they first left, if their status in the community has decreased, or if their perceptions do not acknowledge their realities' (Koser and Kuschminder, 2015, p.15). Finally and for the very first time thus far in both the academic and the policy realms, the authors wished to clearly and purposively distinguish between reintegration and sustainable return, because 'people may return to their country of origin and stay long enough to be considered sustainable but without actually reintegrating' (Koser and Kuschminder, 2015, p.15), or they could reintegrate while still craving re-emigration. Although Koser and Kuschminder did not see reintegration and sustainable return as synonymous, they still thought that the former generally led to the latter. Shortly thereafter, Carling's (2002) model on aspiration and ability in migration was applied to the matter of return to differentiate between (un)sustainable return, volatile return and re-migration. This approach importantly differentiated between unsustainable return – for '[t]hose who do not aspire for reintegration but are unable to re-migrate' (Strand and Aalen, 2016, p.11) – and re-emigration for returnees who reject reintegration, yet manage to leave their countries.

At around that time, questions on sustainable return were proliferating. For instance, Kuschminder (2017) asked '[a]fter what period of time should an individual be considered to be sustainably returned? For example, does sustainable return occur after one, two, or three years? Does sustainable return mean the individual should never migrate again? Alternatively, does a time limit need to be placed on sustainable return?' (2017, p.13). Most importantly, the author suggested substituting sustainable return with sustainable reintegration as the latter 'allows for an understanding of a holistic process of reintegration that is sustainable over the long term. This articulates a clear and sound policy goal, versus one of rooting people unsustainably in one place' (2017, p.15), stressing the importance of language in migration management (Cassarino, 2014). The next section indicates that the IOM capitalised upon this suggestion.

## GETTING THE BEST OF BOTH WORLDS: ASSIMILATION IN SUSTAINABLE RETURN AND REINTEGRATION

The circulating innovative and alternative stances on sustainable return were captured and re-rendered by the IOM, hence discursively boosting its initial approach. Black et al. (2004) as well as van Houte and de Koning (2008) were among the references of a report issued by the IOM on the impact of health on sustainable return. A hard-to-achieve combination of access to supportive social networks, economic stability and a reliable health system was said to be necessary for returnees' 'positive focus on their futures' (Mommers et al., 2009, p.106), making sustainable return 'a function of – for lack of a better word – luck' (2009, p.95). Returnees with precarious health conditions – including mental stress – and in unstable political contexts found it more difficult to be employed or direct an enterprise, hence jeopardising their sustainable return (IOM, 2014). In an exposition of assistance programmes from North Africa within the novel focus on return from transit countries, Cassarino (2008) inspired the assertion that AVRR '[a]llows the migrants concerned to freely prepare for their return, enabling them to identify potential opportunities for socioeconomic reinsertion into communities of origin, thereby enhancing the sustainability of their return' (IOM, 2013a, p.14), with the ultimate aim of averting re-emigration.

A general favour for post-economic indicators – like Amartya Sen's capabilities approach – was making inroads in the IOM's domain (IOM, 2013b; Samuel Hall and IOM, 2017). In this theoretically evolved context, a plain case of assimilation occurred in 2015. This year marked the beginning of the alleged migration crisis, especially in Europe, where a considerable entry of migrants established return migration as an effective containment strategy (Slominski and Trauner, 2018). Citing Black and Gent (2006), Cassarino (2008) and Ruben et al. (2009), the IOM engendered a new definition of sustainable return, which

> should be understood either as: (a) successful reintegration in the country of origin, which includes the economic, social and psychosocial aspects and the capacity of the individual to cope with push factors, both old and new, on the same level as the local population or (b) eventual legal re-migration made possible by skills acquired during the reintegration process. (IOM, 2015, p.19)

This definition followed the assumption that reintegration matches sustainable return and goes beyond returnees' economic reinsertion, also contemplating their social and psychosocial conditions. More importantly, acknowledging the central role of mobility in the contemporary world, this report conceded that Europe's view on sustainable return, centred on the absence of re-emigration, was excessively restrictive and declared return could still be judged sustainable if the returnee made use of legal emigration pathways by means of migration-related acquired skills. By connecting further mobility trajectories to the benefits of reintegration assistance for skills-building, the IOM was simultaneously giving voice to the contention that sustainable return wrongly chained returnees to their countries of origin and legitimising its own migration management role. Furthermore, by stressing the legal component of returnees' potential re-emigration, it was preserving the decisional primacy of immigration countries which are generally far from generous in their offer of legal migration opportunities (Baldwin-Edwards, 2008).

In 2017, the IOM defined, for the first time, sustainable reintegration in lieu of sustainable return, referencing Koser and Kuschminder (2015) and addressing existing limitations in the literature (Majidi and Nozarian, 2019). In the 'integrated approach to reintegration', sustainable reintegration corresponded to returnees having reached 'levels of economic self-sufficiency, social stability within their communities, and psychosocial well-being that allow them to cope with (re)migration drivers. Having achieved sustainable reintegration, returnees are able to make further migration decisions a matter of choice, rather than necessity' (IOM, 2017a, p.3). It appears that irregular re-emigration, seen as the product of necessity, would be averted by a sustainable reintegration enabling returnees to choose to move for reasons not related to their survival. However, this view reduces agency, implying that choice and necessity are clear-cut and returnees can be dragged from the latter to the former by means of reintegration assistance. Again on the point of further migration, it was established that '[t]he latter can take place and can still be a choice regardless of whether reintegration is successful, partially successful or unsuccessful' (IOM, 2017a, p.3). To some, this explanation looked like an advancement with regards to returnees' mobility compared to previous approaches (Majidi and Nozarian, 2019; Samuel Hall and IOM, 2017). However, in the same report, it was specified that 'returnees are unlikely to reintegrate if they find themselves in situations whereby moving again or relying on a family member abroad is considered necessary for their physical or socioeconomic survival' (IOM, 2017a, p.3), meaning that a permanent stay was still deemed a positive indicator of sustainability.

The integrated approach to reintegration was composed of individual, community and structural levels and informed a sophisticated measurement tool aimed at facilitating evidence-based policy-making. This consisted in individual- and community-level indicators for sustainable reintegration, streaming into a reintegration score. Validating the assumption that the attention to discourse, language and terminology reflected migration management's attempt at universalising its approaches, such a score allowed for 'an aggregated and standardised understanding of an AVRR beneficiary's level of reintegration' and was meant to 'be integrated globally, in all reintegration monitoring activities in the field of AVRR' (Samuel Hall and IOM, 2017, p.13). The 2017 definition of sustainable reintegration also informed the framework for AVRR released in 2018, which aimed at 'calling for the adoption of coordinated measures, policies, and practices between stakeholders responsible for migration management and development at the international, national and local levels' (IOM, 2018a, p.2). This striving for standardisation and homogenisation materialised in the renewed normalisation of the last terminological and discursive approach to sustainability in return migration.

## REACTIVATING THE LEGITIMISATION CYCLE: A NEW NORMALISATION

Testifying to the intention to consolidate and normalise the IOM's 2017 definition of sustainable reintegration, the latter was embedded and reproduced in all subsequent IOM reports

(IOM, 2017b, 2018b, 2018c, 2019b, 2019c, 2019d). The consistent utilisation of a single conceptualisation paved the way for the entrenchment of sustainable reintegration in the Global Compact for Migration, marking with its regulatory stature the policy objective's ultimate normalisation. Although sustainable reintegration was not defined in the compact's Objective 21 dealing with return migration, it was said to be conditional on the equal access of returnees and the local population to socio-economic and political services, which would enable migrants to accelerate the sustainable development of their countries of origin (Global Compact, 2018). This rather speculative formulation, looking closer to the discourse on sustainable refugee return mainly attributable to the UNHCR, forcefully brought back the previously contradicted association between return and reintegration and development.

The signature of the Global Compact for Migration incentivised the holding of dedicated conferences, such as the 2018 European Dialogue on the return and reintegration of migrants, repeated in 2019 under the name of European Dialogue on Return and Sustainable Reintegration of Migrants. During these events, international political actors, researchers and practitioners exchanged best practices and perspectives for the improvement of reintegration programmes, contributing to the ossification of sustainable reintegration within the boundaries of global migration governance.

## FINAL REFLECTIONS ON (NOT) DEFINING SUSTAINABLE REINTEGRATION

This chapter has retraced the chronological and discursive evolution of sustainable reintegration from its first appearance as sustainable return by linking it to the related normalisation, fragmentation, assimilation and re-normalisation cycle which encompassed authoritative and rigid definitions as well as critical appraisals. Since this policy objective has expanded beyond the narrow field of refugee returns, the IOM has taken the lead in its discursive formulation and advancement, cooperating directly with consultants and academics or re-employing the latter's independent re-definitions and views. Within this 'knowledge network' of researchers and organisations (in)directly connected to each other, migration management's intention to generalise and standardise the way in which return migration is interpreted and acted upon harnessed and rivalled autonomous and divergent interpretations.

It is beyond the scope of this chapter to trace definitive divides between the legitimising processes or to unquestionably and conclusively assign each of the relevant actors to one or more of them. Rather, we sought to exemplify how a concept may become pivotal for policy after being (re-)negotiated and (re-)discussed in various fora and by diverse actors, be the latter formally associated or not.

The net result of the above reconstruction of this evolution of sustainable return into sustainable reintegration and the latter's final formulation is still that 'there is no universally agreed definition of sustainable reintegration' (IOM, 2019a, p.11). Some have tried to fill this gap, as terminological unison is seen as useful for operational and explanatory purposes. However, a fixed and standardised definition of sustainable reintegration could ossify the predicaments which have been highlighted with respect to assisted-return and migration management, namely, the fact that it speaks to a hypothetical world lacking transnational asymmetries, socio-economic inequalities and multifarious political barriers (Oelgemöller, 2017; Pécoud, 2015). Other shortcomings are its technical and economic nature (Ashutosh and Mountz,

2011; Strand et al., 2008), its sedentary bias (Jeffery and Murison, 2011) and its inattention towards returnees' sense of belonging (Lietaert et al., 2017). Return migration experiences are hard to generalise or standardise, as situations of wellbeing and struggle can occur simultaneously, with migrants' views on their own return and reintegration experiences varying over time (Lietaert et al., 2017).

In this regard, some interesting insights can be borrowed from the extensive discussions on sustainability within the literature on sustainable development, where the term has already been caught in the contest between terminological determinacy and flexibility. In parallel to the engendering of authoritative definitions of sustainable development mainly within the United Nations (Du Pisani, 2006), several scholars have approached the concept of sustainability critically. Although discursive precision is thought to lead to clearer policy and research outcomes (Armstrong and Kamieniecki, 2019), debating over the meaning of sustainability is considered as an act of reaction to the 'imperatives of necessity, desirability and universality' (Luke, 2005, p.230) that mainstream discourse entails. Sustainability, development and similar elusive concepts always stand for particular worldviews or 'complex constellations of ontological presuppositions, epistemic capacities, and ethical and aesthetic values that converge to dynamically organize a synthetic apprehension of the exterior world and one's interior experience' (Hedlund-De Witt, 2014, p.8315). In this context, rather than a purportedly universal cloak for the partiality and relativity intrinsic to any policy concept, sustainability should be a 'dialogue of values' harbouring the unending dialectics of irreducible points of view (Ratner, 2004). A genuine and inclusive interaction of values, views and interpretations across sectors and geographical locations could result in mutable and widely accepted conceptualisations of sustainable reintegration, susceptible to creating more democratic and beneficial approaches to the topic of return migration. This might be particularly important for the next phase of global migration governance corresponding to the implementation of the Global Compact for Migration, whose clause on sustainable reintegration, echoing previously normalised associations, could stimulate bottom-up and unorthodox reflections on the policy objective.

## REFERENCES

Armstrong, J.H. and Kamieniecki, S. (2019) 'Sustainability policy research: a review and synthesis', *Policy Studies Journal*, **47** (S1), S45–S56.

Ashutosh, I. and Mountz, A. (2011) 'Migration management for the benefit of whom? Interrogating the work of the International Organization for Migration', *Citizenship Studies*, **15** (1), 21–38.

Atkinson, S. and Joyce, K.E. (2011) 'The place and practices of well-being in local governance', *Environment and Planning C: Politics and Space*, **29** (1), 133–48.

Bakewell, O. (2008) 'Research beyond the categories: the importance of policy irrelevant research into forced migration', *Journal of Refugee Studies*, **21** (4), 432–53.

Baldwin-Edwards, M. (2008) 'Towards a theory of illegal migration: historical and structural components', *Third World Quarterly*, **29** (7), 1449–59.

Betts, A. and Kainz, L. (2017) *The History of Global Migration Governance*, Oxford: University of Oxford, Refugee Study Centre Working Paper No. 122, https://www.rsc.ox.ac.uk/publications/the-history-of-global-migration-governance (accessed 27 February 2021).

Black, R. (2001) 'Return and reconstruction in Bosnia-Herzegovina: missing link, or mistaken priority?', *SAIS Review*, **21** (2), 177–99.

Black, R. and Gent, S. (2006) 'Sustainable return in post-conflict contexts', *International Migration*, **44** (3), 15–38.

Black, R., Koser, K., Munk, K., Atfield, G., D'Onofrio, L. and Tiemoko, R. (2004) *Understanding Voluntary Return*, London: Home Office, Online Report 50/04, https://webarchive.nationalarchives.gov.uk/20110220155644/http:/rds.homeoffice.gov.uk/rds/pdfs04/rdsolr5004.pdf (accessed 27 February 2021).

Boswell, C., Geddes, A. and Scholten, P. (2011) 'The role of narratives in migration policy-making: a research framework', *British Journal of Politics and International Migration*, **13** (1), 1–11.

Carling, J. (2002) 'Migration in the age of involuntary immobility: theoretical reflections and Cape Verdean experiences', *Journal of Ethnic and Migration Studies*, **28** (1), 5–42.

Cassarino, J. (2004) 'Theorising return migration: the conceptual approach to return migrants revisited', *International Journal on Multicultural Societies*, **6** (2), 253–79.

Cassarino, J. (ed.) (2008) *Return Migrants to the Maghreb Countries: Reintegration and Development Challenges*, Florence: European University Institute, https://cadmus.eui.eu/bitstream/handle/1814/9050/MIREM%20_General_Report_2008.pdf?sequence=1&isAllowed=y (accessed 27 February 2021).

Cassarino, J. (2014) 'A case for return preparedness' in G. Battistella (ed.), *Global and Asian Perspectives on International Migration*, Cham: Springer, pp. 153–65.

Cherti, M. and Szilard, M. (2013) *Returning Irregular Immigrants. How Effective is the EU's Response?*, London: Institute for Public Policy Research, https://www.ippr.org/files/images/media/files/publication/2013/02/returning-migrants-EU-130220_10371.pdf (accessed 27 February 2021).

Chimni, B.S. (1999) *From Resettlement to Involuntary Repatriation: Towards a Critical History of Durable Solutions*, Geneva: UNHCR Working Paper No. 2, https://www.refworld.org/pdfid/4ff59a392.pdf (accessed 27 February 2021).

Danish Refugee Council (2008) *Recommendations for the Return and Reintegration of Rejected Asylum Seekers. Lessons Learned from Returns to Kosovo*, Copenhagen: DRC, https://www.refworld.org/pdfid/484022172.pdf (accessed 27 February 2021).

Danish Refugee Council (2011) *Long-Term Sustainability of Return of Rejected Asylum Seekers to Kosovo*, Copenhagen: DRC, https://flygtning.dk/media/5626436/evaluation-of-the-kosovo-programme.pdf (accessed 27 February 2021).

DRC (2004) *The Sustainability of 'Voluntary Assisted Return': The Experience of the Balkans*, Brighton: University of Sussex, Development Research Centre on Migration, Globalisation and Poverty, https://assets.publishing.service.gov.uk/media/57a08cc740f0b652dd00155a/SustainableReturnBalkans.pdf (accessed 27 February 2021).

Du Pisani, J. (2006) 'Sustainable development: historical roots of the concept', *Environmental Sciences*, **3** (2), 83–96.

European Commission (2002) *Green Paper on a Community Return Policy on Illegal Residents*, https://op.europa.eu/en/publication-detail/-/publication/e89b0243-035c-46cf-8eda-2d2cb509d6c7/language-en (accessed 27 February 2021).

European Commission, ECRE, ICMPD and Matrix Insight Ltd (2012) *Comparative Study on Best Practices to Interlink Pre-Departure Reintegration Measures Carried Out in Member States with Short- and Long-Term Reintegration Measures in the Countries of Return*, https://op.europa.eu/en/publication-detail/-/publication/a933ce1d-c68e-48ce-a2fc-4a42645e37c0 (accessed 27 February 2021).

European Migration Network (2016) *Guidelines for Monitoring and Evaluation of AVR(R) Programmes*, https://emnbelgium.be/sites/default/files/publications/guidelines_for_monitoring_and_evaluation_final_jan2016.pdf (accessed 27 February 2021).

European Parliament (2017) *Reintegration of Returning Migrants*, https://www.europarl.europa.eu/RegData/etudes/BRIE/2017/608779/EPRS_BRI(2017)608779_EN.pdf (accessed 27 February 2021).

Filipi, G., Galanxhi, E., Nesturi, M. and Grazhdani, T. (2013) *Return Migration and Reintegration in Albania*, Tirana: INSTAT and IOM, https://albania.iom.int/sites/default/files/publication/15.%20Return%20Migration%20and%20Reintegration%20in%20Albania%202013.pdf (accessed 27 February 2021).

Fransen, S. (2017) 'The socio-economic sustainability of refugee return: insights from Burundi', *Population, Space and Place*, **23** (1), e1976.

Geiger, M. and Pécoud, A. (eds) (2010) *The Politics of International Migration Management*, London: Palgrave Macmillan.

Global Compact (2018) *Global Compact for Safe, Orderly and Regular Migration 2018*, https://refugeesmigrants.un.org/sites/default/files/180711_final_draft_0.pdf (accessed 27 February 2021).
Gmelch, G. (1980) 'Return migration', *Annual Review of Anthropology*, **9**, 135–59.
Graviano, N. and Darbellay, N. (2019) 'A framework for assisted voluntary return and reintegration', *Migration Policy Practice*, **9** (1), 9–14.
Hedlund-De Witt, A. (2014) 'Rethinking sustainable development: considering how different worldviews envision "development" and "quality of life"', *Sustainability*, **6** (11), 8310–28.
Hsieh, H.-F. and Shannon, S.E. (2005) Three approaches to Qualitative Content Analysis', *Qualitative Health Research*, **15** (9), 1277–88. https://doi.org/10.1177/1049732305276687
IOM (1998) 'IOM return policy and programmes: a contribution to combating irregular migration', *Refugee Survey Quarterly*, **17** (3), 79–87.
IOM (2000) *World Migration Report 2000*, Geneva: International Organization for Migration.
IOM (2002) *The Return and Reintegration of Migrants to the South Caucasus: An Exploratory Study*, Geneva: International Organization for Migration, https://publications.iom.int/system/files/pdf/return_southcaucasus.pdf (accessed 28 February 2021).
IOM (2003) *World Migration Report 2003*, Geneva: International Organization for Migration.
IOM (2004a) *Profiling of Irregular Migrants and Analysis of Reintegration Needs of Potential Returnees from Kosovo (Serbia and Montenegro), Albania and FYROM in Belgium, Italy, the United Kingdom and Germany*, Vienna: International Organization for Migration, https://austria.iom.int/sites/default/files/IOM_research_report_Profiling_of_irregular_migrants.pdf (accessed 28 February 2021).
IOM (2004b) *Return Migration: Policies and Practices in Europe*, Geneva: International Organization for Migration and the Advisory Committee on Aliens Affairs, The Netherlands, https://publications.iom.int/system/files/pdf/returnmigration.pdf (accessed 28 February 2021).
IOM (2004c) *Glossary on Migration*, Geneva: International Organization for Migration, https://publications.iom.int/system/files/pdf/iml_1_en.pdf (accessed 28 February 2021).
IOM (2005) *World Migration Report 2005*, Geneva: International Organization for Migration, https://publications.iom.int/system/files/pdf/wmr_2005_3.pdf (accessed 28 February 2021).
IOM (2008) *World Migration Report 2008*, Geneva: International Organization for Migration, https://publications.iom.int/system/files/pdf/wmr_1.pdf (accessed 28 February 2021).
IOM (2010a) *AVVR Annual Report of Activities*, Geneva: International Organization for Migration, https://www.iom.int/jahia/webdav/site/myjahiasite/shared/shared/mainsite/activities/regulating/AVRR-Annual-Report-2010.pdf (accessed 28 February 2021).
IOM (2010b) *International Dialogue on Migration*, Geneva: International Organization for Migration, https://publications.iom.int/system/files/pdf/idm14.pdf (accessed 28 February 2021).
IOM (2013a) *Assisted Voluntary Return and Reintegration Handbook for the North African Region*, Geneva: International Organization for Migration, https://publications.iom.int/system/files/pdf/avrr_handbook.pdf (accessed 28 February 2021).
IOM (2013b) *World Migration Report 2013*, Geneva: International Organization for Migration, https://publications.iom.int/system/files/pdf/wmr2013_en.pdf (accessed 28 February 2021).
IOM (2014) *Challenges in the Reintegration of Return Migrants with Chronic Medical Conditions*, The Hague: International Organization for Migration, https://publications.iom.int/system/files/pdf/country_assessment_challenges_of_reintegration.pdf (accessed 28 February 2021).
IOM (2015) *Reintegration: Effective Approaches*, Geneva: International Organization for Migration, https://www.iom.int/files/live/sites/iom/files/What-We-Do/docs/Reintegration-Position-Paper-final.pdf (accessed 28 February 2021).
IOM (2017a) *Towards an Integrated Approach to Reintegration in the Context of Return*, Geneva: International Organization for Migration, https://www.iom.int/sites/default/files/our_work/DMM/AVRR/Towards-an-Integrated-Approach-to-Reintegration.pdf (accessed 28 February 2021).
IOM (2017b) *Enhancing Migrant Well-Being Upon Return Through an Integrated Approach to Reintegration*, Geneva: International Organization for Migration, https://www.iom.int/sites/default/files/our_work/ODG/GCM/IOM-Thematic-Paper-Integrated-Approach-to-Reintegration.pdf (accessed 28 February 2021).
IOM (2018a) *A Framework for Assisted Voluntary Return and Reintegration*, Geneva: International Organization for Migration, https://publications.iom.int/system/files/pdf/a_framework_for_avrr_en.pdf (accessed 28 February 2021).

IOM (2018b) *AVRR 2017 Key Highlights*, Geneva: International Organization for Migration, https://www.iom.int/sites/default/files/our_work/DMM/AVRR/avrr-2017-key-highlights.pdf (accessed 28 February 2021).

IOM (2018c) *A Framework for Assisted Voluntary Return and Reintegration and Indicators for Measuring Sustainable Reintegration*, Geneva: International Organization for Migration, https://governingbodies.iom.int/system/files/en/scpf/23rd/S-23-6%20-%20A%20framework%20for%20assisted%20voluntary%20return%20and%20reintegration%20and%20indicators%20for%20measuring%20sustainable%20reintegration.pdf (accessed 28 February 2021).

IOM (2019a) *Reintegration Handbook*, Geneva: International Organization for Migration, https://publications.iom.int/system/files/pdf/iom_reintegration_handbook.pdf (accessed 28 February 2021).

IOM (2019b) *2018 Return and Reintegration Highlights*, Geneva: International Organization for Migration, https://publications.iom.int/system/files/pdf/avrr_2018_kh.pdf (accessed 28 February 2021).

IOM (2019c) *Biannual Reintegration Report*, Geneva: International Organization for Migration, https://ec.europa.eu/trustfundforafrica/sites/euetfa/files/eu-iom-ji_cartographie_reintegration_report.pdf (accessed 28 February 2021).

IOM (2019d) *Report on a Reintegration Sustainability Survey among Voluntary Returnees from Finland*, Geneva: International Organization for Migration, https://migri.fi/documents/5202425/0/2019-10-29+IOM+Finland_Monitoring+Report_Auda.pdf/4e072ae6-0bbf-4014-3079-3386efe4a086/2019-10-29+IOM+Finland_Monitoring+Report_Auda.pdf (accessed 28 February 2021).

Jeffery, L. and Murison, J. (2011) 'The temporal, social, spatial, and legal dimensions of return and onward migration', *Population, Space and Place*, **17** (2), 131–9.

Koser, K. (2001) *The Return and Reintegration of Rejected Asylum Seekers and Irregular Migrants*, Geneva: International Organization for Migration, https://publications.iom.int/system/files/pdf/mrs_4_0.pdf (accessed 28 February 2021).

Koser, K. and Kuschminder, K. (2015) *Comparative Research on the Assisted Voluntary Return and Reintegration of Migrants*, Geneva: International Organization for Migration, https://www.iom.int/files/live/sites/iom/files/What-We-Do/docs/AVRR-Research-final.pdf (accessed 28 February 2021).

Kuschminder, K. (2017) *Taking Stock of Assisted Voluntary Return from Europe. Decision-Making, Reintegration and Sustainable Return: Time for a Paradigm Shift*, Florence: European University Institute, http://hdl.handle.net/1814/47064 (accessed 28 February 2021).

Lietaert, I. and Van Gorp, L. (2019) 'Talking across borders: successful re-entry in different strands of re-entry literature', *International Migration*, **57** (4), 105–20.

Lietaert, I., Broekaert, E. and Derluyn, I. (2017) 'The boundaries of transnationalism: the case of assisted voluntary return migrants', *Global Networks*, **17** (3), 366–81.

Luke, T.W. (2005) 'Neither sustainable nor development: reconsidering sustainability in development', *Sustainable Development*, **13** (4), 228–38.

Macrae, J. (1999) *Aiding Peace ... and War: UNHCR, Returnee Reintegration, and the Relief–Development Debate*, Geneva: UNHCR, https://www.odi.org/sites/odi.org.uk/files/odi-assets/publications-opinion-files/4967.pdf (accessed 28 February 2021).

Majidi, N. and Nozarian, N. (2019) 'Measuring sustainable reintegration', *Migration Policy Practice*, **9** (1), 30–9.

Mesić, M. and Bagić, D. (2010) 'Serb returnees in Croatia: the question of return sustainability', *International Migration*, **48** (2), 133–60.

Mommers, C., Eijkhout, H., Iyamuremye, P. and Maiyo, J. (2009) *Health, Hope and Home? The Possibilities and Constraints of Voluntary Return for African Rejected Asylum Seekers and Irregular Migrants Living with HIV in the Netherlands*, The Hague: International Organization for Migration, https://migrationhealthresearch.iom.int/health-hope-and-home-possibilities-and-constraints-voluntary-return-african-rejected-asylum-seekers (accessed 28 February 2021).

National Contact Point Austria (2006) *Return Migration in Austria*, Vienna: International Organization for Migration and European Migration Network, https://www.emn.at/wp-content/uploads/2017/01/PS_III_Return_FINAL_ENG_lr.pdf (accessed 28 February 2021).

Nay, O. (2014) 'International organisations and the production of hegemonic knowledge: how the World Bank and the OECD helped invent the Fragile State Concept', *Third World Quarterly*, **35** (2), 210–31.

Oelgemöller, C. (2017) *The Evolution of Migration Management in the Global North*, London: Routledge.

Official Journal of the European Union (2008) *Directive 2008/115/EC of the European Parliament and of The Council on Common Standards and Procedures in Member States for Returning Illegally Staying Third-Country Nationals*, https://eur-lex.europa.eu/LexUriServ/LexUriServ.do?uri=OJ:L:2008:348:0098:0107:EN:PDF (accessed 27 February 2021).

OHR (1999) *RRTF Action Plan*, Sarajevo: Office of the High Representative, http://www.ohr.int/?ohr_archive=1999-rrtf-action-plan (accessed 28 February 2021).

Özerdem, A. and Payne, L. (2019) 'Ethnic minorities and sustainable refugee return and reintegration in Kosovo', *Conflict, Security and Development*, **19** (4), 403–25.

Pécoud, A. (2015) *Depoliticising Migration. Global Governance and International Migration Narratives*, Basingstoke: Palgrave Macmillan.

Ratner, B.D (2004) '"Sustainability" as a dialogue of values: challenges to the sociology of development', *Sociological Inquiry*, **74** (1), 50–69.

Rogers, R. (1981) 'Incentives to return: patterns of policies and migrants' responses', *International Migration Review*, **15** (1S), 338–413.

Ruben, R., van Houte, M. and Davids, T. (2009) 'What determines the embeddedness of forced-return migrants? Rethinking the role of pre- and post-return assistance', *International Migration Review*, **43** (4), 908–37.

Samuel Hall and IOM (2017) *Setting Standards for an Integrated Approach to Reintegration*, Geneva: International Organization for Migration, https://www.iom.int/sites/default/files/our_work/DMM/AVRR/IOM_SAMUEL_HALL_MEASURE_REPORT%202017.pdf (accessed 28 February 2021).

Schinkel, W. (2018) 'Against "immigrant integration": for an end to neocolonial knowledge production', *Comparative Migration Studies*, **6** (31), 1–17.

Slominski, P. and Trauner, F. (2018) 'How do member states return unwanted migrants? The strategic (non-)use of "Europe" during the migration crisis', *Journal of Common Market Studies*, **56** (1), 101–18.

Stepputat, F. (2004) *Dynamics of Return and Sustainable Reintegration in a 'Mobile-Livelihoods' Perspective*, Copenhagen: Danish Institute for International Studies Working Paper No. 10, https://www.files.ethz.ch/isn/18448/Dynamics_of%20_Return.pdf (accessed 28 February 2021).

Strachan, A.L. (2019) *Reintegration of Returnees*, Brighton: Institute of Development Studies, https://www.gov.uk/dfid-research-outputs/reintegration-of-returnees (accessed 28 February 2021).

Strand, A. and Aalen, L. (2016) *Programmes for Assisted Return to Afghanistan, Iraqi Kurdistan, Ethiopia and Kosovo: A Comparative Evaluation of Effectiveness and Outcomes*, Bergen: Chr. Michelsen Institute, https://www.cmi.no/publications/5801-programmes-for-assisted-return-to-afghanistan#author-details (accessed 28 February 2021).

Strand, A., Wimpelmann, T. and Suhrke, A. (2008) *Return with Dignity, Return to What? Review of the Voluntary Return Programme to Afghanistan*, Bergen: Chr. Michelsen Institute, https://www.cmi.no/publications/3055-return-with-dignity-return-to-what (accessed 28 February 2021).

UNHCR (1997a) *Review of UNHCR's Phase-Out Strategies: Case Studies in Selected Countries of Origin*, Geneva: United Nations High Commissioner for Refugees, https://www.unhcr.org/research/evalreports/3ae6bd448/review-unhcrs-phase-out-strategies-case-studies-selected-countries-origin.html (accessed 28 February 2021).

UNHCR (1997b) *Reintegration in the Transition from War to Peace*, Geneva: United Nations High Commissioner for Refugees, https://www.refworld.org/pdfid/3ae6b31f8.pdf (accessed 28 February 2021).

UNHCR (2001) *Refugee Protection and Migration Control: Perspectives from UNHCR and IOM*, Geneva: United Nations High Commissioner for Refugees, https://www.unhcr.org/3b3892256.pdf (accessed 28 February 2021).

UNHCR (2004) *Handbook for Repatriation and Reintegration Activities*, Geneva: United Nations High Commissioner for Refugees, https://www.unhcr.org/411786694.pdf (accessed 28 February 2021).

UNMIK (2003) *Manual for Sustainable Return*, Pristina: United Nations Interim Administration Mission in Kosovo, https://reliefweb.int/sites/reliefweb.int/files/resources/A5C2DEEB4D4222C3C1256DDC0034CB9E-Refugees_UNMIK_January03.pdf (accessed 28 February 2021).

van Houte, M. and Davids, T. (2008) 'Development and return migration: from policy panacea to migrant perspective sustainability', *Third World Quarterly*, **29** (7), 1411–29.
van Houte, M. and de Koning, M. (2008) *Towards a Better Embeddedness? Monitoring Assistance to Involuntary Returning Migrants from Western Countries*, Geneva: International Organization for Migration, https://returnandreintegration.iom.int/en/resources/report/towards-better-embeddedness-monitoring-assistance-involuntary-returning-migrants (accessed 28 February 2021).
Van Wijk, J. (2010) *European Cooperation on the Sustainable Return and Reintegration of Asylum Seekers*, Vught: HIT Foundation, http://hitfoundation.eu/docs/EU_Cooperation_Return_final_report.pdf (accessed 27 February 2021).
Whyte, Z. and Hirslund, D.V. (2013) *International Experiences with the Sustainable Assisted Return of Rejected Asylum Seekers*, Copenhagen: Danish Institute for International Studies, https://www.diis.dk/files/media/publications/import/extra/rp2013-13-sustainable-assisted-return_web.jpg.pdf (accessed 28 February 2021).
Williams, R.C. (2006) 'The significance of property restitution to sustainable return in Bosnia and Herzegovina', *International Migration*, **44** (6), 40–61.

# 13. Corruption and return migration
### Erlend Paasche

## INTRODUCTION

This chapter proceeds from the observation that corruption is a structural force that has not received the scholarly interest it merits in the study of return migration. Overall, the estimated number of international migrants in 2019 was 272 million (UN DESA, 2019a, 2019b). Even as an approximate figure, this would indicate that a large chunk of the world's population relates to return to the country of origin as a possible future scenario. For some, return will be no more than a theoretical possibility. For others, return visits or more long-term return journeys 'home' will bring opportunities and challenges alike. Yet one thing is fairly certain. Where the 'home country' that they will return to is significantly more corrupt than the country of residence from which they return, corruption is likely to play a role in structuring the opportunities available and the obstacles to seizing them.

Of those 272 million international migrants, we can presume that more than three quarters go to a country with a higher level of human development than their country of origin (UNDP, 2009, p.2). Countries with lower levels of human development tend to have higher levels of corruption (Akçay, 2006, p.46) – to the extent that perceptions and experiences of corruption can be measured. If we accept this premise, the logical corollary, put very simply, is that most international return migrants will go back from a relatively less corrupt host state to a relatively more corrupt origin state.

The state level of analysis is not always the most meaningful for migrant-centric analysis. For instance, a trafficked Bangladeshi labour migrant working in the UK's informal sector may not perceive the country as a beacon of transparent accountability. Vice versa, a migrant from sub-Saharan Africa may cherish the lack of brown envelopes in London without being aware that hundreds of billions of dirty pounds are whitewashed on an annual basis through British banks by cartels, mafias and kleptocrats. Both examples illustrate the pitfalls of sweeping generalisations. At the same time, it would be misguided to overlook the 'transparency gap' that migrants cross – so rarely foregrounded in the scholarly treatment of return migration – and the labels we use routinely to define countries and contexts of return are not much better, just more common.

It is quite common for migration scholars to speak of origin states as 'conflict affected', 'developing' or 'low-income'. By contrast, it is exceedingly rare to see a migrant-producing state described as 'endemically corrupt', even in cases where this would be accurate. The way we, as migration scholars, frame the countries and places which we study inescapably sensitises us to certain structural features rather than others, of course. The point here is that migration scholars have not historically been very tuned in to corruption as a structural force that governs return migration – from return decision-making to reintegration dimensions and outcomes. It is an innovative perspective which opens up, for some, new and interesting perspectives in a field where studies have mushroomed over recent decades and old wine has filled new bottles.

Corruption exists everywhere but takes various forms and is not uniformly distributed. This chapter will explore corruption as a phenomenon which has received little scholarly attention in the study of return migration yet is, in fact, closely intertwined with it. The next section will first briefly sketch out what corruption is. Then I examine the various ways in which it features in the study of return migration. The conclusion summarises the key points of the chapter and draws together some implications for the field of return studies.

## CORRUPTION: DEFINITIONS AND DEBATES

Corruption comes with heavily normative connotations that complicate analytical definitions. This is partly because it is associated with immorality and partly because it is believed to have a pernicious impact on development and democracy. It is known, for instance, to disproportionately incur social, political and economic costs for those who do not benefit from it (OECD, 2014). Corrupt acts of bribery, embezzlement, nepotism and state capture increase the cost of doing business and distort markets, lead to waste or inefficient use of public resources, exclude poor people from public services, perpetuate poverty, corrode public trust, undermine the rule of law and ultimately delegitimise the state (OECD, 2014; Rothstein and Uslaner, 2005; World Bank, 2020).

A distinction is often made between grand and petty corruption. The former tends to involve decision-makers and huge sums of money, often changing hands behind closed doors. Ordinary people more often engage in petty corruption, such as bribing officials with small sums of money to navigate bureaucracy and cut red tape. Yet that distinction is far from a definition and the debate is not settled. One long-standing definition that covers both grand and petty corruption is that of political scientist Nye (1967, p.419), who defines it thus:

> Corruption is behavior which deviates from the formal duties of a public role because of private-regarding (personal, close family, private clique) pecuniary or status gains; or violates rules against the exercise of certain types of private-regarding influence. This includes such behavior as [bribery, nepotism and misappropriation].

Two strands of corruption research have expressly built on this definition, which seemingly takes for granted a clear distinction between private and public roles and spheres. First, there are rational-actor models that emphasise individual costs and benefits. Second, there are structural models that examine external factors such as public sector size, the lootability of resources, hydrocarbons and policies, while couching corruption in a correlational logic and studying it through large-n data sets and cross-country comparisons.

Policy definitions tend to be shorter. The non-governmental organisation Transparency International defines corruption more simplistically as 'the abuse of entrusted power for private gain', a definition adopted by the World Bank and others. This widely adopted definition, however neat, is not always easily applicable in the plethora of political, social and cultural contexts in which said 'abuse' takes place. It generally works less well, for instance, in contexts where corruption can be said to be 'endemic' rather than 'incidental'. Similar to the distinction between grand and petty corruption, this is a crude conceptual distinction rather than a quantitative one. It does not rely on prevalence alone but on whether or not a norm of legal-rational authority is strong or weak (Lovell, 2005). If the norm is strong, the social costs of corruption are higher and sanctions for transgressions are more likely. If it is weak, the social costs are lower, at times lower than for non-corrupt behaviour, as corruption becomes more easily justifiable and less risky to the individual – who may, nonetheless, condemn it as a societal phenomenon.

What a corrupt transaction is, in other words, depends in part on the normative context in which it takes place – which in turn means that there are cultural isomorphisms at play and that agents of corruption may face normative ambiguity. Individuals and institutions alike face dilemmas, for instance where norms of transparency and role-fulfilment clash with the principle of in-group solidarity. Norms compete, as the norm of legal-rational authority often does with the norm of helping dear ones. Red tape and low salaries can easily compound the dilemma for potential agents of corruption. This is the premise for the anthropologist de Sardan's (1999) definition of a 'corruption complex', in which corruption is culturally embedded in a moral economy. Here, it includes not only bribery, nepotism and misappropriation – as in Nye's definition – but also abuse of power more broadly, as well as embezzlement, influence-peddling, prevarication, insider trading and abuse of the public purse (de Sardan, 1999, p.29). Such a definition of corruption, broad yet disaggregated, seems particularly relevant in contexts where simplistic policy definitions fail. More precisely, it seems particularly apt in contexts where corruption is endemic, boundaries between public and private spheres blur and legal-rational institutions weave seamlessly into neopatrimonial informality (Paasche, 2016).

How, then, do migrants experience the dramatic changes in their normative environment when they return from settings where the abuse of entrusted power is incidental, to settings where it is endemic? How does corruption affect return and vice versa? An embryonic literature offers some tentative answers.

## CORRUPTION IN THE STUDY OF RETURN MIGRATION

While incidental corruption may be more of an isolated 'factor' in returnees' lives, returning to a 'corruption complex' means returning to a place where corruption is ingrained into everyday life and the very fabric of society. If this is a 'factor' it is one that conditions many other factors. It may be more productive, however, to think of it as integral to the *framework* for returnees' post-return lives rather than as a *factor* in them.

It is interesting, then, that the classic literature on the study of return (e.g. Ghosh, 2000; Koser and Black, 1999; Long and Oxfeld, 2004; Markowitz and Stefansson, 2004) hardly considers it. The same largely applies for return studies more broadly. In an earlier article (Paasche, 2016) I reviewed 819 broad-spanning academic studies on return and reintegration, identified from a systematic bibliography on return (Carling et al., 2011). None of them foregrounded corruption for structured analysis. Several underlined its relevance but typically without using the conceptual toolkit of corruption studies. Few demonstrated any kind of analytical ambitions of teasing out the theoretical implications.

### Corruption and Return Decision-making

Some scholars find that corruption affects return decision-making in the diaspora. For instance, one study found that refugees interviewed in the UK cited the corruption they encounter upon return visits as a reason not to return permanently. Yet this analytical observation, largely unexplored in the study of return decision-making, was merely mentioned in passing (Muggeridge and Doná, 2006). In another study, in which corruption is alluded to rather than singled out for study, even the thought of corruption deters the diaspora from considering return. Tsuda (2009) describes how Japanese-Brazilian migrants in Japan could not be incentivised to return by government reforms in Brazil during the late 1990s because corruption was perceived as too entrenched and the reforms as too little too late and lacking credibility. In general, the government needs to build trust in such contexts, both through and in addition to reforms, if they want to attract diasporic return and investment. King and Vullnetari's (2009) recommendation that policy-makers in Kosovo do so could easily be transferable to most post-conflict settings.

Other studies have found corruption to affect return decision-making during visits home. Oeppen's (2009, p.159) interviews with Afghan returnee visitors from the United States in the late 2000s interestingly suggested that 'corruption was one of the most commonly given reasons as to why they had not stayed longer [in Afghanistan], even more so than insecurity'. This finding – quite surprising given Afghanistan's violent imbroglio at the time – is not dwelled upon. What does come across in Oeppen's (2009) study is that corruption appears to affect return not so much in the abstract realm of political preferences as through corruption's tangible and mundane effects on everyday life. Corruption deters return through acting as a time-consuming bureaucratic obstacle for returnees who intended to set up humanitarian projects, establish a business, sell land or work with the government.

## CORRUPTION AND RETURNEES' PSYCHOSOCIAL REINTEGRATION

Anthropological research, while wary of portraying corruption as a pathology of the Other, confirms that corruption has different social meanings in different social models (Blundo and de Sardan, 2006; Haller and Shore, 2005; Smith, 2008). Migrants traverse social models which differ in their norms, institutions, organisations and values (Collier, 2013), at times to such an extent that it is hard for migrants to adapt while maintaining a coherent and positive sense of self. While the psychosocial dimension of reintegration remains generally understudied, there is even less knowledge about the role which corruption differentials play in 'the sociocultural dissonance that return exposes' (Vathi, 2017, p.2). For returnees who move back from incidentally to endemically corrupt settings, however, corruption has been found to affect psychosocial wellbeing.

As Pedersen (2003) points out, places are always defined – and sometimes idealised – in relation to each other. For Lebanese returnees going back after a bloody civil war, the Northern European state in which they had sought refuge 'came to symbolize a political system devoid of the corruption and clientelism that is so widespread in Lebanon' (Pedersen, 2003, p.37). Pedersen's study only briefly considers the impact of corruption on the fluid and ambiguous identity of the returnees she interviews but it is enough to demonstrate why this is a worthwhile undertaking.

One of returnees' predicaments is that they may well themselves have internalised a strong norm of legal-rational authority during a prolonged stay abroad (or, indeed, even before their departure) but return to find themselves in a context where the norm is weak. In the expansive sense of the term 'return', second-generation 'returnees' offer an illustrative glimpse into what this means. Based on more than 50 semi-structured interviews in Germany and Greece, Christou and King (2010, p.643, my emphasis) note that:

> Virtually all our second-generation 'returnees' told similar stories of the objective difficulties of living in Greece, where chaos, corruption, rudeness and clientilism frustrate so many aspects of life (not least finding a decent job), and *are contrasted* with the order, efficiency, politeness and meritocracy of society in Germany.

While second-generation returnees are analytically somewhat distinct from other returnees, this quote illustrates how the 'here' and 'there' are co-constructed through a bifurcated lens. In general, the bifurcated lens through which returnees experience their place of origin, relative to their place of (former) residence, appears to de-naturalise corruption and intensify it as *relative* to the lived experience of democratic accountability. One need not have travelled to or lived in a liberal democracy to become sensitive to corruption or recognise that systematic differences in governance exist across and within different parts of the world. Yet the journey across social models and back can easily alter one's perspective of corruption – and tolerance of it. Using Appadurai's (2004) terms, returnees may have developed, through personal exposure to a different social model, 'a capacity to aspire' for democratically accountable transparency, in a way that many non-returnees do not.

My own case study of Iraqi Kurdish returnees going back from Europe (Paasche, 2016) demonstrates linkages between the capacity to aspire for accountability and the psychosocial costs of frustration with corruption. Psychosocially, corruption was said to alienate interviewees from the ideology of the Kurdish nation-building project, challenge their identities as law-abiding citizens committed to collective values and undermine their sense of belonging and security. The idea of kleptocratic political elites and state capture did not square well with the idea of returning to help in the process of state-building with foreign-earned skills, capitals and ideas. Moreover, in a small, landlocked quasi-autonomous country with a history of victimisation and wedged in between powerful autocracies like Iran, Turkey, and Iraq, returnees' low trust in the national leadership did not inspire confidence in the future (Paasche, 2016).

## Corruption and Economic Reintegration

For the Iraqi Kurds I interviewed at the height of an oil-fuelled boom in Iraqi Kurdistan, corruption was often described as a major practical obstacle to their economic reintegration. Corruption was said to obstruct entrepreneurship, to produce a widespread sense of relative deprivation in spite of general economic progress and to determine employability in non-meritocratic ways that offered a highly uncertain premium on foreign-earned skills. Corrupt bureaucrats with ties to the dominant political parties had immense power, in returnees' narratives, to either prevent start-ups from being able to compete with oligarchic monopolies or to allow entrepreneurship in exchange for a percentage of the profit. Employability was described as contingent on good relations with the political parties, which had been at war with each other during the 1990s and subsequently transitioned into powerful patrons whose control of the formal and informal economy was near hegemonic. The dampening effect of corruption on entrepreneurship in general has been examined in a number of studies (e.g. Anokhin and Schulze, 2009; Avnimelech et al., 2014; Dutta and Sobel, 2016). It is less explored in the study of return migration, even though returnees have long been known for their engagement in entrepreneurship (King, 2000; see also Sinatti, Chapter 24).

Returnees are often eager to invest in a business as a marker of their newfound social status. A lucrative business is a good, visible and profitable symbol of successful migration and return. International migrants are known for being more prone to risk-taking. Returnees who have accumulated capital and skills abroad are often celebrated as agents of development by scholars and policy-makers alike. It is commonly thought that they can stimulate local and national economies through their entrepreneurship and foment innovation and trade through transnational social networks. Yet any discussion of returnees' contribution to economic growth and development must factor in the intermediate and typically constraining effect of corruption, as I noted in Paasche (2016, p.1086).

First, corruption can quash the feasibility and rewards of entrepreneurship. Second, in a highly corrupt environment, entrepreneurship can take the shape of unproductive rent-seeking, here understood simply as any redistributive activity that takes up resources. Rent-seeking is not necessarily illegal, but endemic corruption breeds strong incentives for government bureaucrats to abuse their entrusted discretionary power to extract rent from the private sector. Monopolies and demands for bribes are especially hurtful to entrepreneurs in the process of establishing businesses.

If endemically corrupt emigration countries want returnees to serve as agents of development, it is not enough to build trust through confidence-building measures alone. The policy of capitalising economically on return migration in places of endemic corruption will have to overlap with anti-corruption reforms and checks and controls to prevent returnee entrepreneurs from being exploited through extortive practices by corrupt actors.

## CORRUPTION AND SOCIAL REMITTANCES

Staying in Iraqi Kurdistan for a third topic, I also explored whether or not Iraqi Kurdish returnees could bring back a kind of 'social remittance' that could affect non-migrants' understandings and experiences of corruption (Paasche, 2017). The term social remittances was pioneered by Levitt (1998) at a time when the developmental impact of economic remittances was high on the migration research agenda. Emphasising transnational flows between migrants and non-migrants in a shared social space, Levitt referred to the norms, values, identities and social capital that migrants 'remit' to non-migrants. A substantial literature subsequently examined social remittances on the more-or-less explicit premise that return migrants from the global North to the South could have a positive impact on local development and democratisation (e.g. Jones, 2011; Levitt and Lamba-Nieves, 2011; Levitt and Nyberg-Sørensen, 2004).

In my study I found that the returnees I interviewed certainly tended to express frustration with corruption and view themselves as potential agents of transparency and democratisation. This was unsurprising, as returnees often do (King, 2000). Yet their aspiration to 'socially remit' their perspectives on the pernicious impact of corruption in Iraqi Kurdistan – the rewards of transparency and the need for reforms – was not matched by their ability to do so. As one of my interviewees put it, no reintegration was possible in the absence of client–patron relationships.

> The corruption here, it's so high. Whatever you do, you cannot defeat it. There are a few people [in the diaspora]. They go there with a very good idea, to establish a new life there, to give something to the community in a good way that serves people there. They can't. The political parties there, the

government, they don't allow these people to go there unless they [profit from it themselves]. You have to join them. You have to work for them.

Such a resigned narrative resonated with the data overall. Most interviewees stressed their limited ability to speak freely on the subject matter with non-migrants and the lack of space for critical dissent – for a lack of shared cultural and political references, fears of being dismissed as arrogant Westerners and the fear of reprisals from a kleptocratic political elite. While there are more foundational conceptual flaws in the concept of 'social remittances' (see Paasche, 2017), the point here is merely to nuance the notion of returnees as agents of anti-corruption.

## Corruption and Health Services

Corruption has also been found to obstruct returnees' access to basic health services. This is a largely unstudied field, but Neerup Handlos et al. (2016) found, on the basis of semi-structured interviews with 33 refugee returnees going back from Denmark to Bosnia, that corruption seriously affected returnees' health. They struggled to obtain health care at affordable prices because 'doctors considered them to be better endowed financially [than they were] and therefore demanded larger bribes from them than they did from those who had remained in Bosnia' (2016, p.924). This was not exclusively a question of financial capital either, as the authors observe that returnees had lost the social capital that could have helped them sidestep the corruption.

> Only a minority of the returnees interviewed in this study knew anyone in the healthcare system they could ask for favors, and they therefore only rarely benefitted from special treatment from friends or relatives. On the contrary, they were at a disadvantage compared to individuals who had not been away from the country. During their long period of absence from the country, many returnees lost the connections they had had before they left Bosnia. (Neerup Handlos et al., 2016, p.931)

The study is instructive in the sense that it demonstrates how social capital and economic capital intersect for these returnees. They navigate health care systems which they do not understand and are expected to pay for services with money they do not have. More broadly, different 'types' of migrants return home with different types of health need (Davies et al., 2011). Marginalised migrants who have acquired unhealthy lifestyles abroad without accumulating wealth may well face a predicament similar to these Bosnian refugee returns, whereas healthy retired professionals with dual residency can re-return for treatment in a more transparent economy where medicines are more quality-controlled and medical qualifications are better certified.

## Corruption and the Assisted Return of Rejected Asylum-seekers

Rejected asylum-seekers and irregular migrants are increasingly incentivised to return within a context of coercion. While the increased emphasis on 'Assisted Voluntary Return Programmes' (here referred to as 'assisted return') is global, it is especially observable in Europe (see Lietaert, Chapter 8). Applicable across most of the continent, the European Return Directive (2008/115/EC) promotes the return of rejected asylum-seekers and, more specifically, the use of assisted-return programmes to facilitate return without the physical force applied in deportation (cf. Desmond, Chapter 10). These programmes typically offer transport free of charge, pre-departure counselling and a modicum of cash and/or in-kind assistance (e.g. offering material support for business start-ups, subsidised job placement or vocational training) in the country of citizenship. In Europe, the main implementing partner for assisted return is the International Organization for Migration (IOM).

Corruption and its conceptual twin, anti-corruption, are almost completely overlooked in the study of assisted return and are urgently in need of more scholarly attention. Ambitious programmes that promise rejected asylum-seekers 'tailor-made' and 'individualised' in-kind support upon their return are implemented in asylum-producing states – that is, operational environments that, for the most part, tend to be characterised by high levels of corruption. Endemic corruption *directly* represents a challenge to these programmes' uptake and performance.

Regarding the uptake in assisted return, one unpublished study (Paasche and Leerkes, under review) finds that high levels of perceived corruption in origin countries do have an impact and that this impact is variegated across distinct demographics and conditional on certain migrant characteristics. Regarding programme performance, endemic corruption imposes obvious in-house risks of fraudulent practice within the IOM and other service-providing agencies (Paasche, 2018). More specifically, corruption directly affects programme design. According to an Organisation for Economic Co-operation and Development (OECD) study, cash could theoretically be more appropriate in some contexts (OECD, 2020, p.55) yet could also be seen as putting the returnee at risk from criminals or corrupt officials if it is known that they carry large sums with them on return or will receive cash transfers in the following months (OECD, 2020, p.54).

Less obviously, such service-providers have introduced a number of anti-corruption mechanisms to prevent returnees from engaging in fraudulent practices – which also challenges programme performance (Paasche, 2018). Returnees entitled to in-kind assistance to establish a business, for instance, need to produce substantial paperwork. This may include business plans, tenancy agreements, contracts with eventual business partners, licences and certificates, as well as three quotes from suppliers invited into a competitive bidding process (Paasche, 2018; see also Paasche et al., 2016). In theory, such measures reduce the risk of fraud. One study (Strand et al., 2011; see also Strand et al., 2016), however, found that returnees with little business experience, limited motivation and little education who try to navigate in an informal economy were easily confused and frustrated by formalistic procedures. Ironically, this was observed to give rise to rumours of in-house corruption among returnees, transnationalised through migrant networks as part of a feedback loop which, in turn, may have undermined programme uptake and performance.

## DISAGGREGATING CORRUPTION AND RETURN

The focus thus far has predominantly been on the return of refugees and rejected asylum-seekers. While an exhaustive treatment of all 'types' of return and all 'types' of corruption is beyond the scope of this chapter, I started this latter with the critique that migration scholars have not historically been very sensitised to corruption as a structural force that governs return migration. If this is correct, it is perhaps useful to present a couple of contexts of return in which corruption is particularly likely to merit scholarly attention quite irrespective of legal-bureaucratic categories.

First, scholars of return should be sensitive to country-level structural features that are associated with corruption. Corruption is, for instance, more likely to be endemic in conflict-affected states. Post-conflict return tends to take place amidst post-conflict corruption. Corruption thrives in post-conflict settings where weak states rarely commit to sanction illicit transactions and may well weaken further if they do. Conflict tends to reduce the state's ability to regulate markets, among other things by straining resources, debilitating public institutions and corroding the social structures, sense of shared identity and trust that bind individuals together (Van Hear and McDowell, 2006; World Bank, 2011). Corruption is often systemic in such contexts. This can partly be attributable to the inflow of foreign aid (Billon, 2008). More fundamentally, corruption tends to become systemic because the informal actors and structures 'which precede and/or emerge during the conflict (such as tribal or clan structures, war lords, and criminal and smuggling networks), ... both complement and compete with formal institutions' during the post-conflict phase (Berdal and Zaum, 2013, p.5). When returnees in post-conflict contexts refer to 'the system', such analytical observations can and should help to give meaning to that term.

Second, the origin country's political economy also matters in other ways, absent conflict. Economies that are predominantly based on natural resources, for instance, are statistically associated with higher levels of corruption. There are various possible causal pathways for this. Some studies highlight the 'resource curse' (e.g. Dimant et al., 2013), whereby an abundance of natural resources and inadequate governmental checks and balances 'leave room for favoritism, clientilism, political capture and interference, conflict of interest, bribery and other corrupt practices' (OECD, 2016, p.15). Entrepreneurial activity tends to gravitate towards unproductive rent-seeking in economies which, in turn, breeds strong incentives for public officials to abuse their entrusted power to extract rent from entrepreneurs (Murphy et al., 1993).

Other studies highlight the 'rentier state theory', which posits that corruption and authoritarianism are inherent to the rentier political economy because governments use abundant resources, such as oil, to co-opt opposition through patronage or repress it with authoritarian measures (Basedau and Lay, 2009). Both of these causal accounts receive mixed support in empirical studies but the correlation between hydrocarbons and other extractive industries with corruption is clear. The question for migration scholars, largely ignored, is how 'homecoming' to hydrocarbons affects reintegration. How does it condition entrepreneurship, for instance, to which we know that returnees are prone?

Studies of return migration to post-conflict and naturally resource-rich states could meaningfully draw on the political-science literature on corruption for contextual understanding and informed research questions. Now, turning the analytical focus onto the returnees themselves, which of their characteristics are likely to condition their return and encounters with corruption? Clearly it matters whether you have been able to return with accumulated wealth that enables you to buy your way in or whether you go back empty-handed as a rejected asylum-seeker or a victim of trafficking. Moving beyond resources accumulated abroad and the legal category of migration aside, two frequently overlapping themes will suffice here.

First, *duration of absence* is probably one key factor, as alluded to above in the section on health and return. Reverse culture shocks describe the process of 'readjusting, reacculturating, and reassimilating' into the place left behind prior to a sojourn in far-away lands (Gaw, 2000, p.83). As the anthropological literature reminds us, the engagement with corruption is a particular kind of dance where the steps follow norms and rules. Knowledge of how bribes can be negotiated and through what cultural repertoire they can be countered makes it easier to navigate the personal and institutional landscape of corruption. Losing those skills can have pecuniary costs and, as discussed in the section on psychosocial health, above, non-pecuniary costs.

Second, a related factor of significance could be the extent and nature of *transnational practices* while abroad. Duration of absence is not an absolute category but one that can be socially negotiated between migrants and non-migrants. The dual challenge of carving out a place for oneself in the host state while maintaining membership 'at home' is tricky but balancing the two can be a prerequisite for a successful future return. As Hernández-Carretero (2015, p.2036) puts it, migrants' pursuit of reconciling the two involves 'fixing remittances, limiting contact to reduce incoming requests or adapting the rhythm of return visits to balance social and financial priorities. These negotiation processes shape transnational social ties and migrants' ability to save and invest back home.' Corruption offers a prism on these negotiation processes, because opaquely imperfect markets in endemically corrupt states offer an uncertain premium on foreign-earned skills and capital alone. If employability and access to markets are conditional on having friends in high places, whether patrons in the bureaucracy or oligarchic cliques, access to those friends needs to be transnationally negotiated. In corrupt settings, 'woe betide the one who has no-one, either directly or indirectly' (de Sardan, 1999, p.41).

While there are undoubtedly other factors at play, including the usual suspects of age, gender and class, they represent some possible points of departure for theoretical advances in future studies of the role of corruption in return and reintegration. Notably this includes overly cheerful accounts of highly skilled and entrepreneurial returnees' developmental impacts, in systems that are not conducive to merit-based rewards.

## CONCLUSION: KEYWORDS, BUZZWORDS AND WAYS FORWARD

This chapter has proceeded from the observation that corruption is a structural force that has not received the scholarly interest it merits in the study of return migration. This should not be taken to mean that it is absent from the literature. What is lacking is in-depth treatment. Many refer to it quickly and in passing, but very few draw on the literature on corruption or use the conceptual and analytical toolkits it offers.

If one sees corruption as yet another isolated *factor* in 'returnees' lives, it does not necessarily merit more focused study than any of the other factors. However, as I argue above and as my empirical discussion has hopefully illustrated by now, there are often solid grounds for, instead, thinking of it as integral to the *framework* for return and reintegration. The brief empirical discussion I have sketched out here, much of it based on my own work, has included such phenomena as return decision-making, the psychosocial and economic dimensions of reintegration, the aspiration and ability to transmit social norms, ideas and practices to non-migrants, access to basic public goods exemplified by health services and return policies exemplified by assisted return.

This discussion hopefully serves to demonstrate the plethora of interlinkages at play in the nexus between corruption and return migration. Following the logic presented in this chapter, I posit that corruption above threshold values fundamentally conditions return patterns and reintegration outcomes, especially in cases where migrants return from a place where corruption is incidental to a place where it is endemic. It does so by shaping the pros and cons of return and by determining real-world success criteria beyond neoclassical economic theory and the new economics of labour migration (though the latter may more easily accommodate it). This is quite a paradigm shift, in a sense. It means that 'successful reintegration' may be elusive without successfully playing the game of corruption and that studies of return and reintegration in endemically corrupt places will hardly give a full account of the opportunities and challenges that return brings without looking at them through the looking-glass of corruption.

Corruption is a sensitive issue and intensely morally charged. Scholars have shied away from it on the basis that they do not want to pathologise countries where corruption is rife. One of the leading experts on corruption in Nigeria, for instance, acknowledges his reluctance to write *A Culture of Corruption* for fear of 'perpetuating common misrepresentations of Africa' (Smith, 2008, p.xii). Scholars interested in the corruption–migration nexus face a similar challenge and likewise need to bring analytical clarity and boldness to it. They should engage in careful self-reflection, read critical corruption studies for a dive into the politicisation of the term 'corruption' and the political economy in which it has emerged as a buzzword. They would be wise to avoid the pitfall of thinking that corruption is a problem of the non-Western world while also not denying that, where the Weberian norm of disinterested public scholars is weak, the norm of in-group solidarity is strong and corruption governs everyday life – an account of return that treats it as distinct from corruption will simply miss out.

The intense moral connotations to corruption can also mask the fact that some returnees benefit from it. We habitually think of corruption as something negative. Yet it may not be a bad thing by the individual returnee if there is big profit to be made from a small bribe or if a demanded favour or access to powerful patrons open up doors to better life chances. Social class patterns corruption's costs and benefits. In this sense, corruption is also a prism on inequality. Who enjoys more power, better social protection and access to counterstrategies may well be able to benefit more from systemic corruption than those who do not. Put bluntly, the rich are likelier to benefit from corruption, while the poor will more probably suffer from it. Wealth begets social capital, facilitating grand and petty corruption 'across explicit, formal or institutionalized power, or authority gradients in society' (Szreter and Woolcock, 2004, p.655). Gender is also highly relevant in this regard and offers a rich terrain for empirical and theoretical advances.

On a concluding note, corruption was never something I intended to study for its own sake. For me it has offered an interesting analytical toolkit, a stepping-stone to more migrant-centric perspectives and more innovative analytical approaches, which I find offer fuller accounts of the structural forces in migrants' lives and of the society and state in which these forces are embedded. The intersectional impact of corruption on migrants will depend on group-level and individual variables. Are they rich or poor? Men or women? Young or old? However, in many contexts, it will be profound. Corruption offers plenty for scholars of return migration to sink their teeth into.

## ACKNOWLEDGEMENT

This work was supported by the Research Council of Norway under the grant Research Programme on Welfare, Working Life and Migration (VAM) and through the project

Transnationalism from Above and Below: Migration Management and How Migrants Manage (MIGMA), project number 247622.

## REFERENCES

Akçay, C. (2006) 'Corruption and human development', *Cato Journal*, **26** (1), 29–48.
Anokhin, S. and Schulze, W.S. (2009) 'Entrepreneurship, innovation, and corruption', *Journal of Business Venturing*, **24** (5), 465–76.
Appadurai, A. (2004) 'The capacity to aspire: culture and the terms of recognition' in V. Rao and M. Walton (eds), *Culture and Public Action*, Palo Alto: Stanford University Press, pp. 59–84.
Avnimelech, G., Zelekha, Y. and Sharabi, E. (2014) 'The effect of corruption on entrepreneurship in developed vs non-developed countries', *International Journal of Entrepreneurial Behavior and Research*, **20** (3), 237–62.
Basedau, M. and Lay, J. (2009) 'Resource curse or rentier peace? The ambiguous effects of oil wealth and oil dependence on violent conflict', *Journal of Peace Research*, **46** (6), 757–76.
Berdal, M. and Zaum, D. (2013) 'Power after peace' in M. Berdal and D. Zaum (eds), *Political Economy of Statebuilding: Power after Peace*, London: Routledge, pp. 1–14.
Billon, P. (2008) 'Corrupting peace? Peacebuilding and post-conflict corruption', *International Peacekeeping*, **15** (3), 344–61.
Blundo, G. and de Sardan, J.-P.O. (2006) *Everyday Corruption and the State: Citizens and Public Officials in Africa*, London: Zed Books.
Carling, J., Mortensen, E.B. and Wu, J. (2011) *A Systematic Bibliography on Return Migration*, Oslo: Peace Research Institute Oslo (PRIO).
Christou, A. and King, R. (2010) 'Imagining "home": diasporic landscapes of the Greek-German second generation', *Geoforum*, **41** (4), 638–46.
Collier, P. (2013) *Exodus: How Migration Is Changing Our World*, New York: Oxford University Press.
Davies, A.A., Borland, R.M., Blake, C. and West, H.E. (2011) 'The dynamics of health and return migration', *PLoS Med*, **8** (6), e1001046.
de Sardan, J.-P.O. (1999) 'A moral economy of corruption in Africa', *The Journal of Modern African Studies*, **37** (1), 25–52.
Dimant, E., Krieger, T. and Meierrieks, D. (2013) 'The effect of corruption on migration, 1985–2000', *Applied Economics Letters*, **20** (13), 1270–4.
Dutta, N. and Sobel, R. (2016) 'Does corruption ever help entrepreneurship?', *Small Business Economics*, **47** (1), 179–99.
Gaw, K.F. (2000) 'Reverse culture shock in students returning from overseas', *International Journal of Intercultural Relations*, **24** (1), 83–104.
Ghosh, B. (2000) 'Return migration: reshaping policy approaches' in B. Ghosh (ed.), *Return Migration: Journey of Hope or Despair?*, Geneva: International Organization for Migration, pp. 181–226.
Haller, D. and Shore H. (eds) (2005) *Corruption: Anthropological Perspectives*, London: Pluto Press.
Hernández-Carretero, M. (2015) 'Renegotiating obligations through migration: Senegalese transnationalism and the quest for the right distance', *Journal of Ethnic and Migration Studies*, **41** (12), 2021–40.
Jones, R.C. (2011) 'The local economic imprint of return migrants in Bolivia', *Population, Space and Place*, **17** (5), 435–53.
King, R. (2000) 'Generalizations from the history of return migration' in B. Ghosh (ed.), *Return Migration: Journey of Hope or Despair?*, Geneva: International Organization for Migration, pp. 7–55.
King, R. and Vullnetari, J. (2009) 'Remittances, return, diaspora: framing the debate in the context of Albania and Kosova', *Southeast European and Black Sea Studies*, **9** (4), 385–406.
Koser, K. and Black, R. (1999) 'The end of the refugee cycle?' in R. Black and K. Koser (eds), *The End of the Refugee Cycle? Refugee Repatriation and Reconstruction*, New York: Berghahn, pp. 2–17.
Levitt, P. (1998) 'Social remittances: migration driven local-level forms of cultural diffusion', *International Migration Review*, **32** (4), 926–48.
Levitt, P. and Lamba-Nieves, D. (2011) 'Social remittances revisited', *Journal of Ethnic and Migration Studies*, **37** (1), 1–22.

Levitt, P. and Nyberg-Sørensen, N. (2004) *Global Migration Perspectives*, Geneva: Global Commission on International Migration, Working Paper No. 6.

Long, L.D. and Oxfeld, E. (eds) (2004) *Coming Home? Refugees, Migrants, and Those Who Stayed Behind*, Philadelphia: University of Pennsylvania Press.

Lovell, D.W. (2005) 'Corruption as a transitional phenomenon: understanding endemic corruption in postcommunist states' in D. Haller and H. Shore (eds), *Corruption: Anthropological Perspectives*, London: Pluto Press, pp. 65–83.

Markowitz, F. and Stefansson, A.H. (eds) (2004) *Homecomings: Unsettling Paths of Return*, Lanham MD: Lexington Books.

Muggeridge, H. and Doná, G. (2006) 'Back home? Refugees' experiences of their first visit back to their country of origin', *Journal of Refugee Studies*, **19** (4), 415–32.

Murphy, K.M., Schleifer, A. and Vishny, R.W. (1993) 'Why is rent-seeking so costly to growth?', *American Economic Review*, **83** (2), 409–14.

Neerup Handlos, L., Fog Olwig, K., Bygbjerg, I.C. and Norredam, M. (2016) 'Return migrants' experience of access to care in corrupt healthcare systems: the Bosnian example', *International Journal of Environmental Research and Public Health*, **13** (9), 924.

Nye, J.S. (1967) 'Corruption and political development: a cost–benefit analysis', *American Political Science Review*, **61** (2), 417–27.

OECD (2014) *The Rationale for Fighting Corruption: Background Brief*, Paris: OECD, https://maritimecyprus.files.wordpress.com/2017/09/oecd.pdf (accessed 3 April 2021).

OECD (2016) *Corruption in the Extractive Value Chain. Typology of Risks, Mitigation Measures and Incentives*, Paris: OECD, http://www.oecd.org/dev/Corruption-in-the-extractive-value-chain.pdf (accessed 3 April 2021).

OECD (2020) *Sustainable Reintegration of Returning Migrants: A Better Homecoming*, Paris: OECD, https://doi.org/10.1787/5fee55b3-en.

Oeppen, C. (2009) *A Stranger at Home: Integration, Transnationalism and the Afghan Elite*, Brighton: University of Sussex, unpublished PhD thesis.

Paasche, E. (2016) 'The role of corruption in reintegration: experiences of Iraqi Kurds upon return from Europe', *Journal of Ethnic and Migration Studies*, **42** (7), 1076–93.

Paasche, E. (2017) 'A conceptual and empirical critique of "social remittances": Iraqi Kurdish migrants narrate resistance' in M. Nowicka and V. Šerbedžija (eds), *Migration and Social Remittances in a Global Europe*, London: Palgrave Macmillan, pp. 121–41.

Paasche, E. (2018) *Corruption and Migrant Returns. Managing Risk in Assisted Return Programmes*, Oslo: U4 Anti-Corruption Resource Centre, Chr. Michelsen Institute (U4 Brief 2018: 1).

Paasche, E. and Leerkes, A. (under review) 'Corruption and assisted return from the Netherlands', unpublished manuscript.

Paasche, E., Plambech, S. and Skilbrei, M-L. (2016) *Assistert retur til Nigeria* [Assisted Return to Nigeria], Oslo: Department of Criminology and Sociology of Law, Faculty of Law, University of Oslo.

Pedersen, M.H. (2003) *Between Homes: Post-War Return, Emplacement and the Negotiation of Belonging in Lebanon*, Geneva: UNCHR, New Issues in Refugee Research Working Paper No. 79.

Rothstein, B. and Uslaner, E.M. (2005) 'All for all: equality, corruption, and social trust', *World Politics*, **58** (1), 41–72.

Smith, D.J. (2008) *A Culture of Corruption: Everyday Deception and Popular Discontent in Nigeria*, Princeton NJ: Princeton University Press.

Strand, A., Bendixsen, S., Paasche, E. and Schultz, J. (2011) *Between Two Societies Review of the Information, Return and Reintegration of Iraqi Nationals to Iraq (IRRINI) Programme*, Bergen: Chr. Michelsens Institutt.

Strand, A., Bendixsen, S., Lidèn, H., Paasche, E. and Aalen, L. (2016) *Programmes for Assisted Return to Afghanistan, Iraqi Kurdistan, Ethiopia and Kosovo*, Bergen: Chr. Michelsens Institutt.

Szreter, S. and Woolcock, M. (2004) 'Health by association? Social capital, social theory, and the political economy of public health', *International Journal of Epidemiology*, **33** (4), 650–67.

Tsuda, T. (2009) 'Introduction: diasporic return and migration studies' in T. Tsuda (ed.), *Diasporic Homecomings. Ethnic Return Migration in Comparative Perspective*, Stanford: Stanford University Press, pp. 1–18.

UN DESA (2019a) *International Migrant Stock 2019*, New York: United Nations Department of Economic and Social Affairs.
UN DESA (2019b) *World Population Prospects 2019 Highlights*, New York: United Nations Department of Economic and Social Affairs.
UNDP (2009) *Overcoming Barriers: Human Mobility and Development. Human Development Report*, New York: UNDP.
Van Hear, N. and McDowell, C. (2006) *Catching Fire: Containing Forced Migration in a Volatile World*, Lanham MD: Lexington Books.
Vathi, Z. (2017) 'Introduction: the interface between return migration and psychosocial wellbeing' in Z. Vathi and R. King (eds), *Return Migration and Psychosocial Wellbeing: Discourse, Policy-Making and Outcomes for Migrants and Their Families*, New York: Routledge, pp. 1–18.
World Bank (2011) *Conflict, Security, and Development*, Washington DC: The World Bank.
World Bank (2020) *Enhancing Government Effectiveness and Transparency: The Fight Against Corruption*, Washington DC: The World Bank.

# PART III

# EXPERIENCES OF RETURN AND REINTEGRATION

# 14. Reintegration strategies
*Katie Kuschminder*

## INTRODUCTION

The challenges of returnees' processes of reintegration post-return have received increasing attention in the academic literature (e.g. Guzman Elizalde, 2017; Koser and Kuschminder, 2015; Lietaert, 2016). There is an increasing consensus that reintegration is a multidimensional process that is influenced by the entirety of the migration cycle (Bilgili et al., 2018; Cassarino, 2014; Kuschminder et al., 2021) and, moreover, that it is a long-term process that may be more difficult than the initial integration experience. This recent research builds on central findings in the 1990s that highlighted the complexity of return and the long-term challenges of reintegration (Hammond, 1999; Koser and Black, 1999; Rogge, 1994).

This chapter presents the 'reintegration strategies' framework for analysing and understanding the process of reintegration. The framework conceptualises the process of return from a multidimensional perspective that accounts for the role of different actors and countries of return and for the heterogeneity of return migrants themselves (see King and Kuschminder, Chapter 1). Reintegration is an increasingly salient issue, as return flows increase and return migrants seek to re-establish themselves in different societies around the world. Unsuccessful reintegration can lead to marginalisation and vulnerability, creating new challenges in countries of return or possibly leading to an impetus to re-migrate. Therefore, understanding the process of reintegration is of significance for developing policies and programmes to assist returnees. The reintegration strategies framework aims to shed light on the factors that influence the process of reintegration.

The chapter is organised into five sections. First, the definition of reintegration is presented. Second, the reintegration strategies approach is detailed and discussed. This is followed by the third section, which links the reintegration strategies framework with processes of social change and development. The fourth section reflects on the question: Why use the reintegration strategies approach? The final section provides a conclusion.

## DEFINING REINTEGRATION

The literature on reintegration has increased significantly over the past two decades; however, despite this growth, there remains a lack of consensus regarding the definition and understanding of reintegration processes (see Marino and Lietaert, Chapter 12, for an overview). A first challenge is that reintegration is often considered differently for the various types of return migrant – such as refugee returnees, deportees or assisted voluntary returnees – as compared to returnees who are students, labour migrants or lifestyle migrants (among others). These types of return migrant often have different expectations placed on them in the reintegration process by society, policy-makers and locals. This is not necessarily ill-construed, as return migrants have different rights and entitlements on return and different needs in their reintegration processes. It does, however, maintain the challenge of a lack of harmonisation across the return field and brings forth the requirement that it is necessary, within a theory of reintegration, to be able to encompass the reality of the heterogeneity of return migrants.

Perhaps the most commonly used definition for reintegration within academia is: 'the process through which a return migrant participates in the social, cultural, economic and political life in the country of origin' (Cassarino, 2008, p.134). This definition stresses the importance of the process of reintegration itself. The International Organization for Migration (IOM), the largest international actor in the field of return migration, defines reintegration broadly as 'Re-inclusion or re-incorporation into a group or a process, e.g. of a migrant into the society of his [sic] country of origin' (2004, p.54). The IOM further proposed that there are three dimensions of reintegration – social, economic and cultural reintegration (2004) – and more recently includes the psychosocial dimension (2015). This definition highlights the inclusionary element of the reintegration process and that a returnee must be accepted by the local society.

One element that current definitions do not distinguish is the question of whose responsibility it is to reintegrate the returnee. In the reintegration strategies approach, it is argued that reintegration must be viewed as a bidirectional responsibility between the community of return and the return migrant. Within this view, reintegration is defined in the reintegration strategies approach as: 'the process in which return migrants are supported in maintaining their cultural and social identities by the host society and the whole population acquires equal civil, social, political, human and cultural rights' (Kuschminder, 2017, p.43). Recognising the bidirectional accountability of both returns and the receiving society is central to viewing reintegration as a more holistic process.

## WHAT ARE REINTEGRATION STRATEGIES?

Reintegration strategies represent a multidimensional approach to the process of reintegration based on four dimensions: cultural maintenance, social networks, self-identification and access to rights, institutions and the labour market in the country of return. *Cultural maintenance* reflects the value systems of the return migrant and his/her orientation towards the values of the country of migration or the values of the country of origin/return. The choice of cultural orientation reflects the desire or not for cultural maintenance of the values adopted from the country of migration (Berry, 1997). *Social networks* reflect the type of network of the return migrant: whether it is comprised of returnees, locals, cross-border networks or a combination of the three groups. The network of the return migrant will determine the access to resources and social capital that the network can provide. *Self-identification* is the returnees' subjective view and self-definition of their own identity. Return migrants can identify themselves as having one of the following: a unidirectional orientation towards the country of origin/return, a unidirectional orientation towards the country of migration or a transnational bidirectional orientation towards both the country of migration and of origin/return. Levitt and Glick Schiller (2004) term the last option a *transnational way of belonging*. The final component is the *access to rights and institutions* in the country of return that are available to the return migrant. This includes the position and statuses that the return migrant can achieve in institutions such as the labour market, citizenship rights, political institutions and housing rights and within the education system (Heckmann, 2001). These factors are not absolutes and can be envisioned as different degrees along a spectrum.

From these four dimensions the reintegration framework puts forth four reintegration strategies, as illustrated in Table 14.1. The first strategy is termed 'reintegrated'. The reintegrated returnee has been abroad for a longer duration (more than five years), has a high preparedness for return (cf. Cassarino, 2014) and possesses skills and/or a comfortable level of wealth. In this strategy the return migrant has maintained aspects of the culture from the country of migration but has also adjusted to the culture of the local context. The return migrant has a wide social network that includes locals, other returnees and the maintenance of their cross-border network from the country of migration. Such a broad social network allows the return migrant access to both bridging and bonding social capital, thus being able to access a wide array of resources.[1] The return migrant identifies him- or herself as being transnational or belonging simultaneously to two cultures and country contexts. From this reintegration strategy the return migrant is able to acquire certain rights in the country of return – an ability which will be largely dependent on the latter's citizenship policies. For instance, if the country allows dual citizenship, then the return migrant will have the same rights as citizens. If the country of return does not allow for dual citizenship and the return migrant opts to maintain their citizenship from the country of migration, although being a resident of the country of return, their rights in the country of return will be limited. In terms of access to the labour market, the reintegrated returnees should have strong access due to their skills and adaptability. Finally, their access to the core institutions of the country will also be dependent upon their citizenship choices and thus may be limited.

The second strategy is termed the 'enclave' strategy. Return migrants in the enclave strategy are similar to those in the reintegrated strategy in that they have been abroad for a longer duration (more than five years), have a high preparedness for return and possess skills and/or a comfortable level of wealth. The enclavists, however, maintain the culture of the country of migration and do not adapt to the local culture. Indeed, they may have cultural clashes with the local population. The social network of the enclavists is primarily comprised of other returnees and the maintenance of their cross-border networks, with limited ties to the local community. The enclavists thus have strong bonding social capital but weak bridging social capital. They maintain an exclusive network to which it is difficult for outsiders to gain access. The enclavists also define themselves as transnational. Like the reintegrated, the enclavists will have limited rights in the country of return if the country does not allow for dual citizenship. Unlike the reintegrated, who may opt to give up their citizenship from the country of migration, the enclavists would not give up their citizenship from the country of migration as they identify with that country and want to ensure the maintenance of their connection with it. Thus, their rights would be limited in a country of return that does not allow for dual citizenship, with enclavists probably having limited access to key institutions such as political membership (if this is not allowed for non-citizens); however, they should have access to the labour market, educational institutions and housing.

The third strategy is the 'traditionalist'. The traditionalist has typically been abroad for a shorter amount of time (3–5 years) and has a medium level of preparedness for return and a lower social status than the enclavists or the reintegrated, although having enough status that they can acquire positions of medium power upon return. The traditionalist has fully adapted to the local culture and rejects the culture of the country of migration. Either the traditionalist does not maintain the cultural changes that they adopted from the country of migration and

Table 14.1  Reintegration strategies

| | Reintegrated | Enclaves | Traditionalists | Vulnerable |
|---|---|---|---|---|
| Return migrant | • abroad for longer duration<br>• voluntary return<br>• high return preparedness<br>• economic success | • abroad for longer duration<br>• voluntary return<br>• high return preparedness<br>• economic success | • abroad for shorter duration<br>• voluntary return<br>• medium preparedness<br>• economic stability | • abroad for shorter duration<br>• forced return (deportees)<br>• no return preparedness<br>• economically vulnerable |
| Cultural orientation | • value the culture of both the country of migration and the country of origin/return | • value the culture of the country of migration | • value the culture of the country of origin/return | • rejection of the culture of the country of migration<br>• rejection from dominant society in country of origin/return |
| Social network | • locals, returnees and cross-border ties | • returnees and cross-border ties | • locals | • ties to kin and other vulnerable groups |
| Self-identification | • transnational | • transnational | • unidirectional | • unidirectional |
| Access to rights and institutions | • limited or full access to rights in country of return (depends on citizenship choices)<br>• limited access to key institutions in country of return | • limited access to rights in country of return<br>• limited access to key institutions in country of return | • full access to rights in country of return<br>• full access to key institutions in country of return | • full access to rights in country of return<br>• limited access to institutions in country of return |

*Source:* Kuschminder (2017).

rejects these changes in the return migration strategy or the traditionalist adopted a segregated integration approach in the country of migration wherein they had limited contact with locals and did not venture beyond their cultural environment, thus not acquiring new cultural capital in the country of migration. The traditionalists' social network is primarily comprised of locals with minimal to no interaction with other return migrants and cross-border networks from the country of migration. The network thus has limited access to resources and the traditionalist has weak bridging social capital due to the lack of maintenance of transnational ties. The traditionalist defines himself or herself as entirely oriented towards the country of return. The traditionalist has typically maintained the country of origin/return citizenship and would have full access to rights and institutions there.

The final reintegration strategy is the 'vulnerable'. The vulnerable have been abroad for a shorter duration (less than two years), have a low preparedness for return and are often low skilled, with low social status. The vulnerable have generally had an unsuccessful migration experience and may have been forcibly returned as a deportee. The vulnerable do not associate with the culture of the country of migration. Simultaneously, the vulnerable are often rejected by the dominant culture in the country of origin/return. This is due to the lack of social acceptance of deportees in the country of origin/return. The low social position of the vulnerable places them on the periphery of society and leads to social exclusion, with limited access to local institutions for employment, even though they are full citizens of their country of origin. The vulnerable have limited social networks that are comprised of locals or other returnees. They do not maintain cross-border networks developed during migration, as they generally do not have a network in the country of migration to maintain. The vulnerable are at risk of experiencing the negative aspects of social capital, such as 'downward levelling norms', as their network is comprised of other vulnerable people. The vulnerable identify themselves with a unidirectional orientation towards the country of origin.

The reintegration strategies outlined above are not permanent and return migrants may adopt different strategies at various stages of their return. For example, upon initial return an individual might adopt the enclave strategy; however, with time, as they become accustomed to the culture and country of return, they may change to adopt a reintegration approach. Factors that can impact on a change in reintegration strategy would include a shock to the economic position of the individual, a change in the family situation, a negative or positive experience with the country of origin/return or a change in the relationship with the country of migration. For instance, the relationship with the country of migration could decrease over time and the returnee may choose to move from a reintegrated strategy to more of a traditionalist strategy as they lose connections with the country of migration. On the other hand, the connection with the country of migration may strengthen and a returnee who was initially a traditionalist may re-engage with the country of migration and move to the reintegrated strategy. The returnee may even choose to re-migrate, thus no longer maintaining a return status. Finally, the reintegration strategies are conceptualised to provide overall categorisations and it is possible that individuals may portray aspects representing different categories. Thus, the categorisations may not be mutually exclusive.

The reintegration strategies combine with the structural and cultural environment of return within the origin-country context. The structural and cultural environment is essential to the reintegration experience and ability to enact an individual's strategy as it contextualises the degree of openness to returnees within the receiving society. Following from the central definition guiding the reintegration strategies approach, reintegration is viewed as a two-way process. Thus, in order to be able to enact the strategy of 'reintegration', for instance, there is a need for openness from the country of origin.

Table 14.2 provides an overview of the four categories considered within the framework of the structural and cultural environment and the characteristics that lead to a favourable or open environment, an adverse or negative environment for returnees or a neutral environment for return migrants.

*Table 14.2   Structural and cultural environment for return*

|  | Favourable | Adverse | Neutral |
|---|---|---|---|
| Government | • encourages return migration<br>• implements policies to support returnees' reintegration/participation | • discourages return migration<br>• no policies to support returnees | • ambivalent towards returnees |
| Local population | • inclusive attitude towards returnees<br>• open to cultural diversity | • exclusive attitude towards returnees<br>• closed towards cultural diversity | • ambivalent towards returnees |
| Private sector | • inclusive attitude towards returnees | • exclusive attitude towards returnees | • ambivalent towards returnees |
| Return migrant flows | • medium flow of return migrants | • flow is too large and overwhelms local population<br>• flow too small to be noticed | • small to medium flow of returnees (does not affect local population's daily lives) |

*Source:* Kuschminder (2017).

The structural environment of return is an essential component in considering the possibilities of reintegration. Four variables are considered: first, the *government's position towards returnees*. In a favourable environment, the government would implement policies to support returnees and encourage return. Both India and China have been examples of countries having strong policies to encourage skilled returnees (Siddiqui and Tejada, 2014; Xiang, 2016). A favourable environment would also support unskilled and vulnerable returnees. Sri Lanka's labour policy has been a good example of a reintegration policy seeking to support vulnerable returnees. If the government does not support returnees or discourages return, this would be viewed as a negative return environment.

Second, *attitudes of the local population* towards returnees are a vital component for returnees being able to reintegrate. In a positive return environment, locals have inclusive attitudes towards returnees and are open to cultural diversity. In a negative environment, locals have exclusionary and even hostile attitudes towards returnees and are closed to cultural diversity. This has been found in many return contexts where locals stigmatise returnees with negative slang (see Oeppen, 2009; Stefansson, 2004).

Third, the *private sector's attitudes* towards returnees also influences the structural environment. The private sector plays a pivotal role in employing returnees and being a part of economic reintegration processes. Thus, as above, a positive attitude towards returnees is important in facilitating the reintegration process.

Finally, the *size of the return migrant flows* also affects the reintegration environment. If the flows are too large they can overwhelm the local population, creating adversity. However, if the return flows are negligible then they perhaps have no impact on the locals' lives. This is not necessarily negative but may create more challenges for the returnee in their reintegration, as they are 'innovators' in the reintegration process. Finally, if the flows are of a medium size, this suggests that, if aligned with the other structural factors above, a positive environment can be created to support returnees' reintegration processes.

## LINKING THE REINTEGRATION STRATEGIES, SOCIAL CHANGE AND DEVELOPMENT

As stated above, in order for reintegration to occur, host communities must have accepting attitudes towards returnees. Returnees themselves often recognise this and reintegration thus means working to bridge the divide between locals and returnees. Guzman Elizalde (2017) found that returnees to Mexico stated that one of their roles could be to make Mexican society more inclusive by bringing respect for gender equality and cultural diversity. This approach of bringing new ideas relates to social remittances – the ideas, behaviours, identities and social capital that migrants export to their home communities (Levitt, 1998). However, these ideas only lead to social change when they are translated into ways that locals accept and embrace the new ideas as their own, a process that has been termed vernacularisation (Levitt and Merry, 2009).

Return migrants who are able to act as vernacularisers have the potential to contribute to social change and development. This, however, is no small feat. It requires first having had the opportunity to gain new skills and ideas abroad (often through integration experiences and/or education) and being able to communicate these new ideas in a way that locals accept. There are five conditions that enable return migrants to be vernacularisers: first, they must have demonstrated the ability to integrate while abroad; second, returnees must have engaged in voluntary return and have had a high level of preparedness for return; third, upon return, returnees must maintain transnational networks that enable them to continue the circulation of ideas and information; fourth, returnees must be willing to work with locals and have the ability to frame discussions and topics in a way that key messages can be meaningfully communicated to locals; and fifth, returnees must occupy positions with high status in return, demonstrating prestige and according mutual respect for others (Kuschminder, 2017). Being able to vernacularise requires a fine balance between not being viewed with a negative stigma (as above) and gaining the trust of locals so that they will listen and engage. Within the four reintegration strategies discussed earlier (also Table 14.1), the reintegrated are the most likely to have the potential to contribute to vernacularisation.

The challenge of this process should not be underestimated, although returnees do develop strategies to be able to achieve this. As noted above, framing is a key part of the process. One female returnee whom I interviewed in Ethiopia stated:

> ... to get accepted, you have to act like a local ... Most of the time they [the locals] will not accept you. If you are diaspora they always think, like – different kinds of directions. They have to believe you. You have to really change yourself, like, 'Oh I am one of you'. You have to convince them, you have to be really strong ... It takes time, but after that, like, you will become OK. Most of the diaspora, they do not have local friends. (Kuschminder, 2017, p.172)

This reflects how returnees need to frame their language and ideas in a way that locals accept in order to have the potential to vernacularise.

Stigmatisation towards returnees is common in many country contexts. Mueller and Kuschminder (forthcoming) find in a temporary return programme for knowledge transfer (see also Mueller, Chapter 23) that many returnees expect to experience stigmas and develop strategies for overcoming these barriers in order to be able to create trust and share their knowledge and expertise. These strategies include adapting to the local context and trying to act more like locals for acceptance, signalling commonalities to bridge differences between them and actively working to address stereotypes and misconceptions (Mueller and Kuschminder, forthcoming). These strategies are important in being able to gain trust and vernacularise knowledge transfer within this setting.

The potential and ability of returnees to act as vernacularisers and contribute to social change and development processes are thus predicated both upon their own strategies and ambitions and upon the structural and cultural environment of the country of return. Table 14.3 illustrates this combination and stresses that a high possibility for vernacularisation, social change and development only occurs in the combination of an open and favourable structural and cultural environment and the returnee following the reintegrated strategy.

Table 14.3    *Potential to vernacularise based on the reintegration strategy and conditions of the structural and cultural environment*

| Structural and cultural environment | Reintegrated | Enclaves | Traditionalists | Vulnerable |
|---|---|---|---|---|
| Favourable | High | Medium | None | None |
| Adverse | Medium | Low | None | None |

Source: Kuschminder (2017).

A notable case often cited as a large success in attracting returnees for development and social change is India. India has the largest diaspora in the world, which is also largely a professional diaspora, at least in terms of more recent migration waves and the descendants of previous waves. Since the mid-2000s, India has actively worked to promote a welcoming policy towards the diaspora and encourage return for *brain gain*. It has been highlighted as successful in this approach and stimulating the Indian IT sector, primarily with connections to Silicon Valley. In a survey of 527 skilled returnees in India, 47 per cent reported being able to have 'a lot of influence' on the people around them (Siddiqui and Tejada, 2014). Of interest, women were 77 per cent more likely to state they had a lot of influence on people around them (Siddiqui and Tejada, 2014). This suggests that skilled returnees in India commonly view themselves as being able to influence social change processes and exert influence if they choose to do so.

At the same time, there has been a critique that India's skilled returnees do not contribute to overall development in the country. Elite returnees have been criticised for channelling their resources into their own communities and furthering class and caste divides (Balaji, 2018). The result has been an increasing inequality, rather than gains for the country's large population living in extreme poverty.

It is important to stress that vernacularisation and the potential to contribute to social change and development is a difficult process. In my original study of returnees in Ethiopia, only 14 per cent of returnees were identified as having the potential to contribute to social change and development (Kuschminder, 2017). Research by van Houte (2016) has a similar finding in Afghanistan – that there is a misalignment in funding for return migrants to contribute to development. Funding from the Netherlands focuses on assisted voluntary returnees who do not have the capacity to act as vernacularisers and contribute to development in Afghanistan (van Houte, 2016; also Chapter 11).

Research on deported returnees and assisted voluntary returnees to Afghanistan has stressed their high levels of vulnerability upon return (Schuster and Majidi, 2013). This, combined with an adverse structural and cultural environment, not only means that these returnees are unable to contribute to development but, more importantly, shows their heightened vulnerabilities in return. Deportees and unsuccessful returnees have been referred to as 'contaminated' after an unsuccessful migration abroad and are ostracised by community members who do not want to associate with them (Schuster and Majidi, 2013). This leaves returnees vulnerable, whereby they are experiencing a dual rejection of the culture and society from the country of migration and the country of origin. They lack structural support from institutions in Afghanistan to assist them to reintegrate and/or to re-migrate on dangerous irregular journeys and are vulnerable to poverty and deprivation.

The potential of returnees to act as vernacularisers and contribute to development and social change is highly contextual according to the individual returnees' own reintegration strategy and the structural and cultural environment of return. Only when there is alignment between the reintegrated strategy and a positive structural and cultural environment of return can there be an expectation for development and social change. Recognising that several conditions are necessary for this to occur, it is essential to not overestimate the development potential of return migration and place undue expectations on all return migrants (see King, Chapter 22).

## WHY REINTEGRATION STRATEGIES?

The reintegration strategies framework provides an analytical lens to approach the differentiated experiences of return migrants' reintegration processes. It enables a framework for analysing the process of reintegration, the interaction of returnees with their structural and cultural environment and the resulting potential for returnees to contribute to social change and development in their countries of origin. From an academic perspective, the reintegration strategies approach incorporates the multiple components of reintegration, including the spatial, temporal, social, structural and multidimensional aspects (Lietaert and Kuschminder, 2021). It stresses the need for a bidirectional approach to reintegration that recognises the role of returnees, locals, the government and institutions in supporting cultural diversity and accepting returnees.

In an analysis of skilled returnees to Ghana, Olivier-Mensah (2019) examines how returnees share their implicit and explicit knowledge acquired in Germany. The author describes how one returnee 'had to put on his gloves' when returning to Ghana in order to be able to fit in – an experience that chimes with the 'traditionalist' strategy of seeking to fit back in. Similarly, in my own research, one respondent in Ethiopia stressed that you need to be able to 'wear both hats' and she could switch between her 'America hat' or her 'Ethiopia hat' depending on the context. Both of these allegories represent the challenge of returnees having to cope with the conflicting situations of return: they have to merge their new ways of being and knowing with the structural and cultural environment of the country of return. The reintegration strategies allow a framework to capture the different ways in which returnees can enact reintegration and make choices of 'taking the gloves on or off' or 'wearing both hats or only wearing one'.

In discussing reintegration in New Zealand, Humpage (2020) notes that returnees experience xenophobia but are also part of the solution by contesting these beliefs and acting for change. Humpage (2020, p.51) states 'to realise the diversity dividend and respond to enduring social problems in innovative ways, New Zealand should embrace – not ignore or disparage – returnees'. The reintegration strategies echo this sentiment and advocate for such an approach that focuses on the value added of returnees and promoting cultures of openness and tolerance for new ideas.

From a policy perspective, the reintegration strategies are also important in highlighting the heterogeneity of returnees and eliciting both the potential strengths as well as the limitations of return migrants' capacities within migration and development debates. The ability of returnees is not only dependent on their skills and knowledge; it is also essential to consider their willingness and desire to vernacularise, as well as the openness and ability of the receiving society to welcome new ideas and changes. Furthermore, policy-makers must also acknowledge that returning vulnerable returnees to adverse structural and cultural environments can – and may only – exacerbate their vulnerability. This framework of analysis can therefore inform policy-makers of the differentiating potential impacts of policies on different return migrants. It is increasingly well recognised in policy environments that a return policy that works well in one context may not work in another. Hence, the need to understand the cultural and structural environment towards returnees in order to optimise policies that can both prevent further marginalisation of vulnerable returnees and support skilled returnees who aspire to be vernacularisers.

## CONCLUSION

Research on reintegration has increased greatly over the past two decades and a large contingent of current research on reintegration lies within the space of the politicisation of return (see, e.g., Lietaert and Kuschminder, 2021). The strength of the reintegration strategies framework is that it enables a comparative approach that accounts for the heterogeneity of return migration from highly skilled and elite voluntary returnees, on the one hand, to deportees, on the other. A weakness is that it does not allow enough nuance and depth, particularly within the category of the vulnerable, where more information is necessary to support this group. The approach does lead to several questions for further exploration.

First, how can those in the enclavist category be motivated to move to the reintegrated category? What policies could support this in order to bring further social cohesion between skilled returnees and locals? Second, how can vernacularisation be increased? Is there a possibility for training and programmes to be able to increase the capacity of returnees to act as vernacularisers? At the same time, a third central line of questioning is how can communities and countries of return increase their openness to returnees? How can communities engage and work with their returnees for collective benefits?

Migration is becoming increasingly temporary – often through an imposed or forced temporariness – highlighting an increased importance for reintegration policies and programmes. The Covid-19 pandemic has increased unexpected returns in several countries where preliminary evidence shows that returnees are struggling to reintegrate (Sapkota, 2021). Governments with high numbers of unexpected returnees due to Covid-19 are struggling to invest billions into employment programmes to create job opportunities for economic reintegration

(Henderson, 2021; Sapkota, 2021). This suggests that reintegration policies and programmes will continue to grow in the future. The reintegration strategies approach assists in explaining and understanding complex reintegration processes that can inform academic debates as well as policy and practice.

## NOTE

1. Bridging social capital is defined as networks that are 'outward looking and encompass people across diverse cleavages' and bonding social capital as 'inward looking [networks that] tend to reinforce exclusive identities and homogenous groups' (Putnam, 2000, p.22).

## REFERENCES

Balaji, A. (2018) 'Elite return migration and development in India', LSE Blog, https://blogs.lse.ac.uk/internationaldevelopment/2018/07/30/elite-return-migration-and-development-in-india/ (accessed 15 April 2021).

Berry, J.W. (1997) 'Immigration, acculturation, and adaptation', *Applied Psychology: An International Review*, **46** (1), 1–68.

Bilgili, Ö., Kuschminder, K. and Siegel, M. (2018) 'Return migrants' perceptions of living conditions in Ethiopia: a gendered analysis', *Migration Studies*, **6** (3), 345–66.

Cassarino, J.P. (2008) *Return Migrants to the Maghreb, Reintegration and Development Challenges*, San Domenico di Fiesole: European University Institute (EUI), Robert Schuman Centre for Advanced Studies.

Cassarino, J.-P. (2014) 'A case for return preparedness' in G. Battistella (ed.), *Global and Asian Perspectives on International Migration*, Florence: Springer International Publishing, pp. 153–65.

Guzman Elizalde, L. (2017) *Return to Mexico: Exploring the (Re)integration Experience*, Brighton: University of Sussex, unpublished PhD thesis.

Hammond, L. (1999) 'Examining the discourse of repatriation: towards a more proactive theory of return migration' in R. Black and K. Koser (eds), *The End of the Refugee Cycle? Refugee Repatriation and Reconstruction*, Oxford: Berghahn, pp. 227–44.

Heckmann, F. (2001) *Effectiveness of National Integration Strategies Towards Second Generation Youth in a Comparative European Perspective*, Brussels: European Commission, Final Report.

Henderson, S. (2021) 'Returning "heroes": Filipino migrant workers met with a devastated economy', *Pandemic Borders*, https://www.opendemocracy.net/en/pandemic-border/returning-heroes-filipino-migrant-workers-met-with-a-devastated-economy/ (accessed 15 April 2021).

Humpage, L. (2020) 'New Zealanders returning from overseas: how their experiences of xenophobia could help us respond to superdiversity', *Kōtuitui: New Zealand Journal of Social Sciences Online*, **15** (1), 38–53.

IOM (2004) *Glossary on Migration*, Geneva: International Organization for Migration, https://publications.iom.int/system/files/pdf/iml_1_en.pdf (accessed 16 April 2021).

IOM (2015) *Reintegration – Effective Approaches*, Geneva: International Organization for Migration, https://www.iom.int/files/live/sites/iom/files/What-We-Do/docs/Reintegration-Position-Paper-final.pdf (accessed 16 April 2021).

Koser, K. and Black, R. (1999) 'The end of the refugee cycle?', in R. Black and K. Koser (eds), *The End of the Refugee Cycle? Refugee Repatriation and Reconstruction*, New York: Berghahn, pp. 2–17.

Koser, K. and Kuschminder, K. (2015) *Comparative Research on Assisted Voluntary Return and Reintegration*, Geneva: International Organization for Migration.

Kuschminder, K. (2017) *Reintegration Strategies: Conceptualizing How Return Migrants Reintegrate*, Cham: Palgrave Macmillian.

Kuschminder, K., Ogahara, Z. and Rajabzadeh, I. (2021) 'Evaluations of return within a mass deportation: Ethiopians' experiences of return after expulsion from Saudi Arabia', *International Migration*, **59** (2), 167–85.

Levitt, P. (1998) 'Social remittances: migration driven local-level forms of cultural diffusion', *International Migration Review*, **32** (4), 926–48.

Levitt, P. and Glick Schiller, N. (2004) 'Conceptualizing simultaneity: a transnational social field perspective on society', *International Migration Review*, **38** (145), 595–629.

Levitt, P. and Merry, S. (2009) 'Vernacularization on the ground: local uses of global women's rights in the Peru, China, India, and the United States', *Global Networks*, **9** (4), 441–61.

Lietaert, I. (2016) *Perspectives on Return Migration: A Multi-Sited, Longitudinal Study on the Return Processes of Armenian and Georgian Migrants*, Ghent: Ghent University, Faculty of Psychology and Educational Sciences, unpublished PhD thesis.

Lietaert, I. and Kuschminder, K. (2021) 'Contextualizing and conceptualizing reintegration processes in the context of return', *International Migration*, **59** (2), 140–7.

Mueller, C. and Kuschminder, K. (forthcoming) *Beyond 'Just Comes' and 'Know-it-alls': Exploring Strategies to Deal with Returnee Stigma during Diaspora Return Visits for Knowledge Transfer*, unpublished manuscript under review.

Oeppen, C. (2009) *A Stranger at Home: Integration, Transnationalism and the Afghan Elite*, Brighton: University of Sussex, PhD thesis.

Olivier-Mensah, C. (2019) '"Be the change": action strategies and implicit knowledge in transnational return migration' in R. Anghel, M. Fauser and P. Boccagni (eds), *Transnational Return and Social Change. Hierarchies, Identities and Ideas*, London: Anthem Press, pp. 123–40.

Putnam, R.D. (2000) *Bowling Alone: The Collapse and Revival of American Community*, New York: Simon and Schuster.

Rogge, J. (1994) 'Repatriation of refugees' in T. Allen and H. Morsink (eds), *When Refugees Go Home*, Geneva: United Nations Research Institute for Social Development.

Sapkota, C. (2021) 'As Covid brings migrants home, how can Nepal reintegrate returning workers?', *Pandemic Borders: Opinion*, https://www.opendemocracy.net/en/pandemic-border/covid-brings-migrants-home-how-can-nepal-reintegrate-returning-workers/ (accessed 15 April 2021).

Schuster, L. and Majidi, N. (2013) 'What happens post-deportation? The experience of deported Afghans', *Migration Studies*, **1** (2), 221–40.

Siddiqui, Z. and Tejada, G. (2014) 'Development and highly skilled migrants: perspectives from the Indian diaspora and returnees', *Revue Internationale de Politique de Développement*, **5** (2).

Stefansson, A. (2004) 'Sarajevo suffering: homecoming and the hierarchy of homeland hardship' in F. Markowitz and A. Stefansson (eds), *Homecomings: Unsettling Paths of Return*, Lanham MD: Lexington Books, pp. 54–75.

van Houte, M. (2016) *Return Migration to Afghanistan: Moving Back or Moving Forward?* Cham: Palgrave Macmillian.

Xiang, B. (2016) *Emigration Trends and Policies in China: Movement of the Wealthy and Highly Skilled*, Washington DC: Migration Policy Institute, https://www.migrationpolicy.org/research/emigration-trends-and-policies-china-movement-wealthy-and-highly-skilled (accessed 27 April 2021).

# 15. Labour migrants and the retirement–return nexus
*Claudio Bolzman*

## INTRODUCTION

This chapter explores the question of return for labour immigrants confronted with retirement. It studies the decisions and practices of older immigrants from Southern Europe (Italy, Spain, Portugal) living in Switzerland with respect to their country of origin and proposes a typology that takes into account, in particular, issues of return combined with transnational geographical mobility practices.

Issues related to return are classic in migration studies (King, 2000). Indeed, important migration theories consider temporary stays and return as significant dimensions of migration flows (Piore, 1979; Stark and Blum, 1985). For these theories, return to the home country after some years of emigration was completely integrated into the migratory project. Why, then, establish a nexus between return and retirement? Because things did not happen as immigration societies and the migrants themselves had expected. There are two different reasons for this. The first is that, after some time abroad, many migrants suffered from the separation from their families. They did everything to obtain family reunification. Thus, their move changed from a work migration to a settlement migration (Sayad, 1991) and the idea of return therefore became more of a long-term project. The second reason is that many migrants, thanks to their remittances, became the 'social security' of their families who stayed in the origin country. As de Haas (2008) shows, these migrants could no longer return in the short or medium term if they wanted to guarantee an acceptable standard of living for their families. Their return was therefore postponed, very often until retirement.

From a life-course perspective, retirement thus appears as a relevant transition (Bengtson et al., 2005) that reactivates the idea of return. Indeed, retirement brings about significant changes in migrants' lives – modifying their social status. The migrants themselves start a new stage in their lives, ceasing to be workers and becoming pensioners. Work is no longer the main reason for their presence in the host society. In this new configuration, the question of their country of residence can be reconsidered (Bolzman, 2013; Bolzman and Bridji, 2019; Bolzman et al., 2017).

However, this chapter questions whether it is possible for migrant workers to return after so many years living in another country. If the answer is yes, what are the motivations and factors that influence the decision? If it is not possible to return, what are the alternatives? In particular, is geographical mobility an option enabling migrants to escape the dilemma of returning versus staying? Moreover, is it possible to combine different options like return and mobility or staying and mobility?

In order to answer these questions, the chapter proposes a typology of alternatives that are available for older migrants confronted with retirement, taking into account two dimensions: returning versus staying and geographical mobility versus immobility. Drawing on three qualitative case studies using in-depth interviews and carried out over the last 16 years with retired migrant workers from Italy, Spain and Portugal who live or who lived in Switzerland (Bolzman et al., 2008; Bolzman et al., 2017; Fojo and Fernandez, 2004), it explores their experiences of return/non-return and geographical mobility/immobility.

In the first section, I present the theoretical framework and propose a typology that combines the two main perspectives concerning the issue of the institutional perspective on the one hand and the new transnational mobilities perspective on the other. In the second section, I present the context of migrant workers from Southern Europe in Switzerland who are nearing retirement or are already retired. In the third section, I apply the typology to concrete case studies and, in the conclusion, discuss the main results and their theoretical implications.

## RETIREMENT FOR MIGRANT WORKERS AND THE QUESTION OF RETURN: TOWARDS A TYPOLOGY

The question of the return to the country of origin of migrant workers near retirement or when retired has given rise to an abundant literature in the social sciences, with many dimensions of the issue having been studied. Some scholars have focused on explanatory factors affecting migrants' intentions or decisions relative to their return or non-return (Attias-Donfut, 2006; Baykara-Krumme, 2013; Bolzman et al., 2006; Ciobanu and Ramos, 2016; de Haas and Fokkema, 2010; Hunter, 2011). Others are interested in how legal frameworks influence migrants' return and mobility practices (Ackers and Dwyer, 2004; Böcker and Balkır, 2012; Ciobanu and Hunter, 2017; Gehring, 2017). Yet others analyse the experience of return to the home country (Gualda and Escriva, 2014; Pino and Verde, 2006; Rodriguez et al., 2002). However, much remains to be explored (Cassarino, 2004; Percival, 2013). In particular, the return–mobility nexus and the dynamics of return/no-return processes over time are the two main issues that I examine in this chapter.

Two paradigms that conceive of return differently and predominate in the migration literature are the institutional and the new mobilities (or transnational) paradigms. The first highlights political sedentariness as the norm (Dietzel-Papakyriakou, 2001; Sayad, 1999), the second, mobility as the norm (Cresswell, 2010; Sheller and Urry, 2006). If return is analysed from an institutional perspective, it should of necessity be perceived as the conclusion of the migratory process, since it means returning to the starting point prior to migration. On the other hand, if return is analysed from a new mobilities perspective (or a transnational one), it becomes part of a broader mobility dynamic which includes social processes that lead individuals constantly to cross national borders, either physically or virtually.

If we come back to the institutional perspective in more detail, for Sayad (2001) the desire for return can be explained mainly by the fact that, in a world organised into states, international migration is not considered as 'normal' behaviour. Migrants must justify their decision to remain in the host state for reasons defined as 'acceptable' by these states and their immigration policies. Despite the fact that immigrants can settle in a new state, conditionality and their lack of full citizenship may lead them to think that their 'real place', the place where they are fully considered as human beings, is their home state (Takai and De Guzmán, 2015). However, according to Sayad (1999), for migrant workers the structural conditions for return are seldom fulfilled and they risk experiencing a 'double absence'. They are trapped in a dream of return that they cannot implement and then they postpone it until retirement, a period which they consider as a significant social moment at which to reactivate their initial projects.

Instead, according to transnational and new mobilities perspectives, the situation of migrants is characterised by a 'double presence' (Cresswell, 2010), in which the lives of migrants are organised across borders. They live both here and there simultaneously (Portes, 1996; Pries, 2001). Return can be part of that broader process of cross-border lives. However, these forms of transnational mobility have been especially observed among economically active skilled migrants and entrepreneurs (Solano, 2019) or among lifestyle older migrants (Lardiès Bosque et al., 2016) and have seldom been analysed as former migrant workers near retirement or retired who have resided in European countries.

Now, migration and return are not isolated phenomena in people's lives; they are part of complex biographies that are located in time and space. In this sense, it is important to place the problem in a life-course perspective, which can be conceptualised as 'a sequence of transitions linked to age that are integrated in social institutions and history' (Bengtson et al., 2005, p.493). Moreover, from this perspective, individuals are considered as actors who have expectations, who can choose – to a certain extent – and act intentionally, in relation to the opportunities and limitations structured by institutional contexts. Thus, they develop 'agency within structures' (Spini et al., 2017) in a context related to the retirement period.

In fact, retirement is a normative event (i.e. it is socially expected that individuals cease to work at a certain age) that can have an important impact on a migrant's life course. The need to work to have an income no longer retains migrants in the society of residence. In many cases, they can draw their retirement pension in their home society and live in the house or flat which they own there. Nevertheless, new conflicting roles can emerge at this stage of their lives. On the one hand, they have an opportunity to show to significant others from their reference group in the home society that they are returning after a successful life abroad. They can finally go back with their 'heads held high' (Bolzman and Bridji, 2019). On the other hand, new priorities can arise in relation to new social roles, like duties towards the family they created in the host society: they have, for example, the opportunity to play a role as a parent and grandparent to subsequent generations (Percival, 2013), most of whom have no desire or intention to live in their parents' native country. Moreover, as 'older people', they also have new health issues and concerns about the ease of access to care, which can influence their decision about where to live in this period of their lives (Böcker and Balkır, 2012; Gualda and Escriva, 2014; Hunter, 2011).

If the two evoked paradigms (institutional and new mobilities) are taken into account, then return and non-return related to retirement can be conceived in different ways – ways in which these processes may or may not be combined with forms of mobility. Starting from this basis, one could try to integrate the two perspectives through a typology, which would be an interesting contribution to account for the complexity of migrant workers' lives in a globalised world. Indeed, much empirical research focuses on three alternatives: returning, staying or going back and forth (Baykara-Krumme, 2013; Bolzman et al., 2006; De Coulon and Wolff, 2006; Zontini, 2015). Instead, in its simplest binary form, the proposed typology could include two dimensions that take into account both theoretical perspectives: return versus non-return (the institutional perspective) and transnational geographical mobility versus transnational geographic immobility (a new mobilities and transnational perspective). The combination of these two dimensions would give rise to four situations that are presented in Table 15.1.

*Table 15.1    Typology of return migration and transnational geographical mobility*

| Return migration/transnational geographical mobility | Yes | No |
|---|---|---|
| Yes | Transnational return | Transnational geographical mobility |
| No | Settlement return | Settlement in the country of immigration |

*Transnational return* would be a situation in which the return is part of a geographic mobility project, which means going back and forth between the home country and the former host country. Instead, the *settlement return* would correspond to the institutional perspective of analysis of this process in which retired migrants return 'home' to rebuild their lives, without moving again from that space. *Transnational geographic mobility* would be a situation of circulation between several countries but without any 'official' return. Finally, *settlement in the country of immigration* would represent a renunciation of the intention to return and no more geographical mobility towards the country of origin.

The purpose of this chapter, then, is to examine, on the one hand, whether these four types of possibility appear empirically in the study of retired migrant workers from Southern Europe in Switzerland and, on the other, whether the four types are sufficient to account for what happens in the observed reality. The analysis of situations cannot be static but requires a longitudinal perspective – in terms of the life course – as we have indicated above. In effect, it is the temporal dynamics, taking into account certain contexts and individual resources, that allow us to account for any possible transformations at the spatial level.

## MIGRANT WORKERS FROM SOUTHERN EUROPE IN SWITZERLAND AND RETIREMENT: THE CONTEXT

Older immigrants from Southern Europe came to Switzerland as young adult workers within the frame of guestworker migration policies (Piguet, 2006). The first generation of immigrant workers was mainly recruited during the period spanning the 1950s and 1970s from Italy and Spain and, later, from Portugal, Turkey and the former Yugoslavia. Nowadays, according to the Swiss Federal Statistical Office, Italians are the most numerous (319,300 at the end of 2018), followed by the Portuguese (263,300) and the Spanish (83,700) (OFS, 2019). The majority worked in manual professions in industry, construction, hotels, restaurants, cleaning, care etc. Even though some had upward social mobility in their careers, the majority were still working in unskilled or manual professions just before retirement: this was the case for around 70 per cent of the Spaniards, Italians and Portuguese, while only a third of Swiss workers occupied these professional positions (Bolzman and Vagni, 2018). Now retired or approaching retirement in an era of globalisation, the advent of low-cost flights and the freedom of circulation between European Union (EU) countries and Switzerland mean that transnational living is a more probable option for them. Therefore immigrants who spent 20 to 40 years of their adult lives as guestworkers in Switzerland, harbouring the idea that, one day, they would probably return to their home country, have progressively discovered other options – such as mobility between countries – which enable them to live a transnational life and to be in regular contact with their home country without completely leaving Switzerland (Bolzman and Bridji, 2019; Bolzman et al., 2017). However, at the same time, they discover that there are structural factors (such as the size of their retirement pensions or the quality of health services), relational factors (like the location of family members in one or several countries) and institutional factors (such as the risk of losing their permanent resident status if they leave Switzerland for more than six months or to lose some forms of monetary support if they leave the country for more than three months) that are a source of hesitation, making it difficult to determine their options with respect to the choice of country of residence after retirement. It is thus interesting to know what proportion actually do leave Switzerland on retirement.

The Swiss Federal Statistical Office reports annually both the number of permanent residents in Switzerland and the number of permanent residents who leave the country, by citizenship, canton of residence and age group. Table 15.2 displays an extract of this for Italian, Portuguese and Spanish citizens aged between 40 and 79 years old and living with a residence permit in the canton of Geneva. The period covered is 2011–16.

Table 15.2   *Share of Italian, Portuguese and Spanish immigrants leaving Switzerland (Geneva) between 2011 and 2016\* (average annual scores)*

| Citizenship | | | | | |
|---|---|---|---|---|---|
| 40–64 years old | | | 65–79 years old | | |
| Emigration | Permanent immigrant residents* | Share of immigrants leaving Switzerland | Emigration | Permanent immigrant residents* | Share of immigrants leaving Switzerland |
| No. | No. | % | No. | No. | % |
| *Immigrants with Italian citizenship* | | | | | |
| 132 | 6 923 | 1.91 | 38 | 4 483 | 0.85 |
| *Immigrants with Portuguese citizenship* | | | | | |
| 178 | 14 543 | 1.22 | 45 | 585 | 7.69 |
| *Immigrants with Spanish citizenship* | | | | | |
| 141 | 5 637 | 2.50 | 47 | 1 780 | 2.64 |

*Note:* * Number of immigrant permanent residents (or their children) without Swiss citizenship.
*Source:* Swiss Federal Statistical Office, Switzerland; Bolzman and Bridji (2019).

According to Table 15.2, very few foreign nationals from Italy, Portugal and Spain did actually leave Switzerland (Geneva) between 2011 and 2016 after retirement (the 65–79-year-old age group). Nonetheless, it is worth noting that relatively greater numbers of older immigrants from Portugal leave Switzerland than of those from Italy and Spain. Hence, almost all older immigrants from Italy and Spain and most of the older immigrants from Portugal decide to remain in Switzerland on retiring – with only a few of them returning to their country of origin. In order to control for a potential age bias, we looked at foreign nationals of 'pre-retirement' age (40–64 years old). As shown in Table 15.2, the share of foreign nationals from Southern Europe leaving Switzerland before retiring was very small between 2011 and 2016, even for Portuguese nationals.

In Switzerland, the economic crisis did not have the same impact as it did in other European countries. Unemployment rates are among the lowest in Europe (3 per cent before the coronavirus crisis) and wages are high from an international perspective. According to the neoclassical paradigm, this socio-economic context was ideal for the return to the home country of these older migrants because their purchasing power could be very high in their countries of origin (Hunter, 2011). However, the figures show that the number of departures during retirement is low, which is somewhat surprising from a purely rational perspective and probably indicates that older immigrants have other motivations for staying than a mere rational economic choice.

Moreover, these figures do not say anything about the transnational geographical mobility of those who decided to stay in Switzerland. In the following empirical section, based on qualitative interviews, detailed information is given about the factors that influenced return (or non-return) decisions and the geographical mobility of older immigrants.

## RESULTS: THE TYPOLOGY CONFRONTED WITH THE EMPIRICAL CASES

Insofar as Switzerland has been the destination of a very large labour migration flow from Southern Europe, it is possible to observe an important diversity in the ways of dealing with the issue of return. In addition, due to Switzerland's geographic proximity to the countries of origin of the migrants and an efficient transport infrastructure between them, the possibilities of developing forms of geographic mobility without migrants necessarily returning to their country of origin are high. The cases presented here show the diversity in the ways in which retired migrants position themselves with respect to the issues of return and mobility over time. From this angle, these cases also allow us to examine the typology from the perspective of empirical reality.

**Transnational Return**

This option means that the return to the country of origin goes together with transnational geographic mobility between the country of origin and the former host country. The basic reason for this mobility is to regularly visit children and grandchildren who have remained in the host country. This option has been very little studied because return has often been considered as a definitive resettlement in the country of origin.

This type of return was practised by Maria, an Italian woman who arrived in Switzerland at the age of 30 and worked there for 34 years, first as a caregiver and then as a nursing assistant. She returned to Italy at retirement age (64 years old) since her pension was too low for her to live on comfortably in Switzerland. For her, return was thus an option *par default* for economic reasons. In actual fact, she was not well informed about possibilities of economic support for the elderly in Switzerland. She had bought an apartment in Alassio on the Italian Riviera and her Swiss old-age pension was sufficient for her to have a good quality of life there. Moreover, she had enough savings to take the train and to visit her daughter and three grandchildren in Switzerland at least twice a year (in the summer and at Christmas) and sometimes up to five times a year. For her this was a good compromise, allowing her to maintain an independent economic life and close contact with her family in Switzerland. She travelled like this between Italy and her daughter's home for ten years, until the age of 73. However, after her health deteriorated, she was no longer able to travel by train alone and decided to move back to Switzerland and spend the rest of her retirement years near her daughter and grandchildren. The whole process took her several months (selling her apartment in Italy and again obtaining a residence permit in Switzerland). As she explains:

> I had to leave (Switzerland), because I did not have enough retirement pension. I was short by 200 francs every two months. And I had to go [to Italy]. But I missed my daughter and my grandchildren. Then, they (INCA Patronato, trade union social service) explained to me that, since my daughter lived in Switzerland, I could come back here.

She received a new residence permit as a '*rentier*' (annuitant) in Switzerland, the condition for which was to show a monthly income of at least 2,600 Swiss francs.

In this example, transnational return becomes a reverse return for health reasons. Indeed, difficulties with geographical mobility and the discovery of the possibility for economic support in Switzerland influenced the decision.

## SETTLEMENT RETURN

This is the classic return model whereby migrant workers, after many years living in the host country, return to their home country to spend their retirement there. Different studies show that return intentions concern a minority of migrant workers. In my previous studies, men are more interested in return than women.[1] Return intentions are stronger among the middle-aged (55–59 years) and diminish when the age of retirement (60–64) approaches (Bolzman, 2013; Bolzman et al., 2006). Return intentions drop drastically after the age of retirement (65 years or more). This is particularly the case for Italian and Spanish older immigrants and less for Portuguese (Bolzman and Bridji, 2019; Bolzman et al., 2017). Factors that favour return intentions are a strong symbolic attachment to the culture and language of the home country and the aspiration to recover a full citizenship status (Bolzman et al., 2006).

An interesting example is the case of Francisco and Elvira.[2] They arrived in Switzerland as manual workers in the 1960s with their two small children. During the first few years, they thought that they would settle there definitively as the country gave them the opportunity to escape unemployment in Spain. However, in 1970, the xenophobic 'Schwarzenbach initiative' demanded a drastic reduction in the number of aliens in the country, which gave these latter the impression that they would never be fully accepted in Switzerland. As Elvira explains:

> Our hearts became cold because, even if the Schwarzenbach initiative was rejected, we knew that others would come. So we decided to start saving for our future return. We didn't say anything to the kids because we didn't want to disrupt their schooling.

Francisco explains that he would have liked to be considered as a full citizen and not as a half citizen:

> One of the things that I missed the most in this almost 30 years of life in Switzerland was the possibility to vote or to be able to give my opinion but we were considered only as workers. They thought that our needs were limited to eating and having a roof and that was all. They did not think that we could also have ideas, an opinion.

Finally, Francisco and Elvira decided to return to Spain a few years before retirement in order to become citizens again and to enjoy a better quality of life. They settled in a small town in Andalusia and did not return to visit their children in Switzerland. In that sense, it is clearly a settlement return. However, this was indirectly a transnational life, because their children and grandchildren came from Switzerland to visit them every year in the holidays.

## TRANSNATIONAL GEOGRAPHICAL MOBILITY

Transnational geographical mobility means permanent settlement in Switzerland during retirement with some time spent during the year in the country of origin. This option has been experienced by most migrant workers from Southern Europe during their working years in Switzerland. They return at least once or twice a year – sometimes more – to their home country during the holidays. Thus, it was not surprising that many of them wanted to continue with this option after retirement. It is actually the most popular option for the retired: survey data show, in fact, that a significant number (more than 70 per cent) still spend some time in their home country – particularly Italians and Spaniards, among whom around 80 per cent spend some time there (Bolzman et al., 2017). Zontini (2015) also found a preference for this option in her research on older Italians in England.

This coming and going allows former migrant workers to feel constantly connected to both the societies that are relevant in their lives (Bolzman et al., 2006). For Southern European immigrants, this practice is not too expensive thanks to low-cost flights (or trains) and is feasible from an institutional perspective because Switzerland is part of the Schengen space. However, there are also constraints: they cannot be absent continuously for more than a few months if they want to have access to non-contributive financial support in Switzerland. This solution also requires access to housing in the home country and good health, which allows them to go back and forth (Bolzman et al., 2017).

Time spent in the home country each year and configurations of mobility within the family can be quite diverse. Nevertheless, pendularity is often a compromise within the couple: men are more in favour of return whereas women prefer to stay in the society of residence (Bolzman et al., 2001). One example is this Spanish family with Geneva as their main place of residence. Lorenzo and Teresa, who arrived (aged 25 and 18, respectively) in the early 1970s, knew each other and married in Switzerland, where they had one daughter. Lorenzo worked first for a cleaning company and then as a caregiver, which he found more rewarding. Maria worked as a cashier in a supermarket for many years and also, later, as a caregiver for elderly people. With their savings, they were able to buy a house in Spain after a few years. Lorenzo decided to take early retirement when he was 60, while Teresa, much younger, is still employed. Lorenzo spends about six months of the year in Spain. Teresa and their daughter join him during the summer holidays. Teresa explains:

> He has all his brothers and sisters over there. He always had it in his mind to return but since I am still working and our daughter is still studying, he leaves for Spain between May and September. It is not a question of his not loving Switzerland but he is more nostalgic than me.

In their living arrangements, Lorenzo and Teresa take into account the constraints of Swiss legislation, according to which a foreigner holding a long-term residence permit is not allowed to leave Switzerland for more than six months if he/she wants to maintain his or her status as a permanent resident. Teresa thinks that, even after her retirement, they will continue to come and go between Spain and Switzerland because she likes to live in Geneva and their daughter wants to work in Switzerland after finishing her studies.

Another interesting case is that of Victoria, a single Spanish woman who spent most of her adult life working in Switzerland. After retirement, she decided to stay in Switzerland where she had many friends and a rich associative life. Her weekly agenda was full of her volunteer activities and her social life. However, she also travelled several times a year to Spain to visit her brothers, sisters and nephews, with whom she had a very good relationship. She practised for many years a 'double presence' between Switzerland and Spain. However, after the age of 75, she started to have health problems and had to stop many of the weekly activities she had in Geneva. As she explains:

> Suddenly I didn't have the same energy to keep seeing my friends and doing volunteer activities as often. I started spending a lot more time alone in my apartment. It was then that I said to myself, 'I have no family here and, with age, I will have to spend more and more time alone in my apartment. If my health problems get worse, who will take care of me here? In Spain I have at least family, I will be better surrounded when I can no longer go out'. This is why I decided to return to my country of origin. I never imagined that one day I would make this decision but, when we get older, we see things differently.

In the first example, transnational geographical mobility is clearly a compromise between Lorenzo and Teresa that takes into account the needs of the family – each one of them – as well as the institutional constraints. In the second example, a longitudinal perspective allows us to understand that many decisions concerning return and geographical mobility are not static but are influenced by life events. Victoria changed her mind and moved from transnational geographical mobility to a settlement return – health limitations and family support being decisive in her decision.

**Settlement in the Country of Immigration**

In this fourth option of the typology, former immigrant workers settle definitively in Switzerland after retirement and do not sojourn regularly in their country of origin. They visit their home country only occasionally because of health problems that limit their geographical mobility and/or because of economic difficulties that do not allow them to spend their money on frequent travel. Moreover, the majority of them do not have accommodation in their country of origin, which also limits their travel options. In our surveys, we found that this was the case for around a third of respondents aged 55–64 (Bolzman et al., 2006) and about 20 per cent of those aged 65–79 (Bolzman et al., 2017).

In the following example, settlement in Switzerland without geographical mobility becomes progressively an obligation for the wife in this couple. Indeed, the spouses used to embody transnational geographical mobility but, for health reasons, the woman had to stop travelling to Spain and to settle definitively in Switzerland. Maria arrived at the age of 20 in Switzerland, where her brothers were already working, at the end of the 1960s. She found a job first cleaning in a nursing home and later in a private school. This was also the case for her future husband, José. They met while working together at this school, had two children and settled in Geneva. Like many other Spaniards, they used to visit their home country during the holidays and even bought an apartment there. Their plans for retirement were to spend part of the year in Switzerland with their daughters and part of the year in Spain in their apartment. However, Maria started to have severe back pain and had to stop working at the age of 57, a few years before retirement; she received a disability pension two years later. José is in good health and likes to travel to Spain. However, for Maria, her bad health became an important limitation to her geographical mobility. She experienced considerable pain when travelling and found herself confronted with the question of immobility: 'It is not possible for me to travel to Spain any more. The pain is too strong and I can no longer bear travelling, even by plane, even less by car.' Maria said that she keeps in touch with her family in Spain but now it is only by phone or virtual forms of communication.

In the second example, Luis, a retired Portuguese worker aged 67, had settled definitively in Switzerland and had almost stopped travelling to Portugal. Luis arrived in Geneva, where he worked in construction, at the age of 37. He worked for ten years and then had an accident, had to stop working and received a disability pension until his retirement. He divorced his wife, who returned to Portugal, leaving their two children in Switzerland. Luis remarried a Latin-American woman and they were together for seven years until she died and he was left a widower. He has a house in Portugal but now his former wife is living there. He explains that he prefers to live in Switzerland because his situation is more comfortable compared to Portugal and he no longer feels any links to the country. In his words:

> I am not interested in going to Portugal at all. Really not! As I was saying, here I have the doctor close, 10 minutes' walk away; if I need to purchase something, it is 5 minutes. In Portugal I have to walk miles and miles and pay for a taxi. The doctor in my area in Portugal is 18 km away, the bus is just twice a day, sometimes once a day, and now it is not even every day ... I'm not interested in anything from Portugal, nothing! When I go, it is because I am 'forced' to by my children, it is because my son asks me a lot of times. However, I feel more like a foreigner in Portugal. I have been living away from Portugal for 44 years. When I was 20 years old, I went to Guinea, then I went to France, then to Portugal and from Portugal, I came here ... And now I have no money either; when I worked I had more money, now I have to live on very little and save for some eventuality if something is left.

In both these cases, the original projects were not necessarily to settle permanently in Switzerland. In the first example, the idea was to alternate between the two countries but health problems led Maria to give up on that project and to settle in Switzerland near her daughters. In the second case, life circumstances – divorce, an accident, disability, widowhood and economic problems – led Luis to settle in Switzerland where he feels more protected against health problems and old age.

## CONCLUSION

A typology combining institutional and new transnational mobilities perspectives allows migrants to consider at least four options at the moment of retirement: transnational return, settlement return, transnational geographical mobility and settlement in the country of immigration. Quantitative empirical findings show that the majority of retired migrants decide to keep their main place of residence in the society where they have spent most of their adult life and that only a minority intend to – or do effectively – return to the country of origin (Bolzman and Bridji, 2019; Bolzman et al., 2006; Ciobanu and Ramos, 2016). In fact, most retired migrants practise transnational geographical mobility, going back and forth between the two countries, while keeping their main residence in the country of immigration (Bolzman et al., 2017; Ciobanu and Hunter, 2017; Hunter, 2011). Some practise pendularity while having their main residence in their country of origin (transnational return).

Moreover, the relationship between these different options is complex and cannot be reduced to binary combinations that would give rise to a limited number of possibilities. In fact, there is a space in between the categories of transnationalism, mobility, return and settlement that deserves more exploration, a space related to the fluidity of migrants' lives and characterised by transformations linked to social circumstances, ageing or retirement. Indeed, the empirical case studies show that the reality for retired migrants presents conjunctions that introduce other modalities that should be integrated into a typology and theoretical reflection.

First, a typology would need to integrate the temporal dimension, relying on a life-course perspective (Vlase and Voicu, 2018). In fact, as we have seen in the cases studied, what appears to be a definitive transnational return to the country of origin can be transformed into a reverse return to the immigration country while maintaining transnational geographical mobility. This latter can be transformed into return over time, in settlement without mobility or in other alternatives. This longitudinal dimension constitutes one of the most significant empirical and theoretical contributions of this chapter to studies on return and transnational mobility.

Social complexity is also a central dimension within which to understand return, settlement and circulation among former migrant workers. Factors such as gender, health, finances, family location, care and support exchanges influence migrants' pre- and post-retirement projects and practices regarding return, mobility, settlement or other options. These social variables provide resources and constraints according to the circumstances. For example, among the interviewees, women – in their projects – appear more sensitive than men to the spatial location of their family, particularly their children and grandchildren. Health status can also influence geographic mobility possibilities, both as a resource and as an impediment. Access to housing, in both the countries of immigration and of origin, can also be a powerful factor facilitating geographical mobility. We then observe that individual and family resources (and limitations), as well as the logics of resource mobilisation, influence decisions and behaviour. The relative importance of mobility/immobility is also influenced by different institutional and geo-economic factors.

At the institutional level, immigration and nationality policies, the existence of return aid programmes and bilateral social-security agreements do or do not facilitate a space of free movement, of portability of social rights. Thus, for example, older Southern European migrants who do not hold a Swiss passport have to consider, in their mobility strategies, constraints related to the maximum length of absence from Switzerland in order to keep their right to permanent residence there. On the other hand, the fact of having dual citizenship facilitates mobility decisions because it makes return potentially reversible if there are difficulties in reintegrating the country of origin. From this perspective, nationality becomes a form of legal capital that can be converted into mobility capital. Because of bilateral social-security agreements, retired Southern Europeans living in Switzerland also benefit from the portability of social rights such as retirement and old-age pensions. However, retired migrants receiving non-contributory pensions related to place of residence cannot be absent from Switzerland for more than a limited amount of time if they want to keep their right to receive these complementary pensions.

With regards to geo-economic factors, geographical distance, as well as the frequency, quality and price of transport, also influence the possibilities for mobility depending on retired migrants' resources. In the case of Southern European immigrants in Switzerland, transport infrastructures and relative short distances favour – in most of the cases – transnational geographical mobility.

The example of retired Southern European migrants in Switzerland has certain peculiarities with respect to the above-mentioned factors. It would be interesting to compare this example with others in order to analyse whether the modalities of return/settlement and mobility/

immobility, as well as the factors that influence them, are similar to or different from those of retired migrants in other countries.

## NOTES

1. The broader evidence for this gendering of return migration is presented by King and Lulle, Chapter 4 of this Handbook.
2. This case is based on the film *Album de famille* (Family Album) by Fernand Melgar (1993), who interviewed his own parents on their return to Spain.

## REFERENCES

Ackers, L. and Dwyer, P. (2004) 'Fixed laws, fluid lives: the citizenship status of post-retirement migrants in the European Union', *Ageing and Society*, **24** (3), 451–75.

Attias-Donfut, C. (2006) *L'Enracinement. Enquête sur le Vieillissement des Immigrés en France*, Paris: Armand Colin.

Baykara-Krumme, H. (2013) 'Returning, staying, or both? Mobility patterns among elderly Turkish migrants after retirement', *Transnational Social Review*, **3** (1), 11–30.

Bengtson, V.L., Elder, G.H. and Putney, N.M. (2005) 'The life course perspective on ageing: linked lives, timing, and history' in M.L. Johnson (ed.), *The Cambridge Handbook of Age and Ageing*, New York: Cambridge University Press, pp. 493–509.

Böcker, A.G.M. and Balkır, C. (2012) *Migration in Later Life: Residence, Social Security and Citizenship Strategies of Turkish Return Migrants and Dutch Retirement Migrants in Turkey*, Nijmegen: Radboud University Nijmegen, Nijmegen Migration Law Working Paper Series.

Bolzman, C. (2013) 'Ageing immigrants and the question of return: new answers to an old dilemma?' in J. Percival (ed.), *Return Migration in Later Life*, Bristol: Policy Press, pp. 67–87.

Bolzman, C. and Bridji, S. (2019) 'Older immigrants living in Switzerland and ambivalence related to return around the retirement period', *International Journal of Comparative Sociology*, **60** (1–2), 14–36.

Bolzman, C. and Vagni, G. (2018) '"And we are still here": life courses and life conditions of Italian, Spanish and Portuguese retirees in Switzerland' in I. Vlase and B. Voicu (eds), *Gender, Family, and Adaptation of Migrants in Europe: A Life Course Perspective*, Cham: Springer International, pp. 67–89.

Bolzman, C., Fibbi, R. and Vial, M. (2001) 'La famille: une source de légitimité pour les immigrés âgés après la retraite?', *Revue Européenne des Migrations Internationales*, **17** (1), 55–78.

Bolzman, C., Fibbi, R. and Vial, M. (2006) 'What to do after retirement? Elderly migrants and the question of return', *Journal of Ethnic and Migration Studies*, **32** (8), 1359–75.

Bolzman, C., Hirsch-Durret, E., Anderfuhren, S. and Vuille, M. (2008) 'Migration of parents under family reunification policies. A national approach to a transnational problem: the case of Switzerland', *Retraite et Société*, **55** (3), 39–69.

Bolzman, C., Kaeser, L. and Christe, E. (2017) 'Transnational mobilities as a way of life among older migrants from Southern Europe', *Population, Space and Place*, **23** (5), e2016.

Cassarino, J.P. (2004) 'Theorising return migration: the conceptual approach to return migrants revisited', *International Journal on Multicultural Societies*, **6** (2), 253–79.

Cerase, F.P. (1974) 'Expectations and reality: a case study of return migration from the United States to Southern Italy', *International Migration Review*, **8** (2), 245–62.

Ciobanu, R.O. and Hunter, A. (2017) 'Older migrants and (im)mobilities of ageing: an introduction', *Population, Space and Place*, **23** (5), e2075.

Ciobanu, R.O. and Ramos, A.C. (2016) 'Is there a way back? A state-of-the-art review of the literature on retirement return migration' in U. Karl and S. Torres (eds), *Ageing in Contexts of Migration*, London and New York: Routledge, pp. 96–107.

Cresswell, T. (2010) 'Mobilities I: catching up progress', *Progress in Human Geography*, **35** (4), 550–8.
De Coulon, A. and Wolff, F.-C. (2006) *The Location of Immigrants at Retirement: Stay/Return or 'Va-et-Vient'?*, Bonn: Institute for the Study of Labor, IZA Discussion Paper.
de Haas, H. (2008) *Migration and Development. A Theoretical Perspective*, Oxford: University of Oxford, International Migration Institute Working Paper No. 9.
de Haas, H. and Fokkema, T. (2010) 'Intra-household conflicts in migration decision-making: return and pendulum migration in Morocco', *Population and Development Review*, **36** (3), 541–61.
Dietzel-Papakyriakou, M. (2001) 'Elderly foreigners, elders of foreign heritage in Germany', *Revue Européenne des Migrations Internationales*, **17** (1), 79–99.
Fojo, L. and Fernandez, A. (2004) *Trois Familles Espagnoles entre Ici et Là-Bas*, Geneva: University of Geneva, Faculty of Economic and Social Sciences, unpublished Master's dissertation in Sociology.
Gehring, A. (2017) 'Pensioners on the move: a "legal gate" perspective on retirement migration to Spain', *Population, Space and Place*, **23** (5), e2007.
Gualda, E. and Escriva, A. (2014) 'Diversity in return migration and its impact on old age: the expectations and experiences of returnees in Huelva (Spain)', *International Migration*, **52** (5), 178–90.
Hunter, A. (2011) 'Theory and practice of return migration at retirement: the case of migrant worker hostel residents in France', *Population, Space and Place*, **17** (2), 179–92.
King, R. (2000) 'Generalisations from the history of return migration' in B. Ghosh (ed.), *Return Migration: Journey of Hope or Despair?*, Geneva: International Organization for Migration, pp. 7–55.
Lardiès Bosque, R., Guillén, J.C. and Montes-De-Oca, V. (2016) 'Retirement migration and transnationalism in Northern Mexico', *Journal of Ethnic and Migration Studies*, **42** (5), 816–33.
Melgar, F. (1993) *Album de Famille*, Lausanne: Climage.
OFS (2019) *Age et Nationalité. Population Résidante Permanente selon l'Âge et la Nationalité*, Neuchâtel: Office fédéral de la statistique.
Percival, J. (2013) '"We belong to the land": British immigrants in Australia contemplating or realising their return "home" in later life' in J. Percival (ed.), *Return Migration in Later Life*, Bristol: Policy Press, pp. 113–39.
Piguet, E. (2006) *Einwanderungsland Schweiz: Fünf Jahrzehnte half geöffnete Grenzen*, Bern: Haupt.
Pino, M.R. and Verde, C. (2006) 'Emigración de retorno: análisis de la situación a través de historias de vida', *Migraciones*, **20**, 201–30.
Piore, M. (1979) *Birds of Passage. Migrant Labor and Industrial Societies*, New York: Cambridge University Press.
Portes, A. (1996) 'Globalization from below: the rise of transnational communities' in W.P. Smith and R.P. Korczenwicz (eds), *Latin America in the World Economy*, Westport CT: Greenwood Press, pp. 151–68.
Pries, L. (2001) 'The approach of transnational social spaces: responding to new configurations of the social and the spatial' in L. Pries (ed.), *New Transnational Social Spaces. International Migration and Transnational Companies*, London: Routledge, pp. 3–33.
Rodriguez, V., Egea, C. and Nieto, J.A. (2002) 'Return migration in Andalusia, Spain', *International Journal of Population Geography*, **8** (3), 233–54.
Sayad, A. (1991) *L'Immigration ou les Paradoxes de l'Altérité*, Brussels: De Boeck-Wesmael.
Sayad, A. (1999) *La Double Absence. Des Illusions de l'Émigré aux Souffrances de l'Immigré*, Paris: Seuil.
Sayad, A. (2001) 'La vacance comme pathologie de la condition immigrée: le cas de la retraite et de la pré-retraite', *Revue Européenne des Migrations Internationales*, **17** (1), 11–36.
Sheller, M. and Urry, J. (2006) 'The new mobilities paradigm', *Environment and Planning A*, **38** (2), 207–26.
Solano, G. (2019) 'The mixed embeddedness of transnational migrant entrepreneurs: Moroccans in Amsterdam and Milan', *Journal of Ethnic and Migration Studies*, **46** (10), 2067–85.
Spini, D., Bernardi, L. and Oris, M. (2017) 'Vulnerability across the life course', *Research in Human Development*, **14** (1), 1–4.
Stark, O. and Blum, D.E. (1985) 'The new economics of labor migration', *The American Economic Review*, **75** (2), 173–8.
Takai, Y. and De Guzmán, M.G. (2015) 'Ambivalence of return home: revaluating transnational trajectories of Filipina live-in domestic workers and caregivers in Toronto from 1970 to 2010' in D. Hoerder,

E. van Nederveen Meerkerk and S. Neunsinger (eds), *Towards a Global History of Domestic and Caregiving Workers*, Leiden and Boston: Brill, pp. 222–41.

Vlase, I. and Voicu, B. (2018) *Gender, Family, and Adaptation of Migrants in Europe. A Life Course Perspective*, Cham: Palgrave Macmillan.

Zontini, E. (2015) 'Growing old in a transnational social field: belonging, mobility and identity among Italian migrants', *Ethnic and Racial Studies*, **38** (2), 326–41.

# 16. Return migration and psychosocial wellbeing
## Zana Vathi

## INTRODUCTION

Issues of psychosocial wellbeing are often overlooked in migration research as the study of migrants' identity, integration and impact on welfare have taken precedence (Vathi, 2017). Recently a turn in migration studies and policy-making is observable, wherein different stakeholders have taken an interest in wellbeing and social-protection provisions and practices for migrants (Svasek, 2010; Vrabiescu and Kalir, 2018). The increasing focus on affect across the different social-science disciplines makes psychosocial wellbeing a more natural topic of inquiry (Boccagni and Baldassar, 2015; Wright, 2012).

Nonetheless, across the spheres of academia, policy-making and service provision, it is easier to speak about migrants' vulnerability than their wellbeing. The former is more in line with public discourses on migration, which ordinarily build around the deservingness (or lack) of migrants' access to welfare (Crawley and Skleparis, 2018). When wellbeing *is* emphasised, it is within the framework of migrants' independence and productivity. The situation is not very different in the countries of origin, particularly where economic migrant returnees are concerned. Often the focus is on migrants' economic viability and contribution to development rather than on their human rights, which leaves psychosocial wellbeing at the end of policy-makers' list of concerns in relation to returnees.

Migrants' vulnerability and wellbeing are therefore contentious concepts; they can be easily mobilised for political leverage. Ultimately, the perceived vulnerable status of migrants and its legal acknowledgement shape the interventions of the state and other welfare service-providers (Brown, 2012). Indeed, research on forced migration has highlighted the extremes of testing assessments performed on migrants, who may be granted state support only on the basis of bodily marks of violence (Fassin, 2012).

Despite the prominence and sensitivity of the concepts of vulnerability and wellbeing within the public discourse, both terms remain ambiguous and require further conceptualisation (Brown, 2012; Dodge et al., 2012; Fletcher et al., 2016). In the context of migration, Sabates-Wheeler and Waite (2003) identified three determinants of vulnerability: spatial, socio-cultural and socio-political. These three dimensions aim to encompass the well-documented difficulties that migrants experience with access to resources, the institutional discrimination against them and the varying cultural tensions between them and the 'host' society. A distinction is drawn in the literature between vulnerability *as experienced* and vulnerability *as defined* for state purposes, with it being a negotiated status between migrants, the state and service-providers (Fineman, 2010).

Similarly, wellbeing is a complex concept; the literature gives a variety of definitions and, at the same time, notes the difficulty of adequately capturing its meaning (Vathi, 2017). Dodge et al. (2012) put a strong emphasis on homeostasis, defining wellbeing as a balance point between an individual's resource pool and the challenges that he or she faces, despite the caveat in the definition that life events and challenges are key to this concept's definition and measurement. However, a clear lack of focus on subjectivity in determining and defining wellbeing – and on its cultural sensitivity – is noticeable (Wright, 2012). Furthermore, the focus on homeostasis makes the definition of wellbeing not quite compatible with the very impactful experience of migration. Thus, mainstream definitions consider the temporal dimensions of wellbeing but not the transnational ones, which are key to the understanding and experiencing of wellbeing among migrants.

The definition of psychosocial wellbeing in this chapter, therefore, encompasses both the subjective and the objective aspects of wellbeing (Wright, 2012), resting on a high regard for contextual features and their impact on migrants' lives. Paying close attention to the interlinkages between psychological and social experiences (Wessells, 1999), psychosocial wellbeing is a person-centred concept that emphasises the value of interactions, social and emotional consonance and the individual experience.[1]

For a long time – until the 1970s onwards – returnees were not seen as vulnerable, not least because of the lack of systematic focus on return migration and on 'outcomes' for returning migrants and their families (Cerase, 1974; Gmelch, 1980). Sporadic research has highlighted the mental-health issues of returnees but these clinical approaches leave out the processes that lead to vulnerability and ill-health. Some work on diaspora homecoming (Markowitz and Stefansson, 2004) has included the impact of return on the wellbeing of diasporic returnees (Black and Koser, 1999). Research is even revisiting classic concepts, such as the myth of return, to delve deeper into the processes of migrants' return-thinking and identity-building in the broader framework of wellbeing (Bolognani, 2016).

However, even in the existing body of literature, an important assumption held strongly among policy-makers and some academics is that vulnerability and psychosocial issues are mainly predominant among 'forced' migrants, whose categorisation involves those who were subjected to state-related violence. Other forms of violence (intimate, cultural) are ineligible for justifying the vulnerability of migrants (Vathi, 2017). Forced versus voluntary return is a significant, if problematic divide, even in very recent research in the field (Hagan and Wassink, 2020; see also Erdal and Oeppen, Chapter 5). Indeed, the literature on forced returns with a particular focus on deportation (regimes, procedures, actors etc.) is burgeoning (e.g. Dreby, 2012; Drotbohm, 2015; Majidi, 2018; Rodkey, 2018; also Lemberg-Pedersen, Chapter 9). In the context of deportation, the disregard of states towards migrants' wellbeing shows how sovereignty, security and national identity – in the case of receiving states – and acute issues of economic deficit and unemployment in the case of countries of origin, take priority over human rights (Drotbohm and Hasselberg, 2015).

The analysis of vulnerability based on its determinants in order to enable a 'structural, long-term perspective rather than just a remedial perspective' (Sabates-Wheeler and Waite, 2003, p.15) does little to shed light on returnees' experiences. As returnees are not seen as susceptible to social exclusion nor to structural discrimination, the focus on the structural when migrant vulnerability is concerned makes them widely considered as not vulnerable, as structural determinants do not work against them – at least formally speaking. Ideally, vulnerability assessment and support should aim at prevention, which means that they should start in the host country (Zevulun et al., 2017). However, often assessments of vulnerability go hand-in-hand with punitive measures for those groups which fail to integrate and are excluded or even deported. A gap also exists between the formal definition of vulnerable groups and practice on the ground, with service-providers emerging as major stakeholders who may impose mainstream normative standards to the evaluation which then disadvantage migrants (Vrabiescu and Kalir, 2018).

The turn towards returnees' wellbeing has been evident recently in both academic and policy spheres and is closely linked with a stronger focus on reintegration (see Kuschminder, Chapter 14). At the policy level, the inclusion of wellbeing on the agenda of major actors (IOM, 2013) paved the way for the relevant programming. Nonetheless, while vulnerability has traditionally been studied in terms of the sustainability of return or the conditions that would make returnees disinclined to re-migrate, a much bolder approach to it is needed in order to capture the full spectrum of the impact that return to the country of origin has on migrants. Even recent reviews of the return migration literature overlook the growing importance of considering psychosocial wellbeing in its context and the warranted focus that psychosocial wellbeing has taken in academic and policy writings. Studies of return migration that focus on resource accumulation and mobilisation often ignore the social processes of which these resources are a part (Hagan and Wassink, 2020). The psychosocial turn in the study of return migration argues that, first, these processes are fraught with tension and second, resources that are crucial to the process of return, adaptation and reintegration should encompass those closely linked to wellbeing for a more holistic approach to the topic (Vathi, 2017).

In this chapter, three main aspects of return and psychosocial wellbeing are analysed: intersectionality, health and wellbeing, and reintegration, mobility and transnationality. These are selected not only for their prominence in the growing literature on the topic but also for their implications for policy-making and service provision in this area, with clear implications for the return migrants' lives. The chapter thus proceeds with an analysis of intersectionality and the extent and ways to which it has been utilised in this area. Further, the chapter highlights the privileging of health over wellbeing in the research on return and establishes a link between them, as they are often positively correlated in the context of return since health and wellbeing are very relational in the context of migration. In the last analysis section, the chapter focuses on the impact that reintegration and its sustainability have had on the acknowledgement of wellbeing as an important variable, as well as the direct links between wellbeing and reintegration in contexts around the world. The chapter concludes that structural approaches to return and reintegration are inadequately placed to address returnees' wellbeing and that migrant-centred approaches underpinned by human rights' considerations are needed.

## THE INTERSECTIONALITY OF RETURNEES AND WELLBEING 'OUTCOMES'

The concept of intersectionality refers to the joint impact of key characteristics – or, rather, social divisions – such as race, age, gender and class, that determine a person's positioning in the social hierarchy (Anthias, 2012; Crenshaw, 1994). Return migration is a complex process in which different characteristics of returnees such as gender and age hierarchies and power positionalities at different scales all materialise to determine its dimensions: timing, logistics, location of settlement upon return and re-migration (Vathi, 2017). Therefore, returnees' vulnerabilities have an intersectional nature although research and practice in the field have adopted a generic taxonomy of vulnerability, listing as the most vulnerable groups children and young people, single women and ageing migrants. Class and ethnicity have appeared less often in research on return. Indeed, class has been largely ignored, despite its early highlighting as a vulnerability factor among returnees (Longino, 1979), whereas ethnicity has been discussed primarily in post-conflict settings (Özerdem and Payne, 2019; Zevulun et al., 2017). Each of the categories – age, gender, class and ethnicity – intersect significantly with one another to determine returnees' wellbeing or at least the strategies which they employ against adversity.

The wellbeing of unaccompanied minors (UAMs) and of the children of returnees in the context of family return is an underestimated topic but one with symbolic importance for the reintegration agendas of the different stakeholders, whether migrants, policy-makers or service-providers. It could serve as a fulcrum for a more comprehensive discussion of wellbeing in the return process, tying together humanitarian, economics and human rights principles and agendas. For a long time, however, research on children, migration and psychological wellbeing has mostly looked at the experience of children in the receiving countries, referring primarily to immigration in the global North (Ní Laoire et al., 2011). Children's migration to the parents' country of origin in the context of families' return migration was rarely studied until recently and certainly not from the perspective of the children. The few studies that existed on this topic saw the migration of children as part of families' return as psychologically 'safe', with few exceptions (King, 1977). The assumption that 'returning home' is a psychologically safe process for migrants and, therefore, for their children (see, e.g., Koliatis et al., 2003) does not consider children as autonomous and children's opinions as worthy of scientific analysis, reinforcing a long-standing trend in migration research (Dobson, 2009).

However, the category of child migrant is very diverse in itself. Aside from these intersectional characteristics, such as age, ethnicity and the form of migration, the overall transnational process of return matters in terms of the overall wellbeing of children but concern for children's wellbeing in the return process is hampered by the incoherent links and (lack of) cooperation between migration management and child protection systems (Vathi and Richards, 2019). Even when both areas – migration management and the welfare system – are high on international agendas, which bind countries of origin to different international obligations (e.g. EU accession for the Western Balkans), the realisation of wellbeing for the children of returnees or UAMs tends to fall through the cracks of the two systems.

The focus on children's wellbeing in the context of return is even more important when we consider the very diverse reactions and outcomes for them (see Grosa, Chapter 17, on children's reintegration). Evidence suggests that girls and older adolescents experience return as a largely traumatic experience leading to severe mental-health problems (Neto, 2010; Vathi and Duci, 2016). Zevulun et al. (2017) focused on the return of rejected asylum-seekers to Albania and Kosovo and found that the most vulnerable groups of children were those who experienced irregular migration, had a Roma ethnic-minority background and were older adolescents. Thus, immigration status appears to be the most significant determinant in some settings. Loughry and Flouri (2001) found that, among the repatriated Vietnamese children who had lived unaccompanied in South Korea, the main determinants of wellbeing were their living conditions and immigration status. Return migration appears to exacerbate psychiatric symptoms among children and adolescents in the long term, affecting girls less if they moved before puberty (Vuorenkoski et al., 1998).

However, the intersection of age and gender in the context of return is far more complex. Decision-making on return and on re-migration are very gendered and also linked to the difference in levels of integration between female and male migrants, often making women less inclined to return (Sampaio, 2017; Vathi, 2011). Other evidence suggests that the effects of migration and return on the lives of women can be far-reaching; they appear as key actors in the return process, starting with the logistics of preparing for return (Majidi, 2017). Chen et al. (2010) researched rural–urban return migration in China and observed that women moving back to rural areas adopted positive family planning, reproductive health practices and overall gender attitudes, which have significant potential to shape China's family-planning policy.

The intersection of age and gender is also impacted by relationality, both to people and to place, which emerges as a strong characteristic of ageing migrants. Return migrants are deeply affected by relationality and, crucially, their wellbeing is often seen as a function of significant others, with the concept of linked lives (Elder, 1994) being an important dimension of their migration and return decision-making. Therefore, the theme of transnationality and post-return mobilities appears as paramount in the later life of migrants and returnees, with crucial implications for their wellbeing (Cela, 2017). These themes are important not least because return migrants tend to be negatively selected on socio-economic characteristics relative to other migrants (Longino, 1979), though recent research has found otherwise (see Wahba, Chapter 2, on the economics of return migration).

As mentioned above, later life exposes issues with integration and social support, while emotional ties with partners, children and grandchildren that pull towards different directions lead elderly migrants and returnees to prefer back-and-forth trips between their country of long-term residence and that of origin (Hunter, 2011; see also Bolzman, Chapter 15). Jauhiainen (2009) emphasised this when reporting on Finnish elderly people returning from Sweden, showing that remaining contacts and summer cottages in the countryside positively influenced the return decision and their appraisal of their wellbeing upon return. In line with these findings, Leavey et al. (2004) discussed the experience of older Irish migrants living in London, the process of ageing and the myth of return as linked to the lack of integration in later life and the less-than-optimal option to return home, which appears to affect ageing migrants' appraisal of life satisfaction.

Dealing with vulnerable groups in countries of origin that have low levels of welfare services and a shortage of resources is particularly problematic, especially in the context of intense return waves. Often these countries deal with a complex typology of returnees: forced migrants, economic migrants and 'economic asylum-seekers' – as has been the case of Balkan countries in the past decade. When minorities are part of these waves as well, the reintegration challenges for receiving states are paramount. Arenliu and Weine (2016) researched this in the context of Kosovo, which did not have policies and programmes in place on the vulnerability of returnees. Groups of returnees from the outmigration waves of the wars reported a high prevalence of post-traumatic stress disorder and other common mental-health problems – much more significant among women, minority groups and those with low levels of education. Among those migrating after the war, the most significant vulnerabilities were observed among those who had a longer period of stay abroad, forcibly repatriated migrants and the Roma.

While the focus on the vulnerability of returnees is a positive development in the field of policy-making in return migration, the issue of the (re)integration of minorities is little talked about in the literature on integration. This issue, however, puts a double emphasis on the two-way nature of integration, which would entail both cultural preservation and a willingness to integrate from both 'mainstream' and minority returnees. Vathi (2019) focused on the migration from and return of the Roma to the Western Balkans – a minority distinctly marginalised and discriminated against across the region. A crucial challenge for the Roma is adaptation after having experienced different lifestyles and a sense of dignity in the host countries in the European Union (EU) and then reconciling their expectations with the standards they (re-)experience upon return to the Western Balkans. However, the return and reintegration of minorities has been treated primarily in the context of post-conflict societies. Research on return is showing that conflict is not only a key factor of the wellbeing and mental health of forced migrants but also has serious implications for the adaptation and wellbeing of return migrants (Özerdem and Payne, 2019).

## HEALTH, WELLBEING AND INTERLINKS WITH RETURN

Health is a better-documented variable in the context of return when compared to wellbeing, first, due to more systematic data collection in this domain and, second, perhaps due to a more intense and larger-scale scholarship in clinical research. Though health, wellbeing and return are interlinked in different ways, health concerns among migrants can be a key determinant in return decision-making, leading to return migration and its impact on the wellbeing of other members of migrant families as well. This is documented to be the case both in the context of voluntary return (Conze and Müller, 2004), especially in later life (Hall et al., 2017), as well as in the context of assisted voluntary returns (Kalir, 2017). Repatriation and health, on the other hand, are negatively correlated and this is by far the least ambiguous part of the research in this area, with some studies documenting all-encompassing health issues for the forced returnees that go beyond psychosocial and mental ill-health issues (Fu and Vanlandingham, 2010).

Furthermore, health issues that lead migrants to return are seen to represent only the tip of the iceberg when it comes to the health conditions of the migrant population in the receiving country. Wong and Gonzalez (2010) focused on the effect of disability and wealth on return migration and adaptation in Mexico. They observed significant gender differences, with returnee women more likely to be disabled and returnee men to be wealthier than the average non-migrant. This finding signals a higher incidence of health issues among Mexican returnees, considering the pace of feminisation of migration from Mexico. In other contexts, research has tried to document the ripples of health problems of ageing parents on the children and the impact that this has on return, which often takes place against the will of the children (Zimmer and Knodel, 2010).

In the case of repatriation, a clearer continuation is observed between health and wellbeing problems in the country of origin, poor living conditions, an irregular status in the receiving country and a lack of control over the decision to return. Sundquist and Johansson (1996) adopted a comparative methodology to check the health outcomes of repatriated refugees to Latin America against those of migrants remaining in Sweden. Material factors and lifestyle could not explain the entire spectrum of mental ill-health which they observed, as psychological distress and illness, torture, discrimination and not feeling secure were prevalent among the returnees. These findings are concerning when we consider that repatriation is accompanied with low health scores even two years after the conflict in the country of origin, suggesting that return in post-conflict contexts exacerbates trauma (e.g. Kosovo, see Toscani et al., 2007). Research with migrants going back through assisted return programmes in a similar context (ex-Yugoslavia) reported comparable findings. While the prevalence of mental-health disorders prior to return was moderate at 53 per cent, upon return it increased to 88 per cent, with living conditions in Germany and the willingness to return being major determinants, alongside living conditions and overall levels of welfare upon return (von Lersner et al., 2008).

Sometimes return is for healthcare and wellbeing; the need to access healthcare in the country of origin is more common among women and the elderly. Bergmark et al. (2010) researched the health behaviour of Mexican immigrants in the US and found that access to health systems in the country of origin is seen as a factor that improves overall wellbeing because of the continuity of care but also as a factor that has implications for the healthcare of the country of origin and for border policies. Health also appears in a converse relationship with integration and reintegration. For Mexican women living in the US, integration appeared to lead to lower maternal and infant health, labelled as the 'acculturation paradox'. Ceballos and Palloni (2010) concluded that integration in the country of destination can affect health behaviour, which may lead to selective return migrants.

In turn, access to and (dis)satisfaction with health services informs a general sense of (lack of) welfare among returnees and can trigger re-migration (Vathi et al., 2019). The situation is particularly dire in the case of elderly migrants. Due to the rigidity of the welfare and health systems – which often condition access to their services on long-term residence in the country of origin – and also in the absence of a global and transnational social-protection system (Levitt et al., 2017), elderly migrants may remain in limbo (e.g. ageing Mexican migrants without insurance in the US, see Ross et al., 2006), even in the context of intra-EU migration (British elderly returning from Spain, see Hall et al., 2017).

Health problems among migrants who are forced to return are exacerbated by the uncertainty of life upon return and the lack of quality health services in the country of origin (Junjan et al., 2011). Conze and Müller (2004) draw attention to the continuum between adaptation stress and major mental-health disorders such as schizophrenia. Furthermore, implications for the country of origin and health systems are even more significant in the case of migrants living with HIV. Mommers et al. (2009) highlight that such returns cannot be fully voluntary in view of the serious health implications, with some migrants considering return as a 'death sentence'. Across the board, upon return, migrants facing ill-health fear both overburdening their families and also marginalisation due to the stigma attached to mental ill-health. In turn, family health issues can actually trigger return to the country of origin (Eelens, 1988; Fong, 2008).

The very wide spectrum of returnees' experiences with health and wellbeing, varying from problems of initial adaptation to serious mental-health issues, may also lead to health transnationalism. For Mexican migrants in the US, going home for health services was seen as an alternative to the lack of health insurance in the US (Bergmark et al., 2010). In turn, migrants returning to Albania from Greece utilised the geographical proximity and the freedom of movement to travel back and forth for medical services (Vathi et al., 2019). However, psychosocial issues with adaptation and an incidence of mental-health issues are also observed among highly skilled youth in countries with well-resourced health systems. Furukawa (1997) observed issues among students returning to Japan even six months after their arrival. Gaw (2000) reported similar results with American students and raised the issue of psychological support for them, since reverse culture shock levels were negatively correlated with their proneness to seek professional help.

These strands are intertwined in the context of COVID-19, as evidenced by growing recent research. Return migration and COVID-19 appear to be closely linked; many migrants decided – or accelerated their plans – to return due to the loss of jobs or the risk of infection. The pandemic erected borders formerly permeable by migrants and generated waves of return, particularly among seasonal workers, whose mobility was enabled on the basis of bilateral agreements between neighbouring countries (IFRC, 2020). The International Organization for Migration (IOM, 2020) reports that 230,000 undocumented Afghans returned from Iran and Pakistan between 1 March and 30 May 2020. Pilot research is showing that returnees' households are significantly more affected by the pandemic (Mobarak, 2020).

## REINTEGRATION WITHOUT MOBILITY AND TRANSNATIONALITY?

Structural approaches have consistently been central to the study of reintegration; indeed, an underlying assumption of major stakeholders is that reintegration is mostly for migrants who engage with state-sponsored return schemes and the infrastructure in place. The IOM (2018, p.3) defines reintegration as a process of re-inclusion across the economic, social and psychosocial dimensions and considers it sustainable when 'returnees have reached levels of economic self-sufficiency, social stability within their communities and psychosocial well-being that allow them to cope with (re)migration drivers'. These approaches, following on the footsteps of the sustainable return agenda, look at migrants as contributors to development and are directly concerned with re-migration. At the same time, they are increasingly recognising the importance of political and economic institutional structures for the role which they play in enabling or hampering returnees' resource mobilisation upon return. State policies and programmes that lead to deportation, stigmatisation and criminalisation are seen as barriers to returnees' development potential (Hagan and Wassink, 2020, p.15).

Increasingly, the study of reintegration is moving towards more holistic approaches that emphasise its multiple dimensions (Kuschminder, Chapter 14). Other strands of migration research, such as transnationalism and social networks, have been helpful in framing reintegration as a topic worth researching in its own right, independent of governmental and intergovernmental agendas on the prevention of re-migration. Reintegration is currently widely recognised as a challenging and highly contextualised process (Carling and Erdal, 2014; Vathi, 2017). Aside from the complex temporal dimension, across the board the characteristics of returnees and the modes of return appear as major determinants of reintegration (Cassarino, 2004; Kuschminder, 2017).

Therefore, the traditional stance, which sees return and its 'outcomes' for the returnees in terms of homecoming and discusses the interface between return and psychosocial wellbeing within the framework of home, belonging and home-making, poses three issues. First, it sees home from a static perspective, equating it with the country of birth, which obsures the multiple challenges that returnees face. Despite theoretical developments on transnationality and mobility, the fixity notion is stronger in the context of return migration, because of a rarely questioned assumption about the country of origin as the ultimate home (Malkki, 1995). Second, broader governmental and institutional agendas on the desired sustainability of return (Black and Gent, 2004) and more recently on reintegration have also assumed this framework. Third, this framework presumes reintegration to be a smooth linear process, overlooking the importance of return mobilities within a broader framework of the prevention of re-migration.

Crucial to the decision and the overall experience of return and its intersection with psychosocial wellbeing is the citizenship of returnees. Returnees who hold 'enabling citizenships' (Vathi, 2017) of developed nations, which allow further mobility if needed, are less likely to experience trauma and negative psychosocial outcomes upon return. Indeed, various stakeholders are emphasising the need to consider post-return mobilities within the framework of wellbeing – access to transnational mobilities, as well as comprehensive options for legal migration (Erdal and Oeppen, 2017). Even though the experience of post-return transnational ties and mobilities varies among returnees, van Meeteren et al. (2014) identified the positive impact of maintaining transnational contacts post-return but only among returnees with specific return motives. In the case of children and young people who have limited mobility autonomy and rights, these ties may expose a disturbing sense of disruption and loss (Vathi and Duci, 2016).

Migrants-as-agents is an important goal in the context of reintegration. This stance is supported by both the sustainability of the return agenda – which focuses on migrants' investment in the sending countries' economy and the prevention of re-migration – and more coherently so by the newer agenda on the sustainability of reintegration. As agency and wellbeing link closely with humans' autonomy and self-realisation, it is not surprising that this more recent agenda has a stronger focus on wellbeing (IOM, 2017). Psychosocial support post-return features strongly in recent evidence-based studies on reintegration – for example, Fonseca et al. (2015) list psychosocial support for returnees at least 12 months after arriving in the country of origin as key to the sustainability of reintegration. According to the IOM (2018), assistance for returnees is key to Assisted Voluntary Return and Reintegration (AVRR) programmes, regardless of the type of involvement of migrants with such programmes; such assistance should also encompass the needs of the receiving communities. However, research on the ground has found that psychosocial wellbeing in the context of return has a strong non-linear temporal nature (Lietaert et al., 2017), which makes the traditional, linear and cumulative understandings of wellbeing and reintegration unsuitable in the return context.

Thus, reintegration depends not only on whether and how migrants adapt their material, emotional and logistic resource mobilisation strategies in response to adversity but also on the characteristics of return contexts (Hagan and Wassink, 2020; Lietaert, 2016). Through raising and maintaining barriers to access to information, resources, sociability, recognition and identity, social exclusion appears as an important framework 'for understanding the political, economic, social and institutional context that shapes human vulnerabilities' (Babajanian, 2013, p.6). Social exclusion upon return is gaining prominence in research on the topic, with the issues linked to stigma having heralded this dimension (Potter and Phillips, 2006). Its links with returnee wellbeing are signalled both by theoretical writings on the concept of exclusion and by research on the ground. Especially in the case of the children of migrants and young returnees, these experiences are particularly emphasised (Vathi and Duci, 2016), while the adequacy of reintegration for the experiences of the children who have loose ties with their families' country of origin is questioned widely in burgeoning research in the field (Miah and King, 2018).

Transnational differences in terms of wellbeing (Wright, 2012) also apply, perhaps even more, to the return context. Differences exist among the key stakeholders – policy-makers, service-providers, migrants and receiving communities – in terms of the conceptualisation of wellbeing and the programming that is required or even put in place ad hoc. Policy-makers and service-providers are ordinarily concerned with the establishment of an institutional cooperation and the programming of resources and effectiveness on the ground but, at a broader conceptual and ideological level, the issues of wellbeing and social protection are fraught with tension due to transnational and transtemporal discontinuities (Vathi et al., 2019). The transnational dimension of the return process is, however, largely overlooked, especially when human rights and service provision are concerned. The discontinuities observed are due to significant differences in the welfare regimes of destination, transit and origin countries, as well as in the registers of need, vulnerability and wellbeing upheld by major stakeholders (migrants, communities of origin and reception, policy-makers, service-providers). In the rapidly increasing flows of return migration worldwide and the precarity and significant changes due to COVID-19, these staggered registers have implications for policy-making on return and (re)integration (IOM, 2017, 2020).

The relationship between reintegration (as structurally defined) and wellbeing can enhance the visibility of other issues in the return migration area. Some of the most distinct are, for example, the need for better data collection and standardisation, systematic transnational cooperation, a focus on temporalities and a stronger rationale for longitudinal designs, the reconciliation of returnees' vision and standards with those of the receiving communities, and an ethics of research with returnees. In the absence of a specific institutional structure on return migration in the Global Compact for Migration (GCM), these constructive links become more essential for the elaboration of better standards and an overall understanding of the return process.[2]

The GCM shows a move towards a more holistic conceptualisation of states' obligations in the field of migration and return. On reintegration, it aims to bring in closer cooperation on return in the countries of destination, transit and origin at the global level. In addition, it emphasises systematic data collection to increase cooperation and accountability in the framework of reintegration programming. The GCM focuses on wellbeing as a dimension of, as well as a factor for, reintegration (IOM, 2018). However, the human rights approaches would require that all returnees be regarded as vulnerable, not just those returned as part of AVRR, which would make the latter serve as a legitimating instrument for returnee status and the provision of state support. Also, this formal focus on reintegration excludes the availability of and access to legal migration routes as part of wellbeing post-return.

The embedding of reintegration in the 2030 Agenda and its Sustainable Development Goals (SDGs) is a progressive step across migration management and development areas of policy and practice. Among the numerous direct and indirect references to migration, the SDGs refer clearly to the obligation of states to receive their citizens in a due manner (e.g. Target 10.7, to 'facilitate [the] orderly, safe, and responsible migration and mobility of people'). While this does not roll out an international system of reception for returnees[3] it does bring return to the overall framework of development work with which countries of origin are engaged. Seen as a key part of migration management, reintegration assistance plays an important role in addressing any challenges that states may experience with return migration and reintegration (IOM, 2018).

## CONCLUSIONS

This chapter has analysed the literature on return migration, health and wellbeing and contends that, for a long time, the structural focus on the sustainability of return has obscured the very wide range of psychosocial issues and mental ill-health symptoms that returnees experience, based on intersectional features such as age, gender, ethnicity and class. A shift towards the sustainability of reintegration and a stronger academic focus on it as a topic worth exploring in its own right both shed light on the importance of psychosocial wellbeing at all stages of the migration and return process.

However, even in the recent turn towards reintegration with a focus on social protection and service provision, particular areas of concern are considered to be access to essential services such as healthcare, shelter, education or justice but these confine the reintegration definition and actions within a strong structural perspective. A (human) rights-based approach that recognises the need to 'develop integrated models that reflect the contextual and individual heterogeneity inherent to return migration and resource mobilization' (Hagan and Wassink, 2020, p.15) best addresses reintegration, with a focus on returnees' wellbeing at its core. The psychosocial strand of return and reintegration (Vathi, 2017) arguably combines the contextual and the individual in a migrant-centred perspective, which is crucial to ensuring that specific attention is paid to the rights and needs of the individual returnees.

The chapter concludes that migrant-centred approaches underpinned by human rights considerations are best positioned to enable the integration of psychosocial wellbeing onto policy-making agendas and in service provision, considering this aspect of return as key to enhancing migrants' agency and the deployment of their resourcefulness in the countries of origin post-return.

## NOTES

1. For a discussion of the definition of psychosocial wellbeing, please see Vathi (2017).
2. European Dialogue on Return and Sustainable Reintegration of Migrants, Berlin, 18 October 2020.
3. Ibid.

## REFERENCES

Anthias, F. (2012) 'Intersectional what? Social division, levels of analysis and intersectionality', *Ethnicity*, **13** (1), 3–19.
Arenliu, A. and Weine, S.M. (2016) 'Reintegrating returned migrants to Kosovo', *Psychological Research*, **19** (1), 61–73.
Babajanian, B. (2013) *Social Protection and Its Contribution to Social Inclusion*, London: Overseas Development Institute.
Bergmark, R., Barr, D. and Garcia, R. (2010) 'Mexican immigrants in the US living far from the border may return to Mexico for health services', *Journal of Immigrant and Minority Health*, **12** (4), 610–14.
Black, R. and Gent, S. (2004) *Defining, Measuring and Influencing Sustainable Return: The Case of the Balkans*, Brighton: University of Sussex, Sussex Centre for Migration Research Working Paper No. T7.
Black, R. and Koser, K. (eds) (1999) *The End of the Refugee Cycle? Refugee Repatriation and Reconstruction*, London: Berghahn.
Boccagni, P. and Baldassar, L. (2015) 'Emotions on the move: mapping the emergent field of emotion and migration', *Emotion, Space and Society*, **16**, 73–80.
Bolognani, M. (2016) 'From myth of return to return fantasy: a psychosocial interpretation of migration imaginaries', *Identities*, **23** (2), 193–209.
Brown, K. (2012) 'Re-moralising "vulnerability"', *People, Place and Policy Online*, **6** (1), 41–53.
Carling, J. and Erdal, M.B. (2014) 'Return migration and transnationalism: how are the two connected?', *International Migration*, **52** (6), 2–12.
Cassarino, J.-P. (2004) 'Theorising return migration: the conceptual approach to return migrants revisited', *International Journal on Multicultural Societies*, **6** (2), 253–79.

Ceballos, M. and Palloni, A. (2010) 'Maternal and infant health of Mexican immigrants in the USA: the effects of acculturation, duration, and selective return migration', *Ethnicity and Health*, **15** (4), 377–96.

Cela, E. (2017) 'Migration and return migration in later life to Albania: the pendulum between subjective wellbeing and place' in Z. Vathi and R. King (eds), *Return Migration and Psychosocial Wellbeing*, London: Routledge, pp. 203–20.

Cerase, F. (1974) 'Expectations and reality: a case study of return migration from the United States to Southern Italy', *International Migration Review*, **8** (2), 245–62.

Chen, J., Liu, H. and Xie, Z. (2010) 'Effects of rural–urban return migration on women's family planning and reproductive health attitudes and behavior in rural China', *Studies in Family Planning*, **41**(1), 31–44.

Conze, B. and Müller, F. (2004) *Voluntary Return with a Schizophrenic Disorder. Research Report*, The Hague: International Organization for Migration.

Crawley, H. and Skleparis, D. (2018) 'Refugees, migrants, neither, both: categorical fetishism and the politics of bounding in Europe's "migration crisis"', *Journal of Ethnic and Migration Studies*, **44** (1), 48–64.

Crenshaw, K.W. (1994) Mapping the margins: intersectionality, identity politics, and violence against women of colour' in M.A. Fineman and R. Mykitiuk (eds), *The Public Nature of Private Violence*, New York: Routledge, pp. 93–118.

Dobson, M.E. (2009) 'Unpacking children in migration research', *Children's Geographies*, **7** (3), 355–60.

Dodge, R., Daly, A.P., Huyton, J. and Sanders, L.D. (2012) 'The challenge of defining wellbeing', *International Journal of Wellbeing*, **2** (3), 222–35.

Dreby, J. (2012) 'The burden of deportation on children in Mexican immigrant families', *Journal of Marriage and Family*, **74** (4), 829–45.

Drotbohm, H. (2015) 'The reversal of migratory family lives: a Cape Verdean perspective on gender and sociality pre- and post-deportation', *Journal of Ethnic and Migration Studies*, **41** (4), 653–70.

Drotbohm, H. and Hasselberg, I. (2015) 'Introduction. Deportation, anxiety, justice: new ethnographic perspectives', *Journal of Ethnic and Migration Studies*, **41** (4), 551–62.

Eelens, F. (1988) 'Early return of Sri Lankan migrants in the Middle East', *International Migration*, **26** (4), 401–15.

Elder, G.H. Jr (1994) 'Time, human agency, and social change: perspective on the life course', *Social Psychology Quarterly*, **57** (1), 4–15.

Erdal, M.B. and Oeppen, C. (2017) 'Forced to return? Agency and the role of post-return mobility for psychosocial wellbeing among returnees to Afghanistan, Pakistan, and Poland' in Z. Vathi and R. King (eds), *Return Migration and Psychosocial Wellbeing: Discourses, Policy-Making and Outcomes for Migrants and their Families*, London: Routledge, pp. 39–55.

Fassin, D. (2012) *Humanitarian Reason: A Moral History of the Present*, Berkeley, Los Angeles and London: University of California Press.

Fineman, A.M. (2010) 'The vulnerable subject and the responsive state', *Emory Law Journal*, **60**, 1–41.

Fletcher, D.R., Flint, J., Batty, E. and Mcneill, J. (2016) 'Gamers or victims of the system? Welfare reform, cynical manipulation and vulnerability', *Journal of Poverty and Social Justice*, **24** (2), 171–85.

Fong, V.L. (2008) 'The other side of the healthy immigrant paradox: Chinese sojourners in Ireland and Britain who return to China due to personal and familial health crises', *Culture Medicine and Psychiatry*, **32** (4), 627–41.

Fonseca, A., Hart, L. and Klink, S. (2015) *Reintegration: Effective Approaches*, Geneva: International Organization for Migration.

Fu, H. and Vanlandingham, M.J. (2010) 'Mental and physical health consequences of repatriation for Vietnamese returnees: a natural experiment approach', *Journal of Refugee Studies*, **23** (2), 160–82.

Furukawa, T. (1997) 'Sojourner readjustment: mental health of international students after one year's foreign sojourn and its psychosocial correlates', *Journal of Nervous and Mental Disease*, **185** (4), 263–8.

Gaw, K.F. (2000) 'Reverse culture shock in students returning from overseas', *International Journal of Intercultural Relations*, **24** (1), 83–104.

Gmelch, G. (1980) 'Return migration', *Annual Review of Anthropology*, **9**, 135–59.

Hagan, J.M. and Wassink, J.T. (2020) 'Return migration around the world: an integrated agenda for future research', *Annual Review of Sociology*, **46** (7), 1–20.

Hall, K., Betty, C. and Giner, J. (2017) 'To stay or to go? The motivations and experiences of older British returnees from Spain' in Z. Vathi and R. King (eds), *Return Migration and Psychosocial Wellbeing: Discourses, Policy-Making and Outcomes for Migrants and Their Families*, London: Routledge, pp. 221–39.

Hunter, A. (2011) 'Theory and practice of return migration at retirement: the case of migrant worker hostel residents in France', *Population Space and Place*, **17** (2), 179–92.

IFRC (2020) *Chile: Return Migration to Bolivia (COVID-19 Context)*, Geneva: International Federation Red Cross and Red Crescent Societies, Information Bulletin No. 1.

IOM (2013) *World Migration Report 2013: Migrant Well-Being and Develoment*, Geneva: International Organization for Migration.

IOM (2017) *Towards an Integrated Approach to Reintegration in the Context of Return*, Geneva: International Organization for Migration.

IOM (2018) *Enhancing Migrant Well-Being upon Return through an Integrated Approach to Reintegration*, Geneva: International Organization for Migration.

IOM (2020) *Return of Undocumented Afghans. Weekly Situation Report, May 24–30*, https://afghanistan.iom.int/sites/default/files/Reports/iom_afghanistan-return_of_undocumented_afghans-_situation_report_24-30_may_2020.pdf (accessed 6 April 2021).

Jauhiainen, J.S. (2009) 'Will the retiring baby boomers return to the rural periphery?', *Journal of Rural Studies*, **25** (1), 25–34.

Junjan, V., Popescu, C.A., Sfetcu, R., Miclutia, I. and Ciumageanu, M. (2011) 'What does circular migration cost for the sending country? Evidence of mental health costs after return to Romania', *Journal of Mental Health Policy and Economics*, **14**, S13–S14.

Kalir, B. (2017) 'State desertion and "out-of-procedure" asylum seekers in the Netherlands', *Focaal: Journal of Global and Historical Anthropology*, **77**, 63–75.

King, R. (1977) 'Problems of return migration: case-study of Italians returning from Britain', *Tijdschrift voor Economische en Sociale Geografie*, **68** (4), 241–5.

Koliatis, G., Tsiantis, J., Madianos, M. and Kotsopoulos, S. (2003) 'Psychosocial adaptation of immigrant Greek children from the former Soviet Union', *European Child and Adolescent Psychiatry*, **12** (2), 67–74.

Kuschminder, K. (2017) *Reintegration Strategies: Conceptualizing How Return Migrants Reintegrate*, Cham: Palgrave Macmillan.

Leavey, G., Sembhi, S. and Livingston, G. (2004) 'Older Irish migrants living in London: identity, loss and return', *Journal of Ethnic and Migration Studies*, **30** (4), 763–79.

Levitt, P., Viterna, J., Mueller, A. and Lloyd, C. (2017) 'Transnational social protection: setting the agenda', *Oxford Development Studies*, **45** (1), 2–19.

Lietaert, I. (2016) *Perspectives on Return Migration: A Multi-Sited, Longitudinal Study on the Return Processes of Armenian and Georgian Migrants*, Ghent: Ghent University, Faculty of Psychology and Educational Sciences, unpublished PhD thesis.

Lietaert, I., Broackaert, R. and Derluyn, I. (2017) 'Time heals? A multi-sited, longitudinal case study of returnees in Armenia' in Z. Vathi and R. King (eds), *Return Migration and Psychosocial Wellbeing: Discourses, Policy-Making and Outcomes for Migrants and Their Families*, London: Routledge, pp. 165–81.

Longino, C.F. (1979) 'Going home: aged return migration in the United States 1965–1970', *Journal of Gerontology*, **34** (5), 736–45.

Loughry, M. and Flouri, E. (2001) 'The behavioral and emotional problems of former unaccompanied refugee children 3–4 years after their return to Vietnam', *Child Abuse and Neglect*, **25** (2), 249–63.

Majidi, N. (2017) 'The return of refugees from Kenya to Somalia: gender and psychosocial wellbeing' in Z. Vathi and R. King (eds), *Return Migration and Psychosocial Wellbeing: Discourses, Policy-Making and Outcomes for Migrants and Their Families*, London: Routledge, pp. 149–64.

Majidi, N. (2018) 'Deportees lost at "home": post-deportation outcomes in Afghanistan' in S. Khosravi (ed.), *After Deportation*, Cham: Palgrave Macmillan, pp. 127–48.

Malkki, L. (1995) 'Refugees and exile: from "refugee studies" to the national order of things', *Annual Review of Anthropology*, **24**, 495–523.

Markowitz, F. and Stefansson, A.H. (eds) (2004) *Homecomings: Unsettling Paths of Return*, Lanham MD: Lexington Books.

Miah, Md.F. and King, R. (2018) 'Memoryscapes of the homeland by two generations of British-Bangladeshis' in S. Marschall (ed.), *Memory, Tourism and Migration*, London: Routledge, pp. 213–33.

Mobarak, A.M. (2020) *Mobility and Migration during COVID-19. Yale Research Initiative in Innovation and Scale*, Washington DC: The World Bank, http://pubdocs.worldbank.org/en/735771589469963131/MobilityMigrationCOVID-19-MushfiqMobarak.pdf (accessed 6 April 2021).

Mommers, C., Eijkhout, H., Iyamuremye, P.C. and Maiyo, J. (2009) *Health, Hope and Home? The Possibilities and Constraints of Voluntary Return for African Rejected Asylum Seekers and Irregular Migrants Living with HIV in the Netherlands*, The Hague: International Organization for Migration, Research Report.

Neto, F. (2010) 'Mental health among adolescents from returned Portuguese immigrant families', *Swiss Journal of Psychology*, **69** (3), 131–9.

Ní Laoire, C., Carpena-Mendez, F., Tyrrell, N. and White, A. (2011) *Childhood and Migration in Europe: Portraits of Mobility, Identity and Belonging in Contemporary Ireland*, London: Ashgate.

Özerdem, A. and Payne, L. (2019) 'Ethnic minorities and sustainable refugee return and reintegration in Kosovo', *Conflict, Security and Development*, **19** (4), 403–25.

Potter, R.B. and Phillips, J. (2006) '"Mad dogs and transnational migrants?" Bajan-Brit second-generation migrants and accusations of madness', *Annals of the Association of American Geographers*, **96** (3), 586–600.

Rodkey, E. (2018) 'Making it as a deportee: transnational survival in the Dominican Republic', in S. Khosravi (ed.), *After Deportation*, Cham: Palgrave Macmillan, pp. 169–86.

Ross, S.J., Pagán, J.A. and Polsky, D. (2006) 'Access to health care for migrants returning to Mexico', *Journal of Health Care for the Poor and Underserved*, **17** (2), 374–85.

Sabates-Wheeler, R. and Waite, M. (2003) *Migration and Social Protection: A Concept Paper*, Brighton: University of Sussex, Development Research Centre on Migration, Globalisation and Poverty Working Paper No. T2.

Sampaio, D. (2017) 'Is this really where home is? Experiences of home in a revisited homeland among ageing Azorean returnees' in Z. Vathi and R. King (eds), *Return Migration and Psychosocial Wellbeing: Discourses, Policy-Making and Outcomes for Migrants and Their Families*, London: Routledge, pp. 240–73.

Sundquist, J. and Johansson, S.-E. (1996) 'The influence of exile and repatriation on mental and physical health: a population-based study', *Social Psychiatry and Psychiatric Epidemiology*, **31** (1), 21–8.

Svasek, M. (2010) 'On the move: emotions and human mobility', *Journal of Ethnic and Migration Studies*, **36** (6), 865–80.

Toscani, L., DeRoo, L.A., Eytan, A., Gex-Fabry, M., Avramovski, V., Loutan, L. and Bovier, P. (2007) 'Health status of returnees to Kosovo: do living conditions during asylum make a difference?', *Public Health*, **121** (1), 34–44.

van Meeteren, M., Engbersen, G., Snel, E. and Faber, M. (2014) 'Understanding different post-return experiences: the role of preparedness, return motives and family expectations for returned migrants in Morocco', *Comparative Migration Studies*, **2** (3), 335–60.

Vathi, Z. (2011) 'A context issue? Comparing the attitude towards return of the Albanian first and second generation in Europe', *Journal of Mediterranean Studies*, **20** (2), 343–64.

Vathi, Z. (2017) 'The interface between return migration and psycho-social wellbeing' in Z. Vathi and R. King (eds), *Return Migration and Psychosocial Wellbeing: Discourses, Policy-Making and Outcomes for Migrants and Their Families*, London: Routledge, pp. 1–18.

Vathi, Z. (2019) *Barriers to (Re)Integration: The Roma Return to the Western Balkans*, Brighton: University of Sussex, Sussex Centre for Migration Research Working Paper No. 95.

Vathi, Z. and Duci, V. (2016) 'Making other dreams: the impact of migration on the psychosocial wellbeing of Albanian-origin children upon their families' return to Albania', *Childhood*, **23** (1), 53–68.

Vathi, Z. and Richards, E. (2019) 'Every child matters? Ambivalences and convergences in migration management and child protection in Albania', *Child Care in Practice*, **27** (1), 19–34.

Vathi, Z., Dhembo, E. and Duci, V. (2019) 'Social protection and return migration: the role of transnational and transtemporal developmental gaps in the Albania–Greece migration corridor', *Migration and Development*, **8** (2), 243–63.

von Lersner, U., Rieder, H. and Elbert, T. (2008) 'Mental health and attitudes towards returning to the country of origin in refugees from former Yugoslavia', *Zeitschrift fur Klinische Psychologie und Psychotherapie*, **37** (2), 112–21.

Vrabiescu, I. and Kalir, B. (2018) 'Care-full failure: how auxiliary assistance to poor Roma migrant women in Spain compounds marginalisation', *Social Identities*, **24** (4), 520–32.

Vuorenkoski, L., Moilanen, I., Myhrman, A., Kuure, O., Penninkilampi, V. and Kumpulainen, E. (1998) 'Long-term mental health outcome of returning migrant children and adolescents', *European Child and Adolescent Psychiatry*, **7** (4), 219–24.

Wessells, M.G. (1999) 'Culture, power and community: intercultural approaches to psychosocial assistance and healing' in K. Nader, N. Dubrow and B. Stamm (eds), *Honoring Differences: Cultural Issues in the Treatment of Trauma and Loss*, New York: Routledge, pp. 276–82.

Wong, R. and Gonzalez, C. (2010) 'Old-age disability and wealth among return Mexican migrants from the United States', *Journal of Aging and Health*, **22** (7), 932–54.

Wright, K. (2012) 'Constructing human wellbeing across spatial boundaries: negotiating meanings in transnational migration', *Global Networks*, **12** (4), 467–84.

Zevulun, D., Post, W.J., Zijlstra, A.E., Kalverboer, M.E. and Knorth, E.J. (2017) 'Migrant and asylum-seeker children returned to Kosovo and Albania: predictive factors for social–emotional wellbeing after return', *Journal of Ethnic and Migration Studies*, **44** (11), 1774–96.

Zimmer, Z. and Knodel, J. (2010) 'Return migration and the health of older aged parents: evidence from rural Thailand', *Journal of Aging and Health*, **22** (7), 955–76.

# 17. The return migration of children: (re)integration is not always plain sailing
*Daina Grosa*

## INTRODUCTION

This chapter provides a review of the literature on the representation, roles and experiences of children within the return migration literature, focusing on a particular area of Europe that is currently experiencing return migration – Central Eastern Europe. In this region, with its lingering post-Soviet legacy in mentality and traditions, in the education sector in particular, the smooth reintegration of migrants who originated from this part of Europe is impeded by the lack of adequate support for their children. A deeper insight can be gained by focusing on one country in the region – in this instance, Latvia; however, the challenges faced by families there are not unique and are just as evident in neighbouring Baltic countries and those further south in Eastern Europe. The chapter focuses only on children returning in family contexts (with the families returning voluntarily) and not on unaccompanied minors or forced migration settings.

The return migration of children who accompany their parents back to the latter's country of origin is an area of emerging international migration research which is still largely uncharted territory. It has been looked at only fleetingly, as family return (voluntary return, in particular) has, up until now, been considered 'psychologically safe' (Kolaitis et al., 2003). 'Safe' implies a family setting, hence the assumption that children have returned to a supportive and familiar environment. Yet this assumption can be erroneous – even close family members may have little knowledge about the inner world of the child. In general, there is scant research on the subjective perspective of children in migration studies, even less on this topic in return migration scenarios. In 2005, Knörr and Nunes argued that children have something original to say regarding childhood and 'therefore their experiences, representations, feelings and expressions should be considered a valid object of social research' (2005, p.14), while James and James (2004, cited in Knörr and Nunes, 2005, p.14) stated that 'childhood agency is not yet fully recognized'. Since then, some child-centred studies into the psychosocial wellbeing of children have been conducted, including some with children themselves having agency in the research (Cena et al., 2018; Ní Laoire, 2011; Vathi and King, 2021).

Hatfield (2010) has drawn attention to the fact that two elements of the experience of migration have been 'masked' despite the large numbers which fall in these categories. One is the experiences of children and young people upon migration; the other is return migrants. The crossover of both – the subjective view of children and young people who experience return migration – is still an embryonic research field within migration studies.

To date, studies have looked implicitly at the return of children mostly from the perspective of their parents; looking at their motivation for return and various factors that influence the decision to make a family return move. Some studies have found that having a family can be the catalyst for ending plans to return to the country of origin. Looking from a behaviourist perspective, Dustmann (2003) highlights return intentions and realisations with regard to the perceived long-term social and material benefits to children of remaining in or leaving the host country behind. Tsuda (2004) echoes this sentiment – that having a family produces a greater commitment to the host society, leading to more willingness to become permanent or long-term residents.

There is also a counter-argument by scholars who suggest that starting a family can actually be the deciding factor for return. Ní Laoire (2011) points out that lifestyle benefits for young families – namely, 'safety, spatial freedom, quality of life and ideas of childhood innocence' (2011, p.1258) – are seen by Irish migrants as the reason for returning, while Saar and Saar (2020) stress Estonian returnees' desire to return to a slower pace of life in order to facilitate active and involved parenting.

In her study of families returning to Ireland, Ní Laoire (2011) categorises the narratives of returning migrant children themselves and how these relate to those of their parents. Although, when interviewed, some children mirror their parents' narratives of 'innocent Irish childhoods' regarding freedom, space and safety, others draw out the negatives – among others, the spatial confinement after returning because of poor public transportation and a lack of entertainment opportunities in comparison with the previous place of residence in England. Children do not always see the world in the same way that their parents do and this subjective view, although often a selective interpretation of elements of their parents' narratives, is done in a way that has meaning to them and the reality of their daily life.

The return of Italian families with children from Great Britain 'back home' to Italy and their experience of integrating into the local community were mentioned in an early paper by King (1977), who spoke of the difficulties faced particularly by school-aged children and teenagers who found it hard to cope with the change in environment, in this case a switch from urban England to small and remote hill villages in southern Italy. For many returnee children, the move is actually not a return but, rather, a migration, since they were born in the host country (Knörr, 2005). Szydlowska et al. (2019) found this to be the case for Polish children who experience acculturation difficulties on return; schools, too, have problems coping, primarily due to the lack of Polish language skills of the returning children, which are not addressed adequately in the education system.

Vathi and Duci (2016), Vathi and King (2017, 2021) and Cena et al. (2018) all focus on the children of returning Albanian migrants, examining the integration of these children from different perspectives. The psychosocial wellbeing aspect is tackled in these studies, as well as diasporic belongingness as a precursor to a later sense of attachment to the source country. Feelings of 'othering' and 'othering' practices in Vathi and King (2021) show the double-bind that return migrant children can end up in: a sensation of being in 'no man's land'. Ironically, the migrant children were 'othered' in Greece (the main destination country for post-1990 Albanian migration) because of their 'Albanianness' and then othered upon return to Albania because of their attributed 'Greekness'. Cena et al. (2018) studied the everyday places and social relations that play a central role in alleviating the stress of acculturation in a return situation. These are the quite rare studies that have focused on the wellbeing of return migrant children from a perspective of belonging and integration. The Albanian case will be picked up later, given that it offers some parallels to the case of Latvia, which I focus on towards the latter part of this chapter.

## MOTIVATION FOR RETURN

From interviews with return migrants in their source country, scholars have found a number of reasons for return and not all are associated with bettering the migrant's financial position (Callea, 1986; Saar, 2018). Many returning nationals are motivated by a sense of nostalgia, a longing for the familiar – including the natural environment – and a desire to rejoin the country where they can feel 'at home' and accepted. For some, the motivating trigger is their children reaching school age and a desire for their children to attend school in their country of origin. The reasons for this could be many and varied, for instance because they do not want their children to forget their mother tongue or because they feel the education system in their country is better than that in the host country.

A new way of looking at return is from a lifestyle perspective (see Walsh, Chapter 19). Previous studies of return and lifestyle migration have focused on relatively affluent individuals who migrate to countries with a warmer climate, a slower pace of life and a lower cost of living (Akerlund and Sandberg, 2015; Benson and Osbaldiston, 2014). Janoschka and Haas (2013) have outlined certain distinguishing factors associated with lifestyle migration. First, this is a privileged form of mobility and not undertaken for economic reasons. Second, this form of migration is predominantly evident in wealthy Western societies, where individuals can choose to migrate to locations with a lower cost of living. Third, lifestyle migrants, after moving, end up enjoying a better standard of living than the locals.

Saar and Saar (2020) argue that, in the case of the return migration of Eastern Europeans, there can also be an element of lifestyle migration involved, yet this mobility does not necessarily have the previously mentioned features. The decision to return back to the source country becomes a lifestyle choice, made at the time that a migrant couple begins to consider starting a family (or, alternatively, their children start approaching school age) and as they weigh up the pros and cons of living family life abroad. Living life in a big metropolis, away from close family, with much time spent travelling long distances to work, may no longer seem so appealing when children and their needs have to be factored in. For this reason, the Estonians researched by Saar and Saar chose to return to Estonia so that they could enjoy this stage of life in a more peaceful setting with a slower pace of life.

The prospect of enrolling their children in schools in the host country, which will expose them to what are perceived as 'unfavourable' social classes, can also make migrants consider other options. Other factors that concern young parents when imagining their future life as a family are a clean environment, a proximity to nature and life with less 'hustle and bustle'. All these different factors may have a pivotal role in determining whether a family will remain abroad or return. In addition, the perspective of the returning children themselves is of key importance, as the prospect of school attendance in their parents' country of origin may be met with ambivalence, if not with outright hostility.

## THE PSYCHOSOCIAL WELLBEING PERSPECTIVE

A holistic wellbeing approach is now increasingly being taken by researchers and policymakers in migration destination countries to get a full understanding of the whole gamut of emotions experienced by migrants and their families. A person's wellbeing has been categorised as having 'objective' and 'subjective' dimensions. The former is a dimension that can be verified by an external observer (housing, level of education, income), while the latter reflects a more internal, individual look at the concept – concerning the thoughts and feelings of the subjects in question (White and Blackmore, 2015). Subjective wellbeing or self-reports of the life satisfaction of migrants and their children will be the focus of the remainder of this chapter. Adding in the psychosocial component, the 2018 World Health Organization online guidelines explain 'psychosocial' as:

> The inter-connection between psychological sub-components – such as emotions, thoughts and behaviours, including coping strategies – and social sub-components, such as interpersonal relationships, social roles, norms, values, traditions and community life, that contribute to the overall well-being of a person.

So, at the crux of the matter is the symbiotic relationship between the two: the way a person copes psychologically with a situation in their life, in conjunction with the social components within their life and their connection to the external world. Walking the well-balanced tightrope between the two will ensure healthy psychosocial wellbeing.

A study in Norway in 2015 conducted by Carling et al. refers to this in reference to return migration:

> Return migration is a phenomenon that pervades life in two significant ways. First, the reality is that many migrants do go back. In Norway … half of all immigrants leave within ten years of their arrival, many returning to their country of origin. The realities of return migration concern who returns, how they experience it and what impact their return has on others. Second, all migrants can relate to the possibility of return. For many, it touches on deeper existential issues. (Carling et al., 2015, p.1)

The above-mentioned approach to return migration delves into the emotional side of mobility. It puts a human face on it, looks into the motivation behind individual actions, explores the uncertainty of migrants' feelings and their dual allegiance to two (or perhaps more) countries, revealing that the hope of return to the country of origin is, for many, an ever-present dream that may or may not materialise. This emotional aspect, including the lived realities of migrants and their subjective feelings, illuminates the often unseen side of migration. In other words, the stories behind the statistics – not merely those of the adults making the decisions but also their dependents.

These issues have come to the fore as families return to their countries of origin and are prone to experiencing the very real challenges of re-entry, sometimes known as 'reverse culture shock'. Often adult returnees, as well as various institutions, mistakenly assume that a return to the home country will be seamless and easier than adapting to another culture (Stroh et al., 1998). Those who return to the country of origin have imagined and have the expectation that they will return to exactly the same country that they left a number of years ago. For some, their expectations are met or, possibly, they do not worry much if life does bring different, unpredictable challenges – they just deal with them. Others are not prepared for and are frustrated by the changes that their home country may have undergone in the meantime.

In addition to the disappointment experienced by adult returnees, there is a 'misperception that children are irrelevant to migration studies … compounded by a focus on the economic, and an understanding that only adults are of economic significance' (Dobson, 2009, p.355). Children also undergo a period of readjustment which could be for an entirely different reason.

Their 'return' may actually not be a case of reacquainting themselves with the familiar but, rather, an emigration of sorts.

Zúñiga and Hamann (2015), having surveyed Mexican schoolchildren born in the USA who returned to Mexico, found that it would be misleading to call these children *retornados* (returnees) because they did not return to Mexico; rather, they immigrated there. The return in this context is a 'disruptive geographical relocation' (even when desired). Zúñiga and Hamann's research concludes that '[c]hildren generally experience this disruption as an assemblage of ruptures, both in institutional settings – like schools – and non-institutional ones like neighbourhoods' (2015, p.645). Children experience 'return' as a break from existing social ties (school, neighbourhood, possibly some family) and face the need to forge new relationships in an often unfamiliar setting. So the disruption is not only a physical one but also emotional and it impacts on their psychosocial wellbeing.

The psychosocial wellbeing of returning migrants, including children, has been tackled from a number of angles in a collection edited by Vathi and King (2017). The introduction to the collection provides a considered definition of the concept of psychosocial wellbeing. Bringing together concepts of migration and mobility, psychosocial wellbeing and the various factors (physical, health, socio-cultural and economic) that affect it and looking at their subjective and objective aspects provides a multi-faceted and nuanced insight into this field of return migration (Vathi, 2017). This book is one of the few scholarly publications that look at return migration from this perspective, yet studies with children and students as the focus comprise only a small proportion of the research presented in the volume (see Gonda, 2017; Lulle, 2017).

An important aspect that needs to be considered is the sense of belonging of return migrant children to the source country of their parents, which also partly determines their envisaged future selves. If the children (and their parents) see their future – for the purposes of education and future career prospects – as being outside of the country of origin of their parents, then return to the source country may only serve as an interim measure with no permanency. If their national identity is not embedded firmly in one place, there is a strong likelihood that they will feel a weak sense of attachment to the country they return to and will eventually move back to the previous host country or to another country that could be valuable in terms of study or work options.

This impermanence of residence and this dual or fragmented sense of belonging can be especially prevalent in transnational European Union (EU) families. If the family returning to the country of origin has changed their country of residence numerous times or if the parents' occupation has involved frequent travel (and temporary residence) between the countries of residence and of origin and the children also frequently visit the country of origin, then they have a sense of belonging to both countries. Family members may even consider themselves as 'European' or 'global' citizens, an identity repertoire which could rub off on the children.

This kind of cross-border living, where close social ties with the country of origin are maintained via active involvement in diasporic life in the host country, by sending remittances to relatives in the country of origin, frequent travel and possibly business activity in both countries, all contribute to a fragmentation of identity, making it possible to feel loyalty to two nations or, possibly, the opposite – to none. 'In short, transnational ties can be understood as occupying a continuum from low to high – that is, from very few and short-lived ties to those that are multiple and dense and continuous over time' (Faist et al., 2013, p.16). The impact of this complex lifestyle can play out in the lives of the children in these families – with differing outcomes in regard to their psychosocial wellbeing.

## A SENSE OF BELONGING AND CHILDREN'S AGENCY ARE ALSO CRUCIAL

Vathi and Duci (2016), looking at the return migration of children to the homeland of their parents, in this case Albania, found that if 'diasporic belongingness' is lacking, then the wellbeing of children is affected on return. This sense of belonging is not always shaped by a single frame of reference. After longitudinally examining the children of Albanian return migrants, Cena et al. (2018) postulate the importance of everyday places and social relations in influencing their adjustment to life in their parents' country of origin. If the scarcity of accessible everyday spaces for playing and a lack of acceptance by their peers posed a challenge initially, data collected a year later already showed that the same children had familiarised themselves with their new surroundings; their memories of the previous country had faded, proving that the attachment they feel to places is not fixed and changes over time. By providing social support and local knowledge, families and local communities can be central as mediators for children's adjustment.

Vathi and King (2021) look at the same national scenario – that of return migrant children from Greece to Albania – and, in particular, at belongingness from an 'otherness' perspective with reference to return to an ancestral homeland. In school situations, these children are singled out as 'foreign' because of their Greek accents and birthplace, while the returnee children engage in othering practices themselves because the local children seem too rough and discriminatory. The returnees suffer a 'double othering' as they had also felt as though they did not fit in when they were in Greece either. Ultimately, they can end up with a reaction of 'decoupling of identity from place' (Trew, 2009, p.308), as was the case of one respondent who wanted to declare neutrality and said 'I am from no place' (Vathi and King, 2021, p.206).

Place-belongingness may be different when it comes to the views of the various family members. Parents may have one view and their children another. In the case of minors in a household, their opinion is not always sought or may be considered of lesser importance in the decision-making process when a family unit considers migration. Bushin (2009), referring to children's agency in migration decision-making, argues that children should have some involvement in and be consulted in decision-making regarding relocation. Involvement is dependent, of course, on the children's age and on parental perceptions of their children's best interests. Socio-cultural changes in family structure and mobility, placed within a children's-rights framework, has led to a 'children-in-families' approach to researching migration. Bushin claims that it is time for the 'adultist lens on much research and theorization of family migration decision-making to be readjusted so as to recognize the kaleidoscope of family migration contexts and allow for the possibility that children are actively involved' (Bushin, 2009, p.440). Consequently, a child-centred body of research has been initiated over the past decade.

The agency of the children of migrants is a complex area, fraught with challenges when it comes to return. Some adolescent children of migrants experience such homesickness, dissatisfaction with their 'lot' in life and lack of a sense of belonging in the host country that they persuade their parents that, for the final years of their schooling, they wish to return to the source country. To illustrate this, Lulle (2017) outlines the story of one returnee, Zanda, now an adult who, after living abroad for three years, moved back from Finland as an adolescent to live with her grandparents in Latvia for her higher-secondary-level schooling. She returned back to her previous class and found it challenging academically, although she managed to pass all her exams and tests. Yet she realised that her classmates had changed, as had she. She no longer found their jokes amusing, nor could they understand hers. This was very painful to experience and consequently she took on the role of a silent observer in the classroom as she found it difficult to express her emotions freely.

In Zanda's case, understanding and being able to make jokes with schoolmates epitomises 'fitting in' to a culture. Fooling around with friends and idle, good-natured banter are activities that go hand-in-hand with feeling accepted and 'acculturated'. Here, agency ended up being a double-edged sword; on the one hand, making one's own decisions in adolescence regarding one's country of residence may be a heart-led act which is character-building and a sign of maturity yet, on the other hand, if it leads to encountering difficulties with reintegration and an experience of reverse culture shock where the familiar elements of 'home' are no longer considered familiar, then the return becomes bitter-sweet.

## 'THIRD CULTURE KIDS' – AND CONTRIBUTING FACTORS TO INTEGRATION

The mobile 'third culture kid' (TCK), a term originally coined by John and Ruth Hill Useem in the 1950s but later widely disseminated by Pollock and van Reken (2009), refers to children who have lived in two or more cultural environments for a significant period of time during childhood – those of the home and the host countries. However, in the typical formulation of TCKs, the children are not well integrated in the host country where their parents live and work but, rather, inhabit a kind of 'expat bubble', since they are the children of military personnel, business executives, missionaries, development workers and other mobile professions (Knörr, 2005). Studies have found that, on re-entry to the home country, these children have experienced difficulties with identity formation, grief for the host country environment and relationships that they have lost and loneliness and isolation in the home country (Storti, 2001). Researchers have argued, however, that, for TCKs, 'homecoming' would be more akin to expatriation than to re-entry (Szkudlarek, 2008).

Successful integration into a new environment also concerns preparation before return – which is just as pertinent to migration as it is to return migration, including for children and TCKs (Cassarino, 2004; Gmelch, 1980; Pollock and van Reken, 2009). A lack of preparation for the children of migrants who have assimilated substantially into the host country's culture will probably mean that they experience negative psychosocial consequences upon return. Vathi and Duci (2016) argue that 'identification patterns prior to experiencing (return) migration play an important role in children's and young people's adaptation in their parent's homeland' (2016, p.65).

Another important factor that contributes to the (re)integration of return migrant children is their migrant 'generation'. As some returnee children were born in the country of origin, they are considered to be 1.5-generation migrants, while those born abroad are deemed to be second generation. This slight generational difference between the two types of return migrant is the most evident in the difference in language skills of the country of origin (Mieriņa,

2016). Children of the 1.5 generation may have better language skills than those of the second generation (but not always, depending on the length of time they have spent living outside the country of origin). This nuance may also affect the children's differential sense of belonging and attachment to the host as opposed to the source country, depending on the memories of life back in the latter, their attachment to grandparents and the frequency of visits. This is also important when return migrant children enter the school environment on going back and may affect their academic achievement and level of support required.

Kolaitis et al. (2003) looked at the psychosocial adaptation of immigrant Greek children from the former Soviet Union attending school in Athens, Greece. These families (of Greek origin) had migrated to Greece within the previous three years and were compared to a matching control group of 'native' or non-migrant children. Although no statistically significant differences were observed between the immigrant and the native children in terms of psychopathology and social adaptation, there were differences between the groups in language-related academic performance and a recommendation was made for language enrichment classes to be offered. In this particular scenario, the children under scrutiny, although of Greek origin, were actually from 'roots' migrant families who had migrated to Russia a few generations ago – the generation that was return-migrating actually had no living memory of life in Greece. Even though their national identity and roots were Greek, moving to Greece was like moving to a foreign country.

This 'living memory' aspect is important as it provides contextual information for the return migrant and some form of psychological security for the family. If memories of the homeland are only of a time long gone (an imagined homeland in the form of 'narratives of belonging'), then the life forged in the country of return is built from the ground up, as the nostalgia of previous generations can only function as motivators and markers but serves little practical assistance on arrival in the homeland. Wessendorf (2007), discussing the experiences of a cohort of 'roots migrants' from Switzerland to Southern Italy, reveals that, for younger migrants (in contrast to slightly older ones with families), 'the dreams of living in the parents' homeland are revealed as somewhat naïve. They are faced with both the harsh economic conditions and the social and cultural expectations imposed on women ...' (2007, p.1095). Cultural differences can be a shock to the system and the harsh face of reality can mar the 'return' migration experience. Contrasting gender norms between Switzerland and the Italian South are a particular obstacle encountered by returning girls and young women.

Other factors that come into play are the length of time that has passed since return (the more time has passed, the better the coping mechanisms), as well as the stages of migration and settlement – with different stressors at the different stages (Bhugra, 2004); these are all potentially important in determining the type and intensity of symptoms of a psychosocial nature.

There is a very complex interplay of different factors that contribute to the psychosocial wellbeing of a child. These include individual personality traits, their sensitivity to change, their natural ability to socialise and cope in new circumstances and their natural resilience and ability to cope with challenging situations, whether socially, academically or emotionally. Goldstein and Brooks (2013) unpack resilience and its various dimensions and, in their introduction, cite Cowen (1991), who proposes a wellness framework which 'emphasizes the interaction of the child in the family, academic setting, with adults outside of the home and with peers' (Goldstein and Brooks, 2013, p.4).

Resilience is often overlooked as a contributing factor, yet a 'resilient mindset', according to Brooks and Goldstein (2001), is a trait that is an asset to all youth in general. Wright et al. (2013) highlight examples of promotive and protective factors for resilience (in families in general and not related specifically to immigration), providing a 'short list' (originally created by Masten, 2001), in the form of a set of broad correlates of better adaptation among children at risk – a host of child, family, community and cultural or societal characteristics that influence children's resilience.

## INTEGRATION: A CHALLENGE IN POST-SOVIET COUNTRIES

When returning to countries in Eastern Europe, there are additional confounding factors that make reintegration more of a challenge for both parents and children. These countries are former Soviet republics or satellite states and, even though many are now EU member states, a post-Soviet mentality still prevails in this geographic space in many areas of life. Although 30 years have passed since the fall of the Iron Curtain and a whole generation has been raised since these countries regained their independence or reinstated democratic governments, the mentality of the people is slow to change. This has been noted by Municio-Larsson (2012) who states, referring to family life, 'repertoires are different in former Soviet republics versus countries in the West' (2012, p.276).

Emigrés (in this case, return migrants) who were born during the Soviet era and migrated abroad, experienced life and grew accustomed to the mentality and cultural values of other countries – those of 'old Western Europe' or of traditional 'settler' immigration countries such as the USA, Canada or Australia. On return, they are now no longer satisfied with norms that may have seemed acceptable (or at least familiar) to them when they were living in these origin countries some five, ten or even twenty years ago. Their lived experience abroad also includes gaining familiarity with the education system of the host country, often in stark contrast to what they experienced in their childhood. Yet this category of people are the new 'desired migrants' for Latvia – co-ethnics either with degrees obtained at universities in 'old Western Europe' and/or experience in Western work environments, often with innovative ideas for Latvia in the public or private sectors.

As mentioned previously, for the children of returnees, however, encounters with the Latvian education system may not be classified as a return, either because their memory of life in Latvia as young children has faded or disappeared entirely or because they were born abroad and this is their first encounter with life in their parents' homeland.

Regarding the education sector, one striking legacy from Soviet times is the low prestige and salaries of teachers in the state system. Many pedagogues are aged 50+ and a proportion work well into retirement age because of the meagre pensions. Job satisfaction in the teaching profession is not high and teachers are quite resentful of working at their jobs. Unfortunately, this contributes to making the school environment somewhat depressive and uninspiring (Paula and Priževoite, 2019). Of course, not all teachers are overworked, underpaid and tired, yet there is a stereotypical air of despondency in the school environment. It is into this somewhat depressed educational setting that return migrant children enter when they move with their parents to post-Soviet countries – unless the parents choose alternative or private schools for their offspring to make acculturation easier.

A few studies have been undertaken in Latvia regarding returnee children. Taking a retrospective perspective regarding the situation of these returning Latvian nationals, Lulle (2017) dissects the internal dialogues of returning migrant children on their actions, coping strategies and reflections regarding relocation. In this case, the adult youths interviewed were born in Latvia, migrated at some time during their childhood and, as adults, have made their own choices regarding their preferred country of residence. As adults, they were invited to look back at their inner thoughts following return to their homeland either while still children or later on in their life-course. Among her conclusions, Lulle highlights a link between return migration and psychosocial wellbeing, 'shaping individual and social identity with references from different places, times and systems' (2017, p.198).

There is no doubt that moments of deep self-reflection looking back at any migration experience can uncover home truths that may or may not be positive. Lulle documents stories where participants see the lessons learnt from the experience and put a positive spin on things (one's personality has changed for the better because of increased empathy) which can be all it takes for a former child-migrant to see that migration has actually impacted on them in a good way.

Lulle also takes her findings one step further and recommends that they be accommodated into policies regarding the education and socio-cultural adaptation of returnee children. Her argument is not only that the returnee children themselves need to adapt but that systems within the country of origin should also:

> recognize that 'difference' and mobility experiences constitute a prime human condition ... [and] that places in Europe nowadays are both global and local, [and] we can create more ethical social systems, where a child is embraced to realize his or her potential and not just used as an object that fits or does not fit into the pre-determined standards of a certain grade in a school. (Lulle, 2017, p.199)

In a small qualitative study of returning migrants, Ose (2015) summarises specific suggestions that pupils in Latvia have made regarding return. Their varied migration experiences show that each individual scenario is different – ranging from age at the time of outward migration, length of time spent abroad, level of maintenance of the Latvian language, support measures provided in the host country and the type of support measures provided by the school on return.

The students (some of whom returned to Latvia, having spent the early part of their childhood there; for others, this would be classed as immigration as they were born abroad) also mention culture shock with regard to the difficulties faced when socialising with peers in the school environment, as well as dealing with the attitudes of teachers. Although some teachers were welcoming, seeing newcomer pupils as 'Latvians – the same as us, after all', the opposite mindset, if encountered, was disheartening: that teachers would have to work with 'spoilt half-foreigners with weaker preparedness, on average, to that of local pupils' (Ose, 2015, p.189).

Other issues involve the teaching of the language of instruction of the country of origin. Accent-related issues and terminology in subjects such as mathematics make it difficult for some to follow the lessons or express their thoughts. The challenges to acculturation are felt doubly if there is still a vivid memory of how integration was 'tackled' following migration to the host country. In one case, the experience at an international school in another country was a glaring contrast, as classroom assistants kept a close eye on newcomers and helped to explain or translate if they deemed it necessary. This type of assistance is not freely available in every government school in Latvia (it requires additional funding) and the child may often need to be more independent with regard to understanding the curriculum content.

The use of teaching assistants and other support staff (such as translators and interpreters) to facilitate communication and ease integration are support measures that are transferable to a return migration situation with similar language acquisition issues to migrant scenarios where this type of assistance is used frequently (European Commission, 2019). Many support measures used in migrant scenarios may be just as effective in a return migrant situation; they need to be identified as vitally necessary by those who have returned. Language support is one initial need, as well as the acquisition of terminology for other school subjects.

Less obvious are cultural norms, unwritten codes of conduct, traditions and subtle cues that can only be picked up and understood as time goes by and certain situations arise. For instance, the concept of 'play dates' for children (arranged by parents for pre- and primary-school-aged children) may not be customary in other countries and parents, following relocation, may erroneously feel like their children are being excluded from socialising, which may not be the case at all. The comparison of cultural norms as well as close emotional ties to the homeland, as found by Assmuth and Siim in a 2018 study of Estonian migrants in Finland, can lead to frustration, which may be experienced by both parents and children alike. Making comparisons between education systems and the cultural norms of the previous country of residence can create dissatisfaction because of the contrast.

## CONCLUDING REMARKS

Returning 'home' for migrants is a concept that can have different meanings for different people within one family unit. If this return is based on an imagined reality that turns out to be idealised because of a lengthy absence (the phrase 'absence makes the heart grow fonder' is very apt here), then the return will be problematic, as places may have profoundly changed, as have the migrants themselves. If the return, however, is well researched, well prepared for by the returnees, approached with an open mind, and realistic in terms of expectations of the country of origin, then the new beginning will stand a better chance of success.

Source countries on the receiving end of return may have policies in place to encourage the return of certain migrant groups, such as highly skilled migrants with specific education and skills acquired in the host country. Return integration policies are just as important as they are for migrants in host countries. Children and youth who return with their families have particular needs that may be overlooked because of the expectation that they should seamlessly slot into the parents' familiar surroundings.

Although the current literature touches on different aspects of return migration and children (feelings of 'otherness', sense of belonging, language issues, identity, acculturation), thus far there has not been a holistic approach – looking through a broad lens, including all 'actors' involved in the return process; on an individual and family level (personality, resilience in times of change), an institutional level (school, extra-curricular activities), a neighbourhood level (friends, neighbours, extended family) and also a wider level (national discourse on return migration, institutional response). Taking such a research path, encompassing the different aspects that constitute the whole 'picture' – the sum of its parts – for the return migration scenario to be pieced together coherently and with a specific purpose – helps to ensure the psychosocial wellbeing of the children involved.

A gap in research also exists with regard to the return of Eastern European migrants from old Western European countries back to their homeland. As the number of returnees steadily increases (recently, Brexit and Covid-19 have become triggers to encourage a move back to the source country) and those who have spent a number of years living abroad, for various reasons, are now packing their bags and returning, the psychosocial impact on their children becomes increasingly important. As mentioned earlier in this chapter, studies to date have started to include children and youth as active agents in migration research to help target and identify the needs and challenges faced on return. By giving return migrant children a greater voice and coupling this with the opinion of their parents and teachers and school support staff, a robust insight can be gained into the true nature of the return migration scenario. This can serve to improve source-country return migration policy – to make it more practical and relevant – by both the source-country governments, to reduce re-migration back to the host country and to improve the psychosocial wellbeing of the returnee children involved.

## ACKNOWLEDGEMENT

This chapter was written as part of a research project titled 'Exploring Wellbeing and Social Integration in the Context of Liquid Migration: A Longitudinal Approach', funded by the Latvian Science Council (LSC grant No. LZP-2018/1-0042).

## REFERENCES

Akerlund, U. and Sandberg, L. (2015) 'Stories of lifestyle mobility: representing self and place in the search for the "good life"', *Social and Cultural Geography*, **16** (3), 351–70.

Assmuth, L. and Siim, P.M. (2018) 'School as institution and as symbol in Estonian migrant families' lives in Finland' in L. Assmuth, M. Hakkarainen, A. Lulle and P.M. Siim (eds), *Translocal Childhoods and Family Mobility in East and North Europe*, London: Palgrave Macmillan, pp. 163–92.

Benson, M. and Osbaldiston, N. (eds) (2014) *Understanding Lifestyle Migration: Theoretical Approaches to Migration and the Quest for a Better Way of Life*, Basingstoke: Palgrave Macmillan.

Bhugra, D. (2004) 'Migration, distress and cultural identity', *British Medical Bulletin*, **69** (1), 129–41.

Brooks, R. and Goldstein, S. (2001) *Raising Resilient Children: Fostering Strength, Hope and Optimism in Your Child*, New York: Contemporary Books.

Bushin, N. (2009) 'Researching family migration decision-making: a children-in-families approach', *Population, Space and Place*, **15** (5), 429–43.

Callea, S. (1986) 'Different forms, reasons and motivations for return migration of persons who voluntarily decide to return to their countries of origin', *International Migration*, **24** (1), 61–76.

Carling, J., Bolognani, M., Bivand Erdal, M., Tordhol Ezzati, R., Oeppen, C., Paasche, E., Vattne Pettersen, S. and Heggli Sagmo, T. (2015) *Possibilities and Realities of Return Migration*, Oslo: The Peace Research Institute Oslo (PRIO).

Cassarino, J.P. (2004) 'Theorising return migration: the conceptual approach to return migrants revisited', *International Journal of Multicultural Societies*, **6** (2), 253–79.

Cena, E., Heim, D. and Trandafoiu, R. (2018) 'Changing places: children of return migrants in Albania and their quest to belong', *Journal of Ethnic and Migration Studies*, **44** (7), 1156–76.

Cowen, E.L. (1991) 'In pursuit of wellness', *American Psychologist*, **46** (4), 404–8.

Dobson, M.E. (2009) 'Unpacking children in migration research', *Children's Geographies*, **7** (3), 355–60.

Dustmann, C. (2003) 'Children and return migration', *Journal of Population Economics*, **16** (4), 815–30.

European Commission/EACEA/EURYDICE (2019) *Integrating Students from Migrant Backgrounds into Schools in Europe: National Policies and Measures. Eurydice Report*, Luxembourg: Publications Office of the European Union.

Faist, T., Fauser, M. and Reisenauer, E. (2013) *Transnational Migration*, Cambridge: Polity Press.

Gmelch, G. (1980) 'Return migration', *Annual Review of Anthropology*, **9**, 135–59.
Goldstein, S. and Brooks, R.B. (eds) (2013) *Handbook of Resilience in Children*, New York: Springer US.
Gonda, M. (2017) 'Roots migration to the ancestral homeland and psychosocial wellbeing: young Polish diaspora students' in Z. Vathi and R. King (eds), *Return Migration and Psychosocial Wellbeing: Discourses, Policy-Making and Outcomes for Migrants and Their Families*, London and New York: Routledge, pp. 75–92.
Hatfield, M. (2010) 'Children moving "home"? Everyday experiences of return migration in highly skilled households', *Childhood*, **17** (2), 243–57.
James, A. and James, A. (2004) *Constructing Childhood: Theory, Policy and Social Practice*, New York and Basingstoke: Palgrave Macmillan.
Janoschka, M. and Haas, H. (eds) (2013) *Contested Spatialities, Lifestyle Migration and Residential Tourism*, London: Routledge.
King, R. (1977) 'Problems of return migration: a case study of Italians returning from Britain', *Tijdschrift voor Economische en Sociale Geografie*, **68** (4), 241–6.
Knörr, J. (2005) 'When German children come "home": experiences of (re)migration to Germany – and some remarks about the "TCK" issue' in J. Knörr (ed.), *Childhood and Migration: From Experience to Agency*, Bielefeld and Somerset NJ: Transcript and Transaction Publishers, pp. 51–76.
Knörr, J. and Nunes, A. (2005) 'Introduction' in J. Knörr (ed.), *Childhood and Migration: From Experience to Agency*, Bielefeld and Somerset NJ: Transcript and Transaction Publishers, pp. 9–21.
Kolaitis, G., Tsiantis, J., Madianos, M. and Kotsopoulos, S. (2003) 'Psychosocial adaptation of immigrant Greek children from the former Soviet Union', *Child and Adolescent Psychiatry*, **12**, 67–74.
Lulle, A. (2017) 'The need to belong: Latvian youth returns as dialogic work' in Z. Vathi and R. King (eds), *Return Migration and Psychosocial Wellbeing: Discourses, Policy-Making and Outcomes for Migrants and Their Families*, London: Routledge, pp. 185–202.
Masten, A.S. (2001) 'Ordinary magic: resilience processes in development', *American Psychologist*, **56** (3), 227–38.
Mieriņa, I. (2016) *Bērnu Valodu Prasme un Latviešu Valodas Zudums/Zuduma Intensitāte Jaunajās Mītnes Zemēs* [*The Language Skills of Children and Latvian Language Attrition/ Intensity of Attrition in New Host Countries*], Report, https://dokumen.tips/science/bernu-valodu-prasme-un-latviesu-valodas-zudumszuduma-intensitate-jaunajas.html (accessed 12 April 2021).
Municio-Larsson, I. (2012) 'Doing parenting in post-socialist Estonia and Latvia' in H. Carlbäck, Y. Gradskova and Z. Kravchenko (eds), *And They Lived Happily Ever After: Norms and Everyday Practices of Family and Parenthood in Russia and Eastern Europe*, Budapest: Central European University Press, pp. 273–96.
Ní Laoire, C. (2011) 'Narratives of "innocent Irish childhoods": return migration and intergenerational family dynamics', *Journal of Ethnic and Migration Studies*, **37** (8), 1253–71.
Ose, L. (2015) 'The teacher factor: pedagogues in dialogue with children and adolescents who have returned to Latvia' in A. Lulle and E. Kļave (eds), *Creating Opportunities for Development: Diaspora Children and Youth*, Rīga: Latvijas Universitāte, pp. 185–204.
Paula, L. and Priževoite, I. (2019) 'The status of the teaching profession in Latvia: views of the teachers', *Problems of Education in the 21st Century*, **77** (1), 126–41.
Pollock, D. and van Reken, R. (2009) *Third Culture Kids: Growing Up Among Worlds*, Boston and London: Nicholas Brealey Publishing.
Saar, M. (2018) 'To return or not to return? The importance of identity negotiations for return migration', *Social Identities*, **24** (1), 120–33.
Saar, M. and Saar, E. (2020) 'Can the concept of lifestyle migration be applied to return migration? The case of Estonians in the UK', *International Migration*, **58** (2), 52–66.
Storti, C. (2001) *The Art of Coming Home*, Yarmouth ME: Intercultural Press.
Stroh, L.K., Gregersen, H.B. and Black, J.S. (1998) 'Closing the gap: expectations versus reality among repatriates', *Journal of World Business*, **33** (2), 111–24.
Szkudlarek, B. (2008) *Spinning the Web of Reentry. (Re)connecting Reentry Training Theory and Practice*, Rotterdam: University of Rotterdam, Erasmus Research Institute of Management, unpublished PhD thesis.

Szydlowska, P., Durlik, J. and Grzymala-Moszczynska, H. (2019) 'Returning children migrants: main challenges in school environment', *Studia Migracyjne–Przeglad Polonijny*, **45** (1), 171–92.

Trew, J.D. (2009) 'Migration in childhood and its impact on national identity construction among migrants from Northern Ireland', *Irish Studies Review*, **17** (3), 297–314.

Tsuda, T. (2004) 'When home is not the homeland: the case of Japanese Brazilian ethnic return migration' in F. Markowitz and A. Stefansson (eds), *Homecomings: Unsettling Paths of Return*, Lanham MD: Lexington, pp. 125–45.

Vathi, Z. (2017) 'Introduction: the interface between return migration and psychosocial wellbeing' in Z. Vathi and R. King (eds), *Return Migration and Psychosocial Wellbeing: Discourses, Policy-Making and Outcomes for Migrants and Their Families*, London: Routledge, pp. 1–18.

Vathi, Z. and Duci, V. (2016) 'Making other dreams: the impact of migration on the psychosocial wellbeing of Albanian-origin children and young people upon their families' return to Albania', *Childhood*, **23** (1), 53–68.

Vathi, Z. and King, R. (eds) (2017) *Return Migration and Psychosocial Wellbeing: Discourses, Policy-Making and Outcomes for Migrants and Their Families*, London: Routledge.

Vathi, Z. and King, R. (2021) 'Memory, place and agency: transnational mirroring of otherness among young Albanian "returnees"', *Children's Geographies*, **19** (2), 197–209.

Wessendorf, S. (2007) '"Roots migrants": transnationalism and "return" among second-generation Italians in Switzerland', *Journal of Ethnic and Migration Studies*, **33** (7), 1083–102.

White, S.C. and Blackmore, C. (2015) *Cultures of Wellbeing: Method, Place, Policy*, Basingstoke: Palgrave Macmillan.

WHO (2018) *Mental Health Promotion and Mental Health Care in Refugees and Migrants: Technical Guidance*, Copenhagen: WHO Regional Office for Europe.

Wright, M.O., Masten, A.S. and Narayan, A.J. (2013) 'Resilience processes in development: four waves of research on positive adaptation in the context of adversity' in S. Goldstein and R.B. Brooks (eds), *Handbook of Resilience in Children*, New York: Springer US, pp. 15–38.

Zúñiga, V. and Hamann, E. (2015) 'Going to a home you have never been to: the return migration of Mexican and American-Mexican children', *Children's Geographies*, **13** (6), 643–55.

# 18. Student mobility: between returning home and remaining abroad

*Elisa Alves*

## INTRODUCTION

Imagine that you are a young higher education (HE) student in your early 20s from Bulgaria, single with no children, wondering whether you should stay studying in your country or leave and embrace an international student mobility (ISM) experience. What are the questions that immediately come to your mind? Probably, the main pros and cons of each situation would be at the top; and if you are willing to opt for mobility, you would certainly ask where to go and for how long. Keeping that in mind, imagine that you are still that single young HE student but now from Angola and wondering exactly the same thing: should I stay or should I go? Your questions are probably the same as before – and your answers to those questions, would they be the same whether you are Bulgarian or Angolan?

To finalise this exercise, imagine either that you are that Bulgarian student and that you went abroad to Denmark or that you are that Angolan student and you went to Portugal. What are the odds of you returning to your origin country or remaining abroad after graduation? Am I wrong in saying 'It depends'? On what does it depend?

The question of whether students who decide to study abroad will return to their home country after completing their studies has profound implications – for themselves, for their families and for the skilled labour markets of their countries of origin. Bulgaria – one of the poorest countries in the European Union (EU) – and Angola, a fast-developing country in the Global South, are just two typical settings where the series of questions posed above are highly relevant. They are hypothetical cases but illustrative of wider and diversified contexts.

In this chapter, I consider the return projects of international students by focusing on three key moments. The first moment approaches the students' motivations, expectations, aspirations and characteristics, trying to answer the dual question *Should I stay home or should I go abroad*? Possible answers follow a macro, meso and micro perspective (van Mol and Timmerman, 2014). This moment explains part of the above-mentioned cases with the Bulgarian and Angolan students, suggesting that age, familial status and country of origin impact similarly or differently on students' projects and decisions. The aim is to establish a relation between the impetus for departure and the return project upon completion of studies. Returning home or remaining abroad are here defined as future mobility projects, which might be set by students at the moment at which they decide to go abroad, be postponed for a future day or changed over the migration course. Ultimately, they might be fulfilled or not (Findlay et al., 2017).

The second moment is focused on the students' intentions and choices upon graduation, asking themselves *Should I return or should I remain*? The answer is related to their initial expectations and projects, to personality, to unexpected events – for instance, finding a job or a significant other (Mosneaga and Winther, 2013) – and, overall, to social, cultural, political and economic conditions. Factors implicated in the decision process are deeply entwined, revealing the importance of a holistic perspective to fully understand student mobility projects. Therefore, the introductory cases went a little further, suggesting Denmark and Portugal in order to highlight not only the role of the destination-country context but also of the relationship between home and host countries – respectively student mobility within the EU and in a post-colonial context.

The chapter continues with a third moment that discusses the main *impacts of returning home or remaining abroad*. The analysis will bring to light the perspective of the students themselves, of the home and destination countries, questioning the results of ISM in terms of personal fulfilment, brain drain/gain/waste/circulation and consequent relations with social and economic development.

I start with a brief methodological reflection on how to measure international students' return rates. Then, the three moments will each be analysed in turn, followed by final remarks.

## GROWING INTERNATIONAL STUDENT MOBILITY; AND THE RETURN?

According to UNESCO, ISM has grown considerably over the years. In 2004, almost 2.7 million individuals had crossed a national border for the purpose of education and were enrolled outside their country of origin. By 2017, numbers had almost doubled to around 5.3 million.[1] However, the distribution is far from balanced. In 2017, student net flows[2] showed the US, the UK, Australia, Russia, France and Canada at the top, with the largest net inflows, against China, India, Vietnam, Kazakhstan, Colombia and Indonesia at the bottom, with the largest net outflows. The top ten inbound countries hosted 60 per cent of all international students, while the top ten outbound countries concentrated 38 per cent. This reveals that flows have their main origin in the wide spectrum of the Global South, towards a highly concentrated Global North.

While the number of international students is known (despite difficulties in harmonising data and concepts), the same cannot be said about those who return (or not) upon completion of their studies. Measuring the return or staying rates of international students is hard. First, this is due to the flexible and dynamic characteristics of this flow, where students and/or graduates usually have some sort of freedom to change their status and mobility projects over time (Weisser, 2016). This is especially true for those enrolled in degree mobility, since those in credit mobility are expected to return to their home countries to complete their degrees. Second, it is hard when we consider circular migration and the difficulty of knowing the real dimension of stay or return rates. Finally, the different ways of measurement make it difficult to estimate. The staying rate usually considers the number of status changers (e.g. from student visa to having a work or residence permit) but at least two ways of calculating it are found: according to the number of international/foreign students/graduates (Weisser, 2016); and the number of international students not renewing their student permit (Sykes and Chaoimh, 2012). Regardless of the method, staying-on rates depend also and to a considerable extent on the (changeable) administrative and legal frameworks of states, resulting much more in an estimation of those who were allowed to legally remain, rather than of those who would like to do so (Weisser, 2016).

Within the OECD in 2008–09, on average, 25 per cent of international students were staying on after graduation, although Canada, France, Australia, the Czech Republic, the Netherlands and Germany were above average (Sykes and Chaoimh, 2012). Within the EU (excluding EU students), in the early 2010s, Armenian international students had the highest stay rate (80 per cent), followed by others from North and West Africa, South-East Asia and the Commonwealth of Independent States (Weisser, 2016). In New Zealand, estimations pointed to staying rates of 27 per cent (Soon, 2010). However, to a great extent, data are not comparable, given the different sources and methods.

## SHOULD I STAY HOME OR SHOULD I GO ABROAD?

### Social, Economic and Political Pressure

In knowledge-based societies, investing in HE has become a large public and private goal, based on the relations between knowledge, social development and economic growth (Gürüz, 2008). All over the world, states set their agendas and develop policies to expand their HE and research systems, with the purpose of increasing their international and global competitiveness.

ISM emerges as a new stage in this global competition. Motivated by the quest for profit or concern over HE institutions' survival, by the expansion of academic models or attracting the 'brightest and best' or even by the need to satisfy labour market demands, national and regional governments in the Global North, along with private institutions, have been promoting ISM as a key issue in individuals' curricula (Geddie, 2015; Knight and de Wit, 1995). The insufficient supply of educational resources and infrastructures in developing countries, as is still the case in many African countries, also pushes students overseas (Kritz, 2015a). In this general context, studying abroad or on an international campus is 'sold' as a better way to learn or improve skills, embrace new cultures and enhance autonomous and creative thinking and so on, all valuable competences needed (supposedly) to be successful in personal lives and careers. This quest has first and foremost been promoted by Anglophone and Francophone countries but new players in Europe, Asia and the Middle East are rising, challenging the dominant direction of student mobility flows to the Global North (Bhandari and Blumenthal, 2011).

### Context of Departure, Motivations and Expectations

Acknowledging the importance of education for their professional, economic and social integration and mobility, individuals look for more and better qualifications. Following human capital theory, investment in higher education is seen as a way to access better opportunities, qualified positions and higher salaries (Perkins and Neumayer, 2014). While HE is still a component of social and professional distinction, its massification has opened the door to other avenues of individuals' distinctiveness. In this context, ISM emerges as an answer to improve individuals' CVs.

Despite this more 'general' motivation, the unbalanced distribution of international students across the world suggests some patterns. According to Börjesson (2017), it is possible to identify three poles – the *Pacific pole*, the *Central European pole* and the *French-Iberian pole* – each of them respectively associated with different logics – market, proximity and colonial.[3]

This means that economic, geographic and historic factors have different levels of attraction considering the origin and destination countries (Perkins and Neumayer, 2014). In summary, the following factors can be considered as influencing students' choices and, ultimately, their plans for future mobility:

- *Personal*: age, civil/familial status (having children or not) and personality traits (Bilecen, 2016; Sykes and Chaoimh, 2012). Usually international students are young, single, and with no children; and they are more ambitious and outward-looking.
- *Academic*: in the origin countries, the existence or not of national HE institutions in sufficient numbers and of the right quality to meet home demand; in the destination countries, language, world rankings, reputation and fees (Findlay et al., 2011; Perkins and Neumayer, 2014; Rosenzweig, 2006).
- *Socio-cultural*: cultural experience, adventure, family emancipation or childhood dream (Alves et al., 2022; António, 2013; King and Ruiz-Gelices, 2003); national diaspora, pre-existing stock of migrants and networks and past colonial links (Beine et al., 2014; Berriane, 2015; França et al., 2018); gender (Sondhi and King, 2017); family background/ social class, and parents' *international habitus* (Brito, 2004; King et al., 2011).
- *Economic*: family and/or students' incomes/savings; countries'. income/development levels (Kritz, 2015b; Perkins and Neumayer, 2014); and perceptions of further opportunities to work.
- *Political/institutional*: civil conflicts, dictatorial regimes or a lack of freedom (Zijlstra, 2015); the creation of and access to mobility programmes, grants and visas (Iorio and Fonseca, 2018).
- *Geographic*: distance and connectivity between origin and destination; weather conditions.

Whether ISM is a dream or not, it can be said that, mostly, it is a project regarding the future, which might include plans for further social and geographic mobility, through return home or not.

## SHOULD I RETURN OR SHOULD I REMAIN?

### Country Conditions and Professional Opportunities

Focusing on home countries' conditions, Rosenzweig (2006) established two models to determine whether students are more prone to return or to remain abroad after graduation: the *school-constrained model*, where students come from countries with poor academic conditions but high returns to education and are, therefore, more prone to return; and the *migration model*, where returns to education are lower and studying abroad might be a first step towards longer migrations. In the latter case, students look for professional integration overseas and return will be more or less likely in a situation of unemployment or employment, respectively; whereas in the *school-constraint model*, employment in the host country will hardly affect the return. Findings on Latin American PhD students in Barcelona seem to support the Rosenzweig theory (Mendoza and Ortiz, 2016). Apart from cases where students were granted fellowships in the origin countries and hence had an obligation to return, the lack of professional opportunities in Spanish universities played a key role in pushing them back home. Similarly, considering the case of Bulgarians and Romanians who went to study in the UK and

Spain, Marcu (2015) found that the odds of return were greater for those studying in Spain and smaller for those in the UK, given the more numerous and higher professional opportunities and incomes in the UK compared to Spain.

This (un)employment influence is to some extent contested by Bijwaard and Wang (2016), who studied foreign students in the Netherlands. Despite verifying that unemployment increased the odds of returning home, employment had a different effect depending on the students' country of origin. For students from developed countries it hardly affected their return. However, for those coming from less-developed countries, it increased the odds of return, due to the home countries' high valorisation of professional experience in the Netherlands, besides education.

Sykes and Chaoimh (2012), in a study with international Masters' and PhD students in Germany, France, the Netherlands, the UK and Sweden, observed that international job experience and employment opportunities were important factors for those planning to stay on after graduation. These were followed by quality of life, earnings, cost of living, opportunities for further education, lifestyle, ease of travel, mobility within Europe and good prospects of obtaining a work/residence visa. Overall, most participants agreed with the idea of remaining at least six additional months after graduation. Defined as 'stayers', they showed higher levels of satisfaction with their experience and better information about the required procedures to stay. They also revealed that, for their motivation to remain abroad, it was important to initially decide on the country of study, highlighting a relation between previous motivations and future mobility projects. Chinese, Eastern European and Turkish students revealed more desire to stay, while those coming from English-speaking countries, North and Latin America and Africa revealed less desire.

Despite this result with Chinese students, a study in the US showed, to some extent, different results. While, in the 1990s, only around 30 per cent of Chinese students in the US were planning to return home, recently numbers seem to be increasing (Kellogg, 2012). China's economic expansion, students' perceptions of more prestigious positions back home and the wish to be part of China's resurgence appear as the main determinants. On the other hand, for Iranian students in Turkey, their dissatisfaction with the home country's political regime, as well as the legal obstacles to moving to Western countries (first-choice destinations), seem to extend or set up their residence there (Zijlstra, 2015).

## Students' Socio-demographic and Academic Profiles

Age, gender, socio-economic background and academic characteristics also influence the 'return or remain abroad' decision. Still, studies show a range of results not always aligned, revealing high subjectivity and complexity when analysing this issue.

Studying Polish graduates, mostly engaged in Erasmus programmes, Bryła (2019) concluded that being male and having graduated in education sciences decreased the likelihood of them remaining abroad. On the contrary, graduation in STEM (Science, Technology, Engineering and Mathematics), following studies in Germany or France, having been engaged in academic associations while abroad and in student mobility for the doctorate increased the probability of them staying abroad.

Sykes and Chaoimh (2012) also found that STEM students were more interested in remaining abroad, possibly due to the different levels of demand regarding language competence and better job opportunities. However, they found a larger percentage of 'stayers' among Masters' students rather than PhDs and no relation with gender. The 'stayers' were younger, with longer residence and with work experience in the country of study, corresponding usually to their first choice. Despite this, through a logistic regression model, they observed no effect of the study level nor of the first-choice destination on the likelihood of staying. They confirmed, however, that social-science students – older and with children – were less likely to remain abroad, in line with Lin and Kingminghae (2017). They also found that students with longer residence and work experience in the study country were more likely to stay.

Comparing the effect of cultural, economic and social capital on the decision to return or not of Israeli STEM early-career researchers, Israel et al. (2019) found no effect of each form of capital, individually. However, the combination of economic and social capital seems to improve the likelihood of return, as it gives opportunities to apply the accumulated cultural capital. Beyond this, the authors found no effect of gender, academic discipline, duration of academic training abroad, ethnicity or marital status. Despite this, as the next subsection will explore, this last factor seems determinant in different situations.

**Different Forms of Integration**

When deciding the future, being married or having a partner is usually highly relevant. According to Mendoza and Ortiz (2016), the decision on further migration is taken not individually but by both parties. Kim's (2015) findings, in a southern US university, showed that married students have greater intentions to remain, compared to singles. However, the decision seems also to depend on where the students got married, to whom and where the partner lives. Getting married in the host country seems to make international students more prone to remain, except for those coming from developed countries, possibly because they marry other foreigners and are more open to moving to either country of origin (Bijwaard and Wang, 2016). Focusing on Thai students in China, Lin and Kingminghae (2017) found that, unsurprisingly, married students with spouses in Thailand were more likely to return, whereas those with spouses in China were more prone to remain. Additionally, those with business parents were also more prone to remain, regardless of their larger or smaller attraction for Thai or Chinese cultures. The authors saw it as part of a familial economic strategy to expand business in China. If so, they seem to follow a fourth mobility project, which might be added to the following three identified by Marcu (2015).

Marcu (2015) found a strong relation between motivations to move abroad, the role of family and expected future mobility projects, identifying three kinds of project: (i) *mobility as a platform for permanent migration and family reunification*, where ISM is a familial investment, whose returns are expected afterwards for all members, regardless of place; (ii) *uncertain mobility as a tool for competition*, where students keep migrating to study and find better conditions abroad; and (iii) *mobility for return*, aimed towards family reunion at home and having a patriotic duty of 'giving back' to the home country.

In research on postgraduate students in London and Toronto (Geddie, 2013), several female participants said it was possible that they would follow their partners, compromising their own scientific careers. In the same research, parenthood conditions (including not having children at the time) was another important factor in choosing 'where to go' after graduation. Geddie's results are in line with the analysis carried out by Sondhi and King (2017), who followed the trajectory of Indian students in the UK and Canada and found that (i) the Indian patrifocal family puts greater pressure on males to return and (ii) the Indian male-dominated labour market suppresses women's opportunities after the return (see also Moskal, 2020 regarding Asian postgraduates). However, in Japan in contrast, the pressure to return falls mainly on the first-born, regardless of gender (Alberts and Hazen, 2005).

Exploring the meaning of home for international students in Canada, Wu and Wilkes (2017) found a greater desire to stay among those who saw 'home' in their new *host* country, feeling integrated in Canada and no longer in the origin country. On the other hand, a stronger pull towards return was found among those who saw home as *ancestral*, were experiencing integration difficulties abroad and wanted to be with their family again. More open migration projects were found among students with *cosmopolitan* or *nebulous* conceptions of home. Despite sharing multiple international and multicultural experiences, the former feel as though they fit in anywhere, while the latter experience identity confusion and displacement.

**Overall, a Process under Construction**

In the US, Alberts and Hazen (2005) found that, after completing their studies, most international students felt divided between the options of stay or return. A mix of feelings and some lack of self-belonging explain this ambivalence. Factors increasing the odds of remaining abroad were mainly professional, although some home countries' conditions contributed to that too, for instance a lack of freedom or political and economic instability. On the contrary, societal and personal factors enhance the chances of return. Han and colleagues (2015), also in the US, concluded that the main reasons to stay among international STEM students were job and professional opportunities, salaries and the quality of life, whereas the reasons for returning were related to family, friends and cultural issues (cf. also Sykes and Chaoimh, 2012).

Soon's (2012) results from research with international students in New Zealand showed that the majority intended to return. The students having that initial intention, good perceptions of the lifestyle and the work environment at home, as well as strong familial ties, increase the probability of that outcome. However, the longer they stay in New Zealand, the less likely the return. The odds of moving to another foreign country increased for PhD students and those with work experience. Against the expectations of the author, there was no effect of the previous migratory path, nor of wage competitiveness. These findings are quite in accordance with Sykes and Chaoimh (2012) but are, to some extent, counter to those of King and Ruiz-Gelices (2003), who found that English students who had spent a year abroad were much more likely to engage in further international mobility, for instance through an international career overseas. However, as I argued in the opening paragraphs of this chapter, findings on student mobility pathways are highly contingent on *context* – geographical, developmental – and on level (Bachelors, Masters, Doctoral) and subject (e.g. STEM vs social sciences and humanities). Most critically, the possibility to stay on in the host country is dependent on the legal ability to do so: some countries positively encourage international students to remain; others compel them to leave once their studies are complete.

Questioning Angolan and Cape Verdean students in Portugal, Alves et al. (2022) underline that mobility projects are processes under construction. Despite students' initial intentions to return home soon after graduation, follow-up interviews revealed changes. Based on this, four mobility profiles were identified:

- the *maximisers*, who want to return but who, before they do, aim to improve their social and cultural capital as much as they can through academic and professional experience in

Portugal, as well as acquiring Portuguese nationality, both of which are highly valuable back home;
- the *dreamers*, who would like to remain due to the better living conditions but, considering the lack of fair professional opportunities for black Africans in Portugal, as well as family circumstances, scholarship terms or study leaves, have to return;
- the *world citizens*, for whom finding good professional opportunities or following a partner is more important; and
- the *runners*, who left home with the idea of remaining abroad to live an adventure, achieve family emancipation or avoid poverty, partially following the *migration model* of Rosenzweig (2006, 2010), where ISM is a kick-off for further migration.

Despite their diversity, the studies analysed here reveal a tendency for two kinds of association, one between economic factors and staying intentions and another between social factors and the desire to return. These associations are not linear. Life-course events, a feeling of belonging and a sense of self-fulfilment, among other intrinsic and extrinsic conditions, also shape students' and graduates' decisions. Thus, to a great extent, it might be said that there are different levels of return preparation, especially considering Cassarino's concepts of resource mobilisation and preparedness (2004). A higher level of preparedness might be attributed to the *stayers* (Sykes and Chaoimh, 2012) and the *maximisers* (Alves et al., 2022), who tend to stay abroad for longer periods and (expect to) return after an accurate and positive evaluation of the benefits already acquired vs the benefits to be collected at home. Lower levels of preparedness also seem to be present among the *dreamers*, whose project of remaining abroad might not be achieved. Difficulties in mobilising new cultural capital in the host country, alongside external conditions, prevent them from staying and force them to return.

## AFTER GRADUATION: GAINS OR LOSSES AND FOR WHOM?

### Graduates' Experiences: Returnees and Non-returnees

International graduates might 'harvest' the great advantages of living and studying abroad but they may also face a deskilling or degree mismatch, highlighting ISM inequalities not only in terms of opportunities but also of outcomes (Bilecen and van Mol, 2017). According to Baláž and Williams (2004), Slovakian students who returned home following studies in the UK felt several benefits from their ISM experience, especially related to language and soft skills. However, returnees who reported better advantages were working in the private sector, against those in the public, who reported a lack of recognition and a poor assessment of their foreign experience. This situation might have changed since 2004 but, nevertheless, contrary to what could be expected (or desired), the state as a recruiter seemingly valued an international experience less than the private market did.

Lulle and Buzinska (2017) also showed a negative and somewhat unexpected result of Latvian graduates' return. The lack of networks and the persistence of cronyism within local institutions were the main reasons for a difficult professional integration back home, emphasising a devaluation of their international cultural capital. Thus, instead of returning and contributing to the country's development, as several of them wished to do, they looked for better opportunities abroad.

Non-EU/European Economic Area (EEA) students in Finland (Maury, 2019) and Eastern European students in Denmark (Wilken and Dahlberg, 2017) also revealed significant labour exploitation and discrimination regarding their nationality. These negative effects of ISM might compromise students' projects, especially of those who decide to remain and face degree mismatch, 'caught in the low-skill loop' (Wilken and Dahlberg, 2017, p.1356).

Alves and King (2021) found that the Angolan and Cape Verdean students in Portugal were occupying precarious financial and working positions during their studies and facing difficulties in finding a job in Portugal which corresponded to their skills after graduation. The limited offers of jobs matching students' expectations strongly explains their desire to return home, where they hoped for better prospects and opportunities. In fact, several graduates who had returned found this match at home. Others admitted that they would probably accept the 'mismatch' in Portugal, valuing the new lifestyle they had and the better access to services and goods (social welfare, the Internet, water, electricity and public security).

Berriane's (2015) research with sub-Saharan African students in Morocco showed ISM as a first step into longer and second migrations. Despite the fact that France, Canada, the US, the UK, Belgium and Portugal constituted their most desirable destinations, most ended up by remaining in Morocco for a longer period and only a smaller fraction actually left. Those who remained faced difficulties with professional integration, due to Moroccan legal restrictions with residence permits, occupying precarious positions in call centres or hired as trainees.

**Retaining International Students**

Global competition for talents has changed the perspective of most destination countries towards incoming students. According to Alboim:

> Until recently, Canada did not view international students as future citizens. On the contrary, in order to obtain a visa to study ..., applicants had to demonstrate that they had no intention of remaining in the country. International students were not allowed to work off-campus and had to leave the country if they wanted to apply for permanent residence. Today governments and post-secondary institutions actively encourage international students to come to Canada to study, work and apply for permanent residence from within the country. The main reason for this change ... is the view that international students comprise a pool of skilled, educated and young 'potential immigrants' who could successfully integrate and contribute to Canada's economy. (2011, p.15)

In Canada, federal changes reducing work restrictions for international students and graduates and provincial nomination programmes have been some of the actions taken (Alboim, 2011; Lowe, 2011). The same had happened before in Australia, through the promotion of so-called 'two-step' migration, where migrants can easily enter the country as students and then remain as permanent residents (Hawthorne, 2010). Portugal had changed its legislation too, improving students' chances of working during their studies.[4]

Aiming for the attraction and retention of international 'brains', most OECD countries have been developing job-search permits. In Canada it may be granted for a maximum of three years and four years in Australia, which is quite 'friendly' compared, for instance, to Portugal, which has established a limit of one year (OECD, 2016, p.336).

Particularly in the European context, demographic issues have been threatening the sustainability of HE institutions. International students are seen not only as a future base for the recruitment of high-skilled migrants but also as a great source of 'clients'. Considering their attraction and retention, the EU has been revising its policies; the *Agenda for Research and Innovation*, the *Agenda for Higher Education* and the *Europe 2020 Strategy* are examples.

Despite the belief that international students will be more successful in terms of professional integration in the host society compared to other migrants, data in Australia show that the former have a worse performance in terms of relative salaries and job satisfaction, rather than the latter (Hawthorne, 2010). Also in Canada, in the international graduates' study–work transition, professional experience in the country is more valued than the degree (Alboim, 2011). These cases, as well as those referred to in the previous subsection, point out that retention of international students might lead not only to a situation of brain drain at the origin but to brain waste too, considering the number of graduates working in so-called 3D jobs abroad: dull, dirty and dangerous (Wilken and Dahlberg, 2017, p.1353).

**The Importance of Return for the Origin Countries**

Origin countries expect to benefit from their nationals' ISM. First, there are diminishing educational costs, especially when students are self-funded (Rosenzweig, 2010). Second, increased human capital should accrue through their return, which will ultimately contribute to the home countries' social and economic development. These are, at least, some of the main arguments behind mobility, cooperation and development programmes, through scholarships, exemption or the reduction of tuition fees and other supportive actions (França et al., 2018).

In fact, going back to Alves et al.'s already-cited study (2022), several of the Angolan and Cape Verdean graduates who returned were former grantees of their origin countries or had benefited from Portuguese cooperation programmes. Post-return, they were all working in their field of study, mostly in academia as faculty and research staff. They said that these opportunities were, to some extent, 'easily' found back home, either because they left the country with that promise (and/or obligation) or due to a lack of high-skilled human resources in the study area. This situation was particularly found among the Angolans, who also revealed a more privileged social background. Therefore, it might be said that participation in mobility programmes and better social capital at home, as well as good economic and professional conditions in the origin countries, increase the odds of return (Kellogg, 2012).

However, nowadays, '"Education for aid" gave way to "education for trade", as countries and their educational institutions realized that international students could be a source of income and skills' (OECD, 2011a, p.13). To avoid brain drain, several states, of which Argentina, Brazil, Chile, China, Israel, Moldova, Russia, South Korea, South Africa, Thailand and Turkey are examples (Han et al., 2015), have developed programmes to encourage the return of their nationals, especially STEM graduates. Programmes usually require return after graduation – with or without a minimum period of 're-settlement' in the homeland – and might include tax breaks and job placement services. Despite this, these programmes' effect seems limited, considering the multiple determinants of migration, increasing the risks of non-return and brain drain (Cohen and Kranz, 2015).

It has been estimated that one in four international students stay in the host countries, providing an increasingly important source of skilled workers (OECD, 2011b). If so, this will not only compromise the development of the home countries but will also increase socio-economic and skill gaps between nations (see King, Chapter 22). Host countries or countries of post-graduation migration – usually developed ones – will keep benefiting from high-skilled human capital, increasing their chances of brain gain. However, as mentioned before, data also suggest trends of brain waste, where international graduates do not find a professional occupation overseas that matches their level of education.

## CONCLUSION

The current phenomenon of ISM is characterised by a context of individual and institutional competitiveness and an uneven geographical distribution. It depends on multiple factors, such as the academic, social, political and economic conditions of sending and hosting countries, as well as students' own characteristics, resources, motivations and expectations. To return or not after graduation is the result of the interaction of many factors, which intersect and also change over time.

Several studies have pointed out that students from Eastern Europe, Turkey, Northern and Western Africa, the Commonwealth of Independent States, China and South-East Asia were more likely to remain overseas. Counter to this, those from Anglophone countries and Latin America were more prone to return. If this is so, this highlights that ISM from South to North and from East to West tends to contribute to a global-scale brain drain.

Having or not having professional opportunities in the home or the host country might change the outcome. While unemployment or a lack of opportunities in the country of study increases the odds of return, employment might also lead to return when students are from fast-developing countries, due to high returns to professional experience besides education. Additionally, a willingness to give back to the homeland, better social origins, studying social sciences, being women, older and with children all look to improve the odds of return, while longer periods of residence overseas, having married abroad or having the spouse in the country of study seem to increase the odds of staying put. The pull of family might have a 'return effect' but it might also push students into longer stays overseas, seeing ISM as an economic strategy that will benefit all, for instance via regular remittances.

Whether profiling as *maximisers*, *dreamers*, *world citizens* or *runners* (cf. Alves et al., 2022), the fact is that most students seem to have an initial project of return and only a few see ISM from the outset as a step towards onward migration. However, after some time out, their intentions might no longer be the same, demanding a long and exhaustive exercise of measuring the pros and cons. Thus, it might be said that the initial project for the future and its (final) accomplishment is not always aligned. As Baláž et al. (2004) noticed, there is a relationship between temporary migration and a subsequent disposition to permanent migration, since individuals' motivations change and social networks expand.

In Geddie's words (2013, p.205), 'In many instances, students felt pulled in multiple directions upon graduation, in line with their career aspirations and the various transnational relations that they hold and wish to maintain.' In this sense, a circular or transnational mobility could also be expected. However, the fact is that little is known about international graduates' trajectories and how they are related consequentially to their prior itineraries of study.

International graduates are often seen as desired migrants, although some research has revealed cases of deskilling, due to labour market displacement. This contributes to a brain drain in the origin country and a no brain gain in the host country – thus to a general brain waste. Policies aiming for the attraction and retention of international students/graduates should consider this negative effect.

Revisiting the introductory cases, being from Bulgaria or Angola and studying in Denmark or Portugal is not enough to determine future trajectories, although it seems to increase the odds of remaining abroad. In order to understand which factors have a greater weight on actual return and the dimension of this flow, qualitative and quantitative regional and longitudinal studies would be appreciated, through harmonised indicators. More investigation is needed to elicit how home countries value ISM on public and private labour markets.

## NOTES

1. Two caveats considering ISM data: (i) origin might be measured through country of prior education, secondary education, nationality or residence; and (ii) students might be enrolled in degree mobility (for an entire course) or credit mobility (shorter/ exchange programmes). UNESCO publishes national statistics, meaning they are not uniform and hamper international comparisons (Bhandari and Blumenthal, 2011). Having the EU as an example, until 2016 countries could have reported country of prior residence or nationality. From 2016 onwards, they were asked to report country of prior education. Despite this, variations are still present. For instance, Austria, Denmark and Portugal exclude credit mobility from the ISM numbers, while Czechia, Norway and Spain include it (https://ec.europa.eu/eurostat/cache/metadata/en/educ_uoe_enr_esms.htm, accessed 18 September 2021).
2. The number of tertiary students from abroad studying in a given country minus the number of students at the same level from a given country studying abroad (http://data.uis.unesco.org, accessed 18 September 2021).
3. Taking up the introductory cases, the Bulgarian students in Denmark and the Angolans in Portugal follow the second and third poles.
4. Act 23/2007 of 4 July, amended by Act 102/2017 of 28 August, which establishes the conditions and procedures on the entry, stay, exit and removal of foreign citizens from Portuguese territory.

## REFERENCES

Alberts, H.C. and Hazen, H.D. (2005) '"There are always two voices...": international students' intentions to stay in the United States or return to their home countries', *International Migration*, **43** (3), 131–54.

Alboim, N. (2011) 'From international student to permanent resident: policy considerations', *Canadian Diversity Magazine*, **8** (5), 15–19.

Alves, E. and King, R. (2021) 'Between international student and immigrant: a critical perspective on Angolan and Cape Verdean students in Portugal' in R. Brooks and S. O'Shea (eds), *Reimagining the Higher Education Student*, London: Routledge, pp. 223–39.

Alves, E., King, R. and Malheiros, J.M. (2022) 'Are you just going to study or do you plan to stay on? Trajectories of Angolan and Cape Verdean students in Portugal' in D. Dedgjoni and C. Bauschke-Urban (eds), *Student Mobilities from the Global South*, London: Routledge (in press).

António, M. (2013) 'Os estudantes angolanos do ensino superior em Lisboa: uma perspetiva antropológica sobre as suas motivações e bem-estar subjetivo', *Analise Social*, **48** (208), 660–82.

Baláž, V. and Williams, A.M. (2004) '"Been there, done that": international student migration and human capital transfers from the UK to Slovakia', *Population, Space and Place*, **10** (3), 217–37.

Baláž, V., Williams, A.M. and Kollár, D. (2004) 'Temporary versus permanent youth brain drain: economic implications', *International Migration*, **42** (4), 3–34.

Beine, M., Noël, R. and Ragot, L. (2014) 'Determinants of the international mobility of students', *Economics of Education Review*, **41** (2014), 40–54.

Berriane, J. (2015) 'Sub-Saharan students in Morocco: determinants, everyday life, and future plans of a high-skilled migrant group', *Journal of North African Studies*, **20** (4), 573–89.

Bhandari, R. and Blumenthal, P. (2011) 'Global student mobility and the twenty-first century silk road: national trends and new directions' in R. Bhandari and P. Blumenthal (eds), *International Students and Global Mobility in Higher Education. National Trends and New Directions*, New York: Palgrave Macmillan, pp. 1–23.

Bijwaard, G.E. and Wang, Q. (2016) 'Return migration of foreign students', *European Journal of Population*, **32** (1), 31–54.

Bilecen, B. (2016) 'International students and cosmopolitanisms: educational mobility in a global age' in A. Amelina and K. Horvath (eds), *An Anthology of Migration and Social Transformation: European Perspectives*, Cham: Springer, pp. 231–44.

Bilecen, B. and van Mol, C. (2017) 'Introduction: international academic mobility and inequalities', *Journal of Ethnic and Migration Studies*, **43** (8), 1241–55.

Börjesson, M. (2017) 'The global space of international students in 2010', *Journal of Ethnic and Migration Studies*, **43** (8), 1256–75.

Brito, Â.X.D. (2004) 'Habitus de herdeiro, habitus escolar: os sentidos da internacionalização nas trajetórias dos estudantes brasileiros no exterior' in A.M.F. Almeida, L.B. Canedo, A. Garcia and A.B. Bittencourt (eds), *Circulação Internacional e Formação Intelectual das Elites Brasileiras*, Campinas SP: E. da Unicamp, pp. 85–104.

Bryła, P. (2019) 'International student mobility and subsequent migration: the case of Poland', *Studies in Higher Education*, **44** (8), 1386–99.

Cassarino, J.-P. (2004) 'Theorising return migration: a revisited conceptual approach to return migrants', *International Journal on Multicultural Societies*, **6** (2), 253–79.

Cohen, N. and Kranz, D. (2015) 'State-assisted highly skilled return programmes, national identity and the risk(s) of homecoming: Israel and Germany compared', *Journal of Ethnic and Migration Studies*, **41** (5), 795–812.

Findlay, A., King, R., Smith, F.M., Geddes, A. and Skeldon, R. (2011) 'World class? An investigation of globalisation, difference and international student mobility', *Transactions of the Institute of British Geographers*, **37** (1), 118–31.

Findlay, A., Prazeres, L., McCollum, D. and Packwood, H. (2017) '"It was always the plan": international study as "learning to migrate"', *Area*, **49** (2), 192–9.

França, T., Alves, E. and Padilla, B. (2018) 'Portuguese policies fostering international student mobility: a colonial legacy or a new strategy?', *Globalisation, Societies and Education*, **16** (3), 325–38.

Geddie, K. (2013) 'The transnational ties that bind: relationship considerations for graduating international science and engineering students', *Population, Space and Place*, **19** (2), 196–208.

Geddie, K. (2015) 'Policy mobilities in the race for talent: competitive state strategies in international student mobility', *Transactions of the Institute of British Geographers*, **40** (2), 235–48.

Gürüz, K. (2008) *Higher Education and International Student Mobility in the Global Knowledge Economy*, Albany: State University of New York Press.

Han, X., Stocking, G., Gebbie, M.A. and Applebaum, R.P. (2015) 'Will they stay or will they go? International graduate students and their decisions to stay or leave the U.S. upon graduation', *PLoS One*, **10** (3), 1–19.

Hawthorne, L. (2010) 'How valuable is "two-step migration"? Labor market outcomes for international student migrants to Australia', *Asian and Pacific Migration Journal*, **19** (1), 5–36.

Iorio, J.C. and Fonseca, M.L. (2018) 'Estudantes brasileiros no ensino superio português: construção do projeto migratório e intenções de mobilidade futura', *Finisterra*, **53** (109), 3–20.

Israel, E., Cohen, N. and Czamanski, D. (2019) 'Return on capital? Determinants of counter-migration among early career Israeli STEM researchers', *PLoS One*, **14** (8), 1–20.

Kellogg, R.P. (2012) 'China's brain gain?: attitudes and future plans of overseas Chinese students in the US', *Journal of Chinese Overseas*, **8** (1), 83–104.

Kim, S. (2015) 'The influence of social relationships on international students' intentions to remain abroad: multi-group analysis by marital status', *International Journal of Human Resource Management*, **24** (14), 1848–64.

King, R. and Ruiz-Gelices, E. (2003) 'International student migration and the European "year abroad": effects on European identity and subsequent migration behaviour', *International Journal of Population Geography*, **9** (3), 229–52.

King, R., Findlay, A.M., Ahrens, J. and Dunne, M. (2011) 'Reproducing advantage: the perspective of English school leavers on studying abroad', *Globalisation, Societies and Education*, **9** (2), 161–81.

Knight, J. and de Wit, H. (1995) 'Strategies for internationalisation of higher education: historical and conceptual perspectives' in H. de Wit (ed.), *Strategies for Internationalization of Higher Education: A Comparative Study of Australia, Canada, Europe and the United States of America*, Amsterdam: European Association for International Education, pp. 5–32.

Kritz, M.M. (2015a) 'International student mobility and tertiary education capacity in Africa', *International Migration*, **53** (1), 29–49.

Kritz, M.M. (2015b) 'Why do countries differ in their rates of outbound student mobility?', *Journal of Studies in International Education*, **20** (2), 99–117.

Lin, Y. and Kingminghae, W. (2017) 'Factors that influence stay intention of Thai international students following completion of degrees in China', *Asia Pacific Education Review*, **18** (1), 13–22.

Lowe, S. (2011) 'Welcome to Canada: immigration incentives may not be enough for international students to stay', *Canadian Diversity Magazine*, **8** (5), 20–4.

Lulle, A. and Buzinska, L. (2017) 'Between a "student abroad" and "being from Latvia": inequalities of access, prestige, and foreign-earned cultural capital', *Journal of Ethnic and Migration Studies*, **43** (8), 1362–78.

Marcu, S. (2015) 'Uneven mobility experiences: life-strategy expectations among Eastern European undergraduate students in the UK and Spain', *Geoforum*, **58**, 68–75.

Maury, O. (2019) 'Between a promise and a salary: student-migrant-workers' experiences of precarious labour markets', *Work, Employment and Society*, **34** (5), 1–17.

Mendoza, C. and Ortiz, A. (2016) 'Student on the move: academic career and life transitions of foreign PhD students in Barcelona (Spain)' in J. Domínguez-Mujica (ed.), *Global Change and Human Mobility*, Singapore: Springer Singapore, pp. 249–63.

Moskal, M. (2020) 'Gendered differences in international graduates' mobility, identity and career development', *Social and Cultural Geography*, **21** (3), 421–40.

Mosneaga, A. and Winther, L. (2013) 'Emerging talents? International students before and after their career start in Denmark', *Population, Space and Place*, **19** (2), 181–95.

OECD (2011a) *50th OECD Anniversary: International Migration and the SOPEMI*, Paris: OECD Publishing.

OECD (2011b) *International Migration Outlook: SOPEMI 2011*, Paris: OECD Publishing.

OECD (2016) *Education at a Glance 2016: OECD Indicators*, Paris: OECD Publishing.

Perkins, R. and Neumayer, E. (2014) 'Geographies of educational mobilities: exploring the uneven flows of international students', *Geographical Journal*, **180** (3), 246–59.

Rosenzweig, M.R. (2006) 'Global wage differences and international student flows' in S.M. Collins and C. Graham (eds), *Brookings Trade Forum 2006: Global Labor Markets?*, Washington DC: Brookings International Press, pp. 57–96.

Rosenzweig, M.R. (2010) *Global Wage Inequality and the International Flow of Migrants*, New Haven CT: Yale University, Economic Growth Center Discussion Paper No. 983.

Sondhi, G. and King, R. (2017) 'Gendering international student migration: an Indian case-study', *Journal of Ethnic and Migration Studies*, **43** (8), 1308–24.

Soon, J.-J. (2010) 'The determinants of students' return intentions: a partial proportional odds model', *Journal of Choice Modelling*, **3** (2), 89–112.

Soon, J.-J. (2012) 'Home is where the heart is? Factors determining international students' destination country upon completion of studies abroad', *Journal of Ethnic and Migration Studies*, **38** (1), 147–62.

Sykes, B. and Chaoimh, E.N. (2012) *Mobile Talent? The Staying Intentions of International Students in Five EU Countries*, Berlin: Sachverständigenrat Deutscher Stiftungen für Integration und Migration.

van Mol, C. and Timmerman, C. (2014) 'Should I stay or should I go? An analysis of the determinants of intra-European student mobility', *Population, Space and Place*, **20** (5), 465–79.

Weisser, R. (2016) *Internationally Mobile Students and their Post-Graduation Migratory Behaviour: An Analysis of Determinants of Student Mobility and Retention Rates in the EU*, Paris: OECD, Social, Employment and Migration Working Paper No. 186.

Wilken, L. and Dahlberg, M.G. (2017) 'Between international student mobility and work migration: experiences of students from EU's newer member states in Denmark', *Journal of Ethnic and Migration Studies*, **43** (8), 1347–61.

Wu, C. and Wilkes, R. (2017) 'International students' post-graduation migration plans and the search for home', *Geoforum*, **80**, 123–32.

Zijlstra, J. (2015) 'Iranian student mobility in Turkey: a precursor to permanent immigration?', *Journal of Business Economics and Political Science*, **3** (5), 1–16.

# 19. Returning lifestyle migrants
## Katie Walsh

## INTRODUCTION

Lifestyle migration is a term that has been used to explain the migration of individuals from developed countries 'as a route to a more fulfilling way of life, especially in contrast to the one left behind … an anti-modern, escapist, self-realization project, a search for the intangible "good life"' (O'Reilly and Benson, 2009, p.1; see also Benson and O'Reilly, 2009a, 2015). Researchers have focused on lifestyle migration as a *comparative* project in understanding the choices which lifestyle migrants make to reorientate themselves: those of working age are able to access a more relaxed and slower-paced daily life by leaving careers and mortgages behind while, conversely, a more active phase of retirement and ageing is enabled by warmer climates and increased leisure opportunities (e.g. Benson, 2010; Benson and Osbaldiston, 2015; King et al., 2000; O'Reilly, 2000; Oliver, 2008). The concept has since been further developed, especially in the work of Michaela Benson, as an intervention to understand the migration of the *relatively* affluent, in which accessing a different lifestyle through migration is a way in which *relative* privilege is negotiated and articulated by migrants (Benson, 2018, p.25; also Benson, 2013, 2014, 2015). Indeed, lifestyle migration is not simply the choice of individuals but is facilitated, as Croucher (2015, p.161) argues, by 'socio-spatial reconfigurations taking place in the context of macro-level economic, political and demographic factors – namely neoliberalization and the ageing populations of the US and Western Europe'.

There has been a burgeoning of research on lifestyle migrants, yet very little exploration of their return movements. However, more is known about their anticipated return and it is possible to observe at least three prominent debates in the 'lifestyle migration' literature in relation to return: (1) the relationship between ageing and return, which highlights how social norms and the accessibility of health and social care can inform lifestyle migrants' decisions to stay or return; (2) the relative privilege of lifestyle migrants in relation to global inequalities, considering how their routes and settlement are shaped by structural factors and, consequently, how return migration may arise in situations of unanticipated precarity; and finally (3), the reintegration experiences of lifestyle migrants following their return. However, before turning to these three concerns, the next section critically examines the concept of 'lifestyle migration' and its edges.

## WHOSE RETURN? FURTHER EXPLORING LIFESTYLE MIGRATION

The privilege of lifestyle migrants is not just an economic assessment based on a collective or individual comparison. Although lifestyle migrants are often absolutely or relatively affluent and certainly benefit from lower costs of living in their country of settlement, the privilege of lifestyle migrants is also racialised through whiteness (Benson, 2013, 2018; Fechter and

Walsh, 2010; Lafferty and Maher, 2020). This extends beyond the overt practices of lifestyle migrants to the way in which they are implicitly understood and conceptualised as distinct from other migrants in the wider literature. In spite of the nuanced sociological thinking evident in some uses of the term, lifestyle migrant is frequently used as shorthand for particular migration nationalities undertaking migration to specific destinations, especially by those not working on lifestyle migration themselves. The scholarly imagination of lifestyle migration was, at first, almost entirely restricted to the intra-European mobilities of Britons and other Northern Europeans moving to Southern Europe (Benson and O'Reilly, 2009b; King et al., 2000). However, other routes, noticeably all 'north–south migrations' (Croucher, 2015), have since been examined through this theoretical framework: in particular, US and Canadian movements to Central and South America (Benson, 2013; Benson and O'Reilly, 2018; Hayes, 2014) and 'Westerners' and Japanese retirees in Southeast Asia (Benson and O'Reilly, 2018; Botterill, 2016a, 2016b; Toyota, 2006; Toyota and Xiang, 2012).

While the definitions above help us to understand how debates on lifestyle migration define and frame lifestyle migrants, the boundaries of this terminology are debated for several reasons. As one example, not all those now labelled as lifestyle migrants share the sense of their own migration as a journey of self-realisation, with Stones et al. (2019) asserting that, while 'the good life' remains a valuable distinguishing feature of lifestyle migration, this quest may also be found in notions of 'pragmatic contentment'. As such, Western counter-culture ideals of self-realisation may not be as significant in many lifestyle migrations, which can, instead involve 'a concern with various permutations of relaxation, the sensuous, familial closeness and care, and sometimes the desire for adventure, exploration, and the broadening of horizons, but all typically centred on the prosaic everyday' (Stones et al., 2019, p.48). The comparative methodology of their paper allows them to demonstrate how this is shared by both British lifestyle migrants in Thailand and Hong Kong lifestyle migrants in mainland China.

The distinction between lifestyle and economic/labour migration is more blurred than the separateness of these literatures in Migration Studies would infer. On the one hand, those who are recognised as 'lifestyle migrants' often perceive mobility in terms of entrepreneurial opportunities and work as 'accountants, hairdressers, landlords, lawyers, real estate agents, restaurateurs, therapists' (Croucher, 2015, p.162; Huete et al., 2013). On the other hand, among (highly) skilled professionals, many accept postings, actively choose to relocate for international career opportunities or seek paid employment *only* in destinations which they see as also offering them distinct improvements in lifestyle. Such migrations are, therefore, about employment opportunities and are often primarily understood in terms of labour migration but they are not only about economics: lifestyle may be an important consideration factored into both migration and return. In my own research on British migrants in Dubai, for example, interviewees highlight how economic and lifestyle factors are thoroughly entangled in the narrative of it offering 'tax-free sunshine' (Walsh, 2018a). Likewise, Britons of working age in New Zealand, whose employment allows them to migrate and take up residence, may frame their relocation as lifestyle-oriented (Higgins, 2017). Huete et al. (2013) convincingly question the boundaries of a lifestyle migrant versus an economic migrant. Reviewing empirical literatures where British migrants in Spain are labelled as 'lifestyle migrants', they argue that, leaving aside the motivational reasons expressed by these migrants, they are extremely heterogeneous, including young families with children, retirees in later life and varying settlement patterns determined by work and family responsibilities. Furthermore, they argue, it is not easy to find objective features that are distinctive enough to justify categorising them separately from other kinds of migrant, including labour migrants, with the exception that 'these individuals come from countries with higher levels of economic development than Spain' (Huete et al., 2013, p.332). As such, the authors suggest that lifestyle migrants are often implicitly identified as such by researchers from their nationality and economic factors play a greater role in their migration than is often acknowledged. Moving from European countries where the cost of living is more expensive to countries (in Europe or beyond) where it is less expensive increases the affordability of a desirable lifestyle, via property ownership, reduced working hours, entrepreneurialism or retirement (Huete et al., 2013). Therefore, economic factors play a role that is not fully acknowledged in the lifestyle migration literature.

Further evidence of the necessity of rethinking these categorisations comes from research on return migration as more conventionally understood. Marta Bolognani (2014) demonstrates how the 'return imaginary' of first- and second-generation British Pakistanis is now dominated by lifestyle considerations, as a sense of agency emerges in relation to their current mobility. She notes how economic, political and relational reasoning are still present in their decision-making, as they are for other lifestyle migrants but, unlike earlier migrations to the UK, lifestyle factors become prevalent and key to decisions. Indeed, for British Pakistanis, migration 'home' has become a comparative project, with the identification of a more relaxed pace of life, closer contact with nature, more pleasant weather, domestic help for women and the availability of religious education as key advantages of Pakistan. Bolognani (2014, p.32) argues that this reflects a 'process of change (in class, status, power and position in respect to the both country of origin and the country of settlement)' such that 'the capacity to desire, aspire and dream' has emerged in the community. Such evidence points to the difficulties of working with fixed boundaries between conceptual frameworks of diaspora, labour migrants and lifestyle migrants. Recognising how these kinds of return could also be framed as British lifestyle migration brings into question the very categories that Migration Studies frequently employs.

To avoid overlap across this edited volume, however, the focus in this chapter is on those who are more typically framed as lifestyle migrants in the wider literature. Unfortunately, there are very few discussions of returning lifestyle migrants where return has taken place prior to the research. Even research papers that highlight and foreground discussions of return in relation to lifestyle migrants tend to explore *anticipated* future migration trajectories. Eimermann (2017), for example, explores the return reasoning among Dutch lifestyle migrant families, yet the interviews are mainly about family life in Hällefors, Sweden; it is only in the discussion of 'everyday life in the near and distant future' that we see a more deliberate attempt to capture return more explicitly in interviews as part of a broader research design. It is perhaps not surprising that researchers of lifestyle migration have adopted this approach, since it is much more straightforward to recruit participants within their more structured and obvious communities of lifestyle migrants in their country of destination.

Therefore, I also draw on broader discussions of lifestyle migration that help us to understand the place of return in the narratives, practices and migration experiences of lifestyle migrants globally. In common with the wider literature on return, our understanding of the 'magnitude and configuration' of lifestyle return is constrained by a lack of large-scale quantitative data (see Cassarino, 2004). However, existing research does provide us with important insights into lifestyle migrants' return with respect to how it is anticipated or resisted by those still resident in their migration destination. Most notably, there is now significant understanding of how return features in the lives of British retirement migrants in Spain in the later stages of older age (Giner-Montfort et al., 2015; Hall and Hardill, 2016; Hall et al., 2017; Huete et al., 2013; Oliver, 2004, 2008, 2016). In fact, it is essential to capture those who are attempting or desiring return, because they may not achieve this. Given that an estimated half a million Britons over the age of 50 live in Spain, with 14 per cent over 70 (Hall et al., 2017, drawing on Finch et al., 2010), it is perhaps not surprising that their return migration has also been noticed and discussed. I also draw on my own research with British migrant returnees in the decades after return (Walsh, 2018b, 2019), a study which includes those who return from Mediterranean retirement communities and emigration destinations, as well as those who return from professional working lives in lifestyle-oriented communities of Westerners in postcolonial global cities.

## AGEING AND RETURNING LIFESTYLE MIGRANTS

The relationship between health, care, ageing and lifestyle migration is complex. For lifestyle migrants, return in older age is not a predictable or an inevitable outcome of ageing. The lifestyle migration literature has widely documented how ideas about ageing 'well' and 'active ageing' are central motivations for lifestyle migration after retirement, so ageing may not be considered as a factor until illness is experienced (Oliver, 2008). Furthermore, communities of lifestyle migrants often have extensive and highly organised networks of charities and volunteers devoted to supporting those with health problems in older age (Benson and O'Reilly, 2018; Oliver, 2017). The prevalence of formal and informal support may even be exaggerated among migrants, since people share the experience of being away from family and state support (Benson and O'Reilly, 2018; Oliver, 2017). The need to return may also be removed by the financial accessibility of home-based care in some regions. Kate Botterill's (2016) research, for example, demonstrates that some British migrants relocating to Thailand consider the affordability of live-in care in their decision about where to grow older. Male lifestyle migrants in relationships with younger Thai women also considered that their care needs in later life would be met in return for financial security (Botterill, 2016a, 2016b).

Nevertheless, the later stages of older age can often bring decreased resources for independent living and thereby more often encourage return migration in efforts to access familial support, as well as state and private provisions of health and social care (Giner-Montfort et al., 2015; Hall and Hardill, 2016; Hall et al., 2017; Oliver, 2008; Percival, 2013). While lifestyle migration is framed around 'active ageing', ageing can also bring increasing health concerns, unexpectedly or in the later stages – embodied in conditions such as frailty, chronic illness, physical impairment or dementia, which all increase the challenges of ageing in place. As Giner-Montfort et al. (2015, p.797) summarise, as people age, returning may become more of a consideration due to associated issues, 'such as the death of a partner, loneliness, physical and social isolation, loss of purchasing power, disabilities, the need for health care and/or social care'. Such decisions are also made in relation to others and children may insist that parents return when they become more dependent on healthcare provision (Benson and O'Reilly, 2018). A decrease in public spending since the 2008 financial crisis and rising numbers of older people have also generated a crisis of adult social care in the UK and the reduction of services, including home care, so return is not a straightforward option (Oliver, 2017).

Furthermore, expectations that ageing may bring illness and impairment can also shape plans for returning in the future, long before an actual return becomes desirable or necessary, thereby undermining a sense of permanence to their international residence. As an illustration, many British migrants *anticipate* returning from Spain when they experience ill-health and make plans to do so (Betty and Hall, 2015). Others do not plan to return but feel compelled to do so when faced with the expense of care, a crisis in care or a sudden decline in health that removes their independence (Hall and Hardill, 2016). Frequently lifestyle migrants do not register for health and social care in Spain, fearing the loss of welfare rights in the UK (Giner-Montfort et al., 2015). Language concerns, as well as perceptions of the quality of healthcare provision, are also a primary concern in lifestyle migrants' decisions to return (Betty and Hall, 2015; Walsh, 2018b). In such circumstances, return migration enables access to state-provided routine and emergency healthcare, as well as residential care homes funded through a mixture of state and private finance. In contrast, many of the Southern European countries popular with Northern European lifestyle-oriented retirement migrants still have a 'familialistic' care culture where personal care is provided by family members in the home or, increasingly, where families can afford it, migrant care-givers take their place under the supervision of relatives (Escrivá, 2016). As lifestyle migrants reach older age, therefore, their own ideas about 'good' care provision may be confronted by social norms in their country of residence, triggering a desire to return to models of care that are more familiar and more practical than transnational family arrangements would allow. Retirement in a place where lifestyle migrants are already living may also be prohibited by the cost of health insurance previously covered by an employer, especially as rates rise with age (Walsh, 2018b).

For others, return only becomes an option when anticipating or dealing with death. In her analysis of a British retirement community in Spain, Caroline Oliver (2004, p.238) observed that 'most migrants seemed to have planned what they wanted to do in the eventuality of death'. Many chose cremation in Spain for practical and financial reasons, since repatriating a body by air is expensive, with a spouse or family member then scattering the ashes in the UK. Many others requested that their ashes were scattered in Spain, consistent with claims of their feeling at home there, especially those with weak kin ties in the UK. However, for others, especially those with children in the UK, 'the very nature of disposal in Spain may be too much to manage and they return to the UK before this eventuality' (Oliver, 2004, p.252). Spousal bereavement may also lead to return migration, especial if due to practical concerns – life can become suddenly or unexpectedly challenging if the spouse who dies was the partner who drove or spoke the local language more confidently (Rutter and Andrew, 2009). Others return to be nearer children during a time of grief, because their partner managed their social relations or because they had previously wanted to return. Oliver (2016) notes that, for lifestyle migrants, return requires an imaginative recasting of the country of origin from a place where risk-averse peers have been left behind to a place of comfort and safety. Nevertheless, while it is clear that the emotional orientation towards home may shift in older age with bereavement and ill-health, many choose not to return and instead make adjustments in the face of change (Oliver, 2016).

## PRIVILEGE, PRECARITY AND RETURNING LIFESTYLE MIGRANTS

Recently, Benson and O'Reilly (2018, p.15) reflected that lifestyle migration scholarship has focused to such an extent on migrant subjectivities that structural considerations have been mostly overlooked. This was possible precisely because lifestyle migrants narrate their mobilities in terms of choice and agency when accounting for decisions about their search for 'the good life'. Yet, lifestyle migration does not exist in a vacuum but is facilitated and channelled by state policy, shaped by the ongoing inequalities of postcolonial space (Fechter and Walsh, 2010) and emerging neoliberal processes (Croucher, 2015; Ono, 2015). Discussions of retirement and care needs in the previous section hinted at the way in which the relative financial benefits of residence in different countries help to shape lifestyle migrants' decisions about return. This section explores in more depth the impact of global inequalities and variations by country of the (perceived, actual and relative) affordability of particular lifestyles for migrants as a consequence. Since lifestyle migration can be understood as a '*comparative* project' (Benson and O'Reilly, 2009a), when life in their new country of residence is no longer perceived as 'better' due to changing structural conditions or the need to access welfare support, lifestyle migrants will choose to return.

The global economic crisis also increased the precarity of lifestyle migrants in Europe. Huete et al. (2013) explored the impact on British lifestyle migrants in Spain when the pound was devalued (as the currency of their pension), unemployment of younger migrants in Spain increased and the Spanish real-estate market crashed. Following this crisis, British lifestyle migrants in the province of Alicante behaved in a very similar way to migrants of other nationalities who were categorised as labour migrants, suggesting that economic factors and material considerations are more significant in their decision-making than the terminology of 'lifestyle migrant' infers. Their quantitative analysis shows that, in 2005, there were 1.5 departures of British nationals for every 100 entries but that, by 2010, there were 54.2 departures for every 100 entries (Huete et al., 2013, p.342). Therefore, in spite of leisure being the explanatory lifestyle rationale for relocation to Spain, British 'lifestyle migrants' responded to the economic crisis by returning in much higher numbers, in spite of return being made more difficult by the devaluation of British-owned housing in Spain. Indeed, for many of those who wished to sell and move back to the UK it became impossible to do so (Betty and Hall, 2015; see also Fotheringham, 2012).

Kate Botterill (2016a) argues that the perceived privilege of lifestyle migrants in the Global South may also obscure their precarity. From the late 1990s, countries in Southeast Asia began to issue special visas for foreign retirees (Toyota, 2006). For example, in the aftermath of the 1997 Asian financial crisis, the 'Malaysia My Second Home' programme offering ten-year visas was intended to attract affluent migrants who would then invest in property (Benson and O'Reilly, 2018; Ono, 2015). Botterill's research in Hua Hin, a beach-city resort in Thailand, focused on British migrants resident on a retirement visa, a visa which is available to those over 50 years of age with more than 800,000 Bahts (approximately 25,000 US dollars in 2020) invested in a Thai bank at the point of application. Two thirds of the interviewees were male and, of this group, nearly all were in a relationship with a Thai woman (suggesting that further critical examination of lifestyle migration should include gender and sexuality). However, Botterill (2016a, p.5) reveals that some British lifestyle migrants are experiencing financial insecurity due to a freeze on UK state pensions at the point of emigration. This was exaggerated by the global economic crisis of 2007–08, which saw unfavourable changes in the exchange rates and the devaluation of private pensions and investment portfolios. Younger migrants also cannot work due to the restrictions of the retirement visas. Botterill (2016a) also found that half of the interviewees did not have medical insurance, so the expense of health and social care in Thailand as they age may further reduce the affordability of lifestyle migration, leading to return. Indeed, the lack of provision of state-funded medical care and care homes prompted some interviewees to plan to return in later life. The precarity of their financial situation is exaggerated by their political status as guests in Thailand because, as non-citizens, they feel fragile without any 'safety net' (Botterill, 2016a).

Precarity can also be exaggerated when lifestyle migrants live away from their country of origin for long periods, investing all their resources in their country of residence; it may thus become difficult to access the financial resources to return if they want to. Lafferty and Maher (2020, p.1636) note that lifestyle migrants in Thailand include retirees living off modest state and private pensions, those who work as English teachers or in local companies and entrepreneurs in the tourism industry. As an illustration, Lafferty and Maher (2020) introduce us to Bill, who was married to a Thai spouse and now had a young child; Bill had lived in provincial Thailand for 12 years. He explains that, if money were not an issue, they would live together in the UK but that, in Thailand, he can better fulfil his 'masculine' role as 'provider' for this family that is so critical to his relationship. However, lifestyle migrants' options to return become increasingly limited due to their lack of savings and limited job and housing prospects in the UK, leading Lafferty and Maher (2020) to describe their talk of return as 'wishful thinking'. They also reveal that, when relationships fall apart, men have to relinquish any property to their wives (as land and property can only belong to Thai nationals by law) and some men cannot return to their home countries because they have no savings to fund the plane ticket and are more likely to have fines from overstaying their visa if they have been economically marginal for some time.

Although lifestyle migration begins as a voluntary choice to relocate, lifestyle migrants do not necessarily retain this agency over their mobility and many do not have the resources to return (Lafferty and Maher, 2020; Oliver, 2008). In Thailand, Western lifestyle migrants can end up as street homeless (Lafferty and Maher, 2020, p.1640). In other contexts, charities such as the British Community Assistance Fund in Dubai (Walsh, 2018a) or Age Concern España (Hall and Hardill, 2016) may support and fund repatriation where needed. Some leave considerable debts in their countries of migration. Hall et al. (2017) reproduce a blog post claiming that many handed the keys of their homes back to the bank in the aftermath of the financial crisis in Spain. In Dubai, expensive cars were left abandoned at the airport by those unable to sustain their lifestyle and fleeing illegal debts in the aftermath of the financial crisis (Bond, 2012). Others return when investments in property go wrong, depleting their life savings, so that their country of origin becomes a place of safety in comparison to the risk of lifestyle migration (Walsh, 2019, p.191). Hall et al. (2017) note that experiences of return are shaped by the level of choice and control that returnees feel in relation to their decision, with unwanted involuntary returns leaving people feeling vulnerable and unhappy. The next section explores experiences of return and reintegration in more detail.

## EXPERIENCES OF RETURN AND REINTEGRATION

From the discussion in the chapter thus far, it is clear that lifestyle migrants may narrate decisions about the permanency of their move on departure but that these are subject to an ongoing process of re-evaluation within the constraints and possibilities which they encounter. Thereby, temporary relocations may become a lifetime of settlement, while those who imagined themselves as emigrants may return when things do not work out. Furthermore, any return migration may not be conclusive and migrants may choose to attempt another migration back to where they had been living or to a new destination. There is also a sense in which, for some lifestyle migrants, returns are part of everyday life, if we recognise the active transnational social field that many construct from their attachment to both their place of origin/return and their place of current residence. For Stones et al. (2019, p.50), 'even in those cases where the lifestyle migrant does not physically return to the old world, the two worlds still co-exist in their habitus, memories and imaginations and, for most, in a range of transnational activities'. Examples of transnational practices include visiting and contacting friends and family online, maintaining property, investments or remittances and paying taxes and insurance. Many lifestyle retirees resident in Spain are 'transmigrants' according to Karen O'Reilly's (2000) detailed ethnographic study, maintaining ongoing mobilities and personal relationships in both Spain and the UK. She noted that few British migrants in Spain followed current affairs or voted in UK elections; however, the referendum on Brexit has surely led to increased transnational political engagement according to Higgins (2019).

Experiences of actual physical return and reintegration are varied among lifestyle migrants, revealing both the privilege and the precarity discussed earlier in this chapter. Key factors include the extent to which their return is voluntary or dictated by financial or health concerns, the length of their residence away from their 'home' country and the extent of any engagement with transnationalism while 'away'. Such influences clearly resonate with the way in which Cassarino (2004) highlights how the preparedness of other return migrants is shaped by their resources for return; however, there is very little research with those who have been lifestyle migrants after they have returned to their country of origin. Unlike lifestyle migrant communities that are often clearly visible to researchers, with social organisations and networks allowing easier access to action qualitative research methodologies, returnees will usually disperse into existing communities without such obvious markers of their presence. Furthermore, lifestyle migrants are often highly mobile and rarely register in their country of residence; their movements back and forth overlap with those of tourists and second-home owners (Giner-Montfort et al., 2015). However, the absence of studies on returning lifestyle migrants may also be an epistemological oversight. Giner-Montfort et al. (2015) suggest that there is such an emphasis on the positive dimensions of retirement migration that scholars may have ignored the return dimension. Indeed, the construction of retirement migrants as affluent people accessing a better quality of life voluntarily as an active ageing strategy leaves little space to consider the difficulties or needs that may arise and lead to return. This argument can surely be extended to lifestyle migrants more widely.

Financial and economic resources are considered hugely significant in return decisions, preparedness for return and reintegration (Cassarino, 2004). Most lifestyle migrants are fortunate to be able to plan their return and have access to financial resources to navigate the costs of relocating their belongings and accessing a new residence more easily. Among those returning to the UK, for example, home ownership is higher than among the general population (Rutter and Andrew, 2009). Returnees may already own property in the country to which they are returning (having rented as lifestyle migrants or owning multiple homes) or plan their return so that they can move into a property they purchase shortly after arriving (Walsh, 2019). The category of property ownership is, however, extremely diverse and hides the heterogeneity of their experiences: some own multiple large furnished properties in expensive locations, perhaps complementary rural and urban locations, while others purchase a one-bedroom flat in sheltered housing in a provincial town (Walsh, 2018b). The property markets in each country can facilitate or obstruct return, so that people are not always able to relocate to places in which they used to live or they may need to 'downsize' (Hall et al., 2017). Those who need to rent may find themselves subject to much higher housing costs than they are able to sustain over time.

Lifestyle migrants can also experience difficulties with reintegration when trying to *access welfare benefits and social care*. In the UK context, the Habitual Residence test determines people's entitlement to benefits and those who have spent time overseas are considered no longer 'ordinarily resident' in the UK, removing their eligibility for healthcare, residential care and other welfare on their return (Hall and Hardill, 2016; Oliver, 2017; Rutter and Andrew, 2009). The test, demonstrating proof of residence and the intention to stay in the UK, can take a number of months to organise, even for those who are very frail or vulnerable, with subsequent further delays to benefit payments (Hall and Hardill, 2016, p.570; Hall et al., 2017). Return migrants may assume that they will receive immediate support (Hall et al., 2017), find information difficult to access or understand and experience personal hardship as a consequence (Rutter and Andrew, 2009). Furthermore, those who had settled in another country for much of their working lives and failed to maintain their National Insurance payments may have no access to a pension (Rutter and Andrew, 2009).

Many returning lifestyle migrants choose to return to places with which they are already familiar from their lives before emigration and have maintained intimate connections. For example, many women, especially, wish to return when their grandchildren are born, viewing digital technologies as insufficient to support their children and develop new bonds with grandchildren (Betty and Hall, 2015; Hall et al., 2017). Others return for personal reasons but to places where they have siblings, cousins or friends who may ease the experience of starting afresh. The possibility of renewing close social connections more quickly is very important, especially for those who are recently bereaved, divorced or otherwise single (Hall et al., 2017). In my own research, I interviewed Linda, who was returning from the Gulf after retirement. Linda chose to buy a house in Yorkshire, where she had grown up and where her siblings still lived, explaining: 'By this time I was on my own, I didn't have a partner, so I felt quite vulnerable, as you can imagine' (cited in Walsh, 2019, p.191). Those returning after the death of a spouse or when they or their spouse are ill may also experience a heightened sense of vulnerability (Giner-Montfort et al., 2015).

The difficulties of return can also be exaggerated by the length of residence (Cassarino, 2004, p.259, drawing on King, 2000). As Linda reflects, 'It took me an awful long time to adjust to life in England, because I'd been living abroad for more than thirty years. I felt like a complete, um, foreigner really, coming back to England: I didn't know what people were talking about, I didn't know the rules' (cited in Walsh, 2019, p.192). Those returning after retirement do not have their employment through which to reintegrate, so are relying on pre-existing and new social relations made through other channels. Linda's account also reveals the difficulties of building a new social network and making new friends, difficulties that returning lifestyle migrants often comment on in contrast to the more open sociality of 'living abroad' (Walsh, 2018b, 2019, p.193). In contrast, Patricia relocated with her husband to a middle-class village where there were many newcomers and older people among whom they felt welcome and where they could find their comfortable social place: 'They're all retired professionals ... They're all very worldy people I think' (cited in Walsh, 2019, p.193). The importance of continuing friendships established in other places upon return or finding other people who had been lifestyle migrants to socialise and build community with *even if they were not known previously while living away* was mentioned by all my interviewees and is indicative of the perception among lifestyle migrants of the transformative impact of their experiences and the possibilities of investing this (classed) social capital on return. I use my own research here in the absence of wider studies exploring the experiences of lifestyle returnees but there is clearly more to understand about the place of return in the mobilities of lifestyle migrants.

## CONCLUSION: A RESEARCH AGENDA ON RETURNING LIFESTYLE MIGRANTS

For many lifestyle migrants, especially the more affluent, return can be conceived as part of an ongoing comparative project of migration: since lifestyle migrants often do not intend their move to be permanent, they routinely evaluate when it is more advantageous for them to return (Hall et al., 2017; O'Reilly and Benson, 2009). Such migrants are more likely to have maintained considerable transnational connections with their country of origin and may still consider it one of multiple homes, easing their transition to returnees. However, it is clear from the discussion in this chapter that many lifestyle migrants experience less agency over their return than this would imply, leaving them feeling compelled to return, whether due to visa restrictions surrounding retirement (Walsh, 2018b), family transitions and change (such as divorce or becoming grandparents), unexpected ill-health or bereavement (Hall et al., 2017; Walsh, 2018b) or to financial precarity (Botterill, 2016a; Huete et al., 2013; Lafferty and Maher, 2020). The increased health and social care needs and bereavements associated with ageing is a widely recognised factor, although the impact of ageing on return will vary depending on the accessibility and affordability of care provision in both their country of residence and their country of citizenship (e.g. Giner-Montfort et al., 2015; Hall and Hardill, 2016; Oliver, 2008). Returns are also gendered: for example, male lifestyle migrants in Thailand often factor in the unpaid care of their Thai spouse in facilitating their continued residence (Botterill, 2016a). Decisions to return and experiences of reintegration are also classed, with lifestyle migrants demonstrating varied degrees of agency in navigating structural economic processes and events that impact on their finances (Botterill, 2016a; Huete et al., 2013; Lafferty and Maher, 2020; Walsh, 2018b, 2019). Marital status, the extent to which people engaged with transnational practices while living elsewhere and the social networks which they retain or make anew also inform the diversity of return.

While lifestyle migrants are people who voluntarily choose their relocation, the choice to return is a product not only of individual agency and resource constraints but also of structural factors and events. Shaped by life-course transitions, return may be either planned for or unanticipated as desires and circumstances change. Oliver (2008) notes that return can seem like a sudden decision to the communities which lifestyle returnees leave behind. When lifestyle migrants feel their choices are limited by financial factors, it can be deeply felt and shocking, since it goes against the taken-for-granted entitlements of privileged mobilities and the middle-class performance of their migration project. It thereby limits their preparedness to return and consequently may transform their experiences of it. It is therefore important that studies of return are designed to include the perspectives of those who have already returned and are able to reflect not only on the anticipated role of return in their lives but also, more directly, on what return has been like for them. Research with retirement migrants by Hall et al. (2017) in which five interviewees are returnees is exceptional in this regard but their voices must be heard alongside those of 25 interviewees still in Spain and who are planning a return (see also Walsh, 2018b, 2019). More studies are urgently needed, requiring innovative recruitment techniques and methodologies that document the longitudinal patterns and experiences of returnee lifestyle migrations. It is often helpful to elucidate a distinction between the different kinds of returnee (see Cassarino, 2004) and important to expand such typologies of return to include lifestyle migrants. However, the significance of lifestyle in return decisions, narratives and practices is not restricted to these relatively niche movements of those typically labelled as lifestyle migrants and may help us to understand return more widely.

## REFERENCES

Benson, M. (2010) 'The context and trajectory of lifestyle migration', *European Societies*, **12** (1), 45–64.
Benson, M. (2013) 'Postcoloniality and privilege in new lifestyle flows: the case of North Americans in Panama', *Mobilities*, **8** (3), 313–30.
Benson, M. (2014) 'Negotiating privilege in and through lifestyle migration' in M. Benson and N. Osbaldiston (eds), *Understanding Lifestyle Migration*, Basingstoke: Palgrave Macmillan, pp. 47–69.
Benson, M. (2015) 'Class, race, privilege: structuring the lifestyle migrant experience in Boquete, Panama', *Journal of Latin American Geography*, **14** (1), 19–37.
Benson, M. (2018) 'Constellations of privilege: the racialised and classed formations of Britons living in rural France' in P. Leonard and K. Walsh (eds), *British Migration: Privilege, Diversity, Vulnerability*, London: Routledge, pp. 23–39.
Benson, M. and O'Reilly, K. (2009a) 'Migration and the search for a better way of life: a critical exploration of lifestyle migration', *The Sociological Review*, **57** (4), 608–25.
Benson, M. and O'Reilly, K. (eds) (2009b) *Lifestyle Migration. Expectations, Aspirations and Experiences*, London and New York: Routledge.
Benson, M. and O'Reilly, K. (2015) 'From lifestyle migration to lifestyle in migration: categories, concepts and ways of thinking', *Migration Studies*, **4** (1), 20–37.
Benson, M. and O'Reilly, K. (2018) *Lifestyle Migration and Colonial Traces in Malaysia and Panama*, London: Palgrave Macmillan.
Benson, M. and Osbaldiston, N. (eds) (2015) *Understanding Lifestyle Migration: Theoretical Approaches to Migration and the Quest for a Better Way of Life*, Basingstoke: Palgrave Macmillan.
Betty, C. and Hall, K. (2015) 'The myth of no return? Why retired British migrants in Spain return to the UK' in K. Torkington, I. David and J. Sardinha (eds), *Practising the Good Life: Lifestyle Migration Practices*, Newcastle-upon-Tyne: Cambridge Scholars Publishing, pp. 123–36.
Bolognani, M. (2014) 'The emergence of lifestyle reasoning in return considerations among British Pakistanis', *International Migration*, **52** (6), 31–42.
Bond, A. (2012) 'Dumped in Dubai: the luxury high performance cars left abandoned by British expats who fear being jailed because of debts', *The Daily Mail*, 30 August.
Botterill, K. (2016a) 'Discordant lifestyle mobilities in East Asia: privilege and precarity of British retirement in Thailand', *Population, Space and Place*, **23** (5), e2011.
Botterill, K. (2016b) 'Diminished transnationalism? Growing older and practising home in Thailand' in K. Walsh and L. Nare (eds), *Transnational Migration and Home in Older Age*, Oxford: Routledge, pp. 99–111.
Cassarino, J. (2004) 'Theorising return migration: the conceptual approach to return migrants revisited', *International Journal on Multicultural Societies*, **6** (2), 253–79.
Croucher, S. (2015) 'The future of lifestyle migration: challenges and opportunities', *Journal of Latin American Geography*, **14** (1), 161–72.
Eimermann, M. (2017) 'Flying Dutchmen? Return reasoning among Dutch lifestyle migrants in rural Sweden', *Mobilities*, **12** (1), 116–35.

Escrivá, A. (2016) 'Transforming conceptions of care at home: ageing Moroccan and Peruvian migrants in Spain' in K. Walsh and L. Nare (eds), *Transnational Migration and Home in Older Age*, Oxford: Routledge, pp. 201–13.

Fechter, A.-M. and Walsh, K. (2010) 'Introduction: examining "expatriate" continuities: postcolonial approaches to mobile professionals', *Journal of Ethnic and Migration Studies*, 36 (8), 1197–210.

Finch, T., Andrew, H. and Latorre, M. (2010) *Global Brit: Making the Most of the British Diaspora*, London: Institute for Public Policy Research.

Fotheringham, A. (2012) 'Any expats who could move back to the UK already have, the rest of us are trapped', *The Independent*, 18 April.

Giner-Montfort, J., Hall, K. and Betty, C. (2015) 'Back to Brit: retired British migrants returning from Spain', *Journal of Ethnic and Migration Studies*, 42 (5), 797–815.

Hall, K. and Hardill, I. (2016) 'Retirement migration, the "other" story: caring for frail elderly British citizens in Spain', *Ageing and Society*, 36 (3), 562–85.

Hall, K., Betty, C. and Giner, J. (2017) 'To stay or to go? The motivations and experiences of older British returnees from Spain' in Z. Vathi and R. King (eds), *Return Migration and Psychosocial Wellbeing*, London: Routledge, pp. 221–39.

Hayes, M. (2014) '"We gained a lot over what we would have had": the geographic arbitrage of North American lifestyle migrants to Cuenca, Ecuador', *Journal of Ethnic and Migration Studies*, 40 (12), 1953–71.

Higgins, K. (2017) 'Lifestyle migration and settler colonialism: the imaginative geographies of British migrants to Aotearoa New Zealand', *Population, Space and Place*, 24 (3), e2112.

Higgins, K.W. (2019) 'National belonging post-referendum: Britons living in other EU member states respond to "Brexit"', *Area*, 51, 277–84.

Huete, R., Mantecón, A. and Estévez, J. (2013) 'Challenges in lifestyle migration research: reflections and findings about the Spanish crisis', *Mobilities*, 8 (3), 331–48.

King, R. (2000) 'Generalizations from the history of return migration' in B. Ghosh (ed.), *Return Migration: Journey of Hope or Despair?*, Geneva: United Nations and International Organization for Migration, pp. 7–55.

King, R., Warnes, A. and Williams, A. (2000) *Sunset Lives. British Retirement Migration to the Mediterranean*, Oxford: Berg.

Lafferty, M. and Maher, K. (2020) 'Transnational intimacy and economic precarity of Western men in Northeast Thailand', *Journal of Ethnic and Migration Studies*, 46 (8), 1629–46.

O'Reilly, K. (2000) *The British on the Costa Del Sol: Transnational Identities and Local Communities*, London and New York: Routledge.

O'Reilly, K. and Benson, M. (2009) 'Lifestyle migration: escaping to the good life' in M. Benson and K. O'Reilly (eds), *Lifestyle Migration: Expectations, Aspirations and Experiences*, Aldershot: Ashgate, pp. 1–14.

Oliver, C. (2004) 'Cultural influence in migrants' negotiation of death: the case of retired migrants in Spain', *Mortality*, 9 (3), 235–54.

Oliver, C. (2008) *Retirement Migration: Paradoxes of Ageing*, London: Routledge.

Oliver, C. (2016) 'Ageing, embodiment and emotions in orientations to home: British retirement migration in Spain' in K. Walsh and L. Nare (eds), *Transnational Migration and Home in Older Age*, Oxford: Routledge, pp. 188–98.

Oliver, C. (2017) 'Peer-led care practices and "community" formation in British retirement migration', *Nordic Journal of Migration Research*, 7 (3), 172–80.

Ono, M. (2012) 'Searching for care: international retirement migration and medical tourism in Malaysia among elderly Japanese', *Journal of Asia-Pacific Studies*, 18, 253–67.

Ono, M. (2015) 'Commoditization of lifestyle migration: Japanese retirees in Malaysia', *Mobilities*, 10 (4), 609–27.

Percival, J. (2013) *Return Migration in Later Life*, Bristol: Policy Press.

Rutter, J. and Andrew, H. (2009) *Home Sweet Home? The Nature and Scale of the Immigration of Older UK Nationals Back to the UK*, London: Age Concern and Help the Aged.

Stones, R., Botterill, K., Lee, M. and O'Reilly, K. (2019) 'One world is not enough: the structured phenomenology of lifestyle migrants in East Asia', *British Journal of Sociology*, 70 (1), 44–69.

Toyota, M. (2006) 'Ageing and transnational householding: Japanese retirees in Southeast Asia', *International Development Planning Review*, **28** (4), 515–31.

Toyota, M. and Xiang, B. (2012) 'The emerging transnational "retirement industry" in Southeast Asia', *International Journal of Sociology and Social Policy*, **32** (11), 708–19.

Walsh, K. (2018a) *Transnational Geographies of the Heart: Intimate Subjectivities in a Globalising City*, Chichester: Wiley.

Walsh, K. (2018b) 'Materialities and imaginaries of home: geographies of British returnees in later life', *Area*, **50** (4), 476–82.

Walsh, K. (2019) 'Returning at retirement: British migrants coming "home in later life"' in P. Leonard and K. Walsh (eds), *British Migration: Privilege, Diversity, Vulnerability*, Oxford: Routledge, pp. 182–98.

# 20. Revisiting second-generation 'return' migration to the ancestral homeland
*Nilay Kılınç*

## INTRODUCTION

This chapter provides an overview of the return migration phenomenon for the next-generation descendants of first-generation migrants – the 'second generation'. A dual conceptual problem immediately arises both with the term 'second-generation (im)migrant' – as these individuals were born in the host country where their parents had settled – and with the notion of 'return', as these second-generation protagonists are not going back to where they once were before. Hence, for the parents, return entails going back to the original homeland whereas, for the second generation, moving to the ancestral homeland is migration in its own terms. On the other hand, the move to the parental homeland, whilst not statistically recorded as a return migration to the country of birth, is nevertheless *felt* by many second-generation protagonists as a 'return' of sorts, perhaps at a deeper ontological level. The chapter will address these paradoxes and argue that the second generation's 'return' migration needs to be evaluated as a new migratory *chronotope* (i.e. time–space event). As the chapter will further demonstrate, for the second generation the ancestral homeland is a new context; despite their imagined ties, diasporic belonging and transnational links, they are in effect entering a new social field full of uncertainties and surprises.

Accordingly, return migration concepts and theories which were initially based on the return of the first generation (i.e. neoclassical economics, new economics of labour migration and structural approaches; Cassarino, 2004) have obvious shortcomings in capturing the second generation's diverse return imaginings and experiences. The second generation experiences more problematic and paradoxical relationships with the 'ancestral homeland' and more ambiguous notions of 'identity', 'home' and 'belonging', compared to their parents (Carling and Erdal, 2014; Reynolds, 2008). These paradoxes and re-conceptualisations are dealt with in more detail in the next part of the chapter. After a brief overview of the main global geographical settings for second-generation 'return' migration, the chapter then focuses on the transnational identities, practices and cross-border social networks of the second generation and how these may translate into 'return' migration decisions with certain imaginings and expectations of life in the ancestral homeland. Finally, possible post-return outcomes will be discussed.

## 'SECOND GENERATION' AND 'RETURN': PARADOXES AND RE-CONCEPTUALISATIONS

The construction of the phenomenon of the 'second generation' is closely linked to the distinct yet overlapping connotations of the term 'generation'. Following Kertzer (1983, p.126), the notion of generation can take on four distinct meanings: (a) *kinship descent* refers to the genealogical aspect (parents and their children); (b) *life stage* is about a certain phase of life such as childhood, adulthood, younger generation, older generation and so on (not necessarily with a genealogical relation); (c) a *cohort* generation refers to a group of persons born during a specific span of time – such as 'baby-boomers' or 'millennials'; and (d) *historical period* implies people sharing specific historical events during their life course, for instance the 'wartime generation'. When it comes to migrant generations, canonical definitions of the notion of 'second generation' have come from research based on migrant groups in the United States (Child, 1943; Portes and Zhou, 1993; Rumbaut, 2004). Portes and Zhou (1993, p.75) defined the second generation as 'native-born children with at least one foreign-born parent or children born abroad who came to the United States before the age of 12'. Rumbaut's (2004) widely referenced research on migrant families in the United States introduced a typology of distinct generational cohorts defined by age and life stage at migration which is summarised in Table 20.1. These distinctions based on age and life stage have proved useful for examining differences in educational and occupational attainment, language proficiency and other aspects of integration and acculturation processes in the host country.

Nevertheless, the definitions are either not detailed enough to cater for all circumstances,[1] or are too precise in a way that it is not applicable to other case studies. Hence, scholars often tailor these distinct definitions based on their unique migrant community, acknowledging that different meanings of the term 'generation' play out in shaping the phenomenon of 'their' second generation. Thomson and Crul's useful review article covering the American–European comparative context proposed that the second generation are 'children born in the host country of one or more immigrant parents or those who arrived before primary-school age' (2007, p.1038).

*Table 20.1    A classification of migratory generations*

| Generation | Description |
| --- | --- |
| 1st generation | Born in the country of origin; arrived in the host country age 18 or older |
| 1.25 generation | Born in the country of origin; arrived in the host country between the ages of 13 and 17 |
| 1.5 generation | Born in the country of origin; migrated to the destination country between 6 and 12 years of age |
| 1.75 generation | Born in the country of origin; arrived in the host country before the age of 6 |
| 2nd generation | Born in the country of destination with at least one migrant parent |
| 2.5 generation | Born in the country of destination with one native-born parent (who is second generation) and one foreign-born parent (who is first generation) |
| 3rd generation | Born in the country of destination to two parents who were also born in the destination country and with grandparents born in the country of origin |

*Source:* Author's own creation, based on definitions from Rumbaut (2004).

However, modifications have been ever-present in empirical research. For instance, King and Kılınç (2013) argued, for the Turkish-German second generation, that the historical aspect had to be taken into account, as Turkish guestworkers migrated to Germany in large numbers in the 1960s, as did non-labour migrants who moved in smaller numbers to Germany in different time periods. These authors narrowed their conceptualisation of the Turkish-German second generation within the labour migration flows of 1961–73 to Germany. Thus, definitions of the notion can be narrowed or stretched depending on the country context. In fact, 'second generation' is not a universally utilised term: Germany uses 'persons with a migration background' (Elrick and Farah Schwartzman, 2015) and the UK and Australia refer to 'ethnic heritage' or 'migrant heritage' (Aveling and Gillespie, 2008). Elsewhere, by contrast, the term is used to denote a strong second-generation identity, for example, 'Swiss-Italian *secondos*' (Wessendorf, 2007).

Hence, evaluating return migration in the case of the second generation also requires an examination of the historical development and status of a particular diaspora group or transnational community in a host society. The classical understanding of diaspora referred to a 'scattering' followed by traumatic exile from a historical homeland, as in the Jewish and Armenian diasporas. Victims of this kind of forced dispersal cherish memories about their original homeland, combined with feelings of loss and victimisation and a desire for return to the historical homeland (Safran, 1991). The conscious maintaining of collective memory was a primary component of classical diasporas, sustained by reference to an 'ethnic myth', a shared historical experience and ties to a geographic place whilst collectively retaining 'boundary-maintenance' vis-à-vis the host society (Vertovec, 1997). However, such understanding of diasporas based on sameness through a focus on common origins has changed due to the stretching of the term 'diaspora' to include immigrant, refugee, guestworker, expatriate and exile communities (Tölölyan, 1996); in Brubaker's (2005) critique, the diasporisation or 'scattering' of the very meaning of diaspora.

The 'transnational turn' and associated shifts in theories and methodologies of migration (Glick Schiller et al., 1992) led scholars to examine diaspora groups in relation to cultural hybridisation as well as heterogeneous and multiple ties and belongings (Blunt, 2007). In this context, the second generation's 'return' migration slips into the 'interstices between [the] literatures on second-generation, return migration, transnationalism and diaspora' (King and Christou, 2010, pp.168–70). These authors highlighted the 'reflective ambiguity' of second-generation 'return', using it as a lens to question the boundaries of certain dichotomies that the second generation's lives juxtapose, such as 'here' and 'there', 'indigenousness' and 'foreignness' and 'homeland' and 'hostland'. In her pioneering monograph on second-generation Greek-Americans' 'return' migration, Christou (2006, p.60) described return migration, with these dichotomies and nuances in mind, as 'the process of migrants' return to the country/place of origin, parental/ancestral extraction or to the "symbolic homeland"'. This detailed yet broad description hinted that 'returning to homeland' does not always entail a straightforward 'homecoming' for the second generation.

Indeed, the second generation's 'return' migration appears to be an ontological paradox, if not a complete anomaly. To start with, in the case of the second generation's 'return' migration, scholars have commonly presented the term 'return' in quotes, as this is not a regular form of return migration but, in fact, can be taken as a 'new' migration in its own terms. The question thus becomes: *How can we call it 'return' when individuals settle in a country that they were not even born and raised in?* Some therefore suggest that 'return' is actually another migration and therefore that the 're' prefix needs to be removed from terms like 'return' and 'readjust' (Hammond, 1999). This adjustment is related to evaluating the concept of return within theories of cyclical migration and transnationalism in which return emerges as a migratory journey in its own right – rather than simply the reversal or end of another one (Ley and Kobayashi, 2005).

Overall, recent empirical findings reflect a paradigm change regarding the second generation's distinct experiences; they are perceived as a progressive generation with dual lives and transnational attachments; therefore they represent a 'post-immigrant generation' (Rumbaut, 2002). Moreover, their networks, activities and patterns of life encompass both their place of residence (the so-called 'hostland' where they were born and raised) and the ancestral homeland (their parents' country of origin, of which they have limited lived experience). Hence, they are believed to acquire a 'dual frame of reference' (Vertovec, 2004, p.974). This can be seen as a positive endowment but some studies also focus on their state of 'in-betweenness' which can cause identity struggles (Christou, 2006; Phillips and Potter, 2006; Stroink and Lalonde, 2009).

Other empirical findings suggest that such multiple tensions and 'in-betweenness' lead the second generation to become reflexive actors who respond to their 'multi-sited embeddedness' (Horst, 2018) by crafting their own 'positioned belongings' through negotiating 'the self' vis-à-vis the two socio-cultural and geographical components of their hyphenated identities (e.g. King and Kılınç, 2014 on second-generation Turkish-Germans). These points in relation to the second generation's 'return' migration trajectories, expectations, post-return experiences and re-considerations of identity and belonging will be further evaluated in the upcoming sections.

## GEOGRAPHIES OF THE SECOND GENERATION'S 'RETURN'

In terms of timeframe and geographical scope, contemporary return migration emerged as a post-World War II phenomenon, when individuals from the global South and other relatively poor and peripheral countries, such as those in Southern Europe, migrated to the economically and socially prosperous global North as 'labour migrants' and became the 'first generation' of their respective migrant community. In the case of the second generation's 'return', empirical evidence comes from a variety of geographical settings; importantly from the North American and European context (e.g. Christou, 2006 on Greek-Americans' 'return'; Sardinha, 2011 on Portuguese-Canadians' 'return'). The phenomenon has also gained significant attention in the American-Asian context (e.g. Kim, 2010 on Korean-Americans; Tsuda, 2003 on Japanese-Brazilian '*Nikkeijin*') and there has also been an important clutch of studies on second-generation 'return' to the Caribbean (Duval, 2004; Potter, 2005; Potter and Phillips, 2006; Reynolds, 2008).

In the intra-European context, there is now an extensive literature – for instance Christou and King (2010) on Greek-Germans' 'return', King and Kılınç (2013) on Turkish-Germans' 'return', Wessendorf (2007) on Italian-Swiss '*secondos*' and Cook-Martín and Viladrich (2009) on 'return' to Spain. Furthermore, the post-colonial optic with regards to the second generation's 'return' is also rapidly gaining attention: for instance, Ali and Holden (2006) and Bolognani (2014) on Pakistan and Potter and Phillips (2006) on Barbados. Empirical research also covers the Middle East region – such as that by Abbasi-Shavazi et al. (2008) on 'return' to Afghanistan – as well as 'return' in the post-Soviet era, for example Kulu (2002) on 'ethnic return' to Estonia.

It is impossible to cover the whole geographical scope of the second generation's 'return migration' in this chapter, as empirical research has expanded intensely in the last decade. The above citations are a sample of the most significant and diversified studies.

## 'RETURN' PREPAREDNESS AND REASONS

There is no one type of return and, for return migrants, individual factors are central to social and economic reintegration in the ancestral homeland. Simply put, two decisive questions help to classify the type of returnee (Cassarino, 2004): Is the individual willing to return? (i.e. 'willingness to return'); Is the individual capable, ready, well-equipped, and well-informed to return? (i.e. 'readiness to return'). In this chapter I mainly focus on voluntary return migration; these second-generation diaspora members have an explicit intention to return even though some of them may lack social networks and skills such as knowledge of the culture and language. However, it has to be noted that there is an expanding literature on involuntary return migrants; individuals who are subjected to deportation programmes (on the basis of criminal offences or having no legal residence status) and voluntary assisted-return (VAR) programmes whereby host countries may offer a 'return premium' to encourage certain migrant groups to return to their home countries.

These latter studies on 'forced' return illustrate multiple situations: (1) *deportation* – for instance, the US-Mexican context (Gratton and Merchant, 2013) or the German-Turkish context (Kılınç, 2019); (ii) *asylum and forced return* to conflict and post-conflict areas – for instance, Saito (2007) on second-generation 'return' to Afghanistan; and (iii) the *semi-forced (or semi-voluntary) return* foisted upon children by their families' return, in which the children may have no say or only a limited influence on the return decision – see, for instance, Lee (2016) on the Tongan second generation (see Grosa, Chapter 17). Research points out that involuntary return can be a serious obstacle for personal development and reintegration as these individuals frequently face marginalisation and psychological problems (Ghanem, 2003; Vathi and King, 2017).

Overall, since migration gained complexity with the flows of asylum-seekers, refugees, undocumented migrants, highly skilled migrants, family reunifications and the return migration of 'guestworkers', migrants started to be understood as being a part of a continuum of human mobilities where the return migration is not an end but an ongoing journey embedded in complex connections and practices across borders (Cassarino, 2004; Dustmann and Weiss, 2007; Levitt, 2009). Scholars placed emphasis on 'transnational social fields' (Levitt and Glick Schiller, 2004) wherein return migration processes and experiences are evaluated next to identity formations and negotiations, simultaneous constructions of home and belonging, family ties and border-crossing; yet all of these are also seen as localised social relations (Ahmed et al., 2003; Morley, 2000; Nowicka, 2007). Transnational approaches in understanding return migration decision-making and post-return lives have been increasingly reflected in the case of the second generation.

Taking a step back, the second generation's 'return' migration calls attention to another set of theoretical questions: *How come the second generation desire to settle in a country that their parents once left for a more economically and socially prosperous life elsewhere? What are the motivations and expectations that lead the second generation to undertake this counter-intuitive form of migration in which the push–pull factors that drove the first generation are violated?* This duo of questions indicates, in the case of the second generation, that 'return' is a complex and multidimensional phenomenon which cannot be limited to a macro-level framework of analysis, wherein return decisions are tied to economic opportunity structures. Individual values, lifestyle choices and expectations on a micro level and kinship, social ties and networks on a meso level also affect decision-making processes.

A large body of research findings on the second generation's 'return' is premised on ideas of individual choice, professional and educational strategies, marriage, cosmopolitan openness to the world or the search for a lifestyle and adventure. It should be noted, however, that these different aspects can overlap and also be entangled with structural reasons such as, first, economic transitions and, second, home/host governments' preferential immigration and nationality policies. Between the first generation's original emigration and the second generation's 'return', several decades may have passed and the country of origin may have evolved from a low to a higher level of development, perhaps through the expansion of tourism and a buoyant service sector. Drawing on some of the literature cited in the previous section, the Caribbean (notably Barbados and Trinidad) and Southern Europe (Portugal, Greece and Turkey) are cases where this economic transition occurred between the early postwar decades of first-generation departure and second-generation 'return' in much more recent years. Second, where homeland governments have a strong ethno-nationalist identity, policies may be put in place to preferentially encourage 'the diaspora' to return. Greece and Japan are two cases which have been studied intensively, respectively by Christou and King (2014) and by Tsuda (2003).

On the whole, the literature recognises that there is a clear difference between the first generation's more economically driven motivation to migrate to a different country and then, perhaps, return to their homeland upon retirement and the second generation's more lifestyle and existential motivations (King, 2002; Teerling, 2011). To have a better quality of life in terms of peace and quiet, sense of security, climate and cuisine, as well as the desire to have freedom and autonomy, are strong themes in the contemporary second-generation 'return' literature. For example, Phillips and Potter (2009) write about the search for a 'quality of life' by second-generation Bajan-British 'returnees' from Britain to Barbados. As other research shows, some of these lifestyle factors flourish when those of the second generation travel to the ancestral homeland as adults and encounter a realisation that the culture and traditions of the homeland are older, richer and somehow superior to those of the host country. These elements emerge strongly, for instance, in Bhimji's (2008) research on second-generation British-Muslim women travelling to South Asia and Ní Laoire's (2007) work on return to rural Ireland.

Nevertheless, there are no specific theories or typologies for the second generation's 'return' migration and empirical studies often adopt well-known templates and typologies which were constructed based on the first generation's return migration experiences (see Cassarino, 2004; Cerase, 1974; Gmelch, 1980; King, 1986). Hence, when the second generation's 'return' is concerned, push–pull theories remain inadequate to understand different factors affecting the second generation's 'return' decisions. In addition, pre-supposing that they would acquire 'ideal' or 'perfect' information about life in the ancestral homeland prior to 'return' appears as an oversimplification. Even when they have visited the parental homeland and hence have acquired some familiarity with it, such visits often yield a distorted picture, since they usually coincide with holidays when everybody is hospitable and in a good mood and the weather is also good. Settling in the homeland long-term and all-year-round often turns out to be a different story – as will be seen in the next section of the chapter.

Second-generation 'returnees' may be acting independently in deciding to move to the ancestral home country but, in many cases, the imprint of the first generation's homeland orientation may be highly influential for the second generation, helping to frame the 'return' decision as 'ancestral', 'ethnic' or 'roots' migration (see Jain, 2013; King and Christou, 2008;

Tsuda, 2009; Wessendorf, 2007). However, when those of the second generation acquire some experience of living in the ancestral homeland, they may develop their own way of perceiving and processing 'homing' desires and belonging. In some cases, this may even result in returning back to their 'home' country, which was the destination country for their parents (White, 2014).[2] Hence, the second generation goes through a constant reassessment of their belonging and expectations throughout the 'return' journey and it is difficult to estimate how 'prepared' they are when they decide to settle in their ancestral homelands (Asiedu, 2005; Erdal and Oeppen, 2013; Lulle, 2014).

Most studies indicate that the second generation is relatively more well-off and better-educated (compared to the first generation) and its members are thus able to push their imagination to think of mobility and settlement in richer ways. Frequent transnational contacts also assist in smoothing the 'return' decision – and the actual return itself. For instance, within the growing literature on second-generation 'return' to the Caribbean, repetitive visits to the ancestral homeland and transnational practices and links play an important role in driving 'return' decisions (Duval, 2004; Thomas-Hope, 1999). Nevertheless, this does not mean that all second-generation groups act as 'transnational agents of change' (Conway and Potter, 2007); 'return' experiences may lead to disillusionment, feelings of being 'stuck' and constant negotiations of identity – points which are further evaluated in the next section.

## AFTER 'RETURN': OUTCOMES AND RE-INTEGRATION PROCESSES

Empirical research points to two common outcomes of the second generation's condition of having a sense of attachment to an idealised ancestral homeland but lacking local connection. First, the second generation's construction of the mythical homeland is challenged once they get a lived experience of it upon 'return' (Christou, 2006; King and Christou, 2010; Markowitz and Stefansson, 2004; Tsuda, 2003; Wessendorf, 2007). Second, this disillusionment, together with the practical hardships of fitting into the society and structural system, mean that the second generation's idealisation for place is reversed and this time they develop a feeling of longing for the country they left, interpreted as an intensification of 'reverse transnationalism' (King and Christou, 2014). Therefore, the second generation's 'return' creates challenges over the labelling of the directionality of migration, and further demands innovative perspectives on the nature of transnationalism and contestation of the notions of 'home', 'identity' and 'belonging' (Bolognani, 2007).

King and Christou (2008, 2014) introduced the notion of 'counter-diasporic migration' to specifically examine the Greek-American and Greek-German second generation's relocation to Greece. Their findings illustrate that searching for 'home' and a sense of belonging were emotional drivers for the 'return' decision:

> The second generation's 'return' is ... an existential journey to the source of the self, as a return to the 'cradle' of a cathartic mission to reclaim its sacred sites and to re-enter its mythic space and time. (King and Christou, 2008, p.17)

However, the authors demonstrate that the second generation does not always experience a welcoming embrace at 'home'; instead, experiences of return often invoke feelings of disillusionment and rupture. This finding is also corroborated in King and Kılınç's (2013) research on Turkish-German 'returnees', many of whom experience difficulties in adapting to Turkey due to the loss of friends and the change of environment, as well as being stigmatised against by local Turks for 'having lost their Turkishness' and being too 'German-like'.

Wessendorf's (2007) work on second-generation Italians' 'return' from Switzerland to Southern Italy utilised the concept of 'roots migration'. Her findings illustrate that roots migration is related to the second generation's transnational practices whilst growing up and the nostalgic imagination fostered about their parental homeland. However, once they return and face the realities of life in the Italian South, returnees struggle to integrate themselves into a society and culture that they had always perceived as their own. In Tsuda's (2009) edited volume, which focuses on several 'ethnic return' groups in Europe and East Asia, different cases reflect similarities with Wessendorf's work: homecomings often prove to be ambivalent or negative experiences. The returnees face marginalisation as cultural foreigners and are relegated to low-status jobs; in turn, they redefine the meanings of 'home' and 'homeland' – an accentuated reconstruction process especially for those who had aspired to 'rediscover their ancestral roots' (e.g. Cook-Martín and Viladrich, 2009 on 'return' to Spain; Song, 2009 on Korean-Chinese 'return').

These examples show that living between the blurred lines of 'homeland' and 'hostland' appears to be a characteristic of the second generation; hence their lives evolve within a 'syncretic notion of culture' (Kaya, 2007, p.483) which also indicates the problematic nature of 'return' and the complexity of return migration trajectories. Even when second-generation 'returnees' are not perceived as 'immigrants' in their ancestral homelands, they still experience stigmatisation by their co-nationals, based on how they are dressed, how they speak their 'native' tongue (or in some cases not at all) and how they lead their lives in terms of lifestyle, mentality, work habits and so on (King and Christou, 2010; Potter and Phillips, 2006; Tsuda, 2003).

Other examples signal that this gap between the second generation's 'return' imaginings and the actual realities of 'return' may lead to considerations of further emigration (Ley and Kobayashi, 2005; Lidgard and Gilson, 2002; Tsuda, 2001). For instance, second-generation Turkish-German 'returnees' who relocated to their parental villages and home towns remobilised themselves to put their quest of having a better life into action and further resettled in Antalya, a Mediterranean tourism hub in Turkey which is associated with lifestyle migration (Kılınç and King, 2017).

Levitt's (2009) seminal paper on 'roots and routes', which was an attempt to 'understand the lives of the second generation', argued that the second generation are raised in a transnational social field. Hence the importance of understanding the mobility trajectories of the second generation through family structures, gender relations, religious identity, class differences and kin-based strategies. Levitt further argued that the second generation also have access to ideas, social networks and social capital in their ancestral homelands (their 'roots') that can strongly influence their life trajectories or 'routes'. With vignettes drawn from interviews with second-generation Indian-, Pakistani-, Brazilian- and Irish-Americans, Levitt's study evaluated 'return' in terms of the future possibilities and intensification of transnational identities and links. Her findings resonate in other studies, whether in relation to returnees constructing their own 'third' spaces distinct from both the 'hostland' and the 'homeland' (Teerling, 2011) or through utilising their 'transcultural capital' (Meinhof and Triandafyllidou, 2006) to improve their social and economic lives upon 'return' (Kılınç and King, 2019).

As a part of this 'routes to roots' approach which focuses on innovative and in-flux ways of being and dwelling, Teerling's work on British-born Cypriot 'return' migrants in Cyprus is particularly instructive. She finds that the British-Cypriot returnees not only 'pointed out the disadvantages of feeling like "a stranger" [but] they emphasised some of the benefits of being "a foreigner", whilst at the same time choosing which parts of their Cypriot heritage to enjoy' (Teerling, 2011, p.1080). She argues for evaluating the notions of 'home' and 'belonging' beyond the conventional dualistic ethnic, national and primordial cultural boundaries. Moving beyond such binary oppositions, she suggests that the second generation create 'third-cultural spaces of belonging' through shared experiences, knowledge, interests and values. King and Kılınç (2014) push this line of thinking one stage further and argue that second-generation Turkish-German returnees construct a fourth socio-cultural space that is distinct from German society, from Turkish society and from the enclaved Turkish immigrant community in Germany, a space wherein they strategically switch and negotiate between their multiple identities depending on their social contexts.

## REVISITING THE SECOND GENERATION'S 'RETURN'

With these recent studies providing empirical findings from different geographical contexts, the second generation's 'return' migration is reconfigured as an ongoing journey, in which the idea of 'home' becomes blurry and contested and the returnees' identities, as well as their sense of belonging, are re-shaped. Thereby, understandings of 'return-place as home(land)' and 'return as homecoming' are challenged, along with the taken-for-granted assumption that returnees' expectations of being reinserted into a familiar and secure home are assured upon return (Blunt, 2005; Christou, 2006; King and Kılınç, 2014; Wessendorf, 2007).

There is a growing interest, through qualitative research in particular, in further exploring the specific experience of return migration vis-à-vis the second generation's reconstruction of identities and belonging. 'Return' experiences often lead to contesting self-definitions for second-generation 'returnees', signalling that diasporic 'homeland orientation' and emotional ties fostered by family narratives and childhood nostalgia of holidays are insufficient to maintain the romanticised idea of 'homeland' once they confront the lived experiences of 'return' places (Kılınç and King, 2018; King et al., 2011; Reynolds, 2010). Such anxieties and ambivalences over the 'return journey' are often associated with the duality of 'home': on the one hand, the second generation long for a discretely defined 'home', discursively constructed and imagined in their 'diaspora space'; on the other, they translocally live and experience places as multiple and uprooted (Sardinha, 2011; Teerling, 2011).

Scholars increasingly highlight the importance of locality as the place where migrants touch ground (Ley, 2004), hence arguing that 'transnational social fields' (Levitt and Glick Schiller, 2004) should be understood in relation to spatial questions in Migration Studies – with a focus on translocalism (Brickell and Datta, 2011; Dahinden, 2009). This reconfiguration comes from the idea that return migration inevitably involves specific locales, because individuals not only return to a country of origin but, in reality, experience distinct spatial settings such as cities, villages and coastal towns (Hatfield, 2011; Ní Laoire, 2007). Thus, an alternative way would be to evaluate the second generation's multiple identities and belongingness within the context of 'translocal social fields' – a space wherein a proliferation of identities subverts the knowledge–power nexus that sustains binary representations, making new kinds of 'becomings' possible (Ralph and Staeheli, 2011).

Hence, researchers stress that, although 'the national' aspect is significant, place/locale also needs to be one of the components of the analytical framework (Guarnizo and Smith, 1998; Hannerz, 1996). For instance, King and Kılınç's (2013) research on second-generation Turkish-German 'return migrants' illustrates that some informants have a strong 'Istanbul identity' and they cannot think of living elsewhere in Turkey, even though they are also aware of the negative aspects of big-city life such as choking traffic, high living expenses and a dense population. In their more recent work on Turkish-German 'returnees' in the Mediterranean coastal city of Antalya, the same authors showed the importance of locality and its characteristics for the second generation – the availability of jobs in tourism and the constant 'holiday-like' environment, as well as a slower and cheaper way of life compared to big cities like Istanbul, were decisive factors of settlement (Kılınç and King, 2017).

As with all studies of social processes – including migration – and therefore also the chronotope of second-generation 'return', intersectionality can be highlighted. Within Migration Studies, Anthias (2012) has pioneered this approach, with particular reference to the gender aspect. In the specific field of second-generation 'return', evidence suggests that women and men show different levels of agency; whilst women are subject to higher expectations by their families regarding following the family plans, adaptability and integrating into the social fields of their ancestral homeland, men can get out of these familial and cultural structures more easily (King and Kılınç, 2016; Pessar and Mahler, 2003). Christou and King's (2011) research on second-generation Greek-Americans' and Greek-Germans' 'return' to Greece found that diasporic imaginaries and mobilities, including rootedness and rootlessness, are experienced differently by women and men. Their research illustrates two important findings: first, that return as a 'searching for self' is more widespread amongst men and, second, that women more commonly narrate 'return' as an escape from an oppressive and patriarchal family environment.

There are other examples in migration research which point out that often men present their migratory decisions as autonomous, whilst women view migration as a collective endeavour and represent the experience within the family context (Reynolds, 2008; Vlase, 2013). However, gender relations are always mediated by other socially constructed categories such as class, age, 'race' and ethnicity (Phillips and Potter, 2006). Whilst research shows that it is not only gender but also other forms of capital (mainly economic and social) which act as enablers or obstacles for second-generation 'returnees', gender still plays a vital role in the way it determines a person's active or passive agency (Christou, 2006; Christou and King, 2011; Jain, 2013; King and Kılınç, 2016; Reynolds, 2008).

## CONCLUSION

The second generation's 'return' is a specific migration chronotope which throws up new definitional and conceptual challenges. Consider, for example, the dichotomous statements 'origin is destination', 'return is first-time immigration' and 'the co-ethnic is the foreigner'. Second-generation return demonstrates the blurring that exists over these dualities and even challenges how they should be framed (King and Christou, 2010, p.181). Thus, analysing the second generation's more reflexive paths through the 'return' project constitutes a conceptual puzzle in which macro and structuralist theories are inadequate to grasp individuals' agencies in searching, finding or re-inventing themselves and a sense of 'home'.

Nevertheless, there is no single theoretical model that can grasp all the underlying motivations, aspirations and circumstances of individuals regarding return migration. Hence a focus on a life-course analysis in relation to specific return localities and the intersectionality of identities is necessary. In this way, we can also bring in a more nuanced understanding to the chapter's key theoretical and semantic question of whether the second generation's settlement in the ancestral homeland is *return* or *migration in its own terms*. A macro-level analysis from the point of view of nation states may suggest that those of the second generation who were born in the 'home' country and taken abroad as young children technically return to their country of birth. However, as the empirical examples in this chapter have shown, the second generation who were born in the 'host country' may still 'feel' that they are engaging in some kind of ontological return, even though their settlement in the ancestral homeland is not statistically considered as return.

As with all forms of migration, it is not sufficient to observe and analyse just the movement itself; its effects on the second generation's lives and trajectories must also be considered. As King argues (2012, p.136), 'migrants are not constantly on the move, but what defines them as migrants is that they are ... looking for a place to stop and settle down'. This 'stability within movement' (Halfacree, 2012) is the uniqueness of migration compared to other human mobilities. Hence, this chapter has also argued that the second generation's return forms 'grounded attachments, geographies of belonging, and practices of citizenship' (Blunt, 2007, p.687).

Moreover, the second generation's 'return' is increasingly seen as driven by individualistic and self-oriented aspirations and trajectories. Lifestyle choices, the desire for freedom and searching for self-development all transform the act of migration into an existential 'projection of an individual's identificatory experience beyond what are perceived as the restricting confines of his or her own country' (King, 2002, p.95). In other words, the second generation's 'return migration' can be also explored as an active and agency-oriented endeavour – a 'reflexive project of the self' (Giddens, 1991).

The second generation's transnational-translocal ties and practices provide a space for reflexivity, in which the 'given' and 'static' understandings of 'who they are' and 'where they belong' can be transcended. Nevertheless, certain cases show that their understanding of the plural dimensions and fluidity of norms does not prevent the second generation from longing for a coherent sense of self and acceptance from their societies. However, such longing for living in a *dolce domum* is not always a conscious aspiration or evident motivation for return; it habitually manifests itself because of interactions with the ancestral homeland, experiencing warmth and acceptance in their ancestral community. Undoubtedly, the idea of the second generation experiencing the ancestral homeland as a 'haven' is an oversimplification; it is, rather, an imagined community wherein their membership is ambivalent. Hence upon 'return' they keep negotiating their identities in relation to their daily practices and interactions. In that sense, their belonging and homing desires represent a dynamic process, 'involving acts of imagining, creating, unmaking, changing, losing and moving "homes"' (Al-Ali and Koser, 2002, p.6).

The second generation's hybrid condition and capacity for reflexivity portends two important principles for the study of migration and mobility in the current era. First, this chronotope challenges and subverts fixed or 'container' categories of nation, space, citizenship, ethnic identity, homeland and belonging. Second, for the second generation (and arguably for all migrants), 'return' migration is a journey where the goal is not to arrive at a destination called 'home' or at an 'identity' which is teleologically finally 'achieved' but, rather, a fluid and open-ended project for developing one's personal life – including both material and existential aspects – for the better, at least for a while.

## NOTES

1. For instance, the definition of the second generation to include 'at least one migrant parent' produces two potentially very different socialisation contexts, depending on whether both parents are foreign-born or only one.
2. Here we see the challenging nature of using (perhaps unavoidably) terms such as 'return' and 'home country'. In the case quoted here, the 'return' is a kind of 'return from the return' or a 're-return' and the 'home country' is the country of their birth and early socialisation, not their ancestral home country.

## REFERENCES

Abbasi-Shavazi, M.J., Glazebrook, D., Jamshidiha, G., Mahmoudian, H. and Sadeghi, R. (2008) *Second-Generation Afghans in Iran: Integration, Identity and Return*, Kabul: Afghanistan Research and Evaluation Unit.

Ahmed, S., Castañeda, C., Fortier, A.M. and Sheller, M. (eds) (2003) *Uprootings/Regroundings: Questions of Home and Migration*, Oxford: Berg.

Al-Ali, N. and Koser, K. (2002) 'Transnationalism, international migration and home' in N. Al-Ali and K. Koser (eds), *New Approaches to Migration? Transnational Communities and the Transformation of Home*, London: Routledge, pp. 1–14.

Ali, N. and Holden, A. (2006) 'Post-colonial Pakistani mobilities: the embodiment of the "myth of return" in tourism', *Mobilities*, **1** (2), 217–42.

Anthias, F. (2012) 'Transnational mobilities, migration research and intersectionality', *Nordic Journal of Migration Research*, **2** (2), 102–10.

Asiedu, A. (2005) 'Some benefits of migrants' return visits to Ghana', *Population, Space and Place*, **11** (1), 1–11.

Aveling, E.L. and Gillespie, A. (2008) 'Negotiating multiplicity: adaptive asymmetries within second-generation Turks' "society of mind"', *Journal of Constructivist Psychology*, **21** (3), 200–22.

Bhimji, F. (2008) 'Cosmopolitan belonging and diaspora: second-generation British Muslim women travelling to South Asia', *Citizenship Studies*, **12** (4), 413–27.

Blunt, A. (2005) 'Cultural geographies of home', *Progress in Human Geography*, **29** (4), 505–15.

Blunt, A. (2007) 'Cultural geographies of migration: mobility, transnationality and diaspora', *Progress in Human Geography*, **31** (5), 684–94.

Bolognani, M. (2007) 'The myth of return: dismissal, survival or revival? A Bradford example of transnationalism as a political instrument', *Journal of Ethnic and Migration Studies*, **33** (1), 59–76.

Bolognani, M. (2014) 'The emergence of lifestyle reasoning in return considerations among British Pakistanis', *International Migration*, **52** (6), 31–42.

Brickell, K. and Datta, A. (2011) 'Introduction: translocal geographies' in K. Brickell and A. Datta (eds), *Translocal Geographies: Space, Place, Connection*, Farnham: Ashgate, pp. 3–23.

Brubaker, R. (2005) 'The "diaspora" diaspora', *Ethnic and Racial Studies*, **28** (1), 1–19.

Carling, J. and Erdal, M.B. (2014) 'Return migration and transnationalism: how are the two connected?', *International Migration*, **52** (6), 2–12.

Cassarino, J.P. (2004) 'Theorising return migration: the conceptual approach to return migrants revisited', *International Journal on Multicultural Societies*, **6** (2), 253–79.

Cerase, F.P. (1974) 'Expectations and reality: a case study of return migration from the United States to Southern Italy', *International Migration Review*, **8** (2), 245–62.

Child, I.L. (1943) *Italian or American? The Second Generation in Conflict*, New Haven CT: Yale University Press.
Christou, A. (2006) *Narratives of Place, Culture and Identity: Second-Generation Greek-Americans Return 'Home'*, Amsterdam: Amsterdam University Press.
Christou, A. and King, R. (2010) 'Imagining "home": diasporic landscapes of the Greek-German second generation', *Geoforum*, 41 (4), 638–46.
Christou, A. and King, R. (2011) 'Gendering counter-diasporic migration: second-generation Greek-Americans and Greek-Germans narrate their "homecoming" to Greece', *Journal of Mediterranean Studies*, 20 (2), 283–314.
Christou, A. and King, R. (2014) *Counter-Diaspora: The Greek Second Generation Returns 'Home'*, Cambridge MA: Harvard University Press.
Conway, D. and Potter, R.B. (2007) 'Caribbean transnational return migrants as agents of change', *Geography Compass*, 1 (1), 25–45.
Cook-Martín, D. and Viladrich, A. (2009) 'Imagined homecomings: the problem with similarity among ethnic return migrants in Spain' in T. Tsuda (ed.), *Diasporic Homecomings: Ethnic Return Migration in Comparative Perspective*, Palo Alto CA: Stanford University Press, pp. 133–58.
Dahinden, J. (2009) 'Are we all transnationals now? Network transnationalism and transnational subjectivity: the differing impacts of globalization on the inhabitants of a small Swiss city', *Ethnic and Racial Studies*, 32 (8), 1365–86.
Dustmann, C. and Weiss, Y. (2007) 'Return migration: theory and empirical evidence from the UK', *British Journal of Industrial Relations*, 45 (2), 236–56.
Duval, D.T. (2004) 'Linking return visits and return migration among Commonwealth Eastern Caribbean migrants in Toronto', *Global Networks*, 4 (1), 51–67.
Elrick, J. and Farah Schwartzman, L. (2015) 'From statistical category to social category: organized politics and official categorizations of "persons with a migration background" in Germany', *Ethnic and Racial Studies*, 38 (9), 1539–56.
Erdal, M.B. and Oeppen, C. (2013) 'Migrant balancing acts: understanding the interactions between integration and transnationalism', *Journal of Ethnic and Migration Studies*, 39 (6), 867–84.
Ghanem, T. (2003) *When Forced Migrants Return "Home": The Psychosocial Difficulties Returnees Encounter in the Reintegration Process*, Oxford: Refugee Studies Centre, RSC Working Paper No. 16.
Giddens, A. (1991) *Modernity and Self-Identity: Self and Society in the Late Modern Age*, Stanford: Stanford University Press.
Glick Schiller, N., Basch, L. and Blanc-Szanton, C. (1992) 'Transnationalism: a new analytic framework for understanding migration', *Annals of the New York Academy of Sciences*, 645, 1–24.
Gmelch, G. (1980) 'Return migration', *Annual Review of Anthropology*, 9, 135–59.
Gratton, B. and Merchant, E. (2013) 'Immigration, repatriation, and deportation: the Mexican-origin population in the United States, 1920–1950', *International Migration Review*, 47 (4), 944–75.
Guarnizo, L.E. and Smith, M.P. (1998) 'The locations of transnationalism' in L.E. Guarnizo and M.P. Smith (eds), *Transnationalism from Below: Comparative Urban and Community Research*, New Brunswick NJ: Transaction Publishers, 3–34.
Halfacree, K. (2012) 'Heterolocal identities? Counter-urbanisation, second homes, and rural consumption in the era of mobilities', *Population, Space and Place*, 18 (2), 209–24.
Hammond, L. (1999) 'Examining the discourse of repatriation: towards a more proactive theory of return migration' in R. Black and K. Koser (eds), *The End of the Refugee Cycle? Refugee Repatriation and Reconstruction*, Oxford: Berghahn, pp. 227–44.
Hannerz, U. (1996) *Transnational Connections: Culture, People, Places*, London: Routledge.
Hatfield, M.E. (2011) 'British families moving home: translocal geographies of return migration from Singapore' in K. Brickell and A. Datta (eds), *Translocal Geographies: Space, Place, Connection*, Farnham: Ashgate, pp. 55–70.
Horst, C. (2018) 'Making a difference in Mogadishu? Experiences of multi-sited embeddedness among diaspora youth', *Journal of Ethnic and Migration Studies*, 44 (8), 1341–56.
Jain, S. (2013) 'For love and money: second-generation Indian-Americans "return" to India', *Ethnic and Racial Studies*, 36 (5), 896–914.

Kaya, A. (2007) 'German-Turkish transnational space: a separate space of their own', *German Studies Review*, **30** (3), 483–502.
Kertzer, D.I. (1983) 'Generation as a sociological problem', *Annual Review of Sociology*, **9**, 125–49.
Kılınç, N. (2019) 'From vagabond to tourist: second-generation Turkish-German deportees' narratives of self-healing and well-being', *Nordic Journal of Migration Research*, **9** (2), 239–55.
Kılınç, N. and King, R. (2017) 'The quest for a "better life": second-generation Turkish-Germans "return" to "paradise"', *Demographic Research*, **36** (49), 1491–514.
Kılınç, N. and King, R. (2018) 'Translocal narratives of memory, place and belonging: second-generation Turkish-Germans' home-making upon "return" to Turkey' in S. Marschall (ed.), *Memory, Migration and Travel*, London: Routledge, pp. 234–56.
Kılınç, N. and King, R. (2019) 'Translocal "return", social change and the value of transcultural capital: second-generation Turkish-Germans in Antalya' in R.G. Anghel, M. Fauser and P. Boccagni (eds), *Transnational Return and Social Change: Social Hierarchies, Ideas and Social Identities*, London: Anthem Press, pp. 159–79.
Kim, J.H.J. (2010) 'Transnational identity formation of second-generation Korean-Americans living in Korea', *Torch Trinity Journal*, **13** (1), 70–82.
King, R. (1986) 'Return migration and regional economic development: an overview' in R. King (ed.), *Return Migration and Regional Economic Problems*, London: Croom Helm, pp. 1–37.
King, R. (2002) 'Towards a new map of European migration', *Population, Space and Place*, **8** (2), 89–106.
King, R. (2012) 'Geography and migration studies: retrospect and prospect', *Population, Space and Place*, **18** (2), 134–53.
King, R. and Christou, A. (2008) *Cultural Geographies of Counter-Diasporic Migration: The Second Generation Returns 'Home'*, Brighton: University of Sussex, Sussex Centre for Migration Research Working Paper No. 45.
King, R. and Christou, A. (2010) 'Diaspora, migration and transnationalism: insights from the study of second-generation "returnees"' in R. Bauböck and T. Faist (eds), *Diaspora and Transnationalism: Concepts, Theories and Methods*, Amsterdam: Amsterdam University Press, pp. 167–85.
King, R. and Christou, A. (2014) 'Second-generation "return" to Greece: new dynamics of transnationalism and integration', *International Migration*, **52** (6), 85–99.
King, R. and Kılınç, N. (2013) *'Euro-Turks' Return: The Counterdiasporic Migration of German-Born Turks to Turkey*, Malmö: University of Malmö, Willy Brandt Series of Working Papers in International Migration and Ethnic Relations No. 2/13.
King, R. and Kılınç, N. (2014). 'Routes to roots: second-generation Turks from Germany "return" to Turkey', *Nordic Journal of Migration Research*, **4** (3), 126–33.
King, R. and Kılınç, N. (2016) 'The counter-diasporic migration of Turkish-Germans to Turkey: gendered narratives of home and belonging' in R. Nadler, Z. Kovacs, B. Glorius and T. Lang (eds), *Return Migration and Regional Development*, London: Palgrave Macmillan, pp. 167–94.
King, R., Christou, A. and Teerling, J. (2011) '"We took a bath with the chickens": memories of childhood visits to the homeland by second-generation Greek and Greek Cypriot "returnees"', *Global Networks*, **11** (1), 1–23.
Kulu, H. (2002) 'Socialization and residence: ethnic return migrants in Estonia', *Environment and Planning A*, **34** (2), 289–316.
Lee, H. (2016) '"I was forced here": perceptions of agency in second generation "return" migration to Tonga', *Journal of Ethnic and Migration Studies*, **42** (15), 2573–88.
Levitt, P. (2009) 'Roots and routes: understanding the lives of the second generation transnationally', *Journal of Ethnic and Migration Studies*, **35** (7), 1225–42.
Levitt, P. and Glick Schiller, N. (2004) 'Conceptualizing simultaneity: a transnational social field perspective on society', *International Migration Review*, **38** (3), 1002–39.
Ley, D. (2004) 'Transnational spaces and everyday lives', *Transactions of the Institute of British Geographers*, **29** (2), 151–64.
Ley, D. and Kobayashi, A. (2005) 'Back to Hong Kong: return migration or transnational sojourn?', *Global Networks*, **5** (2), 111–27.
Lidgard, J. and Gilson, C. (2002) 'Return migration of New Zealanders: shuttle and circular migrants', *New Zealand Population Review*, **28** (1), 99–128.

Lulle, A. (2014) 'Spaces of encounter-displacement: contemporary labour migrants' return visits to Latvia', *Geografiska Annaler: Series B, Human Geography*, **96** (2), 127–40.

Markowitz, F. and Stefansson, A.H. (eds) (2004) *Homecomings: Unsettling Paths of Return*, Lanham MD: Lexington Books.

Meinhof, U.H. and Triandafyllidou, A. (2006) 'Beyond the diaspora: transnational practices as transcultural capital' in U.H. Meinhof and A. Triandafyllidou (eds), *Transcultural Europe: Cultural Policy in a Changing Europe*, Basingstoke: Palgrave Macmillan, pp. 200–22.

Morley, D. (2000) *Home Territories: Media, Mobility and Identity*, London: Routledge.

Ní Laoire, C. (2007) 'The "green green grass of home"? Return migration to rural Ireland', *Journal of Rural Studies*, **23** (3), 332–44.

Nowicka, M. (2007) 'Mobile locations: construction of home in a group of mobile transnational professionals', *Global Networks*, **7** (1), 69–86.

Pessar, P.R. and Mahler, S.J. (2003) 'Transnational migration: bringing gender in', *International Migration Review*, **37** (3), 812–46.

Phillips, J. and Potter, R.B. (2006) '"Black skins–white masks": postcolonial reflections on "race", gender and second generation return migration to the Caribbean', *Singapore Journal of Tropical Geography*, **27** (3), 309–25.

Phillips, J. and Potter, R.B. (2009) 'Quality of life issues and second-generation migration: the case of "Bajan-Brit returnees"', *Population, Space and Place*, **15** (3), 239–51.

Portes, A. and Zhou, M. (1993) 'The new second generation: segmented assimilation and its variants', *The Annals of the American Academy of Political and Social Science*, **530**, 74–96.

Potter, R.B. (2005) '"Young, gifted and back": second-generation transnational return migrants to the Caribbean', *Progress in Development Studies*, **5** (3), 213–36.

Potter, R.B. and Phillips, J. (2006) '"Mad dogs and transnational migrants?" Bajan-Brit second-generation migrants and accusations of madness', *Annals of the Association of American Geographers*, **96** (3), 586–600.

Ralph, D. and Staeheli, L.A. (2011) 'Home and migration: mobilities, belongings and identities', *Geography Compass*, **5** (7), 517–30.

Reynolds, T. (2008) *Ties That Bind: Families, Social Capital and Caribbean Second-Generation Return Migration*, Brighton: University of Sussex, Sussex Centre for Migration Research Working Paper No. 46.

Reynolds, T. (2010) 'Transnational family relationships, social networks and return migration among British-Caribbean young people', *Ethnic and Racial Studies*, **33** (5), 797–815.

Rumbaut, R.G. (2002) 'Severed or sustained attachments? Language, identity, and imagined communities in the post-immigrant generation' in P. Levitt and M.C. Waters (eds), *The Changing Face of Home: The Transnational Lives of the Second Generation*, New York: Russell Sage Foundation, pp. 43–95.

Rumbaut, R.G. (2004) 'Ages, life stages, and generational cohorts: decomposing the immigrant first and second generations in the United States', *International Migration Review*, **38** (3), 1160–205.

Safran, W. (1991) 'Diasporas in modern societies: myths of homeland and return', *Diaspora*, **1** (1), 83–99.

Saito, M. (2007) *Second-Generation Afghans in Neighbouring Countries. From Mohajer to Hamwatan: Afghans Return Home*, Kabul: Afghanistan Research and Evaluation Unit.

Sardinha, J. (2011) '"Returning" second-generation Portuguese-Canadians and Portuguese-French: motivations and senses of belonging', *Journal of Mediterranean Studies*, **20** (2), 231–54.

Song, C. (2009) 'Brothers only in name: the alienation and identity transformation of Korean Chinese ethnic return migrants in South Korea' in T. Tsuda (ed.), *Diasporic Homecomings: Ethnic Return Migrants in Comparative Perspective*, Palo Alto: Stanford University Press, pp. 281–304.

Stroink, M.L. and Lalonde, R.N. (2009) 'Bicultural identity conflict in second-generation Asian Canadians', *Journal of Social Psychology*, **149** (1), 44–65.

Teerling, J. (2011) 'The development of new "third-cultural spaces of belonging": British-born Cypriot "return" migrants in Cyprus', *Journal of Ethnic and Migration Studies*, **37** (7), 1079–99.

Thomas-Hope, E. (1999) 'Return migration to Jamaica and its development potential', *International Migration*, **37** (1), 183–207.

Thomson, M. and Crul, M. (2007) 'The second generation in Europe and the United States: how is the transatlantic debate relevant for further research on the European second generation?', *Journal of Ethnic and Migration Studies*, **33** (7), 1025–41.

Tölölyan, K. (1996) 'Rethinking diaspora(s): stateless power in the transnational moment', *Diaspora*, **5** (1), 3–36.

Tsuda, T. (2001) 'From ethnic affinity to alienation in the global ecumene: the encounter between the Japanese and Japanese-Brazilian return migrants', *Diaspora*, **10** (1), 53–91.

Tsuda, T. (2003) *Strangers in the Ethnic Homeland: Japanese Brazilian Return Migration in Transnational Perspective*, New York: Columbia University Press.

Tsuda, T. (ed.) (2009) *Diasporic Homecomings: Ethnic Return Migration in Comparative Perspective*, Palo Alto: Stanford University Press.

Vathi, Z. and King, R. (eds) (2017) *Return Migration and Psychosocial Wellbeing: Discourses, Policy-Making and Outcomes for Migrants and Their Families*, Oxford and New York: Routledge.

Vertovec, S. (1997) 'Three meanings of "diaspora" exemplified among South Asian religions', *Diaspora*, **6** (3), 277–99.

Vertovec, S. (2004) 'Migrant transnationalism and modes of transformation', *International Migration Review*, **38** (3), 970–1001.

Vlase, I. (2013) '"My husband is a patriot!": gender and Romanian family return migration from Italy', *Journal of Ethnic and Migration Studies*, **39** (5), 741–58.

Wessendorf, S. (2007) '"Roots migrants": transnationalism and "return" among second-generation Italians in Switzerland', *Journal of Ethnic and Migration Studies*, **33** (7), 1083–102.

White, A. (2014) 'Polish return and double return migration', *Europe-Asia Studies*, **66** (1), 25–49.

# 21. Return migration experiences: the case of Central and Eastern Europe
*Anne White*

## INTRODUCTION

This chapter considers the specificity or otherwise of migrants' experiences of return to Central and Eastern Europe (CEE). Like other contributions to this Handbook, the chapter understands return migration as more than merely the end of the migration story. It focuses on that part of the return process taking place in the country of origin. This process is fascinating for qualitative researchers interested in how individuals construct the social world. Returnees understand one set of experiences (often labelled 'reintegration') through the prism of their reflections on experiences in the receiving society. Immediately after return, in particular, they often check whether they made the right decision, comparing the origin country with the foreign one and weighing up their attachments to particular places and individuals in one country and the other. In the words of Ewa[1] (whom I interviewed in 2011 about her return to Poland): 'I realised I was living in fact in two worlds at the same time. A Polish world and an English world ... I couldn't completely shut the door on that English world.' This dual focus is also manifest in their networking: reintegrating into the origin society can be accompanied by a parallel process of maintaining and even extending transnational ties. The phrase 'transnational return' (Anghel et al., 2019) captures the idea of how return takes place within this transnational social space.

The fact that scholars around the world find evidence of such behaviour suggests a commonality of return experiences.[2] Nonetheless, place must matter in shaping return processes. Exactly how it matters can be understood by analysing the features of case-study countries or regions. Differences between receiving (i.e. foreign) countries help to shape the outcomes for returning migrants, as demonstrated, for example, by Carletto and Kilic (2011), who write about the labour market experiences of returnees to Albania from Italy and Greece. However, significant aspects of the receiving-country experience are often not so much connected with that country per se but with the migrant's immigration status and the types of migrant which the country attracts. It would probably be true to say that features of the origin/return location are more important than the receiving society in shaping returnees' experiences.

This chapter considers return to CEE, an area currently experiencing considerable geographical mobility, including returns. This makes it a good case study for understanding contemporary return migration trends. CEE is itself a diverse region; today, in particular, there exist dividing lines linked to European Union (EU) membership – whether a country is in the EU, an EU candidate or Eastern Partnership member or is outside EU structures. Nonetheless, the common legacy of communist party rule and the 1990s transformation remain important both for the impact of return migration on societies of origin (White et al., 2018) and for returning individuals and families, the subject of this chapter. Social change is, to some extent, always part of the backdrop to reintegration experiences; in CEE, social change has been particularly dynamic in recent decades. This chapter explores patterns of decision-making for return, reintegration and social remitting within this specific regional context, while also considering how CEE in some ways exemplifies wider mobility trends within the EU and the world today.

'Reintegration' is a concept commonly used to understand returnee experiences (King, 2000; see also Kuschminder, Chapter 14). In keeping with my earlier research (e.g. White, 2017), I define (re)integration as a process of starts, stops and reversals, taking place at different speeds in different domains – cultural, social, economic and political – and involving accommodation by both the (return) migrant and the (origin) society. One difference between integration and reintegration might seem to be that, following Berry (1997), researchers often understand cultural integration as incomplete assimilation. It is an outcome which most migrants prefer (Neto, 2010). By contrast, publications about the cultural reintegration of returnees often imply that they expect to completely reassimilate. 'Reintegration' seems, therefore, to be used as the equivalent of 'reassimilation'. However, as King points out (2000, p.20), 'there can be no return to the *status quo ante*'. Neto's (2010) article about Portuguese adolescents shows that they wished to retain social connections with and aspects of the cultural identity of the foreign country where they previously lived: they did not want to 'shut the door', to use Ewa's metaphor. Hence reassimilation was not their preferred strategy. In fact, all returnees who maintain strong transnational links, as is so easy for many EU citizens, may often experience moments of rebellion against expectations that they conform to origin-society norms.

Finally, the term 'social remittances' (Levitt, 1998) has often been used in recent publications to analyse the experiences of returnees, often also with an eye to their impact on the wider society. Social remittances research links to older literature on migrants as agents of change (Cerase, 1974); this, in turn, links to literature on migration and development (see King, Chapter 22). Returnees can bring back a changed worldview, becoming more open and confident – an experience reported by many in CEE (White and Grabowska, 2019). Aneta, a Polish returnee from Ireland whom I interviewed in 2019, summed this up with the phrase 'I'm not afraid of the world.' Returnees sometimes also take back with them more specific new ideas, attitudes and skills which may help or impede their reintegration process.

The chapter is based on a combination of secondary literature and original data. I have tried to include as much information as possible about non-Polish returnees. However, English-language scholarship mostly considers the Polish case and these publications represent the tip of the iceberg, since there also exist many Polish-language sources. The chapter also draws on my research from 2007 to 2019, when I conducted in-depth interviews with 104 Polish return migrants – in/from locations across Poland – and 25 Ukrainians. My projects asked different research questions and my interviewees had varying reasons to return but one common finding was that perceptions about reintegration in the return location (the actual place more than the country) were often linked to specifically post-communist characteristics. Unless otherwise stated, interview quotations in this chapter are from my 2019 interviews in Płock with 25 Ukrainian circular migrants and 14 Polish return migrants. I first examine some characteristics of recent CEE migration which have a bearing on return experiences. I then discuss other relevant aspects of the environment to which migrants return and the impact of these on their reintegration experiences, before considering the ability of returnees to socially remit.

## CEE MIGRANTS AND PATTERNS OF RETURN MIGRATION

Modern telecommunications and the Internet enable migrants across the globe to send information to contacts in their origin country, speeding up the formation of informal migration networks. EU citizens additionally benefit from free movement. These opportunities encourage a great variety of mobility aspirations with regard to destination and the duration, regularity and frequency of migration. Many types of CEE citizen are drawn into migration. Although the social complexion of migrant flows from different countries varies to some extent, the mobile CEE population from major sending countries such as Romania, Poland, Slovakia and Lithuania is quite heterogeneous, to the extent that some receiving-country populations, such as UK-based Poles, can almost be considered as microcosms of society in the country of origin (White et al., 2018).

Axes of difference among migrants include age, life-stage, gender, parental status, sexual orientation, educational level, skills, income, social status (at home and abroad), degree and nature of their identification with the country of origin and transnational ties while abroad and upon return. Given that each migrant possesses a different bundle of identities, resources and mobility aspirations, return is an individualised process. There is some quantitative evidence about which types of migrant are more likely to return. For example, Anacka et al. (2013) show that Poles have returned more often to villages than to large cities, probably because circular migrants are more likely to come from villages. Moreh et al. (2020) argue that CEE men more often return than women, again probably linked to the fact that men are more often temporary migrants, migrating without their families. Duda-Mikulin (2018) suggests that Polish women, in particular, may be expected to return for family reasons, so return is also gendered in this respect.

Migration flows in the 1990s, soon after the collapse of the communist regimes, were also mixed. Nonetheless, before 2004 a highly gendered type of circularity – usually by just one parent – typified migration from many countries, especially from smaller and poorer locations. This type of mobile livelihood persisted into the twenty-first century. In particular, it was common in Germany, which maintained labour market restrictions until 2011 for CEE states joining the EU in 2004. It has typified countries like the Netherlands – with its demand for seasonal agricultural/horticultural labour – and Italy, with many jobs for live-in carers which are attractive to women from poorer locations in CEE. It is widespread today for Ukrainians utilising temporary work permits to Czechia, Poland and Lithuania. However, repeated temporary migration does not only result from structural factors in receiving countries. It also reflects some specific features of livelihood strategies in post-communist societies; for example, it is socially acceptable for middle-aged working-class women to leave their older children and work temporarily in care and cleaning abroad – and that middle-aged parents should support their children's higher education in this fashion (Lapshyna and Düvell, 2015; White, 2009). Return visits can be a rest for circular migrants but they can also require awkward temporary reintegration adjustments on both sides – as, for example, Lulle (2014) describes with regard to Latvia. Moreover, upon return, the migrants may need to be on the lookout for new opportunities to go abroad, constantly thinking transnationally as they explore 'various destinations depending on emerging opportunities' (Ciobanu, 2015, p.466 on Romania).

In contrast, migration from CEE to the UK and Ireland at the beginning of the twenty-first century involved many childless young people, including city-dwellers. Lifestyle considerations seemed commonly to combine with economic and/or educational motivations, as across

Europe more widely (King, 2018). A specifically CEE feature of this migration flow was high youth unemployment in some countries at the time: among those aged 25–29 in early 2004 it stood at 24.1 per cent in Poland, 18.9 per cent in Slovakia, 14.3 per cent in Latvia and 12.1 per cent in Lithuania (Eurostat, 2004). Krzaklewska's study of Polish returnees born in the 1980s (2019, p.43) refers to

> a generational story of a cohort entering adulthood in the time of Europe opening its borders for Central-Eastern Europeans, thus creating new chances for experiencing youth and capitalizing on the mobility within transitions to adulthood ... The study participants stressed that 'going abroad was a distinguishing trait for their generation'.

Young people's plans to stay or return were often open-ended, with some apparently pursuing a strategy of 'intentional unpredictability', while others always meant to return (Eade et al., 2007). Among Parutis's sample of young Poles and Lithuanians, it was the most non-conformist in their behaviour – such as LGBT people and unmarried migrants over 30 – who felt more disinclined to return. As one remarked, by remaining in London 'I definitely spared myself a conventional life' (Parutis, 2014, p.168). Nonetheless, many in this cohort have returned, as indicated by the fact that, by 2016, 27 per cent of 25–34-year-old Poles had worked abroad in the previous ten years (Cybulska, 2016).

If they returned to poor locations, they were likely to continue to migrate. However, for Krzaklewska's interviewees, as for many of mine who returned to Polish cities, it seems that living in the UK or Ireland was remembered as a pleasurable one-off experience, sometimes followed in later years by short business trips and holidays. Particularly if they gained soft skills such as foreign language fluency, returnees could slot back into the recovering labour market at home; at the same time, the range of leisure opportunities was expanding in Polish cities, which were becoming increasingly 'fun' places to live. Apsite-Berina et al. (2019) found that their young Romanian and Latvian sample easily reintegrated. Moreover, societies in CEE – especially in large cities – were changing too and alternative lifestyles were becoming more accepted, so that it was easier to rejoin the mainstream. For example, Krzaklewska (2019) mentions that cohabitation was rapidly increasing among this age group in Poland itself.

Return among this cohort also linked to life-stage: as people neared the age of 30 they often felt a need to settle down somewhere. A 29-year-old Estonian interviewed by Saar and Saar (2020, p.59) remarked: 'London is a nice change, but not a place for family. It is a phase of life.' Barcevičius (2016, p.39), writing about Lithuanians, reports 'the feeling that a certain stage in life has come to an end and it is time to make a decision (according to one interviewee, "we either come back now or settle abroad for the rest of our lives")'. However, migrants who returned to settle were assuming that the reintegration would be successful; when it actually compared unsatisfactorily with the foreign country, this could prompt them to re-think their plans, and perform a 'double return', deciding to settle abroad (White, 2014). Settlement abroad also occurred thanks to family reunification. Although families could have open-ended plans initially, they had a tendency to settle, especially those with school-age children who could be expected to experience considerable reintegration problems (White, 2017).

Despite these two quite specific forms of migration (middle-aged circular and open-ended youthful), since EU accession in 2004 and 2007 CEE migration has increasingly diversified. Ireland and the UK began to attract a range of age groups and more ordinary labour migrants, while countries where middle-aged circular migration predominated acquired more young people and professionals (Kowalska and Pelliccia, 2012; Strockmeijer et al., 2019). Returns, when they occurred, were therefore also by a greater range of people. By 2020, a great deal of mobility consisted of educational migration and business trips by residents of flourishing cities, which had little in common with the more 'classic' labour migration of the 1990s and early twenty-first century: reintegration in such cases was often relatively straightforward.

One characteristic of CEE migration has been co-ethnic return. Cold War exiles and their descendants returned East after 1989 (see, e.g., Tomić, 2016 on the Croat and Czech experience). These returnees, despite their sometimes elite status, often experienced mixed success in integrating and enacting their business and other projects. Westward co-ethnic return, particularly of Hungarians and Germans from Romania and Poles and Czechs from the former USSR, is often not easily distinguishable from regular labour or educational migration. Pragmatism rather than a strong sense of 'ethnic affinity' (Brubaker, 1998) often seems to guide behaviour. For example, Jirka (2019) argues that Czechs from Ukraine are mostly hoping to acquire residency in Czechia. Despite formal entitlements, which simplify integration in certain institutional domains (e.g. education), co-ethnics arriving from poorer countries can find themselves not accepted as equals in their diasporic homelands. For instance, a Transylvanian Hungarian reported by Fox (2003, p.457) complained: 'Here [in Romania] we're Hungarians; there we're Romanians.' Similarly, a medical student from Ukraine, quoted in Gońda (2016, p.137), lamented that many Poles 'do not accept that it may happen that a Pole can be born outside Poland'.

Little return to CEE can be classed as 'forced', although EU citizens who cannot support themselves financially can be deported (Maslowski, 2015) and deportations are more frequent in the UK since the 2016 Brexit referendum (Guma and Jones, 2019). Germany and Belgium, too, have tightened welfare restrictions for unemployed EU migrants, forcing them to leave (Barbulescu and Favell, 2020). CEE Roma and people 'perceived as Roma' (Juverdeanu, 2021) have been especially vulnerable, with expulsions from France since 2010 arousing particular scholarly interest. However, these publications mostly focus on receiving countries and the EU and/or public discourse in Romania, rather than on the return experiences of deportees. An exception is Juverdeanu (2021), whose 'perceived as Roma' interviewees actually self-identified as Romanians and exercised their free movement rights to return to France after being expelled.

External shocks, notably the Global Economic Crisis (GEC) of 2008 and Brexit, were expected to produce waves of involuntary return. However, with some exceptions (notably Greece to Albania – see Kerpaci and Kuka, 2019) most authors seem to agree that the GEC did not create return waves (Benton and Petrovic, 2013; Zaiceva and Zimmermann, 2016). Research on Hungarian, Latvian, Polish and Romanian returnees during the GEC found that most 'went back for family reasons or because they had achieved their emigration goals' (Barcevičius et al., 2012, p.1). Perhaps, indeed, return migration waves are not likely to happen within the EU, where EU migrants can sit out crises on welfare benefits or move to more prosperous EU destinations. Similarly, the 'Brexodus' expected by some observers has not occurred on any scale, although (with the exception of Bulgarians and Romanians) new arrivals to the UK from CEE have fallen (Sredanovic, 2020).

Return to non-EU states might more often seem to be 'involuntary', as in the case of migrants from the former USSR working in Czechia and Poland on temporary work permits. Although precise statistics are impossible to determine, this is clearly a large population with, since 2015, at least 1 million Ukrainians located in Poland at any one time (Chmielewska et al., 2016) and over 130,000 in Czechia (CZSO, n.d.). However, the demand for migrant labour makes it easy to renew a work permit, so Ukrainians are not forced to return in a final sense after their permits expire. This is mostly circular migration, including multiple returns. Nonetheless, there are also tendencies towards settlement, partly reflecting the workings of networks and family reunification and the increasing diversification of the Ukrainian population abroad (Andrejuk, 2017; Leontiyeva, 2016).

Voluntary post-conflict return occurred to Bosnia and Herzegovina (BiH) and Kosovo after the wars of 1992–95 and 1999. Voluntary return takes place within official programmes or individually; according to Eastmond (2006), migrants often preferred the latter, so they can make optimal use of social networks. Eastmond also argues that return is often the most 'sustainable' when strong links are maintained with the former country of asylum. 'Continued mobility after an initial return – including circulation and the development of a "transnational" lifestyle – may be more "sustainable" than a single and definitive return to the refugee's place of origin' (Black and Gent, 2006, p.15). Returnees can prefer return to ethnic enclaves, where it is easier to reintegrate (Joireman, 2017 on Kosovo).

Porobić (2016) argues that, because of continuing political conflict in BiH, strong grassroots civil-society organisations, often with transnational connections, play a key role in helping to secure sustainable return. However, this type of collective concern for the sustainability of local communities seems rare in CEE. The mobility of CEE citizens today is ordinarily an individual or family project, fanning out in all directions. Each person inhabits their own transnational social space, unlike the dense collective ties and responsibilities described in Levitt's classic (2001) study of links between Boca Canasta, Dominican Republic and Boston, USA. There appear to exist only a handful of hometown associations: of Moldovans (Cingolani and Vietti, 2018) and Romanian Saxons (Oltean, 2019). Local diaspora organisations in receiving countries rarely consist of people from the same location in CEE and seem mostly concerned with their own affairs (White et al., 2018), rather than forging developmental links with sending locations which could facilitate returnees' reintegration.

As seems common across the different countries (King, 2000), CEE surveys suggest that personal reasons for return predominate, even among economic migrants. This, in turn, contributes to the highly individualised character of return. Nonchev and Hristova (2018, pp.13–14), for instance, found the top motivation in their survey was 'affection for the family and my relatives in Bulgaria'. Similarly, Bakalova and Misheva (2018, p.82) assert that 'non-economic factors have been the leading ones that have prompted the Bulgarian citizens to return to their homeland over the last decade'. Barcevičius (2016) and White et al. (2018) each cite several references to similar Lithuanian and Polish findings. Even target migrants who return because they have fulfilled their economic objectives can be said to return for personal reasons, since they tend to come back to the location where they feel at home.

## STRUCTURAL FACTORS CONDITIONING REINTEGRATION EXPERIENCES

Anghel et al. (2019) argue that return migration generally should be viewed as an 'unsettled process'. Although the concept of 'unsustainability' is usually applied to post-conflict return, surveys in some non-post-conflict countries of CEE suggest that there, too, a large share (in some cases over half) of returnees are prepared to migrate again (see, e.g., Nonchev and Hristova, 2018 on Bulgaria or White, 2014 on Poland). If sending locations are unable to retain the return migrants, this is partly linked to the many opportunities enjoyed by returning EU citizens, with their flourishing transnational networks and ability to keep their options open. However, it also connects to structural impediments to reintegration in the locations of origin.

It seems that unemployment levels are often somewhat higher among returnees than among the local population (see, e.g., Grabowska, 2016 on Poland; Lapshyna and Düvell, 2015 on Ukraine; Zareva, 2018 on Bulgaria). Despite EU convergence policy and considerable investment in infrastructure in recent years, the post-communist region still suffers from regional inequalities.[3] According to various Polish surveys (White, 2014), return is usually to a person's home location; this is likely to be typical for other countries, given the prevalence of return for the personal reasons mentioned above. The fact that migrants return for emotional reasons to depressed locations, where they cannot reintegrate into the labour market, makes them more ready to consider migrating internationally again. When reintegration fails in the origin location, onward migration to a more prosperous location in the sending country might seem an obvious alternative to international migration. However, prejudices against internal migration seem to exist across the region (Bélorgey et al., 2012).[4] In numerous interviews I have been told by Poles and Ukrainians that they preferred to move to friends and family abroad, rather than to a prospering city in their own country where they had no contacts.

Of course, there is no simple divide between wealthy locations where returnees reintegrate into the labour market and peripheral ones from where they migrate again. Social class and education are also factors affecting labour market reintegration. This was illustrated in my study of Płock, a medium-sized city of 120,400 (GUS, 2019), which combines features of the big city with those of a small town. Some returnees had found rewarding, high-powered jobs in the city administration and big companies where they could use their English and 'people skills' gained abroad. As Aneta put it, 'If it hadn't been for Ireland I would be in a different job.' On the other hand, workers without university degrees struggled to find jobs which paid adequately and/or had incurred debts as the result of failed business endeavours which they could not pay off on a local wage. Echoing many of my small-town interviewees from earlier projects, Wojciech, a builder, explained why he preferred circular migration, despite having a family in Płock: 'You go abroad and work hard and long, but your work is rewarded. In Poland you work long and hard but with no effect at all.'

Although informal relations are a global phenomenon, they can be particularly prominent in post-communist societies. Unemployed returnees in my study in the small town of Limanowa in 2013 almost all complained that local jobs were reserved for friends and family. Even in Płock, Jagoda, a poorer interviewee, complained: 'As it's a small town, getting a job depends on who you know, it's hard for the average person.' Ivanova (2015) similarly comments on how highly skilled returnees to Bulgaria and BiH were disadvantaged by the attrition of their social networks while abroad and, in BiH, by corruption.

Structural factors which might imbue the reintegration process with homogeneity nationwide could include support offered by governments to facilitate reintegration. Various countries in CEE have attempted to provide such support: see, for example, Kaska (2013) on Estonia or Ivanova (2015) on Bulgaria and BiH. Government programmes have not always been effectively designed and resourced but problems also seem to stem from widespread scepticism about official initiatives – a common post-communist phenomenon. This has been documented, for example, in Bulgaria by Bakalova and Misheva (2018) and in Poland, Latvia and Romania by Barcevičius et al. (2012). Kerpaci and Kuka (2019, p.114) report that, in Albania, 'almost all of them [the interviewees] laughed in disbelief when we informed them about the government's intention to provide assistance'. Overall, Barcevičius (2016), writing about Lithuania, concludes that return migrants succeed in reintegrating thanks to their own agency, not institutions.

CEE societies are also marked by a mistrust of strangers, although this varies between countries and has tended to decrease somewhat in recent years.[5] One aspect of mistrust is a certain hostility towards returnees on the part of non-migrants – a structural factor with conseqences for reintegration experiences. Nevinskaitė (2016), writing about Lithuania, refers to low 'country receptivity' for returning migrants. Similar attitudes have been reported in Latvia (Barcevičius et al., 2012), Estonia (Anniste et al., 2017) and Poland (Dzięglewski, 2016). However, there are also cases where trust in returnees improves over time. Coşciug shows how, despite the anti-migration stance of the Romanian Orthodox Church, the religious activism of returnees can transform local opinion: 'Within the religious communities I studied, migration is increasingly seen and portrayed as an "acceptable" strategy' (Coşciug, 2019, p.94).

Widespread social conservatism in CEE – together with a legacy of underfunded institutional care – is manifested in the prevailing norm that care for older relatives should be provided within the family. Both survey and in-depth interview evidence shows that family illness and caring responsibilities are common reasons for return to CEE, even to locations where it is hard to find a satisfactory livelihood. However, as Radziwinowiczówna et al. (2018) demonstrate in their monograph on the 'ethnomorality of care' in two Polish small towns, it is hard to generalise about the experiences of returnees in providing care. This is partly because attitudes towards on-the-spot family/institutional and at-a-distance (transnational) care are pragmatic and norms are, in fact, somewhat evolving: 'Cultures of care of countries of origin and destination intertwine' (Radziwinowiczówna et al., 2018, p.89). Krzyżowski (2013) shows that Poles in Iceland and Austria – countries with very different ethnomoralities of care – also have different attitudes towards their caring responsibilities vis-à-vis parents in Poland.

## SOCIAL CHANGE AND SOCIAL REMITTANCES

Social change in this part of Europe is very rapid; hence, despite their often intense transnational ties while they are abroad, returnees can find it hard to readjust. Dzięglewski's (2019) book about Polish return is titled *Coming Home to an (Un)familiar Country*. Vathi et al. (2016) comment, for example, on how returning parents did not understand the changed Albanian school system. Kerpaci and Kuka (2019, p.109) also remark that 'when they returned to Albania they had to adapt to the new way of living in Albania, because during their absence significant changes had occurred in Albanian society'.

Other potential returnees are impressed by the development in their origin locations and this encourages them to return. Saar and Saar (2020) show how their Estonian interviewees chose Tallinn for its quality of life in preference to London. Barčevicius (2016, p.41) writes that Lithuanian return migrants

> also gave some reflection with regard to the quality of public services and quality of life in the capital Vilnius: these were considered acceptable and, in some respects, even better than in foreign countries: for example, more accessible and (or) cheaper but still high quality healthcare, childcare, relatively quick commuting between home and work.

Similarly, some returnees I interviewed in Warsaw and Łódź felt that their home cities were civilisationally 'ahead' of smaller locations where they had worked in the UK and Ireland.

However, reintegrating migrants can also be put off by the reverse phenomenon: a belief that change in the origin society is too slow and a perception of its shortcomings is compared with the destination society. This is partly a personal, subjective matter. There is also empirical evidence that various legacies of the communist (1945–89) and transformation (1990s) periods continue to shape social relations and local economies in the region, particularly in some locations and among some local groups. It is, of course, important not to overstate the significance of such legacies, failing to see similarities with other parts of Europe, stigmatising CEE for being 'behind' and not taking into account the extent to which legacies have been overcome and are no longer relevant (Müller, 2019).

Within the CEE region, EU countries – especially those which acceded in 2004 – have received more investment, are more prosperous and in various respects better functioning than their neighbours. This was reflected in comparisons with Poland made by my Ukrainian interviewees. On visits home, they noticed features of Ukrainian life today which Poles would mostly associate with 1990s Poland. The Ukrainians complained about how their home towns and cities all across Ukraine (though not Kiev) were characterised by discourteous driving, poor roads and public transport, unpleasant shop assistants, the conspicuous consumption of expensive cars and clothes, the enclosure of public space in cities and (most of all) corruption. Lapshyna and Düvell (2015, p.300) make similar observations: for example, quoting one interviewee: 'When they [return migrants] return home, they face the same nasty things here, the rude behaviour of salespeople in a shop, for example. Now this would seem absolutely outrageous to them.' Kubal (2015) notes that some Ukrainian returnees begin to drive more courteously once they return and pick up litter more carefully.

Other communist legacies which seem to bother returnees include hierarchical management styles. They prefer the more egalitarian models which they witnessed abroad. For example, Vathi et al. (2016) report that Albanian returnees preferred the more egalitarian schools they had encountered in Greece. Cieślik (2011, p.1380) cites 'relationships with coworkers and the boss [and] the workplace atmosphere' in the UK as reasons why Poles preferred not to return to Poland. Dariusz, whom I interviewed in 2011, explained why he had returned to the UK with the complaint: 'I couldn't get used to the Polish mentality, how the managers treat people.' Even in 2019, some of my Polish interviewees were struck by this difference, commenting on the informality of worker–boss relations that they had witnessed in the Netherlands and the UK. Interestingly, Ukrainians made similar comments about Poland.

To use Grabowska et al.'s (2017) framework for analysing the stages of social remitting, migrants may 'acquire' social remittances abroad – in the sense of being impressed by what they see – and become correspondingly discontented when they return. However, this does not necessarily translate into their taking action to 'diffuse' those social remittances in an attempt to change their origin societies and economies. A considerable part of return migration scholarship investigates whether and under what circumstances migrants become 'agents of change', using their new skills and ideas. As Levitt (2001) observed, when launching the concept of social remittances, migrants vary in their desire and capacity to act as agents of change. Some are more able than others to exploit their foreign experiences. Cormoş (2017), for example, cites the case of a returnee who became a livestock farmer in a poor part of Northern Romania and succeeded in his business thanks to his German links and ability to tap into EU funds.

Equally important, as mentioned above, is local 'receptivity' (Nevinskaitė, 2016) to migrants and their ideas. Barcevičius (2016, p.39), for example, writing like Nevinskaitė about Lithuania, demonstrates how old-fashioned and suspicious employers preferred locally gained skills: 'When offered a choice between a job applicant with foreign experience and an equivalent applicant who gained the relevant skills in Lithuania, they would overwhelmingly opt for the local experience (78.2 per cent vs 9.3 per cent).' Nonetheless – illustrating the actual complexity of the situation – he also reports that '57.9 per cent of the highly qualified returnees … agreed that migration had helped them to find a job (or start a business)'.

One aspect of social remitting which has particularly interested a number of scholars is gender roles and relations, which are generally more conservative in CEE than in the West, although also changing to some extent, especially among younger people and in cities. Researchers have uncovered a certain amount of evidence that return migrants do change local attitudes: for example, raising the respect accorded to women who migrate alone from poor, conservative rural areas of Poland to work as carers in Italy and become the main breadwinners for their households in Poland (Cieślińska, 2014; Urbańska, 2015). Vlase (2013) shows how some Romanian women who have worked abroad try to encourage their daughters to be more ambitious in their choice of career in Romania.

Another area which has been quite extensively researched – although mostly with reference to migrants still living abroad – is attitudes towards racial diversity and homosexuality. My own interviews with return migrants in Poland between 2016 and 2019 bear out the findings of other scholars that some people become more intolerant as a result of migration, while others become more open-minded. In my sample, the latter included some less well-educated, small-town and older interviewees. In fact, since attitudes are already becoming more liberal among the middle class in Polish cities, for a multitude of other reasons, it is in smaller locations and working-class milieux that social change (in the sense of increasing numbers of more open-minded citizens) can be the most impacted on by the migration experience (White et al., 2018).

## CONCLUSION

How universal are return experiences? It seems obvious that specific features of origin communities must be significant. In the case of CEE, this chapter suggests that legacies of the communist period and transformation can inhibit reintegration. By 2020, these are less marked but remain important in some places. Spatial inequalities persist and returnees can find it hard to integrate into certain labour markets characterised by unemployment, cronyism and (in Ukraine) corruption. Migrants nonetheless return to unpromising local economies, since they often go back for emotional reasons and there is a certain culture of not engaging in internal migration. Mistrust in institutions and strangers is another communist legacy, which can manifest itself in scepticism about government reintegration programmes and employers' reluctance to hire returnees.

However, the 'objective realities' of the origin location are not the only factor conditioning reintegration, which has to be seen in its transnational context (i.e. taking into account the receiving societies, outside CEE). Dissatisfaction with reintegration is often linked to continuing wage gaps between CEE and Western Europe and to other comparisons which returnees make in their everyday lives between the origin location and their foreign home. These often seem to involve, for example, a preference for less hierarchical workplaces or more civility from officials. Some returnees are bothered by gender inequality and homophobia in CEE. Although they acquire these social remittances when living abroad, they can feel frustrated by their inability to diffuse them to others upon their return home. Since they are often able to maintain intense and dynamic transnational ties after their return, these comparisons remain fresh in their minds and encourage thoughts of 'return' abroad. This helps to account for the apparent temporariness of many returns to CEE.

Nonetheless, CEE is a varied and fast-changing part of the world. Socio-economic change there over the past 30 years means that much migration from CEE, especially by educated people from the larger cities, involves relocation to Western cities which are actually quite similar to their geographical and social locations of origin in CEE. This facilitates reintegration, at least as far as local structural factors are concerned. In this sense, mobility from and to CEE is not that different from the mobility of Western Europeans. Hence the specificity of CEE return migration has been somewhat diluted over recent decades and it is probably more helpful to view it nowadays less as conditioned by the communist legacy and more in the context of the highly diverse, dynamic, individualised and transnational mobilities characterising the EU as a whole.

## NOTES

1. All interviewees' names are pseudonyms.
2. Carling et al. (2011) find that reintegration is the most common sub-topic in return migration scholarship. However, this does not seem to be the case with regard to scholarship in English on return to CEE; my impression is that studies of return intentions and motivations are at least as common.
3. https://ec.europa.eu/eurostat/statistics-explained/index.php?title=File:GDP_per_inhabitant,_2017_(EU-28_%3D_100,_index_based_on_GDP_in_purchasing_power_standards_(PPS)_in_relation_to_the_EU-28_average,_by_NUTS_2_regions)_F1_RYB19.png (accessed 12 April 2021).
4. Exceptions include Albania, where returnees prefer to settle in the capital, Tirana (Kerpaci and Kuka, 2019) and BiH, where returning refugees often avoid settling in their places of origin (Porobić, 2016).
5. See, for example, World Values Survey data at http://www.worldvaluessurvey.org/wvs.jsp.

## REFERENCES

Anacka, M., Matejko, E. and Nestorowicz, J. (2013) 'Ready to move: liquid return to Poland' in B. Glorius, I. Grabowska-Lusinska and A. Kuvik (eds), *Mobility in Transition: Migration Patterns after EU Enlargement*, Amsterdam: Amsterdam University Press, pp. 277–308.

Andrejuk, K. (2017) *Przedsiębiorcy Ukraińscy w Polsce. Struktura i Sprawstwo w Procesie Osiedlenia*, Warsaw: Wydawnictwo IFiS PAN.

Anghel, R., Fauser, M. and Boccagni, P. (eds) (2019) *Transnational Return and Social Change: Hierarchies, Identities and Ideas*, London: Anthem Press.

Anniste, K., Pukkonen, L. and Paas, T. (2017) 'Towards incomplete migration: Estonian migration to Finland', *Trames*, 21 (2), 97–114.

Apsite-Berina, E., Manea, M.-E. and Berzins, M. (2019) 'The ambiguity of return migration: prolonged crisis and uncertainty in the life strategies of young Romanian and Latvian returnees', *International Migration*, 58 (1), 61–75.

Bakalova, M. and Misheva, M. (2018) 'Explanations of economic rationality challenged: contemporary return migration to Bulgaria', *Икономически изследвания*, 27 (2), 80–101.

Barbulescu, R. and Favell, A. (2020) 'Commentary: a citizenship without social rights? EU freedom of movement and changing access to welfare rights', *International Migration*, **58** (1), 151–65.
Barcevičius, E. (2016) 'How successful are highly qualified return migrants in the Lithuanian labour market?', *International Migration*, **54** (3), 35–47.
Barcevičius, E., Iglicka, K., Repečkaitė, D. and Žvalionytė, D. (2012) *Labour Mobility within the EU: The Impact of Return Migration*, Dublin: Eurofound.
Bélorgey, N., Garbe-Emden, B., Horstmann, S., Kuhn, A., Stubbs, P. and Vogel, D. (2012) *Social Impact of Emigration and Rural–Urban Migration in Central and Eastern Europe*, Brussels: European Commission.
Benton, M. and Petrovic, M. (2013) *How Free Is Free Movement? Dynamics and Drivers of Mobility within the European Union*, Washington DC: Migration Policy Institute Europe.
Berry, J.W. (1997) 'Immigration, acculturation and adaptation', *Applied Psychology: An International Review*, **46** (1), 5–34.
Black, R. and Gent, S. (2006) 'Sustainable return in post-conflict contexts', *International Migration*, **44** (3), 15–38.
Brubaker, R. (1998) 'Migrations of ethnic unmixing in the "New Europe"', *International Migration Review*, **32** (4), 1047–65.
Carletto, C. and Kilic, T. (2011) 'Moving up the ladder? The impact of migration experience on occupational mobility in Albania', *Journal of Development Studies*, **47** (6), 846–69.
Carling, J., Mortensen, E. and Wu, J. (2011) *A Systematic Bibliography on Return Migration*, Oslo: Peace Research Institute Oslo.
Cerase, F. (1974) 'Expectations and reality: a case study of return migration from the United States to southern Italy', *International Migration Review*, **8** (2), 245–62.
Chmielewska, I., Dobroczek, G. and Puzynkiewicz, J. (2016) *Obywatele Ukrainy Pracujący w Polsce – Raport z Badania*, Warsaw: Naradowy Bank Polski.
Cieślik, A. (2011) 'Where do you prefer to work? How the work environment influences return migration decisions from the United Kingdom to Poland', *Journal of Ethnic and Migration Studies*, **37** (9), 1367–83.
Cieślińska, B. (2014) 'The experience of labour emigration in the life of married women: the case of Podlasie, Poland', *International Migration*, **52** (1), 56–73.
Cingolani, P. and Vietti, F. (2018) '"My children think differently": transnationalism, social remittances, and intergenerational differences among Moldovan migrants in Italy'. Paper delivered at the 2018 IMISCOE annual conference, Barcelona, 2–4 July.
Ciobanu, R. (2015) 'Multiple migration flows of Romanians', *Mobilities*, **10** (3), 466–85.
Cormoș, V.-C. (2017) 'Identity benchmarks and reintegration issues of return migration', *GEOREVIEW: Scientific Annals of Stefan cel Mare University of Suceava*, Geography Series, **28** (1), 32–41.
Coșciug, A. (2019) 'Religion, return migration and change in an emigration country' in R. Anghel, M. Fauser and P. Boccagni (eds), *Transnational Return and Social Change: Hierarchies, Identities and Ideas*, London: Anthem Press, pp. 85–102.
Cybulska, A. (2016) *Praca za Granicą*, Warsaw: Centrum Badania Opinii Społecznej.
CZSO (n.d.) *Foreigners, Total by Citizenship as at 31 December 2018*, Praha: Český Statistický Úřad, https://www.czso.cz/documents/11292/27914491/1812_c01t01.pdf/b03cac12-7eef-419d-a66a-567c97b397ec?version=1.0 (accessed 12 April 2021).
Duda-Mikulin, E. (2018) 'Should I stay or should I go now? Exploring Polish women's returns "home"', *International Migration*, **56** (4), 140–53.
Dzięglewski, M. (2016) 'Return migration and social change in Poland: "closures" to migrants' non-economic transfers', *Central and Eastern European Migration Review*, **5** (2), 167–88.
Dzięglewski, M. (2019) *Powroty do (Nie)Znanego Kraju: Strategie Migrantów Powrotnych*, Krakow: Nomos.
Eade, J., Drinkwater, S. and Garapich, M. (2007) *Class and Ethnicity: Polish Migrants in London*, Guildford: Universities of Surrey and Roehampton.
Eastmond, M. (2006) 'Transnational returns and reconstruction in post-war Bosnia and Herzegovina', *International Migration*, **44** (3), 141–66.
Eurostat (2004) *Unemployment Rates by Sex, Age and Citizenship, First Quarter of 2004*, https://appsso.eurostat.ec.europa.eu/nui/show.do?dataset=lfsa_urgan&lang=en (accessed 13 April 2021).

Fox, J. (2003) 'National identities on the move: Transylvanian Hungarian labour migrants in Hungary', *Journal of Ethnic and Migration Studies*, **29** (3), 449–66.
Gońda, M. (2016) 'Educational mobility as a means of return migration: young Polish diaspora members from the former USSR', *EthnoAnthropoZoom/ЕтноАнтропоЗум*, **15**, 111–47.
Grabowska, I. (2016) *Movers and Stayers: Social Mobility, Migration and Skills*, Frankfurt-am-Main: Peter Lang.
Grabowska, I., Garapich, M., Jaźwińska, E. and Radziwinowiczówna, A. (2017) *Migrants as Agents of Change: Social Remittances in an Enlarged European Union*, Basingstoke: Palgrave Macmillan.
Guma, T. and Jones, R. (2019) '"Where are we going to go now?" European Union migrants' experiences of hostility, anxiety, and (non-)belonging during Brexit', *Population, Space and Place*, **25** (1), e2198.
GUS (2019) *Rocznik Demograficzny 2019*, Warsaw: Główny Urząd Statystyczny.
Ivanova, V. (2015) 'The return migration of highly-qualified workers in Bulgaria and in Bosnia and Herzegovina: policies and returnees' responses', *SEER: Journal for Labour and Social Affairs in Eastern Europe*, **18** (1), 93–111.
Jirka, L. (2019) 'Nationality and rationality: ancestors, "diaspora" and the impact of ethnic policy in the country of emigration on ethnic return migration from Western Ukraine to the Czech Republic', *Central and Eastern European Migration Review*, **8** (1), 117–34.
Joireman, S. (2017) 'Ethnic violence, local security and return migration: enclave communities in Kosovo', *International Migration*, **55** (5), 122–35.
Juverdeanu, C. (2021) 'The different gears of EU citizenship', *Journal of Ethnic and Migration Studies*, **47** (7), 1596–612.
Kaska, V. (2013) 'Emigration from Estonia: recent trends and economic impact' in OECD (ed.), *Coping with Emigration in Baltic and East European Countries*, Paris: OECD Publishing, pp. 30–43.
Kerpaci, K. and Kuka, M. (2019) 'The Greek debt crisis and Albanian return migration', *Journal of Balkan and Near Eastern Studies*, **21** (1), 104–19.
King, R. (2000) 'Generalizations from the history of return migration' in B. Ghosh (ed.), *Return Migration: Journey of Hope or Despair?*, Geneva: International Organization for Migration and United Nations, pp. 7–55.
King, R. (2018) 'Theorising new European youth mobilities', *Population, Space and Place*, **24** (1), e2117.
Kowalska, K. and Pelliccia, A. (2012) 'Wykwalifikowane imigrantki z Polski na włoskim rynku pracy: case study w prowincji Rzymu', *Studia Migracyjne – Przegląd Polonijny*, **38** (3), 73–110.
Krzaklewska, E. (2019) 'Youth, mobility and generations: the meanings and impact of migration and mobility experiences on transitions to adulthood', *Studia Migracyjne–Przegląd Polonijny*, **45** (1), 41–59.
Krzyżowski, Ł. (2013) *Polscy Migranci i ich Starzejący się Rodzice: Transnarodowy System Opieki Międzygeneracyjnej*, Warsaw: Scholar.
Kubal, A. (2015) 'Legal consciousness as a form of social remittance? Studying return migrants' everyday practices of legality in Ukraine', *Migration Studies*, **3** (1), 68–88.
Lapshyna, I. and Düvell, F. (2015) 'Migration, life satisfaction, return and development: the case of a deprived post-Soviet country (Ukraine)', *Migration and Development*, **4** (2), 291–310.
Leontiyeva, Y. (2016) 'Ukrainians in the Czech Republic: on the pathway from temporary foreign workers to one of the largest minority groups' in O. Fedyuk and M. Kindler (eds), *Ukrainian Migration to the European Union: Lessons from Migration Studies*, Amsterdam: IMISCOE/Springer, pp. 133–49.
Levitt, P. (1998) 'Social remittances: migration driven local-level forms of cultural diffusion', *International Migration Review*, **32** (4), 926–48.
Levitt, P. (2001) *The Transnational Villagers*, Berkeley: University of California Press.
Lulle, A. (2014) 'Spaces of encounter-displacement: contemporary labour migrants' return visits to Latvia', *Geografiska Annaler: Series B, Human Geography*, **96** (2), 127–40.
Maslowski, S. (2015) 'The expulsion of European Union citizens from the host member state: legal grounds and practice', *Central and Eastern European Migration Review*, **4** (2), 61–85.
Moreh, C., McGhee, D. and Vlachantoni, A. (2020) 'The return of citizenship? An empirical assessment of legal integration in times of radical sociolegal transformation', *International Migration Review*, **54** (1), 147–76.

Müller, M. (2019) 'Goodbye, postsocialism!', *Europe-Asia Studies*, **71** (4), 533–50.

Neto, F. (2010) 'Re-acculturation attitudes among adolescents from returned Portuguese immigrant families', *International Journal of Intercultural Relations*, **34** (3), 221–32.

Nevinskaitė, L. (2016) 'Social remittances from the professional diaspora: the issue of home-country receptivity', *Central and Eastern European Migration Review*, **5** (2), 135–53.

Nonchev, A. and Hristova, M. (2018) 'Segmentation of returning migrants', *Ikonomicheski izsledvaniya/ Economic Studies*, **27** (2), 3–24.

Oltean, O. (2019) 'Minority institutions, German transnational return migration and social change in Transylvania' in R. Anghel, M. Fauser and P. Boccagni (eds), *Transnational Return and Social Change: Hierarchies, Identities and Ideas*, London: Anthem Press, pp. 43–61.

Parutis, V. (2014) 'Returning "home": East European migrants' discourses of return', *International Migration*, **52** (5), 159–77.

Porobić, S. (2016) 'Bosnian "returnee voices" communicating experiences of successful reintegration: the social capital and sustainable return nexus in Bosnia and Herzegovina', *Südost Europa*, **64** (1), 5–26.

Radziwinowiczówna, A., Rosińska, A. and Kloc-Nowak, W. (2018) *Ethnomorality of Care: Migrants and their Aging Parents*, London: Routledge.

Saar, M. and Saar, E. (2020) 'Can the concept of lifestyle migration be applied to return migration? The case of Estonians in the UK', *International Migration*, **58** (2), 52–65.

Sredanovic, D. (2020) 'Brexit as a trigger and an obstacle to onwards and return migration', *International Migration*, DOI: 10.1111/imig.12712.

Strockmeijer, A., de Beer, P. and Dagevos, J. (2019) 'Should I stay or should I go? What we can learn from working patterns of Central and Eastern European labour migrants about the nature of present-day migration', *Journal of Ethnic and Migration Studies*, **45** (13), 2430–46.

Tomić, C. (2016) 'An easy game? Experiences of "homecoming" in the post-socialist context of Croatia and the Czech Republic' in R. Nadler, Z. Kovacs, B. Glorius and T. Lang (eds), *Return Migration and Regional Development in Europe. Mobility Against the Stream*, Basingstoke: Palgrave Macmillan, pp. 309–30.

Urbańska, S. (2015) *Matka Polka na Odległość. Z Doświadczeń Migracyjnych Robotnic 1989–2010*, Toruń: Nicolaus Copernicus University.

Vathi, Z., Duci, V. and Dhembo, E. (2016) 'Homeland (dis)integrations: educational experience, children and return migration to Albania', *International Migration*, **54** (3), 159–72.

Vlase, I. (2013) 'Women's social remittances and their implications at household level: a case study of Romanian migration to Italy', *Migration Letters*, **10** (1), 81–90.

White, A. (2009) 'Internal migration, identity and livelihood strategies in contemporary Russia', *Journal of Ethnic and Migration Studies*, **35** (4), 555–73.

White, A. (2014) 'Double return migration: failed returns to Poland leading to settlement abroad and new transnational strategies', *International Migration*, **52** (6), 72–84.

White, A. (2017) *Polish Families and Migration Since EU Accession*, Bristol: Policy Press (2nd edition).

White, A. and Grabowska, I. (2019) 'Social remittances and social change in Central and Eastern Europe', *Central and Eastern European Migration Review*, **8** (1), 33–50.

White, A., Grabowska, I., Kaczmarczyk, P. and Slany, K. (2018) *The Impact of Migration on Poland: EU Mobility and Social Change*, London: UCL Press.

Zaiceva, A. and Zimmermann, K. (2016) 'Returning home at times of trouble? Return migration of EU enlargement migrants during the crisis' in M. Kahanec and K. Zimmermann (eds), *Labor Migration, EU Enlargement, and the Great Recession*, Berlin: Springer, pp. 397–418.

Zareva, I. (2018) 'Returning migrants: effects on the labour market in Bulgaria', *Ikonomicheski izsledvaniya/Economic Studies*, **27** (2), 102–14.

# PART IV

# RETURN MIGRATION AND DEVELOPMENT

# 22. Exploring the return migration and development nexus

*Russell King*

## INTRODUCTION

When migrants return to their country of origin, what is their developmental impact? This apparently straightforward question begets many others. How is this impact to be measured and evaluated? How could the impact be increased and maximised? Under what conditions do the migrants return – voluntarily or coerced in some way? What are the returnees' socio-economic and demographic characteristics? Are they positively or negatively selected from the pool of emigrants? Is there an optimum length of time as an emigrant to bring the best developmental results on return? This list of questions is not exhaustive but serves to illustrate the complexities involved when trying to analyse the 'return–development nexus'.

The parameters of the chapter are as follows: it is mainly concerned with international migration between relatively poor countries of origin – to which the return takes place – and relatively rich countries of destination – from which the return originates. The focus is on return as a voluntary or semi-voluntary act and not on forced repatriation. In terms of the chapter's relationship to the rest of the Handbook, this can be framed telescopically in two directions. Macroscopically, Jackline Wahba's Chapter 2 on the economics of return provides a broad lens within which my account here can be viewed. At the other end of the viewfinder, this chapter's overview of the return–development nexus does not deal with two more specific aspects of the relationship between return and development – on diaspora return and knowledge transfer and on return migration and entrepreneurship. These are the subjects of the following two chapters, by Charlotte Mueller and Giulia Sinatti, respectively.

This chapter contains three main sections. In the first, with its multiple subsections, return migration's role in the migration–development nexus is appraised. This section is mainly theoretical, based on a range of interpretations of how return migration can be viewed within wider economic theories of migration. The second section of the chapter delves into typologies of return and how the differing types and mechanisms of return can be related to different development outcomes. Key here are the various motives that shape return decisions, including push and pull factors operating in inverse fashion to the push–pull factors shaping the original migration. The third section reviews selected case studies ranging across a variety of geographic contexts, from early studies in Southern Europe and the Caribbean to more recent evidence in Africa and elsewhere. The lesson here is that the developmental impact of return is highly contingent on the time, place and circumstances of return. This finding is reiterated in the conclusion, which summarises the key arguments of the chapter.

Throughout the chapter, there is an 'elephant in the room'. What is meant by development? There is no space here for a full discussion but some guidelines are surely necessary. In its mainstream, 'common sense' definition, development is an overall improvement of living conditions. Historically, the conceptualisation of development has evolved from early postwar concerns with the simple measurement of economic growth, through considerations of basic needs and poverty reduction, to notions of sustainable livelihoods. The concept of *human development* has taken root, to incorporate more qualitative aspects of life such as security, freedom and choice, as well as taking on board the measurement of various dimensions of inequality. Much of this derives from Amartya Sen's landmark *Development as Freedom* (1999), which argues that development should be about expanding people's *capability* to control their own lives and have access to key resources for an enjoyable and satisfying life. These resources comprise economic capital (income and assets), social capital (connections to other people via friendships, relationships and social networks) and human or cultural capital (knowledge, skills, ideas etc.). This 'capabilities approach' applies both to migration (having the ability and choice to migrate or not, including return) and to the ability to materialise the benefits of migration, including, again, after return. This does no more than summarise the conceptualisation of development in a migration context (for more nuance, see Castles, 2009; de Haas, 2010; Geiger and Pécoud, 2013; Lucas, 2005; Raghuram, 2009). One critical problem remains and echoes throughout this chapter: how to measure the specific contribution of return migration to whatever development, however defined, is taking place.

## RETURN MIGRATION AS PART OF THE MIGRATION–DEVELOPMENT NEXUS

Early discussions on the relationship between migration and development were inconclusive about the significance and directionality of the linkages; indeed, the relationship was explicitly defined as 'unsettled' (Papademetriou and Martin, 1991) and subject to discrepancies between 'myths' and 'realities' (Appleyard, 1989). The complexity and multidimensionality of migration's relationship with development were reimagined in an important collection of papers edited by Van Hear and Sørensen (2003) entitled *The Migration–Development Nexus*. In their state-of-the-art overview paper, Sørensen et al. saw return as the 'natural end-product' of the migration cycle, and the standard development-inducing hypothesis was advanced that 'migrants are expected to have saved capital and acquired skills abroad that can be productively invested in the sending country' (2003, p.14). Later in the same article, the authors made a distinction between low-skilled migrants returning after a short period abroad – who are unlikely to contribute much to development – and return after a longer stay abroad, during which the migrant has been able to accumulate some capital to meet development needs, such as building a better home or investing in a business (2003, p.24).

Since Van Hear and Sørensen's introduction of the term, the migration–development nexus has been taken forward and subjected to further scrutiny. Among the angles explored have been viewing the nexus through a transnational lens (Faist, 2008; Faist and Fauser, 2011), looking at its gendered aspects (Bailey, 2010; Bastia, 2013; Dannecker, 2009), highlighting a temporal perspective (Levitt and Lamba-Nieves, 2013) and exposing the migration–development nexus as a political and social construction, which reflects the ideologies and priorities of 'Western' neoliberal policies of development (Delgado Wise and Márquez Covarrubias, 2011; Geiger and Pécoud, 2013; Raghuram, 2009).

One of the consistent features of these writings has been a more critical perspective on the 'mantra' of migrant remittances as an effective instrument of individual initiative and 'development from below'. Rahel Kunz (2008) pointedly asked: Are remittances really so 'beautiful'? It is true that, during the 'remittances decade' of the 2000s, the volume of remittances grew exponentially until the onset of the global economic crisis. However, the dominance of remittances in the migration–development debate downplayed the role of return migration for the simple reason that, for remittances to flow, migrants have to stay abroad. Return halts the sending of remittances.

## How Is Return Migration Seen by Economic Theories?

As Cassarino (2004) has cogently pointed out in his well-cited paper on theorising return migration, different economic frameworks yield different interpretations of return. In the neoclassical model, whereby individuals move in order to maximise their income-earning capacity and act on the basis of perfect information on job opportunities, wages and the costs and benefits of migration (Todaro, 1969), there is no place for return migration. Those who do return, according to the neoclassical logic, are 'failures' who miscalculated the costs and benefits, which contradicts the assumption of perfect information.

Modifications of the neoclassical approach point to three circumstances which 'allow' return to take place whilst still respecting orthodox economic principles (Dustmann and Weiss, 2007; Lucas, 2005, pp.231–2). The first is that migrants may want to benefit from cost-of-living differences and the higher purchasing power of their foreign earnings in the home country, especially for the consumption patterns which they value the most – for example food, land, accommodation, personal services and so on. The second is the possibility of accumulating financial capital abroad which can be productively invested in a business venture back home. Finally, return may be motivated by the higher returns at home on the skills and training received abroad.

As a significant modification to neoclassical migration theory, the 'new economics of labour migration' (NELM) framework posits an entirely different role for return. Return is intrinsic to the NELM model which is based not on individual migratory behaviour but on the family or household as the fundamental decision-making unit (Stark, 1991; Taylor, 1999). In this optic, families in poor countries have to worry not only about earning an income but also about how to manage risks such as crop failure due to adverse weather or a market-price collapse for their product. One or more members of the family is thus encouraged to migrate in order to secure an income, either sent back as remittances or saved for investment back home. Once the target is achieved, return can take place, although this does not preclude another migration episode at a later date, by the same or by a different member of the household (Constant and Massey, 2002). Rather than failures, returnees in the 'new economics' model are seen as successes.

Macroeconomic changes over time may also stimulate return migration. This illustrates the two-way cause–effect relationship inherent in the return–development nexus. In other words, it is not so much the issue of how return migration can generate development – which is the main question underpinning this chapter – but, rather, the various ways in which development in the home country can attract migrants back. For instance, the development of tourism or industry in the country of origin or the discovery of an important mineral resource may offer improved employment and income opportunities, leading migrants to return. Tourist development in the Mediterranean countries of Southern Europe and in several Caribbean islands has been an important factor in turning them from emigration countries in the 1950s and 1960s into countries of net return migration and immigration from the 1980s on (for the case of Greece, see Fakiolas and King, 1996).

On the other side of the push–pull return coin, there is an abundant literature on the effects of the global economic crisis on migration. Much of this is tangential to the main purpose of this chapter. However, Ghosh (2013, pp.92–7, 142–3) gives a useful historical account of how major global and regional recessions have provoked waves of return migration, including the Great Depression of the 1930s, the oil crisis of 1973–74, the Gulf War of 1990–91 and, in more detail, the global recession in the years following 2008. More localised studies of crisis-triggered return show that, unless they were temporary migrants intending to return anyway, most migrants who were negatively affected by the crisis were reluctant to return. This unwillingness was related to two factors: the economic situation in their home countries, which offered them little prospect of a satisfactory life; and the ongoing process of their family's social stabilisation abroad (Bastia, 2011; Boccagni and Lagomarsino, 2011). On the whole, the developmental impact of crisis-driven return migration has been minimal.

Marxist economics and its derivatives constitute the final economic prism through which return can be viewed. Return does not feature prominently in Marxist and historical-structural framings of migration but the general message is as follows. The current global capitalist system, moving through its Fordist to its post-Fordist restructuring and neoliberal phases over the postwar decades and feeding off and reinforcing spatially uneven development at various scales, ruthlessly exploits 'unfree' supplies of migrant labour. In the words of Delgado Wise and Márquez Covarrubias, 'migration appears [both] as an expression of uneven development and [as] a structural pillar of imperialist [in the sense of capitalist monopoly power] strategies intended to weaken and cheapen the labour force at a global level' (2011, p.57).

Where does return fit into the Marxist political economy model? There is something of a silence on this issue. By inference we can suggest that return takes place when the workers are no longer needed – as in a major recession – or when the workers themselves become unproductive – too old, sick or exhausted. Based on a study of North African migrant workers in the French automobile industry, Samers (1999) used the term 'spatial vent' to denote the mechanism by which 'unwanted' or 'difficult-to-manage' migrant workers are expelled when they threaten the process of capitalist accumulation. Such 'excess' labour is subject to either forced repatriation or incentivised 'return-bonus' schemes. The home countries derive little benefit from these semi-forced returns of surplus, mostly low-skilled, workers.

**Unpacking the Migration–Development Nexus: Competing Visions**

The migration–development nexus can be regarded as a discursive arena for many competing ideas and policies. Delgado Wise and Márquez Covarrubias (2009, p.89) set out two opposing interpretations of the nexus: as a virtuous circle and as a vicious one.

Under the *virtuous* version, migration, including return, is seen as beneficial for development all round. The fabled win–win–win scenario foretells a triple pay-off. The *host country* benefits from the extra supply of ready-made workers for which it has not had to bear the costs of reproduction. This labour is available to drive the economy forward, filling both the low-grade jobs rejected by the 'native' workers and staunching critical gaps in high-skilled professions such as IT and medicine. The *sending country* benefits from being able to export its surplus labour, thereby avoiding the costs of unemployment, whilst also recouping remittances sent by the migrants. Finally, the *migrants* benefit from their access to employment and income and the capability to improve their own and their families' lives. In this positive scenario, when migrants return they contribute various kinds of capital to the development of their home countries: financial capital in the form of savings and accumulated remittances; human capital in the shape of enhanced skills and training acquired abroad; and a more progressive and development-oriented set of attitudes and behaviours, termed by Levitt (1998) as social remittances.

The *vicious* cycle represents the opposite view. Migration and development are cast as antithetical; instead, the nexus is between migration and *under*development. Incapable of inducing development dynamics in the place of origin through return migration, remittances and other feedback loops, migration is associated with adverse effects such as forced displacement, depopulation, brain drain and productive collapse, all of which lead to cumulative underdevelopment and further emigration. The intellectual heritage of the vicious circle argument can be traced to theories of cumulative causation (Myrdal, 1957), dependency theory (Frank, 1967) and the long-term historical articulation of the world economy into a dominant core whose economically hegemonic status is continually reinforced by exploitative ties – including migration – over the periphery (Wallerstein, 1974). In this scenario there is only one winner from the triple-win hypothesis – the host country. The sending countries and the migrants lose out.

**Optimism, Pessimism and Pendulum Swings**

The two competing theoretical frameworks outlined above have found favour at different times over the past 60 years or so, such that their waxing and waning popularity can be likened to the swings of a pendulum. Guided by four key papers (de Haas, 2010, 2012; Faist, 2008; Gamlen, 2014), four phases can be delineated: optimism, pessimism, neo-optimism and neo-pessimism. The optimistic view of the migration–development nexus, which includes a positive role for return migration, reflects the principles of the virtuous circle, whilst the pessimistic view draws on elements of the vicious circle, where return plays a minor or even a negative developmental role.

*Optimistic* views of migration's contribution to development held sway during the labour-migration boom of the 1950s, 1960s and early 1970s, especially in Western Europe. Following the economic equilibrium model (cf. Todaro, 1969), migration was seen as a strategy for achieving balanced growth by transferring workers from mostly poor, labour-surplus regions and countries to those richer economies which were short of labour to fill jobs in construction, manufacturing, hospitals and public services. For the sending countries in Southern Europe and former colonies in Africa, Asia and the Caribbean, the belief was that return migration would stimulate growth through savings invested in agriculture, business and industry and through the return of human capital enhanced by training abroad (Kindleberger, 1967).

From about 1970 until the early 1990s, a more *pessimistic* view took hold, especially after the oil crisis radically upset the nature and scale of the demand for migrant workers. The 'pessimism turn' had both ideological foundations – outlined above in the discussion on the vicious circle – and was fuelled by a range of disappointments based on empirical evidence. Castles and Kosack (1973) documented the widespread exploitation of migrant workers, their inadequate housing, lack of access to civic rights and the racism and discrimination they endured. Sending countries suffered not only from the loss of young manual workers (a 'brawn drain') but also from a 'brain drain' of their highly educated professionals who could pursue more lucrative careers abroad and who were actively recruited and siphoned off by richer countries. International migration, rather than being an equilibrating mechanism between labour-surplus and labour-shortage countries, seemed only to have exacerbated the inequalities and dependencies between emigration and immigration countries (Papademetriou and Martin, 1991, p.2). Conspicuous and wasteful consumption, rather than productive investment, became the dominant trope applied to the way remittances were used (see Rhoades, 1978 on Southern Spain) and returning migrants either came back with no skills (since they had been doing unskilled manual jobs) or with skills that could not be used in the country of origin (Gamlen, 2014, p.584).

The migration landscape changed again in the 1990s, signalled in the title of Castles and Miller's well-known text, *The Age of Migration*, whose first edition was published in 1993, and by the launching of the 'migration–development nexus' by Van Hear and Sørensen in 2003.[1] New forms of migration – including circular migration, seasonal worker migration and cross-border shuttling – and the ideological imprint of the new economics of migration created a renewed impetus for considering migration's developmental impact in a more positive light – *neo-optimism*. According to Brønden (2012), 'migration and development' became 'the flavour of the 2000s', even if some of the rhetorical claims of a win–win–win scenario were dismissed as 'buzz and spin' (Vammen and Brønden, 2012, pp.27–8). As well as the popularity of the NELM approach, with its strong focus on the 'development-from-below' effects of remittances, other key concepts shaped migration and development thinking in the 1990s and 2000s. These included transnationalism (Glick Schiller et al., 1995; Vertovec, 1999), social remittances (Levitt, 1998), and co-development (Faist, 2008). All of them implied increased contact, including return, with the migrants' place of origin; they are considered in more detail in the next subsection.

By the end of the 2000s, coincident with but not necessarily triggered by the global economic crisis, the pendulum was showing signs of swinging to its fourth phase, *neo-pessimism*. This was flagged first by de Haas (2012, p.22), suggesting that 'we might be heading towards a neo-pessimistic backswing of the migration and development pendulum'. Writing two years later, Gamlen (2014, p.586) is more categorical about 'the new pessimism', based partly on disillusionment over migration's impact in the countries of origin and partly on its associated 'hidden agenda' of neoliberal economic reform and immigration control, including the forced or incentivised return of migrants to where they allegedly 'naturally belong' – in their 'home countries'. According to Castles (2011, p.311), the neoliberal ideology of economic efficiency and shared prosperity, to which migration would make its contribution, is a myth. In reality, it 'masks the exploitation of labour on a global scale ... The neoliberal dream is dualistic: a cosmopolitan, mobile world for elites; a world of exploitation ... and differentiation on the criteria of gender, race, ethnicity, origins and legal status ... for the rest.'

## Other Perspectives on Development and Return: Transnationalism, Co-development and Social Remittances

Moving on from the ideological and policy swings of optimism and pessimism, neoliberalism and structuralism and virtuous and vicious circles, there are three other conceptual frameworks within which aspects of the migration–development nexus can be considered, including situations of return.

Thomas Faist (2008, p.26) writes that 'the migration and development story' is really about *transnationalism* and the emergence of migrants as 'transnational agents' in the development process. Alongside remittances as the key element of 'economic transnationalism' (Guarnizo,

2003), return migration and other return mobilities such as periodic visits can be seen as a way of transferring resources across borders to the place of origin. In the case of villages and rural towns in the homeland, development means raising household incomes, improving infrastructure and the enhanced provision of social goods such as health and education. This makes the scale of transnational connections essentially *translocal*. Hometown associations, whereby migrants from a common origin form a collective group, often with philanthropic aims, are an example of translocal development. *Co-development* implies a broader-scale collaboration between migrants, returnees and local populations in sending countries. Like hometown associations, co-development is a somewhat nebulous concept, with varying emphases on remittances, aid, investment, return and knowledge transfer (Faist, 2008, pp.26, 39). Often, it is administered at an inter-state level, as between Spain and Morocco (Boni and Lacomba, 2011).

The concept of *social remittances* – the flow of ideas and practices back to the country of migrants' origin (Levitt, 1998) – makes a significant contribution to unpacking the return–development nexus. Unlike financial remittances, which are dependent on the migrants' ongoing presence abroad to be sustained, social remittances are often brought back by the migrants when they return, either to resettle for good or for shorter-term stays or visits. Unlike financial remittances, which are also relentlessly quantified, social remittances are a qualitative approach to migrant-actioned development.

Vari-Lavoisier (2020, p.125) judges that the optic of social remittances has 'generated original empirical studies and stimulated a productive conversation' within the linked fields of migration, development, transnationalism and return. Yet, there are limitations. First, how can the impact of these social transfers be measured? Second, there are inevitable value-judgements involved in deciding whether social remittances imply positive or negative change in home-country societies and therefore whether they are 'good' for development. Third, the contours of social remittances are unclear. Subsequent research has tended to extend the concept to include, for example, political remittances and to explore the interfaces between social and economic remittances. These are productive expansions of the concept. Political remittances are not just about voting patterns (which can be quantified) but also about ideas of democracy and good governance (see Paasche, Chapter 13). The interconnection between social and financial remittances has been explored by Mata-Codesal (2013), working on the hypothesis that social changes amongst migrants and returnees shape the ways in which remittances are used – less on wasteful consumption and more on productive investment.

## DIFFERENT TYPES OF RETURN PRODUCE DIFFERENT DEVELOPMENT OUTCOMES

The impact of social remittances and other components of return migration is crucially dependent on events shaping the earlier parts of the migration trajectory – the motives guiding the original migration, the length of time spent abroad, the experiences accrued there and the reasons for the return. Some of these elements are incorporated into the developmental model of return migration proposed by Francesco Cerase (1970, 1974) some 50 years ago. This framework remains influential and has been widely quoted, despite its obvious shortcomings.

Cerase sets out a four-stage model based on the time spent abroad prior to the return, the empirical reference-point being return migration from the United States to Southern Italy. The first stage represents the *failure* of the migration project. The migrant fails to adapt to the new life of the destination, return-migrates rather quickly and is reabsorbed into the home-country society with little or no developmental impact. The second stage of return occurs after a few or several years and consists of those who invested their savings 'conservatively', in land and housing, according to the traditional values of rural Southern Italy. This is Cerase's *return of conservatism*, named thus because the returnee has not adopted many of the behavioural norms or social networks of the host society but has remained faithful to those of the origin country. Longer-stay migrants abroad become progressively integrated and attuned to the ways and values of the host country; they might also become economically successful and accumulate significant sums of capital. Nevertheless, the ideology of return never goes away and the migrant eventually, typically after ten years or more (Cerase, 1970, p.224), decides to take these experiences, capital and value-systems back to the home country and forge what is in effect a new life there. This, in Cerase's scheme, is the *return of innovation* – the most favourable outcome developmentally but also, in Cerase's view, the most elusive, not least because entrenched power structures in Southern Italian society tend to stifle innovation (1970, pp.233–7; 1974, pp.258–9). Migrants who stay abroad more than 20 years are either unlikely to return at all or likely to return only upon *retirement*, in which case they seek to live out their final years in the peace and quiet of the home town or village.

There are two main shortcomings of the Cerase model. The first is that it is deterministic, based on the length of time spent in the destination country. It assumes a one-dimensional linear relationship between time, the process of integration, the stages of return and the development effects. Second, it fails to unpack the integration process into its constituent elements; this is hardly surprising since research on the multifaceted nature of integration was in its infancy when Cerase published his research.

Subsequent research has gone some way to addressing these problems, with some findings conflicting with those of Cerase. For instance, in a paper on the return intentions (note: not the actual return) of Moroccan migrants in Europe (N =2,832), de Haas et al. (2015) found that structural integration in terms of labour-market participation and education did *not* significantly influence return intentions. Return intentions *were* positively related to social and economic ties to Morocco (as expected) and negatively related to socio-cultural integration in the host countries, in terms of marriage, friendship networks and the subjective evaluation of belonging. Somewhat similar results were found by de Haas and Fokkema (2011) for African migrants in Spain and Italy (N = 1,883). Socio-cultural integration had a strongly negative effect on return intentions, whereas economic integration had either no effect or a weakly positive one on intention to return. Return intentions, in this study, were not significantly affected by respondents' age or length of stay abroad. Further complexity emerges from Carling and Pettersen's (2014) analysis of the return intentions of various migrant groups in Norway, set against what these authors call the integration–transnationalism matrix.

These contradictory and nuanced results indicate that there is no simple model or mechanism of return migration. Different groups return for different reasons, under different circumstances and exhibit different outcomes in terms of reintegration and impulses for development. Given the lack of research data which tie these variations to concrete development effects in the countries to which the migrants return, the following should be regarded as propositions which either cannot be verified or are supported by partial or even conflicting data.

An initial obvious distinction is between voluntary return and forced repatriation, recognising that these polar opposites obscure many intermediate situations (see Erdal and Oeppen, Chapter 5). Especially when voluntary return reflects the achievements of target migrants, return can be summarily judged a 'success' and the target (typically a sum of money saved) can be used to improve the household's social and economic wellbeing in the country of origin. This mechanism is consistent with the NELM model (Taylor, 1999). A similar conclusion applies to schemes of circular migration, such as seasonal agricultural workers, seen as another variant of the NELM framework and an example of the fabled 'triple-win' outcome (Constant et al., 2013). This may be an optimistic characterisation, given the low wages paid to such workers, their indebtedness to labour brokers and their harsh living and working conditions (see, e.g., Gertel and Sippel, 2014). Often, circular migration is a strategy of survival and poverty alleviation rather than a route to higher-level development (Skeldon, 2012).

Where migrants are forced to return, for instance as failed asylum-seekers or as migrants deemed to be in an irregular situation, the impact on home-country development is likely to be minimal or even negative because of their costs of unemployment and welfare support. To give an example, Kleist (2020) found that involuntary returnees to Ghana fell into three groups: those who were worse off than before they departed, those who were intent on re-emigrating and a minority who succeeded in achieving some socio-economic progress.

Another common circumstance is where legal migrants' migration cycle is 'interrupted' by unforeseen circumstances, such as unemployment due to a recession, illness or injury or a family emergency in the home country. The return takes place in a hurried and unplanned fashion (Cassarino, 2016). In this situation, too, conditions may not be favourable for the returnees to make a tangible contribution to the development of their home community.

Some of the aforementioned speaks to another important conditioning factor for a successful return – returnees' *preparedness* (Cassarino, 2004, pp.271–5; 2008, pp.101–3). Preparedness, according to Cassarino, breaks down into several components: the desire of migrants to return home, their readiness to return – especially their mobilisation of the necessary resources (financial capital, relevant skills, social contacts etc.) – and their knowledge assessment of suitable conditions in the home country. Preparedness applies not only to the returnees but also to the country and the individual locales where they resettle. If there is a large number of returnees and they are highly concentrated within a short time-span, the effects can be of two kinds: either the returnees form a 'critical mass' able to bring about change or the numbers may be overwhelming, leading to difficulties finding employment and accommodation (Bovenkerk, 1974). Evidence of both of these outcomes can be observed with the mass migration of the Portuguese *retornados* from Angola and Mozambique in the wake of these former Portuguese colonies' independence in the mid-1970s. Estimates of the scale of the influx of *retornados* range from 450,000 up to 1 million, the latter figure equivalent to one in ten of the Portuguese population (Lewis and Williams, 1986).

Is there an optimum length of stay abroad or an optimum age at return, in order to maximise returnees' development potential? The study by de Haas and Fokkema (2011) cited above failed to find significant answers to these questions but logic suggests otherwise. Cerase (1970, p.224) suggested 10-plus years for 'innovative' return. Other writers frame the argument in the following terms: an optimum length of absence should be where the period is long enough to enable the migrants to accrue financial, social and human capital and to absorb certain experiences and values, yet sufficiently short that the returnee still has time and energy to utilise the acquired investment capital, skills and attitudes (King, 1986, p.19). Age-wise, returnees should be old enough to have mobilised these resources but young enough to pursue their goals and use their capital to foster home-country development (Lang et al., 2016, p.12).

A final question concerns the selectivity of returnees. Are they the successes or the failures amongst the migrants? Wahba answers this question in Chapter 2 of the Handbook but it is worth re-summarising here. The answer depends on the type of selectivity operating in the initial migration flow. If migrants are positively selected on the basis of skills and education upon departure, the more successful will stay on in the host country and the lesser-skilled will return. Conversely, if emigrants are negatively selected from the home-country population, return migrants will represent a positive selection of the migrants abroad (cf. Borjas and Bratsberg, 1996). However, in a final twist to the story, it is theoretically possible that the 'failures' are more successful than the 'successes' because they are selected from migrant populations with different overall skill profiles. A negative selection of returnees from a pool of high-skilled migrants could be more skilled than a positive selection of returnees from a low-skilled migrant group.

## RETURN MIGRATION AND DEVELOPMENT: EMPIRICAL EVIDENCE

It is impossible to cite all the case studies which examine return migration's impact on development. Instead, I summarise clusters of literature regionally, selecting a few examples for each area.

Much of the early research on return migration was done in *Southern Europe*, based on the return of long-stay migrants in North America (Cerase, 1974; Gilkey, 1967; Saloutos, 1956) and, slightly later, the return of 'guestworkers' from Northern Europe in the wake of the 1973 oil crisis (Böhning, 1975; King, 1979; King et al., 1986; Lewis and Williams, 1986; Rhoades, 1978). The Southern European experience highlights two issues with regards to the development potential of return migration. One is the fact that most migrants originated from rural areas. Typically, they were agricultural workers – peasants and farm labourers – from poverty-stricken villages and agricultural towns. Linked by kinship and emotional ties, these were the places to which migrants returned but such settlements are not fertile environments for economic development, with their often isolated locations and shrinking populations due to continued outmigration. The second issue is closely linked to the first: the vast majority of these postwar labour migrants were poorly educated and their work experiences abroad – as manual labourers on construction sites or in factories – did nothing to enhance their human capital. The result is that returnees to Southern European rural areas brought little developmental impetus, beyond setting up small, economically marginal businesses such as shops and bars. They had little interest in returning to farming – except as a hobby or to buy land to rent out – and the scale of their ambitions and skills did not extend to industrial development. An exception occurred in coastal locations where tourism was developing: returnees were able to invest in small hotels, rooms-for-rent and other tourism-related services (e.g. King et al., 1984).

Visually, the main impact made by returnees in rural areas has been the building of new homes as a self-declaration of their success as migrants. Such houses have ambiguous implications for local development, as Boccagni (2020) observes. On the one hand, they are criticised for being an example of conspicuous consumption and a waste of investment capital that could have been put to more productive use (e.g. Rhoades, 1978). On the other, they may create some employment for local construction workers and traders in building supplies and can act as a platform for the migrant family's engagement in other forms of social and economic development (Boccagni, 2020, p.259).

A second important global arena for return migration has been the *Caribbean*, the source area for large-scale emigration to the UK in the early postwar decades, with parallel migration streams channelled along colonial lines to France and the Netherlands. Subsequently, the United States became an important destination for Caribbean migrants. Most of the research on return migration and development has been on the anglophone Caribbean, especially Jamaica (Nutter, 1986; Thomas-Hope, 1999) and Barbados (Gmelch, 1987, 1992). Also important is the extensive body of research led by Potter (see Potter, 2005; Potter and Phillips, 2006; Potter et al., 2005), much of which focuses on Barbados and the return of second-generation 'Bajan-Brits'.

Two things differentiate the Caribbean return experience from that of Southern Europe and many other settings. The first is the strong development of the economy in many Caribbean territories during the period intervening between the departure of the emigrants and their return. Tourism has been the main driver of this development, aided by the growth of industry in the larger islands as well as financial services and mineral exploitation. The second element is the combined influence of language and postcolonialism. Migration and return took place largely within the circuits of British colonialism and its postcolonial heritage, united by the English language and the British education system. The combination of these factors made it easier for returnees to find good employment and business opportunities and even to exploit their 'British' accents and other aspects of their subjective cultural capital (work ethic, professionalism, punctuality etc.). Generational differences are also noted: retirees bring in substantial capital in the form of savings and pensions but are not generally economically active (except in the sense that their capital circulates in the economy), whereas younger returnees, including the second generation (who, born abroad, are not technically 'returnees'), are more active as employees and entrepreneurs.

*Sub-Saharan Africa* has been a third area for empirical research on return and development; most of this work has been more recent. A major study was completed by Ammassari (2009), based on skilled returns to Ghana and the Ivory Coast. Ammassari hypothesised that 'migrants acquire different forms of capital abroad, which are of use back home; and furthermore that the transfer of these resources has positive development implications in their country of origin' (2009, p.117). Although there are variations between the two countries, the hypothesis is broadly upheld. Ghanaians were generally more effective in stimulating home-country development: they had been abroad longer on average and had acquired higher-level professional qualifications as well as a stronger entrepreneurial spirit. In a parallel study drawn from the same project,[2] Black and Castaldo (2009) confirm the greater success of Ghanaians over Ivorians in post-return business development. Ammassari suggests an optimum duration of absence to maximise the acquisition of various forms of capital – approximately five years. Migrants who stay abroad longer face more difficulties on return (2009, pp.149, 300).

The European Union (EU)-funded MAFE project, 'Migration between Africa and Europe', looked at migration from Ghana, Senegal and the Democratic Republic of Congo (DRC) to Europe, including return migration. Papers from this project give insights into the process and effects of return (Flahaux, 2015; González-Ferrer et al., 2014; Mezger Kveder and Beauchemin, 2015). Amongst key findings are the confirmation that African migration to Europe is primarily a migration of skills but there is evidence not just of brain drain (i.e. non-return) but also of brain waste (i.e. deskilling abroad) as well as brain circulation and return. Those who migrated to study are more likely to return than those who migrated for other reasons – for instance, Congolese who left for political reasons are much less likely to return. Although situations of forced return, for instance of Ghanaians from Libya (Kleist, 2020), generate weak development impacts, MAFE survey data reveal that voluntary return leads to more positive economic outcomes: 70 per cent of the returnees surveyed took up an economic activity after return (those who did not were either retired, unemployed or carers and home-makers). The most important post-return economic status was 'self-employed', a broad category ranging from dynamic entrepreneur to a 'street-trader' survival strategy of last resort following failure to secure any other kind of job. The ambiguity in findings is reflected in the case of Senegal. Whilst Diatta and Mbow (1999) are optimistic about return migration's contribution to development, Sinatti (2015) gives a much more nuanced assessment. She questions the feasibility of the win–win–win scenario, pointing out that Western countries which push this interpretation are also following a policy of promoting return and dampening pressures for further 'unwanted' immigration.

A final source for empirical research on the return–development nexus in Africa is the important edited collection by Åkesson and Baaz (2015), which has chapters on the DRC, Somaliland, Senegal, Burundi and Cape Verde. Most of these case studies focus on business development and they are reviewed and summarised by Sinatti in Chapter 24 of this Handbook. The title of the book by Åkesson and Baaz posits return migrants as 'Africa's new developers'. Whilst not overlooking the many achievements which returnees have made in different countries, the editors and authors cast doubt on the celebratory story of return migration and development. Like Sinatti (2015), Åkesson and Baaz also point out (2015, pp.4–5) that neoliberal policies present migrants as proactive agents of development in their countries of origin through a combination of sending remittances, then returning with money ready to invest and with new ideas and entrepreneurial skills. These are utopian hopes, for two main reasons. First, they ignore the structural constraints operating in the countries of origin, which may block and subvert the initiatives of the returning migrants. Second, is it morally fair to impose on migrants the responsibility for kick-starting their home countries' development process?

Empirical research on return migration and development in other parts of the world is more scattered, with correspondingly varied results. A few examples round off this empirical overview. Studies of contract migration from South Asia (Pakistan, Kerala and Sri Lanka; see Arif and Irfan, 1997; Athukorala, 1990; Nair, 1999) to the Gulf and the Middle East reveal the potential for this kind of migration – especially when it lasts more than a few years – to sustain families back home and enable progress to occur in agriculture and in the establishment of small businesses. However, this type of model implies prolonged separation between the migrant worker and the rest of the family, which questions whether this is 'development' in the broad, social meaning of the term. For Ecuador, Abainza and Calfat (2018) confirm the finding noted above from Boccagni (2020) that the investment of savings brought back by returnees and put into housing improves the quality of life and also acts as a platform for broader developmental initiatives, building on work skills learnt abroad. Jones (2011) also uncovers positive findings for development in his study of the local economic impact of returnees in the Valle Alto region of Bolivia. Comparing return households (where at least one member had returned) with 'active migrant' households (where one or more members was working abroad) and with non-migrant households, he found that the return households invested more in the local economy than the other two household types. This was explained by returnees' greater saved capital, their local embeddedness and their use of social remittances.

## CONCLUSION

Given the inconsistency of evidence, conclusions about return migration's contribution to development are hard to draw, beyond the obvious point that the effects are dependent on context – the development standards of the countries involved, the skill levels and other capital endowments of the returnees, their demographic profile and length of absence, their motivations both for the original migration and the return and the political and social receptiveness of the country of return to incoming migrants' developmental potential. Ghosh (1996, p.103) points out that the benefit of return migration through skills transfer can only be met if three conditions are fulfilled: first, that migrants return home with new skills that are more productive than those which they would have learned at home; second, the skills from abroad are useful to the needs of the home country; and third, returnees must have the willingness and the opportunity to use the skills on return. Savings and remittances may enable returned migrants and their families to achieve a measure of prosperity compared both to their economic situation before migration and to their non-migrant peers but does this contribute to the development of their community and country of origin? An improvement in returnees' socio-economic status may do little more than make the distribution of income more unequal and therefore fuel the desire to migrate amongst more local people.

Returnees comprise both 'successes' and 'failures' but most are somewhere in between. Having said that, the criteria for 'success' are not clear-cut. Contribution to economic development is one criterion but there are others, such as the notion of 'sustainable return', interpreted either as the avoidance of the need to re-emigrate or as the ability to achieve a sustainable livelihood with freedom of choice (Black and Gent, 2006; Nzima et al., 2017; van Houte and Davids, 2008; see also Marino and Lietaert, Chapter 12).

Perhaps the most consistent finding, noted by many authors who synthesise the debate on return migration's role in origin-country development (see, inter alia, Davids and van Houte, 2008; Ghosh, 1996; King, 1986; Swanson, 1979) is that, in order for this exogenous stimulus to development to be effective, the conditions in the home country must be favourable. This means profitable investment opportunities, a stable and growth-oriented economic system, the ability of the returnees to become fully re-embedded socially and, arguably the most important of all, a stable and corruption-free political environment.

## NOTES

1. Their 2003 book was actually a repackaging of papers published in the journal *International Migration* the previous year.
2. This was the Transrede project ('Transnational Migration, Return and Development in West Africa'), funded by the UK's Department for International Development and based at the Sussex Centre for Migration Research, University of Sussex, 2001–03.

# REFERENCES

Abainza, L. and Calfat, G. (2018) 'How sweet home: embracing the return to returnees' migration', *Migration and Development*, **7** (3), 366–87.

Åkesson, L. and Baaz, M.E. (eds) (2015) *Africa's Return Migrants: The New Developers?*, London: Zed Books.

Ammassari, S. (2009) *Migration and Development: Factoring Return into the Equation*, Newcastle upon Tyne: Cambridge Scholars Publishing.

Appleyard, R.T. (1989) 'Migration and development: myths and reality', *International Migration Review*, **23** (3), 486–99.

Arif, G.M. and Irfan, M. (1997) 'Return migration and occupational change: the case of Pakistani migrants returned from the Middle East', *Pakistan Development Review*, **36** (1), 1–37.

Athukorala, P. (1990) 'International contract migration and the reintegration of return migrants: the experience of Sri Lanka', *International Migration Review*, **24** (2), 323–47.

Bailey, A.J. (2010) 'Population geographies, gender, and the migration–development nexus', *Progress in Human Geography*, **34** (3), 375–86.

Bastia, T. (2011) 'Should I stay or should I go? Return migration in times of crisis', *Journal of International Development*, **23** (4), 583–95.

Bastia, T. (2013) 'The migration–development nexus: current challenges and future research agendas', *Geography Compass*, **7** (7), 464–77.

Black, R. and Castaldo, A. (2009) 'Return migration and entrepreneurship in Ghana and Côte d'Ivoire: the role of capital transfers', *Tijdschrift voor Economische en Sociale Geografie*, **100** (1), 44–58.

Black, R. and Gent, S. (2006) 'Sustainable return in post-conflict contexts', *International Migration*, **44** (3), 15–38.

Boccagni, P. (2020) 'So many houses, as many homes? Transnational housing, migration, and development' in T. Bastia and R. Skeldon (eds), *Routledge Handbook of Migration and Development*, London: Routledge, pp. 251–60.

Boccagni, P. and Lagomarsino, F. (2011) 'Migration and the global crisis: new prospects for return?', *Bulletin of Latin American Research*, **30** (3), 282–97.

Böhning, W.R. (1975) 'Some thoughts on emigration from the Mediterranean Basin', *International Labour Review*, **111** (3), 251–77.

Boni, A. and Lacomba, J. (2011) 'The new co-development agenda: official and non-official initiatives between Morocco and Spain' in T.-D. Truong and D. Gasper (eds), *Transnational Migration and Human Security: The Migration–Development–Security Nexus*, Berlin: Springer, pp. 91–101.

Borjas, G. and Bratsberg, B. (1996) 'Who leaves? The outmigration of the foreign-born', *Review of Economics and Statistics*, **78** (1), 165–76.

Bovenkerk, F. (1974) *The Sociology of Return Migration: A Bibliographic Essay*, The Hague: Martinus Nijhoff.

Brønden, B.M. (2012) 'Migration and development: the flavour of the 2000s', *International Migration*, **50** (3), 2–7.

Carling, J. and Pettersen, S.V. (2014) 'Return migration intentions in the integration–transnationalism matrix', *International Migration*, **52** (6), 13–30.

Cassarino, J.-P. (2004) 'Theorising return migration: the conceptual approach to return migrants revisited', *International Journal on Multicultural Societies*, **6** (2), 253–79.

Cassarino, J.-P. (2008) 'Conditions of modern return migrants', *International Journal on Multicultural Societies*, **10** (2), 95–105.

Cassarino, J.-P. (2016) 'Return migration and development: the significance of migration cycles' in A. Triandafyllidou (ed.), *The Routledge Handbook of Immigration and Refugee Studies*, London: Routledge, pp. 216–22.

Castles, S. (2009) 'Development and migration or migration and development: what comes first?', *Asian and Pacific Migration Journal*, **18** (4), 441–71.

Castles, S. (2011) 'Migration, crisis, and the global labour market', *Globalizations*, **8** (3), 311–24.

Castles, S. and Kosack, G. (1973) *Immigrant Workers and Class Structure in Western Europe*, London: Oxford University Press.

Castles, S. and Miller, M.J. (1993) *The Age of Migration: International Population Movements in the Modern World*, Basingstoke: Macmillan.

Cerase, F.P. (1970) 'Nostalgia or disenchantment: considerations on return migration' in S.M. Tomasi and M.H. Engel (eds), *The Italian Experience in the United States*, New York: Center for Migration Studies, pp. 217–39.

Cerase, F.P. (1974) 'Expectations and reality: a case study of return migration from the United States to Southern Italy', *International Migration Review*, **8** (2), 245–62.

Constant, A. and Massey, D.S. (2002) 'Return migration by German guestworkers: neoclassical versus new economic theories', *International Migration*, **40** (4), 5–38.

Constant, A.F., Nottmeyer, O. and Zimmermann, K.F. (2013) 'The economics of circular migration' in A.F. Constant and K.F. Zimmermann (eds), *International Handbook on the Economics of Migration*, Cheltenham, UK and Northampton, MA, USA: Edward Elgar Publishing, pp. 55–74.

Dannecker, P. (2009) 'Migrant visions of development: a gendered approach', *Population, Space and Place*, **15** (2), 119–32.

Davids, T. and van Houte, M. (2008) 'Remigration, development and mixed embeddedness: an agenda for qualitative research?', *International Journal on Multicultural Societies*, **10** (2), 169–93.

de Haas, H. (2010) 'Migration and development: a theoretical perspective', *International Migration Review*, **44** (1), 227–64.

de Haas, H. (2012) 'The migration and development pendulum: a critical review on research and policy', *International Migration*, **50** (3), 8–25.

de Haas, H. and Fokkema, T. (2011) 'The effects of integration and transnational ties on international return migration intentions', *Demographic Research*, **25** (24), 755–82.

de Haas, H., Fokkema, T. and Fihri, M.F. (2015) 'Return migration as failure or success? The determinants of return migration intentions among Moroccan migrants in Europe?', *Journal of International Migration and Integration*, **16** (2), 415–29.

Delgado Wise, R. and Márquez Covarrubias, H. (2009) 'Understanding the relationship between migration and development: toward a new theoretical approach', *Social Analysis*, **53** (3), 85–105.

Delgado Wise, R. and Márquez Covarrubias, H. (2011) 'The dialectic between uneven development and forced migration: toward a political economy framework' in T. Faist, M. Fauser and P. Kivisto (eds), *The Migration–Development Nexus: A Transnational Perspective*, Basingstoke: Palgrave Macmillan, pp. 57–82.

Diatta, M.A. and Mbow, N. (1999) 'Releasing the development potential of return migration: the case of Senegal', *International Migration*, **37** (1), 243–66.

Dustmann, C. and Weiss, Y. (2007) 'Return migration: theory and empirical evidence from the UK', *British Journal of Industrial Relations*, **45** (2), 236–56.

Faist, T. (2008) 'Migrants as transnational development agents: an inquiry into the newest round of the migration–development nexus', *Population, Space and Place*, **14** (1), 21–42.

Faist, T. and Fauser, M. (2011) 'The migration–development nexus: toward a transnational perspective' in T. Faist, M. Fauser and P. Kivisto (eds), *The Migration–Development Nexus: A Transnational Perspective*, Basingstoke: Palgrave Macmillan, pp. 1–26.

Fakiolas, R. and King, R. (1996) 'Emigration, return, immigration: a review and evaluation of Greece's postwar experience of international migration', *International Journal of Population Geography*, **2** (2), 171–90.

Flahaux, M.-L. (2015) 'Return migration to Senegal and the Democratic Republic of Congo: intention and realization', *Population-E*, **70** (1), 65–96.

Frank, A.G. (1967) *Capitalism and Underdevelopment in Latin America*, New York: Monthly Review Press.

Gamlen, A. (2014) 'The new migration-and-development pessimism', *Progress in Human Geography*, **38** (4), 581–97.

Geiger, N. and Pécoud, A. (2013) 'Migration, development, and the "migration and development nexus"', *Population, Space and Place*, **19** (4), 369–74.

Gertel, J. and Sippel, S.R. (eds) (2014) *Seasonal Workers in Mediterranean Agriculture: The Social Costs of Eating Fresh*, London: Routledge.

Ghosh, B. (1996) 'Economic migration and sending countries' in J. van den Broeck (ed.), *The Economics of Labour Migration*, Cheltenham, UK and Brookfield, VT, USA: Edward Elgar Publishing, pp. 77–113.

Ghosh, B. (2013) *The Global Economic Crisis and the Future of Migration: Issues and Prospects*, Basingstoke: Palgrave Macmillan.

Gilkey, G.R. (1967) 'The United States and Italy: migration and repatriation', *Journal of Developing Areas*, **2** (1), 23–35.

Glick Schiller, N., Basch, L. and Szanton Blanc, C. (1995) 'From immigrant to transmigrant: theorizing transnational migration', *Anthropological Quarterly*, **68** (1), 48–63.

Gmelch, G. (1987) 'Work, innovation, and investment: the impact of return migration in Barbados', *Human Organization*, **46** (2), 131–40.

Gmelch, G. (1992) *Double Passage: The Lives of Caribbean Migrants Abroad and Back Home*, Ann Arbor: University of Michigan Press.

González-Ferrer, A., Baizan, P., Beauchemin, C., Kraus, E., Schoumaker, B. and Black, R. (2014) 'Distance, transnational arrangements, and return decisions of Senegalese, Ghanaian, and Congolese migrants', *International Migration Review*, **48** (4), 939–71.

Guarnizo, L.E. (2003) 'The economics of transnational living', *International Migration Review*, **37** (6), 666–99.

Jones, R.C. (2011) 'The local economic imprint of return migrants in Bolivia', *Population, Space and Place*, **17** (5), 435–53.

Kindleberger, C.P. (1967) *Europe's Postwar Growth: The Role of Labour Supply*, London: Oxford University Press.

King, R. (1979) 'Return migration: a review of some case-studies from Southern Europe', *Mediterranean Studies*, **1** (2), 3–30.

King, R. (1986) 'Return migration and regional development: an overview' in R. King (ed.), *Return Migration and Regional Economic Problems*, Beckenham: Croom Helm, pp. 1–37.

King, R., Strachan, A. and Mortimer, J. (1984) 'Return migration and tertiary development: a Calabrian case-study', *Anthropological Quarterly*, **57** (3), 112–24.

King, R., Strachan, A. and Mortimer, J. (1986) 'Gastarbeiter go home: return migration and economic change in the Italian Mezzogiorno' in R. King (ed.), *Return Migration and Regional Economic Problems*, Beckenham: Croom Helm, pp. 38–68.

Kleist, N. (2020) 'Trajectories of involuntary return migration to Ghana: forced relocation processes and post-return life', *Geoforum*, **116**, 272–81.

Kunz, R. (2008) '"Remittances are beautiful"? Gender implications of the new global remittances trend', *Third World Quarterly*, **29** (7), 1389–409.

Lang, T., Glorius, B., Nadler, R. and Kovács, Z. (2016) 'Introduction: mobility against the stream? New concepts, methodological approaches and regional perspectives on return migration in Europe' in R. Nadler, Z. Kovács, B. Glorius and T. Lang (eds), *Return Migration and Regional Development in Europe: Mobility Against the Stream*, Basingstoke: Palgrave Macmillan, pp. 1–22.

Levitt, P. (1998) 'Social remittances: migration driven local-level forms of cultural diffusion', *International Migration Review*, **32** (4), 926–48.

Levitt, P. and Lamba-Nieves, D. (2013) 'Rethinking social remittances and the migration–development nexus from the perspective of time', *Migration Letters*, **10** (1), 11–22.

Lewis, J. and Williams, A. (1986) 'The economic impact of return migration in central Portugal', in R. King (ed.), *Return Migration and Regional Economic Problems*, Beckenham: Croom Helm, pp. 100–28.

Lucas, R.E.B. (2005) *International Migration and Economic Development: Lessons from Low-Income Countries*, Cheltenham, UK and Northampton, MA, USA: Edward Elgar Publishing.

Mata-Codesal, D. (2013) 'Linking social and financial remittances in the realms of financial know-how and education in rural Ecuador', *Migration Letters*, **10** (1), 23–32.

Mezger Kveder, C. and Beauchemin, C. (2015) 'The role of international migration experience for investment at home: direct, indirect, and equalising effects in Senegal', *Population, Space and Place*, **21** (6), 535–52.

Myrdal, G. (1957) *Rich Lands and Poor: The Road to Prosperity*, New York: Harper and Row.

Nair, P.R.G. (1999) 'Return of overseas contract workers and their rehabilitation and development in Kerala', *International Migration*, **37** (1), 209–42.
Nutter, R. (1986) 'Implications of return migration from the United Kingdom for urban unemployment in Kingston, Jamaica' in R. King (ed.), *Return Migration and Regional Economic Problems*, Beckenham: Croom Helm, pp. 198–212.
Nzima, D., Duma, V. and Moyo, P. (2017) 'Theorizing migration–development interactions: towards an integrated approach', *Migration and Development*, **6** (2), 305–18.
Papademetriou, D.G. and Martin, P.L. (eds) (1991) *The Unsettled Relationship: Labor Migration and Economic Development*, New York: Greenwood Press.
Potter, R. (2005) '"Young, gifted and back": second-generation transnational return migration to the Caribbean', *Progress in Development Studies*, **5** (3), 213–36.
Potter, R. and Phillips, J. (2006) 'Both black and symbolically white: the "Bajan-Brit" return migrant as a post-colonial hybrid', *Ethnic and Racial Studies*, **29** (5), 901–27.
Potter, R., Conway, D. and Phillips, J. (eds) (2005) *The Experience of Return Migration: Caribbean Perspectives*, Aldershot: Ashgate.
Raghuram, P. (2009) 'Which migration, what development? Unsettling the edifice of migration and development', *Population, Space and Place*, **15** (2), 103–17.
Rhoades, R.E. (1978) 'Intra-European return migration and rural development: lessons from the Spanish case', *Human Organization*, **37** (2), 136–47.
Saloutos, T. (1956) *They Remember America: The Story of the Repatriated Greek-Americans*, Berkeley: University of California Press.
Samers, M. (1999) '"Globalization", the geopolitical economy of migration and the "spatial vent"', *Review of International Political Economy*, **6** (2), 163–96.
Sen, A. (1999) *Development as Freedom*, Oxford: Oxford University Press.
Sinatti, G. (2015) 'Return migration as a win–win–win scenario? Visions of return amongst Senegalese migrants, the state of origin and receiving countries', *Ethnic and Racial Studies*, **38** (2), 275–91.
Skeldon, R. (2012) 'Going round in circles: circular migration, poverty alleviation and marginality', *International Migration*, **50** (3), 43–60.
Sørensen, N.N., Van Hear, N. and Engberg-Pedersen, P. (2003) 'Migration, development and conflict: state-of-the-art overview' in N. van Hear and N.N. Sørensen (eds), *The Migration–Development Nexus*, Geneva: United Nations and International Organization for Migration, pp. 5–50.
Stark, O. (1991) *The Migration of Labour*, Oxford: Blackwell.
Swanson, J. (1979) 'The consequences of emigration for economic development: a review of the literature', *Papers in Anthropology*, **20** (1), 39–56.
Taylor, J.E. (1999) 'The new economics of labour migration and the role of remittances in the migration process', *International Migration*, **37** (1), 63–86.
Thomas-Hope, E. (1999) 'Return migration to Jamaica and its development potential', *International Migration*, **37** (1), 183–207.
Todaro, M.P. (1969) 'A model of labor migration and urban unemployment in less developed countries', *American Economic Review*, **59** (1), 138–48.
Vammen, I.M. and Brønden, B.M. (2012) 'Donor-country responses to the migration–development buzz: from ambiguous concepts to ambiguous policies?', *International Migration*, **50** (3), 26–42.
Van Hear, N. and Sørensen, N.N. (eds) (2003) *The Migration–Development Nexus*, Geneva: United Nations and International Organization for Migration.
van Houte, M. and Davids, T. (2008) 'Development and return migration: from policy panacea to migrant perspective sustainability', *Third World Quarterly*, **29** (7), 1411–29.
Vari-Lavoisier, I. (2020) 'Social remittances' in T. Bastia and R. Skeldon (eds), *Routledge Handbook of Migration and Development*, London: Routledge, pp. 125–35.
Vertovec, S. (1999) 'Conceiving and researching transnationalism', *Ethnic and Racial Studies*, **22** (2), 445–62.
Wallerstein, I. (1974) *The Modern World System*, New York: Academic Press.

# 23. Diaspora return and knowledge transfer
*Charlotte Mueller*

## INTRODUCTION

Evidence from a variety of contexts has shown that different forms of return by migrants to their country of origin may be used for knowledge transfer and may yield impacts on development (Klagge and Klein-Hitpass, 2010; Kuschminder, 2014; Kuschminder et al., 2014; Wang, 2014; see also King, Chapter 22). Knowledge transfer may be the explicit purpose of the return – as it is in the case of diaspora return or temporary return programmes – or a by-product of return. Diaspora[1] return programmes emerged in the 1970s as a way in which to harness the development potential which policy-makers attributed to highly skilled migrants and diaspora members. Such interventions are based on two main premises: highly skilled migrants' ability to address knowledge gaps in their country of origin and the diaspora's operational advantage due to their familiarity with the language and culture (Mueller, 2020). Despite the popularity of diaspora return or temporary return programmes, little research has been conducted on their effectiveness and the specific modalities that enable diaspora members to achieve successful knowledge transfer that is sustainable over time. The first part of this chapter analyses current debate with regards to diaspora return and knowledge transfer. It then draws on research conducted within the first phase of the programme Connecting Diaspora for Development (CD4D), in order to provide a case study of diaspora return and knowledge transfer. In the discussion section, comparisons are made between the different forms of knowledge transfer and inferences are drawn regarding the strengths and weaknesses of these approaches. The chapter concludes by stressing how a diaspora return programme can be used to channel diaspora contributions to knowledge transfer and capacity development in their countries of origin.

## DIASPORA RETURN, KNOWLEDGE TRANSFER AND CAPACITY DEVELOPMENT: DEFINITIONS AND CAVEATS

In line with transnational approaches to return, diaspora return should be regarded as a 'continuous, ongoing transnational process' (Tsuda, 2019, p.7). Thereby, return can take a variety of forms, including temporary and seasonal movements, short-term visits, longer-term stays or return on a permanent basis (Galipo, 2018; King, 2000; Olsson and King, 2008). Tsuda (2019, pp.4–5) distinguishes two types of diasporic return: ethnic return migration – which refers to the return of migrants' descendants – and *return migration* as the return of first- or 1.5-generation migrants. A characteristic which is specific for diaspora return, especially for ethnic return migration, is the symbolic notion of home and the desire to return. At the same time, upon return, the country of origin may no longer be considered as 'home' by the returnee (see Kılınç, Chapter 20). Ethnic return migrants have never actually been to the country of origin before, while other returnees, especially after longer periods of absence, may no longer be familiar with the country of origin (Hasselberg, 2018; Olsson and King, 2008).

The narrative with regards to return migrants and their development potential has changed over time. In the 1970s and 1980s, scholars attributed little to no development impact to returning migrants (Gmelch, 1980; King, 1986). Gmelch's (1980) review of the literature on the impact of return migration on the introduction of new skills, ideas and attitudes, amongst other contributions, identified that few return migrants had acquired the relevant work experience; when migrants *had* acquired this, most were unable to apply it in the origin country. Likewise, King (1986) also noted that improvements in human capital through return failed to appear in the vast majority of cases. Return migrants had acquired few skills abroad and, if skills *were* acquired, they did not match with the needs of the country of origin's labour market or the migrants lost the skills they had prior to emigration. In addition, more skilled migrants tended to remain in the country of destination while the less skilled returned. Next to these reviews, Cerase's (1974) typology of return, based on his research on Italians returning from the United States, should be highlighted. The third of four types of return, the *return of innovation*, refers to the return of migrants who have acquired new skills in the host country, the application of which they consider to be more useful in their country of origin than in the host country (Cerase, 1974). Yet, this type of return was seldom observed (Cassarino, 2004; King, 1986, 2000).

According to Gmelch (1980), the lack of development impact identified by the vast majority of scholars in the 1970s and 1980s may, in part, be the result of a focus on unskilled migrants from rural areas who worked in unskilled or semi-skilled jobs in the country of destination which required little training. More recent studies have focused on the return of highly skilled migrants and demonstrated evidence of returnee contributions to knowledge transfer (Ammassari, 2004; Klagge and Klein-Hitpass, 2010; Wang, 2014). In a study of highly skilled return migrants to Côte d'Ivoire and Ghana, Ammassari (2004) found that returnees gained additional educational qualifications and, in the case of Ghanaians, also professional experience abroad which allowed them to transfer organisational and managerial knowledge upon return. Klagge and Klein-Hitpass (2010), in their study on highly skilled return migration and knowledge-based development in Poland, found that returnees transferred tacit, managerial knowledge to local companies, such as knowledge about human resource management, project management and international cooperation.

In the 1970s, host- and origin-country governments as well as international organisations began to launch programmes to harness the development potential attributed to diaspora members and highly skilled migrants. While the focus of return knowledge transfer is on permanent return, these programmes have specifically promoted the temporary modality of return as a way to channel the potential attributed to migrants from developing countries and increase local expertise in their country of origin. The United Nations Development Programme Transfer of Knowledge through Expatriate Nationals (TOKTEN) pioneered this approach. Several different programmes for diaspora contributions to development in Africa have emerged since then, most notably the Migration for Development in Africa Programme (MIDA).[2] In a study commissioned by the Centre for International Migration and Development (CIM), Kuschminder et al. (2014) examined the knowledge transfer resulting from the two-year placements of returning experts as part of the 'Migration for Development' programme. Evidence for the occurrence of knowledge transfer was found, yet not always 'at optimal levels' (Kuschminder et al., 2014, p.24). In her case study on knowledge transfer and capacity building through the Temporary Return of Qualified Nationals (TRQN) project in

Afghanistan, Kuschminder (2011, 2014) highlighted that returnees made concrete contributions to individual and organisational capacity development.

Despite existing evidence of returnees' contributions to knowledge transfer, scholars have questioned the return–development nexus and diaspora knowledge transfer as 'too optimistic' (Siar, 2014) and continue to criticise some of the underlying assumptions (Åkesson and Baaz, 2015; Sinatti and Horst, 2015). For instance, Åkesson and Baaz (2015) argue that structural conditions in the country of origin constitute a challenge to returnee knowledge transfer and that African returnees might not acquire new skills in Europe due to labour market discrimination and a predominance of low-skilled jobs. In addition, Åkesson and Baaz (2015, pp.7–8) criticise the assumption that skills gained in Europe are 'universally applicable' and will be useful in the African context. Such critique reveals the importance of understanding under which conditions diaspora knowledge transfer takes place (Conway et al., 2012; Siar, 2014). Bovenkerk's early review essay (1974) identified several factors that may determine whether or not returnees become 'innovators', including the number of returnees, the concentration of returnees in time, the time duration a returnee has spent abroad, social class, differences between the countries or regions of immigration and emigration, the nature of the training or skills acquired and the mode of return. Cerase (1974) found that existing power relations and economic conditions inhibited returnees from becoming 'innovators'. More recent studies have shed light on factors that are at play specifically for returnee knowledge transfer (Ammassari, 2004; Kuschminder, 2011, 2014; Kuschminder et al., 2014; van Houte and Davids, 2014; Wang, 2014).

One aspect which has received attention in more recent studies is the influence of the relationship between the diaspora returnees and their non-migrant colleagues on the knowledge transfer process (Ammassari, 2004; van Houte and Davids, 2014; Wang, 2014). Returnees may encounter mistrust from locals as well as a fear that returning diaspora members may take away local jobs or be a threat to local values (Galipo, 2018; Gmelch, 1980; Hammond, 2015). In addition, returnees might experience general as well as returnee-specific xenophobic attitudes (Wang, 2014). As part of their study on voluntary returnees in Afghanistan, van Houte and Davids (2014) identified that mistrust towards returnees and foreigners impeded change. In his study on interorganisational knowledge transfer, Wang (2014) identified a returnee's 'embeddedness' in the country of origin and destination, as well as the knowledge receiver's positive attitude towards the returnee, as the main factors for successful knowledge transfer.

The case study which follows contributes to the literature on the current lack of research on knowledge transfer and capacity development in the case of a diaspora return programme. The study discusses forms of knowledge transfer and their contributions to individual and organisational capacity development. Comparisons are drawn between the different forms of knowledge transfer and inferences are garnered regarding the strengths and weaknesses of these approaches.

## CASE STUDY: THE IOM'S CONNECTING DIASPORA FOR DEVELOPMENT PROJECT (CD4D) IN ETHIOPIA, SIERRA LEONE AND SOMALILAND

The diaspora return programme Connecting Diaspora for Development (CD4D) has been selected as a case study.[3] This chapter draws on research conducted within the first phase of the programme, administered by the International Organization for Migration (IOM) in the Netherlands from 2016 to 2019. The project enables diaspora members to return to their country of origin for in-person assignments at selected public organisations with the objective of contributing to knowledge transfer and capacity development. The host institutions were selected by IOM and are mostly ministries and higher education institutions. Based on the demand of the host institutions, so-called 'diaspora experts' – individuals who are first- or second-generation migrants, originally from the target countries and who have Dutch residency – were selected to conduct assignments at the host institutions. Assignment lengths ranged from two weeks to three months, in some cases followed by one or two extensions of up to a further three months.

The analysis is based on semi-structured interviews with CD4D diaspora experts and staff at host institutions in Ethiopia, Sierra Leone and Somaliland. This study uses an approach previously applied by Kuschminder (2014) as well as in Mueller (2020). Knowledge transfer[4] is operationalised as 'perceived knowledge transfer', drawing on the experiences of CD4D diaspora experts and their perspective as knowledge senders and the experiences of host institution staff and their perspectives as knowledge receivers. The interviews were conducted with staff at higher management level – henceforth referred to as 'managers' – and staff who worked with the CD4D diaspora experts at selected host institutions, who will be referred to as 'colleagues' throughout this chapter. In Ethiopia and Somaliland, a local IOM staff member accompanied the author to all interviews with host institution staff and served as a translator where necessary. In Sierra Leone, a local staff member also accompanied the author to each institution and facilitated the introduction but was not present during the interviews. While the presence of the local IOM staff members was essential for communication, as few respondents in Ethiopia and Somaliland spoke English, this potentially introduces bias, as interviewees may speak less openly when a staff member of the organisation implementing the programme that is subject to the evaluation is present. Nonetheless, host institution staff also voiced critical opinions.

Diaspora experts were interviewed after having finished one or multiple assignments, either in-person in the Netherlands or via Skype or phone. A few interviews with diaspora experts were also conducted in the assignment countries as participants were still in the country at the time of the researcher's visit. Interviews took place on a voluntary basis and no IOM staff member was present during the interviews with diaspora experts. After transcription, all interviews were coded using the qualitative analysis software NVivo. The codes centred around the respondents' perceptions of knowledge transfer methods, knowledge transferred or gained and changes implemented on an organisational and individual level as a result of CD4D.

**Defining Knowledge Transfer and Capacity Development**

Capacity development[5] is a concept that has been framed by practitioners and can be defined as a process of change that encompasses different levels (Whyte, 2004; Zamfir, 2017), commonly the 'Enabling environment', the 'Organisational level' and the 'Individual level' (UNDP, 2009, 2010). For this study, the focus lies on capacity development at the individual and organisational levels. Following the UNDP's definition, individual capacity development in this study is defined as an individual's 'skills, experience and knowledge that allow each person to perform' (UNDP, 2009, p.11). Organisational capacity development is conceptualised as contributions to 'the internal structure, policies and procedures' (UNDP, 2009, p.11) of an organisation. Here, contributions to resources or materials, for example computers or other equipment, are also considered as an aspect of organisational capacity development.

Knowledge transfer is a central pillar of capacity development as knowledge provides the capacity for individuals to have the skills to be able to perform new tasks and improve their work (UNDP, 2010). For the purpose of this study, knowledge transfer is defined as a multi-stage process of an individual's or group's experiences (here the diaspora expert) affecting another individual or group, in this case staff at the host institutions, also referred to as colleagues (Argote and Ingram, 2000; Bender and Fish, 2000). One characteristic of this process is that it involves a transformation of data and information into knowledge, culminating in the creation of expertise or wisdom (Bender and Fish, 2000; Liyanage et al., 2009; Major and Cordey-Hayes, 2000). The acquisition of knowledge and its application are also key elements of models of organisational knowledge transfer (see, e.g., Gilbert and Cordey-Hayes, 1996; Liyanage et al., 2009; Parent et al., 2007; Szulanski, 2000).

As the term suggests, knowledge is a key element and product of the knowledge transfer process. Knowledge, as defined in this study, includes job- or sector-specific knowledge, scientific or technical knowledge, communication skills and cultural and social skills and behaviours (Mueller, 2020). Knowledge emerges from the individual, as everyone creates their own knowledge based on the information received and their existing stock of knowledge and background, personal experience, belief and values (Bender and Fish, 2000; Court, 1997; Davenport and Prusak, 1998; Fahey and Prusak, 1998; Joia and Lemos, 2010). This conceptualisation of knowledge as *individual knowledge* is by far the most commonly applied definition of it (see, e.g., Bender and Fish, 2000; Glazer, 1998). Knowledge is generally divided into explicit knowledge – which can be codified and transmitted through a systematic language – and tacit knowledge, which is highly personal, context-dependent and complex. These characteristics make tacit knowledge more difficult to transfer (Davenport and Prusak, 1998; Fahey and Prusak, 1998; Goh, 2002; Inkpen, 1998; Joia and Lemos, 2010; King, 2009; Kuschminder et al., 2014; Levin and Cross, 2004; Polanyi, 1966).

The concepts of information and knowledge are closely related. However, the lines between these concepts are blurry and there is no agreement on a common distinction (Bender and Fish, 2000; Davenport and Prusak, 1998; Wang and Noe, 2010). Taking into account the ambiguity in the distinction between knowledge and information and the difficulties in measurement, this study regards both information and knowledge as part of the knowledge transfer process, with information transmission being one stage of it. Drawing on the existing literature (Bender and Fish, 2000; Joia and Lemos, 2010; Nonaka, 1994), information is defined as that which is transmitted from the knowledge sender to the knowledge receiver and knowledge as that which the receiver creates for him- or herself from the information.

**Forms of Knowledge Transfer in CD4D**

During CD4D, knowledge transfer mainly takes place through formal training. This explicit form of knowledge transfer is particularly common in academic settings (Mueller, 2020). Formal training here includes training sessions, seminars or workshops of varying lengths and duration that aim to develop new skills and/or theoretical knowledge and teach participants how to use equipment or new technologies. At universities in Ethiopia, it was particularly common that diaspora experts would come specifically to give a training course of one or two weeks. Some diaspora experts who conducted assignments at higher education institutions in Sierra Leone gave short seminars, for instance, once a month during the duration of their stay.

In the CD4D programme, formal training is an effective method of ensuring that information is transmitted from the knowledge sender to the knowledge receiver, providing staff at the host institutions with insights into new topics or specific aspects of a certain field. Examples include modern teaching and learning techniques, methods of formal or academic writing and website development. Formal training also serves to enable staff members to update their knowledge. For instance, a colleague in Ethiopia explained that the training on soil biology and scientific writing given by a diaspora expert served to update colleagues' knowledge in that area. Similarly, a staff member at a host institution in Sierra Leone, who attended a workshop on quantitative analysis and research methods, was able to refresh his/her own knowledge in this area.

> The [diaspora expert's] workshop was very good. In the sense that ... Of course, I teach research methods. It is one of the modules I teach here. But [the diaspora expert] was able to remind us of the topics, practically, like time series and time square and which are very much forming. They add a lot of value to the knowledge I have had in research, research methods and that kind of thing ... So, working with [the diaspora expert] is learning to me. (Host institution staff 64, Colleague, Sierra Leone)

Formal training can also go beyond colleagues gaining new information and insights by them applying the new knowledge in their work and daily routines. For example, the training which a diaspora expert gave at a host institution in Ethiopia led to knowledge creation, according to most colleagues who were interviewed. They reported that they had gained skills in managing, organising and analysing data using particular statistical software for quantitative analysis. While staff had previous experience with data analysis using different software, the training helped them to manage and use the enhanced features of a software which was new to them.

Other diaspora experts engaged in activities that were not a knowledge transfer method in themselves. In contrast to formal training, which at least ensures information transmission, knowledge transfer may or may not take place during these other activities. Such activities include carrying out research or assessments for the host institutions, drafting a new policy or development plan, curriculum reviews or improving the organisational structure or strategic plan of the host institution. These activities lead to knowledge transfer when diaspora experts interact closely and regularly with local staff while working on the above-mentioned activities. This might include tacit knowledge transfer methods such as co-teaching, on-the-job training or informal teaching. For instance, diaspora experts who conducted assignments at Human Resource (HR) departments in different host institutions in Somaliland contributed to knowledge transfer through such close, daily interaction while drafting documents and policies (see also Mueller, 2020). Colleagues learnt from the diaspora experts how to develop HR documents – such as a leave sheet and special leave forms – or how to establish a filing system and implement standard HR procedures.

Other less common methods of knowledge transfer are classroom observations, discussion meetings and lectures. While these methods are less effective in contributing to knowledge creation and individual capacity development, they allow staff members to gain new ideas and insights. For instance, the public lecture which a diaspora expert gave at a host institution in Ethiopia provided a colleague who attended the lecture with new insights and additional awareness about the use of technology in the field of agriculture – in particular, possible applications of ICT for agroeconomic processes. This was something the respondent had already thought about but the lecture gave the push to take more concrete steps, encouraging the respondent to make plans to implement changes in teaching.

**Individual and Organisational Capacity Development**

For CD4D, capacity development mostly occurs on the individual level (Mueller, 2020). Through knowledge transfer, some of the diaspora experts have been able to address the lack of basic skills and knowledge at an individual level by training selected staff members within particular institutions. Individual capacity development occurs when the information absorbed is transformed into knowledge through personal application – in other words, the knowledge receiver applies the new technique in his or her work. Within CD4D, the knowledge transfer methods that led to individual capacity development were formal training and close, regular interaction. An example of formal training that led to individual capacity development is the training that was given by a diaspora expert in Ethiopia. Except for one respondent, the colleagues who participated in the training on data analysis, highlighted in the previous section, reported that they are now using the software for data analysis, thanks to what they learnt during the training. The quote below illustrates the contribution to knowledge and individual capacity development of staff at that host institution:

> It was really important because nowadays everything is improving in every year or in months' time. So we took the R software, so this was new for us. So now we are using this software for application and our statistical analysis. So now our team is using this software ... Yeah. Yeah, [I am also using the software]. Most of us are using the software, because it is new for us ... The software we were using before this training was very old. So this is going to be very important. (Host institution staff 90, Colleague, Ethiopia)

Similarly, a colleague who attended training given by another diaspora expert reported having gained new software skills which s/he is now applying in his/her doctoral research.

At the same time, some of the cases where diaspora experts worked closely with staff at the host institution to achieve a common goal also led to individual capacity development. This was particularly the case for the assignments that three diaspora experts conducted with HR Departments at host institutions in Somaliland (see also Mueller, 2020). The diaspora experts introduced colleagues to HR procedures that are standard in most contexts – such as the Netherlands – but were not in place at the ministries in Somaliland and supported staff in creating the necessary structure. For instance, one of the diaspora experts helped to make the department function better by establishing a filing system and a timetable while working with staff from the department. One colleague – who worked closely with the diaspora expert – still applies what was learnt in his/her work. These examples illustrate how diaspora experts can contribute to individual capacity development using explicit or tacit knowledge transfer methods.

Knowledge transfer may be accompanied by contributions to organisational capacity development. This is particularly the case for tacit knowledge transfer. The previous section gave some examples of diaspora experts who worked with members of the host institutions' HR departments. Using tacit knowledge transfer methods allowed the diaspora experts to introduce the colleagues to standard HR procedures while, simultaneously, establishing some of these procedures, such as a filing system for employee documents, together with the colleagues. Closely working together also ensured that the end results fitted the specific country context. Host institution management considered the changes an important step towards improving the HR department.

> [The diaspora expert] totally changed the department ... The ministry is new and the HR department is also new ... So they are struggling to do many things. So [the diaspora expert] helped to do those things to at least organise all staff of the ministry, even the regional staff, and make this filing system and establishing templates, work templates ... (Host institutions staff 28, Manager, Somaliland)

In a few cases, diaspora experts nonetheless contributed to organisational capacity development without contributing to knowledge transfer. For example, one diaspora expert's main task was to build a website for the host institution. While this activity did not lead to knowledge transfer according to host institution staff, it contributed to the internal structure, policies and procedures of the host institution. Yet, in such cases, the focus on organisational capacity development limited actual knowledge transfer.

## DISCUSSION

By focusing on temporary return through a diaspora return programme, this chapter analyses a very specific form of return. The previous sections demonstrated that, through this form of return, diaspora experts can contribute to knowledge transfer and capacity development at organisations in their country of origin. The previous sections highlighted examples from cases where knowledge transfer and/or capacity development took place, showing that a diaspora return programme can indeed enhance diaspora contributions. Yet, contributions are by no means guaranteed. There are also cases within CD4D where only a little or even no knowledge transfer and capacity development took place. The case study also shows that the extent to which knowledge transfer and capacity development take place depends on several factors, such as the choice of knowledge transfer method, the organisations' and the colleagues' learning intent, time and the role of the diaspora expert which enable or inhibit contributions. Additionally, the appropriateness of a knowledge transfer method varies across contexts.

Formal training was discussed in the previous section as one of the most common knowledge transfer methods in the CD4D project. A key characteristic of formal training is that it is clear for everyone involved that the intention is to transfer knowledge. In turn, the lack of intention to transfer knowledge is one of the main inhibitors when no formal training sessions are planned. Motivation (on both the sender's and the receiver's side) or 'learning intent' has been identified as a crucial factor for knowledge transfer (Narteh, 2008; Szulanski, 2000). In most cases examined for this study where little or no knowledge transfer took place, the learning intent was low as the focus of the assignment was on activities other than knowledge transfer – for instance to conduct an assessment or research or to teach students, in the case of higher education institutions. Different actors are involved in defining how an assignment takes place within CD4D. Terms of References, developed by the IOM and the host institution, are the basis of the activities of all CD4D diaspora experts. At the same time, some host institutions have urgent capacity gaps which make them favour more immediate interventions. For instance, higher education institutions in Sierra Leone seemed to expect a more direct benefit from letting the diaspora experts lecture their students. By using knowledge transfer methods, such as co-teaching, such assignments could still contribute to knowledge transfer to staff but this has not always been the case within CD4D.

The diaspora expert may play a role in whether knowledge transfer takes place. A few diaspora experts showed an attempt to counteract the host institutions' lack of learning intent to ensure knowledge transfer by advocating a greater focus on knowledge transfer. Due to time constraints, others prioritised the tasks they were given over knowledge transfer. Nonetheless, it should also be acknowledged that, even though the diaspora experts are specialists in a certain area, they are not necessarily experienced knowledge senders and, in many cases, this is their first encounter with the host institutions. Another factor is the individual learning intent of staff at the host institutions. The colleagues' motivation to learn from a diaspora expert enabled information transmission, particularly for tacit knowledge transfer, while a lack thereof or a resistance to change by staff was perceived by diaspora experts to inhibit knowledge transfer as well as cooperation more generally. Some diaspora experts reported that, from their perspective, staff did not see the benefit of the CD4D project for them or for the institution due to the intangible nature of the project's aims. A number of diaspora experts also reported that they were seen by staff as a threat to their jobs, which is a common returnee stigma in the assignment countries. While such stigma may inhibit knowledge transfer and capacity development, diaspora experts adopted strategies to prevent and counteract it. This again highlights the role which diaspora experts may play.

On the other hand, the interviews with colleagues showed that it was favourable for knowledge transfer to take place when colleagues perceived a topic as relevant. The way the training is given also plays a role. Here, interviewees highlighted practical exercises and the lack thereof as a factor which influences knowledge transfer and which plays a greater role for knowledge absorption and individual capacity development, as practical exercises help the colleagues to be able to apply the knowledge gained in their work. Time is another important factor. For the case of the Temporary Return of Qualified Nationals (TRQN) programme, Kuschminder (2014) identified the time frame of an assignment as the main constraint. This aspect was also frequently mentioned during CD4D. Diaspora experts, as well as host institutions, may have an incentive to request longer assignment durations. Nonetheless, this study also shows that whether an explicit or tacit knowledge transfer method is better suited also depends on the time frame of an assignment, as more time is required for diaspora experts to closely work with a colleague than for formal training, while more time-efficient, formal training is also dependent on the attendance of staff members, which might be more difficult to achieve in shorter time frames. In addition, the host institutions in which diaspora experts are placed often constitute substantially new environments for the temporary returnees and thus require adjustment time (see Mueller, 2020).

Furthermore, the different approaches also define the setup for the diaspora expert–colleague relationship and constitute different forms of interaction (Mueller, 2020). For the cases where knowledge was transferred through close daily interaction, diaspora experts worked with one to three colleagues. Formal training generally included a higher number of colleagues and required less one-to-one interaction. Particularly for tacit knowledge transfer to occur, a colleague's perception of the diaspora expert as committed and recognising him or her as an expert helps to create a trustful relationship between them, which in turn enables knowledge transfer. The diaspora expert's familiarity with the country's and the host institution's culture and context influences the relationship insofar as it determines the way in which the diaspora experts interact. At the same time, training could also be a way of establishing the relationship between diaspora experts and colleagues for consequent tacit knowledge transfer and one-to-one interaction such as mentoring, coaching or on-the-job training, if time allows.

## CONCLUSION

This study set out to discuss the ways in which diaspora members transfer knowledge and to assess the methods and tools used by them to contribute to successful knowledge transfer by using the case of the diaspora return programme CD4D. It also discussed managers' and colleagues' perceptions of knowledge transfer and its contributions to individual and organisational capacity development at their organisations. Knowledge transfer within CD4D mostly takes place through formal training and colleagues closely working together with the diaspora expert. This chapter has demonstrated that diaspora experts are able to make contributions to individual and organisational capacity development at the host institutions through explicit as well as tacit knowledge transfer methods.

At the same time, it has to be acknowledged that many capacity development contributions through CD4D remain limited in scale and contributions to knowledge transfer and capacity development are not guaranteed. Furthermore, new or altered procedures will only have longer-term impacts through continuous action by the colleagues and with the support of management staff. Moreover, high staff turnover is not uncommon at many of the host institutions. When staff who were trained by a diaspora expert leave the host institution, their knowledge is lost to the organisation as a result. It is therefore of interest to see whether knowledge gained through a diaspora return programme such as CD4D is sustainable over time. This question has been difficult to answer with the data available for this chapter as a more long-term perspective would be necessary, which may be a point for future research.

Furthermore, the specific context in which diaspora knowledge transfer has been discussed here has to be considered. By focusing on temporary return through a diaspora return programme, this chapter has analysed a very specific form of return. Contrary to other forms of return, the diaspora experts choose of their own volition to participate in the programme and are being supported financially and administratively for the duration of their stay. As diaspora experts are being selected based on their skills, returnees in this study are mostly highly educated with valued expertise in a certain field. Finally, the project follows a demand-oriented approach as the needs were identified with each host institution at the beginning of the project. Even though the programme is designed to provide – to the extent possible – 'ideal' conditions for knowledge transfer and capacity development, contributions are not guaranteed. As a result, successful knowledge transfer is likely to be more challenging to achieve through other modes of return such as spontaneous returns or forced returns.

## ACKNOWLEDGEMENTS

This research was conducted as part of the evaluation for the CD4D Programme for IOM which has been funded by the Dutch Ministry of Foreign Affairs. The author expresses gratitude to everyone at the International Organization for Migration (IOM) who supported and assisted in this research. The author also thanks Julia Reinold and Talitha Dubow for their comments as well as everyone who provided research assistance for this project for their excellent work.

## NOTES

1. The term diaspora is applied in a broad definition here, referring more to migrants in the wider sense. It is assumed that the 'classic' diaspora characteristics, such as dispersion, homeland orientation and boundary maintenance, do not necessarily apply here and that whether a diaspora expert identifies as a diaspora member depends on the individual.
2. See https://www.iom.int/mida.
3. Somaliland refers to the self-declared state of Somaliland, internationally considered as an autonomous region of Somalia. Due to its status as a de facto state, Somaliland will be referred to as a country throughout this chapter.
4. In contrast to the concept of social remittances, which emphasises the circularity of knowledge (Levitt, 1998; Levitt and Lamba-Nieves, 2011), knowledge transfer will only be analysed in a unidirectional manner in this chapter as a transfer from the diaspora expert to colleagues, as this is the direction defined by the temporary return programme. Yet, it should be emphasised that, in practice, knowledge transfer may constitute a multidirectional process, as it does in this case.
5. It has to be noted that international organisations have shifted towards the use of the term capacity development instead of capacity building in an attempt to recognise already existing capacities yet, in practice, the terms capacity building and capacity development are still often being used interchangeably (Zamfir, 2017). The UNDP has adopted a clear distinction between capacity building and capacity development, defining the former as 'a process that supports only the initial stages of building or creating capacities and assumes that there are no existing capacities to start from' (UNDP, 2009, p.54).

## REFERENCES

Åkesson, L. and Baaz, M.E. (2015) 'Introduction' in L. Åkesson and M.E. Baaz (eds), *Africa's Return Migrants: The New Developers?*, London: Zed Books, pp. 1–22.

Ammassari, S. (2004) 'From nation-building to entrepreneurship: the impact of élite return migrants in Côte d'Ivoire and Ghana', *Population, Space and Place*, **10** (2), 133–54.

Argote, L. and Ingram, P. (2000) 'Knowledge transfer: a basis for competitive advantage in firms', *Organizational Behaviour and Human Decision Processes*, **82** (1), 150–69.

Bender, S. and Fish, A. (2000) 'The transfer of knowledge and the retention of expertise: the continuing need for global assignments', *Journal of Knowledge Management*, **4** (2), 125–37.

Bovenkerk, F. (1974) *The Sociology of Return Migration: A Bibliographic Essay*, Amsterdam: Springer Netherlands.

Cassarino, J.-P. (2004) 'Theorising return migration: the conceptual approach to return migrants revisited', *International Journal on Multicultural Societies*, **6** (2), 253–79.

Cerase, F.P. (1974) 'Expectations and reality: a case study of return migration from the United States to Southern Italy', *International Migration Review*, **8** (2), 245–62.

Conway, D., Potter, R. and Bernard, G. (2012) 'Diaspora return of transnational migrants to Trinidad and Tobago: the additional contributions of social remittances', *International Development Planning Review*, **34** (2), 189–209.

Court, A. (1997) 'The relationship between information and personal knowledge in new product development', *International Journal of Information Management*, **17** (2), 123–38.

Davenport, T.H. and Prusak, L. (1998) *Working Knowledge: How Organizations Manage What They Know*, Boston MA: Harvard Business School Press.

Fahey, L. and Prusak, L. (1998) 'The eleven deadliest sins of knowledge management', *California Management Review*, **40** (3), 265–76.

Galipo, A. (2018) *Return Migration and Nation Building in Africa: Reframing the Somali Diaspora*, London: Routledge.

Gilbert, M. and Cordey-Hayes, M. (1996) 'Understanding the process of knowledge transfer to achieve successful technological innovation', *Technovation*, **16** (6), 301–12.

Glazer, R. (1998) 'Measuring the knower: towards a theory of knowledge equity', *California Management Review*, **40** (3), 175–94.
Gmelch, G. (1980) 'Return migration', *Annual Review of Anthropology*, **9**, 135–59.
Goh, S.C. (2002) 'Managing effective knowledge transfer: an integrative framework and some practice implications', *Journal of Knowledge Management*, **6** (1), 23–30.
Hammond, L. (2015) 'Diaspora returnees to Somaliland: heroes of development or job-stealing scoundrels?' in L. Åkesson and M.E. Baaz (eds), *Africa's Return Migrants: The New Developers?*, London: Zed Books, pp. 44–63.
Hasselberg, I. (2018) 'Fieldnotes from Cape Verde: on deported youth, research methods, and social change' in S. Khosravi (ed.), *After Deportation. Ethnographic Perspectives*, Basingstoke: Palgrave Macmillan, pp. 15–36.
Inkpen, A. (1998) 'Learning, knowledge acquisition, and strategic alliances', *European Management Journal*, **16** (2), 223–9.
Joia, L.A. and Lemos, B. (2010) 'Relevant factors for tacit knowledge transfer within organisations', *Journal of Knowledge Management*, **14** (3), 410–27.
King, R. (1986) 'Return migration and regional economic development: an overview' in R. King (ed.), *Return Migration and Regional Economic Problems*, London: Croom Helm, pp. 1–37.
King, R. (2000) 'Generalizations from the history of return migration' in B. Ghosh (ed.), *Return Migration: Journey of Hope or Despair?*, Geneva: United Nations and the International Organization for Migration, pp. 7–55.
King, W.R. (2009) 'Knowledge management and organizational learning' in W.R. King (ed.), *Knowledge Management and Organizational Learning: Annals of Information Systems*, Boston MA: Springer, pp. 3–13.
Klagge, B. and Klein-Hitpass, K. (2010) 'High-skilled return migration and knowledge-based development in Poland', *European Planning Studies*, **18** (10), 1631–51.
Kuschminder, K. (2011) *The Role of the Diaspora in Knowledge Transfer and Capacity Building in Post-Conflict Settings: The Temporary Return of Qualified Nationals to Afghanistan*, Maastricht: Maastricht University, IS Academy Migration Policy Report No. 1.
Kuschminder, K. (2014) 'Knowledge transfer and capacity building through the temporary return of qualified nationals to Afghanistan', *International Migration*, **52** (5), 191–207.
Kuschminder, K., Sturge, G. and Ragab, N. (2014) *Contributions and Barriers to Knowledge Transfer: The Experience of Returning Experts*, Maastricht: Maastricht University, Graduate School of Governance CIM Paper No. 7.
Levin, D.Z. and Cross, R. (2004) 'The strength of weak ties you can trust: the mediating role of trust in effective knowledge transfer', *Management Science*, **50** (11), 1477–90.
Levitt, P. (1998) 'Social remittances: migration driven local-level forms of cultural diffusion', *International Migration Review*, **32** (4), 926–48.
Levitt, P. and Lamba-Nieves, D. (2011) 'Social remittances revisited', *Journal of Ethnic and Migration Studies*, **37** (1), 1–22.
Liyanage, C., Elhag, T., Ballal, T. and Li, Q. (2009) 'Knowledge communication and translation: a knowledge transfer model', *Journal of Knowledge Management*, **13** (3), 118–31.
Major, E. and Cordey-Hayes, M. (2000) 'Knowledge translation: a new perspective on knowledge transfer and foresight', *Foresight: The Journal of Future Studies, Strategic Thinking and Policy*, **2** (4), 411–23.
Mueller, C. (2020) 'Diaspora knowledge transfer in Sierra Leone and Somaliland' in M. Konte, L.M. Mbaye and V. Mazzucato (eds), *Migration and Remittances in Africa: Towards the Sustainable Development Goals*, Abingdon: Routledge, pp. 117–37.
Narteh, B. (2008) 'Knowledge transfer in developed-developing country interfirm collaborations: a conceptual framework', *Journal of Knowledge Management*, **12** (1), 78–91.
Nonaka, I. (1994) 'A dynamic theory of organizational knowledge creation', *Organization Science*, **5** (1), 14–37.
Olsson, E. and King, R. (2008) 'Introduction: diasporic return', *Diaspora: A Journal of Transnational Studies*, **17** (3), 255–61.
Parent, R., Roy, M. and St Jacques, D. (2007) 'A systems-based dynamic knowledge transfer capacity model', *Journal of Knowledge Management*, **11** (6), 81–93.

Polanyi, M. (1966) *The Tacit Dimension*, New York: Doubleday.
Siar, S. (2014) 'Diaspora knowledge transfer as a development strategy for capturing the gains of skilled migration', *Asian and Pacific Migration Journal*, **23** (3), 299–323.
Sinatti, G. and Horst, C. (2015) 'Migrants as agents of development: diaspora engagement discourse and practice in Europe', *Ethnicities*, **15** (1), 134–52.
Szulanski, G. (2000) 'The process of knowledge transfer: a diachronic analysis of stickiness', *Organizational Behavior and Human Decision Processes*, **82** (1), 9–27.
Tsuda, T. (2019) 'Korean diaspora returns' in T. Tsuda and C. Song (eds), *Diasporic Returns to the Ethnic Homeland: The Korean Diaspora in Comparative Perspective*, Basingstoke: Palgrave Macmillan, pp. 3–16.
UNDP (2009) *Capacity Development: A UNDP Primer*, New York: United Nations Development Programme.
UNDP (2010) *Measuring Capacity*, New York: United Nations Development Programme.
van Houte, M. and Davids, T. (2014) 'Moving back or moving forward? Return migration, development and peace-building', *New Diversities*, **16** (2), 71–87.
Wang, D. (2014) 'Activating cross-border brokerage: inter-organizational knowledge transfer through skilled return migration', *Administrative Science Quarterly*, **60** (1), 133–78.
Wang, S. and Noe, R. (2010) 'Knowledge sharing: a review and directions for future research', *Human Resource Management Review*, **20** (2), 115–31.
Whyte, A. (2004) *Landscape Analysis of Donor Trends in International Development*, New York: Rockefeller Foundation.
Zamfir, I. (2017) *Understanding Capacity-Building/Capacity Development. A Core Concept of Development Policy*, Brussels: European Union, European Parliamentary Research Service.

# 24. Return migration, entrepreneurship and development
*Giulia Sinatti*

## INTRODUCTION

In international development discourse, migration has been increasingly conceived as a tool to stimulate homeland development and diasporas have emerged as potential agents of change. This discourse is reflected in the return and development nexus (see King, Chapter 22), with high expectations often placed specifically on the development potential of return entrepreneurs (Åkesson, 2011; Åkesson and Eriksson-Baaz, 2015; Boccagni, 2011; Cohen, 2009; Murphy, 2002; Sinatti, 2015a; Tsuda, 2010). States in migrant countries of origin and destination, international development donors and non-governmental organisations (NGOs) all reach out to (potential) migrant investors, praising them for their contributions to development and/ or supporting them in their activities.

In this chapter, I provide an overview of scholarly discussions about return migration, entrepreneurship and development. This growing and diverse area of interest attracts researchers from various disciplines and with a focus on different geographic areas of the globe (Gruenhagen et al., 2020). To make sense of this variety, I distinguish between two main approaches. The first follows a *state-centred* perspective and frames return migration and entrepreneurship from above; the second follows a *migrant-centred* perspective and frames return migration and entrepreneurship from below. I illustrate how these framings are rooted in different understandings of development and its outcomes.

First is an approach that examines from above 'official discourse and the kinds of interventions that are made in the name of diaspora' (Turner and Kleist, 2013, p.192). This approach – which I review in the next section of this chapter – emphasises states' attitudes towards the relationship between return, entrepreneurship and development. It highlights the often-conflicting interests of both origin and destination countries, as well as of international agencies and NGOs. Most importantly, the literature scrutinising policies and programmes from around the globe concludes that state-driven approaches are rooted in implicit understandings of development as a primarily *economic* affair (Boccagni, 2011; Gamlen et al., 2019; Sinatti, 2019).

A considerable amount of scholarly work mirrors the implicit understanding of development as an economic matter typical of state policies. This literature assesses the outcomes of return migrant entrepreneurship for economic development. On the whole, it criticises policy optimism and shows that return entrepreneurship may yield diversified economic outcomes, which may range from macro-economic growth to micro-level poverty reduction. Often drawing on the broader literature on entrepreneurship, this work points to the different economic results ensuing from innovation- and needs-based entrepreneurs.

Second is an approach that emphasises, from below, the viewpoint and experiences of migrants, their families and their networks. As I illustrate in the next section of this chapter, this approach is inspired by the literature on migrant transnationalism, as a process through which 'immigrants form and sustain multi-stranded social relations that link together their societies of origin and settlement' (Basch et al., 1994, p.6). Following a constructivist approach that sees migrants and diasporas as actors with their own agency, rather than as pawns governed by state policies, this approach considers them as distinct from nation states. Insights into the everyday lives, experiences and perspectives of return migrant entrepreneurs, their families and their communities bring more nuanced understandings of development. The latter is no longer conceived exclusively in terms of transfers of economic capital but also extends to transnational transfers of human, social and cultural capital. Most importantly, migrant-centred understandings of *human* development incorporate attention for the outcomes which the migrants themselves value and which may not be confined to the economic sphere.

After discussing top-down approaches to migration, return and entrepreneurship and emphasising their economic focus, followed by a review of bottom-up, migrant-centred approaches and the social and political development outcomes which can be identified, I offer some conclusions in the last section of this chapter.

## STATE POLICIES AND PROGRAMMES: RETURN AND ENTREPRENEURSHIP FROM ABOVE

The state-centred approach may be described as part of a broader 'response[s] of states to globalization and migration [and] as an effort to extend their power beyond territorial borders. Accordingly, ... "diaspora engagement policies" form part of an effort to ... extend the monopoly of power of the state to nationals residing outside of its territorial borders' (Liu and van Dongen, 2016, p.806, citing Gamlen, 2006, pp.3, 5). In countries of migrant origin around the globe, diaspora institutions and policies targeting emigrant populations have boomed over recent decades (Gamlen et al., 2019; Ho et al., 2015; Østergaard-Nielsen, 2003; Ragazzi, 2009; Turner and Kleist, 2013). In destination countries, too, migration policies have highlighted the development potential of return migrant entrepreneurship (Åkesson, 2011; Sinatti, 2015a).

### Home Countries Courting Their Overseas Diasporas

Homeland policies often attempt to invigorate migrant connectedness by drawing on nationalist sentiments among the diaspora. Israel's return migration strategy, for instance, resorts to ethno-nationalist arguments of visceral belonging to the homeland to encourage the return of Israeli emigrants (Cohen, 2009). Similarly, Ecuadorians abroad have been appealed to as forming the fifth region of Ecuador, thus 'involving emigrant connectedness and affiliation to the motherland' (Boccagni, 2011, p.462). The African Union, too, has referred to its diaspora worldwide as the 'sixth region of Africa' (Kamei, 2013).

Scholars heavily criticise this policy optimism, indicating that countries of migrant origin often take an instrumental and elitist approach: they reach out to entire diasporas while effectively targeting only those return migrants carrying the potential to become successful entrepreneurs back home (Åkesson, 2011; Boccagni, 2011; Cohen, 2009; Ho, 2011; Kleist, 2015; Murphy, 2002; Sinatti, 2015b, 2019). On the African continent, Turner and Kleist (2013, p.201) conclude that 'states reaching out to diasporas as agents of change ... are implicitly reaching out to those expatriates whom they assume have the desired resources in terms of economic and human capital'. In the field of international relations, the emergence of diaspora institutions and related policies has thus been explained following a neoliberal interpretation, based on the 'assumption that origin states are primarily interested in exploiting diaspora resources to pursue national interests' (Gamlen et al., 2019, p.496).

Origin countries, moreover, are found to pursue *economic* aims over other potential interests. Based on a review of diaspora institutions worldwide, Gamlen and his colleagues identify several examples in which policies and measures targeting return entrepreneurship have an explicit economic dimension. They cite cases ranging from Haiti's declared aim 'to facilitate diaspora investment and philanthropy' to Angola's commitment "to 'encourage overseas communities to invest in Angola, including support visits and business trips'" (Gamlen et al., 2019, pp.497–8). Cohen (2009) shows that, while its ethno-nationalist arguments to encourage return address *all* Israeli emigrants, Israel's policy effectively pursues a strategy of economic rationalism. Return schemes – Cohen argues – are structurally biased to target only those groups deemed resourceful for the national economy, thus leading to the segmentation of Israel's emigrant population. These schemes – such as a joint initiative by the Ministry for Immigrant Absorption and Israel's Small and Medium Enterprise Authority, a fund making free advice available to return migrants wanting to invest as business entrepreneurs – draw on neoliberal theories to emphasise 'elements pertaining to economic productivity, entrepreneurial skills and added value to highly specialised market niches' (Cohen, 2009, p.18). Similar conclusions have led other scholars to speak of return policies as predominantly targeting *super-entrepreneurs* (Naudé et al., 2017).

**Other State and Non-state Actors in Diaspora Governance**

Homeland policies should not be analysed with an exclusive focus on the domestic sphere and in isolation but, rather, as part of larger systems of international migration governance (Gamlen et al., 2019). Such a perspective allows the identification of areas of convergence and cooperation between countries of migrant origin, destination states and – more generally – the many intergovernmental and non-governmental organisations making up the so-called migration industry (Andersson, 2014; Gammeltoft-Hansen and Nyberg Sørensen, 2012). Often, homeland diaspora institutions and policies like those described above are developed in the hope that they 'may cultivate "triple wins" for migrants, origin states and destination states' (Gamlen et al., 2019, p.497). Yet several observers have pointed out that origin and destination countries usually have competing interests with regard to return and entrepreneurship policies and programmes. My own work on return, entrepreneurship and development in Senegal, for instance, has shown how triple-win discourses tend to gloss over very different understandings of the advantages that the origin state, the European Union (EU) and the migrants might reap (Sinatti, 2015a). I argue that European institutions largely conceive of return as a means to control exit and entrance by removing unwanted migrants from the country of destination and ensuring a definite closure of their migration cycle. The Senegalese state, instead, shows an interest in encouraging migrant mobility that may boost 'the transfer of significant resources, including remittances, savings, contacts and knowledge that may support new investments' in the home country (Sinatti, 2015a, p.286). Other scholars have taken a similar critical stance, highlighting the competition between the interests of origin and destination countries. In the case of Ecuador, Boccagni (2011) highlights the stark contrast between the '*Plan de Ajuda al Retorno Voluntario*' – promoted by the government of Spain to foster the return of *unem-*

*ployed* migrants – and the '*Plan Benvenido a Casa*' set up by the Ecuadorian government and providing tax exemptions or other financial and practical support to *promising* migrant investors.

The burgeoning interest in return and entrepreneurship at a policy level is reflected in numerous programmes supporting migrant investors implemented by international agencies, NGOs and other actors on the international development scene. The aim of non-state programmes ranges from accompanying migrant entrepreneurs who might boost the economy of the country of origin, to enhancing entrepreneurship as a skill that return migrants are seen to be lacking. While programmes with the former aim set high entry barriers to scout promising entrepreneurs with sound business ideas and their own substantial financial means, programmes with the latter aim tend to view all potential return migrants as beneficiaries in need of capacity-building. Illustrative of the latter approach is a small-scale project funded within the Joint Migration and Development Initiative (JMDI)[1] with activities stretching across Italy and Senegal. A consortium of local associations, trade unions and migrant organisations offered business development assistance to any migrant who was planning to return to the homeland, regardless of the sector, the stage of development of his or her business idea, the size of the investment or the timing of return plans.

The diversity of initiatives supporting return migrant entrepreneurship and the variety of actors promoting them call for a distinction between diaspora *government* and diaspora *governance*. Liu and van Dongen (2016, p.806) write:

> [Following] Anglo-American political theory, 'government' indicates 'the formal institutions of the state and their monopoly of legitimate coercive power', whereas 'governance' refers to 'the development of governing styles in which boundaries between and within public and private sectors have become blurred'. Crucial here is the concern with mechanisms of governance based on the interaction between various actors.

These governance 'networks, from the stake holders, mainly from civil societies, to the so-called Business Incubators ... help entrepreneurs overcome the financial, human, and social capital impediments they face during the business creation', thus bridging home-country governments and migrant entrepreneurs (Zapata-Barrero and Rezaei, 2019, p.1961). In practice, however, with the initiatives of international agencies, NGOs and other private-sector actors largely relying on the financial support of Western donors and with the initiatives of origin governments often sponsored through the same international donor arrangements, it has become increasingly difficult to disentangle whose voice may be behind programmes supporting migrant return and investment. As I have illustrated above, one may conclude that, while homeland policies tend to target desirable return entrepreneurs, policies in destination countries more often facilitate the return of migrants living in marginal conditions. Observations, such as those exemplified above from Senegal and Ecuador, have led some scholars to denounce analytical slippage, in Northern policies, between return and removal from the country of destination (Åkesson, 2011; see also Kalir, Chapter 6).

Whether migrants are seen as needy beneficiaries whose skills should be boosted, or as high-flying investors with innovative ideas, depends on what development outcomes are sought-after. Policies and programmes contain implicit assumptions about what development might mean. Macro-economic growth is often the target of national homeland diaspora policies, whereas poverty reduction and reintegration back home are more often the goals of NGO programmes sponsored by Western donors. At the basis of both interpretations is the assumption that the development implications of return entrepreneurship are primarily economic. Before questioning this as a main limitation contained in policy, in the next section I review the empirical literature in line with such an economic focus. This literature shows that the nature of economic development resulting from migrant investments may be very diverse.

**The Economic Emphasis of Approaches from Above**

In the pursuit of answers to policy-driven questions, emphasis on the economic dimension of development has triggered a considerable amount of research. In countries around the world, scholars have investigated whether return migrants are more entrepreneurial than others (Batista et al., 2017; Démurger and Xu, 2011; Gubert and Nordman, 2011; Hagan and Wassink, 2016; Kilic et al., 2009; Mezger Kveder and Beauchemin, 2015). Research has also shown that, in countries of origin with higher levels of informality, a larger portion of migrant remittances is put towards productive investment (i.e. business creation) instead of consumption (Martinez et al., 2015).

Interesting additional insights come from a relatively small amount of literature that takes into account broader theorisations about (ethnic) entrepreneurship (Barjaba, 2018; Croitoru, 2019; Sinatti, 2015a; Zapata-Barrero and Rezaei, 2019). These works suggest that return migrant entrepreneurs form a varied category ranging from needs-based entrepreneurs who choose self-employment as a survival strategy, to innovation-based entrepreneurs who pursue opportunities for growth, usually changing patterns of production. 'The contrast between necessity- and opportunity-driven entrepreneurship is important because it has been proved that they have a different impact on home countries' economic growth' (Zapata-Barrero and Rezaei, 2019, p.1962). Because they match the policy expectations of macro-economic growth, policies selectively focus on innovation-based entrepreneurs. Needs-based entrepreneurs, instead, may contribute to poverty reduction.

Empirical research about return migration, entrepreneurship and development validates the distinction above, confirming that return migrants fall into different categories. Åkesson (2011) finds that entrepreneurs are only one of several potential kinds of returnee in Cape Verde, next to a majority of pensioners, highly educated migrants and unsuccessful migrants. Usually young and relatively well educated – she writes – they tend to invest in innovative ways, by either starting 'up a business activity that was new to Cape Verde or set[ting] out to improve the quality of already-available services' (Åkesson, 2011, p.73). Referring to a classic typology of return migrants proposed by Cerase (1974), Boccagni finds that many returnees in Ecuador practise a 'return of failure' when they have not reaped the expected benefits from migration or a 'return of conservativism' when they have made some personal progress but lack the resources and critical mass 'to induce wider social changes' (Boccagni, 2011, p.477). Far less frequently, migrants perform a 'return of innovation' in which they invest the financial, human and social capital which they have expanded during life abroad. Recent assessments of return entrepreneurship in Ecuador confirm Boccagni's findings, indicating that many engage in forms of necessity entrepreneurship that new government measures prove inadequate to provide with tailored support (Vancluysen et al., 2017). In West Africa, Black and Castaldo (2009) argue that migrants who, instead of investing in self-employment activities on the informal market, register a business after return contribute to economic growth in Côte d'Ivoire and Ghana by generating tax revenue and adding to the gross domestic product. In my own work in Senegal, I have concluded that the different investment logics of migrants 'reflect different personal dispositions towards national development goals' (Sinatti, 2015b, p.103). Most migrants loosely identify with the agenda of national economic growth set by their governments. The majority feel that, migration being a private project, personal advancement for them and their families should be the desired outcome; others feel committed to promoting homeland development, however with a greater interest for the change they might instil, for instance, in people's values or work ethics.

To conclude, the synthesis of scholarly work reviewed so far suggests that policies and programmes are often based on simplistic assumptions about the linkages between return migration, entrepreneurship and development. I argue that the emphasis on economic development outcomes and, more often, on macro-economic growth leads to a limited understanding of migrants' development potential. Migrants themselves are actors in return and development who also have a voice. I address what the implications might be in the next section.

## BEYOND ECONOMIC DEVELOPMENT: INSIGHTS FROM TRANSNATIONALISM

I have thus far claimed that over-emphasis on the economic dimension characterises policies and programmes either targeting a selection of opportunity-driven entrepreneurs, or wanting to boost the skills of needs-based entrepreneurs. Whether national economic growth or poverty reduction, in short, it is the economic aspect of return entrepreneurship that is seen as constituting its main developmental impact. In contrast with this economic focus, scholarship inspired by a transnational approach to migration has contributed a more nuanced understanding of the development outcomes of return entrepreneurship. We know, in fact, from – largely qualitative – research that development repercussions are also felt in social, cultural and political spheres. Migrants combine economic aspirations with personal aspirations, as well as familial obligations. They transfer non-economic capital alongside economic capital, in the form of social remittances, defined as the 'ideas, behaviors, identities, and social capital that flow from receiving- to sending-country communities' (Levitt, 2001, p.54). In short, the transnational approach allows the various and complex development repercussions of entrepreneurship to be uncovered (Landolt, 2001).

### Human Capital: Innovative Businesses and the Repatriation of Skills

The distinction introduced above between needs-based and opportunity-driven entrepreneurs is mirrored in discussions about migrants' ability to repatriate human capital and skills that can innovate local markets back home.

Early research on return migrant entrepreneurship in West Africa (Ammassari, 2004; Tiemoko, 2004) showed an important difference between unskilled and highly skilled returnees, the former being less innovative in their entrepreneurial projects and the latter carrying greater potential to influence development back home. Later empirical literature from several countries confirms that returnees frequently follow investment trends in largely saturated fields, more often pursuing imitative businesses than investing in new ideas (Åkesson, 2011; Eriksson-Baaz, 2015; Sinatti, 2011, 2015b). Examples of overcrowded sectors from Congo and Senegal include transport, the import–export of various goods, the agricultural sector, the tourism industry and the service industry (Eriksson-Baaz, 2015; Sinatti, 2015b). Among the less numerous opportunity-driven return migrants, there is a strongly felt need to come up with new ideas that can make a difference in home markets. In the Democratic Republic of Congo, for instance, innovative return entrepreneurs have set up businesses as foreign investment brokers, facilitating access to the local market to overseas companies – a niche difficult to access for local entrepreneurs and that feeds on transnational social capital built up during immigration (Eriksson-Baaz, 2015).

Evidence from different African countries shows that innovative migrant entrepreneurs see their country of origin as a land of opportunities 'precisely because they "are not finished", in contrast to Western countries where "everything is done"' (Kleist, 2015, p.73). Return entrepreneurs, however, do not operate in a vacuum. Their endeavours are embedded in the economic and political realities of the home countries, which may favour or hinder investment. In a study about return entrepreneurs to Tunisia, Cassarino (2000) found that their social and economic networks responded to the fallacies of policies and programmes initiated by the Tunisian government to facilitate participatory development. Cassarino supports this finding with an account of structural adjustment programmes supported by the International Monetary Fund and liberal reforms of the Tunisian government following Ben Ali's *coup d'état* and rise to power which, at the end of the 1980s, redefined the relationship between the state and entrepreneurs. Despite these measures contributing to a environment favourable to private investment in the country, return migrants relied heavily on their own transnational networks to ensure greater independence from the state and freedom of action in their pursuit of innovative businesses.

While Tunisia and the other examples just cited are largely concentrated on the African continent, countries elsewhere with economies that have experienced exponential growth offer fertile investment terrain for high-skilled returnees. Saxenian (2006), for instance, researched the businesses established by former Silicon Valley immigrants back in China, India, Israel and Taiwan. Having pursued an evolving policy towards its diaspora, China is a particularly poignant example of how home countries can deliberately invite such forms of investment. In fact, 'while "attracting trade and luring capital" (*zhaoshang yinzi*) constituted the focus of overseas Chinese policy in the first two decades after the reform … "attracting talent and luring knowledge" (*zhaocai yinzhi*) has constituted the catchword for the new policy formulation at a time of China rising' (Liu and van Dongen, 2016, p.820). Since the turn of the millennium, changes in China's policies have thus drawn new generations of diasporic Chinese from the West who have returned and invested particularly in the high-tech sector where they bring technical know-how and exposure to international practices. China's active investment in transnational diaspora governance is largely accountable for this outcome, attracting technology and talent through the establishment of networks and interactive platforms linking state, society and capital (Gruenhagen et al., 2020; Liu and van Dongen, 2016).

Whether investing in stagnant or booming home economies, innovative returnee entrepreneurs largely draw on knowledge and experience gained abroad in their ventures back home. For instance, they may bring new products or technologies onto the market. Examples discussed in the literature include – among others – return entrepreneurs introducing medical scanners which revolutionise the way in which doctors handle emergencies in Albanian hospitals (Barjaba, 2018) or upscaling poultry breeding from a subsistence business to intensive production thanks to imported organisational models and chicken feeding lines in Senegal (Sinatti, 2015b). While repatriated financial and human capital play a key role in such development achievements back home, in the next section I also discuss the importance of social capital among return migrant business-owners.

## Social Capital at Home and Abroad

In an edited volume about return migrants to Africa as development agents (Åkesson and Eriksson-Baaz, 2015), contributors support the argument that, regardless of the financial and human capital that is repatriated in countries of migrant origin, the success of returnees – in particular those investing as entrepreneurs – depends on their ability to *transform* that capital and develop new capital upon return, especially in the form of social capital. Among Burundian return businessmen, for instance, the quality of social relations 'plays a key role in dealing with practical challenges in relation to business development' from assessing the investment market, to finding employees, to attracting customers (Sagmo, 2015, p.109).

Evidence from Cape Verde, the Democratic Republic of Congo, Ghana and Burundi (Åkesson, 2015; Eriksson-Baaz, 2015; Kleist, 2015; Sagmo, 2015) shows the importance for African return migrant entrepreneurs of connections among 'big men'. These are intended to be 'politicians and state agents who can use their positions within the state to enable and regulate business' (Eriksson-Baaz, 2015, p.37) and who can support return migrants with overcoming administrative hurdles and dealing with state authorities. The right connections can literally 'make it or break it' for return migrant entrepreneurs, as testified by Willy, a returnee to the Democratic Republic of Congo eager to invest in solar panels. While this product had a definite market potential in the country, Willy attributed the failure of his project to a lack of suitable contacts in this field (Eriksson-Baaz, 2015). This and other examples show that a solid business idea and human and financial means alone, without the ability to navigate relevant local networks and power structures, are unable to ensure success.

Social capital held back home may thus support entrepreneurship but it may also have a dark side. As many qualitative studies have confirmed, migrants are exposed to taxing demands from families and friends to respect social norms of reciprocity or they may rely heavily on relatives as – not always knowledgeable – sources of information supporting their business choices. Sagmo found that returnees who have spent a considerable amount of time out of Burundi may not only lack connections in the relevant field for their business but may also rely excessively on close ties with family and friends that are imbued with power imbalances, trust relations and expectations of reciprocity. As one of her respondents elegantly put it: 'Your success and failure is not always entirely up to you. It is up to all these people behind you, or not behind you' (Sagmo, 2015, p.122). Sagmo found that many returnee entrepreneurs often club together, offering vital support to each other in dealing with the feelings of frustration, alienation and mistrust which they encounter while setting up businesses back home.

Having just argued for the importance of social capital held at home for entrepreneurs to promote development, I also wish to highlight the importance of social capital held abroad after return, through sustained transnational exchanges. In much policy, entrepreneurial investment back home implicitly points to a severing of ties with the country of immigration (Sinatti, 2015a). Sustaining transnational business connections, instead, is vital to many return enterprises. Cassarino (2000, p.183), for instance, finds that 'cross-border and economic networks ... are intentionally created and intentionally organised' by Tunisia's new entrepreneurs. He highlights the non-ethnic nature of such networks, which are not simply based on common religious or kinship ties but on the deliberate exchange of complementary resources between return entrepreneurs and their European partners. The case of one of his respondents is exemplary: after studying industrial engineering in France, Hédi was employed by a bank to oversee credits granted to large companies in the tech sector. In this position, he gained knowledge and networks with key board members in the corporate world which, together with his Tunisian background, made him the perfect candidate for a fibreglass-producing firm wanting to offshore its production to Tunisia. Hédi managed the Tunisian subsidiary for a few years before setting up his own company in the same sector, supplying local – rather than international – clients and therefore ensuring continued collaboration – rather than competition – with his former employer. As this case illustrates, social and economic ties in the countries of immigration offer essential support for the businesses of many returnees in Tunisia as well as elsewhere. Most importantly in the Tunisian case, by relying on external social and economic networks, return entrepreneurs gain substantial autonomy and ensure limited interference from Tunisian institutions and business associations in their enterprises. By selectively choosing to engage with some networks and avoid others, they position themselves in a distinct in-between space that fosters relationships that are functional to their businesses.

By emphasising *return*, policies underestimate not only the importance of continued transnational ties for businesses established in the homeland but also the development potential back home of migrant enterprises in the country of immigration (therefore with an option of non-return). This goes against a tradition of scholarship that highlights the importance of ethnic entrepreneurship and the transnational dimension of its activities (Rath et al., 2019; Sommer, 2020; Zapata-Barrero and Rezaei, 2019). The import and export of goods and services, in fact, may not require a firm to be formally established in the country of origin and involve forms of transnational mobility that entail shuttling between countries, rather than opting for permanent return (Sinatti, 2011). In the fair-trade sector, for instance, migrants may find a market in the country of immigration for merchandise produced back home. Returnee and overseas-based transnational businesses similarly rely on the upkeeping of social ties abroad; both may promote development in the home country.

Many return migrant entrepreneurs master collaboration across different social fields by combining social capital both back home and abroad. This ability is vital to transform financial and human capital for development. Migrants who successfully bridge what they have learned abroad with resources back home – that they either already had or developed after return – have an added edge.

**Migrant-centred Development**

Empirical research shows that return migrant entrepreneurs often do not share the developmental aims of their governments of origin (Boccagni, 2011; Cohen, 2009; Sinatti, 2015a, 2015b, 2019). Nonetheless, they do 'constitute cultural and development brokers and resources who can – and should – contribute to their countries of origin ... as agents of change' (Turner and Kleist, 2013, p.195). This is confirmed by findings from Ammassari's (2004, 2009) studies in Côte d'Ivoire and Ghana, where returnees have important socio-cultural and political impacts on their home countries. Before following up on this point, it is important to place it in the broader context of the underlying understandings of development, as these differ significantly from the macro-economic development laid out in state policies. Scholars adopting a migrant-centred approach in fact emphasise the importance of a *human* approach to development (Sinatti, 2019). This is understood as the expansion of people's capabilities:

the opportunities people have to do and be what they have reason to value. Such an approach is therefore centred around what return migrants themselves value as important instances of change in their home countries (Sinatti, 2019).

What form such instances of change might take is illustrated by research among return migrant entrepreneurs in various countries. Studies highlight an ambition to change the work culture of others without migration experience so that they are 'able to question and change *doxa*' in Ghana (Kleist, 2015, p.80) or to instil a new work ethic among co-workers in the Democratic Republic of Congo (Eriksson-Baaz, 2015, p.34). In Senegal, my own research shows that returnees owning small companies that give employment to others see this 'as a means to expand the capabilities of other people by influencing both the material resources they have access to and the values that shape what they do with them' (Sinatti, 2019, p.618).

Return migrants in Ghana and Cote d'Ivoire have initiated change beyond their families and work environments, for instance promoting community development initiatives or engaging in advocacy work (Ammassari, 2009). Returnees – Ammassari argues – are often influential figures in their home society with the standing to shape decisions in the public sphere or to initiate societal change through development projects in fields ranging from child education to female empowerment, human rights and democratisation, water and sanitation and healthcare and agricultural innovation. Evidence from both Ghana and Côte d'Ivoire (Ammassari, 2009; Kleist, 2015) shows that, while their businesses tend to concentrate in larger urban areas, the development initiatives of return migrant entrepreneurs often focus on the latter's villages of origin.

The development aspirations shared by return migrant entrepreneurs largely differ from those on the policy agendas of their countries of origin. An important reminder is nonetheless required here: while not necessarily sharing the same development goals, states do still play an important role in shaping the economic and political environment in which their investments take place. As exemplified earlier in this chapter, the structural and institutional conditions they set may sustain or hinder the productive endeavours of return migrants.

## CONCLUSION

In this chapter, I have distinguished between two approaches to return, entrepreneurship and development. I have shown that the first approach, the basis of state-led policies and programmes, emphasises the economic gains brought by migrant business investments back home. The second approach, departing from the experiences and practices of the migrants themselves, shows a more multi-faceted side to development, conceived beyond economic gains and incorporating broader social, cultural and political change. This is inspired by notions of human development, defined by migrants' own values and aspirations. Both approaches result in very different understandings of the benefits that may be reaped from the linkages between return, entrepreneurship and development. Often, they lead to a mismatch between policies and programmes on the one hand and the practices of return migrant entrepreneurs on the other.

In this concluding section, I argue against a dualistic and mutually exclusive vision of these approaches. Instead, I call for the pursuit of the middle ground to exploit the explanatory power of both macro and micro approaches and achieve a better understanding of the complex linkages between return, entrepreneurship and development. I am supported in this idea by

Anghel et al. (2019, p.2) who, in a recent volume about transnational return, emphasise the need for meso-level analysis to acknowledge that 'everyday processes and small-scale changes are as important as macro-economic transformations for understanding the societal impact of migration'. Scholars have recognised that return migration is an engine of social change that should be understood beyond a top-down macro-level focus on remittances and financial gains (Castles, 2010; Dahles, 2015; van Hear, 2010). From the bottom-up, Levitt and Lamba-Nieves (2011, p.1) argue that 'social remittances can scale up from local-level impacts to affect regional and national change and scale out to affect other domains of practice'. Extending this thinking to return entrepreneurship, migrants' transnational involvement across more countries initiates mundane forms of change that may acquire critical mass at the level of families and local communities and within their larger social networks. Yet in the literature – and despite return migrant entrepreneurs being described as important brokers and middlemen between two worlds – their 'transnational dimension … has remained widely unexplored' (Zapata-Barrero and Rezaei, 2019, p.1960). Here, I argue, the joint use of a state-centred and a migrant-centred transnational approach may recognise the role of return entrepreneurship as mobilising more than financial capital and facilitating the transfer of various social remittances. A transnational approach, therefore, recognises the cultural, political and social transformations that – in given state-induced conditions – may emerge as by-products of migrant investments (Zapata-Barrero and Rezaei, 2019).

Development is the outcome of specific interactions between state policies and programmes and the initiatives of return migrant entrepreneurs. The distinction introduced above points not only to the contributions which both these parties might make but also to the different understandings of development with which they may identify. This raises important additional questions with regards to policies reaching out to return migrant entrepreneurs as development agents. One may ask: With whom does the responsibility lie to define what development goals and ambitions should look like? Is it the prerogative of sovereign states? Or should it reside with the migrants? To what extent may a reconciliation between these two responsibilities be possible? If so, what would it look like?

In response to such questions, I suggest here that a meso-level understanding of the linkages between return, entrepreneurship and development would be beneficial. Policies and programmes would reap better results when based on a fuller understanding that both incorporates a focus on structural conditions and consequences at the macro level and acknowledges the potential for change brought by migrants and their transnational practices. A meso-level approach, in short, would add value through an increased capacity to formulate policies and programmes that conceive of development in terms of longer-term processes of economic as well as societal and cultural change.

## NOTE

1. Started in 2008 and continued since then with different funding streams, the JMDI is the largest initiative for migration and development ever to be set up in Europe. See: http://www.migration4development.org. More information about the project mentioned here can be found in Sinatti and Alvarez Tinajero (2011).

# REFERENCES

Åkesson, L. (2011) 'Making migrants responsible for development: Cape Verdean returnees and northern migration policies', *Africa Spectrum*, **46** (1), 61–83.

Åkesson, L. (2015) 'Obstacles and openings: returnees and small-scale businesses in Cape Verde' in L. Åkesson and M. Eriksson-Baaz (eds), *Africa's Return Migrants: The New Developers?*, London: Zed Books, pp. 152–72.

Åkesson, L. and Eriksson-Baaz, M. (eds) (2015) *Africa's Return Migrants: The New Developers?*, London: Zed Books.

Ammassari, S. (2004) 'From nation-building to entrepreneurship: the impact of elite return migrants on Côte d'Ivoire and Ghana', *Population, Space and Place*, **10** (2), 133–54.

Ammassari, S. (2009) *Migration and Development: Factoring Return into the Equation*, Newcastle-upon-Tyne: Cambridge Scholars Publishing.

Andersson, R. (2014) *Illegality, Inc.*, Oakland CA: University of California Press.

Anghel, R.G., Fauser, M. and Boccagni, P. (eds) (2019) *Transnational Return and Social Change. Hierarchies, Identities and Ideas*, London and New York: Anthem Press.

Barjaba, J. (2018) *Exploring Transnational Entrepreneurship among Albanian Migrants and Returnees*, Brighton: University of Sussex, unpublished PhD thesis in Migration Studies.

Basch, L., Glick Schiller, N. and Szanton Blanc, C. (1994) *Nations Unbound: Transnational Projects, Postcolonial Predicaments, and Deterritorialized Nation-States*, Langhorne PA: Gordon and Breach.

Batista, C., McIndoe-Calder, T. and Vicente, P.C. (2017) 'Return migration, self-selection and entrepreneurship', *Oxford Bulletin of Economics and Statistics*, **79** (5), 797–821.

Black, R. and Castaldo, A. (2009) 'Return migration and entrepreneurship in Ghana and Côte d'Ivoire: the role of capital transfers', *Tijdschrift voor Economische en Sociale Geographie*, **100** (1), 44–58.

Boccagni, P. (2011) 'The framing of return from above and below in Ecuadorian migration: a project, a myth, or a political device?', *Global Networks*, **11** (4), 461–80.

Cassarino, J.-P. (2000) *Tunisian New Entrepreneurs and Their Past Experiences of Migration in Europe*, Aldershot: Ashgate.

Castles, S. (2010) 'Understanding global migration: a social transformation perspective', *Journal of Ethnic and Migration Studies*, **36** (10), 1565–86.

Cerase, F.P. (1974) 'Expectations and reality: a case study of return migration from the United States to Southern Italy', *International Migration Review*, **8** (2), 245–62.

Cohen, N. (2009) 'Come home, be professional: ethno-nationalism and economic rationalism in Israel's return migration strategy', *Immigrants and Minorities*, **27** (1), 1–28.

Croitoru, A. (2019) 'No entrepreneurship without opportunity: the intersection of return migration research and entrepreneurship literature', *Social Change Review*, **17** (1), 33–60.

Dahles, H. (2015) 'Reverse diasporas' capital investments at home' in S. Köngeter and W. Smith (eds), *Transnational Agency and Migration. Actors, Movements, and Social Support*, London: Routledge, pp. 67–84.

Démurger, S. and Xu, H. (2011) 'Return migrants: the rise of new entrepreneurs in rural China', *World Development*, **39** (10), 1847–61.

Eriksson-Baaz, M. (2015) 'Successive flops and occasional feats: development contributions and thorny social navigation among Congolese return migrants', *Africa's Return Migrants: The New Developers?*, in L. Åkesson and M. Eriksson-Baaz (eds) London: Zed Books, pp. 23–43.

Gamlen, A. (2006) *Diaspora Engagement Policies: What Are They, and What Kinds of States Use Them?*, Oxford: University of Oxford, COMPAS Working Paper No. 32.

Gamlen, A., Cummings, M.E. and Vaaler, P.M. (2019) 'Explaining the rise of diaspora institutions', *Journal of Ethnic and Migration Studies*, **45** (4), 492–516.

Gammeltoft-Hansen, T. and Nyberg-Sørensen, N. (eds) (2012) *The Migration Industry and the Commercialization of International Migration*, London: Routledge.

Gruenhagen, J.H., Davidsson, P. and Sawang, S. (2020) 'Returnee entrepreneurs: a systematic literature review, thematic analysis, and research agenda', *Foundations and Trends in Entrepreneurship*, **16** (4), 310–92.

Gubert, F. and Nordman, C.J. (2011) 'Return migration and small enterprise development in the Maghreb' in S. Plaza and D. Ratha (eds), *Diaspora for Development in Africa*, Washington DC: The World Bank, pp. 103–26.
Hagan, J.M. and Wassink, J. (2016) 'New skills, new jobs: return migration, skill transfers, and business formation in Mexico', *Social Problems*, **63** (4), 513–33.
Ho, E.L.E. (2011) '"Claiming" the diaspora: elite mobility, sending state strategies and the spatialities of citizenship', *Progress in Human Geography*, **35** (6), 757–72.
Ho, E.L.E., Hickey, M. and Yeoh, B.S.A. (2015) 'Special issue introduction: new research directions and critical perspectives on diaspora strategies', *Geoforum*, **59**, 153–8.
Kamei, S. (2013) 'Diaspora as the "sixth region of Africa": an assessment of the African Union Initiative, 2002–2010', *Diaspora Studies*, **4** (1), 59–76.
Kilic, T., Carletto, C., Davis, B. and Zezza, A. (2009) 'Investing back home: return migration and business ownership in Albania', *Economics of Transition*, **17** (3), 587–623.
Kleist, N. (2015) 'Pushing development: a case study of highly skilled male return migration to Ghana' in L. Åkesson and M. Eriksson-Baaz (eds), *Africa's Return Migrants: The New Developers?*, London: Zed Books, pp. 64–86.
Landolt, P. (2001) 'Salvadoran economic transnationalism: embedded strategies for household maintenance, immigrant incorporation and entrepreneurial expansion', *Global Networks*, **1** (3), 217–41.
Levitt, P. (2001) *The Transnational Villagers*, Berkeley: University of California Press.
Levitt, P. and Lamba-Nieves, D. (2011) 'Social remittances revisited', *Journal of Ethnic and Migration Studies*, **37** (1), 1–22.
Liu, H. and van Dongen, E. (2016) 'China's diaspora policies as a new mode of transnational governance', *Journal of Contemporary China*, **25** (102), 805–21.
Martinez, C., Cummings, M.E. and Vaaler, P.M. (2015) 'Economic informality and the venture funding impact of migrant remittances to developing countries', *Journal of Business Venturing*, **30** (4), 526–45.
Mezger Kveder, C. and Beauchemin, C. (2015) 'The role of international migration experience for investment at home: direct, indirect, and equalising effects in Senegal', *Population, Space and Place*, **21** (6), 535–52.
Murphy, R. (2002) 'Return migration, entrepreneurship, and state-sponsored urbanization in the Jiangxi countryside' in J.R. Logan (ed.), *The New Chinese City: Globalization and Market Reform*, Oxford: Blackwell, pp. 229–44.
Naudé, W., Siegel, M. and Marchand, K. (2017) 'Migration, entrepreneurship and development: critical questions', *IZA Journal of Migration*, **6** (5), 1–16.
Østergaard-Nielsen, E. (ed.) (2003) *International Migration and Sending Countries: Perceptions, Policies and Transnational Relations*, Basingstoke: Palgrave Macmillan.
Ragazzi, F. (2009) 'Governing diasporas', *International Political Sociology*, **3** (4), 378–97.
Rath, J., Solano, G. and Schutjens, V. (2019) 'Migrant entrepreneurship and transnational links' in C. Inglis, W. Li and B. Khadria (eds), *The Sage Handbook on International Migration*, Thousand Oaks CA: Sage, pp. 450–65.
Sagmo, T.H. (2015) 'The role of social capital in post-conflict business development: perspectives from returning migrants in Burundi' in L. Åkesson and M. Eriksson-Baaz (eds), *Africa's Return Migrants: The New Developers?*, London: Zed Books, pp. 109–29.
Saxenian, A. (2006) *The New Argonauts: Regional Advantage in a Global Economy*, Cambridge MA: Harvard University Press.
Sinatti, G. (2011) '"Mobile transmigrants" or "unsettled returnees"? Myth of return and permanent resettlement among Senegalese migrants', *Population, Space and Place*, **17** (2), 153–66.
Sinatti, G. (2015a). 'Return migration as a win–win–win scenario? Visions of return among Senegalese migrants, the state of origin and receiving countries', *Ethnic and Racial Studies*, **38** (2), 275–91.
Sinatti, G. (2015b) '"Come back, invest, and advance the country". Policy myths and migrant realities of return and development in Senegal' in L. Åkesson and M. Eriksson-Baaz (eds), *Africa's Return Migrants: The New Developers?*, London: Zed Books, pp. 87–108.
Sinatti, G. (2019) 'Return migration, entrepreneurship and development: contrasting the economic growth perspective of Senegal's diaspora policy through a migrant-centred approach', *African Studies*, **78** (4), 609–23.

Sinatti, G. and Alvarez Tinajero, S.P. (2011) *Migration and Development: A Bottom-Up Approach. A Handbook for Practitioners and Policymakers*, Brussels: EC–UN Joint Migration and Development Initiative (JMDI).

Sommer, E. (2020) *Social Capital as a Resource for Migrant Entrepreneurship. Self-Employed Migrants from the Former Soviet Union in Germany*, Wiesbaden: Springer.

Tiemoko, R. (2004) 'Migration, return and socio-economic change in West Africa: the role of family', *Population, Space and Place*, **10** (2), 155–74.

Tsuda, T. (2010) 'Ethnic return migration and the nation-state: encouraging the diaspora to return "home"', *Nations and Nationalism*, **16** (4), 616–36.

Turner, S. and Kleist, N. (2013) 'Introduction: agents of change? Staging and governing diasporas and the African state', *African Studies*, **72** (2), 192–206.

van Hear, N. (2010) 'Theories of migration and social change', *Journal of Ethnic and Migration Studies*, **36** (10), 1531–6.

Vancluysen, S., Calfat, G. and Pesántez, B. (2017) 'Return for development or "business" as usual? The Ecuadorian experience', *Migration and Development*, **6** (2), 232–52.

Zapata-Barrero, R. and Rezaei, S. (2019) 'Diaspora governance and transnational entrepreneurship: the rise of an emerging social global pattern in migration studies', *Journal of Ethnic and Migration Studies*, **46** (10), 1959–73.

# Index

Abainza, L. 325
Abarcar, P. 26
Abbasi-Shavazi, M.J. 286
Abrego, L. 85
'acculturation paradox' 232
accumulation hypothesis 26
Achughbabian, Alexandre 143
'active ageing' 273
'active migrant' households 325
adult second generation 9
Afghan asylum-seeker 78
Agambenian biopolitics 129
ageing and lifestyle migrants 273–4
*The Age of Migration* (Castles and Miller) 9, 319
aggregate sustainable return 173
'aggressive behaviour' 143
Åkesson, L. 1, 9, 16, 325, 333, 348
Albanian return migrants 246
Alberts, H.C. 261
Alboim, N. 263
Alcalde, M.C. 63
Ali, N. 286
Alvarez, Hernández 3
Alves, E. 261, 263, 264
Ambrosetti, E. 58
Ambrosini, M. 31
Amelina, A. 16
Ammassari, S. 9, 324, 332, 352
Anacka, M. 301
Andersson, R. 154
Anghel, R. 1, 304, 354
Anthias, F. 292
    *Gender and Migration in Southern Europe: Women on the Move* 53, 65
Appadurai, A. 189
apprehension 158–9
Apsite-Berina, E. 302
Arendt, H. 91
Arenliu, A. 230
AR programmes *see* assisted return (AR) programmes
Article 2(2)(a) Return Directive (RD) 149
Article 4(3) of the Treaty on European Union 142
Article 11(1) and (2) RD 149
Article 15 of the Return Directive 149
Asian financial crisis 1997 26, 275
Asiedu, A. 47, 101
aspiration–ability framework 7
aspiration–ability model 7

assimilation and integration 29
assisted return (AR) programmes 2, 108, 159–61
    assistance 110
    content, meaning and outcome of 117–18
    pre-return assistance 110–117
    of rejected asylum-seekers 191–2
    return 109
    voluntariness 109–10
Assisted Voluntary Return and Reintegration (AVRR) programmes 167, 177, 234
'assisted voluntary return' (AVR) programmes 11, 70, 73, 74, 80, 109, 191
Assmuth, L. 251
asylum-seekers 141–2
AVR programmes *see* 'assisted voluntary return' (AVR) programmes
AVRR programmes *see* Assisted Voluntary Return and Reintegration (AVRR) programmes
Azose, J.J. 1

Baaz, M.E. 1, 9, 16, 325, 333
Bahar, D. 32
Bakalova, M. 304, 305
Baláž, V. 262, 265
Baldassar, L. 97–100, 103
    *Visits Home* 96
Barcevičius, E. 304–6, 308
Barrett, A. 31
Bartram, D. 3, 73
Basch, L. 39
Bastia, T. 55
Batista, C. 30, 33
Battistella, G. 5
Bell, J. 44, 45
Ben Ali 350
Benson, M. 274
Benthamite Panopticon 124
Bergmark, R. 232
Berriane, J. 263
Berry, J.W. 300
Bertoli, S. 34
Bhimji, F. 288
Bijwaard, G.E. 26, 28, 259
bilateral social-security agreements 222
Bilgili, Ö. 6, 10, 15
biopolitical function 128
biopolitics 124, 129
*Birds of Passage* (Piore) 54

Black, R. 176, 324, 348
Boccagni, P. 46, 323, 325, 346
Bolognani, M. 98, 272, 286
Borjas, G. 25, 28
Börjesson, M. 257
Bosnian refugee returns 191
Botterill, K. 45, 273, 275
Bovenkerk, F. 4, 333
  *The Sociology of Return Migration* 39
brain gain 207
Bratsberg, B. 25, 28
British-Caribbean migration system 8
British Community Assistance Fund 276
British retirement community 274
Brønden, B.M. 319
Brooks, R.B. 248, 249
Brubaker, R. 285
Bryła, P. 259
Brzozowski, J. 32
Buffel, T. 45
Bushin, N. 246
Buzinska, L. 262

Calfat, G. 325
'capabilities approach' 315
capacity development 334–5
care visits 100
Carletto, C. 32, 299
Carling, J. 6–8, 17, 41, 175, 244, 321
Cassarino, J.-P. 5–8, 17, 39, 49, 174, 176, 262, 277, 316, 322, 350, 351
Castaldo, A. 324, 348
Castles, S. 154, 318
  *The Age of Migration* (Castles and Miller) 9, 319
CD4D 334, 337, 338, 340 *see* Connecting Diaspora for Development (CD4D)
  knowledge transfer in 335–7
Ceballos, M. 232
CEE *see* Central and Eastern Europe (CEE)
Celaj, Skerdjan 143
Cena, E. 242, 246
Central and Eastern Europe (CEE) 9, 299, 309
  migrants and patterns of return migration 301–4
  social change and social remittances 306–8
  structural factors conditioning reintegration experiences 304–6
Centre for International Migration and Development (CIM) 332
Cerase, F.P. 5, 6, 320–322, 332, 333, 348
Chabé-Ferret, B. 29
Chaoimh, E.N. 259, 261
Chauvet, L. 33
Chen, J. 230

child-centred approach 9
children, return migration of 241–2
  integration 249–51
  motivation for return 243
  psychosocial wellbeing perspective 243–6
  sense of belonging and children's agency 246–7
  third culture kid (TCK) 247–9
'children-in-families' approach 246
Choudhury, P. 32
Christou, A. 6, 16, 39, 59, 189, 285, 288, 289, 292
Cieślik, A. 307
CIM *see* Centre for International Migration and Development (CIM)
civil-society actors 115, 116
civil-society organisations 115, 116, 304
'classic' diaspora characteristics 341
client–patron relationships 190
Co, C. 31
Cohen, N. 346
Cohen, R. 17
Colburn, B. 72
Cole, Phillip 132
*Coming Home to an (Un)familiar Country* (Dzięglewski) 306
communist party rule 299
'comprehensive and cooperative migration management approach' 172
conceptualisation and theorisation of return 9–11
Coniglio, N.D. 32
Connecting Diaspora for Development (CD4D) 331, 333–8
Constant, A. 27
contemporary migration studies 72
Conway, D. 57
Conze, B. 232
Cook-Martín, D. 286
Cordaid 160
Cormoș, V.-C. 307
corporeal visits 96
corruption 185, 195
  definitions and debates 186–7
  and return, disaggregating 192–4
  and returnees' psychosocial reintegration 188–90
  and social remittances 190–192
  in study of return migration 187–8
'counter-diasporic migration' 289
Court of Justice of the EU (CJEU) on the Directive 137, 140, 142, 143, 145, 147–9
Covarrubias, Márquez 317
Cowen, E.L. 248
critical geographical analyses 124
Croucher, S. 270

Crul, M. 284
cultural globalisation and development 15
cultural isomorphisms 187
cultural maintenance 201
cultural obligations 97
cultural reintegration of returnees 300
*A Culture of Corruption* (Smith) 195

'data-craving' in governance structures 128–9
Davids, T. 333
decision-making process 246
'decision to return' 78
De Coulon, A. 31
De Genova, N. 11
de Haas, H. 12, 212, 319, 321, 322
de Koning, M. 176
Delgado Wise, R. 6
demand-oriented approach 340
Democratic Republic of Congo 350, 352
departheid 84, 90–91
    defining 85–7
    uncovering 88–90
'deportability' 11
deportation
    continuum 125
    geopolitics of 123
    markets and technologies 127–9
    regimes 11, 123–5
deportation politics 131
    continuums, actors and corridors in 125–7
    race and postcoloniality in 129–30
deportation studies, contours of 122
    continuums, actors and corridors in deportation politics 125–7
    deportation markets and technologies 127–9
    deportation regimes and sovereign biopolitics 123–5
    feasibility and positionality in liberal deportation ethics 130–132
    race and postcoloniality in deportation politics 129–30
'deportation turn' 122
de Sardan, J.-P.O. 187
destitution and vulnerability 114
detention 86, 87, 88, 91, 138–41, 142, 143, 144–6, 148, 149, 154, 158, 161
*Development as Freedom* (Sen) 315
'development-from-below' effects 319
De Vreyer, P. 31
'diaspora experts' 334
diaspora return and knowledge transfer and capacity development 331–3
    case study 333–8
'diasporic belongingness' 246
Diatta, M.A. 325

*Dienst Terugkeer & Vertrek* 157
'digital biopolitics' 128
'disruptive geographical relocation' 245
'distinctly disposable commodity' 124
Djajic, S. 25
Dodge, R. 226
'double return migration' 17
Drotbohm, H. 60, 126
'dual-track policy' 111, 157
Duci, V. 242, 246, 247
Duda-Mikulin, E. 301
duration of absence 193
Dustmann, C. 25, 29, 30, 241
Dutch Refugee Council 160
Dutch return enforcement structure 162
Dutch return migration industry 153
Dutch return-policy landscape 158
Duval, D.T. 44, 45
Düvell, F. 307
Dzięglewski, M.
    *Coming Home to an (Un)familiar Country* 306

Eastmond, M. 304
ECHR *see* European Convention on Human Rights (ECHR)
economic behaviour 29
economic development 349–53
economic equilibrium model 318
economic reintegration 189–90
'economic self-sufficiency' 171
economics of return migration
    after return 30–34
    empirical challenges 27–8
    empirical evidence 25–7
    before return 29
    theoretical literature 24–5
economic theories 316–17
'economic transnationalism' 319
economic visits 101–2
efficient resource mobilisation 7
Eimermann, M. 272
El Dridi, Hassen 143
Elizalde, Guzman 206
Elmallakh, N. 32
entrepreneurial activity 193
entrepreneurship 30
Erdal, M.B. 3, 6, 7, 41, 44, 45, 72
ERPUM *see* European Return Platform for Unaccompanied Minors (ERPUM)
Ethiopian return migration 65
ethnic return migrants 331
EU Charter for Fundamental Rights 140, 147
EU convergence policy 305
EU-funded reintegration programme 116

EU migration policy 108
EU Return Fund 108
EU return policy 148
European asylum systems 122
European AVVR programmes 171
European Commission's (EC) 2020 Migration Pact 122
European Convention on Human Rights (ECHR) 140
European Court of Human Rights 145
European Migration Network 169, 174, 175
European Parliament 175
European Return Directive (2008/115/EC) 191
European Return Platform for Unaccompanied Minors (ERPUM) 126
European Union (EU)-funded MAFE project 324
European Union Return Directive 108

facilitation and control of return 156–8
'failed' or 'bogus' asylum-seekers 84
Faist, Thomas 319
'false universalism' 131
'familialistic' care culture 274
family-based model of migration 56
family care duties 64
femininities in forced return 60–61
Flahaux, M.-L. 30
Flouri, E. 229
Fokkema, T. 321, 322
Fonseca, A. 234
forced removal and detention *see* detention
forced return
    femininities in 60–61
forced *versus* voluntary return 227
Fordist system 8
formal training 336, 338
Foucauldian governmentality 129
Foucault, M. 124
Fox, J. 303
fragmentation 168
freedom of movement 87, 92
'functional interlinkages' 97
fundamental rights obligations 108
Furukawa, T. 232

Galor, O. 29
Gamlen, A. 12, 319
Gammeltoft-Hansen, T. 154
*Gastarbeiter* programme 56
Gaw, K.F. 232
GCM *see* Global Compact for Migration (GCM)
GEC *see* Global Economic Crisis (GEC)
Geddie, K. 260, 265

*Gender and Migration in Southern Europe: Women on the Move* (Anthias and Lazaridis) 53, 65
'gendered geographies of power' 55
'gendered racial removal program' 60
gendering return migration 53
    changing masculinities and femininities in forced return 60–61
    gendered roles after return 61–4
    gender in migration and return 54–6
    model of shifting gender dynamics 56–7
    motivations and decisions to return 57–9
gender-role attitudes 62
Gent, S. 176
geographical proximity 104
German Socio-Economic Panel (GSOEP) 26
Ghosh, B. 1, 317, 326
Gibson, J. 27
Giner-Montfort, J. 273, 277
Girma, H. 64
Glick Schiller, N. 40, 201
Global Compact for Migration (GCM) 11, 108, 178, 179, 235
*Global Compact on Safe, Orderly and Regular Migration* 167
Global Economic Crisis (GEC) 303
Global South 122
Gmelch, G. 6, 10, 14, 39, 49, 332
Gmelch, S.B. 10
Goggin, J. 31
Golash-Boza, T. 60
Goldstein, S. 248, 249
Gonzalez, C. 231
government's position towards returnees 205
Grabowska, I. 307
Grant, R. 47
grassroots civil-society organisations 157
'Greektown' communities 16
GSOEP *see* German Socio-Economic Panel (GSOEP)
Gu, Q. 47
Guarnizo, L.E. 40

Haas, H. 243
Hall, K. 276, 279
Hamann, E.T. 245
Han, X. 261
*Handbook for Repatriation and Reintegration Activities* 171
Handlos, Neerup 191
'hard-to-reach' target group 113
Hasselberg, I. 126
Hatfield, M. 241
Hazen, H.D. 261
health problems 232

health services 191
health status 222
healthy psychosocial wellbeing 244
Hernández-Carretero, M. 194
Hernández-León, R. 154, 163
Higgins, K.W. 277
Holden, A. 286
homeland policies 345, 346
Hondagneu-Sotelo, P. 60
host-country-specific human capital 29
Huete, R. 271, 275
Hugo, G.J. 154
human capital 349–51
    acquisition 32
    theory 257
human development 315
'humane and safe return' 126
'humanitarian borders' 126
'humanitarianization of child deportation politics' 126
human rights approaches 235
human rights-based approach 236
human rights-based argument for regularisation 147
Humpage, L. 209

ICE *see* Immigration and Customs Enforcement (ICE)
IDM *see* International Dialogue on Migration (IDM)
IDPs *see* internally displaced persons (IDPs)
illegalised migrants 87
'illiberal practices' 85
immigration
    settlement in country of 220–221
Immigration and Customs Enforcement (ICE) 122
Immigration and Naturalization Service (IND) 157
immigration ethics 130
'implementation gap' 131
'incentives to return' 169
IND *see* Immigration and Naturalization Service (IND)
in-depth interviews 213
individual and organisational capacity development 337–8
individual knowledge 335
innovative businesses and repatriation of skills 349–51
'insider theory' 132
'integrated approach to reintegration' 177
'intentional unpredictability' 302
inter-continental visits 98
internally displaced persons (IDPs) 80
international cultural capital 262

international development discourse 344
International Dialogue on Migration (IDM) 172
international knowledge transfer 32–3
international migrants 190
international migration 4, 80
*International Migration Review* 54
international organisations (IOs) 122, 341
International Organization for Migration (IOM) 74, 88, 160, 168, 171, 176, 177, 192, 201, 233, 234, 333–8
international retirement migration 10
international student migration 9
international student mobility (ISM) 255, 257, 265, 266
intersectionality 55
intersectionality of returnees 228–31
'intersectional thinking' 55
IOM *see* International Organization for Migration (IOM)
IOs *see* international organisations (IOs)
'IrisFarm' 127
irregular migrants
    detention of 140–141
ISM *see* international student mobility (ISM)
Israel, E. 260
Itzigsohn, J. 40
Ivanova, V. 305

James, A. 241
Janoschka, M. 243
Janta, H. 97, 99
Jauhiainen, J.S. 230
Jim Crow laws 90
Jirka, L. 303
JMDI *see* Joint Migration and Development Initiative (JMDI)
Johansson, S.-E. 231
Joint Migration and Development Initiative (JMDI) 347
Jones, R.C. 325
Juverdeanu, C. 303

*Kadzoev* 146
*kafala* system 61
Kalir, B. 2, 10, 13, 125, 127, 130
Kaska, V. 305
Kerpaci, K. 305, 306
Kertzer, D.I. 283
Kilic, T. 32, 299
Kılınç, N. 9, 61, 284, 286, 289, 291, 292
Kim, J.H.J. 260
King, R. 1, 3, 4, 6, 10, 15–17, 39, 57, 59, 188, 189, 242, 245, 260, 261, 263, 284, 286, 288–9, 291–3, 300, 332
Kingminghae, W. 260

kinship networks 96
Kirchkamp, O. 25, 30
Kirdar, M.G. 26
Klagge, B. 332
Klein-Hitpass, K. 332
Kleist, N. 60, 322, 345
*Knooppunt Vrijwillige Terugkeer* 157
Knörr, J. 241
knowledge-based societies 257
'knowledge networks' 168
knowledge transfer, diaspora return and
 and capacity development 331–3
 case study 333–8
Kolaitis, G. 248
*Koppelingswet* 156
Kosack, G. 318
Koser, K. 175, 177
Krzaklewska, E. 302
Krzyżowski, Ł. 306
Kubal, A. 307
Kuka, M. 305, 306
Kulu, H. 286
Kunz, Rahel 315
Kuschminder, K. 1, 4, 65, 66, 175, 177, 332–4, 339
Kveder, C.L.M. 30

labour immigrants 28
labour market 27, 202
labour migrants and retirement 212
 for migrant workers and question of return 213–15
 migrant workers from Southern Europe in Switzerland and retirement 215–17
 settlement return 218
 transnational geographical mobility 219–21
 transnational return 217–18
labour migration 56
labour policy 205
Lacuesta, A. 31
Lafferty, M. 276
Lamba-Nieves, D. 354
Laoire, Ní 242
Lapshyna, I. 307
larger-scale managed repatriations 74
Lazaridis, G.
 *Gender and Migration in Southern Europe: Women on the Move* 53, 65
Leavey, G. 230
Lee, H. 287
Leerkes, A. 74
legal status and administrative procedure 112–13
legal violence 85
'legitimacy deficit' 84
leisure visits 102

Levitt, P. 33, 40, 190, 201, 290, 304, 307, 318, 354
liberal democratic states 10, 84–92
liberal deportation ethics
 feasibility and positionality in 130–132
Lietaert, I. 46, 48
life-course events 262
life-cycle migrants 26
life-stage events 77
lifestyle migrants, returning
 ageing and 273–4
 experiences of return and reintegration 276–9
 lifestyle migration 270–273
 privilege and precarity 274–6
 research agenda on 279–80
lifestyle migration 10, 270–273, 275
lifestyle return
 'magnitude and configuration' of 272
Lin, Y. 260
Lithuanian return migrants 306
Liu, H. 347
local population
 attitudes of 205
local social-welfare services 115
logistic regression model 260
Longitudinal Survey of Immigrants 26
Loughry, M. 229
Lulle, A. 15, 99, 247, 250, 262, 301
Lutz, H. 16

*Mahdi* 145–6
Maher, K. 276
Majidi, N. 12, 14
'Malaysia My Second Home' programme 275
male-led migration model 54
'managed return' of migrants 75
Marchetta, F. 34
Marcu, S. 259, 260
marginalised migrants 191
Márquez Covarrubias, H. 6
Marxist-inspired historical-structural model 14
Marxist political economy model 317
Massey, D.S. 27
Masso, J. 32
Mata-Codesal, D. 320
Mazzucato, V. 47
Mbembe, A. 129
Mbow, N. 325
McCormick, B. 30
McKenzie, D. 27
Mediation Agency for Return 160
Mendoza, C. 260
Menjívar, C. 85
mental-health disorders 232
Mercier, M. 33

Mesnard, A. 25, 30
Mestres, J. 29
migrant-centred development 352–3
migrant-centred perspective 344
migrant communities 42
migrants-as-agents 234
migration
    criminalisation of irregular 142–4
migration-and-return process 15
'migration binaries' 17
*Migration Can Fall Apart* (Miller) 60
'migration chronotope' 9
'migration crisis' 144
migration–development nexus 172, 323–6
    'return–development nexus' 314
    return migration as 315–20
*The Migration–Development Nexus* (Van Hear and Sørensen) 315
migration–displacement nexus 72
Migration for Development in Africa Programme (MIDA) 332
'Migration for Development' programme 332
migration industry 155
migration model 258
'migration project' 79
migratory generation
    classification of 284
Milbourne, R. 25
Miller, M.J. 9
    *The Age of Migration* 319
Miller, O.A.
    *Migration Can Fall Apart* 60
Misheva, M. 304, 305
'mixed embeddedness' 174
mobilities framework 7
modern telecommunications 301
Mommers, C. 232
money-making and white supremacy 88–90
Moreh, C. 301
Morokvaśic, M. 54
Mueller, C. 314, 334
Mueller, D. 98
Müller, F. 232
Municio-Larsson, I. 249
'myth of return' 38

Nadler, R. 1
'national order of things' 122
Nay, O. 168
Nazi concentration camps 124
'necropolitics' 129
NELM *see* new economics of labour migration (NELM)
neoclassical approach 5
neoclassical equilibrium theory 14

neo-pessimism 319
Netherlands, return industry in 153, 162–3
    Dutch return industry 156–62
    'industry' of migration and return 154–6
Neto, F. 300
Nevinskaitė, L. 306, 308
new economics of labour migration (NELM) 5, 15, 316, 322
new implications of return 14–16
NGOs *see* non-governmental organisations (NGOs)
Ní Laoire, C. 59, 288
Nisrane, B.L. 61, 65
'non-deportability' 131
non-governmental organisations (NGOs) 88, 125
non-migrant families 34
non-migratory alternatives 73
non-refoulement 73
non-state actors 70, 125–7
non-state sources of coercion 76–7
'north–south migrations' 271
nostalgic 'memoryscapes' 99
Nozick, R. 71, 72
Nunes, A. 241
Núñez-Carrasco, L. 64
Nye, J.S. 186, 187

Obama, Barack 122
occupational mobility 32
O'Connell, P.J. 31
Oeppen, C. 72, 188
Oliver, C. 274, 279
Olivier-Mensah, C. 208
Olsaretti, S. 72–4, 80
*One Way Ticket: Migration and Female Labour* (Phizacklea) 54
'open-ended' approach 115
Operational Management of Large-Scale IT Systems 128
oppressive hegemonic ideology 90
oppressive mobility regime 85
O'Reilly, K. 274, 277
organisational capacity development 334
Organisation for Economic Co-operation and Development (OECD) 31, 192
Ortiz, A. 260
Ose, L. 250
Ottonelli, V. 71, 72, 78

Paasche, E. 190
Palloni, A. 232
Paparusso, A. 58
Parutis, V. 302
Pauli, J. 16, 17
'pay-to-go' schemes 73

Pedersen, M.H. 188
'perceived knowledge transfer' 334
Pettersen, S.V 321
Peutz, N. 126
philanthropic activities
    active involvement in 102
Phillips, J. 16, 286, 288
Phizacklea, A.
    *One Way Ticket: Migration and Female Labour* 54
Piore, M.
    *Birds of Passage* 54
Piracha, M. 30, 31
place-belongingness 246
'*Plan Benvenido a Casa*' 347
Polish labour migrant 76
political/civic activities 40
politicisation of return 11–12
Pollock, D. 247
Porobić, S. 304
Portes, A. 284
positive return environment 205
post-communist societies 305
post-conflict return 173, 193
'post-immigrant generation' 285
post-retirement transnational mobility 2
post-return assistance 110, 116, 119
post-return outcomes 10
post-return reintegration 108
post-soviet countries 249–51
Potter, R. 1
Potter, R.B. 16, 57, 286, 288
'pragmatic contentment' 271
PREMIG project 17
preparedness 202, 203, 204, 206, 262, 277, 287–9, 322
pre-return assistance 110–119
    accessibility 112–14
    field of actors 114–17
    institutional positioning 111–12
pre-return visits 101
private sector's attitudes 205
psychosocial wellbeing 226–8, 242
    forced *versus* voluntary return 227
    health, wellbeing and interlinks with return 231–3
    intersectionality of returnees and wellbeing 'outcomes' 228–31
    perspective 243–6
    reintegration without mobility and transnationality 233–5
push–pull theories 288

'racial cruelty' 87
racialised mobility regime 91

Radziwinowiczówna, A. 306
Raftery, A.E. 1
readmission agreements 123
Refugee Convention 71, 91, 140
refugee crisis 16
Reinhold, S. 31
reintegration 300
    of children 247
    and development 321
    experiences, structural factors conditioning 304–6
    post-return 17
    support 110
    and wellbeing 228
    without mobility and transnationality 233–5
reintegration strategies 209–10
    defining 200–201
    labour market 202
    labour policy 205
    social change and development 206–8
    traditionalists social network 204
're-migration' 17
'rentier state theory' 193
resource inequalities 103
'retirement–return' nexus 2
'return and reintegration' 126
return and transnationalism 38
    defining transnationalism and its dimensions 39–41
    existing research on 41–2
    investigating return through transnational lens 42–6
    post-return 46–8
    return as migration, mobilities and imaginary 39
return assistance 110
return-assistance programmes 160
return counselling 110, 115
return decision 144
return decision-making
    and coercion 79
    corruption and 187–8
    and gender 57
    links with health and wellbeing 231
return–development nexus 9, 12, 314
Return Directive 137, 147
    critique 139–40
    effectiveness of 142–4
    migrants' rights with EU efforts at migration control 140–146
    proposed revision of 148
    structure and content 138–9
    termination of illegal stay in the EU 146–7
'returnee identity' 7
returnee transnationalisms 48

'return imaginary' 272
return industry in Netherlands *see* Netherlands, return industry in
return intentions 218
return-migrant characteristics 16
return migrant flows
    size of 205
return migrants 28, 206
return migration
    defining 3–4
    and development nexus 2
    evolution of growing field 8–13
    impacts and effects of 12–13
    industry 153, 156
    and inequality 14
    new implications of return 13–16
    'return turn' 16
    structural approach to 6
    theorising 5–8
    and transnational geographical mobility 215
    typologies of return 4–5
return mobilities 7, 96, 109
    and imaginary return 43–6
return of achievement 5
return of completion 5
return of conservatism 5, 321
return of conservativism 348
return of crisis 5
'return of failure' 5, 348
'return of innovation' 5, 321, 332, 348
return of retirement 5
return of setback 5
return preparedness 7
'returns to returning' 31
return visits 98, 104
    care visits 100
    defining 97–8
    economic visits 101–2
    leisure visits 102
    pre-return visits 101
    rights visits 100–101
    ritual visits 99
    roots visits 100
    routine visits 99
'reverse culture shock' 244
'reverse transnationalism' 6, 61, 289
rights visits 100–101
ritual visits 99
'roots migration' 290
roots visits 100
Rosenzweig, M.R. 258
Rothberg, M. 129
*Rotterdam Ongedocumenteerden Steunpunt* 159
'routes to roots' approach 291
routine visits 99

Roy, A. 28
Ruben, R. 174, 176
Ruiz-Gelices, E. 261
Rumbaut, R.G. 284
rural–urban internal migration 4

Saar, E. 242, 243, 302, 306
Saar, M. 242, 243, 302, 306
Sabates-Wheeler, R. 226
Saito, M. 287
Sakka, D. 62
Salt, J. 154
Samari, G. 63, 65
Samers, M. 317
Saxenian, A. 350
Sayad, A. 213
Schiller, Glick 6
school-constraint model 258
Schuster, L. 12, 14
'Schwarzenbach initiative' 218
Schweisfurth, M. 47
second-generation 'return' migration 292
    geographies of 286
    outcomes and re-integration processes 289–91
    paradoxes and re-conceptualisations 283–6
    preparedness and reasons 287–9
'securitization of migration' 88
selectivity bias 27–8
self-identification 201
Sen, Amartya 176
    *Development as Freedom* 315
sense-making strategies 61
Setrana, M.B. 47
settlement return 215
short-term visiting mobilities 96
Siim, P.M. 251
simultaneity bias 28
Sinatti, G. 12, 314, 325
small and medium-sized businesses (SMEs) 127
SMEs *see* small and medium-sized businesses (SMEs)
Smith, D.J.
    *A Culture of Corruption* 195
Snel, E. 40, 58
social and political norms 33–4
social capital 210, 351–2
social change 299, 306–8
social class patterns corruption 195
social complexity 222
social exclusion 234
    and non-return 161–2
social mobility 215
social networks 201
social network theory 7

social remittances 61, 190–192, 300, 306–8, 320, 341, 354
social remitting 308
socio-cultural changes in family structure 246
socio-cultural integration 321
socio-demographic groups 2
*The Sociology of Return Migration* (Bovenkerk) 39
Sondhi, G. 57, 260
Soon, J.-J. 261
Sørensen, N.N. 154, 319
    *The Migration–Development Nexus* 315
Southern European immigrants 222
sovereign biopolitics 123–5
'sovereign monocular eye' 132
spatial proximity 98
Spilimbergo, A. 33
spousal bereavement 274
Stark, O. 25, 29
state-centred approach 345
state-centred perspective 344
state policies and programmes
    economic emphasis of approaches from above 348–9
    home countries courting their overseas diasporas 345–6
    state and non-state actors in diaspora governance 346–8
*status quo ante* 64
Stein, J. 154
Stepputat, F. 174
*Stichting Duurzame Terugkeer* 160
stigmatisation 207
Stones, R. 271, 277
structural and cultural environment for return 205
student mobility 255
    country conditions and professional opportunities 258–9
    departure, motivations and expectations 257–8
    different forms of integration 260–261
    graduates' experiences 262–3
    growing international 256–7
    retaining international students 263–4
    return for origin countries 264–5
    social, economic and political pressure 257
    students' socio-demographic and academic profiles 259–60
Sub-Saharan Africa 324
Sundquist, J. 231
super-entrepreneurs 346
Sustainable Development Goals (SDGs) 235
sustainable reintegration 10, 11, 167, 170
    absence of re-emigration 169–72
    embodies 167

    theoretical framework and methods 168–9
sustainable return 2, 46, 169–72
Sykes, B. 259, 261
Szydlowska, P. 242

TCK *see* third culture kid (TCK)
TCNs *see* third-country nationals (TCNs)
Teerling, J. 291
temporary migrants 29
Temporary Return of Qualified Nationals (TRQN)
    programme 339
    project 332
third-country nationals (TCNs) 137–9, 142–8
third culture kid (TCK) 247–9
Thom, K. 31
Thomson, A. 59
Thomson, M. 284
time-dependent criteria and nationality 113–14
Tonah, S. 47
'top-down' programmes 2
Torresi, T. 71, 72, 78
tourism scholarship 97
traditional gender norms 62
'traditional' gender relations 62
traditionalists' social network 204
'traditionalist' strategy 208
transborder household economy 58
'transcultural capital' 290
'translocal social fields' 291
'transnational agents of change' 289
'transnational bubbles' 47
'transnational corridors of expulsion' 126
transnational engagements 43, 47
'transnational entrepreneurs' 47
transnational European Union (EU) families 245
transnational geographical mobility 219–21
transnational geographic mobility 215, 217
transnational identities 40
transnational imaginary 47
'transnational involvement' 40
transnationalism 6, 48, 319, 349–53
'transnationalism–return nexus' 6
transnational migration 96
transnational mobility 214, 352
'transnational patriarchies' 59
transnational practices 277
transnational return 215, 217–18, 299
'transnational social fields' 287, 291
transnational social networks 41
transnational transport infrastructures 123
'transnational turn' 285
'transnational ways of belonging' 40, 201
Transparency International 186
Transrede project 326

Treaty of Amsterdam 137, 148
TRQN *see* Temporary Return of Qualified Nationals (TRQN)
Trump, Donald 122
Tsuda, T. 188, 242, 288, 290, 331
Tuccio, M. 34, 63, 65
Turner, S. 345
'two-step' migration 263

unaccompanied minors (UAMs) 229
UNDP 341
UNESCO 256, 266
United Nations Development Programme Transfer of Knowledge through Expatriate Nationals (TOKTEN) 332
United Nations High Commissioner for Refugees (UNHCR) 74, 75, 80, 127, 169, 171
'unwanted' migrants 2
Urry, J. 53

Vadean, P.F. 30
van Dongen, E. 347
Van Hear, N. 319
　　*The Migration–Development Nexus* 315
van Houte, M. 176, 207, 333
van Meeteren, M. 234
van Reken, R. 247
VAR *see* voluntary assisted-return (VAR)
Vari-Lavoisier, I. 320
Vathi, Z. 1, 10, 230, 242, 245–7, 306, 307
vernacularisation 207
Vertovec, S. 40
Vicente, P.C. 33
Viladrich, A. 286
*Visits Home* (Baldassar) 96
Vlase, I. 62, 308
'voluntarily leave' 85
'voluntarily' return 87
voluntariness 70–72, 109–10
　　decision-making proces 70
　　locating 78–80
　　and managed returns 73–5
　　and non-state sources of coercion 76–7
　　and return in regular and liquid migration contexts 75–6
voluntary assisted-return (VAR)
　　migrants 48
　　programmes 287

voluntary post-conflict return 304
voluntary return 75, 78, 109
　　of migrants 84
　　programmes 88
*Vreemdelingenwet* 156
Vullnetari, J. 188

Wahba, J. 14, 28, 30–32, 34, 63, 65
Wahba, Jackline 314
Waite, M. 226
Waldorf, B. 58, 65
Walsh, Katie 10
Walton-Roberts, M. 59
Wang, D. 333
Wang, Q. 259
Weheliye, A. 129
Weima, Y. 48
Weine, S.M. 230
wellbeing 'outcomes' 228–31
Wessendorf, S. 248, 286, 290
Western deportation corridors 131
Western deportation politics function 130
Western migration politics 129
White, A. 304
White immigration policy 90
White Supremacy 90
Wider reintegration assistance 171
Wilkes, R. 261
Williams, A.M. 262
'willingness-readiness' model of Cassarino 7
Wise, Delgado 317
Wissink, L. 125, 127
Wong, M. 62
Wong, R. 231
Wright, M.O. 249
Wu, C. 261

Yang, D. 26

Zaiceva, A. 27
Zenou, Y. 30
Zevulun, D. 229
Zhou, M. 284
Zimbabwean labour migrant 76
Zimmerman, D. 74
Zimmermann, K. 27
Zontini, E. 45, 219
Zúñiga, V. 245